Environmental Aspects of Real Estate Transactions

James B. Witkin, Editor

The Section of
Natural Resources, Energy, and Environmental Law
and
The Section of Real Property, Probate, and Trust Law

American Bar Association

Printed in the United States of America.

Library of Congress Catalog Card Number 95-77802
ISBN 1-57073-216-7

Discounts are available for books ordered in bulk. Special consideration is given to state bars, CLE programs, and other bar-related organizations. Inquire at Publications Planning & Marketing, American Bar Association, 750 North Lake Shore Drive, Chicago IL 60611.

00 99 98 97 96 95 5 4 3 2 1

CONTENTS

ACKNOWLEDGMENTS

A collaborative book of this scope could not have been published without the assistance of many people. First, I would like to thank the authors, who made the time to write, rewrite, and polish their chapters and to work (largely with good cheer) with me, the peer reviewers, and the ABA publications staff.

Each chapter was peer-reviewed by at least one and as many as four reviewers. The following people served as reviewers: Professor Robert Adler, Ellis L. Andersen, Nancer Ballard, Tom Bartman, Julie C. Becker, Michael Brennan, John Cochrane, Michelle Desiderio, Cheryl Fox, Kevin A. Gaynor, Joseph Giamboi, Thomas F. Goode, Jeanne Gorman, David Governo, Nancy Herman, Kenneth S. Kamlet, Susan Kincaid, J. Brent Kynoch, Colleen Lamont, Steven A. Lauer, Bryan Lee, Lawrence R. Liebesman, James McLaughlin, Betsy Monsalve, Matt T. Morley, Paul C. Nightingale, Lou Novick, John R. Orrick Jr., Peter Patchin, Roger Platt, Ian Portnoy, Ritchenya Anni Shepherd, Ted Tewkesberry, Richard Thometz, Robert Thornton, Joseph D. Uradnik, William L. Want, John Welch, G. Van Velsor Wolf Jr., and Gina M. Zawitoski.

Several chapters were peer-reviewed by lawyers and program officials with federal and state regulatory agencies. Many of these reviewers asked that they not be acknowledged by name, to avoid any implication that their comments represented the views of their respective agencies. The comments received from the public sector reviewers were invaluable. Also, although their names are not included in the list of reviewers, many of the authors also reviewed chapters by other authors.

In addition to the peer reviewers, I wish to thank Daniel M. Singer and Myles B. Hannan, each of whom offered superb editing assistance on several chapters.

I thank my partners at Linowes and Blocher for their assistance and advice while this book was in process. Special thanks to Roger D. Winston and John L. Hollingshead, who shared their experiences from other ABA publishing projects.

Also thanks to Theodore Garrett and Alan J. Robin, the respective Publications Chairs of the ABA Sections of Natural Resources, Energy, and Environmental Law, and Real Property, Probate and Trust Law. Ted Garrett was instrumental in the early planning of this book.

Special thanks to Susan A. Winchurch, who served as the principal editorial assistant on this book and assisted in the editing and review of many chapters. Susan's conscientious and creative assistance was invaluable.

The ABA Publications Planning & Marketing Group ably oversaw the transformation of this book from concept, to manuscript, and finally to the book in your hands. Many thanks to Carol Siedell, Holly Wehmeyer, Ron Mochel, and especially Donald J. Gecewicz, who has been with this project from the start.

Finally, my most important acknowledgment is to my wife, Nancy A. Flickinger, who tolerated the nights and weekends at the office while this book was taking shape, and offered inspiration throughout. I am eternally grateful to her, and to my sons, Daniel and Matthew.

James B. Witkin

ABOUT THE EDITOR

James B. Witkin is a partner and co-chair of the Environmental Practice Group of Linowes and Blocher in Washington, D.C., and Silver Spring, Maryland. Mr. Witkin's practice focuses on environmental issues arising in commercial real estate and business transactions. He has considerable experience in the law of underground storage tanks, asbestos, hazardous materials, and environmental lender liability. His practice includes client representation before environmental regulatory agencies, and compliance counseling.

Mr. Witkin is a frequent author and lecturer on real estate and environmental topics. He has organized, chaired, and participated in ABA, state bar, and industry seminars on many issues relating to environmental issues in real estate and commercial transactions.

His articles have appeared in *Legal Times, The Practical Real Estate Lawyer, The National Law Journal, Probate & Property,* and other publications. He is a member of the editorial boards of *The Practical Real Estate Lawyer, Real Estate/Environmental Liability News,* and the *Underground Storage Tank Guide.*

Mr. Witkin graduated from Harvard College (A.B. cum laude), London School of Economics (M.Sc. with distinction) and Harvard Law School (J.D. cum laude). He was a law clerk for the Honorable Ruth I. Abrams of the Massachusetts Supreme Judicial Court. He is admitted to the bars of Maryland, the District of Columbia, and Massachusetts, and is an active member of the ABA's Sections of Natural Resources, Energy, and Environmental Law and Real Property, Probate and Trust Law.

ABOUT THE AUTHORS

Judith A. Armold is of counsel to Venable, Baetjer and Howard, L.L.P., where she practices environmental and land use law in the firm's Baltimore, Maryland, office. She received her undergraduate degree from Western Maryland College and her law degree from the University of Maryland. From 1977 to 1987, Ms. Armold served as an assistant attorney general of Maryland and as general counsel to the Maryland Department of State Planning.

Harry M. Baumgartner is an attorney with Shanley & Fisher, Morristown, New Jersey, concentrating in environmental and toxic tort litigation, environmental insurance litigation, regulatory enforcement actions, and environmental transactional and compliance issues. He received his bachelor of arts degree from Rutgers University and his law degree, cum laude, from Seton Hall University School of Law. He also attended Fairleigh Dickinson University's Graduate School of Management. Mr. Baumgartner is a member of the American Bar Association and the New Jersey State Bar Association and is active in the latter organization's Environmental Law Section.

Jeffre B. Beatty is a manager in the Financial Advisory Services practice of Coopers & Lybrand, L.L.P., in Phoenix, Arizona. He graduated from Northern Arizona University with a bachelor of science degree in accounting. He specializes in the valuation of commercial real estate and the determination of property value diminution resulting from contamination.

Donald I. Berger received both his bachelor of arts degree and his law degree from the University of California at Los Angeles. Mr. Berger is a partner in the Los Angeles office of Morrison and Foerster and is a member of the firm's Real Estate and Land Use and Environmental practice groups. He is also a member of the Section of Natural Resources, Energy, and Environmental Law of the ABA.

Jeffery R. Berry is counsel in the Investment Practice Group of Law and Regulatory Affairs at Aetna Life & Casualty in Hartford, Connecticut. Mr. Berry's practice focuses primarily on environmental issues arising in Aetna's investment operations. Mr. Berry is a member of the ABA's Real Property, Probate and Trust Law Section and is chair of its Environmental Committee on Indoor Air Quality and Asbestos Issues. Mr. Berry is also a member of the Environmental Policy Advisory Committee of the National Realty Committee and a frequent speaker and author on environmental issues facing real estate investors. He is a 1978 graduate of Middlebury College and received his law degree in 1981 from George Washington University Law School. Before joining Aetna, Mr. Berry worked at the law firm of Williams & Connolly in Washington, D.C., and the law firm of Cleary, Gottlieb, Steen and Hamilton in New York City. He also clerked for one year for U.S. District Judge Oliver Gasch in Washington, D.C.

Carol R. Boman is a principal in the Law Offices of Carol R. Boman, a San Francisco, California, based firm specializing in regulatory issues affecting commercial real estate ownership, with a particular emphasis on environmental aspects of business and commerical real estate transactions. Ms. Boman has a bachelor of arts degree from Idaho State University, a Diplome d'Etudes Superieures from the University of Bordeaux, France, and a master's in French literature from the University of Nevada, Reno. She received her law degree in 1980 from the University of California, Berkeley (Boalt Hall). She is an active member of the ABA in both the Section of Natural Resources, Energy, and Environmental Law (where she serves a co-chair of the Keystone Annual Environmental Law Conference and as a vice chair of the Environmental Quality Committee) and the Section of Real Property, Probate and Trust Law (where she serves as chair of the Conveyancing Committee and as co-chair of the Condition of the Premises [Environmental] Subcommittee of the Commerical Leasing Committee).

Johnine J. Brown is a principal in Brown & Bryant, P.C., a Chicago law firm concentrating in environmental law. The firm represents nationally known manufacturers, banks, and developers and offers a full spectrum of services in environmental law, including litigation counsel. Ms. Brown has practiced environmental law since receiving her law degree from the University of Chicago Law School in 1977. She also has a doctorate in language and literature from the University of Chicago.

Gerard A. Caron is an associate in the Environmental Department at Goodwin Procter & Hoar in Boston, Massachusetts. Mr. Caron received a bachelor of arts degree from Boston College and his law degree from Boston College Law School, where he was executive editor of the *Environmental Affairs Law Review*. He then served as a law clerk to the former Hon. Andrew A. Caffrey, U.S. District Court for the District of Massachusetts. Mr. Caron represents and counsels clients in environmental litigation and enforcement matters as well as environmental compliance, permitting, and transactional matters. He is a coauthor of Goodwin Procter & Hoar's four-volume hazardous waste treatise.

James A. Chalmers is a partner in the Financial Advisory Services practice of Coopers & Lybrand, L.L.P., in Phoenix, Arizona. He earned his doctorate in economics from the University of Michigan and is a candidate in the Appraisal Institute. His professional experience includes regional and urban economics, real estate counseling, and real property valuation, with emphasis in the areas of condemnation and the valuation of contaminated property.

Kathleen M. Courtis is an associate in the Washington, D.C., law firm of Tucker, Flyer & Lewis, where she practices tax planning and controversy. She is a graduate of Georgetown University and New York University School of Law.

Frank B. Cross is a professor of business regulation at the University of Texas at Austin. He holds a law degree, cum laude, from Harvard Law School and a bachelor of arts degree, magna cum laude, in history and economics from the University of Kansas. Mr. Cross has authored eight books and has also written over thirty scholarly articles on environmental law and law and economics. Other publications include seven book chapters and numerous editorials. He currently serves on the editorial board of five journals.

Geoffrey T. Cullen is an environmental specialist with the law firm of Beveridge & Diamond in Washington, D.C. Since 1985 Mr. Cullen has followed legislative and regulatory issues primarily in the area of the Clean Water Act.

Richard S. Davis is a principal of Beveridge & Diamond's Washington, D.C., office, a member of the firm's Clean Air Act Practice Group, and Chairman of the firm's Clean Water Act Practice Group. Mr. Davis represents companies and municipalities on a variety of permit proceedings and enforcement actions under the Clean Water Act. He represents companies and trade associations in rulemaking proceedings and judicial challenges to final rules. He also regularly advises both commercial and municipal clients with respect to permitting strategy in light of rapidly evolving regulations. Mr. Davis frequently lectures on permitting and regulatory strategy under the Clean Air and Clean Water acts. Mr. Davis received his law degree from Columbus School of Law and his bachelor of arts degree from Syracuse University. From 1978 to 1980 he was a member of the Catholic University Law Review. He clerked for The Honorable H. Emory Widener, Jr., U.S. Court of Appeals for the Fourth Circuit, from 1980 to 1981. He has written articles on water pollution control and the Clean Water Act. Mr. Davis was an attorney-advisor to the Joint AMSA/EPA Audits Study Group in 1985. He has also been a professorial lecturer at Columbus School of Law, Catholic University of America. Mr. Davis is a member of the Maryland State Bar Association, the District of Columbia Bar Association, the Federal Bar Association, and the American Bar Association.

John J. Delaney is a partner with the law firm of Linowes and Blocher of Silver Spring, Greenbelt, and Annapolis, Maryland, and Washington, D.C. Before joining Linowes and Blocher in 1965, he was an Assistant County Attorney for Montgomery County, Maryland. He has represented or served as a consultant to developers, municipalities, and other clients in a wide variety of land use cases before federal and state courts and administrative agencies of Maryland and the District of Columbia. He is an adjunct professor of Land Use Law and Local Government Law at The American University, Washington College of Law. He has written extensively in the area of land use regulation and is a co-author of the book, *Handling the Land Use Case,* published by Little, Brown and Company, Boston, Massachusetts. Mr. Delaney is a graduate of Georgetown University and the Georgetown University Law Center and is admitted to the bars of Maryland, the District of Columbia, and the United States Supreme Court. He is also a member of the American Institute of Certified Planners.

Edward C. Dolan is a partner in the Washington, D.C., law firm of Hogan & Hartson, L.L.P. He received his undergraduate degree from Columbia University in 1975 and his law degree from Georgetown University in 1978. Mr. Dolan represents institutional lenders and other creditors in all aspects of debt restructuring, recovery, and collateral liquidation. He is a member of the board of directors and a past president of the Bankruptcy Bar Association for the District of Maryland; a member of the Standing Committee on Local Rules of the United States Bankruptcy Court for the District of Maryland; and a member of the Montgomery County and Prince George's County Bar Associations' Bankruptcy Sections and the Walter Chandler Bankruptcy Inn of Court. Mr. Dolan has written and spoken on commercial workouts, bankruptcy financing, use of cash collateral, lien enforcement, distressed real estate, environmental liability, and lender liability.

Robert B. Ecker is a senior associate in the Financial Advisory Services practice of Coopers & Lybrand, L.L.P., in Phoenix, Arizona. He received his graduate business degree in finance from Carnegie Mellon University, his law degree from the University of Pittsburgh, and his bachelor of arts degree in economics from the University of Pennsylvania. His real estate and financial consulting experience includes the analysis of property value diminution and the quantification of damages to real property due to contamination or hazard. Mr. Ecker is licensed to practice law in Pennsylvania and is also a licensed Pennsylvania real estate salesperson. He is a member of the ABA, the Pennsylvania Bar Association, the Allegheny County Bar Association, and the Maricopa County (Arizona) Bar Association and their environmental sections.

Geraldine E. Edens is an associate in the Washington, D.C., firm of Cadwalader, Wickersham & Taft's Environmental Law Group. Ms. Edens practices in areas involving environmental litigation, regulatory matters, and issues regarding law and science. She has an extensive background in the health and biological sciences and statistics. Ms. Edens graduated from the University of Miami School of Law, magna cum laude and Order of the Coif, where she was a member of the *University of Miami Law Review*. She has a doctorate in higher education, with highest honors, from the University of Florida, and a master's and bachelor's of science from the University of Miami. Ms. Edens is a member of the District of Columbia and Maryland bars. Before joining Cadwalader, Ms. Edens was an associate professor at the University of Miami, where she was a member of the graduate faculty. She has written and presented numerous papers on environmental issues.

David B. Farer is a partner in the Westfield, New Jersey, firm of Farer Siegal Fersko, where he heads the nationally active Environmental Law Department. He has lectured and written extensively on environmental law issues, including transaction-triggered environmental laws and concerns, due diligence, lender liability, contractual protection, and cost-recovery techniques. Mr. Farer's practice concentrates on counseling clients as to the impact of environmental laws on business and transactions around the country, environmental compliance and insurance issues, and litigation arising from those issues. Mr. Farer chairs the annual advanced ALI-ABA course of study, "The Impact of Environmental Law on Real Estate and Other Commercial Transactions," and is also a member of the ALI-ABA Program Subcommittee. Among Mr. Farer's books are *ECRA/ISRA Compliance,* 3d ed. (ICLE 1993) and *New Jersey Underground Storage Tank Law,* 2d ed. (ICLE 1990). He is an annual participant in the ABA SONREEL year-end RCRA/CERCLA update, where he speaks on Superfund defenses, and the Georgetown Advanced Institute in Environmental Law.

David J. Freeman is chair of the Environmental Department at Battle Fowler, a one hundred ten-lawyer firm based in New York City. He is a graduate of Harvard College (cum laude, 1970) and Harvard Law School (cum laude, 1975). Mr. Freeman specializes in hazardous waste site litigation, negotiation and supervision of site cleanups, management and conduct of environmental audits, and compliance counseling. He has written and spoken extensively on environmental law topics. He is a member of the ABA's Section of Natural Resources, Energy, and Environmental Law and the Environmental Litigation Committee; the Section of Litigation; the New York State Bar Association's Environmental Law Committee; and the International Environmental Law Committee of the New York City Bar Association.

Eva M. Fromm is a partner with Fulbright & Jaworski in the firm's Houston office. Before obtaining her law degree from the University of Houston Bates College of Law, she received a bachelor's of science in chemical and environmental engineering from Syracuse University and was employed for several years as an environmental consultant. Ms. Fromm's legal practice focuses on regulatory consulting, enforcement matters, contested permit matters, business transactional issues, and environmental property damage and toxic tort litigation. Ms. Fromm is a coauthor and co-editor of the *Texas Environmental Law Handbook,* 3d ed. (Government Institutes, 1993). Ms. Fromm is a member of the Natural Resources, Energy, and Environmental Law sections of the ABA and the Texas Bar Association and is a past chair of the Houston Bar Association Environmental Law Section.

Bruce W. Galloway received his bachelor of arts degree, with honors, from Claremont Men's College and his law degree from Boalt Hall Law School, University of California at Berkeley. Mr. Galloway is currently of counsel to Morrison & Foerster in Los Angeles and is engaged in a general commercial real property practice, with particular emphasis in leasing.

Robert J. Gilbert is in private practice in Andover, Massachusetts, and specializes in environmental insurance matters. Mr. Gilbert received his undergraduate degree in public affairs from Princeton University (1983) and his juris doctor from Harvard Law School (1987). Mr. Gilbert has served as a legislative aide to Senator Daniel Patrick Moynahan (D.-N.Y.) and as a law clerk to Hon. James K. Logan of the U.S. Court of Appeals for the Tenth Judicial Circuit. In addition to assisting clients in the procurement of environmental insurance coverage for ongoing activities and transactions, Mr. Gilbert's practice includes the pursuit of insurance coverage for CERCLA and other environmental liabilities under policies issued from the 1940s to the present.

Margaret V. Hathaway has her own law offices in Washington, D.C., where her practice emphasizes environmental risks in real estate and financing transactions. Ms. Hathaway was vice chair of the E.50.02 Subcommittee of the American Society of Testing and Materials (ASTM) from 1990–1995 and has written a substantial part of ASTM's standard practices for environmental assessments in commercial real estate transactions. She also serves on the Lawyer's Committee of the Environmental Lender Liability Coalition, formed in Washington, D.C., to support legislation and other public policy to protect innocent lenders and fiduciaries from environmental liability. She represented the American Council of Life Insurance, an intervenor in *Kelley v. U.S. EPA*, the judicial challenge to the EPA's rule on lender liability under CERCLA. She is the coauthor of *The Lender's Guide to Environmental Law: Risk and Liability* (Matthew Bender, 1993). A 1980 graduate of Boalt Hall School of Law, University of California at Berkeley, Ms. Hathaway is a member of the California, District of Columbia, and American Bar Associations. She is vice chair of the Committee on Environmental Aspects of Lender Liability of the ABA's Section on Real Property, Probate and Trust and is a member of the Section of Natural Resources, Energy, and Environmental Law.

Anne Rickard Jackowitz is a senior associate in the Boston law firm of Choate, Hall & Stewart. Ms. Jackowitz is a graduate of Boston College and Boston College Law School. As a member of Choate, Hall & Stewart's real estate department, Ms. Jackowitz's practice consists primarily of loan transactions and asset dispositions and purchases, commercial leasing, real estate workouts, and real estate bankruptcies, including foreclosures, deeds-in-lieu of foreclosure, loan restructurings and forbearance agreements. She is also a member of New England Women in Real Estate, the Massachusetts Bar Association, the Boston Bar Association, and the ABA.

Brigid E. Kenney received her undergraduate degree in chemistry from Goucher College in 1973 and her law degree with honors from the University of Maryland Law School in 1977. After clerking for Hon. Rita C. Davidson on the Maryland Court of Special Appeals, she joined the Baltimore, Maryland, office of the law firm of Venable, Baetjer and Howard, L.L.P. A partner in the firm's Environmental Practice Group since 1986, she concentrates on matters involving hazardous and solid waste.

Laurence S. Kirsch is a partner in Cadwalader, Wickersham & Taft in Washington, D.C. He practices in the area of environmental law, including CERCLA, RCRA, the Clean Air Act, the Clean Water Act, TSCA, and related state statutes. Mr. Kirsch graduated from Harvard Law School, where he served as managing editor of the *Harvard Environmental Law Review*. He has a master's of science, emphasizing environmental policy, from the University of Pennsylvania, and a bachelor's of applied science, summa cum laude, Phi Beta Kappa, from the College of Engineering and Applied Science of the University of Pennsylvania.

Jill A. Kotvis is Chair of the Environmental Practice Group at the Dallas-based law firm of Hughes & Luce, L.L.P. Her practice includes counseling on environmental issues in real estate, corporate, and lending transactions, Mexican and international environmental law and NAFTA, environmental issues involving the oil and gas industry and counseling, and representation in relation to compliance and enforcement matters before the Texas Natural Resource Conservation Commission and the U.S. Environmental Protection Agency. Prior to joining Hughes & Luce, Ms. Kotvis was Senior Attorney and Environmental Counsel for LTV Aerospace and Defense Company and Division Counsel to a wholly owned subsidiary, AM General Corporation. Ms. Kotvis serves by appointment on the City of Dallas Environmental Health Commission, the City of Dallas Privatization Technical Subcommittee, and the Greater Dallas Chamber Environmental Task Force. She is active in several professional organizations where she is Co-Chair of the Environmental Committee of the Texas-Mexico Bar Association, and Co-Chair of the Networking Committee of the State Bar of Texas, Environmental and Natural Resources Section, and Vice-Chair of several American Bar Association Committees of the Section on Natural Resources, Energy, and Environmental Law. Ms. Kotvis is also an Associate Editor of the Southern Methodist University Law School and ABA International Law Section *NAFTA Journal of Law and Business Review in the Americas* and Editor of their Environmental Symposium Issue. Ms. Kotvis received her law degree from George Washington University in 1981 and her undergraduate degree in 1977 from the State University of New York at Brockport.

Ann Parisi Messer received her law degree from Chicago Kent College of Law in 1988 and her undergraduate degree in biology and chemistry from Northern Illinois University in 1984. As an associate at Brown & Bryant, P.C., in Chicago, Ms. Messer has worked on a wide variety of environmental issues, including Clean Air Act and Clean Water Act (specifically wetlands) issues, and RCRA, CERCLA, and TSCA compliance issues.

I. Leo Motiuk is a partner at Shanley & Fisher, Morristown, New Jersey, and co-chair of the firm's environmental group. He earned his bachelor of arts degree from Dickinson College, his juris doctor degree from Duquesne University School of Law, and his master's degree from New York University School of Law. His activities include involvement with federal and state agencies in seeking permits, handling Superfund and Spill Act claims, defending governmental enforcement actions and private cost-recovery lawsuits, and engaging in transactional and due diligence work. Mr. Motiuk has served as chair of the Environmental Committee of the ABA's Section on Real Property, Probate and Trust Law and as chair of the Environmental Law Section of the New Jersey State Bar Association. He is a member of the board of advisors of the BNA *Toxics Law Reporter* and of Buraff's *Real Estate/Environmental Liability News.*

James P. O'Brien is a partner in the Environmental Department of Chapman and Cutler in Chicago. Mr. O'Brien served as principal editor and an author of the BNA's *Environmental Due Diligence: The Complete Resource Guide* (1989). Mr. O'Brien also served as chief author and editorial coordinator of "BNA's Environmental Due Diligence Guide." He has lectured widely on the topic of environmental law and has testified before the U.S. Congress on proposed environmental legislation. Mr. O'Brien holds a bachelor of science in physics from the University of Notre Dame and a J.D., cum laude, from the University of Wisconsin, where he graduated Order of the Coif.

Catherine A. Potthast is a member in the law firm of Smith, Somerville & Case, L.L.C., in Baltimore, Maryland. She received her undergraduate degree in environmental science from St. Michael's College and her juris doctor from the University of Baltimore School of Law. She is active in the defense of civil litigation with primary emphasis on lead paint defense, insurance coverage disputes, environmental and toxic tort matters, professional liability claims, and appellate practice. Ms. Potthast also represents owners of single and multifamily rental properties in litigation matters and handles regulatory compliance issues. She is admitted to practice in Maryland and the District of Columbia.

J.B. Ruhl is assistant professor of law at Southern Illinois University School of Law, where he teaches environmental law and administrative law courses. He received his juris doctor degree from the University of Virginia School of Law and an L.L.M. in Environmental Law from the George Washington University National Law Center. Before joining the SIU faculty, Mr. Ruhl practiced law with the Austin, Texas, office of Fulbright & Jaworski, L.L.P. His practice and his academic scholarship focus on environmental law issues, particularly endangered species, wetlands, and NEPA topics. He also serves as executive editor of SONREEL's quarterly magazine, *Natural Resources & Environment.*

Judson W. Starr has been a partner at the Washington, D.C., law firm of Venable, Baetjer, Howard & Civiletti since 1988. From 1982 to 1988, he was the first director and then chief, Environmental Crimes Section, U.S. Department of Justice, Environment and Natural Resources Division. He has served or is serving as the co-chair, Subcommittees on Environmental Crimes in the ABA Section of Business Law and Section of Criminal Justice; and as a member of the Environmental Crimes Advisory Group, U.S. Sentencing Commission. A frequent panelist and author on environmental enforcement issues, he was recently honored to be named one of the nation's leading white-collar experts by the National Law Journal. He is a graduate of Washington and Jefferson College and Georgetown University Law Center.

Margaret (Peggy) N. Strand is the author of *Federal Wetlands Law,* a treatise included in the Environmental Law Institute's *Wetland Deskbook* (1993). After a fifteen-year career in environmental litigation at the U.S. Justice Department, she now practices environmental law in Washington, D.C., at the law firm of Bayh, Connaughton, & Malone. Her practice is divided between litigation and counseling on compliance with environmental regulations. Ms. Strand served on the National Academy of Sciences Committee on Wetlands Delineation. She is a frequent lecturer on wetlands law and an adjunct professor of law at George Washington University National Law Center, teaching solid and hazardous waste law. She holds a juris doctor from William and Mary Law School and a bachelor of arts degree from the University of Rochester.

Stefan F. Tucker is a partner in the Washington, D.C., law firm of Tucker, Flyer & Lewis, where he practices in the tax, business, real estate, and estate planning areas. He is a graduate of the University of Michigan and the University of Michigan Law School. In addition to numerous articles on income and estate taxation and business planning, Mr. Tucker is the author of *Tax Planning for Real Estate Transactions* (Clark, Boardman Callaghan, 1989) and was co-editor of *Real Estate Income Taxation* (1982).

Michelle A. Wenzel is an associate in Beveridge & Diamond's Washington, D.C., office, practicing primarily with the firm's wetlands/endangered species and water practice groups. Before joining Beveridge & Diamond, she worked as a software engineer for Martin Marietta Astronautics Group and Litton Guidance & Control Systems. Ms. Wenzel graduated from the University of Michigan with a bachelor of science degree in computer science. She received her law degree from the Washington College of Law at American University, where she was editor-in-chief of *The American University Law Review*.

Barbara L. Worthen serves as general counsel to Fleet Investment Services, which provides fiduciary, investment advisory services, and brokerage services to Fleet Banks throughout New England and New York. Ms. Worthen received her juris doctor from Suffolk University School of Law, and her bachelor of arts degree, magna cum laude, from Salem State College. She is a 1996 candidate for a master's degree in tax law at Boston University School of Law.

Walter G. Wright Jr. is a partner in the law firm of Mitchell, Williams, Selig, Gates and Woodyard, P.L.L.C., in Little Rock, Arkansas, focusing on legislative, regulatory, and transactional issues related to environmental and energy law. He also serves as an adjunct professor at the University of Arkansas at Little Rock School of Law. He is a former assistant general counsel to the Petroleum Marketers Association in Washington, D.C. Mr. Wright received his bachelor of science degree and his law degree from the University of Arkansas and his master's of law degree from the National Law Center of the George Washington University, in Washington, D.C.

FOREWORD

As editor James Witkin points out in his Introduction, environmental law issues have now become so inextricably intertwined with real estate and business transactions law that no commercial real estate transaction can take place without some focus by purchasers on environmental due diligence or by lenders on appropriate environmental protections.

This superb volume provides both environmental lawyers and real estate lawyers with a readable, comprehensive treatment of all the key issues found at the intersection of real estate law and environmental law. It provides a valuable addition to the growing shelf of books on environmental, energy, and natural resource law that the Section of Natural Resources, Energy, and Environmental Law has planned, developed, and brought out to help educate practitioners of varying backgrounds so that their law practices may be as fulfilling and as excellent as possible. We are especially pleased to have participated in developing this book in partnership with the Section of Real Property, Probate and Trust Law, and look forward to additional joint ventures between our two sections as our respective substantive disciplines continue to intersect as well as grow in complexity.

As this is written in early October, 1995, the past year has been rampant with change to practically every area of environmental law. At both the federal and state level, if the legislation didn't change, there were proposals to have it changed. Business saw changes to liability issues, clean-up standards, obligations of property owners, reporting procedures, application of air standards, and environmental penalty schemes. More changes to environmental law are being proposed, in many cases to make the laws more favorable to industry. So it is all the more important for practitioners engaged in commercial real estate matters to have a solid grasp of how the environmental programs, liability regimes, and enforcement practices were developed and how they have evolved.

We all owe a great deal of gratitude to James Witkin for his organizational skill and managerial mastery of all thirty-eight authors, whose combined efforts have produced this first-rate book. Thanks, too, to Ted Garrett, the Publications Officer of the Section of Natural Resources, Energy, and Environmental Law for his creative judgment in the early planning of this book.

Philip A. Fleming
Chair
Section of Natural Resources,
Energy, and Environmental Law

PROLOGUE

At long last, *Environmental Aspects of Real Estate Transactions* brings to real estate practitioners, under one cover, a comprehensive and practical review of environmental laws as they relate to real estate.

This easy-to-read and understandable volume begins with an excellent overview of environmental liability in real estate transactions viewed from the outlook of the parties involved and proceeds to give a practical review of due diligence in commercial real estate transactions. The book includes interesting chapters on selected issues that are of particular interest to real estate lawyers, including underground storage tanks, asbestos, lead-based paint, radon, PCBs, and indoor air pollution. The book then proceeds with chapters designed to aid the practitioner in structuring real estate transactions to best deal with the environmental issues and their implications.

The authors who have contributed to this outstanding work have accomplished the difficult task of refining concepts of environmental law and the complexity of environmental technicalities into very understandable terms for real estate lawyers.

Editor Jim Witkin has, in a particularly sensitive and effective manner, woven together in an organized manner chapters dealing with the entire range of environmental issues.

It is immediately apparent that *Environmental Aspects of Real Estate Transactions* will have a long shelf life with continuous use.

Morton P. Fisher Jr.
Past Chair
Section of Real Property,
Probate and Trust Law

INTRODUCTION

JAMES B. WITKIN

Within recent memory, no issue has had a greater impact on real estate practice than the need to address environmental concerns. Today, it is inconceivable that a sophisticated real estate investor would make a major acquisition without first performing environmental due diligence, or that a lender would close a loan without appropriate environmental protections. Environmental consultants now are as integral to real estate transactions as are surveyors and title insurance companies. Real estate lawyers, whose primary expertise once appeared—perhaps unfairly—to be familiarity with the Rule in Shelley's Case, and the clogging of the equity of redemption, have had to become conversant on electromagnetic fields and the remediation of benzene in groundwater.

This change took place quickly. A mere fifteen years ago, purchasers of properties did not perform Phase I environmental assessments. The transformation has percolated unevenly through the industry: Some lenders have hired sizable environmental engineering staffs to review environmental assessments, while others treat the reports simply as closing checklist items to be filed and forgotten. Few law schools incorporate environmental issues into courses on real estate law, or vice-versa. Re-education of practitioners has been accomplished largely through seminars and CLE courses, with varying degrees of success. This is why two sections of the American Bar Association—the Section of Natural Resources, Energy, and Environmental Law, and the Section of Real Property, Probate and Trust Law—have jointly undertaken to publish a book devoted entirely to environmental issues that arise in commercial real estate transactions.

Concerns about the impacts of environmental matters on real estate began to surface in the 1980s. The groundwork was established in 1980 with the enactment of Superfund, under which a property owner can be held liable for the cost of cleaning up hazardous substances, even if the contamination was caused by previous owners. In 1984, Congress passed Subtitle I of the Resource Conservation and Recovery Act, which authorized EPA to regulate underground storage tanks. Suddenly, a seemingly innocuous fixture of many commercial properties—the lowly gasoline or heating oil tank—became the focus of costly environmental investigation, and even litigation. Failure to comply with tank regulations could result in fines of thousands of dollars per day. Also in the mid-1980s, parties to real estate transactions began to focus on liability related to asbestos.

In 1985, the EPA began to educate the public about radon, a gas that seeps into buildings and is said to be a significant cause of lung cancer. Not long after, the first articles appeared about indoor air quality problems, as well as the dangers allegedly associated with electromagnetic fields. In the 1970s, few lawyers associated commercial real estate transactions with environmental problems; in the 1980s, environmental liability lurked under every deed.

The federal government was not the only source of environmental regulation. In 1983, New Jersey enacted the Environmental Cleanup Responsibility Act (ECRA), which prohibited owners from transferring many commercial and industrial properties prior to performing environmental investigations and submitting clean-up plans. Although no other state has enacted a law as tough as ECRA, other states have passed statutes that require the disclosure of potential environmental liabilities. Even some municipalities began to regulate asbestos and radon.

Suddenly, real estate attorneys handling complex transactions had to become proficient in new areas of the law. The new topics crossed disciplines. Many environmental issues were regulatory in nature and quite different from the transactional issues familiar to real estate attorneys. Understanding consultants' reports required an understanding of scientific and technical concepts last encountered—if ever—in college or high school. Lawyers who could not convert contaminant measurements from parts per billion to parts per million reviewed environmental reports at their own (and their clients') peril.

Similarly, many issues that arose in real estate transactions were beyond the familiarity of the traditional environmental bar, whose expertise lay largely in administrative and regulatory issues. Many environmental lawyers were simply ignorant of lien priority, title insurance, landlord-tenant law, and the other tax and business issues that arise in every real estate deal.

This book attempts to provide, for both the real estate lawyer and the environmental lawyer, a comprehensive treatment of the key issues found at the intersection of the two disciplines. Part I covers basic issues of environmental liability, both statutory and under the common law. Given the importance of lenders to the real estate world, separate chapters on lender and fiduciary liability are included, as well as chapters on environmental disclosure requirements and criminal environmental liability.

Part II focuses on environmental due diligence, with discussions of the mechanics and scope of the Phase I audit process, the proper role of environmental consultants, and the science underlying consultants' reports.

Part III deals with environmental matters in the context of specific transactional issues, including the documentation of environmental risks, taxation, insurance, securities and bankruptcy issues, and the emerging issue of valuing contaminated properties.

Part IV addresses the most common environmental problems, including underground storage tanks, asbestos, lead, radon, indoor air pollution, and electromagnetic fields.

Finally, Part V highlights environmental problems that arise in the development of raw land—wetlands, endangered species, and stormwater issues, as well as the "takings" implications of environmental laws.

Given the relative newness of this field, one may wonder whether these issues will be viewed in a different light after the year 2000. Some changes already have taken place: Over the past several years, the real estate industry's concern about asbestos appears to have diminished, while concerns about lead paint have resurfaced. Although environmental assessments have become routine, and many parties no longer view every petroleum spill as a deal killer, properties are being subjected to increased environmental scrutiny. More information about the environmental status of the country's real estate is coming to light, and must be considered by parties to property transactions.

Finally, although the desired limits of environmental protection will continue to be debated and adjusted by politicians and policy makers, fundamental concerns over environmental protection are still strong in the United States. Although the toxin *du jour* may change over time, the basic issues covered in this book appear to be here to stay.

PART I

An Overview of Environmental Liability

~

CHAPTER 1

Federal Environmental Liability

LAURENCE S. KIRSCH
GERALDINE E. EDENS

For real estate investors, tenants, and lenders, federal environmental laws represent a veritable minefield that must be navigated with care. Real estate professionals should be concerned about environmental laws because the resulting liability, in addition to being unexpected, tends to be broad and absolute.

Liability under federal environmental statutes frequently takes the liable party by surprise because the liability need not be triggered by any action or inaction by that party. A property owner or tenant may be held liable for contamination even if that person did not deposit hazardous substances on the site or knowingly or negligently allow unsafe conditions to persist there. While such overt actions or omissions most likely will trigger liability, a property owner or user may face the prospect of statutory actions regardless of blame, fault, or causation. Liability often attaches solely based on the holding of bare legal title or as a result of a party's holding a non-fee interest in property, such as tenancy, which has some of the characteristics of ownership.

A party that falls within a statutorily designated class of "liable" parties generally cannot invoke traditional tort or contract defenses such as unclean hands, laches, lack of proximate cause, causation by third parties, de minimis involvement, adherence to prevailing standards of care, or compliance with government regulations. Not even the specific assent or direction of governmental entities to practices carried out on the affected property will provide a defense. The government can impose extraordinarily stringent cleanup standards irrespective of necessity or justification. Enforcement authorities generally will give no consideration to the possible inequity of holding a particular party liable or to the fact that the events leading to an environmental problem occurred many years ago. Once liability attaches, it can be virtually limitless.

While liability is sometimes avoidable, its breadth and scope under the environmental laws mandate that parties to real estate transactions exercise substantial scrutiny. This chapter provides a general overview of several sources of liability under federal environmental statutes. Subsequent chapters address these sources individually and in more detail.

Liability Arising from Ownership or Leasing of Real Estate

Two federal statutes create the greatest potential liability in connection with real estate transactions: the Comprehensive Environmental Response, Compensation, and Liability Act of 1980 (CERCLA or Superfund), as amended by the Superfund Amendments and Reauthorization Act of 1986 (SARA),[1] and the Resource Conservation and Recovery Act of 1976 (RCRA), as amended by the Hazardous and Solid Waste Amendments of 1984 (HSWA).[2] Each of these statutes creates liability in a slightly different manner, but all relate to the cleanup of hazardous waste already released into the environment. In situations of environmental contamination that have not been addressed by Congress in a specific environmental statute, common-law liability for environmental contamination of property may arise. (See Chapter 2.)

The Comprehensive Environmental Response, Compensation, and Liability Act

CERCLA is perhaps the best known and most widely feared environmental statute from the perspective of real estate professionals. The statute is notorious because it can be used to impose prohibitively expensive cleanup liability on unsuspecting purchasers, tenants, and lenders but provides these parties with few defenses. Largely because of the threat of CERCLA liability, most real estate transactions today incorporate a process of environmental due diligence aimed at averting the acquisition of contaminated properties. Parties to most real estate transactions also attempt to allocate liability contractually and provide for indemnifications in the event that contaminated property is acquired.

In response to public outcry over environmental catastrophes at Love Canal and Times Beach,[3] Congress passed CERCLA in the last month of the Carter administration. The statute was signed into law on December 11, 1980. CERCLA is popularly known by the same name as the $8.5 billion federal fund it created, the Superfund,[4] which is derived from industrial taxes, Congressional appropriations, and recovered cleanup costs and penalties. The Superfund was originally intended to be a revolving fund used for the cleanup of hazardous waste sites. The statute created a program to identify sites where hazardous substances had been released into the environment or where such releases appeared imminent and to respond to those releases or threatened releases. As the regulated public has learned, however, CERCLA is anything but a public works project. On the contrary, the statute has been used to compel private parties to remediate contaminated sites, to recover from those parties "response costs" incurred by the government in responding to a release of hazardous substances, and to assess and recover damages to natural resources caused by such a release.

CERCLA authorizes the U.S. Environmental Protection Agency (EPA) to respond to releases or threatened releases in two ways. First, the agency may conduct short-term "removal actions," involving, for example, the removal of drums or soil, securing of the site, installation of water lines, or building of dikes to prevent contaminants from escaping.[5] Second, the EPA may conduct longer term and more expensive "remedial actions," such as the installation of an underground slurry wall to cut off groundwater flow to or from the contaminated area, pumping and treating of groundwater, or placement of an engineered clay cap over the contaminated surface to prevent rain water from washing contaminants into groundwater.[6] In addition to CERCLA's statutory provisions, the National Contingency Plan (NCP)[7] sets forth procedures for discovering sites, ranking them on the National Priorities List (NPL),[8] and selecting and implementing remedial actions.

Scope of CERCLA Liability

CERCLA's underlying policy is to shift away from taxpayers the ultimate responsibility for cleaning up hazardous substances. The statute establishes four categories of "potentially responsible parties" (PRPs) on whom liability may be imposed.

- The current owners and operators of a facility where hazardous substances were released or are in danger of being released
- The owners or operators of a facility at the time hazardous substances were disposed of at the facility (commonly referred to as "generators")

- Persons or entities who arranged for the treatment or disposal of hazardous substances at the facility
- Persons or entities that transported the hazardous substances to the facility[9]

Any person or entity that falls into one or more of these categories is liable for responding to a release of "hazardous substances." CERCLA's definition of hazardous substances is quite broad. It includes substances typically found in industrial and manufacturing settings as well as more common substances such as paint, batteries, solvents, drain cleaners, and photographic chemicals.[10]

The EPA may issue administrative orders directing PRPs to clean up sites under Section 106 of CERCLA, or it may perform the response actions itself and recover the cleanup costs from PRPs under Section 107. Much of the EPA's authority has been delegated to state governments.[11] CERCLA further authorizes private parties to recover response costs from PRPs. This authorization extends to PRPs themselves, who may sue other PRPs for response costs under Section 107(a)(4)(B) or for contribution under Section 113.[12]

Liability of Owners, Operators, and Generators

CERCLA defines an "owner or operator" as the "person" owning or operating a facility or, if the facility has been abandoned, as a "person who owned, operated, or otherwise controlled activities at such facility immediately prior to such abandonment."[13] This rather circular definition has been interpreted by the EPA and the courts in such a way that current owners may be found liable even though no hazardous substances were disposed of during their ownership.[14] A person may also be held liable as an "owner" if that person held title for as little as one hour.[15] Moreover, a person holding equitable title to property may be deemed an owner.[16] Thus, it would seem that anyone signing an agreement to purchase property may be subject to CERCLA liability upon signing. Courts have also ruled that lessees fall within the statutory definition of owner.[17] In addition, officers and employees of companies operating a facility may be treated as owners or operators and, in some cases, held personally liable even when they were performing the work of their employer.[18]

The definition of "facility" also is very broad, covering any location "where a hazardous substance has been deposited, stored, disposed of, or placed, or otherwise come to be located."[19] The term clearly is not limited to sites that might commonly be thought of as dump sites. Indeed, CERCLA liability has been extended to such "facilities" as roads or dragstrips on which hazardous substances were sprayed,[20] residential developments,[21] and even individual homes to which hazardous substances had been transported on the clothing of factory workers.[22]

CERCLA's Strict, Joint, and Several Liability Scheme

Courts have uniformly held that CERCLA imposes strict liability,[23] irrespective of fault. Under the existing precedent, a CERCLA plaintiff has a relatively light burden of proof. Plaintiffs in a CERCLA suit (e.g., the EPA, state regulatory agencies, and other PRPs) need not prove that a release of a particular defendant's hazardous substance caused the incurrence of response costs[24] but only that the defendant disposed of the same type of hazardous substances as those found on the site. Moreover, the plaintiff does not have to prove that a particular defendant's waste was present at the site and had been the subject of removal or remedial measures or that the defendant selected the site at which the hazardous waste was dumped. Nor does the plaintiff have to prove that the release was of the same substance or even of the same type of substance as that disposed of by the defendant.[25] As a result, the courts have tended to impose liability on CERCLA defendants that fit into one of the PRP classes and cannot raise one of the limited defenses set forth in CERCLA.[26]

CERCLA liability is also retroactive.[27] Entities that disposed of hazardous substances or owned contaminated property before the statute's enactment have been held liable for the resulting response costs.

The courts have also held that CERCLA liability is joint and several where the harm is indivisible.[28] Thus, each PRP at a Superfund site is subject to being held liable for the entire cleanup cost if it is not possible to apportion the responsibility for the harm accurately. Originally, CERCLA did not provide for contribution among responsible parties held jointly and severally liable, but the courts inferred that the right of contribution was intended by the statute's overall scheme or by federal common law.[29] SARA codified the statutory right of contribution among responsible parties,[30] which was consistent with SARA's overall goal to "encourage quicker, more equitable settlements, decrease litigation, and thus facilitate cleanups."[31] The ability to sue for contribution under CERCLA facilitates settlement between the EPA and PRPs by allowing PRPs to pursue contribution against other PRPs.

Allocation of Responsibility to Landowners

As the preceding discussion illustrates, the wide net cast by CERCLA can snare a large number of PRPs at a given site. These are usually past and present owners and operators and, in some cases, large numbers of "generator" PRPs. In the EPA's view, each of these parties is just as strictly, jointly, and severally liable as any other. In practice, however, liability is rarely shared equally among the PRPs.

In most cases involving a Superfund site, the PRPs form a steering committee or trust group that negotiates with the EPA, administers the cleanup and, perhaps most critically, negotiates the allocation of liability among the PRPs. It is through the steering committee (or, in some cases, through dueling steering committees or subcommittees representing distinct interests) that allocation disputes are usually resolved, allowing cleanup or reimbursement settlements with the EPA to proceed.

When information on volume is available, liability among generator PRPs is most commonly allocated on a volumetric basis. When "waste-in" information does not exist, parties either (1) reconstruct volume figures by examining various factors, such as production or number of employees, or (2) allocate liability on a tiered basis or some other basis. Even when volumetric information does exist, parties with large volumes may seek adjustments based on cost or the toxicity or mobility of different waste streams.

Allocation among owners and operators on the one hand and generators on the other hand can be much more difficult. Each group obviously seeks to impose a larger share of costs on the other group. In any case, negotiations often deteriorate. As a result, case law has begun to address the allocation of cleanup costs among PRPs through contribution claims filed by PRPs against one another. The courts have found apportionment to be difficult, particularly at a site where hazardous substances have been present for an extended period and where the substances possess diverse characteristics. Some courts have placed on the defendant the burden of proving that there is a reasonable basis for apportionment.[32]

ALLOCATION AMONG SUCCESSIVE OWNERS OR OPERATORS. In *BCW Associates Ltd. v. Occidental Chemical Corp.*,[33] the U.S. District Court for the District of Pennsylvania apportioned cleanup costs equally among a prior owner/operator, a current owner, and a current operator. The current owner was allocated a one-third share of the costs primarily because the owner purchased the site "as is" (contaminated with lead dust) and received substantial collateral benefits from the cleanup. The prior owner, who actually caused the contamination, was allocated one-third of the costs, and the current occupant-lessee also was allocated a one-third share because it also received a financial benefit from the cleanup.

Similarly, in *In re Sterling Treating, Inc.*,[34] the U.S. Bankruptcy Court for Michigan allocated response costs equally between the bankruptcy estate and the purchaser of the debtor's property. The property was auctioned "as is," along with a trailer containing hazardous wastes. Neither the bankruptcy trustee nor the purchaser was aware of the trailer's contents, but the court held the purchaser liable for two reasons: (1) the purchaser was familiar with the debtor's operations and therefore should have suspected that hazardous wastes may have been present on the site and (2) the purchaser failed to inspect the property before purchase. Thus, in the contribution context, when a property buyer will benefit from a cleanup, courts are likely to impose substantial cleanup costs on the buyer who fails to conduct an adequate prepurchase investigation of the property.

ALLOCATION AMONG LANDOWNERS AND TENANTS. In *South Florida Water Management District v. Montalvo*, the U.S. District Court for the Southern District of Florida allocated 25 percent of cleanup costs to an owner and 75 percent to a tenant who was responsible for the disposal of hazardous substances on the leased property.[35] Toxic pesticides used in the tenant's business contaminated the land. Even though the landowner was not the source of the contamination, the court held that the landowner and tenant were jointly and severally liable.

The Florida court considered several factors.[36] For example, the court noted that the tenant used state-of-the-art techniques to minimize contamination and that it clearly profited from the pesticide operation. With respect to the landowner, the court focused on the fact that the land was purchased with full knowledge that a pesticide operation was on it and that the landowner understood the risks associated with the operation. Further, the landowner was intimately familiar with the tenant's operation and knew of the applicable environmental laws and regulations pertaining to pesticides. Moreover, the landowner purchased the property without conducting a survey or inspection. The court also considered the fact that the landowner did not have an interest in the tenant's business (other than collecting rent) and the landowner did not pay less for the land because of the contamination. Therefore, the court concluded that the landowner did not financially benefit from buying contaminated land.

The court in *South Florida* held that "[e]quity demands that the [tenant] pay the lion's share of any costs finally incurred. Equity equally demands that [the landowner] share in the cleanup by virtue of [its] acquiescence in [the tenant's] activities."[37]

In *Weyerhaeuser Co. v. Koppers Co., Inc.*, the landowner was allocated 40 percent of cleanup costs and the tenant was allocated 60 percent.[38] The landowner also had leased his property to a tenant whose business was the sole source of contamination.[39] The U.S. District Court for the District of Maryland held that the tenant and landowner were jointly and severally liable. The court stated that it was "not limited to any specific equitable factors but may consider those factors relevant to the circumstances of the case."[40] Factors that could be considered included "the degree of involvement of the parties in the transportation, treatment, storage, or disposal of hazardous substances."[41] In addition, the court noted that other courts have considered

1. The ability of the parties to distinguish their contribution to the discharge, release, or disposal of hazardous waste;
2. The amount of hazardous waste involved;
3. The degree of toxicity of the hazardous waste;
4. The degree of care exercised by the parties with respect to the hazardous waste; and
5. The parties' willingness to cooperate with the government to prevent harm to the public or the environment.[42]

These factors are useful in allocating costs among defendants in the same class (such as between numerous generators at a site). On the other hand, they may not be applicable to apportioning liability among different *classes* of defendants (such as between an owner and a generator).[43]

Consequently, the *Weyerhaeuser* court stated that "more relevant to the present case are the benefits received by the parties from the contaminating activities and the knowledge and/or acquiescence of the parties in the contaminating activities."[44] The court held that the landowner was 40 percent responsible because he not only knew of and acquiesced in the tenant's wood treatment activities but actually made the continuation of those activities a condition of the lease agreement. Therefore, the landowner benefited from the tenant's activities.

In another recent case, a court allocated 50 percent of the cleanup costs to a landowner and 50 percent to a generator.[45] In *Ellman v. Woo,* the site was contaminated with perchloroethylene (PCE) from the lessee (a dry cleaner) and with petroleum hydrocarbons, the origin of which was unknown. In allocating half the cleanup costs to the landowner, the court relied primarily on the fact that the owner knew about the PCE and petroleum contamination at the time he acquired title. The court, therefore, concluded that the owner knowingly assumed the risk of environmental liability.

Corporate Liability under CERCLA

Some courts have disregarded the corporate form and imposed CERCLA liability on parent corporations, related subsidiaries, and shareholders, either directly, as owners or operators, or indirectly, by piercing the corporate veil. Successor corporations also have incurred CERCLA liability for the acts of their predecessors under the traditional common-law doctrine of successor liability.

DIRECT LIABILITY. In general, the courts have imposed direct liability only when a person's ownership, control, or ability to control could be traced through the organizational chain to the facility where hazardous substances were located.[46] For example, in *United States v. Northeastern Pharmaceutical and Chemical Co. (NEPACCO I)*,[47] the U.S. Court of Appeals for the Eighth Circuit, noting CERCLA's twin objectives of promoting timely cleanup of abandoned waste sites and ensuring that the costs are borne by the responsible parties, concluded that "owner or operator" should include anyone with the "power to direct the activities of persons who control the mechanisms controlling pollution."[48] Thus, the *NEPACCO I* court held that two officer-shareholders were liable for a contractor's improper disposal of wastes that were generated by the individual defendants' corporation. The court noted that one of the officers had approved the disposal site.

This "capacity to control" test was used by another federal district court to impose liability on a parent corporation because of the corporation's capacity to control its subsidiary's waste management practices.[49] In *Idaho v. Bunker Hill Co.*, the U.S. District Court for Idaho concluded that the parent corporation was

> intimately familiar with hazardous waste disposal and releases at the Bunker Hill facility; had the capacity to control such disposal and releases; and had the capacity, if not total reserved authority, to make decisions and implement actions and mechanisms to prevent and abate damage caused by the disposal and releases of hazardous wastes at the facility.[50]

In numerous opinions since *Bunker Hill*, federal courts have applied one of two tests to impose direct liability: (1) "actual control" or (2) "capacity," "authority," or "potential" to control. As the law in this area has begun to be settled, the two tests appear to be merging into one, with a number of courts indicating that the "actual control" standard should be construed to require general control of a subordinate entity's affairs but not proof of actual control of the entity's waste management practices. In contrast, some courts that have applied the "capacity to control" test have based their rulings on evidence of actual, pervasive control of a subordinate entity. At least one court using this test has required evidence that the liable party had the specific authority to control hazardous substances.[51]

INDIRECT LIABILITY: PIERCING THE CORPORATE VEIL. Some courts have pierced the corporate veil to hold parent corporations indirectly liable as "owners" under CERCLA for the acts of their subsidiaries.

Since a key objective of CERCLA is ensuring that response costs are borne by the parties responsible for creating the hazards, several courts have stressed the importance of a parent's control, or capacity to control, a polluting subsidiary.[52] To evaluate the extent of a parent's control, courts have looked at many of the same factors used in holding CERCLA defendants constructively liable as "operators."[53]

In one of the earliest CERCLA cases to address the issue of piercing the corporate veil, *In re Acushnet River & New Bedford Harbor Proceedings Re Alleged PCB Pollution*,[54] the court rejected the government's argument that there must be "an extremely low threshold" for piercing the veil.[55] Instead, the court considered the following traditional factors in light of the statutory purposes of CERCLA, "[i]n approximate descending order of importance":

1. Inadequate capitalization in light of the purposes for which the corporation was organized;
2. Extensive or pervasive control by the shareholder or shareholders;
3. Intermingling of the corporation's properties or accounts with those of the owner;
4. Failure to observe corporate formalities and separateness;
5. Siphoning of funds from the corporation;
6. Absence of corporate records; and
7. Nonfunctioning officers or directors.[56]

The *Acushnet* factors were consider by the U.S. Bankruptcy Court for the Southern District of New York, which—having ruled that a parent corporation was liable as a "generator" and a "transporter" of hazardous substances because it controlled its wholly owned subsidiary—noted in dictum that the parent would also be liable under veil-piercing standards.[57] The court noted that veil piercing was appropriate based on the following facts: the parent's involvement in and control over the subsidiary was pervasive; the parent was aware of its subsidiary's waste dumping activities; the subsidiary's board of directors, which was composed of the parent's officers and directors, never met; the subsidiary's customers occasionally communicated directly with the parent; the parent paid the salary of the subsidiary's president; the parent contributed over $3 million to the subsidiary's operations; and the parent's approval was required for all the subsidiary's major financial undertakings.[58]

In *Joslyn Manufacturing Co. v. T.L. James & Co.*,[59] the U.S. Court of Appeals for the Fifth Circuit rejected the argument that corporate officers or parent corporations could be held liable solely on the basis of language in environmental statutes. Emphasizing the importance of the policies underlying the corporate form, the court found no "express congressional directive" in CERCLA to ignore that form. Thus, the court applied a traditional veil-piercing analysis and found that the subsidiary and parent were distinct entities in substance as well as form and there was no justification for piercing the corporate veil to impose liability on the parent.[60]

The *Joslyn* court stated that "veil-piercing should be limited to situations in which the corporate entity is used as a *sham* to perpetrate a fraud or avoid personal liability."[61] This approach is in direct contrast to *United States v. Mottolo*,[62] in which the U.S. District Court for New Hampshire held that CERCLA "places no importance on the corporate form" and refused to acknowledge the application in the CERCLA context of "the more rigorous standard imposed by common law alter ego doctrine."[63] Accordingly, parent corporations whose subsidiaries are involved in CERCLA enforcement actions, anywhere other than possibly the Fifth Circuit, should recognize that courts may disregard the corporate form more readily than traditional notions of corporate law dictate.

LIABILITY OF SUCCESSOR CORPORATIONS. CERCLA does not expressly state whether or under what circumstances a company that merges with, acquires, or purchases some or all of the assets of another company succeeds to the liabilities of the predecessor company. Thus, a majority of courts have applied the common-law doctrine of successor liability in the CERCLA context. For example, in *Smith Land & Improvement Corp. v. Celotex Corp.*,[64] the U.S. Court of Appeals for the Third Circuit, after examining CERCLA's legislative history and purpose, held that "congressional intent supports the conclusion that, when choosing between the taxpayers or a successor corporation, the successor should bear the cost [of cleanup]." The court further explained that

> In resolving the successor liability issues here, the district court must consider national uniformity; otherwise, CERCLA aims may be evaded easily by a responsible party's choice to arrange a merger or consolidation under the laws of particular states which unduly restrict successor liability. The general doctrine of successor liability in operation in most states should guide the court's decision rather than the excessively narrow statutes which might apply in only a few states.[65]

While the law since *Smith Land* makes clear that successor liability will be imposed under CERCLA, it is not clear whether federal courts will apply the law of successor corporations of the state in which they sit or whether the courts will apply a federal common law as called for by the Fifth Circuit.[66] Some courts have applied state law, while other courts have opted for application of a federal common law, reasoning that hazardous waste disposal is a nationwide problem that calls for a uniform national solution.[67]

Liability of Lenders

Financial institutions that lend money to companies that own or operate property contaminated with hazardous substances have long relied on the so-called "secured creditor" or "security interest" exemption to shield them from liability under CERCLA.[68] The secured creditor exemption excludes from the definition of "owner or operator" any person "who, without participating in the management of a . . . facility, holds indicia of ownership primarily to protect his security interest in the . . . facility."[69]

Court decisions establishing lender liability under CERCLA fall into two main categories: (1) those in which the lenders foreclose on a mortgage and take legal title to a property and (2) those in which the lenders exercise control over the property or the operations of the borrower. A 1990 decision of the Court of Appeals for the Eleventh Circuit caused great alarm in the lending community when it greatly increased the potential exposure of lenders by narrowing the scope of CERCLA's secured creditor exemption.[70] The EPA responded by issuing a rule intended to narrow the scope of a lender's liability, but the D.C. circuit reversed that rule as *ultra vires*. (For a complete discussion of these issues, see Chapter 4.)

Costs for Which the Landowner or Purchaser Is Liable

CERCLA provides for recovery of removal or remedial action costs incurred by the United States or the individual states[71] or of necessary response costs incurred by any other person.[72] Response costs incurred by the federal or state government must be "not inconsistent with the National Contingency Plan."[73] Response costs incurred by any other person must be "consistent with the National Contingency Plan."[74] This small difference in wording has been construed to mean that in government enforcement cases the burden of proof is on the defendants, who are attempting to prevent the government from recovering cleanup costs, to show that specific costs are not consistent with the plan. In contrast, in litigation between private parties plaintiffs attempting to recover cleanup costs bear the burden of proving that the costs they incurred are consistent with the plan.[75]

Various courts have held that the term "response costs" includes the costs of removal, remedial action, monitoring, testing, site investigation, medical evaluations, relocation, provision of alternative water supplies, and interest. Cleanup costs also include government oversight costs.[76] In *United States v. Rohm and Haas Co.*,[77] however, the

Third Circuit held that the EPA is not entitled to recover costs associated with overseeing cleanup activities conducted and paid for by private parties.

The *Rohm and Haas* court determined that CERCLA allows the EPA to recover costs associated with removal actions, which the court defined to include "direct actions by the government to investigate, evaluate, or monitor a release, threat of release, or a danger posed by such a problem."[78] In addition, removal actions include activities "intended to enable EPA to formulate a position on what would be the most appropriate response action at a given facility."[79] The court found that Congress did not intend to include oversight costs within the definition of removal.[80] Thus, "if what the government is monitoring is not the release or hazard itself, but rather the performance of a private party, the costs involved are nonrecoverable oversight costs."[81] Costs that are not recoverable include "the costs of contractors hired by EPA to review the plans and work of a private party or its agents executing a response action."[82]

The circuits are split on whether response costs include attorney's fees.[83] Moreover, in addition to response costs, PRPs are also liable for natural resource damages of up to $50 million.[84] Under certain circumstances this monetary cap does not apply,[85] and the PRP may be liable for the full amount of the natural resource damages.

Defenses to CERCLA Liability

Parties to CERCLA lawsuits have attempted to employ a variety of defenses. Almost invariably those efforts have failed. For example, although some courts have allowed equitable defenses, such as unclean hands, in CERCLA actions,[86] others have rejected such defenses as being contrary to congressional intent.[87] In particular, courts have rejected the caveat emptor defense under CERCLA.[88]

CERCLA explicitly provides for three statutory defenses: an act of God, an act of war, or an act or omission of a third party.[89] Of these, the third-party defense has been the most widely litigated.

To establish that the contamination was caused solely by a third party, all three elements of CERCLA Section 107(b)(3) must be met: (1) no direct or indirect relationship, contractual or otherwise, exists between the defendant/landowner and the third party who (allegedly) caused the contamination; (2) upon discovery of hazardous substances, the landowner must have exercised due care; and (3) the landowner must establish that he or she took precautions against the acts or omissions of the third party.[90] SARA defined the term "contractual relationship" as including "land contracts, deeds, or other instruments transferring title or possession," unless certain narrow showings can be made.[91] Thus, the property owner may not assert the third-party defense based on the actions of a prior landowner unless certain limited conditions are satisfied. These conditions have come to be known as the "innocent purchaser" or "innocent landowner"[92] defense of CERCLA.

THE INNOCENT LANDOWNER DEFENSE. Under CERCLA's innocent landowner provisions, a defendant may avoid liability only if he or she is able to show that the property was acquired after hazardous substances were disposed on it and either (1) the defendant did not know or have reason to know of the hazard when the land was acquired; (2) the defendant is a government body that acquired the property by escheat, any involuntary transfer, or through exercise of eminent domain; or (3) the property was inherited.[93] Thus, in most cases, defendants have the burden of proving that they did not know and had no reason to know of the contamination.

The statute sets forth the criteria for establishing that the defendant had no reason to know of the contamination.[94] CERCLA indicates that the defendant must have undertaken, at the time of acquisition, "all appropriate inquiry" into the previous ownership, consistent with good commercial practice.[95] This translates into a requirement for some type of preacquisition property audit or survey to identify potential environmental hazards.[96] CERCLA left to the courts the task of determining whether a purchaser claiming to be an innocent landowner under CERCLA has made all appropriate inquiry. To date, however, the courts have not articulated a standard, nor has the EPA issued any guidance, that meaningfully deals with what constitutes an "appropriate inquiry" under CERCLA.[97] Factors that have been considered by the courts include: special knowledge on the part of the buyer; whether the purchase price was related to the existence of contamination on the property; the level of diligence of the purchaser's inquiry; and the ease with which the contamination could have been detected. To provide some assistance to real estate buyers and sellers, the American Society for Testing and Materials (ASTM) has released two standards for conducting environmental assessments,[98] both of which are intended to satisfy the "all appropriate inquiry" required under CERCLA. (For a more complete discussion of the ASTM standards, see Chapter 8.)

The EPA has published a policy for taking action against residential property owners.[99] The agency states that it will refrain from taking action against a home owner on property subject to CERCLA cleanup unless the home owner (1) acts in a way leading to a release or threat of release of hazardous substances resulting in the taking of a response action; (2) fails to cooperate with the EPA's response actions; or (3) uses the residential property in a manner inconsistent with residential use or the development of residential property leads to a release.[100] The policy points out, however, that the policy is not law and does not provide an exemption from CERCLA liability.[101]

DE MINIMIS SETTLEMENTS UNDER CERCLA. Purchasers who may not be able to avail themselves of the absolute defense under CERCLA Section 101(35) may nevertheless be able to minimize their liability by being characterized as de minimis parties. SARA added to CERCLA a provision allowing de minimis settlements.[102] Under the provision, the EPA may settle with a PRP if "the settlement involves only a minor portion of the response costs at the facility concerned" and the PRP falls into one of two categories:[103] (1) PRPs for whom the amounts or toxic effects of their contribution of hazardous substances to the site are minimal in comparison to other hazardous substances at the site;[104] and (2) owners of the real property on which the facility is located who did "not conduct or permit the generation, transportation, storage, treatment, or disposal of any hazardous substance at the facility, and did not contribute to the release or threat of release of a hazardous substance at the facility.[105] In addition, the property owner must establish that he or she purchased the property without actual or constructive knowledge of the presence of hazardous substances.[106]

In implementing this settlement provision, the EPA has often required landowners to meet the due diligence requirements of the innocent landowner defense under CERCLA Section 107(b)(3).[107] Typically, the landowner has the burden of demonstrating the following: the condition of the property at the time of purchase; documentation of and representations at time of purchase regarding prior use of the property; the purchase price; the fair market value of comparable property; and any relevant information regarding specialized knowledge of the landowner. Nonetheless, CERCLA Section 122(g)(1)(B) offers landowners an opportunity to settle with the EPA early in the controversy and to avoid litigation over the availability of the defense, often in exchange for access to the site, cooperation with the EPA, or a cash payment.

Resource Conservation and Recovery Act

RCRA was enacted in 1976 as an amendment to the Solid Waste Disposal Act.[108] As originally enacted, RCRA and CERCLA served two separate and distinct purposes. CERCLA was backward-looking—it was a nonregulatory statute enacted to address lingering problems with former disposal sites and to impose liability for the cost of those cleanups. By contrast, the original RCRA was forward-looking—it was intended to provide a comprehensive regulatory program for the active management of hazardous wastes from the point of generation to ultimate disposal (cradle to grave). Thus, RCRA was of lesser significance for real estate professionals and lenders, except on properties where active hazardous waste facilities were located. The Hazardous and Solid Waste Amendments of 1984, however, served to blur the distinction between CERCLA and RCRA by adding to RCRA enhanced provisions for requiring the cleanup of former hazardous waste sites.[109] In addition, the 1984 amendments added a new federal program for the regulation of underground storage tanks (USTs). These amendments thus made RCRA more important for real estate professionals and lenders.

Currently, RCRA prohibits open dumping; encourages recycling and treatment of hazardous wastes; establishes standards for hazardous waste management; regulates cleanup of active facilities; restricts land disposal of hazardous wastes; provides technical requirements for disposal facilities; controls use of USTs; and establishes hazardous waste permit review procedures for storage, treatment, or disposal facilities. RCRA regulations prescribe detailed requirements for anyone who generates, transports, treats, stores, or disposes of hazardous wastes.[110] Disposal is defined as the discharge, deposit, injection, dumping, spilling, leaking, or placing of any solid or hazardous waste on the land or water in such a way that the waste enters the environment.[111]

The two types of RCRA regulation of greatest significance to real estate professionals are the regulations governing hazardous waste and USTs. RCRA hazardous waste regulation, in turn, generally takes one of two forms: regulation of the generators of hazardous waste; and regulation of the owners and operators of facilities for the treatment, storage, or disposal of hazardous waste. This chapter, which focuses on the liabilities associated with real estate ownership and operation, emphasizes the regulation of the owners or operators of hazardous waste facilities.

RCRA imposes two basic types of liabilities on violators: civil penalties generally amounting to $25,000 per day, with criminal penalties available under certain circumstances; and certain obligations to perform or finance "corrective actions" or cleanups or to remedy imminent and substantial endangerments to health or the environment.[112] Thus, unwary purchasers, occupiers, or financiers of real estate may find themselves liable for penalties, cleanup costs, or both.

Landowner Liability for Disposal of Hazardous Substances

RCRA liability has been imposed on landowners for hazardous waste dumped on the property before their ownership. For example, in *United States v. Price*,[113] the United States sought injunctive relief against current and past owners of property on which the past owners had operated a landfill for hazardous chemicals. The government sought to force the landowners to fund an investigation of groundwater contamination attributable to the landfill. Both the past and current landowners denied RCRA liability, arguing that RCRA was designed to prevent future dumping, not to remedy the effects of past waste disposal practices.[114] The court held, however, that the term "disposal" encompassed the leaking of hazardous wastes into the groundwater; therefore, the government was authorized to bring suits under RCRA to prevent continued harm to the environment.

The previous landowners further argued that they were no longer contributing to the disposal of hazardous wastes at the site, but the court rejected this argument, holding them liable because they failed to store chemical wastes properly and to rectify a hazardous condition. Simply put, the court would not allow the previous owners to avoid liability under RCRA simply by selling their property.[115]

The current owners argued that the disposal of hazardous wastes occurred before their ownership and therefore they had not contributed in any way to the disposal of hazardous wastes. The current owners knew the property had been used as a landfill but failed to investigate, before purchase, whether the landfill had been properly closed. At no time did the current owners "actively dispos[e] of any wastes at the landfill or actively contribut[e] to the migration of contaminants from the site."[116] Nonetheless, the court found that the current owners had contributed "merely by virtue of their studied indifference to the hazardous condition" that existed.[117] The court held them liable under RCRA for their failure "to stop the continued leaking of contamination from the site."[118] Thus, the court imposed an affirmative duty on purchasers either to investigate the property before purchase or to accept the property as is, complete with cleanup responsibilities.[119]

In *United States v. Waste Industries*,[120] the U.S. Court of Appeals for the Fourth Circuit followed the reasoning of *Price* and held that disposal under RCRA did not require an affirmative act. Reversing a lower court's decision that disposal under RCRA required "active human conduct," the Fourth Circuit stated that such "a strained reading of that term [disposal] limiting its Section 7003 meaning to active conduct would so frustrate the remedial purpose of the Act as to make it meaningless."[121] Thus, the current owners of the site were liable for its cleanup even though they did not actively dispose of hazardous wastes.[122]

Landowner Liability for Underground Storage Tanks

RCRA is also important to real estate professionals because of its Subtitle I, enacted as part of the 1984 amendments, regulating USTs.[123]

Congress enacted Subtitle I to address the problem of groundwater contamination by leaking USTs.[124] RCRA establishes eight categories of federal standards that apply to "owners" and "operators" of USTs: (1) notification of tank existence; (2) leak detection; (3) records maintenance; (4) release reporting; (5) corrective action; (6) tank closure; (7) financial responsibility; and (8) performance standards for new tanks. (For a complete discussion of potential liability with regard to USTs, see Chapter 18.)

Liability Arising from the Buying or Selling of Real Estate

In addition to ownership and operation of property, real estate transactions are another potential source of environmental liability. Transaction-related liabilities generally relate to disclosure of environmental issues in the course of transferring property. While most disclosure requirements exist under state law, some liability may attach under CERCLA.

Disclosure of Known Releases or Threatened Releases on Property

A general discussion of the common-law or statutory disclosure requirements attendant on the sale of real estate is beyond the scope of this chapter. Nonetheless, there is one specific provision of CERCLA that arguably creates a new kind of liability for nondisclosure of environmental information.

As previously discussed, the four categories of PRPS under CERCLA include current landowners or operators and owners or operators at the time of disposal. Noticeably absent from this list, however, are "interim landowners." These are landowners who first held title after any disposal took place and who transferred title to another party before any EPA proceeding was commenced. By the terms of Section 107(a), absent some continuing act of disposal, such parties do not appear to be liable.

As part of SARA's innocent landowner provision, however, Congress included a curious provision that raises new questions about the liability of interim landowners. In Section 101(35)(C), Congress provided as follows:

> Notwithstanding this paragraph, if the defendant obtained actual knowledge of the release or threatened release of a hazardous substance at such facility when the defendant owned the real property and then subsequently transferred ownership of the

> property to another person without disclosing such knowledge, such defendant *shall be treated as liable under section 9607(a)(1)* of this title and no defense under section 9607(b)(3) of this title shall be available to such defendant.[125]

This provision appears within the innocent landowner provision, and it therefore would seem likely that the provision would only apply to parties already liable under Section 107(a). Nonetheless, it might be argued that the provision's mandatory language[126] modifies Section 107(a), thereby creating a new, fifth type of PRP: an interim landowner who transfers ownership without disclosing any of its knowledge regarding hazardous waste on its property. Whether Congress actually intended to create such a fifth category remains an issue for the courts or Congress to clarify.

In addition to this CERCLA provision, various states have enacted disclosure, assessment, and remediation requirements triggered by sale of property or, in some cases, by transfer of an ownership interest in the parties who own property. The most well known of these state statutes is New Jersey's Environmental Cleanup Responsibility Act (ECRA), now called the Industrial Site Recovery Act (ISRA). (These statutes are discussed in greater detail in Chapter 3.)

Sale of Real Estate as Arranging for Disposal under CERCLA

CERCLA holds liable persons "who by contract or otherwise" arrange for the disposal of hazardous substances.[127] Normally, such persons are hazardous substance generators. Generator liability has dominated CERCLA litigation. The courts have found a surprising array of parties liable as "generators," including companies that sold hazardous materials for profit,[128] entities that brokered waste deliveries,[129] organizations that had their pesticides processed by a third party,[130] and companies that arranged for materials to be disposed of at a site different from the one at which the material was actually disposed.[131]

A property seller may be found to be one who has "arranged for disposal" of a hazardous substance under CERCLA. For example, in *Sanford St. Local Development Corp. v. Textron*,[132] the District Court for the District of New Hampshire held that the sale of property with electrical transformers containing polychlorinated biphenyls (PCBs) at a discounted rate was "arranging for disposal" of a hazardous substance within the meaning of CERCLA. The defendant sold a foundry at a price substantially below fair market value. During the buyer's ownership, the electrical system was disconnected and the PCB transformers were determined to be intact and leak-free by state environmental officials. The property was subsequently sold to a second and then a third buyer. The third buyer conducted a postsale inspection and found PCB-containing oils on the floor surrounding the transformers. The buyer sued the original seller to recover cleanup costs, arguing that the defendant had arranged for the disposal of the transformers when it sold the property.

The court found that the discounted price of the property demonstrated that the defendant believed that the property was not marketable because of the PCB transformers. Thus, the court concluded that the sale was an arrangement for disposal of a hazardous substance. In *CP Holdings v. Goldberg-Zoino Associates*, the court held that the sale of a building with asbestos-containing materials was "arranging for disposal" of a hazardous substance under CERCLA because the seller was aware that the buyer intended to demolish the building.[133]

Conclusion

Federal environmental statutes, particularly CERCLA and RCRA, cast a wide net of potential liability for parties involved in real estate transactions. To minimize liability associated with real estate conveyance and ownership, some important questions should be asked before taking title to property.

- Are there hazardous substances on the property?
- Does the property's history indicate that hazardous substances were sent off the site for storage, treatment, disposal, or recycling?
- What environmental permits regulate activities on the property? Are the permits transferable? What permits are required for the buyer's operations?
- Has soil, groundwater, surface water, or air at the site been tested?
- Is the property identified by the EPA or a state in CERCLIS or another database as a potential problem or Superfund site?
- What role is the lender planning to assume in the management and control of the property?
- Is the property involved in any type of enforcement action, litigation, or regulatory directive?
- Are USTs present on the property?
- Have any liens been imposed on the property as a result of an environmental activity?
- Are there any state or federal prerequisites to conveyance?

In addition, several activities should be conducted before the transaction is finalized. A buyer may avoid CERCLA liability under the innocent landowner defense only if, at the time of acquisition, "all appropriate inquiry" was undertaken. Thus, a due diligence investigation should be conducted in connection with all real estate transactions. A Phase I investigation may include review of title documents, corporate records, government records, and other sources of information as well as a site visit. In some transactions a more extensive Phase II assessment may be necessary, involving sampling and investigation to address specific concerns identified in Phase I. (Chapter 9 discusses how to choose an environmental consultant to assist with these prepurchase activities.)

Finally, environmental liability may also be minimized by allocating responsibility for hazardous materials contamination in the terms, indemnities, and warranties in the purchase contract. (Chapter 11 discusses strategies for structuring the real estate transaction.)

Notes

1. 42 U.S.C. § 9601 *et seq.*

2. 42 U.S.C. § 6901 *et seq.* Regulation of wetlands under the Clean Water Act also creates potential liability in connection with real estate transactions. Wetlands issues are discussed in Chapter 27. Storm water regulations are discussed in Chapter 29.

3. Love Canal was part of a proposed hydroelectric power canal bypassing Niagara Falls that had been excavated in the 1890s but was never completed. The Occidental Chemical Corporation had used the old canal bed for the disposal of chemicals. In the 1970s chemicals were found to be leaking from the canal bed.

4. When enacted, CERCLA created a $1.6 billion fund. With the passage of SARA, this fund was increased to $8.5 billion.

5. CERCLA § 101(23), 42 U.S.C. § 9601(23).

6. CERCLA § 101(24), 42 U.S.C. § 9601(24).

7. 40 C.F.R. § 300.2.

8. The NPL is the list of sites where the EPA may use Superfund money for remedial actions. The EPA is authorized to use Superfund money for remedial actions at sites listed on the NPL and for removal actions at any sites. There are now over 1,200 sites listed on the NPL.

9. CERCLA § 107, 42 U.S.C. § 9607.

10. CERCLA does exclude certain substances, including petroleum, natural gas, natural gas liquids, liquefied natural gas, and synthetic gas usable for fuel. CERCLA § 101(14), 42 U.S.C. § 9601(14).

11. CERCLA §§ 104–06, 42 U.S.C. §§ 9604–06.

12. The distinction between a private party action under Section 107(a)(4)(B) and a contribution action is elusive. *See, e.g.,* Barnhizer, *Joint and Several Liability and Contribution under CERCLA,* 18 Harv. Envtl. L. Rev. 563 (1994).

13. CERCLA § 101(2)(A)(iii), 42 U.S.C. § 9601(20)(A)(iii).

14. United States v. Tyson, 25 Env't Rep. Cas. (BNA) 1897 (E.D. Pa. 1986).

15. United States v. Carolawn, 21 Env't Rep. Cas. (BNA) 2124 (D.S.C. 1984) (court noted that possession of title is not necessarily dispositive with respect to questions of ownership or control). *But see* Robertshaw Controls Co. v. Watts Regulator Co., 807 F. Supp. 144 (D. Me. 1992) (individuals holding title for only one day merely as conduit for passage of title during sale of facility are not liable as "owners").

16. *See, e.g.*, United States v. Wedzeb Enterprises, Inc., No. IP 90-1877C (S.D. Ind. Dec. 9, 1992) (individual holding equitable title under state law while purchase pending is held liable as "owner," despite fact that he paid only 8 percent of purchase price and deed remained in escrow).

17. *See, e.g.*, United States v. South Carolina Recycling & Disposal, Inc., 653 F. Supp. 984, 1003 (D.S.C. 1984) (lessee "maintained control over and responsibility for the use of the property and, essentially, stood in the shoes of the property owners. . . . Accordingly, site lessees . . . should, along with the property owners themselves, be considered 'owners'"), *aff'd in part, vacated in part*, 858 F.2d 160 (4th Cir. 1988), *cert. denied*, 490 U.S. 1106 (1989).

18. *See, e.g.*, New York v. Shore Realty Corp., 759 F.2d 1032, 1052–53 (2d Cir. 1985); Kelly v. Arco Indus., Inc., 17 Chem. Waste Lit. Rep. 114, 117–18 (W.D. Mich. 1989); State of Vermont v. Staco, Inc., 684 F. Supp. 822, 831–32 (D. Vt. 1988), *rescinded in part, vacated in part*, 1989 WL 225428 (D. Vt. 1989); United States v. Bliss, 667 F. Supp. 1298, 1306 (E.D. Mo. 1987); United States v. Mottolo, 695 F. Supp. 615, 624 (D.N.H. 1988); United States v. Medley, 25 Env't Rep. Cas. (BNA) 1314, 1317–18 (D.S.C. 1986); United States v. Conservation Chem. Co., 628 F. Supp. 391, 416–20 (W.D. Mo. 1985).

19. CERCLA § 101(9), 42 U.S.C. § 9601(9)(B). A facility includes any building, structure, installation, equipment, pipe or pipeline, well, pit, pond, lagoon, impoundment, ditch, landfill, storage container, motor vehicle, rolling stock, or aircraft, and any site where hazardous substances have been deposited, stored, disposed of, or placed at that site.

20. United States v. Bliss, 667 F. Supp. 1298, 1305 (E.D. Mo. 1987).

21. *See* Tanglewood East Homeowners v. Charles-Thomas, Inc., 849 F.2d 1568 (5th Cir. 1988).

22. State of Vermont v. Staco, Inc., 684 F. Supp. 822, 833 (D. Vt. 1988), *rescinded in part, vacated in part*, 1989 WL 225428 (D. Vt. 1989).

23. *See, e.g.*, General Electric Co. v. Litton Industries, 920 F.2d 1415 (8th Cir. 1990), *cert. denied*, 499 U.S. 937 (1991).

24. United States v. Wade, 577 F. Supp. 1326, 1331–33 (E.D. Pa. 1983).

25. *Id.* at 1332–33; United States v. Bliss, 667 F. Supp. 1298, 1309–10 (E.D. Mo. 1987).

26. *See* New York v. Shore Realty Corp., 759 F.2d 1032, 1044–45 (2d Cir. 1985); United States v. Price, 577 F. Supp. 1103, 1113–14 (D.N.J. 1983).

27. *See, e.g.*, United States v. Northeastern Pharmaceutical & Chem. Co. (NEPACCO), 579 F. Supp. 823, 844 (W.D. Mo. 1984), *aff'd in part, rev'd in part*, 810 F.2d 776 (8th Cir. 1986), *cert. denied*, 484 U.S. 848 (1987); United States v. Mottolo, 695 F. Supp. 615, 621–22 (D.N.H. 1988).

28. *See, e.g.*, United States v. Chem-Dyne Corp., 572 F. Supp. 802, 809–10 (S.D. Ohio 1983); NEPACCO, 579 F. Supp. 823, 844 (W.D. Mo. 1984); United States v. Mottolo, 695 F. Supp. 615, 629 (D.N.H. 1988).

29. *See, e.g.*, United States v. Chem-Dyne Corp., 572 F. Supp. 802, 805–08 (S.D. Ohio 1983); United States v. New Castle County, 642 F. Supp. 1258, 1269 (D. Del. 1986); United States v. Conservation Chem. Co., 619 F. Supp. 162, 228 (W.D. Mo. 1985).

30. CERCLA § 113(f)(1), 42 U.S.C. § 9613(f)(1).

31. H.R. REP. No. 253(I), 99th Cong., 2d Sess. 59, *reprinted in* 1986 U.S. CODE CONG. & AD. NEWS 4, 2835, 2841.

32. *See, e.g.*, United States v. Ottati & Goss, 630 F. Supp. 1361, 1396 (D.N.H. 1985).

33. 1988 C.W.L.R. 13,606 (E.D. Pa. Sept. 29, 1988).

34. 94 B.R. 924 (Bankr. Mich. 1989).

35. South Florida Water Management District v. Montalvo, No. 88-8038 (S.D. Fla. Feb. 15, 1989).

36. The court noted that the parties were unable to cite and the court was unable to locate any decision that allocated response costs among landowners and generators. Therefore, the court considered the allocation issue a case of first impression. *Id.* at 2.

37. *Id.* at 3–4.

38. Weyerhaeuser Co. v. Koppers Co., Inc., 771 F. Supp. 1420 (D. Md. 1991).

39. The tenant in *Weyerhaeuser* operated a wood treatment plant on the property for over thirty-three years.

40. *Weyerhaeuser*, 771 F. Supp. at 1426.

41. *Id.* (citing United States v. Monsanto Co., 858 F.2d 160 (4th Cir. 1988)). The Fourth Circuit in *Monsanto* never reached the issue of allocating costs. The court, however, stated that

> The site owners limit their joint and several liability argument to the contention that it is inequitable under the circumstances of this case, i.e., their limited degree of participation in waste disposal activities at Bluff Road. As we have stated, such equitable factors are relevant in subsequent actions for contribution.

858 F.2d at 171 n.22.

42. *Id.* (citing United States v. A & F Materials Co., Inc., 578 F. Supp. 1249, 1256 (S.D. Ill. 1984)).

43. Weyerhaeuser, 771 F. Supp. at 1426 n.9. *See also* Montalvo, No. 88-8038 (S.D. Fla. Feb. 15, 1989), at 4 n.2 (factors identified in *A & F Materials* provide little or no assistance in allocating costs between a landowner and a generator; they were clearly intended to distinguish among operators and generators).

44. 771 F. Supp. at 1426. The court relied on *Montalvo* in reaching its decision.

45. Ellman v. Woo, 1991 WL 274838 (E.D. Pa. 1991).

46. *See, e.g.*, CBS, Inc. v. Henkin, 803 F. Supp. 1426 (N.D. Ind. 1992) (minority shareholder of corporation formed for sole purpose of purchasing a subsidiary company that owned a factory did not own or operate the factory).

47. 579 F. Supp. 823 (W.D. Mo. 1984), *aff'd*, 810 F.2d 726 (8th Cir. 1986), *cert. denied*, 484 U.S. 848 (1987).

48. *Id.* (quotation marks and citations omitted).

49. Idaho v. Bunker Hill Co., 635 F. Supp. 665 (D. Id. 1986).

50. *Id.* at 672.

51. Quadion v. Mache, No. 89 C3536, 1991 LEXIS 82221, at *11 (N.D. Ill. June 11, 1991).

52. *See* United States v. Kayser-Roth Corp., 724 F. Supp. 15, 24 (D.R.I. 1989), *aff'd*, 910 F.2d 24 (1st Cir. 1990), *cert. denied*, 498 U.S. 1084 (1991). *Cf.* United States v. Nicolet, Inc., 712 F. Supp. 193, 1202 (E.D. Pa. 1989); City of New York v. Exxon Corp., 112 B.R. 540, 551 (S.D.N.Y. 1990), *aff'd in part on other grounds*, 932 F.2d 1020 (2d Cir. 1991); *In re* Acushnet River & New Bedford Harbor Proceedings Re Alleged PCB Pollution, 675 F. Supp. 22, 33 (D. Mass. 1987).

53. United States v. Kayser-Roth Corp., 724 F. Supp. 15 (D.R.I. 1989).

54. 675 F. Supp. 22, (D. Mass. 1987).

55. *Id.* at 31.

56. *Id.* at 32.

57. City of New York v. Exxon Corp., 112 B.R. 540, 541 (S.D.N.Y. 1990), *aff'd in part on other grounds*, 932 F.2d 1020 (2d Cir. 1991).

58. *Id.* at 552.

59. 696 F. Supp. 222 (W.D. La. 1988), *aff'd*, 893 F.2d 80 (5th Cir. 1990), *cert. denied*, 498 U.S. 1108 (1991).

60. *Joslyn* involved a CERCLA claim for reimbursement by a manufacturing company (Joslyn) against a former company (James Co.) that had held 60 percent of the common stock and all 200 shares of the nonvoting preferred stock of a manufacturing corporation (Lincoln) whose assets had been sold to Joslyn. Lincoln's activities had released hazardous substances at its plant.

61. *Id.* at 93 (emphasis in original).

62. 695 F. Supp. 615 (D.N.H. 1988).

63. *Id.* at 623. *See also* Mobay Corp. v. Allied Signal, Inc., 753 F. Supp. 1248 (D.N.J. 1991) (not requiring "strict veil-piercing" test).

64. 858 F.2d 86, 91 n.2 (3d Cir. 1988), *cert. denied*, 488 U.S. 1029 (1989).

65. *Id.* On the record before it, the court was unable to decide that issue so it remanded and directed the district court to consider national uniformity concerns in applying successor liability principles.

66. The EPA also has taken the position that successor corporations are liable for the acts of their predecessors. Its position was set forth in a 1984 memorandum:

> When corporate ownership is transferred from one corporation to another, the successor corporation is liable for the acts of its predecessor if the new corporation acquired ownership by merger or consolidation. If, however, the acquisition was through the sale or transfer of assets, the successor corporation is not liable unless:
>
> a) The purchasing corporation expressly or impliedly agrees to assume such obligations;
> b) The transaction amounts to a "de facto" consolidation or merger;
> c) The purchasing corporation is merely a continuation of the selling corporation; or
> d) The transaction was fraudulently entered into in order to escape liability.

> Not withstanding the above criteria, a successor corporation may be held liable for the acts of a predecessor corporation if the new corporation continues substantially the same business operations as the selling corporation.

U.S. EPA, Liability of Corporate Shareholders and Successor Corporations for Abandoned Sites under the Comprehensive Environmental Response, Compensation, and Liability Act (CERCLA) 11 (June 13, 1984).

67. For cases in which state law successor liability has been applied, *see* Levin Metals Corp. v. Parr-Richmond Terminal Co., 817 F.2d 1448 (9th Cir. 1987); Anspec Co. v. Johnson Controls, 922 F.2d 1240 (6th Cir. 1991); GNB, Inc. v. Gould, Inc., 1990 WL 207,429 (N.D. Ill. Nov. 30, 1990). For cases in which courts have applied a federal common law of successor liability, *see* Smith Land & Improvement Corp. v. Celotex Corp., 851 F.2d 86, 91 n.2 (3d Cir. 1988), *cert. denied*, 488 U.S. 1029 (1989); Louisiana Pacific Corp. v. ASARCO, Inc., 909 F.2d 1260 (9th Cir. 1990); Mobay Corp. v. Allied-Signal, Inc., 761 F. Supp. 345 (D.N.J. 1991); American National Can Co. v. Kerr Glass Mfg. Corp., 1990 WL 125,368 (N.D. Ill. Aug. 22, 1990).

68. Lenders may also face environmental liability under state laws. For example, a federal district court judge refused to dismiss a suit against a mortgagor brought under Massachusetts's Lead Poisoning and Control Act. The court held that the defendant was an owner within the meaning of the act because the defendant's name appeared on the mortgage papers as a mortgagor. Roman v. Friedland, No. 92-30229-MAP (April 14, 1994).

69. CERCLA Section 101(2)(A) provides in part:

> Such term [owner or operator] does not include a person who, without participating in the management of a vessel or facility, holds indicia of ownership primarily to protect his security interest in the vessel or facility.

42 U.S.C. § 9601(20)(A).

70. *See* United States v. Fleet Factors Corp., 901 F.2d 1550 (11th Cir. 1990), *cert. denied*, 498 U.S. 1046 (1991).

71. CERCLA § 107(a)(4)(A), 42 U.S.C. § 9607 (a)(4)(A).

72. CERCLA § 107(a)(4)(B), 42 U.S.C. § 9607 (a)(4)(B).

73. *Id.*

74. *Id.*

75. Cadillac Fairview/Cal., Inc. v. Dow Chem. Co., 840 F.2d 691, 695 (9th Cir. 1988); Versatile Metals, Inc. v. Union Carbide, 693 F. Supp. 1563, 1574 (E.D. Pa. 1988).

76. *See, e.g.*, United States v. Ottati & Goss, 900 F.2d 429 (1st Cir. 1990).

77. 2 F.3d 1265 (3d Cir. 1993).

78. *Id.* at 1278.

79. *Id.*

80. However, oversight costs associated with remedial investigations and feasibility studies (RI/FS) conducted by private parties pursuant to Section 104(a)(1) of CERCLA were included in the definition of removal.

81. *Id.* at 1279.

82. *Id.*

83. *Compare* Gopher Oil Co. v. Union Oil Co. of California, 955 F.2d 519 (8th Cir. 1992); General Electric Co. v. Litton Business Systems, Inc., 920 F.2d 1415 (8th Cir. 1990), *cert. denied*, 499 U.S. 937 (1991), *with* New York v. SCA Services, Inc., 754 F. Supp. 995 (S.D.N.Y. 1991).

84. CERCLA § 107(c)(1)(D), 42 U.S.C. § 9607(c)(1)(D); Conservation Chem. Co., 619 F. Supp. 162, 222 (W.D. Mo. 1985). Natural resources are broadly defined as "land, fish, wildlife, biota, water, groundwater, drinking water supplies, and other such resources belonging to, managed by, held in trust by, appertaining to, or otherwise controlled by the United States . . . , any State or local government, any foreign government, any Indian tribe, or, if such resources are subject to a trust restriction on alienation, any member of an Indian tribe. CERCLA § 101(16), 42 U.S.C. § 9601(16).

85. The $50 million limitation would not apply where

> (1) the release or threat of release . . . was the result of willful misconduct or willful negligence within the privity or knowledge of [the] person, (2) the primary cause of the release was a violation (within the privity or knowledge of [the] person of applicable safety, construction, or operating standards or regulations; or (3) the person fails or refuses to provide all reasonable cooperation and assistance requested by a responsible public official in connection with response activities under the national contingency plan with respect to regulated carriers . . . or vessels.

CERCLA § 107(c)(2), 42 U.S.C. § 9607(c)(2).

86. *See, e.g.*, Marden Corp. v. C.G.C. Music, Ltd., 600 F. Supp. 1049, 1057–58 (D. Ariz. 1983), *aff'd*, 804 F.2d 1454 (9th Cir. 1986).

87. *See generally* Glass, *Superfund and SARA: Are There Any Defenses Left?*, 12 Harv. Envtl. L. Rep. 385 (1988), for a discussion of authority rejecting defenses to Superfund liability.

88. *See, e.g.*, Smith Land & Improvement Corp. v. Celotex Corp., 851 F.2d 86 (3d Cir. 1988) (if defense were allowed it would improperly shift CERCLA liability from responsible parties to unwitting purchasers), *cert. denied*, 488 U.S. 1029 (1989).

89. CERCLA § 107(b), 42 U.S.C. § 9607(b).

90. CERCLA § 107(b)(3), 42 U.S.C. § 9607(b)(3).

91. *See* CERCLA § 101(35)(A), 42 U.S.C. § 9601(35)(A).

92. It is anomalous that the innocent landowner provisions are referred to as a "defense," given that they are not a defense at all but rather an exception to an exception to the third-party defense.

93. CERCLA § 101(35)(A), 42 U.S.C. § 9601(35)(A). EPA policy memoranda have addressed the scope of the innocent purchaser defense. *See* U.S. EPA Internal Memorandum, Guidance on Landowner Liability under Section 107(a) of CERCLA, De Minimis Settlements under Section 122(g)(1)(B) of CERCLA, and Settlements with Prospective Purchasers of Contaminated Property, 54 Fed. Reg. 34235 (1989).

94. CERCLA § 101(35)(B), 42 U.S.C. § 9601(35)(B).

95. *See* United States v. Sharon Steel Corp., 681 F. Supp. 1492 (D. Utah 1988) (buyer must exercise due care).

96. *See also* Brookfield-North Riverside Water Comm'n v. Martin Oil Mktg., Ltd., 1992 WL 63274 at *11 (N.D. Ill. 1992) (those who buy land without first checking closely for contamination are deemed, in effect, to have purchased it at discount and are liable for cleanup, while those who conduct a thorough environmental audit before taking title may avoid liability under the "innocent purchaser" defense).

97. For cases successfully invoking the innocent landowner defense, *see* United States v. Serafini, 706 F. Supp. 346 (M.D. Pa. 1988) (buyer who fails to inspect property may still be innocent landowner where inspections were not customary practice in 1969); United States v. Pacific Hide and Fur Depot, Inc., 716 F. Supp. 1341 (D. Idaho 1989). For cases where the innocent landowner defense did not prevail, *see* Wickland Oil Terminal v. Asarco, Ltd., 1988 WL 167247 (N.D. Cal. 1988); Washington v. Time Oil Co., 687 F. Supp. 529 (W.D. Wash. 1988); CPC International, Inc. v. Aerojet-General Corp., 777 F. Supp. 549 (W.D. Mich. 1991).

98. *See* ASTM E 1528-93 Standard Practice for Environmental Site Assessments: Transaction Screen Process and ASTM E 1527-93 Standard Practice for Environmental Site Assessments: Phase I Environmental Site Assessment Process.

99. EPA Policy Towards Owners of Residential Property at Superfund Sites, OSWER Directive No. 9834.6 (July 1991).

100. *Id.* at 3, 6.

101. *Id.* at 8.

102. CERCLA § 122(g)(1), 42 U.S.C. § 9622(g)(1).

103. *Id.*

104. CERCLA § 122(g)(1)(A)(i)–(ii), 42 U.S.C. § 9622(g)(1)(A)(i)–(ii). Generally, a PRP that has contributed less than 1 percent of the total hazardous substances is considered a de minimis party. *See* United States v. Rohm & Haas Co., 721 F. Supp. 666, 672 (D.N.J. 1989).

105. CERCLA § 122(g)(1)(B)(i)–(iii), 42 U.S.C. § 9622(g)(1)(B)(i)–(iii).

106. *Id.*

107. *See* U.S. EPA, Guidance on Landowner Liability under Section 107(a) of CERCLA, De Minimis Settlements under Section 122(g)(1)(B) of CERCLA, and Settlements with Prospective Purchasers of Contaminated Property, 54 Fed. Reg. 34,235 (1989).

108. Pub. L. No. 94-580 (1976).

109. In addition, the distinction has been blurred by the EPA's application of the statutes. The EPA has increasingly used CERCLA to address active facilities rather than abandoned dumps.

110. *See* 40 C.F.R. Parts 260–68.

111. RCRA § 1004, 42 U.S.C. § 6903(3).

112. HSWA created the statutory authority for corrective action under RCRA. Section 3004(u) requires corrective action for all releases of hazardous waste or constituents from any solid waste management unit at a treatment, storage, or disposal facility seeking a permit under RCRA. 42 U.S.C. § 6924(u). The EPA may also order corrective action or other response actions at facilities "authorized to operate under section 3005(e)," the interim status provision. RCRA § 3008(h), 42 U.S.C. § 6928. Also, Section 3008(h) has been interpreted to cover

facilities that have lost interim status without obtaining a permit or failed to obtain interim status properly.

113. 523 F. Supp. 1055 (D.N.J. 1981), *aff'd*, 688 F.2d 204 (3d Cir. 1982).

114. *Id.* at 1070.

115. *Id.* at 1072.

116. *Id.* at 1059.

117. *Id.* at 1073.

118. *Id.*

119. *Id.*

120. 734 F.2d. 159 (4th Cir. 1984).

121. *Id.* at 163.

122. *See also* United States v. Ottati & Goss, Inc., 630 F. Supp. 1361 (D.N.H. 1985).

123. Subtitle I defines a UST as

> any one or combination of tanks (including underground pipes connected thereto) which is used to contain an accumulation of regulated substances, and the volume of which (including the underground pipes connected thereto) is 10 per centum or more beneath the surface of the ground.

42 U.S.C. § 6991(1). A regulated substance is any substance defined in Section 101(14) of CERCLA and petroleum but does not include any substance regulated as a hazardous waste under Subtitle C of RCRA.

124. H.R. CONF. REP. NO. 1133, 98th Cong., 2d Sess. 128 (1984), *reprinted in* U.S. CODE CONG. & AD. NEWS 5649, 5699.

125. CERCLA § 101(35)(C), 42 U.S.C. § 9601(35)(C) (emphasis added).

126. The provision requires that certain defendants "shall be treated as liable." CERCLA § 101(35)(C), 42 U.S.C. § 9601(35)(C).

127. CERCLA § 107, 42 U.S.C. § 9607.

128. *See, e.g.*, United States v. Aceto Agricultural Chem. Corp., 872 F.2d 1373, 1381–82 (8th Cir. 1989).

129. *See, e.g.*, O'Neill v. Piccillo, 682 F. Supp. 706, 728 (D.R.I. 1988), *aff'd*, 883 F.2d 176 (1st Cir. 1989), *cert. denied sub nom.*, 493 U.S. 1071 (1990); United States v. Conservation Chem. Co., 619 F. Supp. 162, 176, 240–41 (W.D. Mo. 1985); Missouri v. Independent Petroleum Corp., 610 F. Supp. 4, 5 (E.D. Mo. 1985).

130. *See* United States v. Conservation Chem. Co., 619 F. Supp. 162, 176, 234 (W.D. Mo. 1985); New York v. General Electric Co., 592 F. Supp. 291, 297 (N.D.N.Y. 1984); United States v. A & F Materials Co., 582 F. Supp. 842, 844–45 (S.D. Ill. 1984).

131. *See, e.g.*, United States v. Bliss, 667 F. Supp. 1298 (E.D. Mo. 1987); United States v. Bliss, 16 Chem. Waste Lit. Rep. 1061 (E.D. Mo. 1987).

132. 768 F. Supp. 432 (D.N.H. 1991).

133. 769 F. Supp. 432 (D.N.H. 1991).

CHAPTER 2

Common-Law Causes of Action for Environmental Claims

JAMES B. WITKIN

Modern environmental law is commonly perceived to be statutory law. The federal environmental laws enacted by Congress in the past three decades—the Comprehensive Environmental Response, Compensation, and Liability Act (CERCLA), Resource Conservation and Recovery Act (RCRA), Toxic Substances Control Act (TSCA), Clean Air Act, and Clean Water Act, to name only the most far-reaching—undeniably form the basis of the modern law of environmental protection in the United States.[1] Similarly, many states have enacted important environmental laws. Some state statutes, such as state "Superfund" laws, parallel federal legislation. Others, such as New Jersey's Environmental Cleanup Responsibility Act and Industrial Site Recovery Act, approach environmental issues in novel ways.[2]

However, plaintiffs in environmental impairment and contamination cases, in addition to bringing suits based on federal and state statutes, have relied successfully on centuries-old common-law causes of action. The malleability of common-law tort concepts has allowed judges to apply precedent from preindustrial England to current environmental cases. This chapter provides an overview of the main common-law causes of action on which environmental plaintiffs have relied, especially in cases arising in the real estate context.

Nuisance

Traditionally, nuisances have been characterized as either private or public. The first part of this section concentrates on common-law private nuisance, which is the focus of most nuisance actions that arise in environmental litigation between private parties; the second part discusses public nuisance.

Private Nuisance—Elements

A private nuisance is defined as "a nontrespassory invasion of another's interest in the private use and enjoyment of land."[3] To recover under a private nuisance theory, a plaintiff must prove that the defendant engaged in certain activities or maintained certain conditions that caused an "unreasonable" and "substantial" interference with plaintiff's use and enjoyment of its land.[4] In other words, the "defendant's activity must cause harm that exceeds 'the customary interferences a land user suffers in an organized society,' and be an appreciable and tangible interference with a property interest."[5] Section 822 of the *Restatement (Second) of Torts* provides as follows:

> One is subject to liability for private nuisance if, but only if, his conduct is a legal cause of an invasion of another's interest in the private use and enjoyment of land, and the invasion is either:
> (a) intentional[6] and unreasonable;[7] or
> (b) unintentional and otherwise actionable under the rules controlling liability for negligent or reckless conduct, or for abnormally dangerous conditions or activities.[8]

Many different fact situations may give rise to a successful private nuisance action. In *Frank v. Environmental Sanitation Management, Inc.*,[9] for example, the plaintiff sued for injuries sustained when leachate from the defendant's landfill contaminated the groundwater on plaintiff's property. In *Maryland Heights Leasing, Inc. v. Mallinckrodt, Inc.*,[10] the plaintiffs sued for damages caused to their property by low-level radiation emissions from the defendant's plant. In *Boomer v. Atlantic Cement Co.*,[11] the plaintiffs were injured by dirt, smoke, and vibration from the defendant's cement plant.

These cases provide a sampling of the types of activities that may give rise to a successful nuisance action. As the Michigan Supreme Court has noted:

> There are countless ways to interfere with the use and enjoyment of land, including interference with the physical condition of the land itself, disturbance in the comfort or conveniences of the occupant including his peace of mind, and threat of future injury that is a present menace and interference with enjoyment.[12]

The Balancing Test

The law of nuisance attempts to weigh the defendant's right to carry on its business as it desires against the neighbors' right to be free from interference with the use and enjoyment of their land. To determine whether the defendant's intentional interference was unreasonable, courts balance the competing interests.[13]

A West Virginia court has observed that "[a]lthough balancing tests are always unsatisfactory because they are unpredictable, it nonetheless appears that balancing was at the heart of actions for nuisance from its inception."[14] One commentator has stated, "[b]ecause the facts of each case are unique and the outcome of each dispute depends on balancing of equitable factors, the law of nuisance has been called a 'quintessential judgment-entitlement' rule in contrast to the more 'mechanical' rule of trespass."[15]

The *Restatement (Second) of Torts* lists some of the factors to be considered in determining the gravity of the harm to the plaintiff[16] and the social value of the defendant's activities alleged to cause the harm. *Restatement* Section 827 lists the following "gravity of harm" factors:

> (1) The extent of the harm;
> (2) The character of the harm involved;
> (3) The social value which the law attaches to the type of use or enjoyment invaded;
> (4) The suitability of the particular use or enjoyment invaded to the character of the locality; and
> (5) The burden on the person harmed of avoiding the harm.[17]

Restatement Section 828 lists the following "utility of conduct" factors:

> (1) The social value which the law attaches to the primary purpose of the conduct;
> (2) The suitability of the conduct to the character of the locality; and
> (3) The impracticability of preventing or avoiding the invasion.[18]

Courts have not treated the factors listed in Sections 826 and 827 as exhaustive.[19]

Identifying the Parties

In traditional common-law nuisance cases, landowners generally sued neighboring property owners whose actions (or inactions) had contaminated the plaintiffs' property. In recent cases, however, owners of contaminated property have attempted to recover remediation costs from prior owners or occupiers of the plaintiffs' property. For example, in *Philadelphia Electric Co. v. Hercules, Inc.*,[20] the Philadelphia Electric Company (PECO) relied on public and private nuisance theories in its suit against Hercules, Inc., the corporate successor to a company that had owned and contaminated its land and then subsequently sold the contaminated land to PECO's seller, Gould, Inc. PECO had expended considerable sums cleaning up the property and sought reimbursement from Hercules as a successor of the entity that caused the contamination. The Third Circuit reversed the lower court's judgment that Hercules was liable to PECO on the ground that

> Neighbors, unlike the purchasers of the land upon which a nuisance exists, have no opportunity to protect themselves through inspection and negotiation. The record shows that PECO acted as a sophisticated and responsible purchaser—inquiring into the past use of the Chester site, and inspecting it carefully. We find it inconceivable that the price it offered Gould did not reflect the possibility of environmental risks, even if the exact condition giving rise to this suit was not discovered. . . . Such an extension of common law doctrine is particularly hazardous in an area, such as environmental pollution, where Congress and state legislatures are actively seeking to achieve a socially acceptable definition of rights and liabilities.[21]

Moreover, the Third Circuit explained that this result "is consonant with the historical role of private nuisance law as a means of efficiently resolving conflicts between neighboring, contemporaneous land uses."[22] The *Philadelphia Electric* court held that Pennsylvania common law does not provide a purchaser of property with a cause of action under nuisance against a prior owner for conditions existing on the land at the time of the transfer of ownership.[23]

A California appeals court in *Mangini v. Aerojet-General Corp.*[24] reached an opposite result in interpreting a California nuisance statute. In that case, landowners filed a complaint alleging nuisance, among other common-law theories, against former tenants of a prior landowner who allegedly caused the contamination. Citing treatises on common-law nuisance and the Third Circuit's decision in *Philadelphia Electric,* the defendants argued that nuisances are committed only by "neighbors." The defendants maintained that to be actionable as a "nuisance," the acts causing the claimed injury must be committed by someone outside of the property. The trial court agreed, but the California appellate court reversed with respect to the nuisance action, concluding that California nuisance statutes permitted landowners to recover for direct injury to their property.[25] The *Mangini* court distinguished the authorities on which the defendants' relied on the grounds that

> California nuisance statutes have been construed, according to their broad terms, to allow an owner of property to sue for damages caused by a nuisance created on the owner's property. Under California law, it is not necessary that a nuisance have its origin in neighboring property.[26]

The *Mangini* court pointed out that California courts construed the statutory definition of nuisance to be broad enough "to encompass almost every conceivable type of interference with the enjoyment or use of land or property."[27] The decisions in *Philadelphia Electric* and *Mangini* underscore the importance of analyzing the differences between common law and statutory definitions of nuisance, in those jurisdictions with nuisance statutes.

Public Nuisance

While a private nuisance is defined as an invasion of another's interest in the private use and enjoyment of land, a public nuisance is defined as "an act or omission that unreasonably interferes with or obstructs rights common to the public."[28] In *Copart Industries, Inc. v. Consolidated Edison Co. of New York, Inc.*,[29] the New York Court of Appeals described public nuisance as follows:

> A public, or as sometimes termed a common, nuisance is an offense against the State and is subject to abatement or prosecution on application of the proper governmental agency. It consists of conduct or omissions which offend, interfere with or cause damage to the public in the exercise of rights common to all, in a manner such as to offend public morals, interfere with use by the public of a public place or endanger or injure the property, health, safety or comfort of a considerable number of persons.[30]

A private plaintiff may bring an action under a public nuisance theory only if the defendant's conduct causing a public nuisance also interferes with the plaintiff's use and enjoyment of its private property.[31] The distinction between a public and a private nuisance, therefore, will affect the individual's ability to bring suit for an alleged wrong.[32] To have standing to sue under a public nuisance theory, "one must have suffered harm of a kind different from that suffered by other members of the public exercising the right common to the general public that was the subject of interference."[33]

Although private plaintiffs must demonstrate a special injury to recover under a public nuisance theory, the case law suggests that this requirement is not insurmountable. For example, in *Blair v. Anderson*,[34] in which the plaintiffs claimed injuries stemming from the defendants' adjoining landfill, the Indiana Court of Appeals held that the operation or maintenance of an open dump is a "nuisance inimical to human health" under Indiana statutory law. The court also held, however, that blockage of water flow to the creek on the plaintiffs' property was sufficient special injury to give them standing to bring a private action to abate and enjoin the public nuisance.

Similarly, in *Mangini*,[35] the plaintiffs alleged public nuisance under California statutory law against tenants of the prior owners arising out of the tenants' disposal of contaminants on the property. The defendants argued that the plaintiffs lacked standing to sue for public nuisance. Noting that the plaintiffs had been required by a governmental agency to undertake testing of the property subsequent to their purchase, the court held that the plaintiffs had alleged special injury sufficient to support a public nuisance claim.

In *Philadelphia Electric*, however, the Third Circuit made clear that special pecuniary injury not tied to the common right interfered with does not confer standing upon an individual to sue under a public nuisance theory.[36] PECO sought reimbursement for an expensive cleanup of one of its sites mandated by the Pennsylvania Department of Environmental Resources (DER), arguing that the expense it incurred in cleaning up the offending condition constituted the requisite harm for standing. The Third Circuit disagreed, reasoning that

> Though pecuniary harm certainly may be harm of a different kind from that suffered by the general public, we find in this case no allegation or evidence that PECO suffered this harm "exercising the right common to the general public that was the subject of interference." The public right that was interfered with was the right to "pure water." PECO does not allege that it used the waters of the Delaware River itself, or that it was directly harmed in any way by the pollution of those waters. . . . If [plaintiff]—as a riparian landowner—had suffered damage to its land or its operations as a result of the pollution of the Delaware, it would possibly have a claim for public nuisance. But the condition of the Chester site was not the result of the pollution, it was the cause of it. DER required PECO, as the owner of the Chester site, to remove the sources of the pollution. PECO has been harmed only in the exercise of its private property rights over the Chester site. PECO has suffered no "particular damage" in the exercise of a right common to the general public, and it lacks standing to sue for public nuisance.[37]

Counsel should consider whether a plaintiff has suffered injury different and discrete from that generally suffered by the public, yet tied to the common right interfered with—admittedly a subtle distinction—in determining whether it would be advantageous to sue under both private and public nuisance theories. In some cases, there are procedural benefits to public nuisance lawsuits.[38]

Defenses

Commonly used defenses to nuisance actions include "coming to the nuisance," consent, preemption, primary jurisdiction, and statute of limitations.

"Coming to the Nuisance"

In jurisdictions that follow the reasoning of *Mangini*, a defendant may use the "coming to the nuisance" defense against plaintiffs who acquire property with knowledge that the property is contaminated. The theory is that these plaintiffs knowingly chose to own or occupy contaminated land and, more than likely, were able to lease or purchase the land at a lower price, thereby assuming the risk of remediation. While this defense typically is not an absolute bar to recovery, courts will weigh it as a factor in determining the reasonableness of the defendant's actions.[39] By contrast, in courts that adhere to the logic of *Philadelphia Electric*, no recovery in nuisance is available from prior landowners for conditions existing at the time of transfer of the property.

Consent

A defendant may argue either express or implied consent as a defense to a plaintiff's nuisance claim. Express consent may be argued where the defendant can prove that the plaintiff consented to the defendant's conduct with a clear understanding of the conduct and the risks involved. Implied consent is a viable defense where the defendant can show that the plaintiff failed to object to a nuisance in a timely way. The defense also may be asserted in actions against prior owners or occupiers of the land where the terms of relevant purchase or lease contracts suggest implied consent to the nuisance.[40]

Preemption

Both federal and state legislation can operate to preempt or otherwise preclude nuisance actions brought under state law. Nonetheless, preemption of state nuisance actions rarely occurs at the federal level. In fact, federal and state environmental laws often include a savings clause declaring an intention not to preempt common-law nuisance actions.[41] Even in the absence of such savings clauses, however, courts have been reluctant to find preemption of a private nuisance action. Rather, the cases generally hold that preservation of the common-law actions is consistent with the administrative regulatory scheme for controlling pollution.[42]

Primary Jurisdiction

This defense may be asserted when an administrative body has both the authority and the expertise to decide a nuisance action. The defendant would argue that the plaintiff must seek relief from the appropriate regulatory agency before litigating the nuisance action. While the primary jurisdiction doctrine is potentially applicable to environmental nuisance cases, courts have been reluctant to refer nuisance claims to administrative agencies under this doctrine.[43]

Statute of Limitations

States have adopted statutes of limitations for private nuisance actions, generally ranging from two to five years. Before applying the statute of limitations, the court must decide whether the nuisance complained of is "permanent" or "temporary."[44] If the nuisance is permanent, the statute of limitations begins to run when the nuisance is created and, therefore, a private nuisance action must be brought within the specified period of years after the permanent nuisance was created or occurred.[45] If the nuisance is temporary or continuing, every repetition of the continuing nuisance gives rise to a separate claim for damages and, therefore, a new limitation period commences each day the continuing nuisance persists.[46]

Damages

A successful plaintiff may recover damages for a wide variety of injuries caused by nuisances, including damages for diminution in property value;[47] damages for discomfort, inconvenience, annoyance, and personal injury;[48] damages for loss of profits directly resulting from the nuisance;[49] punitive damages when there is a showing that the nuisance was knowingly and willfully maintained;[50] consequential damages;[51] and damages arising out of remediation costs.[52] A court generally has the power to grant injunctive relief in addition to damages.[53]

Trespass

Common-law trespass is an intrusion or invasion that interferes with an interest in the right of exclusive possession of property. Traditionally, no showing of intent or fault was required to impose liability for trespass, nor was actual damage a prerequisite to recovery. However, under modern trespass theory a plaintiff must prove an intentional, reckless, or negligent intrusion onto his or her property.[54] In the alternative, a plaintiff may prove the existence of an abnormally dangerous activity that supports recovery under strict liability.[55]

Elements

Possession

The plaintiff must demonstrate either actual possession of property or legal title from which constructive possession can be presumed.[56] According to the *Restatement (Second) of Torts*, a possessor is one who

> (a) is in occupancy of land with intent to control it, or
> (b) has been but no longer is in occupancy of land with intent to control it, if, after he has ceased his occupancy without abandoning the land, no other person has obtained possession as stated in Clause (a), or
> (c) has the right against all persons to immediate occupancy of land, if no other person is in possession as stated in Clauses (a) and (b).[57]

Possessors of land include owners, lessees, tenants-in-common of condominium common areas, and successors to a possessor at the time of a continuing trespass.

One who is not a possessor of property has no standing to pursue a trespass claim. For example, in *Hennigan v. Atlantic Refining Co.*,[58] several employees of an independent contractor who were working in the city of Philadelphia's sewer line were injured by an explosion apparently caused by the accumulation of oil in the sewer system. Assuming that the leakage of oil from the defendant's facility into the city's sewer system constituted a trespass, the U.S. District Court for Pennsylvania nevertheless found that the injured third parties had not suffered an invasion of their property rights. However, recovery for damages still may be available to a nonpossessor under negligence or strict liability theories.[59]

A former possessor of the plaintiff's property is not liable in trespass for environmental contamination occurring during the term of its possession. Since trespass requires "an unprivileged, intentional intrusion on land in the possession of another," the Massachusetts Supreme Judicial Court, in *Wellesley Hills Realty Trust v. Mobil Oil Corporation*,[60] held that oil contamination of a former gas station site alleged to have occurred during the period of Mobil's ownership did not form the basis for a trespass action.

> Mobil owned and was in possession of the property when it allegedly released the oil causing the contamination. Thus, Mobil's releases of oil were not unprivileged, and Mobil clearly was not intruding on land in the possession of another. Mobil's releases of oil on its own land, therefore, cannot constitute a trespass.[61]

One may be liable for damages in trespass even though another party may be legally responsible for the trespassing agent. In *Jordan v. Foust Oil Company, Inc.*,[62] the North Carolina Court of Appeals denied the summary judgment motion of a supplier of gasoline where evidence indicated that several deliveries were made into underground storage tanks that the supplier knew, or should have known, were leaking. The court rejected the supplier's argument that, because the tanks were owned by a third party, the supplier was not legally responsible for the gasoline when it escaped from the tanks, and therefore could not be liable in trespass. Evidence that the supplier continued to deliver gasoline into the tanks even though its own records indicated that the tanks were leaking tended to show that the supplier was at least partially responsible for the continued leakage, and was sufficient to support a trespass claim.

Entry

Unlike nuisance, which requires only that the defendant maintain some activity that constitutes a continuing interference with plaintiff's use and enjoyment of its property, trespass requires proof of an actual entry onto the plaintiff's land, either by the defendant or by some physical or observable object resulting from the defendant's actions. While courts traditionally have required evidence of readily discernible physical intrusion, such as flowing water or errant livestock, modern courts have extended the trespass theory to encompass agents that are invisible to the human eye but are scientifically discernible, including airborne particulates and soil and groundwater contaminants.[63]

In *Martin v. Reynolds Metal Co.*,[64] the operator of an aluminum reduction plant was found liable under a trespass theory for damages caused by the emission of fluoride compounds that settled on the plaintiffs' cattle farm, poisoning livestock and contaminating water.[65] The Oregon Supreme Court rejected the defendant's argument that, since the fluoride compounds could not be seen with the naked eye, the plaintiffs' cause of action was grounded in nuisance. The court stated that the important characteristic of a trespassing agent is "the object's energy or force rather than its size."[66] Also, some modern courts have rejected the traditional distinction between "direct" and "indirect" invasions. In a modern trespass action,

> the defendant may be liable for trespass even though a substance was not placed directly on plaintiff's land so long as the force causing the deposit, such as natural flow to the land, was direct. . . . The defendant is liable even though the entry of the "thing" was indirect, rather than direct, so long as the defendant

acted with knowledge that an invasion was "substantially certain" to follow as a result of the defendant's actions.[67]

Moreover, the fact that the plaintiff is unable to prove conclusively which one of several sources of contamination polluted plaintiff's property will not bar recovery from one of the sources.[68]

Actual Damages

Historically a plaintiff could recover under a trespass theory without showing any actual damages. Some modern courts, however, have required the plaintiff to prove some degree of harm. For example, in *Bradley v. American Smelting Corp.*,[69] the Washington Supreme Court required the plaintiff landowners to show actual and substantial damages to property to recover under continuing trespass for the intrusion of airborne toxic particles onto their land from a neighboring copper smelter. The court imposed this requirement to restrict the number of plaintiffs that otherwise might have been able to recover under a trespass theory.

Likewise, in *Borland v. Sanders Lead Co.*,[70] the Alabama Supreme Court required the plaintiffs to prove substantial damages to sustain a trespass action for an intentional, indirect invasion of their property by the settling of microscopic lead particulates and sulfoxide deposits from the defendant's neighboring lead smelter. Other injuries not affecting the property, such as personal injuries, may be actionable under other torts, including nuisance.[71]

Nature of the Trespass

Trespasses may be permanent, temporary, continuing, or renewing. Damages from permanent trespass are measured by the difference in the value of the property before and after the trespass, while damages from temporary trespass are measured by the rental value or reasonable value of the use of the property during the period of trespass.[72] A determination of whether the trespass is continuing or renewing may affect the plaintiff's ability to recover. For example, in *Wilson v. McLeod*,[73] the distinction between a continuing trespass (one that occurs at a particular moment in time and causes a continuing injury) and a renewing trespass (a series of repeating trespasses, each one of which causes separate damage) was important in determining the appropriate statute of limitations. In *Wilson*, a three-year statute of limitations commencing at the date a continuing trespass began was held not to apply to an ongoing seepage of gasoline onto plaintiff's property.

Damages

Plaintiffs may recover damages under a variety of theories, including diminution of property value and personal injury.[74] Plaintiffs traditionally could receive nominal damages and injunctive relief for trespasses that resulted in no actual harm; however, that rule has been abrogated by the modern interpretation of trespass theory, which requires proof of actual damages. In addition, under federal statutory schemes, a plaintiff's action for common-law trespass may be preempted. In *Feikema v. Texaco, Inc.*,[75] plaintiff home owners sued the owner and operator of a gasoline tank farm for both injunctive relief and damages, alleging nuisance and trespass based on soil and groundwater contamination. At the time of the plaintiffs' suit, the defendants were subject to a U.S. Environmental Protection Agency (EPA) consent order that required the defendants to implement an EPA-approved remediation program. The U.S. district court held that the relief prayed for "would conflict with and frustrate . . . the purpose of Congress in its EPA remediation efforts under RCRA."[76] The Fourth Circuit agreed that the injunctive relief sought would conflict with the EPA-required remediation and, therefore, was preempted by the consent order. However, because the consent order did not provide for payment of damages (in fact, the federal statute does not give the EPA the authority to seek damages on behalf of private parties), the court held that the state law claims for damages under nuisance and trespass were not preempted.[77]

Defenses

Defenses to trespass include consent, assumption of the risk, and statute of limitations. The elements of these defenses, when used in trespass cases, are similar to those used in nuisance cases. See the discussion on pages 37–38.

Strict Liability

First delineated in the English case of *Rylands v. Fletcher*,[78] strict liability imposes liability without regard to fault. The rationale is that one who engages in dangerous activity for commercial gain should bear the cost that the activity imposes on society.[79] Section 519 of the *Restatement (Second) of Torts* states the general principle that "[o]ne who carries on an abnormally dangerous activity is subject to liability for harm to the person, land or chattels of another resulting from the activity, although he has exercised the utmost care to prevent the harm."[80] Stated another way, strict liability imposes liability on the defendant regardless of the care with which the activity is conducted.

Courts recognize that strict liability is only appropriate for "dangerous and unusual activities for which negligence is an inadequate remedy or deterrent,"[81] and they have "taken care to limit the application of this doctrine because of the heavy burden it places upon a user of land."[82]

Abnormally Dangerous Activity

Under strict liability, a plaintiff may recover for personal or property injury proximately caused only by an "ultrahazardous" or "abnormally dangerous" activity, defined as an activity that is uncommon (whether because of location or otherwise), and that involves a serious and unavoidable risk of harm in its conduct.[83] According to Prosser, an activity may be deemed abnormally dangerous for two reasons:

> First, because although harm from a mishap may not be very serious, and the social utility of the conduct may outweigh the danger, a mishap resulting in some harm to the plaintiff is very likely to occur; second, because the activity involves an appreciable chance of causing serious injury.[84]

Under the *Restatement (Second) of Torts*, the determination of whether an activity is "ultrahazardous," and therefore susceptible to strict liability, is made by balancing six factors on a case-by-case basis:[85]

> (a) existence of a high degree of risk of some harm to the person, land, or chattels of others;
> (b) likelihood that the harm that results from it will be great;
> (c) inability to eliminate the risk by the exercise of reasonable care;
> (d) extent to which the activity is not a matter of common usage;
> (e) inappropriateness of the activity to the place where it is carried on; and
> (f) extent to which its value to the community is outweighed by its dangerous attributes.[86]

These factors are interrelated. As one opinion states, courts consider these factors as a whole, apportioning weight to each in accordance with the facts in evidence.[87] Although all of these factors are to be considered in determining whether an action in strict liability will succeed, they need not all be present for a court to impose strict liability.

> The essential question is whether the risk created is so unusual, either because of its magnitude or because of the circumstances surrounding it, as to justify the imposition of strict liability for

harm which results from it, even though it is carried on with all reasonable care.[88]

Whether an activity is a "common usage" is closely related to the appropriateness of conducting the activity in a particular location. In *Rylands v. Fletcher*, the English court imposed liability based on its determination that building a reservoir in mining country was both an uncommon and an inappropriate usage of land, rather than on a determination that the activity itself was inherently dangerous.[89] The concept of "common usage" also extends to the magnitude of the activity.[90] The fact that a substance is widely used will not forestall the imposition of strict liability if the quantity of the substance and its location render it a danger to the community. In *City of Northglenn v. Chevron U.S.A., Inc.*,[91] the U.S. District Court for Colorado held that the storage of more than sixteen thousand gallons of gasoline in a residential area warranted the imposition of strict liability.

Case Law

Underground Storage Tanks

Strict liability claims have been brought in many cases arising from contamination from underground storage tanks (USTs) and above-ground storage tanks.[92]

In one of the earliest modern UST cases, the Maryland Court of Appeals held that strict liability was appropriate where a leak from a tank at a gasoline station contaminated the well of an adjoining land-owner.[93] The court focused on the common usage element, stating that, although the operation of a gasoline station does not of itself involve a high degree of risk of harm, "the placing of a large underground gasoline tank in close proximity to the appellees' residence and well does involve such a risk, since it is not a matter of common usage."[94] The court also focused on the appropriateness of the location of the tank, stating that "where the operation of such activity involves the placing of a large tank adjacent to a well from which a family must draw its water for drinking, bathing, and laundry, at least that aspect of the activity is inappropriate to the locale, even when equated to the value of the activity."[95]

The U.S. District Court for the Virgin Islands reached a similar conclusion in *In Re Tutu Wells Contamination Litigation*.[96] The court found that gasoline and solvents that had leaked from USTs had contaminated private and commercial drinking water wells on the island of St. Thomas. As in *Yommer v. McKenzie*,[97] the court refused to hold that the mere operation of a service station gives rise to strict liability. The court stated that the operation of service stations is a matter of common usage, and that it is not unusual to find service stations in residential areas. The court concluded, however, that "where, as here, the risk of seepage is contamination of the area's precious and limited water supply, locating the storage tanks above the aquifer created an abnormally dangerous and inappropriate use of the land."[98]

The court based its holding on the high risk of harm from pollution to the wells; the likelihood that toxic substances would contaminate the aquifer; and the inappropriateness of the location for the activity, because the risks associated with the tanks could not be eliminated. The court applied a societal balancing test, concluding that "the community's interest in a clean water supply far outweighs the benefits of the service stations to the community," and cited in support of its conclusion the clean water legislation enacted by the Virgin Islands Legislature.[99]

Courts that have rejected strict liability claims in tank cases generally have focused on the safety and ubiquity of tanks. In *Arlington Forest Associates v. Exxon Corp.*,[100] the U.S. District Court for Eastern Virginia applied state law and concluded that when "[m]aintained, monitored, and used with due care, underground gasoline storage tanks present virtually no risk of injury from seepage of their contents. They are not abnormally dangerous."[101] The court further found that the presence of filling stations in and near residential areas is widespread and routine and, "although gasoline service stations may not themselves be operated by 'the great mass of mankind,' they are so pervasive as reasonably to be considered 'matters of common usage.' "[102]

Similarly, in *Dominick's Finer Foods, Inc. v. Amoco Oil Co.*,[103] the U.S. District Court for Northern Illinois held that where there was no allegation that tanks were located in a residential area, "the facts alleged do not support that the location of the Facility is inappropriate. Petroleum products are necessary for the functioning of our present society and there must be some means of delivering gasoline and other petroleum products to retail areas."[104]

Hazardous Substance Disposal

Cases arising out of the disposal of hazardous substances have resulted in similarly mixed holdings. In *Richmond, Fredericksburg, and Potomac R.R. Co. v. Davis Industries, Inc.*,[105] the U.S. District Court for Eastern Virginia refused to impose strict liability on a manufacturer of air-conditioning units that was alleged to have improperly disposed of old units containing PCBs. The court reasoned that, although the product (PCBs) was hazardous, the improper disposal of the product did not constitute an "ultrahazardous activity" for purposes of strict liability. Rather, the court found that "the high risk associated with the handling, storing, and disposal of products containing PCBs could have been eliminated through the exercise of reasonable care."[106] As a result, although the plaintiff was barred from recovering under strict liability, the court left open the possibility of recovery based on the manufacturer's negligence.

In contrast, in *Fletcher v. Tenneco, Inc.*,[107] the U.S. District Court for Eastern Kentucky imposed strict liability for groundwater contamination resulting from the improper disposal of wastewater containing PCBs. Tenneco had used PCBs in a fire-retardant lubricant for air compressors in its natural gas pipeline system. The PCB lubricant leaked through the air compressor seals and mixed with condensation that occurred during operation of the air compressors. Tenneco had periodically emptied the PCB-laden condensate either by dumping it on the ground or pouring it down the drain. Relying on the analysis in *New Jersey Department of Environmental Protection v. Ventron Corp.*,[108] the court found the defendant strictly liable, declaring that the improper disposal of the PCB-laden condensate was not a common usage and was not "essential to the continued functioning of Tenneco's gas transmission activities, and thus, the value of this method of disposal to the community is nonexistent."[109]

Identifying the Parties

There are few limitations on the plaintiffs who may recover under a strict liability theory. In *Rosenblatt v. Exxon Co.*,[110] however, the Maryland Court of Appeals recently held that a subsequent occupier of property could not bring a strict liability claim against a previous occupant. Rosenblatt, a current tenant, sued Exxon, a former tenant, alleging that when Exxon's contamination came to light during Rosenblatt's tenancy, Rosenblatt incurred economic damages and lost profits from its planned business. The court held that while it is justifiable to impose the burdens of strict liability in cases of injury to "occupants of neighboring land, who do not benefit and have no way of avoiding the harm to their property," subsequent users of the contaminated property "are able to avoid the harm completely by inspecting the property prior to purchasing or leasing it. Thus, it is not unreasonable to expect subsequent users to bear the risk of such harm."[111]

Potential defendants can include anyone engaging in an abnormally dangerous activity, whether the injuries occur on or off the defendant's property. Concepts of "privity" that are traditionally applicable to product liability cases do not apply to actions in strict liability in torts. As a result, in *T&E Industries, Inc. v. Safety Light Corp.*,[112] the New Jersey Supreme Court permitted a strict liability action between successive landowners for radium contamination. The court reasoned that the defendant seller could not rely on caveat emptor as a shield to liability because the defendant was well aware of the long history of health risks associated with the handling of radium and had failed to disclose to its purchaser the presence of significant quantities of radium by-products on the site.

> Because the former owner of the property whose activities caused the hazard might have been in the best position to bear or spread the loss, liability for the harm caused by abnormally-dangerous activities does not necessarily cease with the transfer of property.[113]

Defenses

In some jurisdictions, a plaintiff's contributory negligence or assumption of the risk may reduce liability to the extent that the plaintiff "knowingly and unreasonably subjects himself to the risk of harm from the activity."[114] Also, consent and caveat emptor may be available defenses under certain circumstances. Further, strict liability will not be imposed for injuries suffered by an intentional or negligent trespasser.[115]

Comparison to Other Torts

As discussed earlier, if the defendant's actions do not constitute abnormally dangerous activities, a plaintiff may still recover under a negligence, trespass, or nuisance theory. In fact, the doctrine of nuisance *per se*, applied in some older cases, closely resembles the modern concept of strict liability. In a 1943 storage tank case, *Bollinger v. Mungle*,[116] the Missouri Supreme Court found no basis for liability under negligence, but it instead relied on nuisance *per se* and described that doctrine as applying to situations where the acts performed on one's own premises *must* result in injury, as opposed to nuisance *per accidens*, where those acts *may* result in injury if not performed properly.

Negligence

Common-law liability for personal injury and property damage resulting from environmental pollution generally is imposed regardless of fault under the theories of nuisance, trespass, and strict liability. When an essential element of one of these no-fault torts is lacking (e.g., continuing condition, a physical invasion of plaintiff's property, or the presence of an ultrahazardous activity), a plaintiff may still be able to recover for damages caused by environmental pollution under a common-law negligence theory.

Elements

To prove a negligence claim, a plaintiff must prove that (1) the defendant owed a duty of care to the plaintiff, (2) the defendant breached that duty of care, and (3) the plaintiff sustained injury that was actually and proximately caused by the defendant's breach of duty.[117] Negligence actions may take a number of forms and target a variety of defendants, including lenders (negligent underwriting);[118] past and present owners of contaminated property (negligent disposal of hazardous materials);[119] property managers (negligent oversight of tenant's operations utilizing hazardous materials);[120] and environmental consultants and others involved in the oversight of environmental cleanup projects (negligent performance of site assessment[121] and negligent misrepresentation[122]).

In *Lippy v. Society National Bank*,[123] the Ohio appellate court upheld a negligence case against a lender where it found that the lender had established an informal fiduciary relationship with the plaintiff by recommending an asbestos consultant to perform a site assessment required as a condition of making an acquisition loan for a former gas station site, and the lender knew or should have known that the consultant was not competent to provide a full site assessment. Moreover, the court held that the plaintiff had sufficiently stated a negligence claim against the consultant where the plaintiff had retained the consultant to perform the site assessment and relied on the consultant's report, which erroneously indicated that the property was free from contamination.[124]

In *Philip Morris, Inc. v. Emerson*,[125] defendant Philip Morris had purchased property from Texaco, Inc., that was later discovered to be a disposal site containing pressurized cylinders of extremely toxic chemicals. During the disposal process, which was conducted with few precautions and in close proximity to a campground and other businesses, chemical fumes escaped, causing one death and serious injury to many others. The Virginia Supreme Court found that Philip Morris had been negligent in retaining the disposal firm without investigating its experience and background. Moreover, the court held that Philip Morris was ultimately responsible for the disposal operations because one of its employees was present at the disposal site and had the authority to stop the work "if he felt that it was being done in an unsafe manner"[126] and had negligently failed to do so. In addition, the court found Texaco to be negligent due to Texaco's own activities in burying the pressurized cylinders and the foreseeability of a negligent disposal operation.[127] The court held that "[t]he evidence is compelling that Texaco's negligent act 'put into operation' Philip Morris' efforts to neutralize and dispose of the cylinders."[128] The court rejected Texaco's argument that its negligence was vitiated by the superseding negligence of Philip Morris and the disposal firm.

In *Russell-Stanley Corp. v. Plant Industries, Inc.*,[129] the assignee of a lease sued its landlord to recover cleanup costs resulting from contamination caused by the previous tenant. The landlord had a long-established practice of conducting weekly inspections of the prior tenant's operations. On appeal, the New Jersey Superior Court held that since the landlord took an active role in overseeing the property, the landlord could be held liable for negligent administration of the property or negligent supervision of its site inspectors.

In *Murlas Living Trust v. Mobil Oil Corp.*,[130] the U.S. District Court for Eastern Illinois held that a claim for negligent misrepresentation was supported by evidence that an environmental consultant, GTI, retained by a former tenant, Mobil Oil, failed to disclose information to Murlas, the landlord, regarding the location and extent of contamination. Murlas relied on the consultant's reports in negotiating with a new tenant and constructing new improvements. Sidestepping the issue of whether GTI owed a duty to the landlord, since its contract was with Mobil, the court noted in a footnote:

> Whether GTI should have known, despite the existence of the confidentiality clause in its contract with Mobil, that some but not all of the information it was generating was making its way to Plaintiffs is a question of fact. The fact that the Mobil-GTI contract contained a confidentiality clause does not prevent Plaintiffs from stating a claim for negligent misrepresentation.[131]

A similar result was reached in *Levy v. Versar, Inc.*[132] In this case, the plaintiff required satisfactory Phase I and Phase II environmental assessments as a condition of purchasing a piece of property. When, in spite of the satisfactory reports, soil and groundwater contamination were later discovered, the plaintiff sued the consultant for negligent misrepresentation in failing to advise the plaintiff as to the true condition of the property. In rejecting the defendant's motion to dismiss, the U.S. District Court for Eastern Illinois found that "[d]espite the carefully worded disclaimer of reliance which accompanies the phase I report, plaintiffs' reliance on the statements in the report was foreseeable."[133]

Reasonable Care

A duty of care is defined as "[a] duty, or obligation, recognized by the law, requiring a person to conform to a certain standard of conduct, for the protection of others against unreasonable risks."[134] This duty is imposed on a defendant only when it is foreseeable that the defendant's actions (i.e., a particular act or omission) will cause injury to another. In an environmental case, the plaintiff seeks to prove "that the defendant owed a duty not to store, emit, dump, or otherwise dispose of toxic chemicals, wastes, pollutants, or contaminants which the defendant reasonably believed, knew, or should have known would cause harm to the plaintiff."[135] Plaintiffs may include owners, occupiers, invitees, and licensees who suffer injuries as a result of toxic contamination on or emanating from a defendant's land. Defendants may include prior owners or occupiers of land, real estate agents,[136] landlords,[137] and tenants, among others, who owed a duty to a particular plaintiff and whose act or omission harmed that plaintiff. For example, in *Sterling v. Velsicol Chemical Corp.*,[138] the inappropriateness of the location of a chemical dump created a high degree of risk, breaching a duty of reasonable care, when the dump later harmed nearby residents and their property.

The theory of negligence is based on the application of a uniform, objective standard of conduct (i.e., reasonable care) to the defendant's actions. The model for this uniform standard of conduct is the so-called "reasonable person," who exercises "reasonable care" under the circumstances. A reasonable person is not expected to avoid *all* risk, and his or her conduct will vary depending on the circumstances. In determining what constitutes "reasonable care" under a particular set of circumstances, the courts weigh a variety of factors, including "the probability that an accident will occur; the severity of harm if such an accident does occur; and the costs of preventing the accident from occurring."[139] The greater likelihood of serious injury or damage generally will translate into a higher standard of conduct required of the defendant, particularly with respect to hazardous materials, even if those materials are of common usage, such as gasoline,[140] and contamination of public resources.[141]

A duty of care or a higher standard of conduct may be imposed by a statute or regulation designed to protect a class of persons that includes the plaintiff. In some states, violation of such a duty constitutes negligence *per se*, meaning that the plaintiff need not offer any additional proof that the defendant failed to exercise reasonable care. In other states, proof of a violation of that duty imposed by statute or regulation will constitute evidence of negligence only, but not negligence *per se*. Notably, mere compliance with a statute or regulation will not prevent a finding of negligence if the plaintiff can prove that a reasonable person would have taken additional actions to prevent a foreseeable injury.

Causation

A plaintiff must establish actual and proximate causation to prove a negligence claim. "The defendant's conduct is a cause of the event if it was a material element and a substantial factor in bringing it about."[142] The requirements of proximate cause limit the scope of causation to the consequences of the defendant's conduct that are foreseeable both as to the type of risk and the class of plaintiff involved. If a cause is too tenuous, or there are substantial intervening factors, the chain of causation is broken, precluding a finding of liability.[143]

The doctrine of *res ipsa loquitur* applies when the event ordinarily would not occur without negligence, the agency or instrumentality causing the event is under the defendant's exclusive control, and the plaintiff did not voluntarily act or contribute to the occurrence. *Res ipsa loquitur* may be particularly valuable in cases involving environmental damage when there is a lack of information about the conduct or events that caused toxic contamination.[144] However, the doctrine may be difficult to establish and sustain even when the facts seem to point clearly to liability. In *Socony Mobil Co. v. Southwestern Bell Telephone Co.*,[145] the absence of a showing that damage to underground telephone cables was caused by an instrumentality under the management and control of the defendant oil company led the Texas Supreme Court to conclude that *res ipsa loquitur* did not apply even though the plaintiff alleged that the damage came from storage tanks, pumps, or lines connecting storage tanks and pumps at service tanks.

Actual Injury

The plaintiff must show that he or she has suffered a real economic or personal injury caused by the defendant's breach of the duty of care. Plaintiffs may recover damages for economic and personal injuries and property damage. However, like negligence actions generally, emotional distress without companion physical injury or property damage is not generally compensable.[146] Where there is proof of physical injury or property damage, the addition of emotional distress may increase a compensatory award, result in punitive damages, or both in cases of gross negligence or willful or wanton conduct.[147]

Defenses

A defendant may argue the following defenses to a plaintiff's claim for negligence: consent; assumption of the risk; contributory negligence; comparative negligence; the statute of limitations; intervening criminal acts of third parties;[148] and, for purchaser-plaintiffs, caveat emptor.[149] In addition, a " 'state of the art' defense can arise when unexpected effects occur or when the release of toxic substances was at a level considered acceptable under past standards."[150] For example, in *Ventron*,[151] the New Jersey Supreme Court found no negligence in the release of mercury into a stream, even though the action was "unreasonable, unwarranted, and unlawful under present standards," because it was within the standards acceptable at the time of the occurrence.[152]

Comparison to Other Torts

A plaintiff who can establish that the defendant knew that pollution was "substantially certain to follow" the defendant's conduct under a trespass or nuisance theory also may be able to prove that the defendant's conduct was unreasonable and the plaintiff's injury foreseeable in a negligence action.[153]

Conclusion

As the cases discussed in this chapter illustrate, the common law of torts has adapted to the environmental realities of the late twentieth century. On the whole, when an environmental injury is significant, courts appear willing to view fact patterns liberally, with the result that traditional limitations on common-law tort actions have been extended to keep pace with scientific advances.[154] These historic causes of action, however, carry with them vestiges from the past and require the careful matching of the facts of a given case to the elements of the given tort. Nonetheless, litigants should not overlook these potential weapons in cases of environmental impairment of real estate.

Notes

The author would like to thank Danielle C. Agee and Margaret McNamara Caputo for their contributions to this chapter.

1. *See generally* Chapter 1 of this book.
2. *See generally* Chapter 3 of this book.
3. Philadelphia Elec. Co. v. Hercules, Inc., 762 F.2d 303, 313 (3d Cir.), *cert. denied*, 474 U.S. 980, 106 S. Ct. 384, 88 L. Ed. 2d 337 (1985); Jersey City Redevelopment Auth. v. PPG Indus., 655 F. Supp. 1257, 1264 (D.N.J. 1987), *aff'd*, 1988 U.S. App. LEXIS 18998 (3d Cir. Oct. 17, 1988); RESTATEMENT (SECOND) OF TORTS § 821D (1977) [hereinafter RESTATEMENT].
4. Hendricks v. Stalnaker, 181 W. Va. 31, 33, 380 S.E.2d 198 (W. Va. 1989).
5. Dunlop v. Daigle, 122 N.H. 295, 444 A.2d 519 (N.H. 1982); *see also* Page County Appliance Ctr., Inc. v. Honeywell, Inc., 347 N.W.2d 171, 175 (Iowa 1984) ("When the alleged nuisance is claimed to be offensive to the person, courts apply the standard of 'normal persons in a particular locality' to measure the existence

of the nuisance. This normalcy standard is also applied where the use of property is claimed to be affected.").

6. At Section 825, the RESTATEMENT defines an intentional invasion as follows:

> An invasion of another's interest in the use and enjoyment of land or an interference with the public right is intentional if the actor
> (a) acts for the purpose of causing it, or
> (b) knows that it is resulting or substantially certain to result from his conduct.

RESTATEMENT § 825, *quoted in* Crest Chevrolet-Oldsmobile-Cadillac, Inc. v. Willemsen, 129 Wis. 2d 129, 137, 384 N.W.2d 692 (Wis. 1986); Hughes v. Emerald Mines Corp., 303 Pa. Super. 426, 450 A.2d 1, 4–5 (Pa. Super. Ct. 1982).

7. The unreasonableness of an intentional invasion is set forth in the RESTATEMENT at Section 826, which provides:

> An intentional invasion of another's interest in the use and enjoyment of land is unreasonable if
> (a) the gravity of harm outweighs the utility of the actor's conduct, or
> (b) the harm caused by the conduct is serious and the financial burden of compensating for this and similar harm to others would not make the continuation of conduct not feasible.

RESTATEMENT § 826; *quoted in Crest Chevrolet*, 129 Wis. 2d, at 138; *Hughes*, 450 A.2d, at 5; *see also* Frank v. Environmental Sanitation Mgmt., 687 S.W.2d 876, 880 (Mo. 1985) ("The easiest way to show a nuisance is to prove defendant's conduct is unreasonable as a matter of law. This category may be called nuisance *per se*.").

8. RESTATEMENT § 822, *quoted in Crest Chevrolet*, 129 Wis. 2d, at 137; *Hughes*, 450 A.2d, at 4.

9. *Frank*, 687 S.W.2d 876.

10. 706 S.W.2d 218 (Mo. Ct. App. 1985).

11. 26 N.Y.2d 219, 257 N.E.2d 870, 309 N.Y.S.2d 312 (N.Y. Ct. App. 1970).

12. Adkins v. Thomas Solvent Co., 440 Mich. 293, 302, 487 N.W.2d 715 (Mich. 1992).

13. "The unreasonable use element of nuisance balances the rights of adjoining property owners." *Frank*, *supra*, at 880.

14. *Hendricks*, 181 W. Va., at 34.

15. Frona N. Powell, *Trespass, Nuisance, and the Evolution of Common Law in Modern Pollution Cases*, 21 REAL ESTATE L. J. 182–215 (1992) [hereinafter Powell].

16. "The factors listed in sec. 827 [of the RESTATEMENT] are not exhaustive. The fact finder may consider other relevant factors in addition to those listed." *Crest Chevrolet*, 129 Wis. 2d, at 141.

17. RESTATEMENT § 827, *quoted in Crest Chevrolet*, 129 Wis. 2d, at 140 (applying the § 827 factors).

18. RESTATEMENT § 828, *quoted in Hendricks*, 181 W. Va., at 34–35 (applying the balancing test to determine that defendant's interference did not constitute a private nuisance).

19. *See Crest Chevrolet*, 129 Wis. 2d, at 140.

20. 762 F.2d 303.

21. *Id.* at 314.

22. *Id.*

23. *See also* Amland Properties Corp. v. Aluminum Co. of Am., 711 F. Supp. 784, 807 (D.N.J. 1989) ("The Restatement (2d) of Torts, § 822, makes clear that the concept of private nuisance has been traditionally confined to instances either of one person's property use interfering with another's use of property, or of property use injuring third parties. . . . The traditional rule in New Jersey is the same."); Sheehy v. Lipton Indus., Inc., 24 Mass. App. Ct. 188, 507 N.E.2d 781 (Mass. App. Ct. 1987) (affirming the lower court's grant of summary judgment in favor of defendants on the ground that a landowner cannot state a cause of action based on private nuisance against a predecessor in title for hazardous materials buried on the property); Rosenblatt v. Exxon Co., U.S.A., 335 Md. 58, 79, 642 A.2d 180 (Md. 1994) ("Courts which have considered [a nuisance claim by a subsequent occupier] have rejected them on the basis that a cause of action for private nuisance requires an interference with a neighbor's use and enjoyment of the land. We are in agreement with these authorities.")

24. 230 Cal. App. 3d 1125, 281 Cal. Rptr. 827 (Cal. Ct. App. 1991).

25. *Id.*

26. *Id.* at 1134.

27. *Id.* at 1135. In addition to California, a number of states have adopted statutory definitions of nuisance. *See, e.g.*, Cal. Civ. Code § 3479, discussed in *Mangini*, 230 Cal. App. 3d, at 1134; Wash. Rev. Code § 7.48.120, discussed in Miotke v. Spokane, 678 P.2d 803, 816 (Wash. 1984); N.D. Civ. Code § 42-01-02, discussed in Rassier v. Houim, 488 N.W.2d 635 (N.D. 1992) ("[T]he common-law nuisance concept does not apply in North Dakota. . . . Where, however, there is no conflict between the common law and a statute, common law remains relevant."); Iowa Code § 675.1 discussed in Pottawattamie County v. Iowa Dep't of Envtl. Quality, Air Quality Comm'n, 272 N.W.2d 448 (Iowa 1978).

28. Wayne County v. Tennessee Solid Waste Disposal Control Bd., 756 S.W.2d 274 (Tenn. Ct. App. 1988); Restatement § 821B; W. Keeton, Prosser and Keeton on the Law of Torts § 90 (5th ed. 1984) [hereinafter Prosser on Torts].

29. 41 N.Y.2d 564, 362 N.E.2d 968 (N.Y. 1977).

30. *Id.* at 567–68 [citations omitted] (*citing* Melker v. New York, 190 N.Y. 481, 488; Restatement, notes preceding § 822, p. 217); *see also* Westwood Pharmaceuticals, Inc. v. Nat'l Fuel Gas Distribution Corp., 737 F. Supp. 1272, 1281 (W.D.N.Y. 1990), *aff'd*, 964 F.2d 85 (2d Cir. 1992) ("With regard to what constitutes a public nuisance under state law, the Second Circuit has held that 'the release or threat of release of hazardous waste into the environment unreasonably infringes upon a public right and thus is a public nuisance as a matter of New York law.' "); Chicago v. Commonwealth Edison Co., 24 Ill. App. 3d 624, 630, 321 N.E.2d 412 (Ill. App. Ct. 1974) ("Earlier cases recognized that the public had a right to clean, unpolluted air and that any deprivation of that right was actionable as a private injury and indictable as a public wrong.").

31. *Wayne County*, 756 S.W.2d, at 283.

32. As Prosser has stated:

> A private nuisance is a civil wrong, based on a disturbance of rights in land. A public or common nuisance, on the other hand, is a species of

> catch-all criminal offense, consisting of an interference with the rights of the community at large, which may include anything from the obstruction of a highway to a public gaming-house or indecent exposure. As in the case of other crimes, the normal remedy is in the hands of the state. The two have almost nothing in common, except that each causes inconvenience to someone, and it would have been fortunate if they had been called from the beginning by different names. Add to this the fact that a public nuisance may also be a private one, when it interferes with the enjoyment of land, and that even apart from this there are circumstances in which a private individual may have a tort action for the public offense, and it is not difficult to explain the existing confusion. [citations omitted]

PROSSER ON TORTS, § 86, at 618.

33. RESTATEMENT § 821C(1), *quoted in Amland Properties*, 711 F. Supp., at 808; *Philadelphia Elec.*, 762 F.2d, at 315; *see also PPG Indus.*, 655 F. Supp., at 1265.

34. 570 N.E.2d 1337 (Ind. Ct. App. 1991).

35. 230 Cal. App. 3d 1125.

36. *Philadelphia Elec.*, 762 F.2d 303.

37. *Id.* at 315 [citations omitted]; *see also Amland Properties*, 711 F. Supp. 784; *PPG Indus.*, 655 F. Supp. 1257.

38. According to Prosser,

> [S]ince the plaintiff does not lose his rights as a landowner merely because others suffer damage of the same kind or even of the same degree, there is general agreement that he may proceed upon either theory, or upon both. Where this is the case, the action founded on the public nuisance may sometimes be preferable, because it is well settled that prescriptive rights, laches and the statute of limitations do not run against it. [citations omitted]

PROSSER ON TORTS, § 90, at 648.

39. On the "coming to the nuisance" defense, the *Mangini* court stated:

> We are aware that, in his Summary of California Law, Witkin remarks that consent is not a defense to an action for nuisance. (11 Witkin, Summary of Cal. Law (9th ed. 1990) Equity, § 150, p. 830.) However, the text accompanying the remark is as follows: "The so-called doctrine of 'coming to a nuisance' has generally been repudiated; i.e., the plaintiff may obtain injunctive relief even though the nuisance was already in operation, with his knowledge, when he acquired his own property." (Ibid.)

Mangini, 230 Cal. App. 3d, at 1138.

40. In *Mangini*, 230 Cal. App. 3d, at 1137, the court briefly discussed the defense of consent. The court held that "where, as here, an owner of property seeks damages for creation of a nuisance by a prior lessee, the lessee has a defense that his use of the property was lawful and was authorized by the lease; i.e., his use of the property was undertaken with the consent of the owner." The court reasoned that consent as a defense is acknowledged by Section 839 of the RESTATEMENT and that consent as a defense is necessary to avoid absurd results.

41. *See, e.g.*, 42 U.S.C. § 6972(f) (savings clause in Resource Conservation and Recovery Act); 42 U.S.C. § 9652 (savings clause in Comprehensive Environmental Response, Compensation, and Liability Act).

42. *See, e.g.*, King v. Western Club, Inc., 587 So. 2d 122, 123–24 (La. Ct. App. 1991); Biddix v. Henredon Furniture Indus., Inc., 76 N.C. App. 30, 331 S.E.2d 717, 724 (N.C. Ct. App. 1985). *But see* Township of Elizabeth v. Power Maintenance Corp., 53 Pa. Commw. 270, 417 A.2d 1285 (Pa. Commw. Ct. 1980).

43. *See, e.g.*, People v. Kerr-McGee Chem. Corp., 142 Ill. App. 3d 1104, 97 Ill. Dec. 344, 492 N.E.2d 1003 (Ill. App. Ct. 1986) (upholding trial court's refusal to stay the action where the defendant argued that the primary jurisdiction over the action lies with the federal Nuclear Regulatory Commission).

44. In *Frank*, the court noted:

> Damages for a permanent nuisances [sic] are measured by the difference in the land's market value immediately before and after injury; damages for temporary nuisances include the decrease in rental or useable value of property during the injury. The character of the source of injury often distinguishes temporary and permanent nuisances. A nuisance is temporary if it may be abated, and it is permanent if abatement is impracticable or impossible.

687 S.W.2d, at 882 [citations omitted].

45. *See Mangini*, 230 Cal. App. 3d, at 1142.

46. *Id.*

47. *See, e.g., Maryland Heights*, 706 S.W.2d, at 221.

48. *See, e.g.*, Atlanta v. Murphy, 194 Ga. App. 652, 391 S.E.2d 474, 476 (Ga. Ct. App. 1990).

49. *See, e.g., Maryland Heights*, 706 S.W.2d, at 222.

50. *Id.*

51. *See, e.g.*, Lunda v. Matthews, 46 Or. App. 701, 613 P.2d 63, 67 (Or. Ct. App. 1980).

52. *Philadelphia Elec., supra.*

53. *See, e.g.*, Dingwell v. Litchfield, 4 Conn. App. 621, 496 A.2d 213 (Conn. App. Ct. 1985).

54. Socony Mobil, Inc. v. Southwestern Bell Tel. Co., 518 S.W.2d 257 (Tex. 1974) (in the absence of proof that omissions by an oil company in maintaining a gas station were willful or intentional, an action for trespass would not be maintained).

55. Powell, at 187.

56. James L. Huitt, Jr., and Roger A. Warin, *Liability and Environmental Problems under Common Law*, at 152, in ENVIRONMENTAL DISPUTE HANDBOOK: LIABILITY AND CLAIMS (David A. Carpenter et al. eds. 1991) [hereinafter Huitt and Warin].

57. RESTATEMENT § 157.

58. 282 F. Supp. 667 (E.D. Penn. 1967).

59. Carroll v. Litton Sys., Inc., No. 92-2219, 1995 U.S. App. LEXIS 2015 (4th Cir. Feb. 1, 1995).

60. 747 F. Supp. 93, 99 (Mass. 1990).

61. *Id.*

62. 116 N.C. App. 155, 447 S.E.2d 491 (N.C. App. 1994).

63. *Litton Sys.*, 1995 U.S. App. LEXIS 2015.

64. 221 Or. 86, 342 P.2d 790 (Or. 1959).

65. By proceeding under a trespass theory instead of a nuisance theory, the plaintiffs were able to avail themselves of a six-year statute of limitations, instead of the two-year statute of limitations applicable to nontrespassory injuries to land. The six-year statute of limitations allowed the plaintiffs to recover additional damages. *Id.* at 88, 791.

66. *Id.* at 794.

67. *Id.* at 188.

68. Wilson v. McLeod, 398 S.E.2d 586 (N.C. 1990) (where there is more than one possible source of gasoline contamination plaintiffs need not prove that some of the contamination came from one of the sources individually).

69. 104 Wash. 2d 677, 709 P.2d 782 (Wash. 1985).

70. 369 So. 2d 523 (Ala. 1979).

71. Huitt and Warin, at 153.

72. *Id.* at 154.

73. *Wilson*, 398 S.E.2d 586.

74. *See* Wardrop v. Manhattan Beach, 160 Cal. App. 2d 779, 326 P.2d 15 (Cal. App. 1958) (a defendant pumped contaminated water onto the plaintiff's property and was held liable on a trespass theory for the plaintiff's developing polio).

75. 16 F.3d 1408 (4th Cir. 1994).

76. *Id.* at 1411.

77. In a concurring opinion, the circuit court is urged to view preemption of the plaintiffs' damages claims "to the extent that those damages arise from conduct regulated by the EPA's Consent Order," thereby preventing the plaintiffs from gaining "indirectly, through the threat of monetary damages, what we have expressly prevented them from gaining directly through an injunction—mandatory cleanup measures that are incompatible with those already approved by the EPA." *Id.* at 1419.

78. 3 H. & C. 774, 159 Eng. Rep. 737 (1865); *rev'd in* Fletcher v. Rylands, L.R. 1 Ex. 265 (1866); *aff'd in* Rylands v. Fletcher, L.R. 3 H.L. 330 (1868).

79. Sterling v. Velsicol Chem. Corp., 647 F. Supp. 303, 312 (W.D. Tenn. 1988) (*citing* C. MORRIS & C.R. MORRIS, MORRIS ON TORTS, Ch. IX, at 231 (2d Ed. 1980)).

80. RESTATEMENT § 519(1).

81. Schwartzman, Inc. *ex rel.* Schwartzman, Inc. v. General Elec. Co., 848 F. Supp. 942, 944 (D.N.M. 1993).

82. *Rosenblatt*, 642 A.2d 180.

83. RESTATEMENT § 520.

84. PROSSER ON TORTS, § 519, *cited in In Re* Tutu Wells Contamination Litig., No. 89-220, 89-224, 1993 U.S. Dist. LEXIS 19167 (D.V.I. Sept. 2, 1993), at *72.

85. New Jersey Dep't of Envtl. Protection v. Ventron Corp., 94 N.J. 473, 468 A.2d 150 (N.J. 1983).

86. RESTATEMENT §§ 519–20.

87. Arlington Forest Assocs. v. Exxon Corp., 774 F. Supp. 387, 390 (E.D. Va. 1991) (*citing* RESTATEMENT § 520, Comment 1).

88. *Velsicol*, 647 F. Supp., at 313 (*citing* RESTATEMENT § 520, Comment (f)). Some courts emphasized the relationship between negligence and strict liability,

namely that if the standard of care under negligence is set high enough, the result is basically strict liability. *See, e.g.*, City of Bridgeton v. B.P. Oil, Inc., 146 N.J. Super 169, 177, 369 A.2d 49 (N.J. Super. 1976) in which the New Jersey Superior Court extended strict liability to the storage of "pollutant substances."

89. More specifically,

> [The court in *Rylands*] said that the principle [of strict liability] applied only to a "non-natural" use of the defendant's land, as distinguished from "any purpose for which it might in the ordinary course of the enjoyment of land be used" [citation omitted]. The emphasis was thus shifted to the abnormal and inappropriate character of the defendant's reservoir in coal mining country, rather than the mere tendency of all water to escape.

Prosser on Torts § 78, at 545–46.

90. More specifically,

> An activity is of common usage if it is customarily carried on by the great mass of mankind, or by many people in the community. * * * Gas and electricity in household pipes and wires [are examples of common usage] as contrasted with large gas storage tanks or high tension power lines.

Restatement § 520, Comment (d), *cited in* Yommer v. McKenzie, 255 Md. 220, 224, 257 A.2d 138, 140 (Md. 1969) (placing petroleum storage tank in close proximity to residential well constituted uncommon usage rendering the storage tank ultrahazardous).

91. 519 F. Supp 515 (Colo. 1981).

92. The varying (and largely irreconcilable) outcomes of these cases may be ascribed both to the highly fact-specific nature of the cases and to the varying judicial—and environmental—temperaments of the judges involved. In *City of Bridgeton*, 369 A.2d 49, 54, the court clearly indicated the policy concerns underlying its opinion:

> As a society we are constantly made aware of the diminishing quantity and quality of our environment. Save, hopefully, in its ideals this is no longer the land of our fathers with its limitless bounty from sea to sea. This generation of Americans has seen its bounty wasted by mindless and reckless misuse. It has further seen the almost unchecked development of products whose misuse or improper employment leads to disfigurement and death. The law is not—or ought not be—so feeble as to exonerate those whose conduct causes harm to others by reason of such use or abuse.

Similarly, in *City of Northglenn*, 519 F. Supp. 515, 516, the court described gasoline as "not merely fuel, but a highly volatile, explosive, and toxic substance as well as one of the most powerful solvents commonly available." Despite the widespread use of gasoline and the common presence of gasoline service stations, the court voiced its opinion that

> [t]hose who store and dispense gasoline for profit, and who attempt to increase that profit by locating their filling stations and incidental stor-

age facilities in or near residential areas, should be held liable for harm resulting to persons or property from gasoline stored at or leaking from those stations.

93. *Yommer*, 257 A.2d 138.

94. *Id.* at 225.

95. *Id.*

96. 1993 U.S. Dist. LEXIS 19167.

97. 257 A.2d 138.

98. *Id.* at *77.

99. *Id.* Other cases that have held defendants in a storage tank case strictly liable include Branch v. Western Petroleum, Inc., 657 P.2d 267 (Utah 1982), and *City of Northglenn*, 519 F. Supp. 515.

100. 774 F. Supp. 387 (E.D. Va. 1991).

101. *Id.* at 390.

102. *Id.* at 391.

103. No. 93-C-4210, 1993 U.S. Dist. LEXIS 17668, at *21 (N.D. Ill. Dec. 15, 1993).

104. *Id.* at *22. Other cases that have reached the same result include Peneschi v. National Steel Corp., 170 W. Va. 511, 295 S.E.2d 1 (W. Va. 1985) (gasoline storage in a filling station is a "natural use of the land" and is not unduly dangerous for purposes of strict liability); Hudson v. Peavey Oil Co., 279 Or. 3, 566 P.2d 175, 177–78 (Or. 1977) (strict liability denied where the evidence did not conclusively show that the harm to be anticipated from underground seepage of gasoline was grave or that the risk of seepage could not be eliminated by the exercise of reasonable care); *Schwartzman*, 848 F. Supp. 942, 944 (strict liability criteria not met where, *inter alia*, the risks can be eliminated through the exercise of reasonable care); Melso v. Sun Pipe Line Co., 394 Pa. Super. 578, 576 A.2d 999, 1003–04 (Pa. Super. 1990).

105. 787 F. Supp. 572 (E.D. Va. 1992).

106. *Id.* at 576 (*citing* Philip Morris, Inc. v. Emerson, 235 Va. 380, 368 S.E.2d 268 (1988)).

107. No. 91-118, 1993 U.S. Dist. LEXIS 3054 (E.D. Ky. Feb. 22, 1993), originally published at 816 F. Supp. 1186, withdrawn from bound volume.

108. 468 A.2d 150.

109. *Tenneco*, 1993 U.S. Dist LEXIS 3054, at *31.

110. 642 A.2d 180.

111. *Id.* at 187. The court applied similar logic to dispose of the plaintiff's counts based on the other common law causes of action.

112. 123 N.J. 371, 587 A.2d 1249 (N.J. 1991).

113. *Id.* at 386, 1257.

114. Huitt and Warin, § 4.4 (*citing* RESTATEMENT § 542(2)).

115. RESTATEMENT § 520(b).

116. 175 S.W.2d 912 (Mo. 1943).

117. PROSSER ON TORTS, § 13, at 69–70.

118. Lippy v. Society Nat'l Bank, No. 92-T-4725, 1995 Ohio App. LEXIS 78 (Trumbull County, January 13, 1995).

119. *Philip Morris*, 368 S.E.2d 268.

120. Russell-Stanley Corp. v. Plant Industries, Inc., 250 N.J. Super. 478, 595 A.2d 534 (N.J. Super. 1991).

121. *Lippy*, 1995 Ohio App. LEXIS 78.

122. Murlas Living Trust v. Mobil Oil Corp., No. 93-C-6956, 1994 U.S. Dist. LEXIS 4777 (E.D. Ill., April 13, 1994); Levy v. Versar, Inc., No. 92-C-4836, 1993 U.S. Dist. LEXIS 14306 (E.D. Ill., Oct. 12, 1993).

123. 1995 Ohio App. LEXIS 78.

124. The court, however, refused to allow the plaintiff to recover damages for economic losses, which the court stated were properly sought in a breach of contract action. *Id.* at *23.

125. 368 S.E.2d 268.

126. *Id.* at 400, 278.

127. Texaco's own employees testified as to the risks of excavating pressurized cylinders containing pentaborane. *Id.* at 397, 277.

128. *Id.*

129. 250 N.J. Super. 478, 595 A.2d 534 (N.J. Super. 1991)

130. No. 93-C-6956, 1994 U.S. Dist. LEXIS 4777 (E.D. Ill., April 13, 1994).

131. *Id.* at *25 n.10.

132. No. 92-C-4836, 1993 U.S. Dist. LEXIS 14306 (E.D. Ill., Oct. 12, 1993).

133. *Id.* at *10.

134. *Id.* at 164.

135. Huitt and Warin, at 147.

136. *See, e.g.*, Cal. Civ. Code § 1102–02.15, 2079 (West 1992) (requiring disclosure of toxic contamination in sales of residential real estate); *see also* Kinney et al. *Remedies Available to Private Parties for Petroleum-Contaminated Property*, ENV'T. COUNS. 7, 10 (Oct. 15, 1992). *But, cf.*, Niecko v. Emro Marketing Co., 973 F.2d 1296 (6th Cir. 1992) at 1302 (stating that seller has duty to disclose only concealed condition posing unreasonable danger).

137. *Russell-Stanley Corp.*, 595 A.2d 534.

138. 647 F. Supp 303 (W.D. Tenn. 1986).

139. Huitt and Warin, at 147 (*citing* RESTATEMENT § 293).

140. Pryor v. Chambersburg Oil & Gas Co., 376 Pa. 521, 103 A.2d 425 (Pa. 1954) ("Gasoline is a highly volatile substance and a higher degree of care is imposed on persons dealing with such a dangerous agency than would ordinarily attach to one conducting a business involving little or no risk. No absolute standard can be fixed by law, but every reasonable precaution commensurate with experience and the known danger ought to be taken.").

141. Masten v. Texas Co., 140 S.E. 89, 90 (N.C. 1927) ("One may no more pollute a subterranean stream than a surface stream. A person has no right to befoul, corrupt, or poison underground water so that when it reaches his neighbor's land it will be unfit for use by either man or beast. . . . This is good morals as well as good law.").

142. PROSSER ON TORTS, at 267.

143. *See, e.g.*, Hennigan v. Atlantic Ref. Co., 282 F. Supp. 667 (E.D. Penn. 1967) (oil leaks from defendant's underground storage tanks did not incur liability for the worker's death caused by an explosion in sewage system where City of Philadelphia's failure to ensure that adequate safety measures were taken by its workers constituted an intervening act).

144. *Id.*

145. 518 S.W. 2d 257 (Tex. Ct. App. 1974).

146. Prosser on Torts, at § 54.

147. *Velsicol*, 647 F. Supp. 303.

148. Avemco Ins. Co. v. Cavanaugh, No. 89-CV-40001-FL, 1991 U.S. Dist. LEXIS 16449 (E.D. Mich. May 13, 1991) (vandalism by disgruntled employee that released acid cloud resulting in property damage to airplanes at nearby facility acted to cut off negligence of defendant, which stored large vats of hydrochloric acid on its premises as part of its business).

149. *See, e.g.*, Preston v. Goldman, 42 Cal. 3d 108, 720 P.2d 476, 480–81 (Cal. 1986).

150. Huitt and Warin, at 147–48 (*citing Ventron*, 468 A.2d 150).

151. *Ventron*, 468 A.2d 150.

152. *Id.*

153. Powell, at 192.

154. *See, e.g.*, *Martin*, 342 P.2d 790.

CHAPTER 3

Transaction-Triggered Environmental Laws

DAVID B. FARER

During the early 1980s commercial transactions became the target of innovative environmental laws that linked real estate deals and other business transactions to government-sanctioned and -monitored environmental audits and cleanups. These "transaction-triggered" (or transfer) statutes marked the end of the era in which environmental issues were considered beyond the purview of real estate lawyers. Combined with stringent federal environmental requirements already in place, the new laws had a wide-ranging effect. Companies suddenly found themselves entangled in lengthy litigation and costly cleanups as a result of compliance requirements, many of which were never contemplated when these parties entered into their agreements.

The landmark transfer legislation was New Jersey's Environmental Cleanup Responsibility Act (ECRA), which became effective at the end of 1983. ECRA was both site-specific and transaction-specific—that is, it was intended to target and ensure the cleanup of hazardous substances and wastes at particular locations when the application of the law was triggered by specific events. The groundbreaking strategy chosen by the New Jersey legislature was to compel current real estate owners, or operators of commercial and industrial businesses, to do everything necessary to obtain a clean bill of health before selling a property or business or closing down or moving an industrial or commercial operation.

ECRA's ingenious approach appealed to regulators, and it appeared early on that ECRA was spawning a nationwide trend toward adoption of transfer laws. However, several states that proceeded to pass transaction-triggered laws modeled on ECRA chose to circumscribe, if not eliminate, the state's pretransaction role in favor of detailed disclosure obligations from seller to buyer and reliance on hefty posttransaction enforcement "hammers" in the event of noncompliance. Those states included Iowa, Oregon, Connecticut, Michigan, Illinois, Indiana, and Ohio. Other states, such as Alaska, California, Delaware, Maryland, Massachusetts, New Hampshire, New York, and Pennsylvania, have debated and rejected ECRA offshoots, particularly in light of relentless criticism of ECRA because of its flawed draftsmanship as well as inadequacies, inefficiencies, and delays in its administration. The criticisms were not lost on the New Jersey Legislature, and an ECRA reform movement led to a significant revamping of the law in 1993 by way of the Industrial Site Recovery Act (ISRA). The innovations of ISRA have led to further national debate on issues such as definitive risk-based cleanup standards and the use of engineering and institutional controls (e.g., capping or a recorded document memorializing restrictions on future use) as alternatives to costly removal or treatment actions.

Other transactional concerns—such as those spawned by the Comprehensive Environmental Response, Compensation, and Liability Act (CERCLA) liability scheme and its innocent purchaser defense, lender vigilance, and "super liens"—have given rise to environmental due diligence practices comparable to those required by ECRA and the various ECRA offshoots. However, the institutionalized transfer law schemes have added a level of regulatory certainty that has not yet been achieved by parties involved in private due diligence activities.

This chapter reviews the various transaction-triggered environmental laws around the country in order of passage (with the exception of Hawaii's Disclosure Act, which is the last of the summaries). In addition to the most often cited of ECRA's progeny, this chapter discusses other transfer laws that carry significant enforcement hammers and thus are distinguishable from laws requiring deed notices or notices on sale of contaminated properties.

New Jersey Industrial Site Recovery Act

The New Jersey Industrial Site Recovery Act (ISRA)[1]—originally titled the Environmental Cleanup Responsibility Act (ECRA)[2]—imposes preconditions on the closure of industrial operations, conveyance of real estate where such operations are located, and transfer of companies owning or operating such real estate. The law, enacted in 1983 and amended in 1991 and 1993, mandates that parties subject to ISRA undertake environmental audits at the time of specified closure and transfer activities and requires that remedial plans be developed if contamination is found. Transactions may not be closed until the New Jersey Department of Environmental Protection (DEP) either approves site conditions or approves a cleanup plan. Cleanups must be financially assured.

Subject Parties

A two-part test defines the "industrial establishments" that are subject to ISRA. First, the place of business or real property where such a business is conducted must fall within particular classifications in the Standard Industrial Classification Manual (SIC Manual), promulgated by the federal Office of Management and the Budget, most of which are within the manufacturing sector.[3] The SIC Manual, which was conceived as a tool for measuring development rates within American industry, was promulgated without any consideration of whether a particular business was a user or producer of hazardous substances or wastes. In delineating industries subject to ISRA, the statute goes no further than to specify the major groups covered.

Second, the business must be engaged in operations (on or after December 31, 1983) involving the generation, manufacture, refining, transportation, treatment, storage, handling, or disposal of defined hazardous substances and wastes, above or below ground. The New Jersey definition of hazardous substances includes petroleum products, so the use of heating oil alone satisfies this part of the definition.

ISRA Triggers

Triggering events are defined as the "closing, terminating, or transferring [of] operations" by the "owner or operator" of "an industrial establishment." This definition includes a long list of proceedings involving either the owner or operator of an industrial establishment or real property where such an establishment is located, including (but not limited to) the following:

- cessation of all or substantially all the operations of an industrial establishment that involve the generation, manufacture, refining, transportation, treatment, storage, handling, or disposal of hazardous substances and wastes, or temporary cessation of all or substantially all operations for a period of two years or more;
- changes in operations sufficient to change the primary SIC number from a subject to a nonsubject classification;
- conveyance of the real property where the establishment is located;
- termination of a lease term;

- any change in ownership of the industrial establishment (except for certain specifically exempted transactions), including (i) a transfer of shares of a corporation that results in a change in the controlling interest of the owner or operator of an industrial establishment; and (ii) the sale of more than 50 percent of assets within any five-year period; and
- initiation of bankruptcy proceedings under Chapter 7 or Chapter 11 of the federal Bankruptcy Code.

Since the conveyance of real property triggers ISRA, it appears that an owner of real estate where an unrelated industrial operation carries on a subject business must comply with ISRA when the real estate is to be sold or when any of the other triggering events concern the ownership entity alone. The DEP has so interpreted and applied the law. Thus, for example, if all shares of a Nebraska company that owns New Jersey industrial real estate are purchased by a California corporation in a transaction negotiated and consummated in Los Angeles, the transaction affects ownership of a subject property and ISRA applies. The Nebraska corporation is considered the "owner" of an industrial establishment, and the DEP considers the "controlling interest" of that corporation to have changed.

ISRA contains various exemptions, including a corporate reorganization not substantially affecting ownership (which is narrowly defined by the DEP regulations as a restructuring or reincorporation that does not diminish the availability of cleanup funds) or certain transfers of shares or assets among entities under common ownership.

The ISRA Process

A subject party must commence the ISRA administrative review process within five days of a triggering event, such as (1) the execution of a sale agreement; (2) the closure of an industrial operation or public release of anticipated closure, whichever occurs first; or (3) the termination of a lease term or notice of termination, whichever occurs first.

The initial filing must contain basic information about the applicant, the ISRA trigger, the nature of the proposed transaction, and the authorized agent designated to work with the DEP. Subsequent tasks must be undertaken as necessary, pursuant to a four-phase procedural scheme.

1. **Preliminary assessment**: A first-phase process involving identification of areas of environmental concern; hazardous substance and waste use; generation, storage, disposal, and

discharge history; cleanup history; and current and historical documentation.

2. **Site investigation**: A second-phase process of data collection, environmental sampling, documentation, and evaluation where warranted by site history.
3. **Remedial investigation**: A third-phase process where contamination has been found and it is necessary to delineate the nature and extent of the problem and develop a cleanup strategy.
4. **Remedial action**: The final phase, comprising all activities necessary to address and resolve the contamination.

Transactions may not be completed until the applicant has done the following:

- completed all required work, submitted a "negative declaration" that there have been no discharges or that all contamination has been cleaned up to the DEP standards, and received a final sign-off from the DEP known as a "no further action letter";
- received DEP approval of a remedial action work plan and established a funding source such as a line of credit or self-guarantee to assure the DEP of the applicant's financial ability to fund the cleanup; or
- entered into a remediation agreement (a form of consent order) with the DEP, before completion of all ISRA obligations, pursuant to which the applicant undertakes to perform whatever sampling and cleanup requirements are thereafter required by the DEP and establishes a funding source to pay for any necessary cleanup.

Finality in cleanups is addressed by ISRA's requirement that once the DEP approves a cleanup plan, it cannot later impose a tougher benchmark unless its cleanup standards have grown stricter by at least an order of magnitude.

Copies of approved negative declarations, remedial action work plans, or remediation agreements must be attached to sale agreements for affected property. If a contract has already been executed, copies of documents must be provided to all other parties to a transfer, specifically including buyers and lenders.

In cases of landlord-tenant disputes, parties may petition the DEP to review lease provisions. If the DEP finds the clauses "clear," it will first require compliance by the party responsible under the lease terms.

Exemption Procedures

Because of the ambiguities in the statute and regulations, as well as buyer and lender concerns, the DEP issues letters of applicability and nonapplicability to concerned applicants who seek confirmation that they either are or are not subject to the ISRA process. Also, there is a "de minimis quantity exemption" for otherwise subject businesses that have used only small amounts of hazardous substances. The use or generation of no more than 500 pounds or 55 gallons of any substance or waste (or 220 gallons for hydraulic and lubricating oils) at any time during the operation will qualify the owner or operator for this exemption.

The ISRA Hammer: Violation and Penalty Provisions

The failure of a transferor to comply with ISRA renders a transaction voidable by the transferee, but only after the transferee provides the transferor with notice of the failure and affords the transferor a reasonable amount of time to comply. In addition, the failure of a transferor to comply with ISRA entitles the transferee to recover damages from the transferor and renders the owner or operator of the subject industrial establishment strictly liable for all cleanup and removal costs and all direct and indirect damages resulting from failure to implement a remedial action plan.

Finally, any person who knowingly gives false information, causes false information to be given, or fails to comply with ISRA is liable for fines of up to $25,000 per violation per day. Any officer or management official who knowingly directs or authorizes violations of ISRA is personally liable for penalties.

Iowa Environmental Quality Act

The Iowa Environmental Quality Act[4] preconditions the sale of, conveyance of, or transfer of title to a hazardous waste or hazardous substance disposal site upon first obtaining the written approval of the state. Subject parties are owners of real property listed in the state registry of hazardous waste or hazardous substance disposal sites.

Before the sale of, conveyance of, or transfer of title to a disposal site listed in the registry, the owner must notify the director of the Iowa Department of Natural Resources. The department must respond to a request for a change in ownership within thirty days of receipt of the owner's notification. If the department believes that this law has been violated or that a violation is imminent, it may institute an action for injunctive relief and for assessment of a maximum penalty of $1,000 per day of the violation.

Connecticut Transfer Act

The Connecticut Transfer Act[5] requires that before the occurrence of specified business and real estate events, a subject party must certify to the transferee that the property in question is environmentally sound. Thereafter the certification must be filed with the state. If the transferor is unable to so certify, then a party associated with the transfer must either: (a) certify that the property is contaminated or that its environmental condition is unknown, and accept responsibility for investigating and remediating; or (b) certify that the property has been remediated except for postremediation monitoring, and agree to take further action as may be necessary.

Subject establishments are those at which:

- on or after November 19, 1980, more than 100 kilograms of hazardous waste per month was generated;
- hazardous wastes generated by others have been handled, used, transported, or disposed of on or after November 19, 1980;
- the process of dry-cleaning was conducted on or after May 1, 1967;
- furniture stripping was conducted on or after May 1, 1967; or
- a vehicle body repair or painting shop is or was located on or after May 1, 1967.

The act's requirements are triggered by any transaction or proceeding through which an establishment undergoes a change in ownership (except for specified exemptions such as corporate reorganizations that do not substantially affect ownership), including the conveyance of real property; the sale of stock (in the form of a statutory merger or consolidation); the sale of a controlling share of assets; a change of corporate identity; and a financial reorganization.

Before transfer of an establishment, the transferor must submit to the transferee a negative declaration stating that either there has been no discharge of hazardous wastes at the premises or that the property has been contaminated but has been cleaned up, and the cleanup has either been approved by the DEP or verified by a licensed environmental professional. Within ten days after the transfer, a copy of the document must be filed with the DEP.

Apart from the certification process, there are no preconditions to transfer, no pretransfer and cleanup plan requirements, no pretransfer state oversight, and consequently no potential state-instigated delays.

Also, there is no provision in the law for determinations of applicability or nonapplicability.

Failure of a transferor to comply with the Connecticut Transfer Act entitles the transferee to recover damages from the transferor and renders the transferor strictly liable for all remediation costs and all direct and indirect damages. Improper filing of information or failure to complete remediation or monitoring may subject the violator to an order or action to prevent or abate any contamination at the site. In addition, any person who knowingly gives false information, causes false information to be given, or fails to comply with the act is subject to a maximum fine of $100,000. However, there is no right under the act for either the state or the transferee to void a transaction.

Oregon Hazardous Waste Removal and Remedial Action Act

The Oregon Hazardous Waste Removal and Remedial Action Act,[6] enacted in 1987 and amended in 1989 and 1991, is intended to ensure that before transfer of ownership or operation of subject real property transferors have disclosed to transferees knowledge of any hazardous substance releases that occurred during the time of a transferor's ownership or operation.

Subject Parties and Property

Subject owners and operators are those who owned, leased, controlled, or exercised significant control over the operation of a "facility." Facilities to which the statute applies include buildings, structures, installations, equipment, tanks, sites, or areas where any hazardous substances have been deposited, stored, disposed of, placed, or otherwise located, but only where a release has occurred or is threatened.

Trigger, Process, and Penalty Provisions

An owner or operator who has obtained actual knowledge of a release that occurred at its facility during the time of its ownership or operation must disclose such knowledge to a transferee before transfer of ownership or operation. Failure to disclose renders the nondisclosing owner or operator strictly liable for all resulting remedial action costs incurred by the state or any other person and for all damages for injury to or destruction of any natural resources caused by a nondisclosed release.

A person who is liable under the statute who fails, without sufficient cause, to conduct a removal or remedial action required by the Oregon Department of Environmental Quality is liable to the state for any remedial action costs incurred by the state, for treble punitive damages, and for the state's reasonable legal expenses incurred in enforcing the law. Failure to comply also subjects violators to civil penalties of up to $10,000 per day.

Illinois Responsible Property Transfer Act

The Illinois Responsible Property Transfer Act (IRPTA)[7] was enacted in 1988 and applies to subject transactions occurring after January 1, 1990. It is intended to ensure that parties involved in certain real estate transactions are made aware of existing environmental liabilities associated with ownership of such properties as well as the past use and environmental status of the properties. IRPTA also aims to ensure that the people of Illinois are protected by a mechanism that provides that parties to a real estate transaction are advised of the environmental status of the property and, therefore, are encouraged to act responsibly in fulfilling the purpose and intent of existing environmental laws.

Subject Parties, Transactions, and Properties

Parties subject to IRPTA are "transferors" of "an interest in real property." Transfers that are subject to the statute are: a deed or other instrument of conveyance; a lease of real property of more than forty years; an assignment of more than 25 percent of the beneficial interest in an Illinois land trust; and a mortgage, trust deed, or collateral assignment of a beneficial interest in an Illinois land trust.

IRPTA contains specific exemptions for a number of conveyances, including confirmatory documents that modify or supplement previously recorded documents; conveyances resulting from foreclosures of mortgages, trust deeds, or other liens on subject properties; and easements.

Subject real property is defined as a "specific and identifiable parcel of land," together with improvements, that has not already been subject to bonding or other financial assurances and thereafter released following compliance with other state environmental laws and that meets one of the following conditions:

- contains one or more facilities subject to the reporting requirements under Section 312 of the federal Emergency Planning and Community Right-to-Know Act of 1986 (EPCRA); or
- is the site of underground storage tanks subject to the notification requirements of the federal underground storage tank law, the Resource Conservation and Recovery Act (RCRA).[8]

IRPTA contains specific exemptions, enacted in 1990, for single-family and multiunit residences, residential condominiums, and other residential properties. The exemptions apply unless these properties contain underground storage tanks subject to RCRA's notification requirements.

The statute defines a "transferee" as a buyer, trustee under a trust deed, owner of a beneficial interest in an Illinois land trust, mortgagee, grantee, or tenant of real property, or an assignee of a greater than 25 percent interest in an Illinois land trust.

The IRPTA Process

For conveyances subject to IRPTA, the transferor must, within thirty days after execution of the contract, and at any date no later than thirty days before the transfer, deliver a "disclosure document" to both the transferee and the lender advancing any funds to be secured by an interest in the property or collateral assignment of beneficial interest in an Illinois land trust holding title to real property.

The disclosure document must be in a form required by IRPTA and must contain specified information regarding the site and its environmental condition. Such information includes a description of past and current operations at the site involving the generation, handling, or treatment of hazardous substances and wastes; the existence of any landfills, surface impoundments, waste piles, underground and aboveground storage tanks, injection wells, septic systems, transfer stations, and other storage and treatment areas; the history of any cleanups on the site; and the ownership history of the site.

If the disclosure document reveals previously unknown environmental defects, or if the transferor fails to deliver the disclosure document within the time constraints imposed by IRPTA and has not obtained a time waiver from the other parties, any of the parties to the transfer (including, by definition, the lender) may at their own discretion, within ten days after demand for or receipt of the disclosure document, void any obligation to accept a transfer or finance a transfer that has yet to be closed or finalized.

Within thirty days after the date of any subject transfer or on recording of the instrument of conveyance, whichever occurs first, the disclosure document must be recorded in the office of the recorder of the county in which the property is located and filed with the Illinois Environmental Protection Agency. Responsibility for recording and filing the disclosure document is placed jointly on the transferor and the transferee. However, failure by any party to comply with IRPTA will not affect any lien or the priority of any mortgage, trust deed, or collateral assignment of a beneficial interest in an Illinois land trust.

Violation and Penalty Provisions

Failure to comply with IRPTA's disclosure requirements renders a party liable for civil penalties of up to $1,000 per day per violation. Any party or transferor who knowingly makes a false statement, representation, or certification in the disclosure document is liable for civil penalties of up to $10,000 per day per violation. Any person who fails to record a disclosure document is jointly and severally liable for civil penalties of up to $10,000.

Finally, any person who suffers damage resulting from an IRPTA violation may sue for monetary damages. In such an action, the court may award reasonable attorney's fees and costs to the prevailing party. However, no action may be taken against a transferee for failure to record a disclosure document if the transferor is in violation of the disclosure document requirements.

Indiana Responsible Property Transfer Law

The Indiana Responsible Property Transfer Law,[9] enacted in 1989 and amended in 1990, applies to transactions entered into after December 31, 1989. In general, it requires that before certain transfers of real property transferors must provide transferees and mortgage lenders with a disclosure document describing the property's environmental history and status. The Indiana law generally follows the Illinois Responsible Property Transfer Act, but the 1990 Indiana amendments include substantive alterations.

Subject Parties and Transactions

Similar to IRPTA's provisions, subject parties under the Indiana statute are "transferors" of subject properties. The statute applies to numerous types of transactions, including conveyances by deed or lease beyond forty years or with a purchase option; mortgages; and certain assignments of a land trust. Certain types of transactions are exempt.[10]

Subject real property is defined exactly as it is in IRPTA, as any specific and identifiable parcel of land, together with improvements, that has not already been subject to bonding or other financial assurances and thereafter released following compliance with applicable state laws. The property must contain one or more facilities subject to the EPCRA reporting requirements, be the site of one or more underground storage tanks subject to registration under RCRA, or be listed on the CERCLA Information System (CERCLIS).

"Transferee" is defined as a buyer, mortgagee, grantee, or tenant of real property; an assignee of a greater than 25 percent interest in a land trust; or, in the case of a transfer to the trustee of a land trust, the owners of the beneficial interest in the land trust. The term includes prospective transferees.

The Indiana Transfer Law Process

The Indiana statute contains a provision similar to that in IRPTA mandating the delivery of a "disclosure document," no later than thirty days before the transfer, to the transferee and any lender providing a loan to be secured by an interest in the property or by an assignment of beneficial interest in a land trust. However, the buyer of a subject property who finances the purchase by way of a mortgage loan is not required to deliver a disclosure document to the mortgagee.

The form of the disclosure document and the information that must be included in the document closely track the provisions of IRPTA. The Indiana statute, however, also requires that the existence of "environmental defects" be included in the disclosure document. Defects requiring disclosure under this provision are defined to include an act, omission, or condition that constitutes a material violation of an environmental statute or regulation; that requires remedial activity under an environmental statute or regulation; that presents a substantial endangerment to public welfare or the environment; or that would have a material adverse effect on the market value of the property or an abutting property.

If the disclosure document reveals previously unknown environmental defects, any party to the transfer, including the lender, may at its own discretion void any obligation to accept a transfer or finance a transfer that has yet to be closed or finalized. The Indiana transfer statute, however, does not permit voiding of obligations following completion of a transaction.

Within thirty days after the date of any subject transfer, the disclosure document, together with any site plan appended to it, must be recorded by the transferor or transferee in the office of the recorder of the county in which the property is located and filed by the transferor with the Indiana Department of Environmental Management.

If a disclosure document has been recorded and the environmental defect is remedied after the recording of the document, a person with a financial interest in the property may record a document reporting the elimination of the environmental defect. The document must be certified by a registered professional engineer who has no financial interest in the property.

Violation and Penalty Provisions

The Indiana provisions are similar to those of IRPTA.

Michigan Natural Resources and Environmental Protection Act

The Michigan Natural Resources and Environmental Protection Act (MNREPA)[11] was originally enacted in 1982 and was substantially amended in 1990. The Michigan environmental laws were recodified in 1994, and again substantially amended in 1995. The primary feature of the law is a requirement that before the transfer of an interest in subject real property, transferors with information about a hazardous substance release must give written disclosure to transferees of the general nature and extent of the release.

Subject Parties and Transactions

Subject parties under MNREPA are transferors of interests in subject real property. Subject properties are those at which hazardous substances in excess of the allowable concentrations have been released, deposited, disposed of, or otherwise come to be located. The portion of a property where a release has occurred is known as a "facility."

Trigger, Process, and Penalty Provisions

A transferor with knowledge or information or who was on notice that a parcel of property is a facility must, before transfer of the property, provide written notice to a transferee that the property is subject and that there has been a release. The notice must be recorded in the county register of deeds if the instrument of conveyance is recorded. The transferor must also disclose any land or resource use restrictions that apply to the real property as part of a remedial action that has been or is being implemented due to the release.

An intentionally false or inaccurate notice renders the transferor subject to prosecution for a felony, with fines of up to $25,000 per violation per day and up to two years' imprisonment. Subsequent conviction renders a transferor liable for penalties of up to $50,000 per day per violation and up to two years' imprisonment.

The Ohio Clean Closure Act

The Ohio Clean Closure Act[12] was enacted to ensure that necessary and appropriate steps are taken to protect health, safety, and the environment due to temporary or permanent discontinuation of operations involving the production, use, storage, or other handling of hazardous substances.

Subject Operations and Parties

The law applies to the permanent or temporary cessation of operations, and transactions or proceedings involving the cessation of operations, at facilities where hazardous substances are produced, used, or stored. However, the law does not apply to oil or gas production operations, equipment, petroleum, or piping owned by a public utility, or underground storage tank systems, provided that those facilities are already subject to closure requirements under Ohio law and regulations.

Trigger, Process, and Penalty Provisions

If an owner or operator intends to temporarily discontinue operations for thirty days to one year, the Ohio Environmental Protection Agency (EPA) must be notified in writing within forty-five days after the discontinuation of the operations as to the date the operations were discontinued, and the owner or operator must certify that the cessation of operations will not exceed one year. An owner or operator who temporarily discontinues operations for more than one year may request a waiver from EPA and must provide EPA with an interim maintenance and operation plan that sufficiently demonstrates that the operations will be resumed and that no unauthorized entry or any contamination will occur during the interim. If EPA does not grant a waiver, the owner or operator may be subject to procedures required for those who permanently cease operations.

If an owner or operator intends to permanently cease all regulated operations, including instances where waivers have been denied or revoked, the owner or operator must submit to EPA and designated local authorities a notice of cessation. Within thirty days of cessation, the owner or operator must secure all buildings and structures on the subject facilities from unauthorized entry until EPA has verified compliance. Within ninety days of cessation, the owner or operator must submit to EPA a copy of the most recent Emergency and Hazardous Chemical Inventory Form, accompanied by a statement indicating whether asbestos materials are present, a current Hazardous Chemical

List or Material Safety Data Sheets, if such owner or operator was required to have the data sheets on file with the state environmental response commission, and a list of every stationary tank, vat, or electrical transformer (vessels) that contain or are contaminated with regulated substances. The owner or operator must indicate which vessels are to remain at the facility, as well as the location of each and an identification of regulated substances that are in or contaminating each. The owner or operator must drain or remove all regulated substances from each vessel and from all piping that will remain at the facility and properly transport, transfer, manage, or remove all regulated substances in compliance with applicable state and federal laws. The owner or operator must additionally remove all debris, nonstationary equipment, furniture containers, and moving vehicles that contain or are contaminated with hazardous substances from the property and properly transfer the substances in compliance with all applicable state laws, and certify to EPA that the draining and removal has been completed in compliance with all applicable laws. Finally, the owner or operator must designate a contact person who will have responsibility for providing EPA with access and information concerning the reporting facility.

A violator could be subject to a civil penalty of up to $10,000 per day, per violation. Initial knowing violations could result in fines between $10,000 and $25,000 or a prison term of two to four years, or both. Subsequent knowing violations could result in fines ranging between $25,000 and $50,000 or a prison term of up to two years or four years, or both. Failure to secure the facility against unlawful entry could result in a civil penalty of up to $5,000 per day, per violation. EPA may request the attorney general to initiate either a criminal prosecution or a civil action for injunction against any person in violation of any provision of the Clean Closure Act.

Hawaii Environmental Disclosure Act

Enacted in 1982, the Hawaii Environmental Disclosure Act[13] requires that subject parties who own voting securities of a Hawaii corporation file an environmental disclosure statement before purchasing additional voting securities or assets of that corporation.

Subject Parties and Transactions

Any party, including a corporation, partnership, or other entity, that beneficially owns 10 percent or more of any class of voting securities of a Hawaii corporation may not purchase more than an additional 5 percent of any such security or 5 percent or more of the assets of such corporation during any twelve-month period without first filing a disclosure statement with the Hawaii Office of Environmental Quality Control.

Certain transactions, however, are exempt. Specifically, these are purchases of any voting securities or assets by a person already owning 50 percent or more of such securities or assets and purchases of voting securities or assets of a corporation having less than one hundred shareholders of record.

Trigger, Process, and Penalty Provisions

A transaction may not be completed until the disclosure statement has been filed, the requisite waiting period has expired, any required hearings have been conducted, and any corrections of the disclosure statement have been completed.

The subject party must file a disclosure statement with the state agency. The statement must contain, among other things, information about the subject business and its compliance with environmental laws. If a subject party fails to file a disclosure statement, or refuses to participate in a hearing or produce relevant documents, the state agency may recommend to the state attorney general that the person be prohibited from completing the transaction within the following year.

If the state agency believes that any person has engaged in or intends to engage in a violation of the law, the agency may refer the matter to the state attorney general, who may commence an action to enjoin the purchase temporarily or permanently, to enforce compliance with the law, and to impose a civil penalty of up to $100,000. Any person, including the target company or its shareholders, aggrieved as a result of a violation of the law, may sue to enjoin any practice constituting a violation. The court is specifically empowered to rescind the transaction, impose a civil penalty of up to $100,000, award attorney's fees, and grant any other available relief.

San Francisco's Ordinance

San Francisco's municipal ordinance,[14] to date the only one of its kind, was enacted in 1986 and amended in 1988. As it currently stands, the law requires building permit applicants to undertake site histories and soil sampling for hazardous wastes as a condition to issuance of certain permits and mandates cleanup of hazardous wastes before issuance of building permits if contamination is found. Subject parties are applicants for building permits when the permit sought is for a construction project involving disturbance of at least fifty cubic yards of soil.

The Process

A subject permit applicant must submit a site history, which is reviewed by, among others, the municipal director of public health. The applicant must then undertake detailed sampling in line with specific sampling parameters outlined in the law and must also undertake further sampling if ordered by the director after the review of the site history. If no hazardous wastes are found, the director provides the applicant with written notification of compliance with the ordinance, enabling the applicant to move forward with the building permit application.

If hazardous wastes are found, the applicant must submit to both the directors of public health and public works a site mitigation report, certified by a qualified professional, either establishing that no cleanup is necessary or proposing a cleanup plan. If a qualified professional concludes that a cleanup is necessary, the cleanup proceeds. The director of public health must determine whether site mitigation is complete. If it is, once the applicant completes a final certification, the director of public health must notify the director of public works, who may then proceed to consider the building permit.

Sellers and sellers' agents involved in the sale of any San Francisco real property must provide a copy of Ordinance 253-86 to buyers and obtain receipts from the buyers acknowledging the copies.

Related State Laws

Other states, while not specifically mandating environmental cleanup as a prerequisite to transactions, require disclosure of certain conditions on real property before a sale or transaction. New Hampshire and Minnesota provide examples.

The New Hampshire Waterfront Property Septic Disclosure Law,[15] for example, requires that before execution of a purchase and sale agreement for any developed waterfront property utilizing a septic disposal system, a site assessment study must be performed and disclosed to the buyer. Failure of the seller or the seller's agent to notify the buyer of the assessment is punishable by a fine of up to $500. In addition, the New Hampshire Water and Sewer Disclosure Law[16] requires that sellers of real property disclose information to purchasers relative to private water supplies and septic and sewage disposal systems.

The Minnesota Well Disclosure Law[17] aims to ensure that before the transfer of subject real property transferors disclose to transferees the status and location of all known wells on the property.

Notes

This chapter is based on materials developed by Mr. Farer over the past eight years for the annual ALI-ABA advanced course of study "The Impact of Environmental Law on Real Estate and Other Commercial Transactions," chaired by Mr. Farer.

1. N.J. STAT. ANN. § 13:1K-6 *et seq.* (1993).

2. Current Rules: N.J. ADMIN. CODE tit. 7, § 26B-1.1 *et seq.*; Unadopted Cleanup Standards Proposal (currently being used as guidance document): 24 N.J. Reg. 373 (February 3, 1992).

3. Major groups 22–39, 46–49, 51, and 76 are subject to ISRA.

4. IOWA CODE ANN. § 455B.430 (enacted 1984); current Regulations: IOWA ADMIN. CODE r. 567-148.1 *et seq.* (enacted 1992).

5. CONN. GEN. STAT. ANN. §§ 22a-134 to 134d (enacted 1985; amended 1987 and 1995).

6. OR. REV. STAT. §§ 465.200–260 and § 465.900 (enacted 1987; amended 1989 and 1991).

7. 765 ILL. COMP. STAT. 90/1–90/7 (enacted 1988; amended 1989, 1990, 1991, and 1992).

8. 42 U.S.C. § 6991.

9. IND. CODE §§ 13-7-22.5-1 *et seq.* (enacted 1989; amended 1990).

10. The statutory exceptions, many of which track IRPTA, include confirmatory documents, conveyances resulting from foreclosures, installment land contracts, and easements.

11. MICH. COMP. LAWS §§ 324.20116, 324.20139 (underlying statute enacted 1982; relevant amendments enacted 1990; recodified 1994; amended 1995).

12. OHIO REV. CODE ANN. §§ 3752.01 to 3752.99 (enacted 1994; effective date amended in 1995; effective January 1, 1996).

13. HAW. REV. STAT. §§ 343D-1 to -11 (enacted 1982).

14. CAL. PUBLIC WORKS CODE art. 20, §§ 1001–15 (enacted 1986 as Ordinance 253-86; amended 1988 by Ordinance 348-88).

15. N.H. REV. STAT. ANN. § 485-A:39 (enacted 1989; effective Jan. 1, 1990; amended 1992).

16. N.H. REV. STAT. ANN. § 477:4-c to 4-d (enacted May 18, 1992; effective Jan. 1, 1993; amended 1994).

17. MINN. STAT. § 103I.235 (enacted 1989; effective July 1, 1990; amended 1991, 1992, and 1994).

CHAPTER 4

Lender Liability Issues

JILL A. KOTVIS

Lenders today must be intimately familiar with environmental laws and regulations. Besides affecting borrowers' financial viability and the value of borrowers' assets taken as collateral, such laws may directly impact lenders as a result of their actions in monitoring, "working out," and foreclosing on loans.[1] The primary environmental risks to lenders are discussed in this chapter.

Lender Risk Considerations under Environmental Laws

Impact on the Value of Collateral and on Borrowers' Financial Capability

Lenders face the risk that the value of real property collateral will decrease because of preexisting contamination or contamination arising during the life of the loan. A lender may be left with no security if its collateral is environmentally impaired. It is even conceivable that the cost of remediating a severe environmental problem will exceed the value of the collateral. In such a case, a lender may be left with a defaulted mortgage and a foreclosed property that requires expensive cleanup to make it marketable.

The borrower's profitability and, consequently, its ability to repay a loan may be significantly affected by the burden of complying with exhaustive federal, state, and local environmental laws and regulations, including the requirement of cleaning up contamination on the borrower's property.[2]

Subordination of Security Interest to Environmental Liens

Under the Comprehensive Environmental Response, Compensation, and Liability Act of 1980 (CERCLA), commonly known as Superfund, as amended by the Superfund Amendments and Reauthorization Act of 1986 (SARA),[3] property can be subject to a federal lien in an amount required as reimbursement for costs incurred in remediating the property. Although this lien takes priority only over subsequently filed liens, in several states environmental "super liens" take priority over prior recorded liens, including deeds of trust. In some states a super lien may extend beyond the remediated property to the other real or personal property of the owner.[4]

Direct Liability of Lenders

Lenders have increasingly become unwilling players in the environmental liability game. Some courts, interpreting CERCLA, have expressed a desire to impose on lenders an obligation to ensure the environmental compliance of borrowers. Hence, lenders may find themselves directly liable for, or immersed in litigation involving, environmental noncompliance and cleanup costs as owners, operators, or arrangers under CERCLA or under various theories of federal, state, and local environmental laws.

Lender Liability under CERCLA

CERCLA's Liability Scheme

Basic Liability Principles

CERCLA poses the principal environmental risk to lenders with security interests in real or personal property. Congress enacted CERCLA primarily to address inactive or abandoned hazardous waste sites. It also wanted to respond to future hazardous substance releases. In general, CERCLA authorizes the U.S. Environmental Protection Agency (EPA) to identify abandoned hazardous waste sites, rank those sites by degree of hazard on the National Priorities List (NPL), clean up the sites, and take enforcement action whenever there is a release into the environment. In addition, private parties are entitled to seek reimbursement of incurred response costs from "potentially responsible parties" (PRPs) if the costs are "necessary" and consistent with the National Contingency Plan (NCP).[5] (See Chapter 1).

Under CERCLA, the four classes of parties that may be liable for the costs of cleaning up contaminated property are: (1) current owners and operators of the property; (2) parties who owned or operated the site at the time of the contamination; (3) parties who produced the hazardous substance causing the contamination or arranged for its disposal, treatment, or transportation; and (4) transporters of hazardous substances.[6]

Security Interest Exemption

Lenders may incur liability under CERCLA primarily as "owners" or "operators." The lending community initially believed it was fully protected from CERCLA liability by the act's "security interest exemption." The CERCLA definition of owner or operator expressly excludes "a person, who, without participating in the management of a . . . facility, holds indicia of ownership primarily to protect his security interest in the . . . facility,"[7] (known alternatively as the security interest exemption, lender liability exemption, and secured creditor exemption). However, the statute failed to define the terms "indicia of ownership," "participating in management," and "primarily to protect his security interest." Congress also failed to provide legislative history or statutory guidance on these points.[8] Thus, the courts began to fill in the definitional gaps.

Case Law Interpretations: Before the EPA Lender Liability Rule

Before the EPA attempted to develop its Lender Liability Rule (discussed later in this chapter), courts interpreting the secured creditor exemption diverged on two key points: (1) whether a lender became an owner upon foreclosure and automatically lost its exemption; and (2) whether a lender became an operator and thereby lost its exemption by having the mere capacity to control, as opposed to actually controlling, the borrower or its operations.

Lender as "Owner"

The first CERCLA case relating to a secured lender involved the repossession of personal property (underground storage tanks) rather than foreclosure on a security interest in real property. The U.S. Bankruptcy Court for the Northern District of Ohio held, in *In re T.P. Long Chemical, Inc.*,[9] that the lender's mere "repossession" of the tanks did not make it an owner or operator of the facility responsible for cleaning up the contamination arising from or caused by the tanks.

The following year, the U.S. District Court for Maryland decided the first case involving liability of a lender as an "owner" upon foreclosure in *United States v. Maryland Bank & Trust Co.*[10] The court held that a lender that foreclosed on a deed of trust, held title for four years, and failed to comply with the EPA's request to clean up preexisting hazardous wastes was liable to the EPA as owner of the facility. At the time of the cleanup, the court concluded that the lender held indicia of ownership to protect its investment in the land rather than merely to protect its security interest. In 1989, the U.S. District Court for the Western District of Pennsylvania decided *Guidice v. BFG Electroplating & Manufacturing Co.*, relying in part on *Maryland Bank & Trust Co.* In *Guidice*, the court denied the lender's motion for summary judgment. The court reasoned that "when a lender is the successful purchaser at a foreclosure sale, the lender should be liable to the same extent as any other bidder at the sale would have been."[11] The bank in that case held the property for eighteen months following foreclosure.

Two subsequent federal appeals court decisions examined whether a secured creditor could be an "owner" based on the degree of the creditor's participation in the management of the borrower's operations. The Ninth Circuit, in *In re Bergsoe Metal Corp.*,[12] held that the mere capacity or unexercised right to control facility operations is insufficient to void the secured creditor exemption. The court reasoned that "there must be some actual management of the facility before a secured creditor will fall outside the exemption." In *Bergsoe*, the defendant, a municipal corporation organized to issue bonds, held title to a lead recycling facility primarily to ensure that the plant operator would meet its obligations under the bonds. The court decided that the defendant held indicia of ownership primarily to protect a security interest in the plant and did not participate in management of the site. The plaintiff argued that the defendant should have been deemed to have participated in management because it negotiated and encouraged building the plant and possessed certain rights to inspect and take possession of the premises. The court rejected these arguments. It stated that, under CERCLA's "participating in management" terminology, the critical issue is not what rights the lender has but, rather, how the lender acts.

In contrast, in the infamous *United States v. Fleet Factors Corp.*,[13] the Eleventh Circuit held that a secured creditor may incur liability as an owner or operator merely by participating in the financial management of a facility to a degree indicating a capacity to influence the corporation's treatment of hazardous waste; by actually becoming involved in the day-to-day operations of the facility; or by participating in management decisions involving hazardous wastes. Under *Fleet Factors*, a lender could be held liable if it had sufficiently broad involvement with the borrower's management to support the inference that it could, if it chose, affect the borrower's hazardous waste disposal decisions. Such control could be inferred from the extent of the lender's involvement in the facility's management. The court concluded that no *inference of control* was necessary in this case because the lender had *actively controlled* the facility's disposal of hazardous waste. The Supreme Court denied Fleet Factors's petition for *writ of certiorari* in January 1991, declining to resolve the Ninth and Eleventh Circuit conflict regarding the secured creditor exemption.

A later case, *Snediker Developers Ltd. Partnership v. Evans*[14] in the Eastern District of Michigan, adopted the reasoning of *Bergsoe*.[15] The *Snediker* court granted summary judgment to land contract vendors of a contaminated facility who retained the deed as security, reasoning that they did not participate in the management of the facility and held legal title solely to protect a security interest.

Lender as "Operator"

The U.S. District Court for the Eastern District of Pennsylvania, in *United States v. Mirabile*,[16] first announced the general rule on when a secured creditor could be considered an "operator" under CERCLA. The *Mirabile* court held that a secured creditor "must, at a minimum, participate in the day-to-day operational aspects of the site" (e.g., in operational, production, or waste disposal activities) before operator liability could be triggered. On that basis, the court granted summary judgment in favor of two of the three secured creditors. It decided that the lender's postforeclosure actions (i.e., securing the property, exhibiting it to potential buyers, and investigating cleanup costs) did not constitute "participating in the borrower's management" but were instead designed to protect its security interest. The court found that the second lender's actions were limited to purely financial aspects of the borrower's operations and therefore did not constitute participation in the borrower's management.

The court, however, denied the summary judgment motion in favor of the third lender. It held that a genuine issue of material fact existed regarding whether that lender's actions constituted participation in management. The court held that the lender's placement of one of its loan officers on the borrower's board would not have been sufficient to qualify for participation in management, since the loan officer's responsibilities extended only to financial matters and did not encompass production or waste disposal issues. However, the lender became increasingly involved in the borrower's day-to-day operations, including supervision of cash collateral accounts, following the borrower's bankruptcy filing.

The 1989 decision in *Guidice*[17] similarly held that a bank became a CERCLA operator by taking "prudent measures" *preforeclosure* to protect its security interest in the property, including: (1) receiving periodic financial statements; (2) meeting with corporate officers after loan default to ascertain status of financial conditions and operations; (3) gathering information on status of accounts, raw material, and personnel changes; (4) contacting state officials regarding the facility's compliance with the waste-water discharge requirements; (5) inspecting the property after the business closed and reporting results to the lender; (6) assisting the borrower in its application for a small business loan; (7) holding a series of meetings regarding loan restructuring; (8) referring a potential lessee to the owners; and (9) agreeing to provide financing to an individual affiliated with the borrower if she were the successful purchaser at the foreclosure sale.

The EPA Lender Liability Rule

Overview and Analysis

After two drafts and a year and a half of comments and modifications, the EPA promulgated the final version of its long-awaited Lender Liability Rule on April 29, 1992.[18] The agency issued the rule largely in response to an aggressive lobbying effort by the financial community. The lack of a clear definition of "participation in management," further exacerbated by the holding in *Fleet Factors*,[19] heightened lenders' apprehensions. The EPA rule sought to reconcile the lenders' needs with the EPA's duty to protect the environment. Accordingly, the EPA, recognizing that "judicial interpretations of the exemption are varied in their articulations of the meaning of 'participation in management,' " issued the rule specifically to "reduce these uncertainties" and to "specify the range of permissible actions that may be undertaken by holders of a security interest within the bounds of the § 101(20)(A) security interest exemption."[20]

The Lender Liability Rule represented an attempt to clarify and expand safe harbors for lenders. Surprisingly, it also represented a retreat by the EPA from some of the more aggressive regulatory and judicial positions on lender liability. The rule provided a pro-lender interpretation, rejecting the *Maryland Bank*[21] and *Guidice*[22] courts' approach, which voided the secured creditor exemption upon foreclosure. In addition, the rule rejected the *Fleet Factors'*[23] capacity-to-influence standard by requiring active involvement as a prerequisite to finding participation in management. In general, the rule coupled new tests with examples of permitted activity. For example, in the preloan period, the rule allowed lenders to conduct any activities deemed necessary without risking CERCLA liability. During the loan term, while the borrower still possesses the property, the rule permitted lenders great latitude in policing the loan, as long as such activities did not amount to actual participation in management of the facility or the borrower's business. The EPA also permitted lenders to wind up the borrower's business and foreclose on property, provided the lenders took only those actions necessary to preserve the assets and did nothing to contribute to or cause environmental contamination. The rule alleviated some of the uncertainty created by the conflicting case law and provided guidance for lenders.

It did not, however, resolve all lender liability issues. Some criticized the rule because it was not retroactive and did not provide guidance for resolving lender liability under other federal statutes, such as the Resource Conservation and Recovery Act (RCRA) (which contains a security interest exemption that applies to owners of underground storage tanks.)[24] Others criticized the rule for the following reasons:

- It did not preempt state hazardous waste laws. A lender therefore might face liability under state laws based on permitted activities under CERCLA and the rule.[25]
- It did not provide certainty to parties using nontraditional financing techniques, such as convertible debt or debt with an equity kicker.
- It allowed the EPA to proceed against a lender and recoup funds without regard to the security interest exemption.
- It implied that the EPA or a third-party claimant has the burden of proving that a lender is not entitled to the secured creditor exemption, contrary to the *Fleet Factors*[26] and *Maryland Bank*[27] cases.[28]
- It was silent as to whether a lender can reestablish the protection of the security interest exemption if the exemption is lost with regard to one environmental issue.

The most significant criticism leveled against the Lender Liability Rule ultimately led to its downfall. In the rule's preamble, the EPA stated unequivocally that the rule applied to all CERCLA activities, whether brought by the government or private parties, because it had adopted the rule as part of the NCP. The EPA thus intended that a private party may recover under CERCLA Section 107(a)(4)(B) only to the extent that such party incurred costs consistent with the NCP. Therefore, any action to recover response costs from a security interest holder would have had to pass muster under the NCP, which exempts lenders under most circumstances.[29] Critics expressed serious doubt about whether the EPA had the authority to revise the NCP to promulgate its Lender Liability Rule, since the NCP's limited purpose is to identify and clean up toxic waste sites.

The Challenge to the EPA's Authority to Issue the Rule

The ink was barely dry in the *Federal Register* when the State of Michigan and the Chemical Manufacturers Association challenged the EPA's authority to issue the Lender Liability Rule.[30] These parties argued that (1) the EPA lacked the authority to issue a rule interpreting the exemption and (2) the interpretation was inconsistent with the language in CERCLA.[31]

On February 4, 1994, two members of a three-judge panel of the U.S. Court of Appeals for the District of Columbia Circuit issued an opinion agreeing with the petitioners, holding that the "EPA lacks statutory authority to restrict by regulation private party rights of action arising under the statute."[32] The court ruled that the EPA could not, by regulation, limit a party's liability under Section 107 of CERCLA; only the judiciary could define Section 107's parameters. Interestingly, the court also refused to sustain the rule as an interpretive regulation for the same reasons it struck down the rule as a legislative regulation. Finally, the majority noted that the EPA had not requested that the rule be sustained as an agency statement of policy. It refused to grant the rule even that minimal status and ultimately vacated it.[33]

Effect of Voidance of the Lender Liability Rule

Case Law Impact

Several cases decided subsequent to the rule's issuance, and based solely on the statute (and not on the rule), offer the lending community some guidance. These cases are important because they appear to reject the *Fleet Factors*[34] "mere capacity to influence" standard as well as the *Maryland Bank and Trust Co.*[35] holding that a lender loses the security interest exemption merely upon foreclosure.

Specifically, in *Grantors to the Silresim Site Trust v. State Street Bank & Trust Co.*,[36] the court ruled that a lender was entitled to the benefits of the security interest exemption because none of its activities constituted participation in management. The lender's mere ability to affect management decisions was insufficient to void the security interest exemption. (At this writing, this case is on appeal to the U.S. Court of Appeals for the First Circuit.)

In *United States v. McLamb*,[37] the U.S. Court of Appeals for the Fourth Circuit narrowed *Maryland Bank & Trust Co.*[38] and provided some security to foreclosing lenders. In this case, the Fourth Circuit ruled in favor of a lender that purchased the collateral property at a foreclosure sale, as the sole bidder, on the basis that the lender "almost immediately placed the property on the market, took no steps to use or manage the land during its ownership, and ultimately sold the property to the first able buyer." The court held that such steps supported the lender's claim "that it held title primarily, indeed exclusively, to protect its security interest." In *Northeast Doran, Inc. v. Key Bank of Maine*,[39] the U.S. Court of Appeals for the First Circuit also upheld the postforeclosure application of the security interest exemption, without relying on the Lender Liability Rule, when a lender "makes a reasonably prompt effort to divest itself of its unwelcome ownership."

Superfund Reauthorization Impact

Congress may yet provide the EPA with the legislative authority required to reissue the Lender Liability Rule. Congressional hearings on Superfund Reauthorization raise this possibility, as does President Clinton's proposed Superfund Reauthorization package. The President's proposal would amend Section 115 of CERCLA to provide the EPA with authority to promulgate regulations that define the terms and scope of all sections of CERCLA, specifically as they apply to "lenders and other financial service providers, and property custodians, trustees, and other fiduciaries."[40] The proposed amendment also withdraws jurisdiction from the courts to review the final rule issued by the EPA.

EPA Policy Impact

Although they provide some level of comfort, the recent lender liability opinions certainly do not provide the same degree of guidance contemplated by the Lender Liability Rule. However, in a March 21, 1994, correspondence from EPA Administrator Browner and then-Treasury Secretary Bentsen to the American Banker's Association, the EPA and the U.S. Treasury Department confirmed that "the policy adopted by the EPA rule remains the policy of this Administration." They further pledged "that the Administration will pursue whatever actions are necessary to ensure that lenders and trustees will not be held liable under the Superfund law because of the actions of their borrowers or principals."

Case Law Interpretations: After the EPA Lender Liability Rule

Cases decided since the issuance of the Lender Liability Rule have begun to provide guidance to lenders as they develop environmental risk management programs.

Lender Activities: Preforeclosure

In a bench ruling, the U.S. District Court for Massachusetts ruled that a lender was entitled to the secured creditor exemption because none of its activities constituted participation in management.[41] The court found that the following actions did not constitute participation in management: (1) the bank's periodic forbearance from collecting on a loan or increasing the line of credit; (2) the demands of the bank with respect to collateral and security (which remain undefined in the opinion); and (3) the bank's direct contacts with those who owed money to the borrower in an effort to collect on accounts receivable that secured the loan.

The court based its decision on the statutory language in the secured creditor exemption rather than the Lender Liability Rule. The court expressly declined to decide the case on the basis of the rule, which it said raised "concerns about whether the agency rule adopted long after all of the events in this case is either binding on this court or should be given some degree of deference by this Court in arriving at an appropriate interpretation of the statute." By way of *dictum*, however, the court noted that "the rule does require more in the way of a relationship to constitute participating in the management in a relevant sense here than at least one might argumentatively read the statute [to require]."

The fact that the court based its decision solely on the statute rather than the rule is significant because the court held, contrary to *Fleet Factors*,[42] that the mere ability to affect management decisions was not sufficient to void the secured creditor exemption. In this case the court found that the lender's financial influence over the borrower did not necessarily influence the borrower's waste disposal practices simply because the borrower operated a waste reclamation plant.

In *Kelley ex rel. Michigan Natural Resources Commission v. Tiscornia*, the State of Michigan sued to recover environmental cleanup costs from a lender.[43] Deciding in favor of the lender on cross motions for summary judgment, the court held that a lender's monitoring of the borrower's financial condition, and management of the company by a bank-recommended workout specialist, did not constitute "participation in the management nor make the lender an operator of the hazardous waste sites." Activities taken by the bank during the life of the loan included lender's representation on the borrower's board and its receipt of financial information concerning the borrower's affairs. Additionally, during the workout period, the lender participated in decisions made by, and attended meetings with, the borrower's officers.

The court concluded that, although the lender exercised some influence over the borrower, its actions did not trigger Superfund liability because the lender had not exercised *actual* control over or engaged in *actual* decision making for the borrower, nor had it exercised control over the borrower's hazardous substance handling or environmental compliance practices. The court further concluded that the lender's workout activities did not constitute participation in management because the borrower was free to disregard the lender's advice (and risk having the loan called). The *Kelley v. Tiscornia* case was not appealed.

In *Reading Co. v. City of Philadelphia*,[44] the city of Philadelphia purchased and leased to Reading Company new railcars that released PCBs onto the rail beds. The court denied the city's motion for summary judgment, finding genuine issues of material fact concerning whether the city held ownership in railcars primarily to protect its security interest and whether it participated in management of the railcars. The court allowed that the Lender Liability Rule shed some light on the meaning of the term "primarily to protect a security interest" and, citing *Fleet Factors*,[45] stated that the city had the "burden of proof with regard to its claimed status as a secured creditor exempt from CERCLA liability." The court stated that: (1) the city may not have held title to the cars solely to protect its security interest because it purchased the cars for the purpose of "improving service to attract ridership to support the downtown areas"; and (2) the city may have participated in management of the cars because the city set the train schedules and the terms of the lease required that the cars be used primarily on city-subsidized lines.

Lender Activities: Foreclosure/Postforeclosure

In *Ashland Oil, Inc. v. Sonford Products Corp.*,[46] the court specifically applied the Lender Liability Rule despite the fact that it was promulgated after the lawsuit was filed. The plaintiff leased a site to the borrower who caused the contamination. The lender had taken a security interest in the borrower's equipment, inventory, and barrels that allegedly leaked. The lender foreclosed on the assets following the borrower's filing of a bankruptcy petition and briefly held title to the assets to facilitate transfer to a prospective purchaser. The court found that, by conducting periodic reviews of the borrower's finances, the lender did not participate in management or exercise decision-making control over the borrower's environmental compliance. Nor did it become an owner or operator by foreclosing on the security interest or selling the "contaminated assets." The court also specifically rejected the argument that the lender had "arranged for disposal" by foreclosure and sale of the contaminated assets.

Waterville Industries, Inc. v. Finance Authority of Maine[47] was the first case explicitly to apply the secured creditor exemption to sale-leaseback transactions and to guarantors of loan obligations. The U.S.

Court of Appeals for the First Circuit dismissed a private party's claim for response costs brought against a state agency acting as a lender-lessor in a sale-leaseback arrangement. The court reasoned that the state agency was not liable as an owner as long as it made a "reasonably prompt effort to divest itself of its unwelcome ownership" when the lessee "by default or otherwise" lost its contractual rights to regain full ownership. The state agency originally guaranteed the loan of a private corporation. The agency later made substantial payments to cure the borrower's defaults and in return received mortgages on the site. Thereafter, the authority accepted a deed in lieu of foreclosing on the property and leased the property back to the borrower, with an option of purchasing the site for one dollar at the end of the lease. During its operation of the site as lessee, the borrower released hazardous waste into two on-site lagoons.

The court rejected the argument that the state authority became the owner of the land through the sale-leaseback arrangement. It reasoned that the authority structured the transaction solely to protect its security interest. The court further noted that when Congress wrote Section 101(20)(A), it had in mind "not only the classic case of the bank mortgage but also equivalent devices serving the same function, such as lease-financing arrangements." Contrary to the decisions in the *Ashland* and *Fleet Factors* cases, the court in *Waterville* expressly did not rely on the EPA rule because the events there took place before the rule's effective date.

Following the issuance of the Lender Liability Rule, the court in *United States v. Fleet Factors Corp.*[48] allowed litigation to resume and, applying the rule retroactively, found the lender liable as an owner and arranger under CERCLA. The court found that the lender's activities before foreclosure did not constitute participation in management because they were taken in the "normal course of business" of lending. It found that those activities fell within what "a reasonable creditor motivated primarily to protect its security interest would have done" and, therefore, they were consistent with activities permitted under the EPA rule. The activities the court deemed to be permitted included the bank's impeding a sale of chemicals that the EPA alleged caused site contamination and the disposal of inventory to mitigate the lender's losses.

Nonetheless, the lender was deemed liable as an owner/operator of the site at the time of the hazardous waste disposal as a result of the postforeclosure activities of its liquidator and salvage crews in failing to comply with Superfund regulations. The court stated that when a secured creditor or its agent undertakes action that it "knows or reasonably should know will severely aggravate a site's environmental problems," such action constitutes control over decisions involving hazardous substances that rises to "impermissible participation in management." The lender's agent handled drums of hazardous waste in a manner contrary to the NCP, backed into and crushed drums of hazardous waste with tractors, scraped asbestos-laden insulation from equipment in violation of environmental laws, and carelessly dismantled the site and assets in a manner causing new hazardous substance problems and severely aggravating existing ones. The court's decision was also based on the fact that, because the lender's agent was present at the site over eighteen months after the borrower's departure, the lender failed to complete its operations in a reasonably expeditious manner.

In *McGuire v. Sigma Coatings, Inc.*,[49] the U.S. District Court for the Eastern District of Louisiana held that the security interest exemption applied to a lender that: (1) acquired an interest in property upon default of the borrower; (2) became an owner under Louisiana law; and (3) thereafter accepted rent from a tenant on the property under an existing lease and agreed to extend the lease. The bank did not become an owner or operator by hiring a consultant to perform site assessments after it became aware of contamination on the property caused by the tenant. The court found no capacity on the part of the bank to control the tenant's hazardous substance handling practices. The court further recognized that the bank acquired its security interest before enactment of CERCLA and therefore could not have anticipated that its foreclosure would result in environmental liability under the statute. The court also found the tenant liable to reimburse the lender for costs incurred in connection with evaluating the site's environmental status and the contamination caused by the tenant while occupying the lender's collateral. The court also stated that lenders are permitted to handle hazardous substances, after and incidental to foreclosure and sale, if done in accordance with the NCP, if consistent with CERCLA's underlying principles, and if for the purpose of protecting the lender's security interests.

Without relying on the Lender Liability rule, the Fourth Circuit in *United States v. McLamb*[50] narrowed the scope of *Maryland Bank and Trust*[51] and provided some measure of security to foreclosing lenders who take title to and expeditiously dispose of *contaminated collateral* in a commercially reasonable manner. In this case, the lender purchased the collateral property at a foreclosure sale as the sole bidder. Thereafter, it quickly sold the property to a group of purchasers who sued the lender as a third-party defendant in an action brought against them by the government. The Fourth Circuit ruled in favor of the lender, stating it "almost immediately placed the property on the market, took no steps to use or manage the land during its ownership, and ultimately sold the property to the first able buyer. Such steps support its claim that it held title primarily, indeed exclusively, to protect its security interest." The plaintiffs also attempted to void the lender's security interest exemption on the basis that it failed to act in a commercially reasonable manner by failing to tell the purchasers about the contamination on the property before purchase. As in the *Northeast Doran*[52] case, the court found that CERCLA imposed no such requirement on a lender.

In a pending case, *United States v. Fidelco Credit Corp.*, the government has sought to recover its expense costs under CERCLA by alleging that the lender is directly liable because it arranged for disposal of waste from the borrower's facility after foreclosure and conducted operations at the facility for a period of time. Although the court has dismissed several defenses to liability asserted by the lender, neither the court's opinion nor the pleadings refer to the secured creditor exemption or the Lender Liability Rule.

Miscellaneous Cases Interpreting Lender Liability

In *O'Neil v. Q.L.C.R.I., Inc.*,[53] an action under the Clean Water Act, the court found that the lender could be liable as an aider and abettor for the borrower's contamination of groundwater, reasoning that the lender participated in a series of questionable conveyances to inflate the value of the collateral. After *O'Neil*, it appears that a non-CERCLA case can be brought against a lender when there is a combination of substantive environmental violations by the borrower and wrongdoing by the lender, even if such wrongdoing is not directly related to the environmental damage caused by the borrower.[54] The decision suggests that the reach of lender liability for environmental problems can extend beyond hazardous waste and into the arenas of air and water pollution, destruction of species' habitat, or ocean dumping.

In *United States v. Norris*,[55] a bank acquired ownership of the property through foreclosure. The court rejected the bank's innocent purchaser contention, stating that "if the bank lent more than a quarter of a million dollars without inspecting the property by which the loan was to be secured, the bank acted imprudently."

In *Resolution Trust Corp. v. Polmar Realty, Inc.*, the U.S. district court allowed the Resolution Trust Corporation (RTC) to enter onto the borrower's contaminated property to conduct an environmental assessment. The court cited *Fleet Factors* and the increased risk of lender liability in support of the RTC's request for court involvement and its need to determine the property's environmental status before foreclosure.

In *Northeast Doran, Inc. v. Key Bank of Maine*,[56] the U.S. District Court for Maine found the security interest exemption does not require a lender to disclose known environmental contamination. The First Circuit affirmed the lower court's ruling that "the right of contribution is a statutory one that turns solely on Key's status as an owner," a status defeated by the security interest exemption.

The court in *Kemp Industries, Inc. v. Safety Light Corp.*[57] ruled that Prudential Insurance Company of America, which held title to property pursuant to a sale-leaseback transaction principally to protect its security interest, was not liable as an owner under CERCLA. The court found: (1) the reason that title was taken, and not the nature of the title, is relevant to determine whether the security interest exemption applies; (2) it was clear that Congress intended the security interest exemption to apply to a party that holds title pursuant to a standard sale-leaseback arrangement; (3) the Uniform Commercial Code (UCC) was the proper guide and Congress intended UCC principles to govern the interpretation of CERCLA's security interest exemption; (4) the determination as to the nature of the transaction should be based on relevant facts and the intentions of the parties at the time the transaction is entered into; and (5) the transaction must be characterized after viewing the totality of the facts surrounding the transactions and relationships created, with no one factor to be determinative, and the inquiry does not require mechanical adherence to some test or the fulfillment of a list of elements.

The court followed *Bergsoe Metal Corp.* and *Mirabile*, finding that there must be some actual management of the facility before a secured creditor will fall outside the security interest exemption. The court held that Prudential was not involved in management merely by participating in the planning of construction on the leased property or periodically inspecting the leased premises.

Federal Deposit Insurance Corporation Environmental Risk Guidelines

On February 25, 1993, the Federal Deposit Insurance Corporation (FDIC) issued its "Guidelines for an Environmental Risk Program."[58] The guidelines require that lending institutions establish and implement environmental risk programs, detail the "appropriate" safeguards and controls that should be contained in a risk program, and require that institutions comply with their own environmental risk programs. The guidelines state that bank examiners will review an institution's environmental risk program as part of the examination of its lending and investment activities. The guidelines provide, in material part, as follows:

- The environmental risk program must be an integral part of the lending institution's overall decision-making process. The environmental risk program should establish procedures for identifying and evaluating potential environmental concerns associated with the bank's lending practices and other actions relating to real property.

- The board of directors is required to review and approve the environmental risk program.
- The board of directors is required to designate a senior officer "knowledgeable in environmental matters" responsible for the program implementation.
- The environmental risk program should incorporate staff training to a level that ensures the program is implemented and followed and that the appropriate personnel have the knowledge and experience necessary to determine and evaluate potential environmental concerns that might affect the institution.
- When appropriate, loan policies, manuals, and written procedures should address environmental issues pertinent to the institution's specific lending activities. For example, the lending manual might identify the types of environmental risks associated with the institution's trade area and provide guidelines for conducting an analysis of environmental concerns and liabilities in such area. Procedures for resolution of environmental concerns might also be developed for credit monitoring, loan workout situations, and foreclosures.
- The environmental risk program should require an environmental review or analysis during the loan application process.
- The environmental risk program should include loan documentation standards. Loan documents should include language to safeguard the institution against potential environmental losses and liabilities.
- The program should require that the environmental risk assessment continue during the life of the loan by monitoring the borrower and the real property collateral for potential environmental concerns.
- Lending institutions should evaluate the potential environmental costs in conjunction with an assessment of the value of collateral in reaching a decision on whether to take title to the property by foreclosure or other means.

Strategies for Avoiding Lender Liability under CERCLA

Avoid Mortgages and Seek Alternate Forms of Security

Perhaps the simplest way for lenders to avoid liability under CERCLA is to avoid taking ownership rights in the borrower's property. Unfortunately, this is rarely a practical solution. In the rare case when a borrower is sufficiently capitalized to support an entire transaction on a credit basis, the lender may decide to issue an unsecured loan or a loan secured only by liens on equipment, inventory, and accounts receivable.[59] Note, however, that foreclosures on security interests in equipment or inventory can also lead to liability if, during foreclosure and subsequent sale, the lender creates or exacerbates an already existing environmental problem at the property where the inventory or equipment is located.

Attempt to Ensure Innocent Purchaser Status

Should a lender step over the line and participate in the management of its borrower to an extent that it loses its claim to the security interest exemption, it should strive to involve the innocent purchaser defense under CERCLA. To qualify for the innocent purchaser defense, the lender will be required to establish that, at the time it acquired the property, it did not know and had no reason to know of the contamination. To meet this standard, a lender must prove it undertook (at the time of acquisition) all reasonable inquiry into the previous ownership and uses of the property consistent with good commercial or customary practice. The due diligence principles applicable to purchasers of property are generally applicable to lenders as well. (See Chapter 8 for a detailed discussion of due diligence issues.) Two questions, however, particularly concern lenders: When should due diligence be performed, and who should perform the due diligence?

On the first question, the Congressional Conference Report on the Superfund Amendments and Reauthorization Act of 1986 makes clear that the level of due diligence required shall be judged "as of the time of acquisition."[60] In the case of a lender, the question arises as to whether "time of acquisition" occurs before making a loan, before acquiring the status of an "owner" or "operator" by "participating in the management," or before foreclosure. The lender's most conservative approach, in light of recent court rulings, would be to perform an assessment at each of the three stages of loan involvement (assuming that the second stage of participating in management is done with the lender's knowledge and deliberation). At a minimum, the lender should perform a preforeclosure assessment. In its preamble to the Lender Liability Rule, the EPA appeared to support the position that, even if a lender does not obtain a preloan assessment, it will be entitled to claim the innocent purchaser defense based on a preforeclosure assessment.[61] Both preloan and preforeclosure assessments were permitted by the Lender Liability Rule without risk of the lender's voiding its security interest exemption.

As to the second question, CERCLA states that it is the "defendant" claiming the innocent purchaser defense who must make the due diligence inquiry. Therefore, due diligence conducted by the borrower may not be sufficient if the court determines that the borrower's environmental consultant performed the work for the borrower only. This may be true even if the borrower conducted the inquiry at the lender's request. Accordingly, lenders should make certain that environmental assessments are conducted on behalf of both the borrower and the lender or separately and directly on behalf of the lender.

To qualify for the innocent purchaser defense, the lender must not only perform due diligence before the acquisition of the property but must also establish that once it became aware of the contamination it (1) exercised due care with respect to the hazardous substance and (2) took precautions against foreseeable acts or omissions of any third party and any consequence that could result from any such acts or omissions.[62] Finally, should a lender sell or otherwise transfer title to property subsequent to foreclosure, knowledge of an actual or threatened release of hazardous substances at the property must be disclosed to any subsequent purchaser. Otherwise, the lender will forfeit the innocent purchaser defense in subsequent litigation or claims.

Establish Environmental Policies and Operating Practices

Policies

Protecting lenders from environmental liability begins with a carefully drafted environmental loan policy. These loan policies, which should appear in institution manuals and management policies, should cover all commercial loan decisions from initial customer contact through foreclosure and the sale of collateral. Environmental loan policies generally cover the following four phases:[63]

- Application phase: Assessment and evaluation of the loan applicant and the collateral.
- Loan documentation phase: Specific environmental indemnification and other language for all loan documents, including commitment letters, evaluation forms, and standard loan documents, including promissory notes and mortgages.
- Loan policing/workout phase: Monitoring status of borrower and its collateral, dealing with environmental issues in prob-

lem loans, and making decisions regarding involvement in the borrower's business.
- Foreclosure/sale of collateral: Making decisions regarding foreclosure and making decisions and procedures for sale of foreclosed real property collateral.

Environmental loan policies should be drafted to reflect compliance with the FDIC's environmental guidelines as well as recent developments provided by case law and the Lender Liability Rule.[64] Also, environmental policies should cover bank-owned facilities such as branches and administrative buildings. Beyond the specific issues discussed above, environmental policies should include guidance on the training of bank employees and qualifications for, hiring of, and contracting with environmental consultants.

Operating Practices

ENVIRONMENTAL QUESTIONNAIRES. Prudent lenders are well advised to take precautionary steps at the earliest stages of loan origination. As their initial step in the due diligence process and as a transaction screening device, lenders should require their borrowers to complete an environmental questionnaire. This questionnaire could be similar to, or an expanded version of, the questionnaire in the site assessments standard developed by the American Society for Testing and Materials (ASTM). (See Chapter 8 for a more complete discussion of the ASTM environmental standards.) This questionnaire is not intended to replace the more exhaustive, subsequent screening device that may be required in the commitment as a condition of the lender's obligation to make the loan. It is intended, instead, to enable a lender at the earliest possible stage to determine if it is prudent to even sign a commitment to a particular borrower.

If the lender enters into a loan commitment based on the answers in the borrower's questionnaire, the lender may want to include in the commitment a requirement for a more thorough transaction screen or environmental assessment.

ENVIRONMENTAL ASSESSMENTS. The primary purpose of a preloan environmental assessment is to determine whether the prospective borrower or its property is, or is likely to become, subject to liability for environmental contamination.[65] Assessments may not be cost-effective in the case of smaller loans, and lenders may decide not to perform Phase I assessments for loans falling below a certain threshold. Lenders should remember, however, that a preforeclosure assessment will be required if they wish to invoke the innocent purchaser defense.

As a condition of the loan commitment and as the next level of investigation, if the need is indicated upon review of the borrower's environmental questionnaire, the lender should perform a Phase I site assessment directly or jointly with the borrower. As discussed earlier, the lender should not request that the borrower perform the assessment because the lender may risk losing the innocent purchaser defense by failing to comply with the literal statutory language requiring the lender to perform due diligence. The lender's environmental consultant should perform the assessment.

If the Phase I uncovers any evidence of existing or potential contamination, the lender should request that the consultant perform a Phase II investigation, taking samples of the soil, surface, and groundwater as necessary to determine whether contamination is present and, if so, to estimate remediation costs.[66] Depending on the amount of existing or potential contamination, the lender may wish to evaluate the borrower's financial viability in detail to determine if the borrower can sustain any remediation costs. Even when there will be no real property to secure the loan, the lender should still obtain information on those aspects of the borrower's operations that may render the borrower liable for exorbitant cleanup costs and, thus, impact its ability to repay the debt.

If the lender discovers contamination, it may elect to terminate the loan commitment or to require the borrower to take corrective measures before closing. The lender may also condition closing on the borrower's contracting with a qualified environmental consulting firm for the remediation work, or it may withhold loan proceeds in an amount sufficient to cover the cost of such work. In addition, the lender should require certification by the environmental consultant upon completion of cleanup work to ensure satisfactory completion of the corrective action. Furthermore, when state or federal agencies are involved, satisfactory completion of remedial action should also satisfy agency review and approval.

The lender should maintain, for a reasonable period of time, all information, records, photographs, appraisals, surveys, and documentation of due diligence. These records may later be required to show that due diligence was performed by the lender, either as lender or as purchaser of the real property at foreclosure. In addition, maintaining comprehensive environmental information about a property will facilitate a subsequent transfer of the property.

LOAN CRITERIA. As part of its environmental operating practices, the lender should establish loan criteria whereby a loan officer considers environmental risks when evaluating a loan.

MONITORING AND POLICING ACTIONS. A lender's operating practices should set forth the specific action that a loan officer can take following the decision to extend financing for an environmentally challenged property. Monitoring and policing activities specifically contemplated by the Lender Liability Rule include the following:

- Requiring the borrower to clean up real property
- Requiring the borrower to comply with environmental laws and regulations
- Monitoring the borrower's business and financial condition
- Requiring the borrower's compliance with representations and warranties
- Exercising rights pursuant to covenants, representations, and warranties in loan documents
- Requiring the borrower to perform an environmental audit and to comply with the recommendations in the audit
- Providing financial or other advice, suggestions, counsel, or guidance

Case law subsequent to (and in some cases interpreting) the Lender Liability Rule also suggests that the following actions may be permissible during the course of the loan: (1) forbearance on the loan *(Silresim)*;[67] (2) increase in the line of credit *(Silresim)*; (3) direct contacts with the borrower's debtors to collect on accounts receivable in which the lender holds a security interest *(Silresim)*; (4) lender's representation on borrower's board, primarily to address financial issues *(Kelley)*;[68] (5) lender's receipt and review of information regarding borrower's financial and employment or labor activities *(Kelley)*; (6) conditioning forbearance on the borrower's cutting expenses *(Kelley)*; and (7) participation in meetings with the borrower *(Kelley)*.

A lender's operating practices should not encompass the cleanup of contaminated collateral, or any other action that indicates the lender's control over the borrower's environmental compliance or day-to-day operations. The lender should be careful to leave all decision making in the borrower's hands, lest it risk losing the secured creditor exemption. Situations in which lenders wish to go beyond those actions specifically provided in case law (which may or may not be conclusive in other jurisdictions where the courts have not ruled on the issue) should be evaluated individually and only with the advice of counsel.

However, in certain situations in which the property is highly contaminated and poses threats of imminent environmental harm and the borrower fails to remediate, a lender may be compelled to assume responsibility for cleanup. CERCLA Section 107(d) will provide such lenders some solace. It states that no person shall be held liable "for rendering care, assistance, or advice" in connection with an environmental problem, even if such actions result in a release, provided the actions are consistent with CERCLA's statutory goals and are in accordance with the NCP or at the direction of an on-site coordinator.[69] In its Lender Liability Rule, the EPA acknowledged that "a [security interest] holder does not participate in the management of a . . . facility by taking any response action under Section 107(d) of CERCLA or under the direction of an on-scene coordinator." The EPA recognized in the preamble to the rule that "if a release" occurred in connection with activities taken at the direction of an on-scene coordinator (under Section 107(d)(1) of CERCLA), then evidence of a release is not relevant to the issue of whether the security interest holder had participated in management. However, the EPA also agreed with commentators that "a holder's actions which result in a release or threat of release of hazardous substances" could indicate that the holder has participated in the facility's management, depending on the circumstances in which the release occurred.[70] For example, if the release occurred in connection with the holder's exercise of decision-making control over the borrower's environmental compliance, the holder has "participated in management."

FORECLOSURE. The Lender Liability Rule provided lenders with carte blanche to foreclose on property without losing the security interest exemption. Subsequent case law reaffirmed that the lender's actions after foreclosure are crucial to determining whether it loses the exemption's protections. Specifically, the Rule permitted lenders to do the following:

- Foreclose on collateral
- Purchase collateral at a foreclosure sale
- Maintain or wind up the borrower's business activities
- Render care or advice in respect of response actions under CERCLA
- Take actions reasonably necessary to protect, preserve, or prepare the property for sale or disposition

Case law subsequent to, and in some cases interpreting, the Lender Liability Rule also suggests that lenders may take the following actions during, or subsequent to, foreclosure:

- Foreclose or sell contaminated collateral equipment (*ARCO*,[71] *Ashland*[72])
- Control and operate the facility (*ARCO*) (but see *McLamb*,[73] in which the court noted favorably that the lender, upon foreclosure of contaminated collateral, took no steps to use or manage the land during its ownership)

- Hire a consultant to perform a site assessment after becoming aware of contamination (*McGuire*)[74]
- Sell property without disclosing known contamination (*McLamb, Northeast Doran*[75]) (but note that a failure to disclose can possibly void the innocent purchaser defense)

A lender that exacerbates existing environmental problems on a property is potentially risking a loss of the security interest exemption. Furthermore, any action on a lender's part to arrange for the disposal or transportation of hazardous substances will subject the lender to potential liability as an arranger under CERCLA.[76]

SALE. A lender's operating practices should set specific guidelines for selling foreclosed properties. Lenders must, at a minimum, take the following actions to maintain the security interest exemption:

- Act to sell or divest the property promptly upon foreclosure
- Use commercially reasonable means for sale or divestiture, or follow the bright-line rule and list the property for sale within twelve months after acquiring the legal right to sell the property
- If the property is purchased at foreclosure, not reject or outbid any offer that is equal to or exceeds the debt owed by the borrower
- Any time after six months following foreclosure, accept any written, bona fide (i.e., cash) offer equal to or exceeding debt within ninety days of receipt.

Cases provide that the lender may maintain the security interest exemption upon foreclosure if (1) it makes a "reasonably prompt effort to divest itself of its unwelcome ownership" (*Waterville*); (2) it immediately places the property on the market, takes no steps to use or manage the property during "ownership," and ultimately sells to the first available buyer (*McLamb*); or (3) it makes "a reasonably prompt effort to divest itself of unwelcome ownership" (*Northeast Doran*).

Carefully Draft Document Provisions

Lenders must carefully draft loan documents to protect themselves from environmental risks while not stepping over the line and participating in the borrower's management. The good news is that the Lender Liability Rule, and the subsequent *Silresim Site Trust*[77] case (which does not rely on the rule), have rejected the *Fleet Factors*[78] finding that the security interest exemption could be lost based solely on loan documents that provided the lender the "capacity to control" the borrower's operation. The rule also specifically confirmed that the lender could obtain protection through indemnities, representations, warranties, and covenants in the loan documents. Even so, a lender should ensure that its documents cannot be construed as giving it control over the borrower or allowing the lender to make decisions on behalf of the borrower with respect to its overall business, hazardous substance handling and disposal practices, and other associated environmental issues.

Loan Commitments

Loan commitments should include some or all of the following provisions:

- The borrower's agreement to perform environmental assessments as required by the lender or to pay for assessments obtained by the lender
- The borrower's cooperation with the lender in the performance of the assessment, including the borrower's agreement to provide access to the property and any required data or documents belonging to the borrower
- The borrower's grant of authority to the lender to contact regulatory authorities and to review government documents relating to the borrower and its activities as well as a waiver by the borrower of any claim arising out of the lender's contact with regulators
- A grant to the lender of the right to refuse to make the loan, or to terminate or revoke the commitment, based on environmental issues
- The borrower's agreement to modify loan terms based on environmental issues discovered by and/or not remediated by the borrower

The documents should allow sufficient time for completing the initial assessment and reviewing the results and should provide for an extension of time if needed.

Loan Documents

Loan documents should describe in detail the lender's rights and the borrower's obligations with respect to environmental issues. The Lender Liability Rule indicated, and subsequent case law holds, that mere capacity to control will no longer be considered participation in management. The *Kelley*[79] and *Silresim Site Trust*[80] cases, in particular, held that a lender will be judged by its actions and not by provisions in its loan documents. However, there is still no crystal clear guidance on this point, particularly in view of the uncertain status of the rule.

Consequently, documents should be drafted to cast the lender in the role of an advisor and observer rather than as a party with power to direct and control the borrower, its operations, its business, and its hazardous waste and remedial activities.

CLOSING CONDITIONS. Although duplicative, it is a good idea to repeat in the closing conditions certain provisions found elsewhere in the loan documents (in the warranties, representations, and covenants sections). This will allow the lender to avoid entering into a transaction if environmental conditions are discovered before closing that are contrary to the representations and warranties. Lenders should consider including the following provisions in the closing section of their loan documents:

- Closing should be conditioned on the lender's approval of the results of any environmental assessment and the borrower's correction of any environmental issues that are discovered during the assessment.
- The borrower should provide copies of all environmental permits and licenses as well as certify that its permits are in full force and effect and that it is in compliance with all such permits.
- Closing should be made contingent upon the borrower's obtaining estoppel certificates on environmental matters from tenants of any of the subject property. Such a certificate should include a statement that the person has no knowledge of any current or past hazardous waste activities on the site, that it is conducting its operations in compliance with all applicable environmental laws, and that it is in compliance with the terms and conditions of all required government permits and licenses.
- The borrower must provide environmental insurance, if available and appropriate, in favor of the lender.

COVENANTS. The loan documents should require the borrower to make affirmative promises that govern its environmental behavior during the life of the loan. Specifically, the borrower should do the following:

- Conduct all future and present operations and maintain any real property in compliance with all present and future federal, state, and local laws and regulations.
- Require any tenants to conduct their operations and maintain the property in compliance with all laws.
- Notify the lender promptly of any unauthorized spills or releases or the discovery of any other violation of environmental law.

- Immediately provide the lender with copies of any environmental notices, complaints, or claims from any governmental agency or third parties relating to the borrower's operations.
- Keep the lender advised of all information relevant to any release, threatened release, or other site contamination related to the property.
- Take all necessary cleanup measures with regard to any release, threatened release, or other environmental contamination on the property, and bring the property back to its prerelease condition in accordance with a specific set of standards to be incorporated in the document. (This provision is recommended because a borrower may negotiate a settlement with a regulatory agency that leaves significant contamination in place and therefore renders the property economically impaired.)[81]
- Report any releases to applicable regulatory agencies in a timely fashion.
- Agree to cooperate with regulatory agency investigations and requests for information.
- Refrain from conducting environmentally "risky" activities on the property (as further defined in the loan documents).
- Agree that the lender may conduct periodic reviews of the borrower's records and the property.
- Agree that the lender has the authority to request and review regulatory agency documents regarding the borrower and its activities.

REPRESENTATIONS AND WARRANTIES. Loan documents should require borrowers to provide environmental representations and warranties regarding the property and the borrower's business operations. These should be drafted to survive the loan repayment—without a "best knowledge" standard—and should include the following provisions:

- That the property is free of environmental liens, hazardous substances, and other on-site conditions of potential environmental concern
- That neither the borrower nor any prior owner of the property is using or has used the property in violation of federal or state environmental laws
- That there are no pending or threatened environmental claims, complaints, or litigation by any government agency or third party
- That the borrower has received no notice of any alleged violations of any environmental law or regulation
- That no hazardous substances or waste have been produced, generated, treated, stored, released, or disposed of on or near

the borrower's property by the borrower except in accordance with all applicable environmental laws and regulations

LENDER'S RIGHTS. Loan documents should also afford the lender certain rights regarding environmental issues affecting the borrower. In particular, lenders should establish specific criteria that the borrower agrees to follow rather than providing the lender with authority to make or control decisions. The provisions should include the following:

- The right to conduct environmental assessments of the collateral at any time during the life of the loan
- The right to enter onto the site to conduct inspections to ensure compliance with environmental laws
- The right to require that the borrower comply with environmental laws and remediate environmental contamination in accordance with environmental laws and agency directives
- Criteria for the borrower to follow in selecting an environmental consultant and in establishing remediation methodologies
- Parameters for leasing and for the borrower's rejecting or approving a lease[82]
- Recourse rights against the borrower (at least to the extent of environmental liability)
- A due-on-sale clause to give the lender an opportunity to reexamine the environmental status of the property should the borrower propose its sale[83]

INDEMNIFICATION. Although an indemnity is only as valuable as the financial health of the indemnitor, lenders should always include indemnification clauses in their loan documents. The indemnification should accomplish the following:

- Define the covered materials broadly to include hazardous, toxic, and any regulated substances and wastes, petroleum, and other pollutants
- Reserve to the lender the right to accomplish remediation in any manner the lender deems appropriate, should such an action be necessary
- Include all expenses incurred by or on behalf of the lender, including those for environmental consultants, laboratories, expert witnesses, counsel, damages to natural resources, damages to real and personal property, injuries to persons, and unforeseen consequential damages
- Reserve to the lender the sole right to defend and settle any claims brought against it by the government or third parties

- Run with the land, thus binding subsequent purchasers (although in some jurisdictions this proviso may not be enforceable)
- Survive repayment of the debt
- Expressly allow for assignment to subsequent purchasers of the loan or of the secured property from the lender

DEFAULT AND REMEDY PROVISIONS. The document should provide certain remedies in case the lender incurs environmental costs or the collateral becomes contaminated. Examples include requirements such as the following:

- That the borrower provide environmental impairment insurance upon the lender's request
- That the borrower reimburse the lender for, or add to the principal of the loan, amounts reflecting costs incurred by the lender because of environmental contamination of the collateral
- That the borrower agree to the lender's demand for additional or different security or loan acceleration, in the case of borrower's noncompliance with environmental laws and regulations or contamination of the collateral

The loan documentation should also explicitly make the breach of any environmental covenants, representations, or warranties an event of default and should limit the cure periods with respect to such events. Finally, the discovery of hazardous substances or waste on the site should be grounds for declaring the loan in default.

Seek Inclusion on Borrower's General Liability Insurance or Obtain Other Insurance

The lender can require that it be added as an additional insured on the borrower's general comprehensive liability (CGL) insurance. The benefit of this action may be limited because of the pollution exclusions in CGL policies. In some cases, courts have construed the pollution exclusion narrowly and have held that the CGL policies cover liability of third persons arising out of pollution occurrences. CGL policies, however, exclude damage to the property owned by the insured, which may defeat any claim by the lender against the insurance for costs incurred with regard to the borrower's property. The lender may also require that the borrower carry adequate environmental impairment liability insurance or "pollution liability coverage." (See Chapter 15 for more on environmental impairment insurance.)

Execute Covenants Not to Sue with Regulators

Lastly, in cases in which a lender discovers it has a nonperforming loan secured by a contaminated property, a lender should consider settlement with the EPA (or a state agency) before foreclosure by way of a covenant not to sue. The EPA will consider entering into a covenant not to sue a prospective purchaser of contaminated property pursuant to the agency's guidance on settlements with de minimis landowners, issued on June 6, 1989.[84] The EPA may enter into a covenant not to sue when (1) an enforcement action is otherwise anticipated, (2) the performance of or payment of cleanup costs would not otherwise be available except from Superfund, and (3) the prospective purchaser participates in the cleanup.

On May 10, 1991, the EPA entered into its first covenant not to sue with a bank. The bank agreed to clean up a property that it intended to acquire by foreclosure and to contribute $350,000 toward remediation of a Superfund site of which the property was a part. Without the agreement, the bank could have been subject to joint and several liability for the estimated $32 million cleanup of Commencement Bay in Tacoma, Washington.[85]

Notes

1. Jeff Civins, *Lender Concerns under Environmental Laws*, 20 St. B. Tex. Envtl. L.J. 93 (Spring 1990).

2. Theodore D. Nering III, *Environmental Liability—A Nightmare for Lenders and Owners, But a Solution Is in the Making*, 4 Dig. Envtl. L. Real Prop. 64, 66 (1991).

3. 42 U.S.C. § 9601 *et seq*. (West 1983 & Supp. 1995).

4. *Supra* note 1, at 95. In such cases, however, no super lien status is provided to the liens on property other than that remediated.

5. 42 U.S.C. § 9607(a)(4)(B) (West 1983 & Supp. 1995).

6. 42 U.S.C. § 9607(a) (West 1983 & Supp. 1994).

7. 42 U.S.C. § 9601(20)(A) (West 1983 & Supp. 1995).

8. Lenders may also incur liability if they arrange for disposal, treatment, or transportation of hazardous substances at, on, or from a borrower's property and its activities cause contamination. 42 U.S.C. § 9607(a)(3) (West 1983 & Supp. 1994). See Tanglewood East Homeowners v. Charles-Thomas, Inc., 849 F.2d 1568 (5th Cir. 1988), wherein the subdivision property owner/plaintiffs charged the lender, along with the developer and construction company, with having arranged for disposal or treatment of hazardous substances in the wake of earthmoving activities that disturbed hazardous waste during development of the site. The Fifth Circuit affirmed the district court's denial of lender's motion to dismiss it from a Superfund cost recovery action even though there were no facts that would support the lender's involvement beyond the financing of the development project that was the subject of the Superfund activity. This holding may, however,

be primarily based on the court's lack of desire to rule on the reach of CERCLA liability without additional facts at hand.

9. 45 B.R. 278 (Bankr. N.D. Ohio 1985).

10. 632 F. Supp. 573 (D. Md. 1986).

11. 732 F. Supp. 556 (W.D. Pa. 1989).

12. 910 F.2d 668 (9th Cir. 1990).

13. 901 F.2d 1550 (11th Cir. 1990), *cert. denied*, 498 U.S. 1046 (1991).

14. 773 F. Supp. 984 (E.D. Mich. 1991). *See also In re* Cuyahoga Equipment Corp. v. United States, 980 F.2d 110 (2nd Cir. 1992). The court held that a lender's assumption of control of a dormant facility and contracting for salvage and sale of materials and equipment pursuant to a court order did not constitute management participation under the EPA's Proposed Lender Liability Rule. The court expressly did not rule as to whether the lender's activities did constitute management participation. However, it did affirm a lower court's approval of a consent decree granting protection and covenant not to sue the bank and the bank's successor, the Resolution Trust Corporation, on the basis that the government compromise of its claim was reasonable in light of doubt concerning the bank's liability.

15. 910 F.2d 668 (9th Cir. 1990).

16. No. CIV. A. 84-2280, 1985 WL 97 (E.D. Pa. Sept. 6, 1985).

17. 732 F. Supp. 556 (W.D. Pa. 1989). *See also* United States v. Nicolet, Inc., 712 F. Supp. 1193 (E.D. Pa. 1989), in which the court stated that the rule of law is that a mortgagee can be held liable under CERCLA only if the mortgagee participated in the management and operational aspects of the facility in question. In this case involving foreclosure and a mortgagee who also held controlling stock of the borrower/polluter, the court, in ruling on motions to dismiss, declined to impose liability on the mortgagee, who did not appear to have actually participated in the management of the borrower's operations and the asbestos-contaminated facility. *See also* United States v. Nicolet, Inc., 712 F. Supp. 1205 (E.D. Pa. 1989), in which the court found that a mortgagee who was a parent of the borrower/polluter fell within one of the four categories of "covered person." This case, however, was probably decided primarily under the shareholder liability and direct participation in management, familiarity with and capacity to control the site, and alter ego theories of liability.

18. 40 C.F.R. § 300.1100 (1994).

19. 901 F.2d 1550 (11th Cir. 1990), *cert. denied*, 498 U.S. 1046 (1991).

20. 57 Fed. Reg. 18,344 (1992).

21. 632 F. Supp. 573 (D. Md. 1986).

22. 732 F. Supp. 556 (W.D. Pa. 1989).

23. 901 F.2d 1550 (11th Cir. 1990), *cert. denied*, 498 U.S. 1046 (1991).

24. The EPA has since issued proposed lender liability rules relating to underground storage tanks. 59 Fed. Reg. 30,448 (1994). See the discussion of these regulations in Chapter 18 of this book.

25. John Noble, *EPA Lender Liability for Environmental Cleanups*, 24 CHEM. WASTE LITIG. REP. 57, 62 (1992).

26. 901 F.2d 1550 (11th Cir. 1990), *cert. denied*, 498 U.S. 1046 (1991).

27. 632 F. Supp. 573 (D. Md. 1986).

28. Kurt Burkholder, *The Lender Liability Rule under CERCLA*, 6 DIG. ENVTL. L. 59, 62 (1993).

29. Peter M. Gillon, Thomas F. Kleissler, and James D. Barnette, *Taking a Walk on the Wild Side? The Path of CERCLA Lender Liability After EPA's Rule*, 24 CHEM. WASTE LITIG. REP. 52, 56 (1992).

30. *Michigan v. EPA*, C.A. No. 92-1312 (Pet. filed July 28, 1992); *Chemical Mfrs. Ass'n v. EPA*, C.A. No. 92-1314 (Pet. filed July 28, 1992); consolidated at *Kelley v. EPA*, 15 F.3d 1100 (D.C. Cir. 1994), *cert. denied*, 115 S. Ct. 900 (1995).

31. David T. Buente et al., *Environmental Law Developments Affecting Lender and Fiduciary Liabilities and Bankruptcy Matters: Legislative and Judicial Developments in 1993*, CFA 49th Annual Convention, Sidley & Austin, 1993, at 3.

32. Kelley v. EPA, 15 F.3d 1100 (D.C. Cir. 1994).

33. A vigorous dissent by Chief Judge Mikva argued that Congress, by the overall structure of CERCLA's statutory scheme and certain specific statutory provisions, had delegated implicitly to the EPA the authority to define which parties fall within the statute's regulatory regime. "In interpreting the statute otherwise," Mikva argued, "the majority renders the EPA powerless to define not only the term 'owner or operator' within the meaning of CERCLA, but 'vessel,' 'facility,' 'transport,' and 'transportation' as well."

34. 901 F.2d 1550 (11th Cir. 1990), *cert. denied*, 498 U.S. 1046 (1991).

35. 632 F. Supp. 573 (D. Md. 1986).

36. 23 ELR 20428 (D. Mass. 1992).

37. 5 F.3d 69 (4th Cir. 1993).

38. 632 F. Supp. 573 (D. Md. 1986).

39. 15 F.3d 1 (1st Cir. 1994).

40. H.R. 3800, 103d Cong., 2d Sess. § 407 (1994).

41. Grantors to Silresim Site Trust v. State Street Bank & Trust Co., 23 ELR 20428 (D. Mass. 1992).

42. 901 F.2d 1550 (11th Cir. 1990), *cert. denied*, 498 U.S. 1046 (1991).

43. 810 F. Supp. 901 (W.D. Mich. 1993).

44. 155 B.R. 890 (E.D. Pa. 1993).

45. 901 F.2d 1550 (11th Cir. 1990), *cert. denied*, 498 U.S. 1046 (1991).

46. 810 F. Supp. 1057 (D. Minn. 1993).

47. 984 F.2d 549 (1st Cir. 1993).

48. 821 F. Supp. 707 (S.D. Ga. 1993).

49. Nos. 91-2076, 91-3098, 92-3187, 1993 WL 329982 (E.D. La. August 19, 1993).

50. 5 F.3d 69 (4th Cir. 1993).

51. 632 F. Supp. 573 (D. Md. 1986).

52. No. 92-0247-B, 1993 WL 313629 (D. Me. June 4, 1993), *aff'd* 15 F.3d 1 (1st Cir. 1994).

53. 750 F. Supp. 551 (D.R.I. 1990).

54. Stephen L. Kass and Michael B. Gerrard, *Minimizing Lender Liability*, 5 DIG. ENVTL. NEWS 50, 51 (1992).

55. 937 F.2d 286 (6th Cir. 1991).

56. No. 92-0247-B, 1993 WL 313629 (D. Me. June 4, 1993), *aff'd* 15 F.3d 1 (1st Cir. 1994).

57. No. 92-95(AJL), 1994 WL 532130 (D. N.J. June 28, 1994).

58. FIL 14-93

59. Bruce E. Prigoff and Elona Lipschitz, *Living with Fleet Factors: A Practical Guide for the Wary Lender*, 1 REAL EST./ENVTL. LIAB. NEWS 9 (1990).

60. H.R. Conf. Rep. No. 962, 99th Cong., 2d Sess. (1986).

61. 57 Fed. Reg. 18353 (1992).

62. 42 U.S.C. § 9607(b)(3).

63. Peter G. Glubiak, *Loan Policies for Environmental Matters*, 6 DIG. ENVTL. L. 29, 30 (1992).

64. Mark J. Bennett, *Financial Institutions Adopting Policies to Tackle Environmental Risk, Survey Shows*, 7 TOXICS L.R. 201 (1993). Loans secured by equipment and inventory, as opposed to real estate, should also be included in bank policies, particularly considering the fact that *Fleet Factors* involved foreclosure on personal property only.

65. Howard B. Epstein and Gail V. Karlsson, *Hazardous Loans: Lender Risks under Superfund*, 1 ENVTL. CLAIMS J. 231, 237 (1988/89).

66. *Supra* note 65, at 238.

67. Grantors to the Silresim Site Trust v. State Street Bank & Trust Co., 23 ELR 20428 (D. Mass. 1992).

68. Kelley *ex. rel.* Michigan v. Tiscornia, 810 F. Supp. 901 (W.D. Mich. 1993).

69. 42 U.S.C. § 9607(d) (West 1983 & Supp. 1995).

70. 57 Fed. Reg. 18,355 (1992).

71. Atlantic Richfield Co. v. OAAS; Nos. CV-90-75-BU-PGH, CV-91-082-PGH, 1992 U.S. Dist. LEXIS 17574 (Mont. 1992).

72. Ashland Oil, Inc. v. Sonford Prod. Corp., 810 F. Supp. 1057 (D. Minn. 1993).

73. 5 F.3d 69 (4th Cir. 1993).

74. McGuire v. Sigma Coatings, Inc., Nos. 91-2076, 91-3098, 92-3187, 1993 U.S. Dist. LEXIS 11934 (E.D. La. August 19, 1993).

75. Northeast Doran, Inc. v. Key Bank of Maine, 15 F.3d 1 (1st Cir. 1994).

76. 42 U.S.C. § 9607(a) (West 1983 & Supp. 1995).

77. Grantors to the Silresim Site Trust v. State Street Bank & Trust Co., 23 ELR 20428 (D. Mass. 1992).

78. 901 F.2d 1550 (11th Cir. 1990), *cert. denied*, 498 U.S. 1046 (1991).

79. Kelley *ex. rel.* Michigan v. Tiscornia, 810 F. Supp. 901 (W.D. Mich. 1993).

80. Grantors to the Silresim Site Trust v. State Street Bank & Trust Co., 23 ELR 20428 (D. Mass. 1992).

81. *Supra* note 54.

82. Debra Pogrund Stark, *Contaminated Loans*, BUSINESS LAW TODAY (Nov./Dec. 1992) (ABA Section of Business Law).

83. *Supra* note 2.

84. EPA Guidance on Landowner Liability under Section 107(a)(1) and De Minimis Settlements under Section 122(g)(1)(B) of CERCLA, and Settlements with Prospective Purchasers of Contaminated Property, OSWER Directive No. 9835.9, June 6, 1989.

85. *In re* BankAmerica Corp., EPA Region 10, No. 1090-11-16-101 (May 15, 1991).

CHAPTER 5

Fiduciary Environmental Liability

BARBARA L. WORTHEN

CERCLA—Circa the Nineteenth Century

The whaling industry has long since disappeared from Cape Cod, but not the whales. They are periodically washed up on the beach where they first attract and later repel the tourist trade. The disposal problem is traditionally solved by waiting until a curious New Yorker approaches near enough to the whale to be charged with possession, and hence title thereof; then requiring the New Yorker as owner to give the whale decent burial under the public health laws. According to the folk lore of the locality the whales usually come ashore in the summer at Wellfleet; but in winter they choose Cohasset because, it is believed, they like to be nearer town.[1]

Ever thus the problem: near enough means possession, possession means title, and title means ownership of the odoriferous whale.

Fiduciary Duty and Fiduciary Liability

The relationship of fiduciary to beneficiary has early historical beginnings and has evolved today to include a wide range of relationships that may be viewed as fiduciary in nature. Contemporary fiduciary roles include probate estate executors, trustees of testamentary trusts, inter vivos trusts or employee benefit plans, court-appointed estate administrators, guardians, conservators, bankruptcy trustees, bond indenture trustees, land trust trustees, and nominee trustees. Competent individuals (as defined by local law) and qualified corporate organizations may generally serve in any of the above fiduciary roles.

Financial institutions such as banks and trust companies, under special powers (trust powers) granted by their primary banking regulator, frequently serve in the fiduciary capacity as executors of wills or as trustees of personal and corporate (bond indenture) trusts.

In the personal trust arrangement the grantor or settlor of the trust creates a plan for the orderly administration of the trust assets and the application of the income earned on those assets. This plan may contemplate either the creation of an inter vivos or a testamentary trust, the difference being that the grantor may create an inter vivos trust during his or her lifetime, and may also fund the trust during life, or the grantor may create a testamentary trust, which becomes effective at the death of the grantor in that it is part of the grantor's will or "testament."

The grantor's plan or trust identifies the beneficiaries of the fiduciary assets and income, and it is to this group of individuals or charitable corporate entities that the fiduciary is obligated to perform its duties. These duties include a duty of loyalty, a duty not to delegate, a duty to exercise reasonable care and skill, a duty to keep the trust assets and income separate from other trusts, and a duty to produce income.

Traditionally a fiduciary's liability was dependent on the fulfillment of its common-law duties. Under early law, a fiduciary's personal liability was limited to two scenarios. First, the fiduciary would be personally liable for torts committed by the fiduciary. In addition, the fiduciary would also be personally liable under a contract entered into on behalf of the trust, subject to indemnification from the trust to the extent the fiduciary acted properly. The Uniform Probate Code and statutes adopted by the states further limited the potential liability of fiduciaries to torts committed by the fiduciary only if the fiduciary was personally at fault.

Under common law, fiduciaries aware of their common-law duties could operate with a certain degree of confidence. Absent a breach of common-law duties, a fiduciary could feel comfortable knowing that personal liability most likely would not attach. However, the environmental liability provisions of the Comprehensive Environmental Response, Compensation, and Liability Act (CERCLA),[2] which are triggered without regard to culpability, have destroyed that comfort.

As noted, the fiduciary has as its primary responsibility a duty of absolute loyalty toward the beneficiaries of the trust and the trust estate. The proper exercise of those responsibilities when contaminated or potentially contaminated real property is involved, however, can expose the personal assets of the fiduciary to unlimited liability.

CERCLA—Circa the 1990s

To establish a *prima facie* case for liability under CERCLA, a plaintiff must prove that a "release" or "threatened release" from the site has occurred that has caused either the government or a private party to incur cleanup costs and that the defendant falls within at least one of the four classes of potentially responsible parties (PRPs).

Liability for response costs under CERCLA is strict, joint, and several (as described in Chapter 1). The four classes of PRPs include owners, operators, generators, and transporters. Fiduciaries are reasonably concerned about fitting within the boundaries of these four classes because the ordinary range of fiduciary activities includes the very same actions that owners may perform in the management of property.

Owner Liability

For example, trustees may, in conjunction with protecting a security interest of the trust, become owners of a property pursuant to foreclosure. Trusts frequently hold shares of corporate entities, typically a closely held business, and trustees frequently take an active shareholder role. Although not advisable, trust officers may serve from time to time as officers or directors of a closely held company to oversee or protect the trust's rights as shareholder. Trusts may hold and trustees may exercise options (as in the case of *City of Phoenix v. Garbage Services Co.*)[3] to purchase real estate. Tenant and landlord relationships are common to trust arrangements. Many trusts hold income-producing real property and trustees enter into lease arrangements with tenants. Trustees and executors are very often charged with the responsibility of selling and leasing real estate. Note that in most states title to the real estate is held in the name of the fiduciary and can only be conveyed by the fiduciary.

In short, fiduciaries own and manage property in a variety of roles because it is their job to do so. In so doing, fiduciaries are vulnerable to CERCLA liability because they act in a capacity identical to that for which CERCLA owner liability has been imposed by the courts in nonfiduciary cases. For example, courts have interpreted foreclosure-owners,[4] officers, directors, and shareholders,[5] optionees,[6] tenants,[7] landlords,[8] and sellers[9] to be PRPs and have imposed liability under CERCLA.

Several cases involving non-personal trust fiduciaries are instructive as well because they demonstrate the court's willingness to extend or limit liability. One court, for example, extended liability to present trustee owners of a site even though the actions of the trustees did not contribute to the environmental hazard.[10]

Statutory trustees, who were also directors and officers of the corporation, were held jointly and severally liable in their capacity as trustees. Liability, however, was limited to corporate property.[11]

In the case of *United States v. Burns*,[12] a defending trustee was unsuccessful in his efforts to seek dismissal in a cost recovery action. The trustee had been, before assuming a fiduciary role, part owner of the hazardous waste site. In addition, the trustee was also a beneficiary of the trust. The court concluded that the trustee could be liable as an owner. Relying on *Burns*, the *Phoenix* case (*Phoenix I*), discussed below, failed to distinguish between a trustee who holds both equitable and legal title to property, as in *Burns*, and a disinterested trustee who holds title for the exclusive benefit of others, as in *Phoenix*.

Control and Other Pitfalls

Potential liability is most probable when the fiduciary was or is either a past or present owner or operator of a facility. It is less probable, though still possible, that a fiduciary may be engaged in the transportation, disposal, or treatment of a hazardous material. A fiduciary may, however, be liable as one who arranges for such activities. Although CERCLA embodies a special exemption for secured lenders who own property simply to protect their security interest, no such administrative exemption exists for a fiduciary. A fiduciary may hold title as a trustee of property that was already contaminated before the fiduciary obtained legal title.

If a fiduciary is not deemed to be an owner under CERCLA, liability may still be imposed if the fiduciary is found to be an operator of a facility. The word "operator" is not defined in CERCLA. Courts have typically looked at the amount of control exerted over the day-to-day management and administration of a facility. The greater the daily managerial participation, the greater the probability that a fiduciary will be held liable as an operator of a facility.[13]

Fiduciaries are advised to review the nature and degree of their control over trust assets that are or may become the subject of an environmental hazard. A trustee who personally participates in conduct that constitutes control and that results in a release may be held personally liable as an operator or manager.[14]

Some courts have based liability on a mere showing of a capacity to control the property.[15] There is no apparent reason for distinguishing these cases from those involving fiduciary management of property.

Note that fiduciaries are charged with the responsibility of managing fiduciary assets. If the fiduciary claims that it had no control of the property, the fiduciary runs the risk of admitting that it has delegated a duty that, under commonly accepted principles of trust law, is not delegable.

The Easy Case

United States v. DiBiase Salem Realty Trust[16] involved an action brought by the United States seeking to recover over $2 million in costs associated with remedial action for the cleanup of a hazardous waste site. The site was owned by DiBiase Salem Realty Trust, of which Ugo DiBiase was the sole trustee and beneficiary. DiBiase did not dispute the fact that if the trust was found to be liable he would be personally and individually liable as sole trustee and beneficiary. DiBiase purchased the site in late 1969. Untreated waste had been deposited on the site since 1946. After purchasing the site, DiBiase did not accept untreated waste at the site. DiBiase admittedly did not undertake anything more than a minimal inspection of the site nor did he take any action to rectify the potential hazard, even at the behest of the Massachusetts Department of Environmental Quality Engineering.

In 1986, the site gained national attention and the U.S. Environmental Protection Agency (EPA) placed it on the National Priorities List of the most potentially hazardous sites. In 1987, hazardous substances migrated from the site and flowed into local wetlands and a brook. The EPA undertook an emergency removal action to clean up the release, incurring substantial costs. The government urged that both DiBiase Salem Realty Trust and DiBiase individually were liable as "owners" and "operators" of the site.

The *DiBiase* court had no trouble finding DiBiase and the trust liable as "owners" of the site. DiBiase individually owned 50 percent of the site from 1969 to 1982 and, after 1982, the entire property was owned by the trust for which DiBiase served as sole trustee and beneficiary. DiBiase and the trust were also held liable as "operators" of the site because they had active involvement in, and control over, the operations of the site.

The court found that DiBiase's claim to CERCLA's innocent landowner defense had no merit because he failed to exercise due care and the trust acquired the site with full knowledge of the contamination. (For a full discussion of CERCLA defenses, refer to Chapter 1.)

DiBiase is the easy case because individually, and later as sole trustee and beneficiary, the fiduciary owned and managed the contaminated site for his own use, benefit, and ultimate detriment. As both legal and equitable title vested with Mr. DiBiase, the court could easily have ignored his fiduciary status and determined that, in light of these dual roles, he constituted the site's true "owner."

Up Against the Whale—The Phoenix *Case*

If *DiBiase* represents the easy case for fiduciary liability under CERCLA, the *City of Phoenix* line of cases creates an analytical minefield.[17] *City of Phoenix*, decided January 19, 1993 (*Phoenix 1*), greatly expanded a true fiduciary's liability for CERCLA response costs for environmental cleanups and sent shock waves throughout the entire professional fiduciary community. In *Phoenix I*, the city of Phoenix, Arizona, sought to recover for response costs incurred in cleaning up a contaminated site. The defendant trustee, Valley National Bank (VNB), moved for partial summary judgment on the ground that it was neither an owner nor an operator of the site.

The background to the *City of Phoenix* line of cases is as follows. In 1965, William Calvin Estes, the owner of a landfill, conveyed the property subject to an option to repurchase. In 1966, VNB was nominated and accepted the position of executor and testamentary trustee of the Estes estate. During that year, VNB, as trustee, exercised the option and acquired legal title to the landfill site. At all times prior and subsequent to VNB's acquisition as trustee, the site was being managed as a municipal landfill by Garbage Service Company (GSC). In 1980, the city instituted a condemnation proceeding and acquired the site. At the condemnation proceeding it was found that VNB, as trustee, was the record owner of the site. In 1989, nine years after the site's acquisition, the city filed an action to recover response costs from VNB as owner or operator of the site.

Phoenix—VNB as Operator

The *Phoenix I* court, quoting a decision of the U.S. Court of Appeals for the Ninth Circuit, adhered to the premise that liability for a former operator "under CERCLA only attaches if the defendant had the authority to control the course of the contamination at the time the hazardous substances are released into the environment."[18] The *Phoenix I* court went on to state that liability as a former operator "attaches only where the defendant had control over the day-to-day management and administration of the facility."[19] The court further determined that VNB did not handle day-to-day administration of the site. Further, VNB did not exercise any decision making or other control over disposal or transportation of any hazardous waste.

VNB did not establish operational procedures or approve procedures regarding the landfill's operations. VNB's Trust Real Estate

Department visited the site once in connection with the city's acquisition of a right-of-way, and two drive-by inspections were made after the landfill closed. No contracts were entered into by VNB in connection with waste disposal at the landfill. No bank employee attempted to ascertain the nature of materials disposed of at the landfill.

VNB's internal procedures prohibited bank employees from serving as officers or directors of a corporation when the bank served as fiduciary of an estate that held corporate stock, and no bank employee ever served as an officer or director of GSC. The bank never exercised any voting rights on behalf of the estate as a shareholder. The bank never advised, influenced, or instructed any officer or director of GSC. The bank exercised no financial oversight or financial control. The bank did, however, inquire as to the filing of corporate annual reports required by Arizona law and, after the landfill was closed, made GSC checks available for the payment of GSC's accountants and annual report fees.[20]

Weighing the lack of managerial participation that VNB exercised over the site, the court held that the bank was not liable as an operator.[21] Unfortunately, the court did not give any clues as to what day-to-day activities would constitute managerial participation in the operation of the facility. Fiduciaries, therefore, may find themselves in a quandary. If the fiduciary does not involve itself in managing the trust property, it may be accused of not managing the trust. However, if it takes an active role in managing the trust, it may incur strict liability under CERCLA.

Phoenix—VNB as Owner

VNB was not to escape liability as a former owner of the facility. In adhering to CERCLA's strict liability mandate, the *Phoenix I* court stated that the only issue left in the case was whether VNB's former status as the holder of legal title made it an "owner" of the site under CERCLA.[22] The court recognized that the only exception from liability for owners under CERCLA is for secured creditors who hold indicia of ownership solely to protect their security interests.[23]

The *Phoenix I* court noted the apparent willingness of the EPA to consider trustees as owners under CERCLA.[24] The court then stated that the EPA's "interpretation of CERCLA provisions is entitled to considerable deference. . . ."[25] The *Phoenix I* court then referred to *United States v. Burns*,[26] in which the trustee was found liable as legal title holder to the property. In citing *Burns*, the *Phoenix I* court failed to distinguish between the facts of that earlier case and VNB's status as an independent and disinterested fiduciary. In conformity with its interpretation of *Burns* and the EPA's position regarding fiduciaries, the *Phoenix I* court found VNB liable as an owner of the facility. However, its ruling was tempered by the court's subsequent order, discussed below.

Phoenix II

On April 5, 1993, the *Phoenix II* court ruled on VNB's motion for an order attempting to limit its liability to the amount of the assets of the trust (*Phoenix II*).[27] VNB argued that since it only owned the site in its capacity as a trustee, it could not be held personally liable and its liability should be limited to the amount of assets in the trust. VNB's position was supported by *amicus curiae* briefs submitted by, among others, the American Bankers Association, the Arizona Bankers Association, and the National Trust Real Estate Association.

The *Phoenix II* court began its analysis by stating that the common law of trustee liability was to be the foundation for its final ruling. The court displayed its willingness to rely on the *Restatement (Second) of Trusts* and focused on Sections 264 and 265 of the *Restatement*. Section 264, Liability of Trustee for Tort, provides: "The trustee is subject to personal liability to third persons for torts committed in the course of administration of the trust to the same extent that he would be liable if he held the property free of trust."

Section 265, Liability of Trustee as Title Holder, provides:

> Where a liability to third persons is imposed upon a person, not as a result of a contract made by him or a tort committed by him but because he is the holder of the title to the trust property, [he] is subject to personal liability, but only to the extent to which the trust estate is sufficient to indemnify him.

Combining the law of trusts with the intent of CERCLA, the *Phoenix II* court fashioned three general rules governing the application of CERCLA liability to trustees of contaminated property.

The first rule involves the situation in which a trustee is held liable under Subsection 107(a)(1) as the current owner of contaminated property. According to *Phoenix II*, in this situation the trustee's liability is not personal, but rather it is limited to the assets in the trust sufficient to indemnify him or her. Subsection 107(a)(1) imposes liability on current owners of property regardless of when or how the property became contaminated. This first rule directly reflects the court's reliance on Section 265 of the *Restatement*, and it helped to alleviate some of the fears within the professional fiduciary community that ensued after the same court indicated that mere ownership alone subjected the fiduciary to unlimited liability.

The second rule fashioned by the *Phoenix II* court involved the situation in which a fiduciary formerly owned the site *at the time* of the disposal of hazardous substances but did not have the authority or power to control the use of the trust property. Liability under this rule is not based on mere ownership of the property but also requires that the fiduciary have had the power to control the use of the property. Under the court's second rule, where the trustee had no authority through the trust instrument to control the property, liability is once again limited to the extent that the trust assets are sufficient to provide indemnification.

The court's third rule again assumes a dual role, that is, prior ownership of the property at the time of disposal and the power to control the use of the trust property. The court indicated in this third rule that liability is also dependent on whether the fiduciary "knowingly" allowed the property to be used for the disposal of hazardous substances. Therefore, liability attaches if the trustee

- owned the property at the time of contamination;
- had the power to control the use of the trust property; and
- knowingly allowed the property to be used for disposal of hazardous substances.

If the above three criteria are met, liability is not limited to the assets in the trust. In this instance, personal liability attaches as if the trustee held the property in his personal capacity and not as trustee.

Turning to the facts of the VNB situation, the court noted that the trust instrument vested in VNB the power to operate and control the trust property. Because VNB was also aware that the property was a disposal site, the court denied VNB's motion to limit its liability to the assets held in the Estes trust.

The court justified the imposition of liability without fault (as opposed to the requirement of fault in the *Restatement*) by noting the strict liability requirements of CERCLA. The culpability standard of the Uniform Probate Code becomes subservient to CERCLA, which imposes liability without regard to fault. *City of Phoenix* is at odds with traditional trust law, which limits the liability of a trustee without fault to the extent that the trustee can be indemnified from trust assets.

Fiduciaries and Beneficiaries: New Controversies

New controversies are bound to arise with respect to the relationships between fiduciaries and beneficiaries. Beneficiaries, for example, may harbor a concern that trust or estate funds will be used to identify environmental problems and, if necessary, to remediate them. Such use of trust assets will undoubtedly lead to complaints from the beneficiaries of the improper use of trust funds, on the theory that such use of the funds was not contemplated by the governing instruments or that the trustee, out of concern for itself, has expended trust assets negligently. It is likely that beneficiaries will be reluctant to incur the costs of site evaluation or remediation absent a clear need, enforcement order, or claim. One concern of beneficiaries may be that a voluntary undertaking to evaluate real property may very well uncover information that diminishes the value of the property. Thus, new law on the probate and trust side of the problem clearly awaits us.

Current Statutory Relief: The States

Conditional Relief for Fiduciaries

In an effort to provide much-needed relief, a number of states have responded by adopting statutes that recognize the special role of fiduciaries. Note that each state's definition of the term "fiduciary" may vary and certain classes of fiduciaries may be excluded from the relief granted under the statute.[28] Note that state statutes are only applicable to state enforcement and private party actions and may not bind the federal government or other CERCLA plaintiffs. The development of these safe harbors by the states, however, may provide needed guidance to federal courts grappling with cases brought under federal environmental law.

The two broad categories of state regulations that have evolved are fiduciary immunity statutes and fiduciary powers statutes. A number of state immunity statutes exclude fiduciaries from the definition of owner or operator under state hazardous waste laws provided the fiduciary did not cause or contribute to the hazard and provided the fiduciary follows state mandatory guidelines. For example, in Massachusetts a fiduciary is not deemed to be an owner or operator of a contaminated site if the fiduciary

(1) does not cause or contribute to the release;
(2) after acquiring title to the site

- notifies the Department of Environmental Protection (DEP) upon obtaining knowledge of a release or threat of a release;
- provides access to the site for response efforts;
- notifies DEP of any insufficiency of trust assets to cover response costs; and
- upon obtaining knowledge of a release, and to the extent that assets are available in the estate or trust, undertakes

> reasonable steps to prevent exposure to third persons, takes action to contain any further release, and takes appropriate short-term protective action measures if an imminent hazard exists.[29]

As detailed in Figure 1, these sixteen states have provided various types of conditional immunity for fiduciaries in their environmental statutes: Florida, Georgia, Illinois, Indiana, Kentucky, Louisiana, Maine, Maryland, Massachusetts, Michigan, New Hampshire, North Dakota, Oklahoma, Oregon, South Dakota, and Vermont.[30]

Although the provisions in these statutes vary significantly in their application to fiduciaries, generally the statutes either exempt fiduciaries from the statutory definition of "owner, operator, or responsible person"[31] or provide fiduciaries with a special defense to liability.[32]

In most cases, the fiduciary may claim immunity only if it did not cause the hazard[33] or did not have any current or, in some cases, prior managerial or participatory control over the contaminated property.[34] Additionally, some states require that the fiduciary also satisfy more extensive requirements designed to protect the public good.[35] These additional measures typically require the fiduciary to notify the department of environmental protection about a possible hazard and to provide the department with access to the affected property. Some of the statutes expressly limit liability to the assets held in the estate or trust.[36]

New Fiduciary Powers

In addition to the fiduciary immunity statutes that typically appear in the environmental law sections of the compilations of various state statutes, a number of states have amended their probate practice sections to provide fiduciaries with special powers in dealing with property that is or may be the subject of an environmental hazard.[37] These statutes generally may permit a fiduciary to

- inspect property it "holds" to determine compliance with environmental law;
- respond to actual or threatened violations of environmental law affecting held property;
- take any action necessary to prevent, abate, or remedy actual or threatened violations of environmental law;
- refuse to accept property contaminated by or used for an activity involving hazardous substances;
- settle or compromise claims involving violations of environmental laws;

FIGURE 1. Summary of Fiduciary Immunity Statutes (as of June 28, 1994)

The following sixteen states have adopted express provisions that relate to the rights and obligations of fiduciaries. Six major elements distinguish these statutes, as shown below.

States		Fiduciary Must Not Cause or Contribute to Hazard	Fiduciary May Have Special Defense to Liability	Fiduciary Exempt as Owner/Operator or Responsible Party	Fiduciary Must Not Exercise Prior Control over Property	Fiduciary Must Comply with Additional Conditions	Liability Is Expressly Limited to Assets of Trust/Estate
Florida	(1)	✓	✓ (1)				
Georgia		✓		✓			
Illinois				✓			✓
Indiana	(2)	✓ (2)	✓				✓
Kentucky		✓	✓		✓	✓	
Louisiana		✓	✓				
Maine		✓		✓		✓	✓
Maryland		✓		✓			
Massachusetts		✓		✓		✓	✓
Michigan		✓		✓	✓		✓
New Hampshire	(3)	✓		✓		✓	✓
North Dakota		✓	✓				
Oregon		✓	✓			✓	
South Dakota		✓	✓				
Vermont		✓		✓		✓	

(1) Financial institution fiduciaries have additional defenses (petroleum products).
(2) Fiduciary is not liable unless actual managerial control is exercised.
(3) Trustees of revocable trusts are excluded from the definition of fiduciary.
NOTE: Oklahoma recently enacted a fiduciary immunity statute, 1994 H.B. 1967, that at the time of the preparation of this chart had not been codified and was unavailable for review.

- disclaim any power that may cause the fiduciary to incur personal liability; and
- decline to serve as fiduciary.

These statutes may also authorize the fiduciary to charge the costs of these actions against the assets of the trust.[38] Figure 2 provides further detail.

Note that two states, Maine and Kentucky, have adopted an immunity statute and a powers statute. In the author's view, this combination most effectively furthers the cause of protecting the environment by insulating fiduciaries so that they may properly evaluate the trust property. In doing so, a fiduciary possibly would discover and remedy contamination that might otherwise have gone undiscovered. In addition, upon the discovery of contaminated property, the fiduciary is under an affirmative obligation to report the contamination to the state environmental agency.

Federal Initiatives

Legislative initiatives also exist at the federal level. Numerous bills have been introduced in Congress, primarily in connection with the reauthorization of CERCLA, with the goal of limiting the CERCLA liability of fiduciaries who own or operate a contaminated property. These bills typically exclude liability for a fiduciary as an owner or operator if that fiduciary did not, before assuming control as a fiduciary, own, operate, or participate in the management of the property. Other proposals include a limitation on the liability of the fiduciary and the imposition of response costs only to the extent that the release is directly attributable to the fiduciary's activities. In its 1994 session, Congress is considering major changes to CERCLA, including measures addressing trustee liability.[39]

Guidelines for Limiting Liability

With the apparent willingness of the judiciary to expand fiduciary liability, it is increasingly important for the professional fiduciary to take precautionary measures in an attempt to limit liability.

Due Diligence before Acceptance

Before accepting an appointment as a fiduciary or obtaining legal title to trust property, the fiduciary is advised to evaluate the potential environmental ramifications. For example, the environmental enforcement history of the property may be documented through a search of

FIGURE 2. Summary of Fiduciary Powers Statutes (as of June 28, 1994)

The following eleven states have enacted legislation providing fiduciaries with additional rights and powers with respect to property held in a fiduciary capacity. Six elements distinguish these statutes, as shown below.

States		No Personal Liability to Beneficiary	Right to Disclaim Certain Powers (3)	Right to Refuse to Accept Property	May Decline to Serve as Fiduciary	Expenses May Be Charges Against Estate/Trust	May Settle Environmental Claims
Alabama	(2)	✓	✓	✓	✓	✓	✓
Arkansas		✓	✓	✓	✓	✓	✓
Connecticut						✓	
Kentucky		✓				✓	
Maine	(1)	✓	✓	✓	✓	✓	✓
North Carolina		✓	✓	✓	✓	✓	✓
Rhode Island	(1)	✓	✓	✓		✓	✓
Tennessee	(2)	✓	✓	✓	✓	✓	✓
Utah		✓	✓	✓	✓	✓	✓
Virginia		✓	✓	✓	✓	✓	
West Virginia		✓		✓	✓	✓	✓

(1) Statute is retroactively applied.
(2) The fiduciary is not considered an owner or operator under the statute.
(3) The fiduciary may disclaim any granted power that may result in personal liability.

state and federal environmental agency files. The environmental compliance records of a facility and any enforcement actions taken against that facility may also appear in the record. The local board of health and fire department personnel may have valuable knowledge of the property at issue even if a file search was unproductive. Interviews with past and current owners or the beneficiaries may also be conducted. A title search may be required to determine past owners and past uses of the property. Issues concerning underground storage tanks and waste disposal may also be explored.

Site Assessment

If preliminary inquiries reveal the potential for environmental problems, the fiduciary may choose to perform or to hire an environmental consulting firm to conduct a more detailed site assessment. A records review, interviews, and a visual inspection of the property may be followed by a more extensive examination, which may include soil and groundwater sampling. Note that the costs associated with, and the authorization for, such testing may be covered in the state's fiduciary powers statute. The fiduciary should check the state's fiduciary statutes to determine if this is a protected activity.

Insurance Coverage

If a potential environmental problem exists, the fiduciary is advised to research and examine all available comprehensive general liability and property damage insurance policies for the subject property. Although modern insurance policies often include pollution exclusions, older policies (possibly in effect at the time of the contamination) typically do not. Even those that do contain pollution exclusions may offer coverage in some states. Note that a number of companies specialize in locating lost or misplaced policies.

Drafting Considerations

Although no indemnity agreement will bind the government or any entity not a party to it, indemnification agreements may allocate risks between the individuals. Therefore, the inclusion of environmental indemnifications and the receipt of other warranties and representations from the settlor or beneficiaries are of substantial value. The governing instrument may be drafted to include protective language and authority to take necessary actions to comply with environmental laws. The new fiduciary powers statutes may provide specific language for drafting such provisions. For example, the inclusion of provisions in the governing instrument that address the fiduciary's authority to expend funds to identify and remediate a hazard, to settle claims, and to be held harmless in connection with these actions may be specifically authorized by such statutory provisions. They would surely be valuable inclusions in the trust document.

Guidelines for Bank Fiduciaries

Although the Federal Reserve and the FDIC have not provided specific guidelines on the issue, the Office of the Comptroller of the Currency (OCC) has acknowledged that "environmental liability has become a critical issue for fiduciaries." The OCC's *Handbook for Fiduciary Activities* states:

> Presently there is limited protection for fiduciaries against possible liability. However, there are a few recommended guidelines for managing trust property which may limit the risk of liability. The following guidelines should be considered:
>
> - Develop a policy for the management of property contaminated by hazardous waste.
> - Identify potential problem real estate properties.
> - Perform on-site inspections of existing property and possible new property.
> - Examine the title history of the property.
> - Examine regulatory agency files, i.e., EPA lists of hazardous waste sites.
> - Perform an environmental audit if concerns are noted.
> - Obtain indemnification from the settlor or beneficiaries of the account.[40]

National Bank fiduciaries will find further guidance in the Comptroller's Regulations and Precedents. Specifically, under Section 9.4120 of the Precedents, the Comptroller has expressed concern that

> unnecessary risks are assumed by bank fiduciaries when they fail to obtain full information on which to base asset management decisions. With respect to real estate, the minimum necessary would include knowledge of the condition, insurance, and the current fair market value of such properties. Without information on the value and condition of a property, compliance with 12 CFR 9.7 (a)(2) would not be possible. That part of the regulation, which was issued in 1963, requires an annual review of all of the assets held in or for each fiduciary account, over which the bank has investment responsibility, to determine the advisability of retaining or disposing of such assets. In effect, Section 9.7 requires real

estate initial appraisals and reappraisals because they are the source of important asset review information.[41]

Conclusion

Strategies for identifying and minimizing environmental liability must be incorporated into the fiduciary's internal control and training program in the aftermath of *Phoenix*. Banking regulators will undoubtedly conduct more comprehensive examination of fiduciary real estate policies and procedures. The ratings of trust divisions may rise or fall in connection with these regulatory audits. The ultimate test is whether fiduciary policies are designed to minimize the risk associated with managing assets that may be the subject of environmental hazards. Clearly, fundamental assumptions about the bank's exposure in dealing with such assets are forever changed in the wake of the *Phoenix* decision.

Resources

Comptroller of the Currency Administrator of National Banks. *Comptroller's Handbook for Fiduciary Activities* 1990.

Fratcher, William F. *Scott on Trusts*. 4th ed. 1992.

Graham, Michael, and Lindquist, Philip M. "Fiduciaries and CERCLA." *ACTEC Notes* 18 (1993): 212–13.

Martin, O.C., Stephens Shi, J., and Vaughn, R.C., Jr. *Environmental Risks for Trustees and Fiduciaries*. ACTEC Notes 77 (1990).

Restatement (Second) of Trusts §§ 264, 265 (1987).

Sliger, Herbert J., Jr. "The Environmental Liability Tar Baby: Is Relief for Fiduciaries Elusive or Illusory?" Presentation to May 2, 1994, Tri-State Trust Conference.

Warchall, James, et al. *Guide to the Environmental Liabilities of Fiduciaries*. 1990.

Notes

1. This subject is referred to in Casner's CASES AND TEXT ON PROPERTY in what appears to be an article titled *Dahl. What. Wore Dahl (1944) and Dahl's Boston (1946)*. A. JAMES CASNER and W. BARTON LEACH, CASES AND TEXT ON PROPERTY 25 (2d ed. 1969); *see also* Ghen v. Rich, 8 F. 159 (D. Mass. 1881).

2. Comprehensive Environmental Response, Compensation, and Liability Act of 1980, Pub. L. No. 96-510, 94 Stat. 2767 (1980) (codified at 42 U.S.C. §§ 9601–75 (1993)).

3. City of Phoenix v. Garbage Serv. Co., 816 F. Supp. 564 (D. Ariz 1993); 827 F. Supp. 600 (D. Ariz. 1993).

4. *See, e.g.*, United States v. Maryland Bank & Trust Co., 632 F. Supp. 573 (D. Md. 1986).

5. *See, e.g.*, United States v. Northeastern Pharmaceutical and Chem. Co., 810 F.2d 726 (8th Cir. 1986), *cert. denied*, 108 S. Ct.. 146, 98 L.Ed. 2d 102 1987) (NEPACCO); New York v. Shore Realty, 759 F.2d 1032, 1052 (2d Cir. 1985).

6. *See, e.g.*, United States v. Carolina Galvanizing, D.S.C. No. 6:89-163-0 1/20/89.

7. *See, e.g.*, BCW Associates Ltd. v. Occidental Chemical Corp., D.C. E. Pa. No. 86-5947, 9-30-88.

8. *See, e.g.*, United States v. Monsanto, 858 F.2d 160 (4th Cir. 1988).

9. *See, e.g.*, Channel Master Satellite Systems, Inc. v. J.F.D. Electronics Corp., 702 F. Supp. 1229 (E.D.N.C. 1988).

10. New York v. Shore Realty Corp., 759 F.2d 1032, 1037 (2d Cir. 1985); United States v. Cauffman, 21 Env't. Rep. Cas. (BNA) 2167 (C.D. Cal. 1984).

11. United States v. Bliss, 667 F. Supp. 1298 (E.D. Mo. 1987).

12. United States v. Burns, No. C-88-94-L, 1991 U.S. Dist. LEXIS 17340, at *1 (D.N.H. September 12, 1988).

13. Edward Hines Lumber Co. v. Vulcan Materials Co., 685 F. Supp. 651, 657, 27 E.R.C. 1904 (D.C.N. Ill. 1988), *aff'd.*, 861 F.2d 155, 28 E.R.C. 1457 (CA 7 1988). *But see* Ecodyne Corp. v. Shah, 718 F. Supp 1454, 30 E.R.C. 1500 (N.D. Cal. 1989); Cadillac Fairview/California Inc. v. Dow Chemical Co., 21 E.R.C. 1108 (C.D. Cal. 1985), *rev'd on other grounds*, 840 F.2d 691, 27 E.R.C. 1313 (CA 9 1988).

14. *See, e.g.*, Riverside Mkt. Dev. Corp. v. International Bldg. Prods., 931 F.2d 327 (5th Cir. 1991), cert. denied, 112 S. Ct. 636 (1991); *see also* Federal Claims Priority Act, 31 U.S.C. § 3713(E)(1) (1993).

15. *See, e.g.*, Kelly v. Thomas Solvent Co., 727 F. Supp. 1532 (W.D. Mich. 1989).

16. United States v. DiBiase SaZem Realty Trust, C.A. No. 91-11028-MA (D. Mass. Nov. 19, 1993).

17. *City of Phoenix*, 816 F. Supp. 564; 827 F. Supp. 600.

18. *City of Phoenix*, 816 F. Supp., at 567 (*quoting* Kaiser Aluminum & Chem. Corp. v. Catellus Dev. Corp., 976 F.2d 1338, 1341 (9th Cir. 1992)).

19. *Id.*

20. *See* Matter of Estate of Estes, 134 Ariz. 70, 79, 654 P.2d 4, 13 (1982) ("the bank's obligation was to act as a prudent shareholder, not to run the corporation").

21. *City of Phoenix*, 816 F. Supp., at 567.

22. *Id.*

23. 42 U.S.C. § 9601 (20) (a) (1993).

24. *City of Phoenix*, 816 F. Supp., at 567.

25. *Id.* at 568.

26. *Burns*, No. C-88-94-L 1991 LEXIS 17340.

27. *City of Phoenix*, 827 F. Supp. 600.

28. New Hampshire currently excludes trustees of revocable trusts from the conditional immunity provisions otherwise applicable to other types of fiduciaries. N.H. REV. STAT. ANN. §§ 146-C:11-a,b,c (1993).

29. MASS. GEN. LAWS ch. 21E (1994).

30. FLA. STAT. ANN. § 376.308 (West 1992); GA. CODE ANN. § 12-8-92 (Michie 1993); III. REV. STAT. 45, 1 5/22.2 (1994); IND. CODE § 13-78.78 (1993); KY. REV.

STAT. ANN. § 244.01-400 (West 1992); LA. REV. STAT. ANN. § 30.2277 (West 1994); ME. REV. STAT. ANN. tit. 38, § 342 B (West 1993); MD. ANN. CODE art. 7 § 201 (1993); MASS. GEN. LAWS ANN. ch. 21E § 2 (West 1992); MICH. COMP. LAWS ANN. § 299.612a (West 1994); N.H. REV. STAT. ANN. §§ 146-C:11a,b,c (1993); N.D. CENT. CODE § 32-40.1-02 (1993); Okla. Sess. Laws 1627, § 8A (1994); OR. REV. STAT. §§ 465.255, 465.400, 465.435 (1993); S.D. Codified Laws Ann. § 34a-15 (1994); VT. STAT. ANN. tit. 10, §§ 6615, 6617 (1993).

31. Georgia, Illinois, Maine, Maryland, Massachusetts, Michigan, New Hampshire, Vermont.

32. Florida, Indiana, Kentucky, Louisiana, North Dakota, Oregon, and South Dakota.

33. Florida, Georgia, Indiana, Kentucky, Louisiana, Maine, Maryland, Massachusetts, Michigan, New Hampshire, North Dakota, Oregon, South Dakota, and Vermont.

34. Kentucky and Michigan.

35. Kentucky, Maine, Massachusetts, New Hampshire, Oregon, and Vermont.

36. Illinois, Indiana, Maine, Massachusetts, Michigan, and New Hampshire.

37. ALA. CODE § 19-3-11 (1990); ARK. CODE ANN. § 28-69-304 (Michie 1993); KY. REV. STAT. ANN. § 386.740 (West 1992); ME. REV. STAT. ANN. tit. 18-A § 1-111 (West 1994); N.C. GEN. STAT. § 32-27 C8.11 (Supp. 1991); R.I. GEN. LAWS § 18 4-26 (1993); TENN. CODE ANN. § 35-50-110 (1993); UTAH CODE ANN. § 75-1 109 (1993); VA. CODE ANN. § 64.1-57 (T) (Supp. 1990); W.VA. CODE ANN. 44 § 5-14 (1993).

38. Note that under the Federal Claims Priority Act, *supra* note 14, fiduciaries may be liable for distributing estate or trust assets that are subject to environmental claims. The same result may be seen in state statutes. *See, e.g.*, MASS. GEN. LAWS ch. 21E (1994).

39. *See* S. 1834 and H.R. 3800 (companion bills).

40. Comptroller of the Currency Administrator of National Banks, Comptroller's Handbook for Fiduciary Activities 37 (Sept. 1990).

41. *Id.* at 240.

CHAPTER 6

Environmental Reporting Obligations

DAVID J. FREEMAN

Your client owns a shopping center with a dry cleaner that has experienced a spill and a gas station where leaking tanks are discovered. Does the client need to report, and if so, to whom? Can you wait to investigate before making the report? What must the report contain? Are there follow-up requirements?

You have completed the due diligence on your client's latest acquisition. You have shared the results of that effort with the seller. Can you simply file the environmental report in your attorney-client or work-product file?

Legal requirements, ethical obligations, and contractual provisions may require that such matters be reported to third parties. You may have to share this information with other parties to a transaction, even if you did not originally intend to do so. You may have to disclose it to the government. If a governmental report is required, there are usually follow-up reports as well. Property owners who discover environmental contamination may be forced by legal or business considerations to clean up any contamination they have found.

These disclosure obligations may conflict with other legal, ethical, or contractual obligations to your client or to the other side in a transaction. Sharing the results may also create confidentiality problems relating to waiver of legal privileges.

The area of disclosure obligations is laden with risk. It does not always receive the attention it deserves. The wrong decisions, however, can create significant legal exposure for companies and their counsel.

Federal Reporting Requirements

Statutory and Regulatory Provisions

The principal federal reporting requirements are imposed under the Comprehensive Environmental Response, Compensation, and Liability Act (CERCLA or Superfund),[1] the Emergency Planning and Community Right-to-Know Act (EPCRA),[2] and the Clean Water Act.[3] In addition, there are reporting obligations imposed by the Toxic Substances Control Act (TSCA)[4] and the Resource Conservation and Recovery Act (RCRA).[5] The requirements of these statutes overlap to a significant degree. However, except where expressly provided, compliance with one statute does not substitute for compliance with the others.

CERCLA Section 103(a)

CERCLA Section 103(a)[6] requires that notification be made for any unpermitted release of a "reportable quantity" of a hazardous substance. The person in charge of a facility where a release has occurred must report it as soon as he or she learns of such a release. The notification is made to the National Response Center,[7] which in turn notifies all appropriate governmental agencies, including the governor of any affected state. As noted in paragraph I.A.3. below, EPCRA requires that the reporting party also notify state and local officials of the incident.

Hazardous substances are defined in Section 101(14) of CERCLA as those designated under these federal statutes:

- Section 311(b)(2)(A) of the Clean Water Act[8]
- Section 102 of CERCLA[9]
- Section 3001 of RCRA[10] (includes both listed substances and those having the characteristics described by Section 3001)
- Section 307(a) of the Federal Water Pollution Control Act[11]
- Section 112 of the Clean Air Act[12]
- Section 7(f) of TSCA[13]

A current list of these chemicals is set forth at 40 C.F.R. Section 302.4.

Not all releases must be reported—only those involving a release within a twenty-four-hour period of a "reportable quantity" of the substance in question. Reportable quantities for each substance have been promulgated pursuant to CERCLA Section 102[14] and are set forth at 40 C.F.R. Sections 302.4 and 302.5. Reportable quantities for some of the most commonly found contaminants are listed in Table 1.[15]

TABLE 1. Reportable Quantities for Commonly Found Contaminants

Hazardous Substance	Reportable Quantity (lb)	(kg)
Acetone	5,000	(2,270)
Ammonia	100	(45.4)
Arsenic	1	(0.454)
Asbestos (friable only)	1	(0.454)
Benzene	10	(4.54)
2-Butanone (MEK)	5,000	(2,270)
Chlordane	1	(0.454)
2-4-D Acid	100	(45.4)
1,2-Dichlorobenzene	100	(45.4)
1,2-Dichloroethane	100	(45.4)
Ethanol, 2-Ethoxy	1,000	(454)
Formaldehyde	100	(45.4)
Heptachlor	1	(0.454)
Hydrochloric Acid	5,000	(2,270)
Mercury	1	(0.454)
Methanol	5,000	(2,270)
Naphthalene	100	(45.4)
Nitric Acid	1,000	(454)
Perchloroethylene	100	(45.4)
Pyridine	1,000	(454)
Sodium	10	(4.54)
Styrene	1,000	(454)
Sulfuric Acid	1,000	(454)
1,1,2,2-Tetrachloroethane	100	(45.4)
Tetrahydrofuran	1,000	(454)
Toluene	1,000	(454)
1,1,1-Trichloroethane	1,000	(454)
2,4,5-Trichlorophenol	10	(4.54)

A report submitted pursuant to CERCLA Section 103(a) should contain the following information:

- The name, amount, and reportable quantity of the substance involved
- The listing used to classify such material
- The geographical location and media into which the substance was released
- The date, time, and duration of the release
- The remedial action(s) taken to control the release
- The name(s) and phone number(s) of any other person(s) notified[16]

The initial report must be supplemented by notice in local newspapers to "potential injured parties."[17]

Penalties for failure to report can be severe. Civil penalties of up to $25,000 per day can be assessed or up to $75,000 per day for a second or subsequent violation.[18] A criminal conviction can result in imprisonment for up to three years, or up to five years for a second or subsequent conviction.[19] Penalties can mount quickly, as evidenced by UNOCAL Corporation's March 1994 agreement to pay a $1.5 million criminal fine for failure to report discharges from its Guadelupe oil field facilities over a five-year period.[20]

CERCLA Section 103(c)

An often overlooked reporting provision is CERCLA Section 103(c),[21] which requires that the administrator of the U.S. Environmental Protection Agency (EPA) be notified of facilities that have treated, stored, or disposed of hazardous wastes. The statute requires notification by December 11, 1980, leading many to assume that facilities discovered after that date are not subject to reporting under Section 103(c).[22] The EPA does not agree. The agency takes the position that the notification requirement attaches anytime a facility of this type is identified.[23]

Notification is made to the EPA, which in turn notifies affected state agencies. The notification must include the amount and type of any hazardous substance found at the facility as well as the known, suspected, or likely releases of such substance from the facility. The penalty for not reporting is a fine of up to $10,000 and/or imprisonment for up to one year.[24]

EPCRA Section 304

EPCRA Section 304[25] requires notification by the owner or operator regarding releases of reportable quantities of "extremely hazardous substances." Substances covered by these requirements, as well as the reporting thresholds, are listed at 40 C.F.R. Section 355, Appendix A.

If no reporting threshold has been set for a substance, the reportable quantity is set by statute at one pound. Releases of substances not deemed extremely hazardous but otherwise reportable under CERCLA must be disclosed to local and state emergency planning committees.[26]

Notification must also be made immediately to the National Response Center and to the emergency coordinators for communities and states likely to be affected by the release. The appointment of such coordinators is governed by EPCRA Section 301(c),[27] which directs each state and local emergency planning commission to designate an official to serve as a coordinator for information received by the commission. (Under certain circumstances, the local officials receiving the reports will be the fire and police departments.) To the extent it is known at the time of the notice, the notification must specify the following:

- The chemical name and identity of the substance
- Whether the substance is on the list of "extremely hazardous chemicals"
- An estimate of the quantity released into the environment
- The time and duration of the release
- The medium or media into which the release occurred
- Known or anticipated health risks associated with the substance as well as medical advice for exposed individuals
- Proper precautions to take regarding the release
- The name and telephone number of the person(s) to be contacted for further information[28]

As soon as practicable after a release, a follow-up report must be made indicating the actions taken to respond to and contain the release, the resulting known or anticipated health risks, and advice regarding medical attention for individuals exposed to the release.[29]

Failure to report can result in a civil fine of up to $25,000 per day ($75,000 per day for a second or subsequent violation) and imprisonment for up to two years (five years for a subsequent violation).[30]

Such releases must also be reported on a facility's Annual Toxic Chemical Release Form (Form R) under EPCRA Section 313.[31]

Clean Water Act Section 311(b)(5)

Section 311(b)(5)[32] of the Clean Water Act requires reporting of unauthorized discharges of oil or hazardous substances in harmful quantities into the navigable waterways, adjoining shorelines, or waters of the contiguous zone, or discharges affecting natural resources belonging to or under the management of the federal government. With respect to oil, the reportable quantity is any amount that violates applicable water quality standards, causes a sheen on the water, or causes a sludge or emulsion on the water surface or shoreline.[33] The reportable quantity of hazardous substances varies by substance and is set forth at 40 C.F.R. Section 117.3.

A report must be made by the person in charge of the vessel or facility as soon as he or she learns of the discharge and determines that it equals or exceeds the reportable quantity. The report is made to the National Response Center, which in turn notifies the relevant state agencies. The information to be reported is the same as that required under CERCLA Section 103(a).

Penalties for nonreporting can be as much as $10,000 per violation (up to a maximum of $25,000) or $10,000 per day (up to a maximum of $125,000).[34] Moreover, in the case of oil spills, failure to report can make inapplicable the liability limits that would apply under the Oil Pollution Act of 1990.[35]

RCRA

RCRA contains a variety of reporting requirements.

A leak from a hazardous waste tank must be reported to the EPA regional administrator by the owner or operator of the tank within twenty-four hours of discovery.[36] The report should include the following:

- The generator's name and address
- The facility's EPA identification number, if applicable
- The date, time, and type of incident
- The quantity of hazardous waste released
- The extent of any injuries
- The quantity and disposition of any materials recovered from the spill

Underground storage tank (UST) leaks of regulated substances other than hazardous waste, such as petroleum products, including gasoline and heating oil, must be reported by owners or operators within twenty-four hours of discovery or any other period required by the relevant state agency. The content of the report is not specified under federal regulations but will typically be governed by state provisions. The owner or operator must take immediate action to prevent further releases (including removal of the substance from the UST, a thorough inspection of the tank, and monitoring) and must act promptly to remediate any contamination from the spill. Follow-up reports are required.[37] (For a further discussion of regulations applicable to USTs, see Chapter 18.)

Under 40 C.F.R. Section 264.56, the emergency coordinator designated by the owner or operator of a facility is required to report a release, fire, or explosion that could threaten human health or the environment outside of the facility in question. The report must be made to the National Response Center or the local government official designated as the on-scene coordinator for the affected area. It must include the following:

- The name and telephone number of the person making the report
- The name and address of the facility
- The time and type of incident
- The name and quantity of material(s), to the extent known
- The extent of injuries, if any
- The possible hazards to human health or the environment outside of the facility

Failure to file a report required under RCRA is punishable by fines of up to $25,000 per day.[38]

TSCA

An emergency incident reporting requirement under TSCA is set forth in a 1978 EPA enforcement policy statement.[39] The policy requires the reporting of "emergency incidents of environmental contamination" that (1) seriously threaten humans with cancer, birth defects, mutation, death, or serious or prolonged incapacitation or (2) seriously threaten nonhuman organisms with large-scale or ecologically significant population destruction.

Since its promulgation this TSCA-based policy has been superseded in large part by more recent, and more comprehensive, reporting requirements under the statutes discussed above. Because no report need be made under TSCA if the EPA has this information from another source,[40] and because it is difficult to imagine an incident fitting this description that is not otherwise reportable, the TSCA spill reporting policy is of limited relevance today.

TSCA's reporting requirements for polychlorinated biphenals (PCBs) are considerably more important. The PCB spill reporting obligation applies to a release of more than ten pounds of material containing more than 50 parts per million (ppm) of PCBs.[41] (Untested mineral oil is presumed to contain more than 50 ppm PCBs.)[42] To be reportable, the release must have directly contaminated surface water, sewers, drinking water, animal grazing lands, or vegetable gardens.[43]

Spills meeting the above criteria must be reported by the responsible party (such as the owner, facility manager, or foreman)[44] as soon as possible and, in any event, within twenty-four hours of discovery.[45] Notification must be made to the National Response Center and the EPA Regional Office's branch of the Office of Pesticides and Toxic Substances.[46] The EPA also interprets TSCA to require reports of fires involving electrical transformers containing PCBs. (For a further discussion of regulations applicable to PCBs, see Chapter 22.)

What Is a Release?

The statutory and regulatory provisions discussed in the first part of this chapter require the reporting of a "release" or "disposal" of a contaminant. Although that requirement may appear to be straightforward, it can be difficult for a landowner to know whether his or her reporting obligation has been triggered.

For example, under CERCLA or RCRA some federal courts have given broad interpretations to the terms "release" and "disposal," including within their definitions the mere migration or leaching of contaminants through the soil, even when the landowner has not taken any affirmative action to introduce the contaminant into the environment. Other courts have taken a narrower view, holding that the mere existence of contamination does not necessarily constitute a release. This divergence of opinion has important consequences in the reporting context: Is discovery of existing contamination a "release" that requires reporting?

All of the federal case law interpreting these two terms has arisen in connection with government attempts to impose liability for cleanup or cleanup costs on the current and prior owners of contaminated land. As of this writing, the author is aware of no federal court that has addressed this issue of interpretation as it relates to reporting requirements. The gloss given to the statutory language in cases involving cleanup costs, however, should put parties on notice that courts may adopt a similarly broad interpretation regarding reporting obligations.

Courts that have addressed the question are split on the issue of whether the terms "release" and "disposal" require active human conduct, with the majority imposing liability for passive leakage. There are differences of opinion within the circuits themselves.

The courts that have imposed liability for passive "release" or "disposal" have focused on both the statutory language and the legislative intent. Many have noted that the definitions of release and disposal include several terms describing how a contaminant can enter the environment, some requiring human action (such as "discharge," "deposit," and "dumping") and others that do not commonly imply an intentional act ("leaking" and "spilling"). These courts have determined that the inclusion of the term "leaking" in the definition was aimed at imposing liability for passive leakage of hazardous substances.[47]

These courts, and others, have supported their conclusions by noting that to condition liability on affirmative human participation in contamination would frustrate the statutes' purposes. The statutes emphasize strict liability, providing only certain limited defenses for innocent landowners and others who did not control the property at the time of the release.[48]

By contrast, the courts that have refused to impose liability on "passive" landowners have expressed concern about the inequity of imposing cleanup costs on landowners who simply happened to own the land while contaminants either leaked from tanks put there by previous owners or migrated through the soil after rainfall.[49] Where the context is reporting requirements rather than imposition of cleanup liability, this reasoning may not be as persuasive.

Several courts have distinguished between the terms "release" and "disposal" in their efforts at interpretation. In *United States v. Petersen Sand & Gravel, Inc.*, for example,[50] the court took a hard look at the language of the CERCLA provisions containing the words "release" and "disposal" and concluded that, although it was "undisputed that a 'release' includes the kind of passive migration at issue here," the word "disposal" was not meant to encompass passive events. This court also noted that the CERCLA reporting requirements create an incentive to clean up that would not be undercut by a limited interpretation of "disposal."

In summary, there is some authority for the proposition that discovery of an existing contamination problem may not always constitute discovery of a release. Currently, however, such a holding would appear to be a minority view. In any event, the conservative approach would be to report any discovery of existing contamination as if it were a release under applicable statutes.

State Law Reporting Requirements

A wide variety of state statutes governs disclosure obligations for environmental contamination. Typically these statutes mirror federal requirements for reporting releases into the environment of hazardous chemicals or discharges from USTs. The variations occur in the quantities that are reportable, how and to whom to make the report, what the report should contain, and follow-up requirements. They neither supersede nor are preempted by federal requirements, so a knowledge of state statutory or regulatory reporting schemes is essential to full compliance in this area.

Unfortunately, the number and variety of state statutes make adequate coverage of state issues impossible here. The reader is referred to the number of excellent reference works that comprehensively track these statutes and their implementation.[51]

Other Considerations

Common-Law Fraud

The doctrine of caveat emptor—"let the buyer beware"—has had a long and illustrious history in real estate transactions. Yet today it is under sustained assault. Courts and juries are often influenced by the inequities that sometimes result from the application of the doctrine. In addition, many states have modified some of its harsher features in consumer protection legislation. Accordingly, it can no longer be counted on as an absolute shield for the seller who fails (knowingly or unknowingly) to disclose an environmental problem.

New York's jurisprudence is not atypical in this regard. Caveat emptor remains the basic rule, at least where the seller has not made any affirmative misrepresentation of environmental conditions on its property.[52] The courts have recognized certain exceptions, however, in situations where there has been an affirmative misrepresentation on the seller's part or where the seller played an active role in causing the environmental problem.[53] In addition, there have been several legislative attempts (although so far none has been successful) to modify the caveat emptor doctrine on a prospective basis.

One reason that attempts to limit caveat emptor have not been more widespread is, ironically, the success of CERCLA and similar federal statutes in mitigating the harshness of the common-law rule. For example, in *Hydro-Manufacturing, Inc. v. Kayser-Roth Corp.*,[54] the Rhode Island Supreme Court rejected the plaintiff-purchaser's attempt to overrule the caveat emptor doctrine, noting that CERCLA and a companion state statute provided the plaintiff with ample avenues for redress.

Suffice it to say that the doctrine retains significant vitality in some states, whereas in others it has been undercut by statute or eroded by court-made exceptions. (Caveat emptor and other common-law doctrines relating to seller liability are discussed in more detail in Chapter 2.)

Status as Innocent Purchaser

CERCLA contains a very limited "innocent purchaser defense." Under Section 101(35)(A), a party that acquires a facility after hazardous substances were disposed of or placed on it is excused from liability if it can establish, by a preponderance of the evidence, that it did not know or have reason to know that such substances were present at the facility. In addition, the party also "must have undertaken, at the time of the acquisition, all appropriate inquiry into the previous ownership and uses of the property. . . ."[55] (For a more complete discussion of CERCLA's innocent purchaser defense, see Chapter 1.)

Much has been written about the almost impossible burden that must be satisfied to qualify for the innocent purchaser defense. The great majority of those attempting to obtain this status fail to do so. But even those few who qualify can lose their privileged status by failing to make full disclosure, in connection with a subsequent sale, of all they learn about the property after their purchase. Section 101(35)(C) provides that "if the defendant obtained actual knowledge of the release or threatened release . . . when [he or she] owned the real property and then subsequently transferred ownership . . . to another person without disclosing such knowledge, such defendant shall be treated as liable under [Section 107(a)(1)]. . . ."

Thus, failure to disclose knowledge of contamination is particularly dangerous for at least one category of owners—those who might otherwise qualify as innocent purchasers under Section 101(35) of CERCLA.

Sentencing Guidelines

While failing to report a release of contaminants puts an individual at risk of criminal liability under a variety of state and federal statutes, the criminal enforcement policies contain "carrots" in addition to "sticks." It is appropriate briefly to discuss these "carrots" from the perspective of reporting issues. (Criminal enforcement matters are addressed in detail in Chapter 7.)

One such incentive to reporting is the possibility of lenient treatment for companies that voluntarily report a problem and proceed voluntarily to remedy it. For example, a 1991 U.S. Department of Justice guidance document[56] provides a "nondefinitive" list of factors to be used in determining when and how to prosecute an environmental criminal matter. Among the factors suggesting that lenient treatment may be warranted are (1) whether the "person" (or violator) made a voluntary, timely, and complete disclosure of the matter under investigation and (2) the degree and timeliness of the person's cooperation (e.g., willingness to make relevant information available to the government).[57] Conversely, failure to report releases as required by law significantly reduces the chances of obtaining prosecutorial leniency.[58]

Similar provisions are found in many state enforcement and penalty policies. The New York State Department of Environmental Conservation's Civil Penalty Policy, for example, permits adjustments to proposed penalties based on culpability and violator cooperation (including timely reporting of noncompliance).[59]

These policies, of course, do not guarantee leniency to companies that voluntarily disclose environmental problems and take corrective action on their own initiative. In practice, however, agencies are often extremely solicitous of companies that do so.

Counsel as Coconspirator

There is a line of cases, exemplified by *United States v. Park*,[60] that stands for the proposition that individuals who are in a position to prevent the violation of a public welfare statute can be held liable if they fail to do so.

This was the standard used by the district attorney in the notorious *InFerGene* case in California.[61] There, a law firm was prosecuted for advising its client, the bankrupt InFerGene Company, to abandon waste at the site rather than to clean it up. The district attorney's office characterized the giving of the advice as criminal abandonment of wastes under the state's Health & Safety Code.[62] The indictment was ultimately dismissed because the outside counsel did not have the requisite "control" over the company's decision. This narrow ground for dismissal, however, gives scant comfort to senior in-house counsel or to outside counsel who serve as directors or officers of corporations.

Environmental counsel are by no means the only ones to feel the effects of the continuing quest for deep pockets to fund cleanup efforts. The lesson of cases such as *InFerGene* is that prosecutors will not hesitate to cast a wide net in an effort to find as many sources as possible to fund a cleanup. Clearly, environmental counsel will not be regarded as off-limits. Therefore, a lawyer should give serious thought to the potential for personal liability before advising a client that reporting of a particular release is not required.

Ethical Considerations

There are ethical obligations embodied in the Code of Professional Responsibility that, perhaps surprisingly, pull in opposite directions with respect to the disclosure of environmental conditions.

One set of rules, for example, prohibits disclosure of client confidences, except those relating to the client's intention to commit a crime.[63] Thus, if the client decides not to disclose an environmental condition, a lawyer generally cannot reveal that information.

Lawyers, however, are forbidden from making false statements of fact.[64] In addition, where a statute places an affirmative obligation on a lawyer to make a disclosure,[65] the lawyer cannot avoid this obligation by invoking the notion of client confidence. Moreover, in a situation where a failure to disclose an environmental condition is deemed to be a criminal violation of the reporting statutes, the prohibition against a lawyer counseling or assisting the client engaged in illegal conduct[66] will come into play, and the lawyer may be obliged to report the environmental condition.

Contractual Obligations

Another consideration potentially arguing against disclosure rights and obligations is the possibility of breaching a contractual obligation to the other side. Typically, transactional documents either expressly require a party to disclose its knowledge of adverse site conditions or contain representations and warranties that all such conditions have been fully disclosed. Breach of any such provision may lead to penalties provided for by contract, including rescission.

On the other hand, parties to such transactions frequently insist on confidentiality. Care must be taken in the drafting of such contracts to permit disclosures that are required by law. Doing so eliminates the dilemma of having to choose whether to comply with a statutory disclosure requirement or to abide by the terms of a confidentiality agreement between the parties.

Waiver of Privilege

While the results of sampling are generally not entitled to confidentiality, the analysis of the results' significance, especially if it contains legal conclusions, may be protected, either as attorney-client communications or work product or both.

What happens to the privilege when an audit report containing such analyses is disclosed to the other side in a real estate transaction or to the government in an attempt to comply with the reporting statutes? Does this disclosure sound the death knell for the confidentiality of those documents with respect to third parties, such as toxic tort plaintiffs, or other potentially responsible parties at a Superfund site?

The relevant federal statutes generally allow public access to any information or records that the EPA collects, unless the person divulging the information can demonstrate that it should be treated as confidential.[67] However, supplying the information under a claim of business confidentiality may waive other claims of privilege, such as attorney-client privilege or work-product immunity.

The attorney-client privilege and the work-product doctrine are the two primary legal privileges that may apply to audit reports. A privilege for self-critical evaluation has been recognized by some courts and has also been the subject of legislative activity in a number of states.

The attorney-client privilege protects communications to an attorney from a client. To invoke the privilege, specific facts demonstrating the existence of the requisite elements of the privilege must be shown. The elements of the privilege are (1) use of an attorney to provide legal advice; (2) a communication between the client and the attorney; (3) confidentiality of the communication; and (4) absence of waiver.[68]

Companies should be aware of particular risks of waiver in the context of environmental audits. The attorney's primary purpose for being involved in the audit should be to provide legal assistance.[69] Distribution of documents should be limited to those who need the information to act on it.

In the case of a due diligence audit shared between the buyer and the seller in a real estate transaction, the attorneys for both parties should memorialize their understandings. The memorialization should demonstrate that each party will keep the information confidential, that the parties have a common interest in resolving the environmental issues, and that the report was prepared so that each counsel could provide its client with legal advice. Finally, the attorney-client privilege may extend to an agent of the attorney on the theory that the agent provides specific expertise, which enables the attorney to provide legal advice. Therefore, the attorney should be the one to hire environmental consultants.[70]

The work-product doctrine protects from discovery an attorney's work product prepared in anticipation of litigation.[71] The two types of work product are (1) opinion work product, such as the attorney's mental impressions, conclusions, opinions, or legal theories, which is absolutely protected in the absence of waiver, and (2) non-opinion work product, which enjoys a lesser degree of protection.[72] The work-product immunity does not apply to documents prepared in the regular course of business.

To invoke this privilege, the audit must be prepared in anticipation of litigation. While a remote prospect of litigation will generally not suffice, an audit prepared after an environmental accident may be protected on the theory that the accident "foreseeably could have been made the basis of a claim."[73] In addition, there must not have been a waiver of confidentiality. Opinion work product is less susceptible to waiver than the attorney-client privilege—only disclosure that is inconsistent with the adversary system will waive the privilege.[74]

The self-evaluation privilege is designed to protect certain internal documents to allow candid and frank self-evaluation. An increasing number of jurisdictions are making this privilege a matter of statutory law.[75] Elsewhere courts that have considered this privilege have used a balancing test, weighing the public benefit of access to the information against the negative effects of disclosure.[76] To assert this privilege, companies must demonstrate that one purpose of the audit has been to further the public interest by improving the facility's compliance with environmental obligations. As with other evidentiary privileges, the self-evaluation privilege can be waived by disclosing the materials to others.[77]

The case law in this area is developing. However, the courts have tended to construe privileges in this type of situation narrowly. In general, any disclosure to the other side in a transaction or to the government presents the risk that any privileged status that might previously have attached to the document may be waived. Counsel should weigh the possibility of such a result when deciding whether to disclose the results of environmental reports in the context of a real estate transaction.

Conclusion

Reporting obligations can put companies, and their counsel, between the Scylla of reporting and having to engage in expensive cleanup, and the Charybdis of not reporting and risking significant civil and criminal penalties. The stakes are very high. Case law and regulatory guidance are often unclear. The variety of issues that must be addressed, and their interrelationship, can present a formidable challenge to even the most knowledgeable and resourceful counsel.

In the real estate context, as elsewhere in environmental law, reporting requirements are becoming a key element in governmental enforcement strategies. Companies and their counsel can expect increasing attention to be paid to these obligations in the years ahead, both by governmental agencies and private interests. Knowing the rules, and anticipating their impact, is of utmost importance in the conduct of business operations and in transactions involving real property.

Notes

The assistance of Greg Belcamino, an associate at Battle Fowler LL.P. in New York City, is gratefully acknowledged.

1. 42 U.S.C. §§ 9601–75.
2. 42 U.S.C. §§ 11001–50.
3. Federal Water Pollution Control Act (FWPCA), 42 U.S.C. §§ 1251–1387.
4. 15 U.S.C. §§ 2601–92.
5. 42 U.S.C. §§ 6901–92k.

6. 42 U.S.C. § 9603(a).

7. The National Response Center was established pursuant to the federal Clean Water Act, 33 U.S.C. § 1321(b)(5) and (6); 33 C.F.R. § 153.203. The center's phone number is (800) 424-8802.

8. 33 U.S.C. § 1321(b)(2)(A).

9. 42 U.S.C. § 9602.

10. 42 U.S.C. § 6921.

11. 33 U.S.C. § 1317(a).

12. 42 U.S.C. § 7412.

13. 15 U.S.C. § 2606(f).

14. 42 U.S.C. § 9602.

15. Special rules apply for mixtures of chemicals and "continuous and stable" releases. *See* 42 U.S.C. § 9603(f). There are also certain other exceptions found in the statute or implementing regulations. They include federally permitted releases, such as those under National Pollutant Discharge Elimination System (NPDES) permits (*see* 42 U.S.C. § 9603(a)); releases that expose only persons in the workplace, such as those in totally enclosed buildings (*see* 42 U.S.C. § 9601(22)(A) (definition of release)); and releases of solid pieces of metal (*see* 40 C.F.R. Table 302.4 at note ††).

16. *See* 40 C.F.R. § 302.6. Again, special rules apply to continuous releases. *See* 40 C.F.R. § 302.8.

17. 42 U.S.C. § 9611(g).

18. 42 U.S.C. § 9609(b).

19. 42 U.S.C. § 9603(b).

20. *See* 24 Env't Rep. (BNA) 2015 (1994).

21. 42 U.S.C. § 9603(c).

22. The person responsible for notification is "any person who owns or operates, or who at the time of disposal owned or operated, or who accepted hazardous substances for transport and selected a facility at which hazardous substances . . . are or have been stored, treated, or disposed of. . . ." 42 U.S.C. § 9603(c).

23. Undated memorandum from Lisa K. Friedman, Associate General Counsel, Solid Waste and Emergency Response Division, to Barry R. Bedrick, Acting Assistant General Counsel, General Accounting Office.

24. 42 U.S.C. § 9603(c).

25. 42 U.S.C. § 11004.

26. 42 U.S.C. § 11004(a)(3).

27. 42 U.S.C. § 11001(c).

28. 42 U.S.C. § 11004(b)(2).

29. 42 U.S.C. § 11004(c).

30. 42 U.S.C. § 11045(b)(2) and (4).

31. 42 U.S.C. § 11023. *See also* Pollution Prevention Act of 1990, 42 U.S.C. § 13106. The information that must be reported on the annual Form R includes the following for toxic chemicals manufactured, processed, or otherwise used in reportable quantities during the previous year: an estimate of the maximum amount of the chemical present at the facility at any time; for each wastestream, the disposal method and estimated treatment efficiency achieved by that method; and the annual quantity of each toxic chemical entering each environmental medium.

32. 33 U.S.C. § 1321(b)(5).
33. *See* 40 C.F.R. §§ 110.3, 110.4, 110.5, 110.11.
34. 42 U.S.C. § 1321(b)(6), (7).
35. 33 U.S.C. § 2704(c)(2)(A).
36. *See* 40 C.F.R. §§ 264.196, 265.196.
37. 40 C.F.R. § 280.62(b).
38. 42 U.S.C. § 6928(a)(3).
39. 43 Fed. Reg. 11,110 (1978).
40. *Id.*, at 11,111–12.
41. 40 C.F.R. § 761.125(a).
42. 40 C.F.R. § 761.123 (definition of spill).
43. 40 C.F.R. § 761.125(a)(1).
44. 40 C.F.R. § 761.123 (definition of responsible party).
45. 40 C.F.R. § 761.125(c)(1).
46. *Id.*
47. *See* Nurad, Inc. v. William E. Hooper & Sons Co., 966 F.2d 837, 845 (4th Cir. 1992), *cert. denied*, 113 S. Ct. 377 (hereinafter *Nurad*); United States v. Waste Indus., 734 F.2d 159, 164–65 (4th Cir. 1984); Pantry, Inc. v. Stop-n-Go Foods, Inc., 796 F. Supp. 1171, 1177 (S.D. Ind. 1992).
48. *See* Lincoln Properties, Ltd. v. Higgins, 823 F. Supp. 1528, 1536 (E.D. Cal. 1992) ("Nor is the 'one source' or 'passive owner exception' . . . supported by the overall structure or purpose of CERCLA. The Act is structured to provide for broad coverage"); *Nurad*, 966 F.2d at 846 (opining that the definition of disposal requires active human conduct is "at odds with CERCLA's strict liability emphasis"). *See also* United States v. Price, 523 F. Supp. 1055, 1073 (D.N.J. 1981), *aff'd*, 688 F. 2d 204 (3rd Cir. 1982) (holding subsequent owners to have been "contributing to the disposal (i.e., leaking) of wastes merely by virtue of their studied indifference to the hazardous condition that now exists"); State of N.Y. v. Shore Realty Corp., 759 F.2d 1032 (2d Cir. 1985) (holding defendants who bought land knowing of the existence of waste storage tanks held to be liable for the tanks' leakage).
49. *See, e.g.*, United States v. CMDG Realty Co., 1995 WL 55378 (D.N.J.); Joslyn Mfg. Co. v. T.L. James & Co., 836 F. Supp. 1264, 1269 (W.D. La. 1993); Snediker Developers Ltd. Partnership v. Evans, 773 F. Supp. 984, 989 (E.D. Mich. 1991); Ecodyne Corp. v. Shah, 718 F. Supp. 1454, 1457 (N.D. Cal. 1989); *In re* Diamond Rio Trucks, 115 B.R. 559, 565 (Bankr. W.D. Mich. 1990).
50. 806 F. Supp. 1346, 1351–52 (N.D. Ill. 1992) (finding defendant liable for leakage/disposal from waste storage barrels that were on the land prior to defendant's incorporation).
51. *See, e.g.*, KENNETH R. MYERS ET AL., ENVIRONMENTAL SPILL REPORTING HANDBOOK (1992); SUSAN M. COOKE, THE LAW OF HAZARDOUS WASTE: MANAGEMENT, CLEANUP, LIABILITY, AND LITIGATION (1994).
52. *See, e.g.*, Banker North Salem Assocs. I v. Haight, 612 N.Y.S. 2d 281 (3d Dep't 1994); Perin v. Mardine Realty Co., 5 A.D.2d 685, 168 N.Y.S.2d 647 (2d Dep't 1957), *aff'd*, 6 N.Y.2d 920, 190 N.Y.S.2d 995 (1959).
53. *See, e.g.*, Tahini Invs., Ltd. v. Bobrowsky, 99 A.D.2d 489, 470 N.Y.S.2d 431 (2d Dep't 1984).
54. 640 A.2d 950 (R.I. 1994).
55. 42 U.S.C. § 9601(35)(A)(B).

56. U.S. Dep't of Justice, "Factors in Decisions on Criminal Prosecutions for Environmental Violations in the Context of Significant Voluntary Compliance or Disclosure Efforts by the Violator" (July 1, 1991).

57. *Id.*, at 3–5.

58. *Id.*, at 12.

59. Civil Penalty Policy, N.Y. State Dep't of Environmental Conservation (June 20, 1990), at 9–10.

60. 421 U.S. 658 (1975). *See also* United States v. Dotterweich, 320 U.S. 277 (1943) (strict liability constitutionally permissible for crimes involving public welfare).

61. California v. Sullivan Roche & Johnson, Cal. Super. Ct. Solano County, No. C-31529 (March 20, 1992); California v. InFerGene Co., Solano County Mun. Ct., No. 096922 (August 16, 1991).

62. *See* CAL. HEALTH & SAFETY CODE §§ 25097(a)(d), 25189.5, and 25865(b)(1).

63. *See* MODEL CODE OF PROFESSIONAL RESPONSIBILITY DR 4-101(B), DR 4-101(C)(3).

64. *See* MODEL CODE OF PROFESSIONAL RESPONSIBILITY DR 7-102(A)(5).

65. *See, e.g.*, N.Y. Envtl. Conserv. Law § 40-0111 (McKinney 1994).

66. *See* MODEL CODE OF PROFESSIONAL RESPONSIBILITY DR 7-102(A)(7).

67. *See, e.g.*, 33 U.S.C. § 1318(b); 42 U.S.C. § 9604(e)(7); 42 U.S.C. § 6927(b).

68. *See* United States v. United Shoe Machinery Corp., 89 F. Supp. 357, 358–59 (D. Mass. 1950).

69. *See* United States v. Chevron U.S.A., Inc., 1989 WL 121616 (E.D. Pa. 1989) (finding certain documents were not privileged because in-house counsel was merely an audit-team member and did not act as the attorney).

70. *See* Upjohn Co. v. United States, 449 U.S. 383 (1981); United States v. Cote, 456 F.2d 142 (8th Cir. 1972).

71. *See* Hickman v. Taylor, 329 U.S. 495 (1947); FED. R. CIV. P. 26(b)(3).

72. *See* FED. R. CIV. P. 26(b)(3).

73. Waste Management Inc. v. Florida Power & Light Co., 571 So.2d 507, 1510 (Fla. Dist. Ct. App. 1990).

74. *See, e.g.*, Permian Corp. v. United States, 665 F.2d 1214, 1219 (D.C. Cir. 1981).

75. As of this writing, fourteen states have enacted legislation establishing a privilege for environmental audits. They are Arkansas (Act. No. 350 of the 1995 Session); Colorado (C.R.S. § 13-25-126.5); Idaho (I.C. § 9-801 *et seq.*); Illinois (415 I.L.C.S. § 5/52.2); Indiana (I.C. § 13-10-3-1 *et seq.*); Kansas (1995 Kan. SB 76); Kentucky (K.R.S. § 224.01-040); Minnesota (1995 Minn. SB 1479); Mississippi (1995 Miss. Laws 627); Oregon (O.R.S. § 468.963); Texas (1995 Tex. HB 2473); Utah (U.C. § 19-7-103 *et seq.*); Virginia (1995 Va. Acts. 564); and Wyoming (W.S. § 35-11-1105 *et seq.*).

76. *See, e.g.*, Reichhold Chemicals, Inc. v. Textron, Inc., 157 F.R.D. 522 (N.D. Fla. 1994); Kansas Gas & Elec. v. Eye, 789 P.2d 1161 (Kan. 1990).

77. *See, e.g.*, COLO. REV. STAT. § 13-25-126.5(3)(a).

CHAPTER 7

Criminal Liability for Environmental Matters

JUDSON W. STARR
JUDITH A. ARMOLD

Before an Environmental Crimes unit was established within the Environment and Natural Resources Division of the U.S. Department of Justice in October 1982, criminal enforcement of environmental laws was rare, even though environmental statutes provided for criminal penalties. However, since federal fiscal year 1983, and particularly since the latter part of the 1980s, criminal indictments, guilty pleas, and convictions have multiplied.

As of April 7, 1995, more than $296 million in criminal fines and penalties had been levied at the federal level and more than 561 years of jail time had been imposed.[1] From the beginning of the Clinton Administration until federal fiscal year 1996, funding for environmental enforcement was substantially increased, and the U.S. Environmental Protection Agency (EPA) has restructured its enforcement effort to provide additional coordination and focus in this area. In accordance with statutory authorization included in the Clean Air Act Amendments of 1990, 42 U.S.C. Section 7413(f), the EPA even announced a proposal to issue rewards of up to $10,000 to citizens who report company violations of the Clean Air Act (CAA),[2] suggesting that even more prosecutions would follow. Whether 1995 Congressional moves to change the direction of the nation's environmental programs, particularly threats to make drastic cuts in funding for enforcement, will alter this direction is not certain.

The trend toward increased criminal enforcement at the federal level is reflected in the states as well. This trend affects real estate transactions, just as it does other activities that may give rise to liability under environmental laws. It is, therefore, increasingly important that lawyers who advise their clients about real estate transactions and operations be aware of at least the basic principles that govern the prosecution and defense of environmental crimes.

Clients who own and manage real property face potential criminal liability—at federal and state levels—in connection with wetland disturbances; asbestos abatement; handling and disposal of PCBs, pesticides, and other hazardous materials (even if the client had nothing to do with placing these substances on the land and simply discovered contamination in the course of or following a real estate transfer); installation, management, and abandonment of underground and aboveground storage tanks; and similar problem areas. Enforcement authorities may elect to pursue environmental violators criminally, especially when their acts or omissions appear particularly willful, when government warnings have been blatantly ignored, or when proscribed actions or the failure to disclose discovered contamination could seriously endanger humans or the environment.

In addition, in connection with the purchase, sale, or lease of real property there are often statutory or regulatory requirements—again, either federal or state—mandating environmental certifications, reports, or notifications (sometimes in deeds or land records), or even requiring the cleanup of known contamination.[3] It is especially important that real estate practitioners be aware of applicable disclosure or cleanup requirements and assure that their clients follow these requirements, because ignorance of the law is unlikely to serve as an effective defense to the imposition of criminal penalties.

The kinds of activities that can lead real estate clients into trouble under environmental laws are discussed in detail in other chapters of this publication. For example, a client may discover hazardous wastes or underground tanks on property that the client is contemplating buying or has just bought. Promptly reporting the discovery and appropriately handling any contamination may determine whether and what enforcement action will be taken. A number of criminal prosecutions have been prompted by landowners' or developers' deliberate filling of known or suspected wetlands. More careful attention to wetlands regulations could almost certainly have prevented these prosecutions, and appropriate response to initial government contacts could likely have mitigated penalties.

Unless recent trends are reversed as a result of Congressional action, enforcement officials are likely to pursue the criminal enforcement option with more frequency and zeal. It is the purpose of this chapter to provide readers with an understanding of some of the major criminal law issues likely to be encountered if their clients are faced with the threat of a criminal prosecution or with an actual indictment.[4]

Introduction

Besides understanding the growing number of criminal prosecutions and the growing size of criminal penalties, practitioners need to appreciate a number of other facts of environmental enforcement. Both individuals and organizations are likely to be targeted for criminal enforcement. Environmental crimes are frequently charged in conjunction with more traditional criminal violations, such as conspiracy, aiding and abetting, false statements, mail fraud, and obstruction of justice.[5] In part because of efforts to shift the responsibility for environmental protection from the federal government to the states, it is very possible that those who commit environmental offenses will face prosecutions at both federal and state levels. Lack of coordination among federal and state agencies, as well as among various arms of the same agency, may result in overlapping administrative, civil, and criminal enforcement actions.

Additionally, notwithstanding the rule of strict construction of criminal laws, the statutes creating environmental crimes are being construed to permit conviction upon evidence of involvement that is less than personal and a state of mind that is less than the classic *mens rea*. This gives prosecutors tremendous discretion. Targets of investigation can influence the exercise of that discretion by convincing the prosecutor that the target is fundamentally law-abiding, notwithstanding the potential violation under investigation. A preexisting auditing program and other due diligence activities can be an effective demonstration of commitment to environmental compliance. In commercial transactions, a thorough environmental assessment of the property and operations before acquisition by the purchaser would be helpful if illegal conditions are later discovered and if they are then addressed or reported promptly.

Finally, if the government obtains an environmental conviction, it is more and more likely that the convicted defendant will receive at least some jail time. Federal sentencing guidelines, in effect since late 1987, severely curtail the sentencing discretion of federal judges, and recommended revisions to these guidelines aimed at organizations convicted of environmental crimes may demand even more severe penalties.

Statutory Overview

There are many environmental statutes, both federal and state, that include criminal enforcement provisions, and it would be impossible to set out or even cite each one here. However, the majority of federal environmental prosecutions have been brought under the CAA, the

Clean Water Act (CWA), the Resource Conservation and Recovery Act (RCRA), and the Comprehensive Environmental Response, Compensation, and Liability Act (CERCLA).

The CAA can be and has been invoked in connection with the release of hazardous air pollutants, such as asbestos, during the course of demolition activities—for example, in *United States v. Louisville Edible Oil Products, Inc.*, 926 F.2d 584 (6th Cir.), *cert. denied*, 502 U.S. 859 (1991), and *United States v. Buckley*, 934 F.2d 84 (6th Cir. 1991). Both *Louisville Edible Oil* and *Buckley* involved the knowing release of asbestos in violation of the CAA and failure to report the release as required by CERCLA. In *Louisville Edible Oil*, the violations occurred in connection with asbestos removal from tanks and piping. The *Buckley* violations occurred in the course of a demolition project.

Under the criminal penalty provisions of the CAA, 42 U.S.C. Section 7413(c), knowing violation of a state implementation plan, an order to comply with such a plan, or any one of a number of listed requirements and prohibitions of the act can lead to a fine of up to $250,000 for an individual or up to $500,000 for an organization.[6] Furthermore, an individual violator is subject to imprisonment for up to five years or to both a fine and imprisonment (42 U.S.C. Section 7413(c)(1)).

Negligent endangerment—that is, the *negligent* release of a hazardous air pollutant that *negligently* places another in imminent danger of death or serious bodily injury—can lead to a fine of up to $100,000 for an individual or up to $200,000 for an organization. An individual violator is subject to imprisonment for up to one year or to both a fine and imprisonment (42 U.S.C. Section 7413(c)(4)).

On the other hand, knowing endangerment—that is, the *knowing* release of a hazardous air pollutant that *knowingly* places another in imminent danger—can lead to a fine of up to $250,000 for an individual or up to $1 million for an organization. An individual violator is subject to imprisonment for up to fifteen years or to both a fine and imprisonment (42 U.S.C. Section 7413(c)(5)(A)).

Knowing failure to pay a fee required by or under the CAA can be prosecuted as a felony under 42 U.S.C. Section 7413(c)(1) or as a misdemeanor, with penalties similar to those for negligent endangerment, under 42 U.S.C. Section 7413(c)(3). Maximum penalties under all of these CAA provisions are doubled for a second or later conviction under the same provision.

Wetlands violations and other offenses involving the release of pollutants to surface water fall under the CWA, criminal penalties for which are set out at 33 U.S.C. Section 1319(c).[7] Misdemeanor penalties are available for negligent violation of a condition in a permit issued under the CWA (including a wetlands permit) or for the unpermitted discharge of a pollutant. The maximum stated fine is $25,000 per day, and an individual violator may be fined, imprisoned for up to one year, or both (33 U.S.C. Section 1319(c)(1)). Felony penalties are available upon a conviction for knowing violation of the CWA. The maximum stated fine is $50,000 per day, and an individual violator may be fined, imprisoned for up to three years, or both (33 U.S.C. Section 1319(c)(2)).

In *United States v. Pozsgai*, No. 88-00450 (E.D. Pa. 1989), a landowner was convicted of filling wetlands on his property without a permit. Upon conviction on forty-one counts, he was sentenced to serve three years in prison and to pay a $200,000 fine, and he was further ordered to restore the site.[8]

In *United States v. Ellen*, 961 F.2d 462 (4th Cir.), *cert.* denied, 113 S. Ct. 217 (1992), the Fourth Circuit upheld the felony conviction of a property manager for intentionally filling wetlands, the exact extent of which was in dispute. The gravamen of the offense, as argued by the government, was that Ellen continued to fill wetlands after the Corps of Engineers had issued several cease-and-desist orders.

Under the CWA, knowing endangerment can result in a stated fine of up to $250,000 for an individual or $1 million for an organization, and an individual may be fined, imprisoned for up to fifteen years, or both (33 U.S.C. Section 1319(c)(3)(A)). As in the case of CAA violations, maximum penalties under the CWA are doubled for a second or later conviction under the same provision.

The criminal penalty provisions of RCRA are set out at 42 U.S.C. Section 6928(d) and (e).[9] Among the acts for which RCRA provides criminal penalties are knowingly: (1) transporting hazardous waste to a treatment, storage, or disposal facility that does not have a permit; (2) treating, storing, or disposing of any hazardous waste without a permit; or (3) violating any permit condition. A violation is a felony punishable by a stated fine of up to $50,000 per day, and an individual violator may be imprisoned for up to five years or both fined and imprisoned (42 U.S.C. Section 6928(d)). The maximum penalties are doubled for a second or later conviction (*id.*), and knowing endangerment convictions can bring even higher penalties (42 U.S.C. Section 6928(e)).

Under CERCLA's criminal penalty provisions, the person in charge of a facility from which a hazardous substance is released in greater than a threshold quantity can incur penalties for failure to notify the National Response Center of the release immediately,[10] for knowingly reporting false or misleading information, or for knowingly destroying or falsifying certain reports (42 U.S.C. Section 9603(b)(3), (d)(2)).[11] The maximum fine is $250,000 for an individual or $500,000 for an organization.[12] An individual violator can be imprisoned for up to three years for a first offense, or up to five years upon a second or later conviction, in addition to or instead of being fined.

A number of environmental statutes at both federal and state levels include reporting provisions, and also call for penalizing false statements or knowing omissions in the required reports. An example is the CAA's provisions in this regard (42 U.S.C. Section 7413(c)(2)). They provide for a fine of up to $250,000 for an individual or up to $500,000 for an organization for knowing false statements or knowing omissions in required records or reports or for tampering with monitoring devices. An individual violator is subject to a fine, imprisonment for up to two years, or both. The maximum punishment is doubled for a second or later conviction under the same provision. Often reports, certifications, or notices are required in connection with or at the time of real estate transactions, so this is an area where real estate clients and their lawyers need to be particularly vigilant. For example, some state hazardous waste laws require deed notices if hazardous wastes are left on the property.

Who May Be Prosecuted?

Questions frequently arise in criminal proceedings as to whether the government has brought its case against the proper party, or whether the defendant (individual or organization) can properly be convicted and punished for criminal acts principally committed by another. Not surprisingly, the cases consistently hold that a corporation, which can act only through its individual agents, may be held liable for an employee's criminal conduct, as long as the acts in question were done on behalf of the corporation and are within the scope of the employee's authority.

Indeed, a corporation may be held criminally liable for the acts of an employee even when express corporate policies prohibit the activities on which a prosecution is based. Thus, in *United States v. Hayes International Corp.*, 786 F.2d 1499 (11th Cir. 1986), the court upheld conviction of a company on the basis of acts committed by the employee in charge of the company's hazardous waste disposal, despite the fact that those acts directly contravened written company policy.

By the same token, prosecution of corporate agents is not limited to officers, directors, and other high-level employees. Most of the criminal provisions in the major environmental statutes impose criminal liability on "persons," a term broadly defined without restrictions relating to status or responsibility. (See 33 U.S.C. Section 1362(5); 42 U.S.C. Sections 6903(15), 7602(e).)

Even in prosecutions brought under CERCLA, 42 U.S.C. Section 9603(b), which imposes criminal liability on the "person in charge" of a vessel or facility, courts have ruled that relatively low-level corporate officials may be convicted. Thus, in *United States v. Carr*, 880 F.2d 1550, 1551 (2d Cir. 1989), a CERCLA prosecution, the court instructed the jury that, "[s]o long as the Defendant had supervisory control or was otherwise in charge of the truck or the area in question, he is responsible. . . . If you find that he had any authority over either the vehicle or the area, this is sufficient, regardless of whether others also exercised control." Likewise, in *United States v. Buckley*, the asbestos case discussed earlier, the court emphasized that even a relatively low-level employee can be held liable for CERCLA violations if that person is in fact in charge of the facility where hazardous substances were released.

In *United States v. Johnson & Towers, Inc.*, 741 F.2d 662 (3d Cir. 1984), *cert. denied*, 469 U.S. 1208 (1985), two employees were convicted for disposing of hazardous waste without a permit, notwithstanding that they were in no position to obtain the required permits. The Third Circuit noted that, while this result might appear harsh, RCRA is regulatory in nature and intended to promote public health and, therefore, must be construed broadly to "effectuate the regulatory purpose" (741 F.2d at 666).

The courts have developed a "responsible corporate officer" doctrine, which in its broadest application imposes criminal liability on a corporate officer for violating a public welfare statute, regardless of the officer's personal participation, as long as the officer is in a position to prevent or correct the violation.[13] The doctrine grew out of the decision in *United States v. Dotterweich*, 320 U.S. 277 (1943), where the Supreme Court held a corporate president strictly liable for criminal violations of the Federal Food, Drug, and Cosmetic Act. Later, in *United States v. Park*, 421 U.S. 658, 673–74 (1975), the Supreme Court declared:

> [T]he Government establishes a prima facie case when it introduces evidence sufficient to warrant a finding by the trier of the facts that the defendant had, by reason of his position in the corporation, responsibility and authority either to prevent in the first instance, or promptly to correct, the violation complained of, and that he failed to do so.

The responsible corporate officer doctrine is based on the policy that the public is entitled to expect corporate officials who deal with threatening or potentially threatening products to act when the law requires them to act.

At least two major federal environmental statutes suggest that Congress specifically intended to adopt the responsible corporate officer doctrine. The CWA imposes liability on "persons," defined to include "responsible corporate officer[s]," 33 U.S.C. Section 1319(c)(6), without, however, defining the latter term.[14] The CAA also uses the term "responsible corporate officer," 42 U.S.C. Section 7413(c)(6), without defining it.

Corporate officers have been found liable in cases like *United States v. Torigian Laboratories, Inc.*, 577 F. Supp. 1514 (E.D.N.Y.), *aff'd*, 751 F.2d 373 (2d Cir. 1984) and *United States v. Dee*, 912 F.2d 741 (4th Cir. 1990), *cert. denied*, 499 U.S. 919 (1991). In the former case, a company president was convicted based on shipments of contaminated intraocular lenses, in part because he took no steps to prevent such shipments when faced with clear warnings of a contamination problem.

In *Dee*, the government brought a RCRA prosecution against the civilian manager of the U.S. Army's Aberdeen Proving Ground and others, alleging that they had committed "knowing" violations. The circuit court upheld trial court instructions that to convict the defendants under the responsible corporate officer doctrine the jury must find the following: first, that each defendant had a responsible relationship to the violation (that is, that the violation occurred under the defendant's area of authority and supervisory responsibility); second, that each defendant had the power or the capacity to prevent the violation; and third, that each defendant acted knowingly in failing to prevent, detect, or correct the violation.[15]

The indictment in *United States v. Pennwalt*, No. CR-88-55T (W.D. Wash. 1989), demonstrates the far-reaching implications of the responsible corporate officer doctrine. In that case, corporate officers were charged with violating the CWA based on their failure to prevent the collapse of a chemical holding tank in the corporation's Tacoma, Washington, facility. Three of the officers charged were in Pennsylvania when the tank collapsed. The case never came to trial because the individual indictments were dismissed in return for a corporate plea. Nevertheless, the prospect that a corporate officer could face criminal charges for a pollution incident from which the officer was so physically remote would surely alarm many executives.

The courts in two more recent cases, *United States v. MacDonald & Watson Waste Oil Co.*, 933 F.2d 35, 55 (1st Cir. 1991), and *United States v. White*, 766 F. Supp. 873, 895 (E.D. Wash. 1991), rejected an expansive reading of the responsible corporate officer doctrine, holding that, for a crime in which knowledge is an express statutory element, a mere showing of official responsibility is not an adequate substitute for direct or circumstantial proof of knowledge.

What State of Mind Is the Government Required to Prove?

Many of the federal criminal cases in the environmental law area have dealt with defendants' arguments that they could not properly be found guilty because the government did not present sufficient proof of the criminal state of mind constituting a necessary element of the pertinent statutory offense. Often the defendant has admitted to actions that were committed knowingly but has argued that the government was also required to prove knowledge of the statute making those actions criminal.

Knowledge of the Law

Supreme Court Precedents in Nonenvironmental Cases

Outside of the environmental arena, the Supreme Court has taken differing positions on whether knowledge of the underlying statute is a necessary element of proof to sustain a criminal conviction, depending on the type of statute involved. In *United States v. Freed*, 401 U.S. 601 (1971), a prosecution for illegal transportation of explosives, the Court declared that a person dealing with dangerous or inherently hazardous materials is presumed to know the controlling regulatory framework. In *United States v. International Minerals & Chemical Corp.*, 402 U.S. 558 (1971), in which the corporate defendant was charged with violating Interstate Commerce Commission regulations for the transportation of corrosive liquids, the Court ruled that proof of knowledge of those regulations was not required to obtain a conviction. Rather, it was sufficient for the government to show general knowledge that the materials being shipped were dangerous. Again, the Court ruled that those handling hazardous materials are presumed to know that their activity is heavily regulated.

Both *Freed* and *International Minerals* dealt with statutes plainly designed to protect the public health, safety, and welfare. The Supreme Court declared in *International Minerals* (402 U.S. at 565):

> [W]here . . . dangerous or deleterious devices or products or obnoxious waste materials are involved, the probability of regulation is so great that anyone who is aware that he is in possession of them or dealing with them must be presumed to be aware of the regulation.

On the other hand, in *Liparota v. United States*, 471 U.S. 419 (1985), a prosecution for food stamp fraud, the Court demanded that the government prove knowledge of the statute making the defendant's acts criminal, because the proscribed conduct was not the "type of conduct that a reasonable person should know is subject to stringent public regulation and may seriously threaten the community's health or safety" (*id.* at 433).

Lower Federal Court Decisions in Environmental Cases

In cases arising under RCRA's criminal enforcement provisions, lower federal courts have differed in their construction of the statutory requirement that a defendant act knowingly. In one of the earlier cases, *United States v. Johnson & Towers, Inc.*, the trial court did not require the government to prove that the defendants knew they were acting in violation of the law. On appeal, the U.S. Court of Appeals for the Third Circuit reversed, holding that the word "knowingly" applied to all elements of the offense. As to the defendants' specific knowledge of the particular law they had violated, however, the appellate court held that "the government need prove only knowledge of the actions taken and not the statute forbidding them" (741 F.2d at 669).

Another circuit court took a somewhat different view in *United States v. Hayes International Corp.* (discussed earlier), where the defendants argued that the *Liparota* rationale should apply and that the government should be required to prove specifically that they knew their actions violated RCRA. The U.S. Court of Appeals for the Eleventh Circuit rejected this argument, holding that knowledge of illegality of the acts committed is not an element of an offense under 42 U.S.C. Section 6928(d)(1) (786 F.2d at 1503). Likewise, in *United States v. Dee* (discussed earlier), the U.S. Court of Appeals for the Fourth Circuit affirmed convictions, holding that the government need not prove either that the defendants knew violations of RCRA were crimes or that there were regulations listing and identifying the chemical wastes they handled as RCRA hazardous wastes (912 F.2d at 745).

Because *Johnson & Towers*, *Hayes*, and *Dee* all dealt with hazardous wastes and were brought under RCRA, a statute readily understood as protecting classic public health and welfare interests, the courts in those cases were easily able to apply the reasoning in *Freed* and *International Minerals* and thus to dispense with knowledge of the law as an element of the crime. However, other environmental statutes may be seen to further less compelling policies, and it has been argued that the *Liparota* rationale, demanding specific knowledge of the statute violated, may be more appropriate for cases brought under those statutes.[16]

Nevertheless, in its decision in a case of first impression construing the knowing violation provisions of the CWA, 33 U.S.C. Section 1319(c)(2),[17] *United States v. Weitzenhoff*, 1 F.3d 1523 (9th Cir. 1993), opinion amended and superseded on denial of reh'g en banc, 35 F.3d

1275 (1994), *cert. denied*, 115 S. Ct. 939 (1995), the U.S. Court of Appeals for the Ninth Circuit rejected this distinction, at least as far as the CWA is concerned. In *Weitzenhoff*, two managers at a wastewater treatment plant were found guilty of instructing employees of the plant to pump toxic sludge directly into an outfall near a public beach. Declaring that the CWA's criminal provisions were "clearly designed to protect the public . . . from the potentially dire consequences of water pollution," the court concluded that those provisions fell within the category of "public welfare" legislation and that the reasoning of *International Minerals* therefore applied (35 F.3d at 1286).[18]

In another criminal case brought under CWA Section 404, 33 U.S.C. Section 1344, *United States v. Ellen*, 961 F.2d 462, 466-67 n.2 (4th Cir. 1992), the appeals court approved (in a footnote) trial court instructions that required the jury to convict only upon proof that the defendant acted knowingly with respect to all four elements of a Section 404 offense, including that the areas where he deposited fill were wetlands and that permits were required.

Knowledge of the Facts

Permit Status

In cases brought under RCRA, CERCLA, and the CWA, federal courts have considered whether it is necessary for the government to prove knowledge of a facility's deficient permit status to convict a defendant of a criminal offense relating to requirements that the facility have a permit. The federal circuits are divided.

In *United States v. Johnson & Towers* (discussed earlier), a case brought under 42 U.S.C. Section 6928(d)(2)(A) for illegal disposal of hazardous waste at an unpermitted facility, the U.S. Court of Appeals for the Third Circuit held that the government must prove that the defendant knew the facility lacked a permit, but that this knowledge might be inferred from conduct, as, for example, from evidence that the defendant "willfully" failed to determine the permit status of the facility (741 F.2d at 669).[19]

Similarly, in *United States v. Speach*, 968 F.2d 795 (9th Cir. 1992), a case brought under 42 U.S.C Section 6928(d)(1) for knowingly transporting hazardous waste to an unpermitted facility, the U.S. Court of Appeals for the Ninth Circuit overturned the conviction of a company president because the prosecutor had not presented proof that the defendant knew the permit status of the facility. The court in *Speach* emphasized that removing knowledge of permit status as an element of the offense set out in Section 6928(d)(1) would criminalize innocent conduct, such as that of a transporter who relied on representations that the facility in question was properly licensed (968 F.2d at 796). The court went on to explain that the requisite knowledge can nonetheless be established through a variety of direct and circumstantial means, as, for example, through evidence showing willful failure to ascertain permit status or knowledge of suspiciously low charges for disposal (*id.* at 797).

In contrast to the *Johnson & Towers* and *Speach* decisions, other decisions have held that knowledge of permit status is not a necessary element of the crimes created by Congress. In *United States v. Hoflin*, 880 F.2d 1033 (9th Cir. 1989), *cert. denied*, 493 U.S. 1083 (1990), the same court that three years later decided *Speach* held that 42 U.S.C. Section 6928(d)(2)(A) (illegal disposal of hazardous waste at an unpermitted facility) did not require knowledge with respect to the permit status element of the crime. The court noted that a *mens rea* requirement was conspicuously absent in this part of the statute (880 F.2d at 1037).

Likewise, in the more recent RCRA cases of *United States v. Dean*, 969 F.2d 187, 191 (6th Cir. 1992), *cert. denied*, 113 S. Ct. 1852 (1993), and *United States v. Laughlin*, 10 F.3d 961, 966 (2d Cir. 1993), *cert. denied*, 114 S. Ct. 1649 (1994), the courts ruled, directly contrary to *Johnson & Towers*, that knowledge of permit status was not a necessary element of a case under 42 U.S.C. Section 6928(d)(2)(A).[20] In addition, in *United States v. Weitzenhoff* (discussed earlier), the U.S. Court of Appeals for the Ninth Circuit decided that a defendant need not know that his or her actions violate a permit or the CWA to be convicted of a knowing violation under 33 U.S.C. Section 1319(c)(2) (see 35 F.3d at 1283-86).

Status of Materials Handled

Another aspect of RCRA criminal knowledge about which questions have arisen is the defendant's knowledge of the RCRA status of materials handled. In the 1971 non-RCRA case of *United States v. International Minerals & Chemical Corp.* (discussed earlier), the Supreme Court held that proof of the defendant's knowledge that materials he handled were generally dangerous was enough to give rise to the presumption that the defendant knew his activities were heavily regulated. The Court did not require the government to prove the defendant's specific knowledge of the regulations he had violated.

In *United States v. Hayes International Corp.*, the U.S. Court of Appeals for the Eleventh Circuit extended the presumption analysis of *International Minerals*. The defendants in *Hayes*, who were charged with unlawfully transporting hazardous waste to an unpermitted facility, argued that they thought the paint waste they shipped was being recycled and therefore was unregulated. The circuit court rejected this argument based on the evidence, but the court recognized the validity of a "mistake of fact" defense. The court indicated that, when a defendant raises this defense, the defendant bears the burden of persuasion; the government need not disprove the defense (786 F.2d at 1506). Rather, the government may overcome the defense by producing evidence from which knowledge of the true facts may be inferred.

More recently, in *United States v. Goldsmith*, 978 F.2d 643, 645 (11th Cir. 1992), the same federal circuit court affirmed a conviction for transporting hazardous waste to an unpermitted facility, holding that the government need not prove that the defendant knew the chemical waste in question had been defined by the EPA as a "hazardous waste." Rather, the government need only prove that the defendant knew "the general hazardous character" of the chemical. The appellate court in *Goldsmith* approved the lower court's instructions, which required the jury to find "[t]hat the defendant knew that the stored material had the potential to be harmful to others or to the environment, in other words, that it was not an innocuous substance like water" (*id.*).

Finally, in *United States v. Self*, 2 F.3d 1071, 1089–92 (10th Cir. 1993), the court considered as an issue of first impression whether knowledge of the regulatory status of materials handled was a necessary element of a cause of action under 42 U.S.C. Section 6928(d)(2)(B) (knowingly treating, storing, or disposing of hazardous waste in knowing violation of a material permit condition). The court ruled that it was not.

The Responsible Corporate Officer Doctrine and Knowledge

The responsible corporate officer doctrine discussed earlier in this chapter raises particularly difficult issues with respect to the traditional notion that criminal liability requires a guilty mind or *mens rea*. The doctrine originated under statutes involving strict liability, where there was no need to inquire into the defendant's mental state. When, however, the doctrine is transferred into the environmental arena, where governing statutes often do demand knowledge, it raises equitable concerns. Taken to an extreme, the doctrine could impute liability to a corporate officer who lacked knowledge of the crime, either active or inferred. However, a more reasoned application of the doctrine might simply raise an inference of knowledge on the part of a corporate officer, based on the officer's position or responsibility.

In *United States v. MacDonald & Watson Waste Oil Co.* (discussed earlier), a conviction was vacated based on the lower court's instruction that, if evidence showed that the defendant, the president of a hazardous waste disposal facility, was a corporate officer responsible for waste disposal, this conclusively established the defendant's knowledge of an illegal shipment. The circuit court held that the defendant could not be convicted solely because of his corporate position under a criminal statute that expressly required knowledge (933 F.2d at 50–55; see also *United States v. White*). Thus, when a defendant is charged with a crime of which knowledge is an express element, merely showing the defendant's official responsibility is probably not an adequate substitute for direct or circumstantial proof of the required knowledge.

Willful Blindness

Another question in this area is whether a defendant can be convicted on the basis of "willful blindness." The courts have consistently held that the knowledge element of a criminal offense can be established both by evidence of actual knowledge and by circumstantial evidence that raises an inference of knowledge.[21] They have also ruled that knowledge can be inferred from a defendant's deliberate avoidance of material facts.

Moreover, the principle that criminal liability may be founded on willful blindness has now been expressly incorporated in the knowing endangerment provisions of major federal environmental statutes—the CAA, the CWA, and RCRA (33 U.S.C. Section 1319(c)(3)(B); 42 U.S.C. Sections 6928(f)(2), 7413(c)(5)(B)). Each of these laws provides that an individual defendant is responsible only for actual knowledge or actual belief but that, in determining whether such a defendant possessed actual knowledge that a violation endangered another person, the court may consider circumstantial evidence, "including evidence that the defendant took affirmative steps to shield himself [or be shielded] from relevant information."

The willful blindness theory originated in nonenvironmental criminal cases, such as those brought for illegal possession of weapons or drugs (e.g., *United States v. Jewell*, 532 F.2d 697 (9th Cir.), *cert. denied*, 426 U.S. 951 (1976)). In these cases, courts decided that the term "knowingly" was not limited to positive knowledge but included the state of mind of one who acted "with an awareness of the high probability of the existence of the fact in question," such as "one who [did] not possess positive knowledge only because he consciously avoided it" (532 F.2d at 700, 702). According to this line of authority, willful blindness requires more than negligence on the part of the defendant—it requires a purposeful act to avoid learning the truth.

In *United States v. Pacific Hide & Fur Depot, Inc.*, 768 F.2d 1096 (9th Cir. 1985), a case involving violation of the Toxic Substances Control Act, 15 U.S.C. Section 2601 *et seq.*, the circuit court reversed a conviction because the lower court's instruction allowed the jury to convict based on the defendant's reckless conduct. The appellate court declared, "It is not enough that defendant was mistaken, recklessly disregarded the truth, and negligently failed to inquire" (*id.* at 1098). On the other hand, in *United States v. Hayes International Corp.*, the court held that a corporate officer's willful failure to determine the permit status of a facility to which hazardous waste was transferred satisfied the knowledge requirement under RCRA.

In *United States v. Buckley*, referenced earlier, a case prosecuted under the CAA and CERCLA for the release of asbestos during the course of a demolition project, the circuit court held that the government need not prove that the defendant knew the legal status of asbestos materials or that he was violating the law, since conscious avoidance of knowledge can be legally equivalent to knowledge (934 F.2d at 88).

Negligence

The CAA and CWA both expressly provide criminal penalties for negligent conduct. Thus, in *United States v. Frezzo Brothers, Inc.*, 461 F. Supp. 266 (E.D. Pa. 1978), *aff'd*, 602 F.2d 1123 (3d Cir. 1979), *cert. denied*, 444 U.S. 1074 (1980), defendants were convicted under pre-1987 provisions of the CWA for discharging pollutants from a mushroom farm. The charges were based on the defendants' negligent maintenance of water pollution control facilities. (See also *United States v. Oxford Royal Mushroom Products*, 487 F. Supp. 852 (E.D. Pa. 1980) (same).) It remains unclear whether proof of simple negligence is sufficient to convict, but standard government instruction maintains that it is.

Knowing Endangerment

Several environmental statutes, including RCRA, the CWA, and the CAA, contain knowing endangerment provisions and impose substantial criminal penalties for a knowing violation that places another person in imminent danger of death or serious bodily injury. There is little case law construing these provisions. However, in *United States v. Protex Industries*, 874 F.2d 740, 744 (10th Cir. 1989), the circuit court approved a trial court's instructions defining "imminent danger" as "the existence of a condition or combination of conditions which could reasonably be expected to cause death or serious bodily injury unless the condition is remedied."

In *United States v. Borowski*, 977 F.2d 27 (1st Cir. 1992), a conviction obtained under the CWA's knowing endangerment provision was vacated because, while the corporate defendant's own employees were endangered by its violations of the CWA and the individual defendant (the corporation's president) knew of this danger, the CWA section that had been violated (33 U.S.C. Section 1317) was aimed at pretreatment violations and was designed to guard against danger downstream, at a publicly owned treatment works.

The court in *Borowski* focused on the statutory requirement that a defendant know at the time of a CWA violation "that he *thereby* places another person in imminent danger" (emphasis added), and, inasmuch as prosecutors never alleged that anyone was put at risk after hazardous materials entered the sewer system, the court concluded that the defendants' violations were not properly linked by causation to the kind of endangerment for which Congress intended to impose criminal penalties. Moreover, the court pointed out that Congress had passed other laws to deal with industrial employee health and safety and with the general handling of hazardous substances.

The Federal Sentencing Guidelines

As a result of the Sentencing Reform Act of 1984,[22] a U.S. Sentencing Commission was established and charged with adopting sentencing guidelines and policies to bring consistency and more fairness to the task of meting out sentences for those convicted in the federal courts. The act and the commission's initial sentencing guidelines generally took effect November 1, 1987.[23]

Under current federal sentencing guidelines, criminal defendants are divided into individuals and organizations, and Chapter 8 of the guidelines sets out special rules for the sentencing of organizations. Chapter 8 took effect on November 1, 1991. On November 16, 1993, an Advisory Working Group on Environmental Offenses submitted to the Sentencing Commission a draft of even more specific proposed sentencing guidelines for organizations convicted of environmental offenses. Although the Sentencing Commission has collected comments on this latest proposal (see 58 Fed. Reg. 65764–65), it has not yet acted to adopt guidelines in this area.

Six of the federal sentencing guidelines for individuals deal specifically with violations of environmental laws, and one deals with violations of conservation and wildlife laws (Guidelines Sections 2Q1.1-2Q2.1). Guideline Section 2Q1.2 (mishandling of hazardous or toxic substances or pesticides; record keeping, tampering, and falsification) is set out in the endnotes.[24]

As with all of the guidelines, each environmental guideline establishes a numerical "base offense level," which is modified by specific offense characteristics. The modified base offense level is then further adjusted by certain factors generic to all crimes subject to the guidelines, such as the role of the defendant in the offense, whether the defendant obstructed the investigation or accepted responsibility and cooperated with authorities, and other similar factors. These factors are set out in Chapter 3 of the guidelines. The resulting offense level is then matched with a sentencing table, published in Chapter 5 of the guidelines, depending on the criminal history of the defendant, computed in accordance with Chapter 4 of the guidelines.

A court may depart from the sentence calculated under the guidelines only if it finds "that there exists an aggravating or mitigating circumstance of a kind, or to a degree, not adequately taken into consideration by the Sentencing Commission in formulating the guidelines that should result in a sentence different from that described" (18 U.S.C. Section 3553(b)). Both upward and downward departures are reviewable—the former on appeal by the defendant and the latter on appeal by the government (18 U.S.C. Section 3742(a),(b)).

Miscellaneous Issues

Although, as indicated at the outset, this chapter cannot hope to cover the multitude of issues that may arise in a criminal proceeding brought under one of the many and varied federal and state environmental laws, it is perhaps appropriate to mention several more issues and to provide the reader with appropriate environmental case citations.

First, when a criminal statute is subject to any ambiguity, that ambiguity is to be resolved in favor of the defendant. (This is sometimes referred to as the "rule of lenity.")

- *Bivens v. Florida*, 586 So. 2d 442, 443 (Fla. App. 1991)
- *United States v. Borowski*, 977 F.2d at 31–32

Second, a defendant may be precluded from challenging the regulations on which a conviction is based, at least on their face, if the defendant had an opportunity but declined to challenge those regulations when they were adopted. (See, e.g., 33 U.S.C. Section 1369(b)(2) (CWA); 42 U.S.C. Section 6976(b) (RCRA); 42 U.S.C. Section 7607(b)(2) (CAA).)

- *United States v. White*, 766 F. Supp. 873, 878 (E.D. Wash. 1991) (challenge to regulations *as applied* not precluded)
- *United States v. Alley*, 755 F. Supp. 771, 775 (N.D. Ill. 1990)

Third, the statute of limitations for federal crimes is five years, except as otherwise expressly provided by law (18 U.S.C. Section 3282).

- *United States v. White*, F. Supp. at 886

Fourth, a criminal prosecution may be foreclosed by the constitutional protection against double jeopardy when previous punitive fines have been levied for the same offense or when the defendant has previously been prosecuted under a different statute for the same acts. However, double jeopardy does not generally prevent federal and state prosecutions for the same conduct, since each sovereign has its own laws and the conduct violates each of these bodies of law separately.

- *United States v. Louisville Edible Oil Products, Inc.*, 926 F.2d at 586–87 (asbestos case)
- *United States v. Halper*, 490 U.S. 435 (1989)

Fifth, when, on the other hand, Congress has expressed an intent to preempt a regulatory field, states may be without authority to prosecute a defendant for the same acts.

- *Sims v. Florida Department of Highway Safety*, 862 F.2d 1449, 1455 (11th Cir.), *cert. denied*, 493 U.S. 815 (1989)

Sixth, ex post facto and retroactivity issues may arise when the government attempts to apply regulations against a defendant with respect to conduct occurring before the regulations became effective or after they were invalidated.

- *United States v. Goodner Bros. Aircraft, Inc.*, 966 F.2d 380 (8th Cir. 1992), *cert. denied*, 113 S. Ct. 967 (1993) (RCRA convictions overturned in light of invalidation of "mixture rule")

Seventh, difficult issues may arise with respect to the ethical obligations of an attorney whose client commits or discovers environmental violations.

- See Model Rules of Professional Conduct Rule 1.6 (1983) (confidentiality of information) (information revealed by a client to his or her attorney is generally confidential and privileged, except that the attorney may reveal such information to the extent the lawyer reasonably believes it necessary to prevent the client from committing a future criminal act that will result in imminent death or substantial bodily harm)

Eighth, conviction of an environmental crime may have unexpected consequences beyond the obvious ones associated with monetary fines and jail terms. A number of states deny environmental permits or renewals to persons or organizations whose histories include past convictions.

Factors Considered by Prosecutors before Filing a Criminal Case

Criminal case selection by the EPA Office of Criminal Enforcement is guided by two general factors: significant environmental harm and culpable conduct.[25] In exercising their discretion on whether criminal enforcement is appropriate, prosecutors are likely to consider such questions as these:[26]

- What is the seriousness of the actual or potential harm to human beings or to the environment?
- Is the defendant a "repeat offender" or one who has received warnings (verbal or written) from the regulatory agency?
- Is this violation part of a pattern of ongoing violations?
- Does the conduct of the defendant undercut the integrity of the regulatory scheme (for example, has the defendant submitted false information on a permit application, falsified a report, or deliberately failed to report changes in processes or spills as required by regulations or by a permit)?
- Has the defendant reaped economic gain or benefit from the violation?
- Is there some articulated reason or motive for the conduct (for example, job security, disdain for the law, or arrogance)?
- Are there other indicia of criminality (for example, has there been obstruction of justice or has the defendant lied to inspectors)?
- Has the defendant kept complete records and performed environmental investigations and audits that demonstrate the intention to discover environmental problems and comply with environmental laws and regulations?

Suggestions

To avoid criminal liability in the first instance, an organizational client can take steps such as these:

- Establish procedures for discovering and promptly correcting environmental problems.
- Document employee complaints and the organization's responses, and handle these complaints quickly.
- Document government contacts and advice obtained from regulatory officials and consultants. (However, it is extremely difficult, if not impossible, to estop the government from an enforcement proceeding based on prior information given by governmental employees.)[27]

- Do not assume that local building permits or zoning approvals are sufficient authorization to proceed.
- Do not assume that the organization can avoid criminal liability by performing activities through consultants, contractors, or other third parties.
- Emphasize environmental compliance as a stated business priority, and establish operating procedures that discipline employees' environmental transgressions.
- Encourage employees to bring problems to the attention of management, without fear of reprisals. (If lower-level personnel discover an environmental problem and deal with it illegally, the organization will likely be liable for their actions.)
- Consider performing environmental audits—if the organization is willing to correct any problems that may be identified.
- Do not assume that audit reports will always be privileged information and kept out of criminal enforcement actions.

Once a criminal investigation has begun, it becomes imperative that any client, individual or organization, act immediately. The client should move quickly at the first hint of government investigatory efforts because witnesses will become increasingly less willing to cooperate once grand jury subpoenas are issued. Early contact with the government is critical, and counsel should not hold back on the assumption that the investigation can be derailed at a later date.

Counsel should determine whether individual clients, or officers and employees of an organizational client, are being contacted because the client is a target of the government's investigation or simply as fact witnesses. Counsel and their clients should recognize that this status could change as the investigation develops.

Organizational clients should consider notifying employees about any criminal investigation and advising them of their rights and obligations in dealing with government investigators; appoint a central contact for responding to government information requests; and interview employees who may have any relationship, no matter how collateral, to the purported criminal activity. To avoid allegations of obstruction of justice, all clients, whether organizations or individuals, should document their responses to government requests for information and should be careful not to "manipulate" contacts with or information provided to government representatives.

When the target of an investigation is an organization, individual officers and employees should consider whether they need separate counsel to protect interests that may conflict with those of the organization.

It is almost always wise to maintain contact with other individuals and organizations that are being investigated or contacted as witnesses. They may be able to provide important clues as to what the government is planning. Although ideally it is preferable to keep any investigation confidential, the publicity afforded to the matter may not be within a client's control. Therefore, the client should be prepared to go public about the investigation if the government's efforts are leaked to the media, neighbors, or customers.

Resources

Block, Joseph, and Voisin, Nancy. "The Responsible Corporate Officer Doctrine—Can You Go to Jail for What You Don't Know?" *The Corporate Analyst* 63 (Business Laws, Inc., May 1994).

DeVaney, Earl E., Director, Office of Criminal Enforcement, to All EPA Employees Working on or in Support of the Criminal Enforcement Program, memorandum. "The Exercise of Investigative Discretion" (Jan. 12, 1994).

Freed, Daniel J. "Federal Sentencing in the Wake of Guidelines: Unacceptable Limits on the Discretion of Sentencers." 101 *Yale Law Journal* 1,681 (1992).

National Association of Criminal Defense Lawyers. "The Nuts & Bolts of Defending an Environmental Criminal Case," Course Materials, June 10–11, 1993 program.

Notes

The authors wish to thank Michael Schatzow and Thomas M. Lingan, their colleagues in the firm of Venable, Baetjer and Howard, LL.P., for assistance in preparing this chapter.

1. *See* U.S. Dep't of Justice Memorandum of P. Hutchins, Paralegal, to R. Sarachan, Chief, Environmental Crimes Section (April 7, 1995).

2. 25 ENV'T REP., (BNA) *Current Developments* (May 6, 1994), at 12. Similarly, 42 U.S.C. § 9609(d) provides for awards of up to $10,000 for information leading to the successful prosecution of any person violating criminal provisions of CERCLA.

3. To facilitate compliance, some notification provisions—for example, the CERCLA provision codified at 42 U.S.C. § 9603(b)—prohibit information revealed in the notification from being used against the provider in any criminal case. Exceptions may be made, as they are in CERCLA, to permit prosecution of the provider for perjury or the giving of a false statement.

4. This chapter does not purport to deal with many important criminal law and criminal procedure issues that are not unique to environmental crimes. Indeed, even with respect to the issues it does touch on, there is a wealth of authority available in treatises and articles that are more concentrated on the field of criminal law.

5. *See, e.g.*, United States v. Self, 2 F.3d 1071 (10th Cir. 1993).

6. Section 7413(c) provides for fines "pursuant to Title 18," and 18 U.S.C. provides for the classification of offenses (§ 3559) and for the maximum fines

available for the several classifications (§ 3571). Under Section 3571, if a violator derives pecuniary gain from the violation or if the violation causes pecuniary loss to another, the violator is generally subject to a fine as high as twice the gross gain or loss, even if that would exceed an otherwise applicable maximum.

7. Again, the Alternative Fines Act, 18 U.S.C. § 3571, permits a court to impose a fine substantially higher than the maximum specified in the CWA itself.

8. The Third Circuit affirmed his sentence without an opinion. 897 F.2d 524 (3rd Cir.), *cert. denied*, 498 U.S. 812 (1990). The lower court reduced his fine to $5,000.00 due to his inability to pay. 22 Envtl. L. Rep. (Envtl. L. Inst.) 20,772 (E.D. Pa. 1990).

9. In the case of RCRA violations as well, the Alternative Fines Act, 18 U.S.C. § 3571, authorizes fines that may significantly exceed the maximums specified in RCRA.

10. *See* United States v. Liebman, 40 F.3d 544 (2d Cir. 1994).

11. Section 9603(d)(2) makes it a crime to destroy or falsify records identified in EPA regulations under Section 9603(d)(1), relating to the location, title, or condition of contaminated facilities and the substances contained or deposited there. Since the EPA has not as yet adopted such regulations, this criminal provision is currently ineffective.

12. Section 9603 calls for fines in accordance with Title 18, and the alternatives provided in 18 U.S.C. § 3571 authorize even higher fines in some cases.

13. *See* Block and Voisin, *The Responsible Corporate Officer Doctrine—Can You Go to Jail for What You Don't Know?*, THE CORPORATE ANALYST 63 (Business Laws, Inc., May 1994).

14. In United States v. Brittain, 931 F.2d 1413, 1419 (10th Cir. 1991), an individual defendant, who had not been prosecuted as a responsible corporate officer but as an individual "person" who had allegedly caused the unlawful discharge of pollutants by an NPDES permittee, argued that Congress's addition of the language "any responsible corporate officer" to the definition of "person" for purposes of the CWA's criminal penalty provisions evidenced legislative intent to restrict potential individual criminal liability to those who were themselves permittees or had been proven to be responsible corporate officers. The court rejected this argument, interpreting Congress's addition as an expansion of liability under the CWA. *See also* United States v. Johnson & Towers, Inc., 741 F.2d at 665 n.3.

15. The jury instructions are not set out in the opinion reported at 912 F.2d 741, but they do appear in the record of proceedings before the district court, No. CR-88-211-HAR (D. Md.). The circuit court opinion specifically endorses the instructions. 912 F.2d at 746 n.8.

16. For example, CWA § 404, 33 U.S.C. § 1344, regulates the discharge of dredge and fill material into navigable waters, including wetlands. A discharge in violation of Section 404 generally does not present the same possibility of danger to the public health and welfare as the discharge or release of hazardous substances.

17. These provisions were added to the CWA in 1987 to replace earlier language providing criminal penalties for "[a]ny person who willfully or negligently violates . . . any permit condition." The earlier language had been construed as not requiring proof of specific intent, and in United States v. Baytank (Hous-

ton), Inc., 934 F.2d 599, 618–19 & n.32 (5th Cir. 1991), and United States v. Frezzo Brothers., Inc., 546 F. Supp. 713, 720–21 (E.D. Pa. 1982), *aff'd*, 703 F.2d 62 (3d Cir.), *cert. denied*, 464 U.S. 829 (1983).

18. *See also* United States v. Brittain, 931 F.2d at 1419 (CWA, like the Federal Food, Drug, and Cosmetic Act, was designed to protect important public health interests).

19. See the discussion of "willful blindness" later in this chapter.

20. In *United States v. Laughlin*, the court extended its reasoning to excuse proof of knowledge of regulatory requirements as a necessary element of the crime of failure to report a release under CERCLA. 10 F.3d at 966–67.

21. *See* United States v. Greer, 850 F.2d 1447 (11th Cir. 1988), where strong circumstantial evidence was ruled sufficient to support conviction of the individual operator of a waste recycling business under RCRA, 42 U.S.C. § 6928(d)(2)(A), for causing the illegal dumping of hazardous waste.

22. Pub. L. No. 98-473, Title II (§§ 211–39), 98 Stat. 1987 *et seq*. (1984).

23. 8 U.S.C. ch. 227; 28 U.S.C. §§ 991–98 (1987).

24. Section 2Q1.2. Mishandling of Hazardous or Toxic Substances or Pesticides; Recordkeeping, Tampering, and Falsification

(a) Base Offense Level: 8

(b) Specific Offense Characteristics

- (1) (A) If the offense resulted in an ongoing, continuous, or repetitive discharge, release, or emission of hazardous or toxic substance or pesticide into the environment, increase by 6 levels; or
  - (B) if the offense otherwise involved a discharge, release, or emission of a hazardous or toxic substance or pesticide, increase by 4 levels.
- (2) If the offense resulted in a substantial likelihood of death or serious bodily injury, increase by 9 levels.
- (3) If the offense resulted in disruption of public utilities or evacuation of a community, or if cleanup required a substantial expenditure, increase by 4 levels.
- (4) If the offense involved transportation, treatment, storage, or disposal without a permit or in violation of a permit, increase by 4 levels.
- (5) If a recordkeeping offense reflected an effort to conceal a substantive environmental offense, use the offense level for the substantive offense.
- (6) If the offense involved a simple recordkeeping or reporting violation only, decrease by 2 levels.

25. Memorandum from Earl E. DeVaney, Director, Office of Criminal Enforcement, to All EPA Employees Working in or in Support of the Criminal Enforcement Program, "The Exercise of Investigative Discretion" (Jan. 12, 1994).

26. U.S. Dep't of Justice, Factors in Decisions on Criminal Prosecutions for Environmental Violations in the Context of Significant Voluntary Compliance or Disclosure Efforts by the Violator (July 1, 1991).

27. United States v. Weitzenhoff, 35 F.3d at 1290–91.

PART II

Environmental Due Diligence in Real Estate and Commercial Transactions

~

CHAPTER 8

The Due Diligence Dilemma: How Much Is Enough?

CAROL R. BOMAN

The undeniable impact that environmental laws have had in recent years on real estate owners and on business and real estate transactions has led to the development of an entirely new industry, one composed of experts in the field of environmental due diligence. Because of the importance of taking environmental laws and regulations into account when structuring an acquisition, sale, leasing, or financing transaction, the parties need to know whether the underlying real estate is contaminated and what effect that contamination will have on the economics of the transaction.

Environmental due diligence has become important for a number of reasons. Buyers, for example, need to assess potential costs that may be associated with environmental contamination, such as leakage from an underground fuel storage tank. Developers need to know if contamination will thwart their plans for the property. The cost of renovation work can be significantly increased if a building contains asbestos.

The Comprehensive Environmental Response, Compensation, and Liability Act (CERCLA), also known as Superfund,[1] has been perhaps the most important influence behind the development of the due diligence industry. Under CERCLA an "owner" or "operator" of a facility where a hazardous substance has been deposited, stored, placed, or disposed of is a potentially responsible party (PRP). Federal court rulings interpreting CERCLA have established that a PRP's liability is strict, joint and several, and retroactive. As a result, property owners and their lenders have become anxious to determine, before entering into a transaction, the amount of environmental risk that they may assume by virtue of being parties to that transaction.

Due diligence is not a new concept. For years cautious purchasers of real property have conducted prepurchase investigations of property, aware that the doctrine of caveat emptor ("let the buyer beware") prevented them from making claims against a seller for defects in a property's condition discovered after the sale. However, before the enactment of laws such as CERCLA that impose liability based solely on one's status as an owner, an investigation for contamination would not have been considered necessary except where the physical presence of a substance could thwart a development or renovation project or increase its cost. For example, even before CERCLA's enactment, a buyer would have wanted to determine whether underground tanks would make soil removal more costly or whether landfill gas would increase the risk of explosion. Due diligence in recent years, however, has acquired greater importance in real estate transactions, particularly because buyers and lenders, while still concerned about the practical effects of contamination, also hope that by ascertaining the environmental condition of a property they can avail themselves of one of the few exceptions to CERCLA liability: the innocent purchaser defense.[2]

The Innocent Purchaser Defense

The innocent purchaser defense was introduced in amendments made to Superfund during the CERCLA reauthorization process in 1986 (Superfund Amendments and Reauthorization Act of 1986, known as SARA) in response to complaints about the unfairness of imposing liability on parties who unwittingly acquired contaminated real property. SARA introduced a clarification of CERCLA's "third-party defense," which exempted a party from liability under CERCLA if the release was caused by a third party with whom the person otherwise liable had no contractual relationship.[3] SARA amended the definition of "contractual relationship" to exclude contracts for the acquisition of real property where the buyer could establish that it had acquired the property after the hazardous substance release had occurred and that, before the acquisition, it had no knowledge nor any reason to know of the contamination, after having conducted "all appropriate inquiry" into the property's environmental condition.[4] So far, there is no clear standard for what constitutes "all appropriate inquiry." The statute only requires that such inquiry be consistent with good commercial or customary practice.[5]

Congress specified that the following factors be taken into consideration in determining whether the inquiry made by a potential buyer was "appropriate": any specialized knowledge or experience on the part of the buyer; the relationship of the purchase price to the value of the property if uncontaminated; commonly known or reasonably ascertainable information about the property; and the ability to detect such contamination by appropriate inspection.[6]

These criteria do not provide much guidance to practitioners or to the courts. The initial hurdle that must be overcome in assessing whether a party qualifies as an "innocent landowner" is to determine whether *any* standards for "appropriate" inquiry into the environmental condition of a site existed before the passage of environmental laws making such inquiry necessary. One could argue that before the enactment and reauthorization of CERCLA no "commercial" or "customary" practice of "appropriate inquiry" into environmental factors existed because, unless the pollution impeded the development or use of a site, its presence alone rarely affected the value or marketability of real property. In fact, it was only the advent of CERCLA and laws with liability schemes comparable to CERCLA that led to any practice of making some inquiry into the environmental condition of a site.

Case Law Interpreting the Innocent Purchaser Standard

This lack of explicit direction in the law placed courts in the position of determining, in retrospect, how much environmental due diligence should have been performed in a particular transaction. In early decisions rendered after the 1986 reauthorization of CERCLA, when buyers and sellers began to recognize the impact that CERCLA's liability scheme could have on real estate transactions, courts grappled with the terminology imposed by the law and attempted to give substance to "all appropriate inquiry" and "good commercial practice." It is not surprising, given the difficulty of this task, that the legal decisions generally provide little assistance in formulating a more specific standard.

In *United States v. Serafini*,[7] decided shortly after CERCLA's reauthorization, the U.S. District Court for the Middle District of Pennsylvania denied the government's motion for summary judgment on the issue of the innocent landowner defense. The U.S. Environmental Protection Agency (EPA) and the Pennsylvania Department of Environmental Response had conducted a removal action on a former landfill and waste disposal site under Section 104 of CERCLA. The agencies had instituted an action to recover response costs against four individuals, and their company, the Empire Contracting Company, who were the current owners of the site. The defendants had acquired the site from the landfill operator, the city of Scranton. In response to the EPA's motion for summary judgment, the owners raised the third-party defense under CERCLA. The EPA responded that a contractual relationship existed between the owners and the city and that the owners should have known about the contamination at the property when they purchased it. The government further insisted that the owners could not claim to be innocent purchasers if they failed to conduct *any* inquiry before buying the property. The court responded that complete lack of inquiry would be "inappropriate" only if the facts of the case warranted such a conclusion. Because the EPA had presented no evidence to prove that the landowner's failure to inspect or inquire was "inconsistent with good commercial or customary practices," the court refused to rule as a matter of law that "appropriate" inquiry necessarily meant at least some inquiry.[8]

The 1989 case of *United States v. Pacific Hide & Fur Depot*[9] produced a similar result. The U.S. District Court for the District of Idaho noted that, if it was to determine, in any specific situation, whether prepurchase inquiries were "appropriate" and "reasonable," its decision must be based on the particular facts before it.[10]

In both *Serafini* and *Pacific Hide*, the courts were asked to rule against the defendants as a matter of law. There is no way of knowing whether, had all the facts been heard and analyzed by either of those courts, it might have been found that no inquiry at all was "appropriate" at the time the property in question was acquired.

In *Wickland Oil Terminals v. Asarco, Inc.*, another case decided contemporaneously with *Serafini*, the U.S. District Court for the Northern District of California examined the type of inquiry required in a commercial context in rejecting the landowner's claim that it had conducted an appropriate amount of inquiry.[11] Wickland Oil Terminals was the current owner of contaminated property, having purchased the land from the defendant in that case, Asarco, Inc., in 1977, after having made some inquiries about the condition of the land that Asarco had used for smelting operations for many years. When the property was placed on the California list of hazardous waste sites, Wickland sued Asarco under CERCLA, seeking indemnification for the remediation of hazardous substances disposed of by Asarco on the land during its smelting operations.

Wickland moved for summary judgment against Asarco, arguing that, because Wickland was an "innocent landowner" under CERCLA, Asarco should be judged wholly liable to Wickland for its cleanup costs at the site. The court, in rejecting Wickland's motion, concluded that either Wickland knew of the condition of the property at the time of its acquisition or should have known about the contamination, because Wickland had known before the purchase that the property had been used for smelting operations, activities likely to cause environmental contamination. In addition, state authorities and environmental experts consulted by Wickland before the purchase had been informed that the property was polluted. Reasonable inquiries by Wickland before the sale and a reasonable analysis of information readily available to Wickland, which was known by Wickland's consulting firm and its legal counsel, would have disclosed the risk of future environmental problems associated with the slag on the site. Thus, the court determined that "even if Wickland could establish that it was unaware of the presence of hazardous waste on the site, [it] had not demonstrated that it conducted all appropriate inquiry."[12] A question raised by this decision is whether, when a property is "at risk" for contamination, a due diligence investigation that fails to uncover that contamination in retrospect will be considered sufficiently thorough.

Although the lack of a specific due diligence standard applicable in all situations may have the merit of maintaining flexibility, it has also increased the risk of liability, which in turn has increased the cost and risk of a real estate transaction. Moreover, because of the difficulty of ascertaining an appropriate level of inquiry, there is no sure way for a buyer to know whether its attempted due diligence was excessive, insufficient, or right. Generally, however, because a truly thorough investigation is both costly and time-consuming, most prepurchase inquiries, examined in retrospect, will appear to be less than adequate.

The result of uncertain due diligence requirements imposed by CERCLA, combined with the prospect of open-ended liability, has been that many risk-averse buyers and lenders have backed away from transactions that carry any potential for contamination. In some situations in which the buyers have been willing to take the chance, their lenders have not.

Lender Liability Concerns

The role played by lenders in the environmental due diligence process has grown exponentially during the past few years, due primarily to lenders' concerns about their own potential liability. When CERCLA was first enacted, few imagined the far-reaching scope of the law and the impact that it would have on lenders. The express language of the statute attempts to exclude lenders from its reach by providing that a person who is an "owner" of a contaminated property merely as a result of holding a security interest in the property is excluded from CERCLA liability unless that person participates "in the management of [the] . . . facility."[13]

Despite this language, certain court decisions interpreting CERCLA and its applicability to secured creditors have disturbed lenders,[14] especially *United States v. Fleet Factors Corporation.*[15] The secured creditor in that case had not foreclosed on any property but nevertheless incurred CERCLA liability by, according to the court, "participating in the financial management of a facility to a degree indicating a capacity to influence the corporation's treatment of hazardous wastes."[16] *Fleet Factors* caused lenders to become increasingly reluctant to lend to borrowers in situations involving the use or disposal of hazardous substances. While the lender in *Fleet Factors* appeared to have taken a more active role than most lenders customarily would take in the management of a borrower's business, the broad language used by the *Fleet Factors* court suggests that CERCLA liability may be imposed on a lender solely by virtue of the lender's having a right, albeit unexercised, in its loan documents to be involved in the management of its borrower's contaminated facility. Increasingly nervous lenders thus began to require that borrowers conduct more thorough environmental due diligence to ensure that the site that was the security for a loan would not turn into a "Fleet Factors" problem.[17] (For further discussion of this issue, see Chapter 4).

Phase I Environmental Site Assessments

Against this legal and practical framework has emerged the concept of the environmental site assessment, or the so-called Phase I environmental site assessment. In the early days of environmental due diligence, the definition of an adequate Phase I environmental assessment depended on who requested that the work be performed. The environmental consultant selected to perform the assessment often had a preconceived notion of what he or she thought had been requested. The party who hired the consultant (either the lawyer or the client) may have had its own established standards for an adequate site assessment, although usually not, and the lender financing the transaction may have developed its own standards that either correlated with or conflicted with those of the borrower. Over time, several large institutional lenders developed fairly comprehensive Phase I site assessment guidelines. In addition, various trade groups representing consultants, such as the National Ground Water Association, developed their own guidelines.

The ASTM Standards

In late 1989, responding to the confusion in the marketplace about the meaning of the term "environmental due diligence," a number of real estate trade groups, including owners and lenders and their counsel, initiated a project to standardize the due diligence process, in much the same way that the title insurance industry has developed customary procedures. A buyer, for example, could order a "Phase I site assessment" for a parcel of real property in much the same way that he or she would order a title insurance commitment from a title company. With the process standardized, the buyer would know in advance what type of product would be delivered.

The group was not so naive as to believe that imposing a comparable level of certainty and uniformity in environmental due diligence would be easily achievable. They sought from the outset of their project to concentrate specifically on the relatively confined goals of formulating a uniform approach to due diligence and establishing a minimum guideline for what would constitute "all appropriate inquiry" for the purposes of CERCLA's innocent landowner defense. More specifically, the group hoped to develop a common terminology for environmental due diligence; to improve the quality of environmental site assessments; to define the roles of the parties associated with commercial real estate transactions; and to develop a standard practice that would be both practical and reasonable.

The informal working group was approached by the American Society for Testing and Materials (ASTM) as a willing sponsor for their efforts. ASTM formed the Subcommittee on Environmental Assessments in Commercial Real Estate Transactions in March 1990.

The relationship between ASTM and the real estate trade groups seems at first glance a rather odd affiliation. ASTM, a highly respected organization, is best known for the formulation of scientific standards. However, the group had valid reasons for agreeing to a relationship with ASTM. ASTM provides procedures for developing standard practices that ensure an intensely open and democratic adoption process. An ASTM standard cannot be issued without a consensus of the membership. In addition, ASTM requires that the committee formulating the standard reflect a broad cross section of the parties affected by the standard.[18] The subcommittee members hoped that, by placing their efforts under the auspices of this respected organization and its rigorous requirements, they would attain for their due diligence standard the same degree of credibility and respect that is afforded to other ASTM standards.

The subcommittee eventually grew to approximately four hundred members, including representatives of environmental engineering firms, real estate owners, trade group representatives, representatives of industrial concerns, and lenders. After several years of lengthy negotiation and compromise among these diverse subcommittee members, ASTM published two standards developed by the subcommittee and made them available for purchase by the general public in May 1993. The second edition of the standards was published in late 1994.[19]

The ASTM standards are intended to be used by buyers, sellers, tenants, appraisers, lenders, insurers, legal counsel, and environmental professionals on a voluntary basis for the conduct of environmental due diligence. In addition to attempting to define the steps that must be taken to qualify for CERCLA's innocent landowner defense, because of the prevalence of underground storage tanks in many real estate transactions, the standard also addresses the presence of petroleum products, notwithstanding the petroleum exclusion of CERCLA.[20] Generally, the subcommittee members hoped to outline prudent business practices for due diligence by a buyer or lender in a commercial real estate transaction. They intended to develop guidelines that were practical and reasonable. For example, "appropriate inquiry" does not mean exhaustive assessment of a site that is likely to be clean. However, it does mean that the amount of due diligence performed will depend on the property involved, the uses of the property, and the risk tolerance of the owner. The standard recognizes that performing environmental due diligence will not completely eliminate uncertainty about the potential for contamination.

The standard is intended to be used for the performance of a Phase I site assessment, which, by definition, does not include actual physical sampling and testing. The work that would be recommended if the Phase I site assessment indicates a need for further investigation is termed a Phase II site assessment. The subcommittee has commenced work on a standard guidance for the performance of a Phase II site assessment and has circulated a draft document among its members. As of this writing, the subcommittee has not completed writing the standard, which then will be circulated to ASTM members for comment and approval.

The Transaction Screen

The two ASTM standards consist of a document known as the Transaction Screen Process and a separate document known as the Phase I Environmental Site Assessment Process. It is anticipated that the Transaction Screen Process[21] can be completed either by the "user" (defined in the standard as the owner of the site, the purchaser, a potential tenant, a lender, or the property manager) *or* the environmental professional. The environmental professional's input, however, is not essential for the completion of the initial Transaction Screen.

Allowing the user alone (without the involvement of the environmental professional) to complete the Transaction Screen was a controversial part of the subcommittee's discussions. Certain members believed that many users lack the requisite skill and knowledge to conduct a due diligence investigation. There was a strong belief among these persons that the input of the environmental professional is essential to the environmental due diligence process, including the initial Transaction Screen. However, the majority of the subcommittee members voted for the development of the separate Transaction Screen Process that could be completed independently of the Phase I Environmental Site Assessment Process. A number of the members held the view that, as a practical matter, buyers, bank officers, and others were already conducting such informal assessments of properties. In addition, because of the relative cost and time involved for a Phase I site assessment, a number of smaller transactions, including many commercial leases, are often completed without any environmental due diligence at all. A complete environmental site assessment, including records searches and site investigation, can cost several thousand dollars and will ordinarily take at least twenty to thirty days. Although not specifically stated as a purpose for the Transaction Screen Process, when parties are reluctant to engage a professional because the expenditure of funds for such activity is not justified by the economics of the transaction or because the timing of the transaction does not allow for thorough due diligence, the Transaction Screen provides an alternative to doing nothing.

The Transaction Screen includes a questionnaire to be completed by the owner of the site or its operator (or both, if called for by the situation); a site visit; and a records review. The questionnaire explores issues such as present and past uses of the land and adjoining properties. For example, was the property the site of an industrial facility, gasoline station, motor repair facility, commercial printing facility, dry cleaner, photo developing laboratory, junkyard, or landfill? It addresses questions such as the current or prior presence of underground storage tanks at the site; evidence of staining that might have been witnessed by the party completing the questionnaire; waste disposal issues; and other issues that might reveal the potential for contamination at the site. It also addresses lawsuits and administrative orders concerning the release or threatened release of hazardous substances on or from the site.

Phase I Environmental Site Assessment Process

The second standard produced by the ASTM subcommittee is the Phase I Environmental Site Assessment Process.[22] The Phase I Environmental Site Assessment Process can be performed independently of the Transaction Screen. In addition, if a Transaction Screen has been completed and if facts derived from performing the Transaction Screen indicate a need for further inquiry, the parties may elect to perform a Phase I site assessment pursuant to the ASTM standard, using an environmental professional, or they can limit further due diligence to one or more particular issues. The two standards exist independently of each other.

The Phase I Environmental Site Assessment Process contains four components: a records review; a site reconnaissance; interviews with current owners and operators; and an evaluation and report. The standard recognizes the role of professional judgment in defining the scope of the environmental assessment. The standard is intended to be site-specific and to leave to the user, who ultimately will bear responsibility for the site, the decision of how much due diligence should be performed. However, in any later dispute over whether "appropriate inquiry" was made, the user has the burden of justifying the reasons for the performance of less due diligence than that called for by the standard.

The records review portion of the assessment is intended to be a search of generally available records concerning the subject property and sites within the "approximate minimum search distance" defined in the Phase I standard,[23] to the extent that such a review can be performed within a reasonable time (generally within twenty days) and at a reasonable cost.[24] The review should cover commonly accessible and customary sources, including a specific list of databases of contaminated or potentially contaminated sites.[25] Use of commercial services to obtain access to such databases is permitted. Such a review generally would not include a visit to the offices of governmental agencies to search their files, although letters to relevant agencies, with follow-up telephone calls to verify information, would be considered part of a reasonable records review.

The subcommittee intended that the four specific parts of the Phase I standard should be used in coordination with each other. For example, if the site reconnaissance does not point to the presence of an underground storage tank but the records review indicates such a possibility, then the reviewer must explore other sources, such as interviews with knowledgeable persons, to arrive at the truth.

Each task for the parties involved in the site assessment process includes an objective, with guidelines and alternatives. However, the Phase I standard specifically stresses the importance of the discretion and judgment of the professional conducting the site assessment. Although not expressly acknowledged in the Phase I standard, it is clear that the usefulness of any checklist or guidance document is limited, despite its drafters' intentions, unless the party implementing it has the understanding and intelligence to make the informed decisions and analysis that good due diligence requires. The standard is set out in a way that emphasizes its goal of uniformity while at the same time recognizing the uniqueness of an individual site and the need for judgment on the part of all parties involved in the process. In addition, the ASTM standard recognizes the fact that both cost and time should be kept at a reasonable level.[26]

The Phase I standard also contains an appendix that provides a suggested format for the report generated by the environmental consultant.[27] This appendix furthers one of the most important goals of the subcommittee: to achieve a measure of uniformity in the environmental due diligence process and the reports generated by environmental consultants. The standard contains several required provisions of the report. First, the report must include all of the due diligence elements required by the Phase I standard, such as the results of records searches. Second, the report must name the environmental professionals who conducted the site assessment and prepared the report and their qualifications, as well as the qualifications of the consulting company.[28] Third, and most importantly, the report must contain findings and conclusions as to whether or not an environmental condition was discovered and, if so, its nature. Unless specifically required to be included in the report by the user in deviation from the standard, the report will not contain recommendations for further work, liability or risk evaluations, or detailed conclusions. These items are beyond the scope of the standard.[29]

The Phase I standard provides for a "team" effort in the conduct of environmental due diligence. The user has specific responsibilities that are enumerated in the standard that generally do not require technical expertise and that will not be performed by the environmental consultant as part of the environmental assessment. For example, the user is expected to conduct any title search for environmental liens against the property. If the user has specialized knowledge or information that could have a significant impact on the work, it is the user's responsibility to communicate this to the environmental professional before the site investigation is performed.[30] The user must consider whether specific additions or deletions from the scope of work should be made, such as including an investigation into the presence of asbestos at the site or electing to perform an environmental compliance audit of the operations of the current owner of the facility.

This involvement of the user differs from the more customary approach to environmental due diligence in which the user "buys" an environmental report in much the same way that one buys a property survey for title insurance purposes. Too frequently the consultant is left to perform the work without being fully informed of the purpose and goals of the client who commissioned the investigation. The ASTM standard provides a means to resolve what has become a major problem facing those involved in the performance of environmental due diligence: the exclusion of the consumer from the process and from the final product.

The ASTM subcommittee included in its membership a substantial number of environmental engineers and other professionals. However, it also included others, such as lenders' representatives, lawyers, and insurance industry representatives, who are significantly affected by the environmental condition of a property. These members understood how important it was that the standard provide for the input of the user into the final product of the environmental due diligence process.

Beyond the Scope of the ASTM Standard

While the ASTM standard represents a significant step toward a more consistent and rational approach to environmental due diligence, it has limitations. The most critical of these relate to the underlying goals of the assessment process, the type of assessment that is conducted, and the scope of issues that are and are not addressed by the standard. The subcommittee limited its objectives for practical reasons: they wanted to reach a consensus in a reasonable time period to establish uniformity in a chaotic marketplace. They considered setting a standard for "good commercial practice" for environmental site assessments in commercial real estate and stating a minimum level of "appropriate" inquiry that is both reasonable and practical and yet sufficient to satisfy CERCLA's innocent landowner defense to be a large enough task to accomplish.[31] However, there are other important reasons for conducting environmental due diligence besides to meet CERCLA's criteria, and the subcommittee was unable to focus sufficient attention on these other reasons. Although the rationale behind the limited scope of the standard is understandable, it makes the standard less useful as a tool that can be uniformly applied in all due diligence situations.

Often, in fact, parties may care little, if at all, about potential CERCLA liability when performing an environmental site assessment. For example, a tenant and landlord may wish to perform a site investigation at the expiration of a lease to determine the current condition of the property. Both parties are technically "owners" and therefore are already potentially responsible parties under CERCLA. These parties are thus potentially liable for contamination already present on the site. They need a site assessment to allocate between themselves whatever expenditures may be required to remediate the property. Similarly, a current owner may wish to undertake a site investigation, either as part of a feasibility study for a proposed development or to become aware, in advance, of any potential conditions that would affect market value.

In any of these situations it is critical that the party requesting a site assessment obtain a thorough and accurate product. The ASTM standard, as currently formulated, may not be adequate to this task.

For example, the Phase I Site Assessment Practice calls for the consultant to conclude whether or not recognized environmental conditions have been discovered and to provide an opinion of their impact. In the situations described above, the parties may already know of the existence of contamination that is likely to affect the property and may only be seeking assistance in quantifying that impact, or they may be seeking remediation alternatives. The scope of work will require modification in those types of situations to ensure that the consultant adequately satisfies the needs and demands of the client.

The ASTM standard is site-specific for a commercial real estate transaction. The report that is produced by performing the Phase I Environmental Site Assessment Process will not address additional issues that may arise in the acquisition or sale of a business, such as the buyer's potential liability for sites previously owned by the seller or for wastes shipped off-site by the seller. However, these issues will be just as (if not more) critical to the transaction as potential liability for the real property currently owned by the seller.

Finally, because the ASTM standard addresses potential CERCLA liability, its scope is limited to those substances that are defined as "hazardous substances" under CERCLA and to petroleum products, because of their pervasiveness. It does not provide guidelines for assessments for the presence of asbestos-containing materials, radon, lead-based paint, lead in drinking water, or wetlands. The subcommittee's reasoning was that these items, although important, should be the subject of future, separate standards. However, to assess fully the potential environmental risks associated with a site, a buyer or lender will likely require information concerning each of these items. One may not incur CERCLA liability through the ownership of a building containing asbestos, but in order to demolish or renovate that building, the presence of the asbestos will have to be taken into account.

It follows that use of the ASTM standard in many instances will not be a simple matter of incorporating it verbatim into an engagement letter or a contract with an environmental consultant. The user will have to be astute enough to instruct the consultant to evaluate items not covered by the standard, and, depending on the nature of the transaction and the ultimate goal of the user, other modifications to the process may also be required.

Consultants and the ASTM Standard

Another problem arising from the use of the ASTM standard is the general inflexibility that many users encounter when dealing with environmental consultants who are asked to perform an assessment pursuant to the standard. Perhaps because they recognize the limitations of the standard's primary purpose of defining "all appropriate inquiry," or perhaps because they fear liability if they stray from the suggested criteria contained in the Phase I Environmental Site Assessment Process, consultants who have been asked to use the Phase I standard with modifications have shown some intransigence. At the same time, consultants, after agreeing to perform a site assessment based on the standard, will frequently produce a report that does not meet its requirements. Although certain modifications to the guidelines, such as reducing the "approximate minimum search distance" for records review, are permitted in the discretion of the environmental professional,[32] the consultant and the user's counsel should advise the user in advance when such a modification is recommended.

In addition, it is not uncommon for a consultant to agree to use the ASTM standard and then to produce a document that is little more than a Transaction Screen accompanied by a database search or other comparable records review. This is common in situations in which the user, because of time and budget constraints, has asked the consultant to perform the work within a time frame unreasonable for a complete Phase I Environmental Site Assessment. While such a modified scope of work may be just what the transaction requires, the user should be informed of the limitations of this type of approach before the work is performed. The inflexibility and unwillingness of many consultants to inform the user at the outset of the investigation of the impracticality of what has been requested may prove to be self-limiting and may have the practical result of making the ASTM standard less valuable.

A frequent critique of the ASTM standard from members of the nonlegal community is that it has been written in a very "lawyerly" style. This complaint is especially common when discussing the Transaction Screen, which is intended to be used by property owners, bank officers, and other persons who may not be completely familiar with the terminology. To some extent, this complexity is the reason for discrepancies between what the Phase I standard demands and the final report provided by a number of consultants. Either the consultant has not fully analyzed the requirements of the standard or does not believe the slight changes that he or she has made will make a difference to the user. It is rare that the user will have the patience to review the full text of the standard to determine whether the report actually contains everything that the standard dictates.

Finally, the ASTM standard may be too little too late. During the nearly three years that the subcommittee was working to develop the standard, certain large institutional lenders as well as the RTC acted to fill the void with their own internal guidelines. As a result, the ASTM standard may not become the uniform model that the subcommittee had hoped. There is some indication that these parties will not abandon the use of their own standards in favor of the ASTM standard unless they are convinced that ASTM improves on what they have already developed. Without the following of major lenders and other users, the ASTM standard will not further the subcommittee's goal of uniformity.

Despite these limitations, the ASTM standard represents the best effort in the standardization of the field of environmental due diligence to date. It offers a measure of certainty that was not previously present. Unlike prior efforts at "standardization" of the due diligence process, the ASTM standard involves in the process the person requesting that the assessment be performed and the lawyer as well. Despite the controversy that this caused within the ranks of subcommittee members, the committee had faith that the owner, the property buyer, the lender, and the lawyer could and should play a role in the performance of environmental due diligence and should be involved in the decisions that were made. This is an important development.

Beyond Standards: The Quality of the Assessment

Ultimately the ASTM standard may help to improve Phase I assessments by forcing consultants to adhere to a standard of quality for both their investigative work and their reporting of results. Historically the lack of consistency and quality in environmental due diligence reports has been a common problem in the consulting industry. The reports prepared by even the most competent environmental consultants may be poorly written and may contain unsubstantiated conclusions, logical inconsistencies, and misinformation. These reports may omit critical details. Too often, the poor quality of the report reflects not only its preparer's lack of meticulousness but also the inadequacy of the investigation itself. It is to be hoped that, through the rigorous application of the ASTM guidelines for both the site assessment and the report of the consultant's conclusions, the overall quality and usefulness of these reports will improve.

Whether or not the ASTM standard, or some other standard, is ultimately used as a guideline for the performance of the work and the preparation of the report of an environmental site assessment, much more than mere adherence to a standard is required to perform sufficient environmental due diligence in a commercial real estate transaction. "Quality," a term that has lately been overused in the business context, is a valuable concept to remember when discussing environmental due diligence. The term denotes work performed according to high professional standards, which should be a fundamental goal of the provider of environmental services.

While the environmental due diligence process has increasingly been standardized, quality is frequently lacking in this field. When reading a series of environmental site assessment reports prepared by the same consulting firm, it is not uncommon to notice a striking similarity among them. The reader might feel as though he or she were reading the same report over and over again. Many times, in fact, this is actually the case. The introduction of computer programs into the consulting industry and the resulting ease of reproduction have increased the likelihood of mistakes. Some of these may be innocent, even amusing, such as reading in three successive reports for sites located in separate geographic areas about the same gasoline station on a certain street corner having unregistered tanks. Such an oversight obviously results from forgetting to edit the text when copying one report into the next. But other mistakes, such as the missed underground storage tank, are potentially disastrous.

The value of an environmental site assessment hinges on the skill of the person in the field who performs the investigation. Too frequently, however, an engineering firm's younger, less experienced personnel will be assigned to perform the site investigation work for the Phase I assessment, leaving the more skilled staff to do the sophisticated (and better compensated) work. This practice frequently enables the consultant to remain within the budget quoted to the client, something that has been critical because of the competition within the industry for site assessment work.

The problem stems from the fact that those hiring environmental consultants often have a tendency to seek the lowest bid, either because they fail to appreciate the fact that quality differences may exist between two assessments or because they view the entire process as one imposed on them by lenders or the government to which only a token response is necessary. The result of either of these attitudes is a tendency not to take the process seriously and to attempt to accomplish it as quickly and as cheaply as possible. The consultant who submits a low bid will be tempted to take short cuts to perform the work and still make money. As a result, less time will be spent analyzing and understanding available information about the site. The site history will be minimal, at best. Finally, the report will be hastily written and poorly developed. Such an assessment will be of minimal value to the client and frequently leave open more issues than it resolves.

Unfortunately, development of the ASTM standard alone cannot solve this problem. To obtain substantial, dependable, and adequate environmental due diligence for a commercial real estate transaction, all involved parties, including the owner, lender, lawyer, and consultant (and staff) must comprehend the importance of the product to be generated and be committed to achieving the goals identified by the property owner or lender. Ideally, these parties will work together in a flexible and cooperative manner as a team throughout the assessment process. The consultant must understand the time frame within which the owner must operate as well as the quality concerns of the lawyer monitoring the process. In addition, both the owner and the lawyer simultaneously must appreciate the fact that imposing unrealistic deadlines will necessarily diminish the quality of the product delivered.

Conclusion

Before environmental due diligence is undertaken, the parties who have commissioned the work must analyze and discuss with the consultant the reasons for performing the due diligence. Being aware of the ultimate goals of the parties in seeking a due diligence investigation will assist all those involved in determining the scope of work, which may or may not incorporate ASTM requirements. It is unlikely that using the ASTM standards in their present format without additional site- and transaction-specific guidelines will provide the parties with all that they are seeking. Modifications to the scope of the work will likely have to be made to assure a complete and adequate report.

Good environmental due diligence requires many things: a clear understanding by all parties involved of the purpose for which the due diligence is being performed and what potential risks require evaluation; selection of a professional who is and will remain committed to the performance of quality work and the production of a complete and understandable report; a clear and full understanding by all parties of the context in which the work is being performed; and other site-specific considerations. In addition, and perhaps most importantly, the parties must remember at all times how all of those interests may have to be compromised because of the time limitations for completing the investigation and the need to keep costs within reasonable limits.

Notes

1. 42 U.S.C. §§ 9601 *et seq.*
2. 42 U.S.C. § 9607(35).
3. 42 U.S.C. § 9607(b).
4. 42 U.S.C. § 9607(35)(A) and (B).
5. 42 U.S.C. § 9607(35)(B).
6. 42 U.S.C. § 9601(35)(B). Aside from the factors specified in the statute, there is little legislative history to explain what Congress intended as a standard

for appropriate inquiry. However, different amounts of investigation were anticipated depending on the type of transaction involved. For example, Congress intended that "those engaged in commercial transactions" be held to a higher standard than residential transactions. H.R. REP. No. 962, 99th Cong., 2d Sess. 187 (1986).

7. 706 F. Supp. 346 (M.D. Pa. 1988).

8. 706 F. Supp. at 353.

9. 716 F. Supp. 1341 (D. Idaho 1989).

10. 716 F. Supp. at 1349.

11. 19 ENVTL. L. REP. (ENVTL. L. INST.) 20,855 (N.D. Cal. Feb. 23, 1988).

12. 19 ENVTL. L. REP. at 20,856.

13. 42 U.S.C. § 9601(20)(A).

14. *See* United States v. Mirabile, 15 ENVTL. L. REP. 20,994 (E.D. Pa. Sept. 4, 1985) (mere foreclosure of a security interest in real property did not make a lender an "operator" of the facility, even though, after purchasing the property at the foreclosure sale, the bank held the property for several months and took certain steps to protect the property, including initiating cleanup activities); United States v. Maryland Bank & Trust, 632 F. Supp. 573 (D. Md. 1986) (where the lender had foreclosed on the property and held it for four years, the court held that, to qualify for the exemption provided for in CERCLA, the lender must hold its security interest at the time of the cleanup, 632 F. Supp. at 579).

15. 901 F.2d 1550 (11th Cir. 1990), *cert. denied*, January 14, 1991.

16. 901 F.2d at 1557.

17. To alleviate some of the lenders' concerns and to clarify the issues, the EPA issued a rule creating certain "safe harbors" for lenders who took certain acts, including foreclosing upon contaminated property, to protect their security interest. 57 Fed. Reg. 18,344 (1992), 40 C.F.R. § 300.1100. After the EPA lender liability rule was issued, it was challenged in the federal courts and struck down in February 1994. Kelley v. EPA, No. 92-1312; Chemical Mfrs. Ass'n v. EPA, No. 92-1314, 1994 U.S. App. LEXIS 1715 (Feb. 4, 1994).

18. According to the ASTM rule book of procedures, committees must be balanced. No more than fifty percent of the membership of a committee formulating a standard can be a "producer" of the product about which the standard is being formulated. At least 50 percent of the committee's membership must be users of the product.

19. The standards are ASTM E 1527 STANDARD PRACTICE FOR ENVIRONMENTAL SITE ASSESSMENTS: PHASE I ENVIRONMENTAL SITE ASSESSMENT PROCESS [hereinafter ASTM E 1527] and ASTM E 1528 STANDARD PRACTICE FOR ENVIRONMENTAL SITE ASSESSMENTS: TRANSACTION SCREEN PROCESS [hereinafter ASTM E 1528]. These publications can be purchased directly through ASTM at 1916 Race St., Philadelphia, PA 19103. ASTM has copyrighted these materials and does not allow any reproduction without the express consent of ASTM. References to these standards will sometimes be made in the singular in the text as the "standard" or the "ASTM standard."

20. The scope of the standards is otherwise limited to investigation for hazardous substances under CERCLA. Consequently, the standards do not address issues such as the presence of asbestos-containing materials, lead-based paint,

lead in drinking water, radon, or wetlands. These items may be the subject of future ASTM standards.

21. ASTM E 1528.

22. ASTM E 1527.

23. ASTM E 1527 at § 7.1.2.

24. ASTM E 1527 at § 7.1.4.2.

25. Examples of databases to be searched include the federal CERCLIS list, the federal RCRA generators list, state lists of hazardous waste sites, and state leaking UST lists.

26. Attached at the back of both of the standards is an appendix discussing the status of the legal background of federal law. ASTM E 1527 and ASTM E 1528, app. X1, Legal Background to Federal Law and the Practices on Environmental Assessments in Commercial Real Estate Transactions.

27. ASTM E 1527, app. X2, Recommended Table of Contents and Report Format.

28. *See* ASTM E 1527 at § 11.4. The standard does not contain a substantial definition of an "environmental professional," other than as a person "possessing sufficient training and experience necessary" to perform environmental due diligence. § 3.3.11. The subcommittee elected to leave the task of determining the technical requirements for training as an environmental professional and the level of technical experience to the consulting industry.

29. *See* ASTM E 1527 at § 11.6.

30. ASTM E 1527 at § 5.3. In addition, it is the user's responsibility to document any reasons for a purchase price lower than the value of comparable properties. § 5.4.

31. ASTM E 1527 at § 1.2.

32. ASTM E 1527 at § 7.1.2.1.

CHAPTER 9

Environmental Consultants

EVA M. FROMM

Parties to real estate transactions are often faced with the task of selecting and supervising environmental consultants to perform various types of environmental assessments. Selection of an environmental consultant is probably the most important step in ensuring that the work is done properly and that the real estate practitioner can rely on the consultant's work product. Unfortunately, while many good environmental consultants are available, it often seems that there are just as many inept or inexperienced consultants who miss crucial problems. The less competent consultants may, for example, use improper analytical techniques, neglect to recommend appropriate follow-up investigations, or miss critical liability issues.

In certain instances, when the seller selects the consultants involved in a transaction, different problems can arise. These consultants may have their scope of work so dictated by the seller that the usefulness of the consultants' reports is considerably reduced. Also, the consultants' reports may be so extensively edited by the seller that much of the important information is omitted or presented in an obscure manner, resulting in significant expertise being required to extract the important information from the reports.

The purpose of this chapter is to assist real estate practitioners in screening and selecting environmental consultants. Guidance is given on how to request a proposal and qualifications from a consultant and on criteria to use in reviewing the consultant's proposal. Contractual concerns also are discussed, including typical contract terms and conditions that should be included to protect the client. Examples of consultants' representations, warranties, and covenants are set forth, along with suggestions for minimum insurance requirements and indemnity provisions.

The chapter also addresses steps that should be taken when supervising a consultant, including determining the scope of work for Phase I and Phase II assessments,[1] report formatting, assignment of key project personnel, and time limitations. In addition, the chapter provides guidance to real estate practitioners on how to review the consultant's final report and to interpret the data provided in the report. Finally, the consultant's liability for the work performed is discussed.

Selecting a Consultant

The Initial Screening Process

Selecting a good environmental consultant at the beginning of the assessment process is the most crucial step that can be taken to achieve a successful outcome. Engaging a consultant should be done only after a careful review of the consultant's expertise, experience, and reputation in the area. Consulting firms that profess to have vast experience in conducting real estate transactional audits are plentiful, while in fact good consultants are difficult to find. Even the simplest transactional audit may require expertise in several areas, including engineering, building practices, geology, hydrology, industrial hygiene safety, and biology. Many consulting firms do not have a great depth of expertise, so careful review of the resumes of the individuals to be assigned to the project is important.

Perhaps the simplest way to select an environmental consultant is to ask for recommendations from an experienced environmental lawyer. An environmental lawyer is more likely to have been exposed to a wide variety of consulting firms and can easily eliminate firms with poor reputations. An environmental practitioner can also provide names of consulting firms that not only have good reputations but are willing to work with the client on the terms of the contract and to include reasonable provisions relating to insurance, representations and warranties, and indemnities.

Absent recommendations from a reputable environmental lawyer, it is advisable to interview and hire larger consulting firms with national (or at least regional) reputations. This is recommended for several reasons. First, national consulting firms generally pay employees higher wages and are therefore more likely to have highly qualified personnel. Larger, well-established firms are also more likely to have good insurance coverage, including excess policies (also referred to as umbrella policies) that are outside the economic reach of many smaller firms. Finally, many larger firms are more apt to indemnify the client above and beyond the limits of the insurance policies for matters not covered by the policies. Smaller firms typically are unable or unwilling to agree to these provisions. Should the worst-case scenario happen—the consultant misses something significant—the larger, well-established consulting firm is more likely to be around to make good on a claim. On the other hand, not all assessments will warrant the costs associated with a larger firm. All these factors should be carefully balanced when selecting the consultant.

Unfortunately, there is not a national licensing program for environmental consulting firms, nor do most states have licensing procedures for consultants. Typically consulting firms are only required to be licensed for certain limited activities, such as asbestos abatement and underground storage tank (UST) removal. In some states, environmental professionals have organized to attempt to establish baseline requirements for environmental consultants. In many instances, however, the requirements are conflicting and there is no assurance that an environmental consultant approved by any particular group is actually competent to provide the work.

When requesting proposals from a consulting firm, it is beneficial to require that the firm include the following with its proposal:

- A list of real estate audits conducted by the consultant and a description of the type of facilities covered by such audits
- The resumes of key personnel
- A copy of the consultant's standard contract (unless you plan to provide your own form contract to the consultant)
- A copy of the typical disclaimer language that the consulting firm includes in its Phase I reports
- A list of references with phone numbers

If you are not familiar with the consultant or have not received a glowing endorsement from a respected environmental lawyer, it is important that each of these items be obtained to ease the selection process.

A list of sample projects previously conducted by the consultant can be extremely useful in narrowing down the available choices. If, for example, a property to be audited primarily consists of oil and gas operations, it would be extremely useful to have a consultant who has conducted prior assessments of such properties. Oil and gas exploration and production sites often have unique problems, such as the possible presence of naturally occurring radioactive materials. Similarly, if the audit will be of shoreline property, the consultant should have experience with the various laws governing coastal properties. Consultants who do not regularly conduct assessments of such sites may not know how to deal with these issues. Selection of the consultant is highly dependent on the nature of the work to be conducted, although other factors, such as the ability to negotiate with lenders, may also need to be considered in the final selection process.

The resumes of the key project personnel also are important. Often the environmental consulting firm will use good marketers or "front men" to make the initial contact. Upon a closer review of the resumes of the project personnel, it may become evident that many so-called environmental consultants have no technical degree and, as a result, are probably not qualified to conduct the work. Another potential pitfall to avoid is the assignment of very junior personnel to the actual site walk-through (also referred to as field work). It is easy for an inexperienced young consultant to miss important problems. Prudence dictates that the actual field work be conducted by a professional with a minimum of three to five years of experience conducting real estate audits.

Obtaining a copy of the consultant's standard contract with the proposal is also a good practice. Many a lawyer has wasted considerable time and effort selecting a consultant, only to find that the consultant's contract was so unreasonable that he or she could not in good faith recommend that the client execute the contract. Obtaining and reviewing the contract at the proposal stage can save considerable time and effort, both of which are at a premium when trying to meet a closing. Even better, see if the consultant will agree to use a standard contract that you have prepared.

Checking the consultant's references is a good practice, although the consultant will probably provide only references who will give favorable reviews. If time permits and the scope of the project is significant, the following types of questions should be asked of the references:

- Were you satisfied with the overall service provided by the consultant?
- Did the consultant complete the project within the prescribed time frame?
- Was the project performed within budget?
- Was the report format adequate?
- Were you happy with the contract provisions agreed to by the consultant?
- Was the consultant willing to work with you on language in the final report?
- Did you experience any problems with the consultant?
- Would you use this consultant again?
- Would you recommend this consultant to others?

When all else is said and done, a meeting with the proposed project personnel is always useful in making the final selection. A face-to-face meeting, in conjunction with probing questions, may serve to eliminate consultants who appear qualified on paper yet in reality lack the expertise required for the project.

Requests for Proposals and Qualifications

Most practitioners will request proposals from several consultants for a Phase I assessment. After a consultant is selected for the Phase I assessment, that consultant typically will be used for any follow-up work. Consequently, comparison of proposals is normally concluded in the Phase I stage.

To allow the lawyer or client to make an accurate comparison of costs, it is crucial that the proposals obtained in this early stage be fairly uniform. There are a number of methods of standardizing bids to reach this goal. Many lenders, for example, will prepare a scope of work that is expected to be covered in each Phase I assessment and then circulate the scope of work to the consulting firms that will be asked to bid on the job. Alternatively, the real estate practitioner can mandate that the scope of work be conducted in accordance with the American Society for Testing and Materials (ASTM)[2] standards for Phase I assessments, although many of the ASTM provisions are not appropriate for every Phase I audit. Another alternative is to use a scope of work such as that set out in this chapter's section on "Supervising the Consultant" (below), specifying such as the minimal scope of work to be included in the Phase I assessment, while including instructions to the consultant that the proposal should include any additional work that the consultant feels is necessary or warranted.

Reviewing the Proposal and Selecting the Consultant

As discussed earlier, obtaining references, statements of qualifications, and the resumes of key personnel are crucial steps that assist the lawyer or the client in the final selection of a consultant. Many times clients will select a consultant based solely on costs, without placing enough emphasis on other factors, such as experience and the consultant's financial viability. Often the smaller consulting firm is the least expensive but also the least likely to be financially viable. While it is not necessary to hire the most expensive firm, nor is the most expensive firm necessarily the best for the project, it is important to consider each of these factors when selecting the consultant: cost; experience of the personnel assigned to the project; experience with the particular type of property to be assessed; insurance; and financial viability. As a practical matter, if the consulting firm is not financially viable and does not have adequate insurance, none of the other factors are important. Without sufficient financial strength and good insurance, it is unlikely that the client will be able to recover any damages resulting from the consultant's negligence. A combination of the foregoing factors should be sought when making the final selection.

Contractual Concerns

General Contract Terms

Contracts with consultants range from the very simple to the very complex. There are, however, certain minimum provisions that should be included in every contract. The easiest course of action is to prepare a standard contract for use with all consultants and insist that consultants use it instead of their own form contracts (which, of course, heavily favor the consultant).

The contract should include an introductory clause specifying that the contract is an agreement for professional services and setting forth the date the contract is executed and the parties who have entered into the contract for obtaining professional environmental services. If the lawyer is hiring the consultant on behalf of his or her client (i.e., to attempt to preserve a privilege), it is best that the client also is a party to the contract or a beneficiary of it so that the client is protected under the contract's indemnity and insurance provisions.

It is not uncommon for the introductory section of the contract to include several recital (or "Whereas") clauses, such as the following:

- WHEREAS, Client intends to retain Consultant to render certain services, including professional environmental services, such as, but not limited to, conducting a Phase I Audit at the property described in Appendix A (hereinafter the "Services" as more particularly described herein).
- WHEREAS, Client has chosen Consultant because of Consultant's experience and reputation in providing real estate assessments.
- WHEREAS, Consultant is willing to provide such services for the consideration and upon the terms hereinafter stated.

The first substantive section of the contract typically is titled "Scope of Services." This section should adequately describe the services to be included in the contract. It is also prudent to refer to the scope of services described in the consultant's proposal and attach the proposal as an appendix to the contract. In addition, this section should set out the fee to be charged for the services and may include a "not to exceed" cost, which cannot be exceeded without written agreement or authorization by the lawyer or the client. To permit flexibility, this section may also include a provision stating that additional services may be performed by the consultant under the terms of the agreement upon written agreement of both parties.

A section describing the terms of payment also may be included in the contract. There are various mechanisms for dealing with this issue. Some contracts provide that the consultant will submit an invoice at the completion of the project and that the invoice will be paid within a certain number of days, typically thirty days after receipt. It is not uncommon for contracts for significant amounts of money to include procedures for handling disputed invoices, such as mediation or arbitration procedures.

The section regarding payment conditions is often followed by the covenants or representations of the contractor, the indemnification section, and the insurance provisions. These issues are discussed below in some detail.

Other provisions that may be included in service contracts with environmental consultants are as follows.

Relationship of Parties and Subcontractors

The contract may provide that the contractor is to be considered an independent contractor and shall have responsibility for and control over the details regarding the services. This provision may also require that the consultant may not use subcontractors without prior written approval from the client. It is prudent to include a provision stating that, for the purpose of the agreement, the negligent acts, gross negligence, errors or omissions, or willful misconduct on the part of any subcontractor of the consultant shall be considered the negligent acts, gross negligence, errors or omissions, or willful misconduct of the consultant.

Sample Preservation

In certain instances, it is important to maintain samples in the event that analyses have to be rerun. In many cases, however, this provision is not necessary.

Reports

It is generally prudent to include a provision that a report will be prepared based on the services performed that will set forth, consistent with the proposal, all pertinent data, findings, and opinions regarding the project that is the subject of the contract. This section of the agreement should specify when the report must be submitted so that it is provided in a timely fashion to counsel, the client, or both.

Consultants may try to include a provision that prohibits the dissemination of any reports prepared for the client to any third parties. When such reports are to be submitted to lenders or regulators, agreeing to this type of provision is generally not recommended. The contractor may also try to insert a provision that the client will indemnify the consultant from any claims made by any third party relying on the consultant's report, when such a report has been submitted to the third party without the consultant's written consent. The client should not agree to this type of provision, since often reports are inadvertently disseminated to third parties by engineers and other personnel of the client who may be unfamiliar with the terms of the contract. The practitioner can explain that the consultant will simply have to rely on the appropriate state law to protect itself in a situation in which it is sued by a third party who has allegedly relied on the consultant's report.

Ownership and Maintenance of Documents

The consultant may try to include a provision stating that all data and information prepared for the client is the consultant's property. To protect the client most effectively, this provision should indicate that data prepared for and paid for by the client shall belong to the client (not the consultant) and, upon completion of the services, shall be provided to the client or its nominee. Notwithstanding this provision, data that was in the contractor's possession before the preparation of the proposal, that was or is in the public domain, or that is furnished to the consultant by others not a party to the agreement can be exempt from this provision.

Confidentiality

It is prudent to include a confidentiality provision stipulating that the consultant shall keep confidential all information received from the client as well as the substance of any report, test, recommendation, or advice the consultant gives to the client in connection with the services provided under the agreement. The consultant should also treat as confidential all maps, data, reports, and other written or oral information relating to the services. The contract may include a caveat stating that, in the event the consultant is required by subpoena or court or administrative order to disclose any information deemed by the agreement to be confidential, the consultant shall give immediate verbal notification to the client upon receipt of that order. A confidentiality provision can ensure that information is not disseminated to others. For business development purposes, consultants often want to use descriptions of the work done for various clients; however, it may not be in the clients' best interest to have such information disclosed. This section can include a sentence specifying that the consultant may not provide the client as a reference to third parties or use the client's name in marketing or promotional materials without the client's prior written approval. Inclusion of a confidentiality provision would allow for a breach of contract suit against a consultant who impermissibly revealed information to third parties.

Services by the Client

The consultant will usually want the contract to include provisions that require the client to grant access to the project site to the consultant and the consultant's employees, agents, and subcontractors. The provision may provide for a minimum notice period that must be given to the client before entry. This provision may also require the client to notify the consultant of any on-site or nearby health or safety hazard or condition of which the client has knowledge.

Suspension of Work

The contract should also include a provision allowing the client, upon verbal or written notice to the consultant, to suspend the performance of the consultant's work at any time and for any reason. This will permit the client to shut down a project immediately if it becomes obvious that the consultant is not competent or is violating environmental, health, or safety regulations. The consultant may want this section to include a clause providing that if payment of undisputed invoices is not maintained on a current basis, the consultant may, with notice to the client, suspend further work until payment is restored to a current basis.

Amendments and Termination

It is advisable to include a provision requiring that any amendments to the agreement be in writing and executed by the authorized representatives of the client and the consultant. This section may also include a provision allowing the client to terminate any or all of the services for its convenience at its option by providing the minimum number of hours of written notice of termination to the contractor. On a larger project, the consultant may insist that only certain triggering mechanisms—such as failure to comply with the regulations, improper safety controls, or failure to perform the work in a competent manner—can be used to terminate the contract.

Other General Terms

Other general terms may be included, such as a provision requiring that neither party can assign the contract without the written consent of the other party; a provision regarding the governing law and venue for the contract; an integrated writing provision; and a provision stating who will receive notices and who will be authorized representatives under the contract. A conflict of interest provision prohibiting the consultant from performing work for potentially adverse parties during the pendency of the work may also be useful.

Consultants' Representations, Warranties, and Covenants

The types of representations, warranties, and covenants that may be included in a consulting contract vary widely. A representation generally is a statement by the consultant that some fact is true and correct. In contrast, a covenant typically refers to a future act. The following are examples of representations desirable in projects in which significant costs are to be expended:

- Consultant and consultant's agents who will perform all or any portion of the services provided for in this contract are fully experienced, qualified, and have expertise in providing Phase I and Phase II assessment investigations.
- Consultant has obtained all permits, licenses, certificates, or approvals required under any environmental law to conduct the services.
- Consultant is a certified (or licensed) asbestos contractor (or UST contractor) and all licenses or certificates required to conduct such work are current, valid, and in effect. (Appropriate for asbestos removal or abatement work or UST removal.)

The covenants are even more crucial to the transaction than representations. The following types of covenants should be included in any consulting contract for professional services:

- Consultant warrants that the services shall be performed within the limits prescribed in this agreement and in a manner consistent with a level of care, skill, practice, and judgment exercised by other professional consulting firms in performing services of a similar nature under similar circumstances.[3] If consultant breaches the foregoing warranty, it shall promptly correct the portion of the services that have not been performed in accordance with such warranty, at no additional charge.
- Consultant further warrants that the services shall be performed in strict accordance and compliance with all federal, state, and local laws and regulations applicable to the services to be performed under this agreement, including but not limited to all laws and regulations applicable to the handling of hazardous substances, wastes, or materials; human health and safety; and environmental compliance.

- Consultant warrants that the work shall be performed in accordance with the requirements, standards, specifications, and schedules set forth or referred to in this agreement.
- Time is of the essence under this agreement. Consultant warrants that it shall perform the work diligently and continuously in accordance with the schedule and shall complete the work within the time constraints specified herein.

Other covenants also may be useful, such as the following:

- In the performance of the services hereunder, consultant shall require that its contractors comply with all applicable federal, state, and local rules, ordinances, regulations, and requirements relating to health, safety, security, and environmental matters. Contractor shall use its best efforts to ensure that all persons and entities entering onto the site shall comply with the foregoing laws, ordinances, rules, regulations, and requirements.
- This work shall be performed in accordance with the following standards: American Society for Testing and Materials, ASTM E-1527 *Standard Practice for Environmental Site Assessments: Phase I Environmental Site Assessment Process* (May 1993), or ASTM E-1528-93 *Standard Practice for Environmental Site Assessments: Transaction Screen Process* (May 1993), as the case may be. (For more on these standards, see Chapter 8 of this book.)
- Consultant will utilize only treatment and disposal facilities that have been issued, as of the date of the execution of this agreement, all permits, licenses, certificates, or approvals required by valid and applicable statutes, ordinances, orders, rules, and regulations of the federal, state, and local governments in which such facilities are located.

Termination or suspension provisions such as those previously discussed may easily be tied to the foregoing covenants and representations. The contract should also provide that the breach of any covenant or representation constitutes grounds for immediate suspension or termination. Additionally, the indemnity clause should provide that the client be indemnified for breaches of any covenant or representation by the consultant.

Indemnity Issues

Along with the insurance requirements discussed below, the indemnity section of the contract is perhaps the most crucial. It must be drafted carefully to protect the client from any negligence, gross negligence, errors or omissions, or willful misconduct on behalf of not only the consultant but the consultant's subcontractors as well. It is not uncommon for a consulting firm to attempt to limit the consultant's liability to the total of the compensation received by the consultant under the contract. This is simply not adequate protection for the client, since even the simplest error by a consultant can cost a client hundreds of thousands of dollars. The following is an example of a fairly simple indemnity provision that should fully protect the client:

> Consultant agrees to defend, indemnify, and hold harmless Client, Client's parent and subsidiary corporations, and their respective officers, directors, employees, agents, representatives, shareholders, successors, and assigns for any and all liabilities, costs, demands, losses, damages, claims, actions, or penalties caused by or arising from (i) the negligence, errors, or omissions, gross negligence, or willful misconduct of consultant or any of its employees, agents, or subcontractors in connection with this Agreement, or (ii) the breach of any representation, warranty, or covenant contained herein.

An alternative provision could allow for an indemnification up to the limit of the consultant's insurance, combined with an indemnity to a maximum cap (e.g., $1 million) by the consultant for matters not covered by the insurance. Because actions that constitute gross negligence or willful misconduct are often excluded from insurance policies, it is possible that some actions taken by the consultant in performing the work may not be covered under insurance. Therefore, an indemnity from the consultant may be necessary to protect the client adequately. In addition, insurance policies often contain high deductibles and the consultant might argue that the indemnity provision would not apply if the damages asserted are less than the deductible.

If a full indemnity such as that set forth above cannot be obtained, the client is best protected by using the second alternative. However, the client's interest will not be protected if the lawyer agrees to limit the amount of the consultant's liability to the amount paid under the contract.

The indemnity should also include a clause providing that indemnity survives the term of the contract. In many cases, a consultant's error may not be discovered until some time after the work has been completed. To protect the client under these circumstances, the indemnity should expressly provide that it survives the term of the agreement.

Finally, an indemnity provision is only as good as the financial viability of the indemnitor. If the services are available to the client, a

Dun & Bradstreet report should be obtained on the consultant. Larger firms may be publicly traded and have available financial reports or other documents typically filed with the Securities and Exchange Commission. Any mechanism that assists the client or counsel in determining the financial strength of the consulting firm should be used, to the extent desired by the client, to ensure that the indemnity is meaningful.

Insurance Requirements

Insurance is an additional layer of protection available to the client. Before entering the contract, the client should determine the minimum insurance requirements that are needed for the project. Many insurance policies contain exclusions for environmental issues, so each policy must be carefully reviewed to verify that it provides the coverage desired.

Types of Insurance

Generally the consultant should have five types of insurance in place, along with the specified minimum limits and coverages.

1. Workers' compensation: Workers' compensation insurance should be provided in the statutory amount required in the state in which the work is to be conducted.
2. Commercial general liability insurance: Commercial general liability insurance covering bodily injury and property damage should be required. This insurance may also include premises and operations coverage; explosion, collapse, and underground property damage coverage; products and completed operations coverage; independent contractor's coverage; broad form property damage liability; personal injury liability; and other specific coverages. The minimum recommended limits are $1 million per occurrence and $5 million aggregate.
3. Comprehensive business automobile insurance: This coverage should ensure that the consultant's owned and rented automobiles are covered for the project. If wastes are to be transported, an MCS-90 endorsement may also be necessary. The typical minimum limit for this insurance is $1 million per occurrence.
4. Professional liability (errors and omissions): This type of insurance covers the errors and omissions of professionals and the performance of their work. This is fairly standard insurance for most consulting firms and should provide a minimum limit of $1 million per occurrence and $5 million aggregate, if

available. Because of the cost of this insurance, some consultants may be limited to coverage of $1 million.

5. Umbrella liability coverage: The consultant may also have umbrella (or excess) coverage, typically in minimum limits of $5 million, which serves as a second layer of coverage for personal injury, explosions, broad form property damage, and other types of liability.

No Right of Subrogation

The above described insurance policies should all contain provisions that the insurance companies will have no right of recovery or subrogation against the client or its agents, directors, officers, employees, or insurers. They should also specify that any deductible provided for in these policies shall be assumed by the consultant.

Named as an Additional Insured

In certain circumstances, being designated as an additional insured on the consultant's policies is desired. This will provide the client with the broadest protection possible. If this provision is included, the client should insist on obtaining copies of the certificates of insurance reflecting the client's status as an additional insured.

Provisions Relating to Subcontractors

The insurance section of the contract can also require that subcontractors maintain the same minimum insurance amounts as those required of the consultant. However, many subcontractors will not be able to obtain these minimum insurance requirements and lesser requirements will have to be established for them. A provision should be included that makes it necessary for the consultant to require that subcontractors' insurers waive all rights of subrogation to the same extent provided in the primary agreement.

Termination Provision

The contract should include a provision requiring notice to the client if the insurance coverage is canceled or expires. In addition, it may be necessary to provide for the termination of the contract upon the expiration or cancellation of the coverage.

Review of Policies

It is good practice to obtain and review the consultant's certificates of insurance *before* the project is initiated. In addition, the underlying insurance policies, such as errors and omissions and commercial general liability policies, should be reviewed to ensure that there are no exclusions for the type of work being conducted by the consultant.

Supervising the Consultant

Determining the Scope of Work for the Phase I Audit

To qualify for the innocent landowner defense under the Comprehensive Environmental Response, Compensation, and Liability Act (CERCLA), an owner must have acquired the property after the disposal of the hazardous waste and prove that he or she (1) exercised due care, (2) took precautions against foreseeable acts or omissions of third parties, and (3) at the time of acquisition did not know and had no reason to know that any hazardous substance had been disposed of on the property.[4] The latter requirement makes the innocent landowner defense difficult to achieve. It requires that the purchaser must have made "appropriate inquiry into the previous ownership and uses of the property consistent with good commercial or customary practice."[5] Among the factors to be considered by the courts in determining whether an "appropriate inquiry" was made is the purchaser's ability to detect the contamination by appropriate inspection.[6] It is commonly thought that, at a minimum, the innocent landowner defense requires the purchaser to conduct a Phase I audit of the property before acquisition.

The scope of work for a Phase I audit (or assessment) should be fairly standard across the industry. Items typically included in Phase I audits are as follows:

1. A site visit and a walk-through of the property to identify areas of visual contamination and other issues of concern
2. A site description, including information on topography, depth to groundwater (if available), proximity to surface water, potential wetlands areas, and surrounding land uses
3. A description of any industrial processes on the property and of USTs, transformers, wells, and waste disposal activities
4. A description of housekeeping problems, spill areas, the condition of storage of chemicals and wastes, discolored soils or waters, and unusual odors or vegetative conditions
5. Interviews of site personnel to develop information on (a) historical activities conducted at the site, including spills and disposal activities, and (b) current discharges of materials or wastes to the soil, air, and water
6. Identification of potential asbestos-containing materials
7. Identification of any equipment that may contain polychlorinated biphenyls (PCBs)
8. A review of prior land uses through a title search, interviews of relevant persons, and review of aerial photographs

9. A review of aerial photographs for indications of problem areas, such as prior disposal areas or oil and gas usage
10. A review of agency records for information about the subject site, including permitting status, spill notifications, enforcement actions, and notifications of waste activities, and discussions with agency representatives when warranted
11. A review of agency files for sites that may affect the subject property, with files including the Comprehensive Environmental Response, Compensation, and Liability Information System (CERCLIS) database (identifies sites at which certain hazardous substances have been disposed of); the National Priorities List (NPL) database (identifies federal Superfund sites); the Leaking Petroleum Storage Tank (LPST) database; state Superfund databases; and the Resource Conservation and Recovery Act (RCRA) notifier list (identifies companies that generate, store, treat, or dispose of hazardous wastes)
12. A search of agency files for well drilling and plugging reports for properties suspected of being used for oil and gas exploration or production
13. The photographing of process equipment and areas of concern, such as visibly discolored soils

It is prudent to provide a detailed scope of work to the consulting firm and advise the firm that the scope of work provided sets forth the *minimum* activities to be conducted during the Phase I assessment. The consultant should also be advised that if, in the consultant's judgment, additional work is necessary, the client and the client's lawyer are to be advised of the same. The lawyer will then have an opportunity to review the consultant's proposal and determine if the additional work is warranted.

One of the most critical areas in a Phase I assessment, often overlooked by both consultants and lawyers, is compliance with regulations. The typical Phase I audit generally concentrates on contamination issues—that is, what contamination is either present on the property or could potentially affect the property that would void the innocent landowner defense or cause the client to incur remediation costs. Compliance issues, however, are equally important, and often just as costly for ongoing operations. If the property to be audited includes an ongoing business operation (anything ranging from a dry cleaner to a factory), a compliance assessment may be warranted to determine if the facility is operating in compliance with applicable rules and regulations. Consultants generally will not include a compliance assessment in a Phase I audit unless specifically requested, often to the surprise of the real estate lawyer. It is potentially devastating for a client to purchase a facility only to learn that a key permit is lacking, meaning the purchaser cannot operate the facility legally until the permit is applied for and obtained (a costly and time-consuming process).

Determining the Scope of Work for the Phase II Audit

The Phase I audit results may indicate that additional work should be performed at the site. At this step the expertise of the consultant and the supervising lawyer are most critical. A Phase II audit is warranted if there is an indication of spills or prior disposal activity. Even the most inexperienced individual will recognize that these factors warrant further investigation. Often, however, it is not as clear to the inexperienced reviewer of a report if additional work is warranted where industrial activities have occurred but there are no obvious indicators of problems. Other factors then become increasingly important, such as the age of the facility (e.g., pre-1980 facilities are more likely to have historical spills or disposal activities that are not readily apparent) or the type of activity conducted on the property (e.g., pipe yards used for the storage of oil field pipe and string may have problems with solvents, lead from threading compounds, or naturally occurring radioactive materials from oil field activities).

The following circumstances dictate that a Phase II investigation be conducted:

- Visible evidence of contamination
- Prior on-site waste disposal
- USTs
- Asbestos-containing materials
- Unprotected soils around equipment containing PCBs
- Unprotected soils around aboveground storage tanks (i.e., no man-made secondary containment)
- Unprotected soils around process equipment pads where run-off of contaminants may have occurred

It may also be prudent to conduct a limited Phase II assessment at any site where significant industrial activity has taken place, regardless of whether the foregoing factors are present, particularly if the site was built before the inception of regulations requiring special handling of solid and hazardous wastes.

It is not feasible to present a scope of work for Phase II audits that will be adequate for any Phase II investigation. However, the inexperienced report reviewer can request information that may allay his or her concerns about the scope of the Phase II investigation recommended by the consultant. When in doubt as to whether the consultant is suggesting the appropriate scope of work for a Phase II, the client or the lawyer should ask the following questions:

- What types of problems are expected for this type of property or industry?
- What chemicals are used, or have historically been used, by this company or by this industry that may cause problems?
- What propensity do such materials have to migrate? (For example, metals typically do not migrate downward significantly, absent a "carrier" such as a solvent, whereas solvents may migrate readily into the groundwater.)
- Would these materials be expected to be confined to surficial soils or is groundwater contamination a concern?
- What analyses are recommended for analyzing the soil and groundwater?
- Will these analyses indicate if the constituents of concern are present?
- What specific problems were revealed by the Phase I audit and will the proposed scope of work address *all* these problems?

If after these questions have been answered the client or the lawyer is still not confident that the consultant has recommended an appropriate scope of work, a "fail-safe" scope of work such as the following may be selected:

1. Install a minimum of three groundwater monitoring wells in the first water-bearing zone and space these wells in areas of suspected concern, but place them far enough apart to determine the direction of groundwater flow. (Note that in some areas of the country, the first water-bearing zone is in excess of fifty feet deep and installation of groundwater wells may be cost prohibitive.)
2. Analyze the groundwater using gas chromatography/mass spectrometry (GC/MS) for a full priority pollutant scan, which includes volatiles, semivolatiles, acid and base-neutral extractables, and pesticides/herbicides. The groundwater should also be analyzed for total metals, PCBs, and total petroleum hydrocarbons. These analyses should detect the majority of the problem chemicals.
3. Obtain soil samples from each of the corings obtained during installation of the monitoring wells and analyze the soils for the above-referenced constituents. Obtain soil samples at regular intervals (i.e., surface, two feet, five feet, and every five feet thereafter until groundwater is reached).

4. Obtain soil samples from other areas of suspected contamination at regular intervals until there is no more visible evidence of contamination or until a field screening instrument such as a volatile organic compound (VOC) analyzer indicates that the soils are clean. Analyze such soils for the same constituents described in item 2 above.
5. Obtain surface water samples, as indicated, where contaminated runoff is an issue. Analyze for the same parameters.

It may be feasible to limit these analytical parameters after the initial sampling event. If, for example, the soils analysis identifies only ten constituents of concern, the groundwater analysis could be limited to those constituents. It would not be anticipated that other constituents would be found in the groundwater if they were not found in the soils. However, this method would not detect contaminants migrating from an off-site source or from another source on the property. Thus, for the initial round of samples, it is more prudent to "over analyze" and limit the parameters for future sample events.

Again, the above-suggested scope of work for Phase II audits should be used only when the practitioner does not have confidence in the consultant or does not feel that he or she has the expertise to determine whether a consultant's proposed scope of work is adequate. The analyses specified in the above scope of work are expensive but should serve to detect most of the typical constituents of concern.

In addition, if the business being purchased has ongoing industrial operations that are also being purchased, the Phase II audit should include an assessment of the company's environmental compliance status. Potential liabilities associated with off-site waste disposal, including potential CERCLA liability, should be addressed as well.

Report Format

The consultant should be given direction as to the type of report format expected at the project's conclusion. Even the most diligent field work is useless unless all relevant data are presented effectively. If possible, one should review prior reports prepared by the consultant and discuss modifications that may be beneficial to the client. Alternatively, one could develop a standard report format and advise the consultant that the format identifies the minimum information desired in the report.

The client or the lawyer should also review the typical disclaimer language that the consulting firm will include in its report. In loan transactions, lenders may balk if the consultant's disclaimer is so strong that the Phase I audit becomes meaningless.

Time Limitations

If time is of the essence in the transaction, the contract should specify the time limitations and require the consultant to indemnify the client if it breaches its warranty that the work will be completed within the time specified. Consultants are notorious for missing deadlines for submitting audit reports. A consultant's failure to submit a report on time could cause the client to lose a loan or an important deal.

The Final Report

Understanding the Report

Once the Phase II audit is completed, the client's counsel will need to advise the client on whether the problems detected during the audit are significant. Assistance from an environmental lawyer is needed at this stage in the negotiation process. With the assistance of environmental counsel and the consultant, the client should determine the following:

- What is the extent of contamination (area and depth) at the property?
- How much will it cost to remediate?
- How long will it take to remediate?
- What other compliance issues—especially lack of permits—have to be addressed?
- Can the facility operate without these permits until the permits are obtained?
- Is it possible that penalties may be assessed for the problems found?
- Did the audit reveal any off-site issues that have to be addressed (i.e., Superfund sites or wastes sent to the wrong sites for disposal)?

Once the foregoing information is determined, it will be necessary to ascertain whether the seller is sufficiently solvent to bear the costs of remedying the problems. It will also be necessary to draft contract provisions that address the seller's liability for the same. Finally, it may be prudent to establish an escrow account or some other mechanism to ensure the seller funds the remediation. (For more on allocating environmental liability, see Chapter 11.)

Protecting a Report from Disclosure

Although it is infrequent in the context of real estate transactions, in certain instances the client may want to protect the environmental audit report from disclosure. Some clients, for example, may want to have a Phase I audit and a compliance audit performed before placing a property or business on the market. Under these circumstances, the client may want the audit protected as privileged.

As a matter of policy, the U.S. Environmental Protection Agency has stated that it will "not routinely request environmental audit reports."[7] If, however, an audit discloses regulatory violations or uncovers conditions that may create environmental problems, a company must determine whether the information must be reported to a government agency or others and whether immediate corrective action is necessary. (Reporting requirements are discussed in more detail in Chapter 6.)

Attorney-Client Privilege

The purpose of the attorney-client privilege is to protect the confidential relationship between the attorney and the client. Consistent with the confidential nature of this relationship, certain communications between an attorney and a client are protected from disclosure. The required elements of this privilege have been described as follows:

> The privilege applies only if (1) the asserted holder of the privilege is or sought to become a client; (2) the person to whom the communication was made (a) is a member of the bar of a court, or his subordinate, and (b) in connection with this communication is acting as a lawyer; (3) the communication relates to a fact of which the attorney was informed (a) by his client (b) without the presence of strangers (c) for the purpose of securing primarily either (i) an opinion on law or (ii) legal services or (iii) assistance in some legal proceeding, and not (d) for the purpose of committing a crime or tort; and (4) the privilege has been (a) claimed and (b) not waived by the client.[8]

To come within the attorney-client privilege, the environmental audit must be conducted under the direction and control of an attorney.[9] This requirement is often difficult to meet when the audit is prepared by an independent consultant because a court may determine that the necessary direction and control by the attorney is not present. In certain instances, an attorney with a technical background may be able to assess regulatory compliance directly and advise the client of compliance problems. Consultants could then be hired through the attorney to remedy any noncompliance.

To attempt to fall within the attorney-client privilege, the environmental audit must be conducted for the purpose of obtaining legal advice.[10] This element of the privilege may create confusion in the context of an environmental audit because the audit frequently serves several different purposes.

The attorney-client privilege can be waived by a failure to maintain the confidential nature of the communication. Disclosure of an audit report to a third party, such as a potential purchaser or lender, waives the attorney-client privilege.

Other Potential Privileges

Other potential privileges can be explored, but they are less helpful in the context of an environmental audit.

WORK PRODUCT DOCTRINE. The work product doctrine applies only if the audit was prepared in anticipation of litigation. Most compliance and transactional audits will not meet this qualification. This doctrine may, however, cover a special investigation.

"CRITICAL SELF-ANALYSIS" PRIVILEGE. This claim of privilege is based on public interest considerations, but it has been rejected in at least one case involving an environmental assessment.[11]

Typical Problems Encountered with Reports

Even when the greatest care has been taken in selecting a consultant, costly mistakes can be made during the audit. Here are some examples of more common mistakes.

Using the Toxicity Characteristic Leaching Procedure (TCLP) as a test method to determine the extent of contamination is a fairly common, and extremely critical, error. TCLP is a test method that requires an extraction procedure. In essence, it dilutes the concentration of contaminants so that some contaminants may go nondetected when they are actually present. TCLP should be used only to determine if a material is a hazardous waste under RCRA, *not* to indicate whether contaminants are present above background levels. A GC/MS analysis or a total metals analysis should be used instead of TCLP. If the wrong analysis method is used, samples obtained in the field will be relatively useless.

Consultants will also err by reviewing one aerial photograph dated before the property's most recent development and assuming from that photograph that the site had not been previously developed. It is incomprehensible that a consultant can extrapolate that information from one such photograph. By failing to look at earlier photographs, the consultant may fail to discover old disposal activities, oil and gas operations, or other industrial activities.

Another common mistake is to interview site personnel but not note names or include interview summaries. On occasion, what was told to a purchaser during an audit later becomes a crucial issue in litigation. Some consultants do not summarize the interviews they conduct, while others only indicate generically that they spoke with someone at the site. Neither practice is acceptable.

Another faulty practice is stating only facts discovered and not providing opinions or conclusions relating to those facts. Some consultants, particularly sellers' consultants, will state information in a report and expect the recipient to read between the lines to gather other critical information. For example, only facts will be given (the waste was placed in the trash) without conclusions being drawn (it was actually a hazardous waste and should not be disposed of in this manner) or recommendations for further work being provided (liabilities may be imposed on a successor corporation for this illegal activity).

Some consultants may test for asbestos but fail to note the location from which the individual samples were obtained. This happens frequently in Phase II audits of apartment complexes. The consultant will indicate that a certain number of samples were obtained from apartments but fail to specify apartment or building numbers. For complexes built in stages, this can be particularly frustrating when test results show friable asbestos in only some of the samples.

In addition, consultants seriously err by failing to immediately advise the client (when the client is the seller or the borrower) when they discover a spill or release that requires reporting to an agency. Consultants often present such information by indicating in a report that spills are present. If an inexperienced practitioner reviews the report and the report does not advise immediate reporting of the spill, the property owner may be in violation of regulations and costly penalties can be imposed.

Consultant's Liability for Work Performed

A carefully drafted contract can be crucial to the success of a lawsuit if it becomes necessary to sue the consultant for the work conducted. If the contract includes appropriate provisions, the client should, arguably, be able to sue the consulting firm under the contract for damages resulting from the consultant's negligence or breaches of covenants or warranties. Unfortunately, consultants' final reports often include disclaimer provisions that attempt to negate the client's ability to rely reasonably on the audit results. Care should be taken to ensure that such disclaimers are not included in the report.

Recent cases have addressed consultant liabilities for economic damages in tort. In *Levy v. Broussard, Inc.*,[12] the purchasers of real property sued Broussard for negligent misrepresentations and breach of contract. Broussard allegedly failed to identify perchloroethylene as a potential source of environmental liability in a Phase I environmental audit of the plaintiff's premises. The issue revolved around the negligent misrepresentation claim and whether an engineer could be classified as being in the "business of supplying information."[13] Ultimately, the court held that the defendant was not "in the business of supplying information" and thus could not be held liable for economic damages in tort.[14]

A more difficult issue is the consultant's liability to third parties for reliance on the report. In *Murlaf Living Trust, et al. v. Mobil Oil Corp. and Groundwater Technology, Inc.*,[15] Groundwater Technology, Inc. (GTI), was sued for intentional misrepresentation and failure to disclose hydrocarbon contamination that existed outside of the perimeter of the plaintiffs' building. GTI had been hired by Mobil Oil Corporation to conduct an assessment. The assessment revealed contamination on the plaintiffs' property, but GTI did not disclose this information to the plaintiffs. On a motion to dismiss, the court refused to dismiss the plaintiffs' claim, which might entitle them to relief under an intentional misrepresentation theory, and stated that the claim was not susceptible to a motion to dismiss. The court indicated that the contract between Mobil and GTI, which contained a confidentiality clause prohibiting GTI from disclosing information to third parties, did not prevent the plaintiffs from stating a claim against GTI for nondisclosure of the information.

There is a fairly extensive body of law concerning third-party beneficiaries (such as lenders) under contract law, and it is important to recognize that many courts have refused to hold a contractor liable for negligence to a third party based on lack of a duty to that party.[16]

Resources

Fevastianos, E. "Recovery of Economic Damages against Environmental Professionals: Another Exception Carved from the Economic Loss Rule." *Real Estate/Environmental Liability News* 5, no. 9 (Feb. 28, 1994).

Hines, A., and Levin, M. "Liability Without End? Consultants, Contracts, and the Limits of Environmental Responsibility." *BNA Environment Reporter* (Sept. 10, 1993).

Levin, M., Hines, A., and Mullaney, S. "Discovery and Disclosure: How to Protect Your Environmental Audit Report." *BNA Environment Reporter* (Jan. 7, 1994).

Notes

1. The terms "assessment" and "audit" are used interchangeably in this chapter.

2. *See* American Society for Testing and Materials, ASTM E 1527-93 Standard Practice for Environmental Site Assessments: Phase I Environmental Site Assessment Process, and ASTM E 1528-93 Standard Practice for Environmental Site Assessments: Transaction Screen Process, in Annual Book of ASTM Standards (1993).

3. It may also be prudent to require that the services be performed under the direction of a registered professional engineer.

4. CERCLA § 101(35)(A), 42 U.S.C. § 9601(35)(A).

5. CERCLA § 101(35)(B), 42 U.S.C. § 9601(35)(B).

6. *Id.*

7. EPA Auditing Statement, 51 Fed. Reg. 25,004, 25,007 (1986).

8. United States v. United Shoe Machinery Corp., 89 F. Supp. 357, 358–59 (D. Mass. 1950).

9. *See* Congoleum Industries, Inc. v. GAF Corp., 49 F.R.D. 82, 84 (E.D. Pa. 1969), *aff'd*, 478 F. 2d 1398 (3rd Cir. 1973) (privilege applies to communications to a patent agent employed by and under the personal supervision of outside counsel).

10. *Compare* Upjohn Co. v. United States, 449 U.S. 383 (1981) (communication to counsel was made for the purpose of securing legal advice and was protected), *with* Diversified Industries, Inc. v. Meredith, 572 F.2d 596, 603 (8th Cir. 1977) (communications not privileged because lawyers were hired to conduct an investigation of facts and to make business recommendations).

11. United States v. Dexter Corp., 132 F.R.D. 8 (D. Conn. 1990).

12. No. 92C-4836 (D.C. Ill. 1993) (Real Estate Environmental Liability News).

13. *Levy*, at 5.

14. *Levy*, at 9.

15. Murlaf Living Trust et al. v. Mobil Oil Corp. and Groundwater Technology, Inc., No. 93 C 6956 (D.C. Ill. 1994), U.F. Dist. Lexis 4777 (April 12, 1994).

16. *See, e.g.*, Lincoln Alameda Creek v. Cooper Industries, Inc., 829 F. Supp. 325 (N.D. Cal. 1992); Sykes v. Propane Power Corp., 541 A.2d 271 (N.J. Super. Ct. App. Div. 1988); U.S. Ecology, Inc. v. Carlson, 638 F. Supp. 513 (C.D. Ill. 1986).

CHAPTER 10

Understanding Environmental Reports: Science Issues for Transactional Lawyers

JAMES P. O'BRIEN

Environmental issues are scientific issues. Contamination is chemistry; site investigation is patterned on the scientific method; and cleanups are aimed at minimizing statistical health risks. This chapter explores several scientific issues that frequently arise in real estate transactions.

Most transactional lawyers first see scientific issues in Phase II environmental assessment reports, which describe soil and water sampling and analysis. The first section of this chapter discusses how Phase II reports should be evaluated.

Since Phase II reports usually include sampling data and laboratory reports, the chapter's second section discusses how to understand the scientific data. Often, Phase II reports show soil or groundwater contamination by chemical compounds, an area about which most lawyers know little.

The chapter then discusses the physical chemistry and toxicity of contaminants. Since the last step for resolving transactional environmental issues is site remediation, the chapter's final section explains how target cleanup levels are established.

Evaluating Phase II Sampling and Analysis Reports

Many environmental investigations include soil and water sampling and analysis. The resulting reports are filled with long chemical names, pages of confusing laboratory reports, and drawings or logs of borings, wells, and geology. Without technical help, many report users cannot critically evaluate the results. This section is a practical guide to evaluating reports on sampling and analysis. First, it examines what the report should tell the user. Next, it discusses what the environmental consultant usually does in the field to generate information. Then, the section focuses on evaluating the results. Lastly, some common Phase II problems are identified.

What the Report Should Tell the User

Most soil and groundwater sampling is performed because an initial review indicates the potential for environmental problems. Typically a Phase I environmental site assessment identifies "flags" of potential problems. Because contamination can rarely be observed, a walk-through assessment can only spot indications that problems exist. To confirm whether the Phase I flag truly represents an environmental problem, a more extensive and intrusive investigation is necessary. The assessment moves to the next level or phase of the process: hence the term "Phase II" assessment.

Phase II work typically involves sampling environmental media, which are air, soil, sediment, and water, and analyzing the samples for contaminants. The number of samples, the methods of sampling, and the analysis performed varies widely. More sampling produces better and more thorough information, but at a greater cost. Limited sampling and analysis can generate data that demonstrate whether soil or groundwater contamination is present. Extensive Phase II work can generate enough data to describe the nature of the contaminants and the extent of the contamination.

In addition to sampling of environmental media, Phase II work can also include sampling of materials, building structures, and equipment. For example, probably the most common Phase II work is sampling building structures for asbestos-containing materials (ACMs). In fact, ACM sampling is so common that many Phase I assessment protocols include sampling suspected ACM. Other common Phase II work includes sampling electrical equipment such as transformers and capacitors for polychlorinated biphenyls (PCBs), sampling building paint and drinking water for lead, and sampling indoor air for radon.

What the Consultant Does in the Field for Phase II

The consultant's job can be stated simply: Find the contamination. Generally contamination is found in soil or water. If soil is contaminated, it can act as a source of continuing contamination to groundwater. If groundwater is contaminated, the contamination can be carried far from the source in a "plume" of contamination. To carry out a Phase II investigation efficiently, the consultant must make assumptions about how environmental problems may have occurred and use professional judgment to design a sampling and analysis program to evaluate these problems.

For example, assume that the Phase I flagged as a potential environmental problem the accumulation of chemical drums on a loading dock and potential leakage from the drums. As part of preparing a Phase II work plan, the consultant will trace the expected flow of liquid from the dock down onto the ground. Usually, once on the ground, the contamination will migrate or leach down through the soils to the groundwater. Once at the groundwater, the contaminant can do one of three things, depending on its chemistry: float on top, dissolve in the groundwater, or continue sinking through the groundwater until the contamination is stopped by tightly packed soils or rocks. Usually some quantity of the contaminant dissolves in the groundwater and is carried away with the groundwater as it moves. Depending on the chemicals involved and the physical properties of the site, the consultant will look for the contaminant at different depths in the soil and groundwater.

Soil Sampling

In planning the Phase II assessment, the consultant will look for soil and groundwater contamination throughout the area of expected impact. To find the contamination, the consultant will pick the spot where liquids from the dock have most likely traveled and then drill into the soil to take a boring. The drilling equipment allows the consultant to extract a column of soil from the hole drilled. Samples of soils at different depths can be taken to find out whether the contamination decreases or stops at a certain depth.

To ensure that a sample is taken from the most heavily contaminated soil, most consultants use field instruments that can detect and measure gross contamination. The most common field instrument is a photoionization detector, usually referred to as a PID or an HNu (which refers to a particular manufacturer). A PID can detect many carbon-containing organic gases, such as gasoline or industrial solvent fumes. By measuring the level of fumes emitted by a contaminated soil sample, the consultant can pick the most heavily contaminated sample for further laboratory analysis.[1]

Groundwater Sampling

After taking soil samples, the consultant can continue drilling down until groundwater is encountered. Once in groundwater, also called the "saturated soil zone," a monitoring well can be installed. Essentially, a monitoring well consists of a long plastic or stainless steel tube with a screen at the bottom. It reaches from the surface down to the groundwater. Water enters through the screen, typically until the level of water in the tube equals the level of water in the soil. Sometimes the level of water in the tube is different than the level of water in the soil, as when, for example, the groundwater is under pressure in a "confined" layer. By measuring the level of the water, the consultant can calculate groundwater elevation. Using elevation data from at least three different monitoring wells, the consultant can determine the direction of groundwater flow at the time of measurement. Once in place, a series of samples and elevation data can be taken from the monitoring wells over time to produce an ongoing picture of the groundwater movement and quality.

Sampling Techniques

Soil and groundwater samples are taken using established procedures. For some contaminants, samples must be taken and the lids closed tightly before the contaminants evaporate. Some contaminants react with common sample jars and bottles. Other samples must be kept cold, so sample jars are packed with dry ice. For many samples, bottles must contain a preservative before introducing the sample. Quality control rules require that the samples be analyzed no later than a certain number of days after being taken. Most Phase II reports include a discussion of the quality assurance and quality control (QA/QC) procedures followed during sampling and transportation. Although the procedures and rules are quite technical and detailed and thus beyond the expertise of most users, the Phase II report should state whether the consultant followed appropriate QA/QC procedures.

Laboratory Analysis

A variety of different instruments and techniques are used to analyze different kinds of contaminants. The consultant must ask for the right kind of method analysis to find the contaminants present in the sample. In the example above, the methods used must take into account the kinds of chemicals found in the drums. Sampling the soils in the drum accumulation area for contaminants that were never stored in the drums does not provide useful information. "Clean" analytical results do not necessarily mean clean soils.[2]

Evaluation of Phase II Results

After chemical analysis of the samples is complete, the consultant usually prepares a report describing the work and the results. The results can be evaluated using the following six steps.

Scope of Work

The first step is to read the scope of work to find out what the report should tell the user. Depending on the scope of work, the amount of work done and the data generated can vary substantially. If the Phase II is intended simply to demonstrate the presence of contamination, borings and wells in potential hot spots are sufficient. If the report is supposed to describe the nature and extent of the contamination, the sampling should be extensive enough to establish the boundaries of the contamination, and a variety of analytical techniques should be used to find all contaminants present.

Many, if not most, reports fall somewhere between these two extremes. The scope of work is typically limited by budget. Although the user wants enough information about the nature and extent of the problem to quantify the cost, most users are willing to accept some uncertainty to save money on the Phase II.

Field Techniques

The second step is to evaluate the consultant's field techniques. This evaluation involves three things. First, the work plan should have placed borings and wells in those areas where other information about the property suggests there may be a problem, and samples should have been taken from the contaminated zones. Also, the consultant should have used proper sampling and sample handling techniques before submitting samples for analysis. Finally, the consultant should have selected analytical methods sensitive to the kinds of contaminants expected.

Laboratory Results

The third step in evaluating the report is to review the laboratory analytical results. Later sections of this chapter discuss the chemistry of contaminants in greater detail. In the meantime, the consultant should highlight the chemicals that present a health threat and describe the concentration levels that give rise to a risk. In addition, the consultant should note which of the concentration levels of the chemicals present are likely to be above agency-established cleanup levels. Consultation with legal counsel is often necessary to determine the applicability or relevance of particular standards.

Nature and Extent of Contamination

The fourth step is to evaluate the nature and extent of the contamination. The report should describe the contaminants' physical behavior, such as whether they are likely to migrate, whether they will dissolve in the groundwater, and whether the concentrations present in different samples indicate the contamination source. In addition, the report should describe how deep the contamination has gone and how far it reaches.

Since many report users are concerned about contamination that must be remediated, the costs associated with the contamination problem are very important. Usually, the cost of a cleanup is driven by the nature of the contaminants and the extent of the contamination. Depending on the client's requirements, the Phase II may need to evaluate cleanup costs with a high degree of specificity.

Site Geology

The fifth step is to evaluate the geology of the soils on the property. Usually the Phase II report includes the boring logs or monitoring well logs prepared at the time of drilling. The logs describe the soils that were encountered at different depths during drilling. More compact or "tight" soils are less permeable to contamination. Thus, tight soils may indicate that a contamination problem is not widespread.

Soils are typically classified in four categories, in order of increasing tightness or decreasing permeability: sandy soil, loamy soil, silty soil, and clay. Beneath the soil is the "bedrock," or the start of the crust of the earth's surface. Most contaminants will not migrate through the bedrock. If the depth to clay or bedrock is small, leaching contaminants should not have migrated far. If contaminants have migrated through fractures in the bedrock, the complexity of the site's environmental problems increases. Tight soils and clay also inhibit the movement of groundwater and may act as a protective liner under the contamination or as a barrier to lateral migration.

The geology of the soils on the property can affect the flow of groundwater. Groundwater moves through more permeable soils more easily, and the flow can be diverted by pockets of less permeable material. In addition, subsurface water can be trapped above tight soil layers and falsely indicate groundwater.[3]

Consultant's Recommendations

The last step in reviewing the report is to consider the consultant's recommendations. Often the recommendations in a Phase II report concern additional sampling and analysis for better answering the questions posed in the scope of work. The consultant usually will not (and indeed should not) make recommendations unless requested. In addition to describing the additional work recommended, the recommendations also identify the "data gaps" or weak areas in the report. If the consultant was sufficiently concerned to recommend additional work, the dimensions of the problem may not be developed fully.

Common Problems with Phase II Reports

Some problems with Phase II work and reports seem to be more common than others. Report users should keep these issues in mind as they review reports.

Laboratory Analytical Results

Many problems seem to involve the laboratory analytical results. Laboratory instruments and techniques can detect extremely small concentrations of chemicals. As a result, the techniques for sampling, sample handling, sample preparation, and analysis can all affect results. In addition, since the detection level for contaminants has decreased steadily, allowing much lower concentrations to be identified, the regulatory standards for allowable concentrations of contaminants has decreased correspondingly. Moreover, the laboratory results are the most crucial portion of a Phase II report; they describe the nature and severity of the contamination problem.

Analytical results can be affected by the sampling technique and handling of the sample. Because many contaminants evaporate in the open air, the longer the sample is exposed, the greater the chance that contaminants have escaped. Similarly, some samples must be prepared specially and transported appropriately. A common technique for assuring that samples were not mishandled is to use "trip blanks" and "laboratory blanks." Trip blanks are samples that have a known material and that are sent along with the consultant during the sampling process. The trip blank is later analyzed along with the other samples, and any unexpected results indicate potential problems with the sampling. In the same way, laboratory blanks are samples with known materials that are analyzed at the laboratory along with the other samples. The presence of unexpected contaminants can indicate a potential problem with the laboratory analysis.

Perhaps the most common laboratory analytical problem is contamination of samples through laboratory chemicals. Most often, samples are contaminated by methylene chloride or acetone, which are commonly used in analytical laboratories. If either of these chemicals is detected in the samples, it is appropriate to review the QA/QC for the sampling, and it may be necessary to resample to ensure an accurate result.

The detection limit of a method or analytical instrument is usually identified as the "method detection limit" (mdl). Laboratory analytical reports usually identify the mdl for each chemical analyzed as part of that method. If the method does not detect the chemical, many laboratories report that the result for that chemical was "below detection limit" (bdl). Different methods and laboratory instruments may have different mdls for the same chemical. It is important to select the appropriate method and instrument to obtain the right mdl for the chemical. For example, if the report indicates bdl for a contaminant using a method that has a 10 parts per billion (ppb) mdl, that report is valuable as long as the regulatory standard is not less than 10 ppb. For a number of chemicals, the drinking water standards are below 10 ppb. If the mdl is 10 ppb, the report is not valuable for a chemical with a 5 ppb regulatory standard. Users should review the mdl for the analytical results in view of the appropriate regulatory standard.[4]

The mdl may also be affected by the concentration levels of different chemicals in the sample. Laboratory instruments are accurate within a range of concentration levels. Very high concentration levels of contaminants in the sample cannot be reported accurately. If a laboratory report indicates concentration levels in the tens or hundreds of thousands, it is likely that the results are not precisely accurate, even though high levels of the contaminant are confirmed. Moreover, high concentration levels of particular chemicals can mask the presence of other chemicals. Lab reports indicating very high concentrations of certain chemicals, and very low concentrations of others, should be closely evaluated.[5]

Finding the Boundaries of the Contamination

Another common problem with Phase II work is the failure to establish the boundaries of the contamination. To evaluate the potential cost of the problem, the extent of the contamination must be known, both horizontally and vertically. To identify the extent of the contamination, the consultant must "bracket" the affected area. If contaminants are detected during field work, additional borings and sampling should be suggested to the user while the consultant is in the field. By continuing to move away from the contamination until clean soils or groundwater are detected, the consultant can identify the extent of the problem. Indeed, perhaps the most common complaint among report users is that the field work did not provide enough information.

Before commissioning Phase II work, however, the user should work with the consultant to ensure that changes in the scope of work can be made while the consultant is in the field. That way, if contamination is encountered, the user can authorize the consultant to continue field work until enough information is obtained and thus avoid the consultant's remobilization costs.

Understanding Environmental Sampling Data and Laboratory Reports

Environmental assessments typically produce many pages of sample analysis data, boring logs, maps, and chain-of-custody records. Often the information seems confusing, or at least unuseful. These documents, however, are a valuable part of an environmental assessment. They describe the nature, concentration, and location of contamination. Understanding this information is necessary to evaluate and understand the environmental issues.

Sampling

The sampling process during a Phase II usually generates four documents in the following order:

- A site map showing where samples were taken, borings were drilled, and monitoring wells were installed
- A boring log or well log describing the boring or well and the geology encountered
- A chain-of-custody record accounting for the handling of the sample
- A laboratory analysis report identifying the substance assay and reporting the concentrations obtained

Site Maps

A site map indicates the location of each sample taken, boring drilled, and monitoring well installed.[6] The purpose of the map is to describe in spatial terms the extent of the investigation and contamination. The map helps the user evaluate the analytical results. For example, if certain borings are contaminated, the map can be used to estimate the volume of impacted soils and the sufficiency of the investigation. More borings may be needed around the contamination "hits" to bracket the affected soils. The Phase II work may produce hits at different locations and different depths. Contaminants may move laterally as well as horizontally. As a result, the extent of contamination can be evaluated in three dimensions using the site map.

A common complaint is that site maps fail to identify sampling locations with sufficient precision to allow the sampling event to be duplicated in the same place later. If that degree of precision is desired, the consultant should be so instructed.

Boring or Well Logs

A boring log is a record of information obtained while the boring was being drilled and samples were being taken. A well log includes the same information and also describes the construction of the well. The purpose of a boring or well log is to provide information about the geology and groundwater to use in evaluating laboratory analysis reports. In addition, the log describes the construction materials and techniques used in the boring or well, which is useful if the data's quality is questioned.

Boring logs typically provide information about four areas: (1) the type of soil or geology present to the depth drilled (e.g., sand, loam, silt, or clay); (2) the characteristics of the soil or geology (e.g., color, odor, and moisture content); (3) the results from field instruments, such as PIDs; and (4) general information about the location and number assigned to the boring, the project number, the person classifying the soils, the rig performing the drilling, and the drilling method used.

Chain-of-Custody Records

A chain-of-custody record accounts for the custody of each sample. Its purpose is to make a permanent record of the identity of each person responsible for the sample, until the sample is analyzed at the laboratory. The record ensures that the sample taken at the site is the same sample, unaltered by anyone or anything, that is analyzed at the laboratory. In addition, the record is part of the foundation for admitting the laboratory analytical report into evidence at a legal proceeding.

Laboratory Analytical Reports

A laboratory analytical report contains the results of the analysis of the sample for chemical compound constituents. The purpose of the report is to set forth the concentrations of the contaminants measured by the laboratory instruments. Understanding the report helps the user understand the environmental problem. To understand analytical results, four preliminary points are important.

Proper Laboratory Analysis Method

First, a sample of soil or groundwater contains hundreds and sometimes thousands of different chemical compounds. Laboratory instruments measure only certain compounds for which the analysis method is sensitive. As discussed earlier, the right analysis method must be selected to find the right kind of chemical. In some cases, the same sample may be analyzed using two or three different methods.

Chemical Compound Concentrations

Second, analytical results are reported for particular chemical compounds or constituents. For example, samples are tested for suspected gasoline contamination by measuring the concentration of benzene, toluene, ethyl benzene, and xylene, commonly referred to as BTEX. The laboratory analysis report does not indicate a concentration level for gasoline.

Physical Properties of Chemical Compounds

Third, the physical properties of the chemicals in question should be discussed. Some compounds evaporate more quickly, while others are more likely to leach through soils. Some compounds dissolve more readily in groundwater, while others float on top or sink. Although the concentrations generally indicate the severity of contamination, to evaluate the nature and extent of the problem, the behavior and physical properties of the chemical compounds are important. The consultant's report should discuss the physical properties of the chemical compounds as part of the review of the laboratory analytical reports.

Reporting of Analytical Results

Fourth, the results of the laboratory analysis are reported as concentrations of the compound in the sample. For example, a laboratory analysis reporting 1 ppb of a compound means that there is one part by weight of the compound for each billion parts by weight of the sample. Groundwater analysis results are sometimes reported as the weight of the compound contained in a certain volume of water. For example, 1 milligram per liter (mg/L) of a compound means that 1 milligram of the compound is contained in each liter of groundwater.[7]

Analytical Laboratories

Analytical work on soil or groundwater samples is performed at a commercial laboratory that specializes in analyzing field samples. The laboratory is normally an entity separate from the firm that drilled the borings and collected the samples, although some consulting firms have their own in-house laboratories or are affiliated with a laboratory. The consultant contracts with the laboratory to analyze the samples. In these instances, the consultant, not the user of the Phase II environmental assessment, is the laboratory's client.

Most commercial laboratories are certified by a professional organization, such as the American Industrial Hygiene Association. In addition, some state regulatory agencies require or operate state registration programs. The U.S. Environmental Protection Agency (EPA) does not operate a general certification program for laboratories, although for Superfund projects the lab must be approved under the contract laboratory program. To meet the certification requirements, laboratories must implement QA/QC programs. As part of a QA/QC program, a laboratory must analyze test samples, keep appropriate records, and perform routine instrument maintenance. Most report users rely on their consultants to select laboratories that have implemented appropriate QA/QC programs.

Analysis Methods and Detection Levels

The EPA has established standard analytical methods for analyzing samples. Some states have developed different analytical procedures. Which method should be followed depends on the circumstances. Most laboratories will use EPA- or state-approved methods in analyzing a sample. The specific method used by the laboratory is indicated on the laboratory report and will depend on the suspected contaminants.

Over the last several years, analytical devices and methods have improved significantly, and laboratories now can detect contaminants in minute quantities. Whereas concentrations were typically reported in parts per million (ppm), contaminants now can be measured in ppb, parts per trillion, and even parts per quadrillion.

Despite the detection levels of these devices, each result has a range of uncertainty that depends on the instrument, method, and contaminant. For example, if a laboratory report states that sample A contains 50 ppb of a compound and sample B contains 60 ppb of the same compound, it appears that sample B has a higher concentration than sample A. If, however, the range of error or uncertainty for the method and compound is equal to or greater than 10 ppb, that may not be an accurate conclusion. In other words, if the range of error is 10 ppb, any reported value that is 10 ppb greater than or less than the reported value for a separate sample may represent the same concentration of a contaminant. Consequently, in comparing the reported value of 50 ppb for sample A, any value for sample B between 40 ppb and 60 ppb may represent the same concentration.

The Physical Chemistry of Contaminants

Laboratory reports produced during an environmental site assessment may indicate contamination. The Phase II environmental site assessment process will then conclude by reporting the extent, identity, and concentrations of contaminants at the site assessed and should interpret these results in light of the contaminants' physical properties and the site's environmental setting to help the report user evaluate the contamination problem.

This section of the chapter addresses the physical properties of contaminants, which relate to how contaminants behave in air, soil, and groundwater.

Contaminant Categories

Contaminants that exhibit similar physical and chemical properties are grouped into categories. This provides a way to understand and label many contaminants. By understanding the physical and chemical properties of particular categories of contaminants, one can draw general conclusions regarding how the contaminants should behave in soils and groundwater (usually called the subsurface).

Common contaminants can be grouped into three general categories based on volatility, which is the tendency to evaporate: (1) volatile organic compounds (VOCs), such as gasoline and solvents; (2) semivolatile organic compounds (SVOCs), such as tars, oils, and pesticides; and (3) inorganics, such as metals. VOCs and SVOCs can be further grouped according to whether the compound contains elements such as chlorine or bromine, known as halogens. Generally, these five groups describe the contaminants commonly found in soils and groundwater: halogenated VOCs, nonhalogenated VOCs, halogenated SVOCs, nonhalogenated SVOCs, and inorganics.

Halogenated VOCs

The primary physical property of halogenated VOCs is a high vapor pressure, which manifests as an increased tendency to evaporate. These chemical properties are due to the presence of halogens, such as chlorine or bromine, which make the compounds less stable and more reactive. Contaminants in this group include carbon tetrachloride, trichloroethylene (TCE), chloroform, methylene chloride, and ethylene dibromide. Halogenated VOCs are commonly found in degreasing solvents. Degreasing solvents are used at automobile repair shops to clean parts, at industrial facilities to clean products before painting, and at commercial facilities to clean equipment and vehicles.

Nonhalogenated VOCs

Nonhalogenated VOCs also are characterized by a tendency to evaporate, but they do not contain any halogens. Examples include various ketones such as acetone or methyl ethyl ketone (MEK) and furans such as tetrahydrofuran. Ketones and furans are commonly found in solvents. Also included in this group are chemical compounds referred to as aromatic compounds (because they evaporate and cause an aroma), including benzene, toluene, and xylene. Aromatics are constituents of hydrocarbon fuel and fuel oils such as gasoline and diesel fuel.

Halogenated and Nonhalogenated SVOCs

Halogenated SVOCs have a relatively lower tendency to evaporate than halogenated VOCs. PCBs, many pesticides, chlorinated benzenes, and phenols fall into this group.

Similarly, nonhalogenated SVOCs have a relatively lower tendency to evaporate than nonhalogenated VOCs. This group includes polyaromatic hydrocarbons (PAHs, also referred to as polynuclear aromatic hydrocarbons or PNAs), such as naphthalene and fluorene, and nonchlorinated phenols, such as cresol and dinitrophenol. PAHs are constituents of low-fraction hydrocarbon products, such as coal, asphalt, and tar.

Physical and Chemical Properties of Contaminants

The physical and chemical properties of contaminants affect their movement through soil and groundwater. Usually called the "subsurface fate and transport" of the contaminants, this information helps to evaluate the problem presented by the contamination.

Subsurface contaminant movement and interaction depends on the physical and chemical properties of the contaminants and on chemical and biological processes affecting contaminants. Physical and chemical properties of contaminants include water solubility, vapor pressure, density, and kinematic viscosity.

Water Solubility

Water solubility is a physical property that refers to the extent to which a contaminant will mix with or dissolve in water. Various factors, such as pH (measuring acidity or alkalinity), temperature, and the presence of dissolved salts or minerals in the water, can affect a contaminant's water solubility.[8]

Chemicals range in solubility from completely miscible compounds, such as some alcohols, to compounds whose solubility is so low that a physical dividing line can be seen between a mixture of water and the low-solubility liquid.

Contaminants that are highly soluble will dissolve in water. Thus, when rainwater infiltrates the soils and percolates toward the groundwater, highly soluble contaminants travel with it. As a result, water soluble contaminants tend to migrate deeper and more quickly into the subsurface than contaminants with low solubility. Water soluble contaminants can cause a more widespread environmental problem.

Vapor Pressure

Vapor pressure refers to how readily vapors evaporate from a contaminant in a pure liquid phase. Vapor pressure is heavily dependent on temperature, with increased temperature causing increased vapor pressure.

A contaminant's volatility is directly proportional to its vapor pressure. Volatility describes a contaminant's tendency to evaporate from the aqueous phase (i.e., when dissolved in water). In contrast, vapor pressure measures a contaminant's tendency to evaporate from its pure liquid phase. Consequently, volatility is measured by dividing a contaminant's vapor pressure by its water solubility.[9]

Density

The density of a contaminant indicates whether it is heavier or lighter than water. Water has a density of 1 gram per milliliter (g/mL). A contaminant with a density greater than 1 g/mL will pass or "sink" through water. Highly water soluble contaminants, however, will dissolve into the aqueous phase while passing through water. Contaminants with densities less than 1 g/mL will "float" on water. Specific weight and specific gravity are equivalent methods of expressing density.

The density of a contaminant is usually described by its behavior in water.

- "Floaters" are low-solubility contaminants that are less dense than water and float on top of water. The density of gasoline is less than water; thus gasoline will float.
- "Mixers" are high-solubility contaminants that have densities near that of water. The density of phenol is at or near water and phenol is soluble; thus phenol will mix.
- "Sinkers" are low-solubility contaminants that are more dense than water. As a result, they sink to the bottom of water. The density of TCE is greater than water; thus TCE will sink.

The density of contaminants, especially contaminants with very low water solubilities, is important for site cleanup. For example, TCE, a commonly encountered solvent, has a density of 1.46 g/mL (greater than water) and is moderately water soluble. As a result, TCE will sink through underground water until it stops at an impermeable geology, such as clay. Because it moves by gravity, TCE may migrate along the impermeable layer, ending up far from the original point of entry.[10]

Kinematic Viscosity

Kinematic viscosity measures a contaminant's resistance to flow in the subsurface. It accounts for the contaminant's density and the ease with which it percolates through the subsurface. The lower the kinematic viscosity of a compound, the greater is its tendency to migrate downward.

The Toxicity of Contaminants

Each day people ingest, drink, or breathe thousands of different chemical compounds. Yet government agencies force private parties to spend substantial sums cleaning up certain compounds. The reason is that these targeted compounds have been shown to be toxic to humans. A contaminant's toxicity depends on (1) the harm it will cause and (2) how much of it will reach the person affected. In environmental practice, the first part is called the "toxicological risk" and the second part is called the "exposure."

Contaminant Toxicity

Contaminant toxicity is evaluated through a toxicity assessment, a necessary step in the risk assessment process at sites where hazardous substances have been released. The risks to human health can be estimated by determining how much of a contaminant an individual will be exposed to from the site and factoring in the extent of harm the contaminant may cause to humans. Contaminants are divided into two categories, depending on the type of harm they may cause to humans: noncarcinogenic contaminants are those that adversely affect the organs of the body without causing cancer, and carcinogenic contaminants are those that present a risk of cancer.

The key term concerning noncarcinogenic effects is "reference dose" (RfD). The greater a contaminant's RfD, the less toxic a contaminant is. Likewise, contaminants with smaller RfDs are more toxic. For carcinogenic contaminants, slope factors are used to estimate the probability of developing cancer after being exposed to a contaminant. Conversely to RfDs, the greater the slope factor, the more toxic the contaminant is. The EPA lists RfDs and slope factors in the Health Effects Assessments Summary Tables (HEAST) and as final work-group-reviewed values on a computer database called the Integrated Risk Information System (IRIS). Contaminant toxicity is a relatively new area, and the EPA is continually reviewing and updating toxicity information on contaminants and their corresponding RfDs and slope factors.

The approach to evaluating contaminant toxicity is similar to the Phase II approach to evaluating contamination. Once a Phase I assessment reports an environmental risk, Phase II environmental assessment work evaluates the nature of the contamination and the extent of the site affected. Similarly, a toxicity assessment evaluates the nature and extent of the risk posed by the contaminants to human health and the environment. Contaminants vary in toxicity, and a toxicity assessment identifies the toxicological risks presented by each contaminant at a site.

The amount of contaminant that a person is exposed to depends on the contaminant's chemical and physical properties and on the site's characteristics. This information is gathered in the exposure assessment.

Exposure Assessment

An exposure assessment estimates how much of a contaminant humans and the environment will receive from the site. The assessment determines who may be exposed to the contaminants, how the exposure will occur (e.g., by way of breathing, eating, and touching a contaminant), how much of the contaminant they will be exposed to, and for how long.

Characterization of Exposure Setting

The first step in an exposure assessment is to evaluate the physical characteristics of the site and identify the relevant population that may be exposed to contaminants. The information collected will help determine by which exposure pathway the human population will contact a contaminant and the quantity to which they may be exposed. The important physical characteristics of a site include climate, vegetation, groundwater hydrology, soil type, geology, and presence of surface water.

To characterize the population at risk of exposure, information must be gathered on how near to the site people are located, what types of activities people are involved in near the site, and whether any individuals are in the vicinity who may be more sensitive to the contaminant than others. Children, the elderly, and pregnant and nursing women are at greater risk because they are either more sensitive to contaminants or exhibit behavior patterns that may increase their exposure. Children, for example, are more likely to eat contaminated soil than adults are.

Identification of Exposure Pathways

The second step in an exposure assessment is to identify the potential human exposure pathways at a site. The exposure pathway describes the means by which individuals are exposed to a contaminant. There are three possible exposure pathways: inhalation, ingestion, or contact with the skin. A contaminant's physical and chemical properties affect its fate and transport in the environment and, consequently, the pathways by which a person would likely come into contact with the contaminant. A consultant conducting an exposure assessment will use his or her knowledge of a contaminant's physical and chemical properties to determine the likelihood of exposure through each pathway.

Quantification of Exposure

The final step in an exposure assessment is to calculate the intake or amount of a contaminant to which individuals will be exposed. In this step, values are assigned to all the qualitative information gathered in the previous steps so as to calculate a number that represents the toxicological risk presented by a contaminant. Intakes are calculated for each contaminant of concern, each exposure pathway, and every class of person at risk. The risk is then calculated for noncarcinogenic and carcinogenic effects. When the risk calculations show unacceptable levels of risk, there are unacceptable concentration levels of the contaminants.

Target Cleanup Levels: How Clean Is Clean?

Environmental laws provide that contaminated soil, sediment, and groundwater must be cleaned up. Inevitably, a key question is how much must be cleaned up, or, just how clean is clean? The last section examined the toxicity of contaminants. Toxicity depends on the amount or dose of the contaminant and the manner of exposure. Because "clean" really means not toxic, a contaminant cleanup standard must ensure that the amount or dose of the contaminant remaining after the cleanup will not be toxic if the contaminant is inhaled, ingested, or absorbed. In plain English, what's left can't hurt.

This section provides a brief overview of the process of establishing target cleanup levels. An example of a target cleanup level is 5 ppb benzene in groundwater. In other words, all the groundwater that has benzene in concentrations greater than 5 ppb must be remediated. Since there are thousands of hazardous substances, this section does not spell out all the possible target cleanup levels. Indeed, because acceptable levels depend on a site's individual characteristics, listing all the target cleanup levels is not possible. Instead, this section summarizes the process of selecting the concentration levels used to clean up dirty, albeit sometimes naturally dirty, contaminated soils, sediment, and groundwater.

Superfund Framework

The Comprehensive Environmental Response, Compensation, and Liability Act (CERCLA), commonly known as Superfund, provides a framework for cleaning up hazardous substances released into the environment. A cleanup level, also referred to as a cleanup goal or a cleanup standard, is the level of contamination that a cleanup must attain in a specific medium, such as soil, surface water, or groundwater, to reduce the environmental and human health threat posed by contamination at a hazardous substance site. Cleanup levels need to be determined for each contaminant present at a site and are typically expressed as a concentration of a contaminant in a particular medium. For example, the concentration of a contaminant in soil is generally expressed in ppm or, equivalently, milligrams per kilogram (mg/kg).

Two important goals for private parties undertaking cleanup are finality and cost recovery. First, private parties want the cleanup to be final so that the EPA or a state agency will not demand further cleanup action in the future. Second, private parties often want to recover some or all of the cleanup costs from other responsible parties. Cleanup costs can be recovered under CERCLA only if the cleanup is consistent with EPA regulations in the National Oil and Hazardous Substance Contingency Plan (NOHSCP/NCP). One problem with reaching these goals is that the EPA has not established generic cleanup levels but instead chooses site-specific cleanup levels.

Consequently, in many instances private parties selecting cleanup levels look to Superfund sites where the EPA has established cleanup levels. Cleanup levels for contaminants at Superfund sites must satisfy two criteria: (1) they must attain legally applicable or relevant and appropriate federal and state requirements, standards, criteria or limitations, often referred to as the ARAR requirement; and (2) they must be protective of human health and the environment, which means that the amount of contaminants remaining will not be toxic. ARARs are substantive environmental protection requirements (e.g., 5 ppb benzene in drinking water) promulgated under federal or state environmental laws or facility siting laws. If an ARAR is not available to establish a cleanup level, an assessment of the risk from the contamination must be performed to establish cleanup levels.

Contaminant-specific cleanup levels, or ARARs, have been promulgated for only a few contaminants. Thus, cleanup levels usually must be set through the risk assessment process. The complex risk assessment process, however, requires numerous risk assumptions and may not predict EPA cleanup levels effectively.

The EPA and some state agencies are attempting to standardize cleanup levels for contaminants. Standardized levels would streamline cleanups by eliminating some of the uncertainty involved in selecting cleanup levels. Standard cleanup levels, however, leave little room for adjusting for site use.

Summary

Cleanup levels are established through the risk assessment process to satisfy applicable federal and state requirements as well as to ensure that the contamination remaining at the site is protective of human health.

Notes

The author gratefully acknowledges the contributions of Jeremy A. Gibson, Kathleen L. Nooney, Robert M. Baratta, Jr., and Robert M. Wood. The author also thanks Woodward-Clyde Consultants for their help with the risk assessment portion of this chapter.

1. A PID can be used in two ways. The "tip" or probe of the instrument can be placed near the sample to analyze the fumes escaping into the open air. Alternatively, the sample can be placed in a jar and the fumes allowed to collect at the top. The tip of the PID is then inserted through the top of the jar to measure the vapors in the "headspace." Headspace analysis is better for detecting lower concentrations of contaminants, but it is still only an indicator of relative levels rather than an accurate measurement of contamination.

2. Publications are available that suggest the "suite" of contaminants that should be investigated depending on the potential source of contamination. *See, e.g.*, U.S. EPA, RCRA Facility Investigation Guidance Document (May 1989). Laboratories usually use sample analysis methods established by the EPA.

3. "Geologic cross sections" of the site can assist Phase II report readers. A geologic cross section is a diagram of the vertical cross section of the geology at a site using the geology information from the boring and monitoring well logs. The diagram helps the user visualize the characteristics of the material through which the contamination and groundwater move.

4. Sample analysis methods also have a "practical qualification level" (pql). The pql is the minimum concentration level that the method or laboratory instrument can practically measure, like the resolution of a telescope.

5. To report high concentration levels accurately, the laboratory technician typically dilutes the sample to measure chemical concentrations within the accurate range of the method or instrument. The laboratory report usually indicates the dilution factor for that sample. Dilution of the sample, however, may also result in dilution of chemical concentrations below the mdl for other chemicals. For example, if the mdl for a chemical is 10 ppb and the sample is diluted by a factor of 10, the mdl for that chemical increases to 100 ppb. To measure low concentration levels of particular chemicals in samples in which very high concentration levels of other chemicals are present, special sample preparation techniques and laboratory methods must be used.

6. As part of the numbering system, a prefix may be included to indicate whether a boring was completed as a monitoring well. Usually, the prefix SB indicates a soil boring, while the prefix MW indicates a monitoring well.

7. Because the metric units for weight and volume of water are equivalent, groundwater samples are reported in both ppb and ppm or ug/L and mg/L, respectively.

8. Contaminants are sometimes described by the "phase" in which the contaminant exists. "Solid phase" refers to the contaminant as a solid. "Liquid phase" refers to the contaminant as a pure liquid; pure contaminant liquid is also referred to as "product" or "product phase." "Vapor phase" refers to the contaminant as a gas in another medium, such as soil or air. "Aqueous" or "dissolved phase" refers to the contaminant in solution with water. "Nonaqueous phase"

refers to the liquid phase of the contaminant in contact with water, where the concentration of the contaminant in the water is at the solubility limit.

9. This relationship is known as Henry's Law Constant and is used to characterize a contaminant's volatility. The greater the Henry's Law Constant, the greater the tendency to volatilize from the aqueous phase.

10. Contaminants that are heavier than water and sink below the aquifer are referred to as dense nonaqueous phase liquids (DNAPLs). DNAPLs pose detection and removal problems because of a tendency to gather in pools far below the aquifer, at locations that depend on local geological conditions. Contaminants that are lighter than water and float on top of the aquifer are referred to as light nonaqueous phase liquids (LNAPLs). Because LNAPLs are usually volatile, they can move along the aquifer and release vapors that can migrate into subsurface structures, such as basements. Gasoline will form an LNAPL and can present an explosion hazard.

PART III

The Transaction: Structural, Tax, and Other Business Issues and Implications

~

CHAPTER 11

Structuring the Transaction to Allocate Environmental Liability

GERARD A. CARON

In any significant real estate transaction or corporate acquisition, parties to the transaction and their counsel must acknowledge and address the substantial environmental risks associated with owning or operating real property and related business activities. While it is certainly true that property associated with manufacturing uses, past or present, often poses the greatest environmental risks, even residential and commercial uses of property may have related environmental risks and liabilities. All interested parties in the transaction should address potential environmental issues right from the beginning to ensure that unattended issues do not threaten the viability of a transaction later in the negotiations. Parties must also understand that many environmental liabilities are different and much more stringent than other types of liabilities and require special attention and special contract terms. Parties cannot assume that general provisions of agreements effectively deal with potential environmental liabilities. For instance, an "as is" clause in a purchase and sale agreement will almost certainly not protect the seller from potential future claims under state or federal Superfund statutes. Moreover, while there are certain general rules that may be followed in dealing with environmental risk and liabilities in a transaction, each transaction is different and requires specific provisions tailored to the particular facts of the given transaction. There is no set formula that will be effective in every transaction.

This chapter is primarily focused on contractual provisions related to the acquisition of property or business operations that may have potential environmental liabilities. The chapter also touches briefly on other types of transactions, such as financing and leasing, which may also involve contractual allocation of environmental liabilities. Finally, this chapter outlines certain methods available to limit the potential environmental liabilities taken on by a purchaser in acquiring property or business operations.

Early Considerations

Even before a potential purchaser proceeds with a formal offer, letter of intent, or acquisition agreement, preliminary investigations may be conducted to identify any known environmental liabilities that may exist with respect to the property or business operations. Particular attention should be paid to any disclosures by the seller in offering memoranda or other promotional materials relating to potential environmental liabilities associated with the subject property or business operations. Follow-up questions may be posed to the seller to get additional information that supports the seller's assessment of the potential magnitude of the problems identified. Even if the seller is convincing in providing its assessment of potential environmental liabilities, the purchaser should understand that the seller's assessment may rest on outdated or otherwise incomplete information characterizing the relevant issues. The potential purchaser should determine right from the beginning whether it has an adequate comfort level with the known environmental compliance aspects of the seller's business and related conditions on the seller's property. In light of the significant costs and time associated with environmental due diligence leading up to an acquisition of property or business operations, the potential purchaser should make an affirmative decision early on that the deal still makes sense notwithstanding the available information on potential environmental liabilities involved in the transaction.

Offer or Letter of Intent Stage

If a party decides to go forward with an offer or letter of intent, both sides must be prepared to negotiate contract terms dealing with environmental liabilities, even at this early stage. Some transactions may proceed right to the acquisition agreement without a formal offer or letter of intent. In such situations, the same issues addressed here would need to be considered in negotiating the acquisition agreement, and particular attention would have to be given to the timing implications of any due diligence requirements.

First, the purchaser should condition its obligations to acquire the property or business operations on satisfactory environmental due diligence. To carry out these investigations, the purchaser will need access to the seller's property and will need the seller to cooperate by providing available documentation on the known environmental issues associated with the property and related business operations. The purchaser may want to retain the right to walk away from the transaction if significant environmental problems are uncovered, even if the seller offers to further investigate and remediate the problems. The purchaser needs to consider its intended use of the property as well as the resale potential of the property. While a particular issue may not be overly troublesome to the purchaser, the purchaser needs to consider whether prospective tenants or future buyers may be concerned about the same issue. Second, the timetable for the purchase agreement and closing must be adjusted to accommodate the need for environmental due diligence. Such investigations would likely include performance of a Phase I environmental site assessment, business records review, and interview of selected current employees in property or environmental management areas and may also include sampling and testing of soil, groundwater, surface water, and indoor air. If testing is necessary, this could require a significant period of time, depending on weather conditions, the availability of consultants, difficulties in gaining access to the property, and other factors. Third, the parties should understand that the purchase price may have to be adjusted in the event environmental investigations uncover material environmental liabilities previously unknown to the purchaser.

The seller must be mindful that any investigations carried out by the potential purchaser or on behalf of the potential purchaser may uncover environmental conditions that trigger notification or other requirements imposed on the current property owner. Moreover, the purchaser or the purchaser's lender may require the seller to satisfy those requirements before transfer of the property. In the event the potential purchaser decides not to proceed with the transaction based on the environmental conditions that are uncovered, the seller may be required to disclose the conditions to the next interested purchaser.

Though the seller or the purchaser may engage the environmental consultant to perform the site investigations, the purchaser may want to retain the consultant directly to ensure that the purchaser receives the information first hand and from a purchaser's perspective. Otherwise, the seller's consultant may attempt to gloss over important environmental issues to maximize the chances of obtaining a quick sign-off from the purchaser. Some potential purchasers would prefer to have the seller engage the environmental consultant to help distance the purchaser from any liabilities uncovered in the investigations and to ensure that the seller will be responsible for funding the consultant's services. If the seller engages the environmental consultant, the purchaser should require a letter from the consultant stating that the purchaser may rely on and have the use of environmental reports produced by that consultant.

As a result of preacquisition diligence, the purchaser may attempt to carve out of the transaction those properties or other assets that carry potential environmental liabilities. The purchaser must consider whether the remaining property, or properties, and other assets are still viable for the purchaser's intended purpose. Moreover, as discussed later on, if the purchaser will be treated under the law as a successor to the seller, the purchaser may be unable to dissociate itself from the potential environmental liabilities.

Acquisition Agreement Stage

If the parties proceed to the purchase and sale or acquisition agreement stage, there are several additional contract provisions that should be negotiated to deal with actual and potential environmental liabilities. A critical goal of both parties should be to ensure that all of the provisions that may pertain to environmental liabilities contained in different sections of the agreement actually fit together in a coherent and consistent manner. Otherwise, a desired contract term contained in one section of the agreement may essentially be undone by another section of the agreement. A second critical goal, and possibly the most important goal for both parties, should be to resolve any ambiguity in the contract terms dealing with environmental risk. Given the large amount of litigation that has occurred over the last few years involving interpretation of contract terms as they might apply to environmental contamination, parties should work hard to agree on language that clarifies the parties' rights and obligations under the agreement. In cases where such rights and obligations are not clearly defined in the agreement, the parties run the risk of having serious disagreements and complications develop on environmental issues even before the closing.

Representations and Warranties

The seller should be expected to provide the purchaser with a number of representations and warranties relating to environmental conditions on the property and environmental aspects of the seller's operations. These representations and warranties would typically include information regarding the following items:

- Violations of environmental and health and safety laws and regulations, including, but not limited to, failure to possess necessary permits, approvals, and other governmental authorizations
- Generation, storage, treatment, handling, processing, and disposal of hazardous waste on the site

- Presence of any hazardous materials or petroleum products on the site
- Existence of any underground storage tanks, underground pipelines, surface impoundments, or dry wells, whether active or inactive, on the property
- Releases of hazardous materials or petroleum products on the site or in the vicinity of the site
- Storage, treatment, and disposal of hazardous materials off the site at a location that is or could be a Superfund site
- Liens imposed by the local, state, or federal government for environmental costs incurred by the government
- Consent decrees, compliance orders, and administrative orders regarding the site and operations thereon
- Notices under citizen suit provisions of any environmental laws
- Requests for information or notices from the local, state, or federal government concerning environmental and health and safety matters
- Complaints, claims, and threats of enforcement action and lawsuits with respect to environmental and health and safety matters
- Notices concerning potential responsibility for Superfund sites in connection with disposal of wastes off the site

The representations and warranties should focus on current operations, conditions, and liabilities as well as past operations and conditions that could reasonably lead to environmental liabilities in the future. A representation should also be included confirming that the seller has made "due inquiry" in collecting the information provided in the environmental representations and warranties. If such a representation is included, the parties will need to agree on the scope of due inquiry and, in particular, whether it requires the seller to make inquires of third parties. The seller should carefully consider whether it has satisfied the due inquiry standard because a failure to conduct due inquiry could result in a breach of the representations and warranties. A representation may also be included confirming that the seller is aware of no information that indicates that the company's ability to comply with environmental requirements may be adversely affected by some imminent change in circumstances.

Materiality Standard

The seller may seek to limit the representations and warranties to a "materiality" standard in light of the plethora and complexity of environmental requirements that may apply under federal, state, and local laws. Particularly in a large transaction involving the transfer of multiple properties, the seller may take the position that perfect compliance with all environmental laws is impossible and that the seller should not have to schedule every exception to broad environmental representations and warranties. Though this position is understandable, such a standard creates some ambiguity in the agreement since there may be substantial disagreement about what is and is not material in a given transaction. The purchaser may agree to narrow the scope of certain representations and warranties in an effort to resist imposition of a materiality standard. One alternative to the materiality standard is an "aggregate materiality" standard whereby issues do not have to be disclosed as exceptions to the representations and warranties unless they are expected to be material, either individually or in the aggregate. The aggregate materiality standard may be particularly appropriate in a multiproperty transaction in which the schedule of exceptions could be unmanageably long and the purchaser's threshold for concern about discrete environmental issues may be somewhat higher than in a small transaction.

Predecessor Operations

The parties to an agreement also need to decide on which operations are covered by the representations and warranties in situations in which predecessors may have conducted operations on the seller's property or where other unrelated parties have conducted operations on the property. On the one hand, the seller may have serious reservations about extending any representations and warranties to the activities of other parties given that it may have only limited information about such activities. On the other hand, the purchaser may be inheriting significant environmental liabilities associated with those other parties and needs to be adequately informed about those potential liabilities. One compromise available to the parties is to limit any representations and warranties regarding other entities' activities to the best knowledge of the seller. This issue is of greatest importance where past uses of the property include manufacturing or other industrial operations.

Best Knowledge

The seller may attempt to limit the environmental representations and warranties to its "best knowledge" rather than have the representations and warranties be absolute. This limitation is arguably more appropriate in a transaction involving large operations or many properties, since the seller may have difficulty commanding all the appropriate information held by many different employees. This limitation may also be appropriate when the seller is expected to provide representations and warranties relating to operations by predecessors or other parties, such as tenants and adjoining landowners. If a best knowledge standard is included, the purchaser should ensure that the seller's knowledge includes any information obtained by its environmental consultants. The purchaser should also understand that a best knowledge standard may substantially limit the effect and value of the seller's representations and warranties and constitutes a major concession to the seller. For instance, the purchaser may have limited recourse against the seller in a situation in which a previously undetected abandoned underground storage tank is discovered on the property after the acquisition if the seller represented to its best knowledge that no underground storage tanks were present on the property. Obviously, if the representations provided were absolute, the seller may be contractually responsible for costs associated with removal of the underground storage tank even after the closing.

Need for Accuracy

The seller should take the representations and warranties very seriously because the purchaser may be allowed to terminate the agreement in the event of a breach of the terms of the representations and warranties. In addition, any environmental indemnity to be provided by the purchaser may be conditioned on the accuracy of the seller's representations and warranties regarding the property and business operations. For example, even though the purchaser may otherwise take responsibility for liability in connection with certain past operations if such operations were carried out in compliance with applicable governmental approvals, the purchaser may be able to disclaim any responsibility for such liability if it later discovers undisclosed historic noncompliance. Moreover, the purchaser should be concerned if the seller is willing to make very broad representations and warranties without any apparent "due inquiry." Such conduct could indicate that any indemnity to be provided by the seller will be of limited practical value. Such a cavalier attitude could also reflect that the seller does not have an appropriate understanding of the significance and scope of applicable environmental requirements.

Duration of Representations and Warranties

The agreement should specify how long the seller's environmental representations and warranties survive after the closing. This may have important implications for the effect of the seller's indemnity, given that the seller's indemnity may be tied to breaches of the representations and warranties. While the seller will attempt to keep the representations and warranties open for as limited a time as possible, the purchaser will obviously attempt to negotiate for a longer time frame. Given that environmental liabilities often develop many years after the underlying operations take place, strong arguments favor keeping the representations and warranties open for an extended period of time. If the representations and warranties are only effective for a limited period of time, the purchaser may have strong incentive to uncover any site conditions early on to have potential recourse against the seller.

Schedule with Exceptions

Environmental representations and warranties generally provide a schedule listing specific exceptions. The parties should make an effort to prepare and review the draft schedule of exceptions to the representations and warranties early in the process. Often the schedule of exceptions raises additional potential environmental liability issues that need to be addressed well before the papers are ready to be signed. Providing the schedule just before execution of the agreement may cause significant and costly delays in the transaction. Moreover, the purchaser may overreact to any newly disclosed issues on the theory that the seller must have been trying to brush over potentially serious environmental issues.

The seller may attempt merely to reference attached documents that contain information that constitutes exceptions to the representations and warranties. This approach may create serious ambiguity about what is actually being excepted out from the representations and warranties and should generally be resisted by the purchaser. It may be very difficult, if not impossible, for the purchaser and its consultants to comprehend fully all the potential implications of items referenced in a group of environment-related business records and reports. The documents may also contain inconsistencies about certain property conditions, thus making it unclear whether those conditions are intended to be exceptions to the representations and warranties. Furthermore, years later it may be difficult to locate all the documents referenced in the schedule, thus making it impossible to interpret or apply the agreement. Again, a critical goal of both parties should be to remove any ambiguities in the agreement about the intended allocation of environmental liabilities between the parties. Achieving this goal may take additional time and effort, but it will help minimize future disagreements between the parties.

Scope of Definitions

Much of the success of the environment-related contract provisions in comprehensively and effectively reflecting the parties' intention will be in the definition of key terms such as "environmental law," "hazardous material," "hazardous waste," and "the company" transferring the property. Typically these terms are defined very broadly in such agreements, unless a particular term is intentionally cut back at the request of one of the parties. With respect to the definition of "environmental laws," the parties should state whether that term is intended to cover only existing environmental requirements or also requirements that may come into existence at a later time. With respect to the definition of "hazardous material," "hazardous waste," and "environmental law," one approach is to provide general, all-encompassing definitions instead of providing a long list of specific pollutants, wastes, and statutory provisions that are covered by those definitions. With respect to the definition of "company," the parties should clarify whether the term is meant to cover all related entities, entities for which the company may be responsible for potential environmental liabilities, or both. If this type of broad definition is adopted, the seller should consider the implications on the scope of its representations and warranties and indemnity.

Covenants

The acquisition agreement may also contain covenants whereby the seller is obligated to take specified actions before the closing. First, a covenant may be included obligating the seller to ensure that all activities and operations on the property will fully comply with all environmental requirements up to and at the time of closing. Second, a covenant may be included obligating the seller to provide the purchaser with any additional documentation in the seller's possession regarding environmental conditions and liabilities in connection with the property or business operations, which documentation has not already been provided to the purchaser. Third, the parties may agree to a covenant obligating the seller to provide timely notice to the purchaser of any development relating to potential environmental conditions and liabilities associated with the property or business operations before the closing.

Contractual Indemnification

A fundamental negotiation point between the parties is to determine what type of environmental indemnifications, if any, will be built into the agreement. A common indemnification in an assets acquisition is for the seller to indemnify the purchaser against all environmental liabilities incurred as a result of the seller's operations before the closing, with a reciprocal indemnity from the purchaser for all liabilities incurred as a result of purchaser's operations after the closing.

Another common environmental indemnification is an indemnity provided by the seller for any breaches in the representations and warranties provided in the acquisition agreement. The parties should ensure that the environmental indemnity fits together with any general indemnification provisions in other sections of the agreement. The parties should clarify the intended effect of any general indemnity on environmental liabilities that are specifically dealt with in an environmental indemnity. Though a general indemnity in an acquisition agreement may be extended to environmental liabilities, the parties should seriously consider drafting a separate indemnity for environmental liabilities. Such a provision can be drafted to address the significance and complexity of potential environmental liabilities. The indemnified party should also carefully consider the financial health of the indemnitor in assessing the value of the indemnity, since the indemnity otherwise has no benefit.[1] Furthermore, receiving an environmental indemnity is no substitute for carrying out adequate environmental diligence before the acquisition. While both types of protection are important, adequate diligence is even more critical than pressing for a broad environmental indemnity.

Deductible or Cap

The parties must determine whether the environmental indemnity should be subject to a deductible or cap. In some agreements, the duty to contribute to certain liabilities will not come about until some specified amount of liabilities has been incurred by the purchaser. In other agreements, no deductible is set but the outside liability is capped at a specific dollar amount. Increasingly, the issue of a cap on environmental indemnities has become a heavily negotiated aspect of most transactions. The battle is really about which party should have to live with the risk of some unknown or unquantifiable environmental liability that may be incurred in the future. The seller may be less concerned with this issue when it believes insurance coverage is available to cover at least some of those potential liabilities. The purchaser should be particularly hesitant to provide an unlimited indemnity that may relate to historic contamination unless it has considerable information about past operations and activities on the properties being acquired.

Predecessor Operations

Particularly in a bright line preclosing or postclosing operations indemnity, it is important to clarify whether "preclosing operations" applies only to the seller's operations or to the operations of predecessors as well. It may be difficult for the seller to provide such an indemnity if it is not a legal successor to the predecessors or if it has inadequate information about the nature of the predecessors' operations and waste disposal practices. Moreover, past manufacturing operations by predecessors may have been conducted before environmental laws pertaining to hazardous waste, treatment, storage, and disposal, and thus may pose a substantial risk of on-site contamination. Arguably, however, the seller as current owner of real property may already have those liabilities and the purchaser may insist that the seller retain all such preexisting environmental liabilities in the transaction. Whatever the final decision is after negotiations, the parties should make sure that the contract language is clear with respect to the scope of preclosing operations referenced in any indemnity.

Losses

A critical point of clarification that should be discussed and reflected in the agreement is whether the environmental indemnity is only intended to cover "losses," that is, liability to third parties and liabilities incurred as a result of governmental requirements, rather than other, discretionary-type costs that may be incurred by the indemnitee. Unless the indemnity makes clear that the parties intend it to apply to other types of costs or expenses as well, the indemnity may be construed to extend only to losses.[2] The indemnitee should understand that courts will carefully scrutinize an indemnification claim regarding losses unrelated to any third-party liability to confirm that the parties intended the indemnity provision to have the unusual effect of covering such expenses. Limiting the indemnity to losses offers an indemnitor much more comfort than having the indemnity extend to other types of costs or expenses, which may be largely discretionary on the part of the indemnitee. If the indemnification is not limited to traditional losses, the parties should consider imposing some standard by which the indemnitee's costs will be measured. Otherwise, the indemnitor's exposure under the indemnity could essentially be limitless, encompassing discretionary-type costs incurred by the seller to improve its property or business operations.

Notification and Opportunity to Defend

Most environmental indemnifications include notification and opportunity to defend provisions with which the indemnitee must comply if it is to assert a successful claim under the indemnification. The indemnitee will be expected to provide timely notice to the indemnitor of any loss for which the party intends to seek indemnification. Often the indemnitee will also be expected to provide the indemnitor with the opportunity of taking over or participating in the defense of any claim asserted for which the indemnitee will look to the indemnitor for recovery. If such provisions are included in the agreement, they should constitute conditions to the indemnitee's right to assert a claim under the indemnity. These provisions are likely to be strictly enforced by courts and therefore should be complied with in a timely manner. The parties may agree to include a provision stating that untimely notice of an indemnity claim will only defeat the claim if the indemnitor is prejudiced by the delay in notice.

Environmental Report

The parties may consider referencing an environmental assessment report in an indemnification provision and having the indemnification extend to liabilities or conditions referenced in the report. Though this option may seem attractive during protracted negotiations to simplify already complicated and time consuming drafting discussions, it may create serious problems down the road in trying to determine what liabilities and conditions fall within or outside of the relevant environmental report. Accordingly, any reference to an environmental report may also be supplemented with a list of action items, which are identified in the report, specifically referenced in the indemnification as the intended scope of the indemnification. In addition, the indemnification should state that all parties to the agreement have reviewed the environmental report. Otherwise, the parties could later have substantial disagreements about the intended scope of the indemnification, particularly where the report includes a detailed discussion of past operations at the property and touches on a number of potentially significant environmental liability issues.

Enforceability of Contractual Indemnifications

A key consideration in understanding the effect of any environmental indemnifications should be the enforceability of such provisions. It is generally accepted that contractual allocation of environmental liabilities between parties is enforceable, notwithstanding that it will not release a party from direct liability to the government under the Comprehensive Environmental Response, Compensation, and Liability Act (CERCLA) or similar state Superfund statutes.[3] Though the majority of courts have upheld the validity of such contractual arrangements, a few courts have held that CERCLA precludes the contractual allocation of liability under that statute.[4] Accordingly, parties should understand that there is no guaranty that contractual indemnifications will be effective to shift all environmental liabilities between the parties. Also, no matter how comprehensive an indemnity, it will not insulate a party from direct liability to the government for environmental investigation and remediation costs.

Mediation Clause

The parties may also agree in an indemnification provision that any disputes regarding application of the indemnity to particular circumstances will be resolved by mediation or some other form of alternative dispute resolution. This type of agreement is particularly beneficial to the indemnitee as it may save substantial time and money in pursuing enforcement of the contract.

Clarification of Ambiguities

Given the amount of disputes and related litigation that develop over the intended meaning of indemnifications pertaining to environmental liabilities, parties should carefully work through any ambiguities in the contract language during negotiations. Parties should not find comfort in ambiguous language, given that subsequent disputes on these issues may be time-consuming and expensive and may disrupt the ongoing relationship between the parties. Rather, parties to the agreement should be sure they have a meeting of the minds on environmental indemnification issues and take the time to have this adequately reflected in the contract language.

Cost-Sharing Provisions

One mechanism for dealing with both known and unknown environmental liabilities in a transaction is to include cost-sharing provisions outlining what percentage or dollar amount each contracting party will be expected to contribute toward environmental costs. A benefit of this approach is that both parties will have an incentive to carry out any necessary work efficiently and cost-effectively. This approach is easier to apply with respect to known, quantifiable environmental liabilities and may be less workable with respect to unknown or contingent liabilities. The party that will actually be carrying out the investigatory and/or remedial work should consider having the other party provide a letter of credit, bond, or some other financial assurance mechanism. Alternatively, the parties may set up an escrow account as part of the agreement to hold funds that will later be applied to the anticipated environmental costs. The amount agreed on should reflect a conservative estimate of what the consultant believes the investigatory and remedial costs will be. The agreement may also include a "hold-back" provision to earmark some of the seller's proceeds from the sale toward environmental cleanup. Any cost-sharing arrangement should specify what role each of the parties will have in approving and carrying out any environmental investigations or remediation, as well as what standards apply to the work. If the seller will have continued involvement in the ongoing activities, then the agreement will have to provide for the seller's continued access to the site.

Miscellaneous Provisions

Other relevant provisions in a standard acquisition agreement may include an acknowledgment of property inspection, an "as is where is" clause, and provisions imposing certain obligations on the seller prior to the closing. A provision acknowledging site inspection may actually list known environmental site conditions to confirm both the condition of the property before transfer and the purchaser's knowledge of those conditions. Such a list may be tied to the representations and warranties, the indemnification, or both, or it may serve as a general reference point for determining whether specific contamination is attributable to the seller's or purchaser's operations. An environmental site assessment and possibly an audit of site operations may be necessary to prepare a thorough list of site conditions. An acknowledgment of site inspection should also reference the current use of the property as manufacturing, commercial, retail, or residential, in the event the purchaser later seeks to upgrade the use of the property and recover from the seller the related costs of improvement.

The seller may insist that the agreement contain an "as is" clause to confirm that the purchaser understands that the property is not perfect. Sellers often argue that such clauses place all risks associated with ownership of the property, including CERCLA liability, on the purchaser. Courts, however, have uniformly rejected this argument on the basis that an "as is" clause only precludes breach of warranty claims, not statutory claims such as those based on CERCLA.[5] Moreover, an "as is" clause will probably not protect a seller that has knowledge of a latent defect and fails to disclose it to the purchaser.[6]

Provisions may be included in the agreement requiring the seller to carry out certain work on the property before the closing. The purchaser's obligation to proceed may be conditioned on the satisfactory performance of the specified work by the seller. As a general rule, requiring performance of the necessary work before closing is likely to minimize potential disputes and complications regarding the seller's obligations. While this arrangement may be appropriate with respect to work that may reasonably be performed over a limited period of time, such as a tank removal or removal of accumulated wastes on the property, it may present problems for work that cannot be completed before the closing. One mechanism for dealing with the latter case is to execute a side agreement regarding any performance of work by the seller after the closing. The seller should ensure that it is granted continued access to the site to carry out the agreed-on work and that the standards for what constitutes acceptable work are fixed and reasonably attainable. Otherwise, the purchaser could later attempt to have the seller finance a "gold-plated" cleanup that goes beyond compliance with relevant government requirements.

Other Types of Agreements

Financing Agreements

Financing agreements between lenders and borrowers may involve similar issues necessitating representations and warranties, indemnifications, and covenants regarding the borrower's expected operations on the property. While the lender's potential environmental liabilities may not be as direct or immediate as a purchaser's, its potential exposure for the borrower's activities is significant and necessitates protective terms in the loan agreements. In addition to representations and warranties about the borrower's property and operations and an indemnity for potential environmental liabilities, the lender should get covenants from the borrower with respect to ongoing and future operations. These covenants should include provisions that essentially carry forward traditional environmental representations and warranties (e.g., compliance with permits, laws, agreements, no tanks, no hazardous wastes). The lender should understand that any indemnification provided by the borrower may not have much value, given that the lender would likely seek to enforce the indemnity in situations in which the borrower is no longer financially viable. Again, an environmental indemnification is not a substitute for requiring adequate due diligence before proceeding far with any transaction.

Lease Agreements

Lease agreements may also contain provisions intended to deal with environmental risk and liabilities between the landlord and tenant. In addition to representations, warranties, and indemnities similar to those described earlier, lease agreements may also include covenants (as in financing agreements) pertaining to environmental compliance issues going forward. (See Chapter 12, which deals extensively with these issues in the landlord-tenant context.)

Side Agreements

In situations in which certain work cannot be carried out before the closing, the parties may decide to enter into a side agreement that deals specifically with seller's obligations after the closing. Though there is no reason why such provisions cannot be set forth in the acquisition agreement, the parties may prefer not to add more complexity to an already lengthy agreement. In addition, a side agreement may be preferable in situations in which the issue of ongoing work develops late in the negotiations, when the draft acquisition agreement is fairly complete and largely agreed on by the parties. In any event, the seller should ensure that it will have continued access to the property to carry out the work, purchaser's cooperation in obtaining regulatory approvals, and fixed standards by which its work will be measured for approval by the purchaser. The purchaser should consider asking for provisions that afford it some meaningful role in reviewing and approving plans for and performance of the necessary work.

Mechanisms to Structure the Transaction

Certain methods are available to limit the likelihood that environmental liabilities will be taken on by a purchaser in acquiring property or business operations. Such methods include structuring the transaction as an assets deal, forming a subsidiary corporation or limited partnership to acquire the assets, or entering into a lease agreement with respect to any real property involved in the transaction. Notwithstanding these mechanisms, however, there is no guarantee that changes in structuring the transaction will insulate the purchaser from taking on environmental liabilities associated with the property or business operations being acquired. Particularly in recent years, courts have imposed environmental liabilities on acquiring entities despite formal structuring techniques that would normally insulate the parties from other types of liabilities of the predecessor. Environmental liabilities have readily been imposed on acquiring entities based on the public policy favoring the cleanup of contaminated property, even where such parties would otherwise not be liable for the actions of predecessors. Therefore, purchasers must understand that while limiting techniques should be considered and adopted when appropriate, they may not be effective if tested in litigation.

Transfer of Assets

One traditional method of limiting the liabilities taken on by a purchaser is to structure the transaction as an assets acquisition, as opposed to a merger or consolidation between the parties. When a company purchases the assets of another company, the purchaser should not be responsible for the seller's liabilities unless:

(1) the purchaser expressly or impliedly assumed the liability at issue;
(2) the transaction amounts to a de facto merger;
(3) the purchaser is a mere continuation of the seller; or
(4) the transaction was entered into fraudulently to escape liability.[7]

In cases in which a successor corporation merges or consolidates with a prior corporation, the prior corporation's liabilities are automatically taken on by the successor.[8] Thus, one of the first considerations should be whether the transaction will be structured as a transfer of assets, as opposed to a merger or consolidation. Federal courts applying successor liability under CERCLA uniformly recognize these four traditional exceptions.

In addition, there is some authority to support the recognition of two additional exceptions to the general rule that liabilities are not taken on by the purchaser of assets. These more recently developed exceptions cover situations in which

(1) the successor undertakes to conduct the same manufacturing operation of the seller's product lines in essentially an unchanged manner or
(2) the successor continues the business enterprise of the seller.[9]

Increasingly, courts look to the substance rather than the form of the agreement and are not hesitant to impose CERCLA liability outside of traditional principles of corporate law.[10] This is particularly true when the effect of the transaction would be to leave behind potential environmental liabilities that exceed the value of the remaining assets and when the purchaser intentionally structured the transaction to avoid known environmental liabilities.

Formation of a Subsidiary

Another potential mechanism to help limit the environmental liabilities of an acquiring entity is the formation of a subsidiary to acquire the property or business operations of the seller. The parent and its subsidiary corporation should be treated as separate and discrete legal entities unless the parent fails to observe corporate formalities and separateness, the subsidiary is inadequately capitalized, or some other special circumstance justifies piercing the corporate veil.[11] Accordingly, the parent may be insulated from at least "owner" liability under CERCLA if the appropriate corporate formalities are maintained. The parent may still, however, be deemed an "operator" under CERCLA, even if the corporate formalities are maintained, in situations in which there is evidence of substantial involvement by the parent in the operations of its subsidiary.[12] Moreover, while the majority ownership of a subsidiary will be evidence of an ability to control its activities, control sufficient to impose CERCLA liability may also be found in the absence of majority ownership.[13]

Limited Partnership

Formation of a limited partnership is another method to limit the potential environmental liabilities of at least some parties investing in the acquisition. Under traditional principles of partnership law, limited partners should not be responsible for the liabilities of a limited partnership beyond the amount of their capital contribution. In the environmental context, however, limited partners may be responsible under CERCLA if they are deemed to be "operators" of the property at issue based on their level of participation in the day-to-day operations of the business. A partnership agreement limiting the authority of the limited partners may not be an effective shield from such liability in cases in which the government could show actual control over relevant business operations. In addition, care must be taken throughout the period of ownership that there is no common identity between the general partner, who would be responsible for the liabilities of the limited partnership, and any of the limited partners.

Lease Agreement

When contamination is discovered on a property, the potential purchaser may consider entering into a lease agreement with the owner instead of making an outright purchase. Though this arrangement will not provide the lessee protection against liability as an operator, it may preclude CERCLA-type liability for contamination that occurred before the time of the lease.[14] As a practical matter, however, if the lessee's activities or operations contribute to any existing contamination on the property, it may be difficult, if not impossible, for the lessee to prove exactly what environmental liabilities are and are not attributable to its own operations. This is particularly true when the lessee's activities on the property are in the same location as the prior activities that caused the existing contamination and when the lessee uses materials similar to those associated with the contamination. The lessee should therefore consider conducting its own environmental diligence before entering into a lease agreement and attempting to obtain an indemnity for any environmental liabilities in connection with the property that are attributable to the activities and operations of other parties.

Conclusion

Considering the enormous potential expense of environmental investigation and cleanup in connection with the ownership and operation of real estate, parties should take seriously the issue of environmental risk in negotiating and drafting agreements. Adequate time should be spent discussing what allocation of responsibility is appropriate in a particular transaction and drafting the agreement to reflect the intent of the parties unambiguously. Parties may save themselves the pain and expense of years of litigation regarding relative allocation issues if they take care to execute clear and comprehensive environmental provisions. Moreover, if risk associated with certain potential environmental liabilities is clearly allocated to one of the parties to the agreement, other aspects of the transaction may be adjusted to reflect that factor.

Resources

Bernstein. "Deal-Makers Beware: Superfund Liability of Parent Corporations and Asset Purchasers." *Chemical Waste Litigation Reporter* 19 (1989): 40.

Coss. "CERCLA Liability of Parent Corporations: Direct (by Control of Subsidiary), Indirect (by Piercing the Corporate Veil)." *Chemical Waste Litigation Reporter* 24 (1992): 750.

Dearing. "Successor and Parent Corporations: Liability for CERCLA Response Costs." *Environment Reporter* 20 (Feb. 9, 1990): 1,764.

DeMeester. "Practical Guidance for Due Diligence Environmental Auditing." *Environmental Law Reporter* 18 (June 1988): 10,210.

Frantz. "Minimizing Environmental Liabilities Associated with the Purchase or Sale of Real Property and Businesses." *Toxic Law Reporter* 2 (Nov. 25, 1987): 723.

Garrett. "CERCLA's Impact on Indemnification Agreements." *Toxic Law Reporter* 7 (May 12, 1993): 1,478.

Gillon. "Toxic Transfers: The Evolving Doctrine of Successor Liability." *Toxic Law Reporter* 5 (Oct. 24, 1990): 696.

Janke and Kurzla. "Current Trends in Asset Purchaser Liability for Environmental Claims." *Toxic Law Reporter* 9 (July 27, 1994): 223.

Kezsbom and Goldman. "Corporate 'Successor' Liability for CERCLA Cleanup Costs: Recent Developments." *Toxic Law Reporter* 7 (Mar. 3, 1993): 1,156.

Light. "Liability and the Corporate Form under the Environmental Laws." *Chemical Waste Litigation Reporter* 17 (1989): 199.

Russell and Richardson. "Avoiding Corporate Successor Environmental Liability." *Chemical Waste Litigation Reporter* 14 (1987): 870.

Notes

1. *See, e.g.*, South Florida Water Mgt. Dist. v. Montalvo, No. 88-8038, 1989 WL 260215 (S.D. Fla. Feb. 15, 1989) ("indemnification agreement is only as good as the assets of the party obligating itself").

2. *See, e.g.*, Atlantic Richfield Co. v. Interstate Oil Transp. Co., 784 F.2d 106, 114–15 (2d Cir), *cert. denied*, 479 U.S. 817 (1986) ("indemnity agreements are generally designed only to protect against liability for damage to third parties"); Schiavone Constr. Co., Inc. v. County of Nassau, 717 F.2d 747, 751 (2d Cir. 1983) (indemnity agreements generally are designed to protect against third-party liabilities); *see also* 42 C.J.S. INDEMNITY § 13, at 94 (1991) ("[a]n indemnity against losses does not cover losses for which the indemnitee is not liable to a third person, and which he improperly pays").

3. *See, e.g.*, Olin Corp. v. Consolidated Aluminum Corp. 5 F.3d 10, 16 (2d Cir. 1993) (contractual indemnity is effective to allocate CERCLA liability between sophisticated parties); Mardan Corp. v. C.G.C. Music, Ltd., 804 F.2d 1454, 1459 (9th Cir. 1986) (seller's release is upheld even without specific reference to CERCLA); Kaufman & Broad-South Bay v. Unisys Corp., 822 F. Supp. 1468 (N.D. Cal. 1993) (parties may enter into agreements to apportion CERCLA responsibility as to each other, but they cannot alter their underlying liability to the government); Chemical Waste Mgt. v. Armstrong World Indus. Inc., 669 F. Supp. 1285, 1291–95 (E.D. Pa. 1987) (CERCLA authorizes indemnity agreements between potentially responsible parties).

4. *See* Harley-Davidson, Inc. v. Minstar, Inc., 837 F. Supp. 978, 983–85 (E.D. Wis. 1993), *rev'd*, 41 F.3d 341 (7th Cir. 1994) (CERCLA precludes indemnity agreements between potentially responsible parties); CPC Int'l, Inc. v. Aerojet-General Corp., 759 F. Supp. 1269, *reh'g denied*, 21 ENVT'L L. REP. 20,805 (W.D. Mich. 1991) (same).

5. *See, e.g.*, Smith Land & Improvement Corp. v. Celotex Corp., 851 F.2d 86, 90 (3d Cir. 1988), *cert. denied*, 488 U.S. 1029 (1989) (caveat emptor is not a defense to CERCLA liability); International Clinical Labs, Inc. v. Stevens, 710 F. Supp. 466, 469–70 (E.D.N.Y. 1989) ("as is" clause does not bar CERCLA claim); Mardan Corp. v. C.G.C. Music, Ltd., 600 F. Supp 1049, 1055 (D. Ariz. 1984), *aff'd*, 804 F.2d 1454 (9th Cir. 1986) (same).

6. *See* Haney v. Castle Meadows, Inc., 839 F. Supp. 753, 757 (D. Colo. 1993) ("[w]hile the parties can contractually alter the allocation of risk as to defects of which neither party has knowledge, a seller who actually knows there is a latent defect on the property and chooses not to reveal this to the purchaser cannot hide behind contract language purporting to shift the risk of nondisclosure to the purchaser").

7. 15 W. FLETCHER, CYCLOPEDIA OF THE LAW OF PRIVATE CORPORATIONS, § 7122 (rev. ed. 1990). *See* Philadelphia Elec. Co. v. Hercules, Inc., 762 F.2d 303, 308–09 (3d Cir.), *cert. denied*, 474 U.S. 980 (1985) (court acknowledges general rule of nonliability for transfer of assets and four exceptions).

8. 15 FLETCHER at § 7117.

9. *See* Louisiana-Pacific Corp. v. Asarco, Inc., 909 F.2d 1260, 1264 n.3, and 1265 (9th Cir. 1990) (court acknowledges "product line" and "continuing business enterprise" exceptions).

10. *See* United States v. Mexico Feed & Seed Co., 980 F.2d 478, 488 (8th Cir. 1992) ("imposition of successor liability under 'substantial continuation' test is justified by a showing that in substance, if not in form, the successor is a responsible party"); Kleen Laundry & Dry Cleaning Serv., Inc. v. Total Waste Mgmt. Corp., 817 F. Supp. 225, 233 (D.N.H. 1993) (court will adopt a common sense test rather than an overly restrictive analysis of corporate transfer rules).

11. *See In Re* Acushnet River & New Bedford Harbor Proceed., 675 F. Supp. 22, 32–34 (D. Mass. 1987) (equitable decision to pierce the corporate veil depends on the facts peculiar to each case).

12. *See* United States v. Kayser-Roth Corp, Inc., 910 F.2d 24, 27 (1st Cir. 1990), *cert. denied*, 498 U.S. 1084 (1991) (corporate status cannot shield a party from operator liability under CERCLA). *But see* Joslyn Mfg. Co. v. T.L. James & Co., Inc., 983 F.2d 80, 82–83 (5th Cir. 1990) (CERCLA does not impose direct liability on parent corporations).

13. *See* United States v. McGraw-Edison Co., 718 F. Supp. 154, 157 (W.D.N.Y. 1989) (percentage of shares of subsidiary owned by parent is not dispositive to operator analysis under CERCLA).

14. *See* United States v. National Bank of Commonwealth, No. 98-2127, 1990 WL 357792 (W.D. Pa. Apr. 23, 1990) (court precludes summary judgment against defendant who was current lessee of premises with preexisting contamination).

APPENDIX

Sample Environmental Representations, Warranties, and Covenants and Indemnification and Audit Provisions

Section 1. Definitions

For the purposes of this agreement, the following words and phrases shall have the following meanings:

"Environment" shall mean soil, surface waters, groundwaters, land, stream sediments, surface or subsurface strata, ambient air, and any environmental medium.

"Environmental Condition" shall mean any condition with respect to the Environment on or off the Site, whether or not yet discovered, which could or does result in any damage, loss, cost, expense, claim, demand, order, or liability to or against Seller or Buyer by any third party (including, without limitation, any government entity), including, without limitation, any condition resulting from the operation of Seller's business and/or the operation of the business of any other property owner or operator in the vicinity of the Site and/or any activity or operation formerly conducted by any person or entity on or off the Site.

"Environmental Law" shall mean any environmental or health and safety-related law, regulation, rule, ordinance, or bylaw at the federal, state, or local level, whether existing as of the date hereof, previously enforced, or subsequently enacted.

"Hazardous Material" shall mean any pollutant, toxic substance, hazardous waste, hazardous material, hazardous substance, or oil as defined in or pursuant to the Resource Conservation and Recovery Act, as amended, the Comprehensive Environmental Response, Compensation, and Liability Act, as amended, the Federal Clean Water Act, or any other federal, state, or local environmental law, regulation, ordinance, rule, or bylaw, whether existing as of the date hereof, previously enforced, or subsequently enacted.

"Permit" shall mean any environmental permit, license, approval, consent, or authorization issued by a federal, state, or local governmental entity.

"Release" shall mean any releasing, spilling, leaking, pumping, pouring, emitting, emptying, discharging, injecting, escaping, leaching, disposing, or dumping into the Environment.

"Threat of Release" shall mean a substantial likelihood of a Release that requires action to prevent or mitigate damage to the Environment that may result from such Release.

Section 2. Seller's Representations, Warranties, and Obligations

Section 2. 1. Seller represents and warrants to Buyer, such representations and warranties to be true and correct on the date hereof and as of the closing date, that:

(a) Seller, and any other person or entity for whose conduct it is or may be held responsible, has no liability under, has never violated, and is presently in compliance with all Environmental Laws applicable to the Site and any facilities and operations thereon, and, to the best of Seller's knowledge, there exist no Environmental Conditions with respect to the Site or any facilities or operations thereon, except as set forth in Exhibit __;

(b) Seller, and any other person or entity for whose conduct it is or may be held responsible, has not generated, manufactured, refined, transported, treated, stored, handled, disposed, transferred, produced, or processed any Hazardous Material or any solid waste at the Site, except in compliance with all applicable Environmental Laws, and has no knowledge of the Release or Threat of Release of any Hazardous Material at or in the vicinity of the Site, except as set forth in Exhibit __;

(c) No lien has been imposed on the Site by any governmental agency at the federal, state, or local level in connection with the presence on or off the Site of any Hazardous Material;

(d) Seller, and any other person or entity for whose conduct it is or may be held responsible, has not: (i) entered into or been subject to any consent decree, compliance order, or administrative order with respect to the Site or any facilities or operations thereon; (ii) received notice under the citizen suit provision of any Environmental Law in connection with the Site or any facilities or operations thereon; (iii) received any request for information, notice, demand letter, administrative inquiry, or formal or informal complaint or claim with respect to any Environmental Condition relating to the Site or any facilities or operations thereon; or (iv) been subject to or threatened with any governmental or citizen enforcement action with respect to the Site or any facilities or operations thereon, except as set forth in Exhibit __; and Seller, and any other person or entity for whose conduct it is or may be held responsible, has no reason to believe that any of the above will be forthcoming.

(e) Seller has all Permits necessary for its activities and operations at the Site and for any past or ongoing alterations or improvements at the Site, which Permits are listed in Exhibit __.

Section 2.2. Seller covenants to Buyer, from the date hereof, that:

(a) Seller shall provide to Buyer, within __ days of the date hereof, copies of all documents, records, and information in its possession or control or available to Seller concerning Environmental Conditions relevant to the Site or any facilities or operations concerning Environmental Conditions relevant to the Site or any facilities or operations thereon, whether generated by Seller or others, including, without limitation, environmental audits, environmental risk assessments, or site assessments of the Site and/or any adjacent property or other property in the vicinity of the Site owned or operated by Seller or others, documentation regarding off-site disposal of Hazardous Materials, spill control plans, and environmental agency reports and correspondence. Furthermore, Seller shall have an ongoing obligation to provide to Buyer copies of any additional such documents that come into the possession or control of or become available to Seller subsequent to the date hereof, within __ days of any such document becoming available to Seller.

(b) Seller shall, at its sole cost and expense, take or cause to be taken all actions necessary to: (i) ensure that as of the closing date the Site, all activities and operations thereon, and all alterations and improvements thereto, comply with all applicable Environmental Laws and with any and all agreements with governmental agencies, court orders, and administrative orders regarding Environmental Conditions; and (ii) satisfy Buyer, no later than the closing date, that relevant governmental agencies are not likely to require any further action to remedy any Environmental Conditions.

Section 3. Seller's Indemnities

Section 3.1. Seller agrees to indemnify and hold harmless Buyer, its officers, employees, agents, successors, and assigns (the "Indemnitees") against and in respect of, any and all damages, claims, losses, liabilities, and expenses (including, without limitation, reasonable legal, accounting, consulting, engineering, and other expenses), that may be imposed on, incurred by, or asserted against any of the Indemnitees by any other party or parties (including, without limitation, a governmental entity), arising out of, in connection with, or relating to the subject matter of: (a) Seller's breach of any of the representations and warranties set forth in Section 2; (b) any Environmental Condition, relevant to the Site or any facilities or operations thereon, existing as of and/or prior to the closing date, even if not discovered until after the closing date; or (c) any violation of an Environmental Law with respect to the Site or any facilities or operations thereon, existing as of and/or prior to the closing date, even if not discovered until after the closing date. Such damages, claims, losses, liabilities, and expenses are hereinafter referred to as "Environmental Liabilities." This indemnity shall survive the closing and shall be in addition to Seller's obligations for breach of a representation or warranty set forth in Section 1.

Section 3.2. If any dispute arises between the parties with respect to: (a) whether an Environmental Condition existed as of and/or prior to the closing date; (b) whether a violation of an Environmental Law existed as of and/or prior to the closing date; or (c) the percentage of an Environmental Liability that is attributable to an Environmental Condition or violation of an Environmental Law existing as of and/or prior to the closing date, such matter shall be resolved by mediation or arbitration.

Section 3.3. Seller's indemnification obligations under this agreement shall be limited as follows: (a) with respect to the indemnification obligations of Seller pursuant to Section 3.1, no such obligation shall arise with respect to any Environmental Liabilities arising or incurred after (i) the receipt of a Certification, as defined hereunder, unless a governmental entity shall order or require further action with respect to an Environmental Condition or violation of an Environmental Law within __ years after the date of the Certification, in which case Seller's indemnification obligations shall remain effective with respect to Environmental Liabilities in connection with any such Environmental Condition or violation of an Environmental Law; or (ii) the receipt of an Agency Letter, as defined hereunder.

For the purposes of the expiration of Seller's obligations pursuant to this Section 3.3, such expiration may occur with respect to any individual Environmental Condition or violation of an Environmental Law, provided that Buyer has received a Certification or Agency Letter that covers such individual Environmental Condition or violation of an Environmental Law. None of Seller's obligations under this agreement shall be extinguished pursuant to this Section 3.3 with respect to any individual Environmental Condition, violation, or group of Conditions or violations for which no Certification or Agency Letter has been received.

For the purposes of this Section 3.3, "Certification" shall mean the issuance of a report by an environmental engineer satisfactory to Buyer, stating that in the opinion of said engineer, all actions likely to be required by the governmental entity or entities charged with the enforcement of applicable Environmental Laws have been taken with respect to any Environmental Condition or violation of an Environmental Law covered by the Certification. The conclusions set forth in any Certification shall be based on consultations by the engineer with such relevant governmental entity or entities.

For the purposes of this Section 3.3, "Agency Letter" shall mean a letter from the governmental entity or entities charged with the enforcement of applicable Environmental Laws stating that: (a) all actions have been completed to the satisfaction of such entity or entities and no further action will be required with respect to any Environmental Condition or violation of an Environmental Law covered by the Agency Letter; or (b) no action will now or hereafter be required by such governmental entity or entities with respect to any Environmental Condition or violation of an Environmental Law covered by the Agency Letter.

Section 3.4. Seller shall be given prompt written notice after any Environmental Liability, with respect to which indemnification is to be claimed hereunder, comes to the attention of Buyer. Notwithstanding the prior sentence, Seller shall not be relieved of its obligations under this agreement if Buyer's failure to notify Seller of an Environmental Liability does not prejudice Seller's rights or materially increase its liabilities and obligations hereunder.

CHAPTER 12

Environmental Issues in the Landlord-Tenant Context

DONALD I. BERGER
BRUCE W. GALLOWAY

In many respects, the environmental issues confronting landlords and tenants are no different than those confronting parties to other types of commercial real estate transactions. The potential presence of hazardous substances on or around the property involved in the transaction poses liability risks that must be allocated between the parties.

From this perspective, a number of the typical transactional mechanisms for allocating risks, including due diligence, representations and warranties (or disclaimers thereof), and indemnities also arise within the leasing context. Just as in a sale, purchase, or financing transaction, the attention devoted to these provisions in a lease transaction will vary depending on the type and usage of the property. For example, a lease of an operating manufacturing facility to a tenant proposing to use large quantities of hazardous materials will present materially different risks—and result in materially different provisions in the lease—than a lease of office space.

In at least one important respect, however, the relationship between a landlord and a tenant is different from that arising in other commercial real estate contexts. Unlike a purchase or financing transaction, in which control of the property is usually conveyed *in toto* at a specific point in time, a lease transaction involves the transfer of *transitional* control over the premises from the landlord to the tenant and back to the landlord.

An important aspect of this transitional control structure is the overlapping liability faced by the landlord, as owner of the leased premises, and the tenant, as operator of the leased premises. Many environmental laws impose strict, joint, and several liability on *both* the landlord and the tenant for costs associated with the presence of hazardous materials on the leased premises. As discussed later in this chapter, these joint legal obligations require negotiation of specific lease provisions to address releases of hazardous materials on or near the leased premises.

Although a number of factors, including the respective leverage of the parties, will dictate the manner in which the lease addresses potential environmental risks, the transfer of control between the landlord and the tenant offers a framework for analyzing how these risks should be allocated. As discussed in the section "Negotiating and Drafting Leases to Address Environmental Issues" (below), the transitions in control over the premises that occur in connection with a lease provide a convenient structural basis for resolving most environmental issues likely to arise in the landlord-tenant context.

The first stage of the parties' relationship is at the time of initial transfer of possession of the premises. At this juncture, the parties must consider the level of due diligence that should precede the transfer, the description and nature of the premises to be leased, the condition of the premises upon occupancy, and the tenant's permissible uses of the premises.

In the second stage of the parties' relationship, the period during which the tenant controls the leased premises, environmental concerns will focus on the operation of the premises and the surrounding property. The lease must address the tenant's compliance with laws; the landlord's entry and inspection rights; alteration, repair, and maintenance of the premises; changes in uses associated with assignment or subletting; the scope of indemnity provisions; and operating costs.

In the final stage of the leasing relationship, possession and control of the premises revert to the landlord. This transfer may occur as a result of a default and the exercise of termination rights arising from a discharge of hazardous materials or a breach of other environmental provisions in the lease. Even when this is not the case, the lease should address the condition of the premises upon surrender and the survival of representations and indemnities.

Overview of Legal Principles Affecting the Landlord-Tenant Relationship

Overlapping Liability as Owner and Operator

Most environmental laws do not specifically regulate landlords and tenants. Instead, the parties' potential liabilities are typically derived from environmental statutes regulating the ownership and operation of property where hazardous materials are located or businesses that generate or handle hazardous substances.

The environmental law that has received the most attention in the commercial context, the Comprehensive Environmental Response,

Compensation, and Liability Act (CERCLA), potentially imposes strict cleanup liability on current owners and operators of a facility, former owners and operators at the time of disposal of a hazardous substance, and generators of the hazardous substance.[1] (See Chapter 1.) Although CERCLA and many state environmental laws provide little guidance as to when a landlord or tenant may be deemed an owner or operator, the courts have consistently held that a landlord may be liable for hazardous substance cleanup costs caused by its tenant even if the landlord does not actively participate in the management of the site[2] and that a tenant that maintains control over the use of the property may be liable as an operator or even, in some cases, as an owner.[3]

Because the landlord maintains fee ownership of the leased premises while the tenant is given possession and control for a specified period of time, owner and operator liability is inherently overlapping in the landlord-tenant relationship. While there is usually little question about the landlord's ownership interest, the scope of the tenant's control over the property on which a release has occurred can be a determining factor in assessing the tenant's liability for the release of hazardous substances.

For example, in *Nurad, Inc. v. Hooper*, [4] the U.S. Court of Appeals for the Fourth Circuit considered the liability of tenants who leased a building in an industrial park adjacent to a parcel that contained a leaking underground storage tank. Noting that the site had been subdivided and that the defendant tenants did not lease any portion of the contaminated parcel, the Court held that the tenants could not be held liable for the contamination unless it could be demonstrated that they had the authority to control the area where the hazardous release occurred. In upholding the tenants' dismissal from the action, the Court found that the trial court had carefully examined the "precise" language of the underlying lease—including the description of the premises, permissible uses, and definition of common areas—and properly concluded that the tenants had no explicit or implied authority to exercise control over the area in which the contamination occurred.[5]

Despite uncertainties as to how the term "control" may be interpreted and applied in a specific instance, as discussed later in this chapter, the legal and regulatory emphasis placed on control mandates caution in how the landlord and tenant define the premises and address rights of access and off-premises uses.

Limitations on the Third-Party and Innocent Landowner Defenses

A principal feature of many environmental statutes, including CERCLA, is the imposition of strict liability "without regard to causation."[6]

The potential imposition of strict liability may, in certain cases, be softened by the so-called third party or innocent landowner defenses.

CERCLA provides that an owner or operator of contaminated property may be exempt from liability if it can demonstrate that the costs associated with the cleanup of the contamination were incurred solely as a result of a third party who is not in "a contractual relationship, existing directly or indirectly with the defendant," and that the owner or operator exercised due care and took precautions against the foreseeable acts or omissions of the third party.[7] However, the extent to which these defenses apply in the landlord-tenant context is questionable. A landlord will not be able to rely on the defense to shield it from liability arising from the release of hazardous substances by its tenants[8] because the courts have consistently held that a lease agreement is a "contractual relationship" under CERCLA, and that the innocent landowner defense applies only to individuals acquiring property *after* the contamination has occurred.

To the extent a tenant acquires its interest under the lease *after the contamination has occurred*, it may be in a better position to assert the innocent landowner defense.[9] However, for several reasons, the tenant clearly cannot assume that it will be protected from potential environmental liability merely by virtue of its contractual relationship with the landlord.

First, depending on the jurisdiction and the nature of the contamination, tenants may be held responsible for cleanup costs attributable to the ongoing migration of contamination within the leased premises.[10] Second, to take advantage of the innocent landowner defense under CERCLA and many state laws, the tenant must demonstrate that it has made "all appropriate inquiry" into the history and use of the leased premises and had no reason to know of any contamination.[11] Finally, regardless of whether the tenant may be directly liable for cleaning up preexisting contamination, the remediation of such contamination on or around the leased premises may be disruptive to the tenant's ongoing operations.

Given the limitations and uncertainties associated with the assertion of defenses to environmental liabilities, both landlords and tenants should conduct reasonable due diligence before the commencement of a lease. The nature of this due diligence is addressed later in this chapter.

Risk Shifting through Indemnities

Although the courts have consistently held that potentially responsible parties (PRPs) may not shield themselves from *governmental* cleanup orders through contractual indemnification and release provisions, the courts generally recognize parties' ability to allocate cleanup costs among themselves pursuant to contract.[12] Even those courts that have allowed parties to a commercial transaction to shift environmental risks from one entity to another, however, have focused carefully on contractual provisions purporting to do so to determine precisely which risks the parties intended to transfer or assume. For example, in *AM International v. International Forging Equipment*,[13] the court found that under Ohio law, even when a release contains unambiguous language that purports to bar claims based on unknown future causes, a release will be not effective with respect to CERCLA cleanup liability unless the evidence "clearly and convincingly establishes" that the parties intended that the release cover such claims.[14]

In the leasing context, indemnification and release provisions allocating environmental liabilities between the landlord and the tenant are commonplace. However, given the courts' tendency to narrowly interpret these provisions, both the landlord and the tenant should be particularly careful in negotiating such provisions. As discussed later, because of the shifts in control of the premises inherent in a lease transaction, particular attention should be devoted to the source, location, and timing of the contamination to avoid uncertainty about who is responsible for future environmental remediation.

Permitting and Disclosure Obligations

In addition to addressing potential liability for the discharge of hazardous substances on the leased premises, the landlord and the tenant will need to consider the impact of various environmental permitting and disclosure laws. The handling of certain hazardous materials or wastes, or the discharge or emission of pollutants, often requires disclosure to, or permits from, one or more governmental agencies.[15]

The parties may also have legal responsibilities to disclose the presence or release of hazardous substances to one another. This duty of disclosure may arise under common-law negligence or misrepresentation principles or under specific statutes. Under the California Health and Safety Code, for example, the failure of a tenant to disclose in writing the release of a hazardous substance on the leased premises "within a reasonable period of time" may entitle the landlord to declare a default under the lease and exposes the tenant to damages and civil penalties.[16]

The permitting and disclosure obligations applicable to landlords and tenants affect not only the parties' due diligence inquiries but also the uses permitted under the lease and the ongoing monitoring of such uses throughout the lease term, as discussed later in this chapter.

Remediation Obligations

Once a hazardous material release occurs, the process of reporting, investigating, characterizing, and remediating begins. Depending on the amount and type of the substance released, the circumstances under which the release occurred (e.g., proximity to groundwater, creation of a public nuisance, etc.), the regulatory agencies involved in the site investigation and cleanup, and the environmental regulations that govern the cleanup, several remediation options may be available, ranging from doing nothing to completely removing all contaminated soils.

Also, the scope of remediation may be dictated by the extent of testing done on the site. Less testing, for example, may result in more conservative estimates of the degree to which soils or groundwater may have been affected and, consequently, more extensive remediation efforts. As discussed in later sections of this chapter, because the respective interests of the landlord and the tenant may not be fully aligned in resolving these issues, consideration should be given to how remediation of contamination will be addressed, both during and after the lease term.

Negotiating and Drafting Leases to Address Environmental Issues

Issues Relating to the Initial Transfer of Possession

Due Diligence

Given the potential impact on a tenant's operations if a release of hazardous substances is discovered after the lease term begins, contractual provisions shifting risks for preexisting contamination to the landlord, while possibly helpful in minimizing the tenant's potential liability, do not obviate the need for due diligence at the inception of the transaction. While it is unrealistic to think that the tenant will always perform a comprehensive due diligence investigation, at least some minimal due diligence is advisable where the potential for preexisting contamination is high. If, for example, the tenant is leasing space in a commercial office park, its investigation may be confined to a review of all the environmental reports in the landlord's possession, including any asbestos survey or Phase I assessment performed when the landlord acquired the property. By contrast, if a tenant is proposing to lease a manufacturing plant that has been operating over a lengthy time period and has a history of intensive hazardous material use, a full-scale environmental audit may be appropriate.[17]

In addition to due diligence with respect to the leased premises, a prospective tenant must decide whether to investigate other tenant activities or other portions of the landlord's property. Particularly in office or industrial parks, where the tenant may be affected by releases from other tenants or may be required to pay for common-area contamination, off-premises due diligence may be appropriate.

Before executing the lease, the landlord also should engage in some due diligence inquiry of the tenant's past use of, and experience in handling, hazardous materials. In many cases, this investigation will begin (and often end) with a questionnaire concerning the tenant's business practices and the types of chemicals and hazardous materials the tenant anticipates using on the premises. When the landlord is leasing industrial property or the tenant is engaged in a business that uses substantial quantities of hazardous substances, or requires numerous environmental permits, the landlord may seek additional information about the tenant's track record with the regulatory agencies with jurisdiction over the tenant's past operations.

In the case of tenants that anticipate handling substantial quantities of hazardous materials, the landlord should consider whether the tenant's financial strength warrants a request for additional security deposits or letters of credit as a precaution against future contamination problems.

Description of Premises and Liability for Releases within Common Areas

Defining the leased premises is typically one of the first business points addressed in the negotiations. Too often, however, the parties ignore potential environmental issues that may arise as a result of the way the premises are defined.

For example, the landlord and the tenant need to address who will bear the cost of remediating contamination of parking facilities and common-access areas. Typically the tenant is not responsible for securing or maintaining these areas. Yet, depending on how the premises are defined in the lease and how the costs of maintaining parking and common-access areas are allocated among the landlord's tenants, a tenant may find itself paying for hazardous material remediation costs unrelated to the operation of its business.

To the extent areas readily accessible to other tenants or the public are included in the description of the premises—for example, where the lease includes the right to use a specific area for parking, storage, or access—the tenant may be directly liable, as an operator, for any hazardous material discharges within this area. The tenant is also likely to be liable for such contamination under the lease, which will usually require the tenant to maintain "the premises" in compliance with all laws, including all environmental laws, as discussed later.

Even if parking and common areas are excluded from the definition of "premises," most net leases contain broad definitions of operating expenses (to be paid by the tenant on a pro rata basis), which include costs incurred in maintaining these areas. Often, costs incurred in remediating hazardous material conditions are either explicitly or implicitly included among those "maintenance" costs for which the tenant will be responsible. From the landlord's perspective, passing through such costs may be justified on the grounds that, since the tenant is benefiting from the use of the common areas, it is fair to allocate to the tenant its proportionate share of liability for such costs.

While most landlords will be reluctant to delete the environmental pass-through provisions completely, the tenant may attempt to carve out those environmental liabilities that (1) existed before the commencement of the lease term, (2) were created solely by a specific tenant (the generator or discharger of the hazardous material), or (3) were attributable to the negligence or willful misconduct of the landlord or its agents. The tenant should also consider adding a provision that limits the remediation cost pass-throughs to a specific amount, and a provision that amortizes remediation cost pass-throughs over the term of the lease or the useful life of the leased building. Such provisions may be more appropriate when remediation costs are spread over a longer period (for example, when ongoing groundwater monitoring is involved).

Use of the Premises

The use clause may be the landlord's most direct means of avoiding environmental issues at the outset. From the tenant's perspective, an outright ban on the use of all hazardous substances or materials will probably be unworkable. At a minimum, a prohibition on the handling of hazardous materials should contain a carve-out for commonly used consumer products containing components that may be classified as hazardous, as long as such materials are used for their intended purpose in compliance with all applicable laws and are not stockpiled in large quantities.

The landlord should avoid open-ended carve-outs from lease restrictions governing the use of hazardous materials. Only in rare instances should the landlord accept a use provision that allows the tenant to handle hazardous materials "as long as tenant complies with applicable permit and regulatory requirements." Such a provision adds little to the compliance with law requirements already present in most leases and does not adequately address the potential that extensive use of hazardous materials or use of particularly toxic materials may expose the landlord to greater liability risks.

For those tenants intending to use a significant quantity of hazardous materials in their ongoing business operations, the parties should include provisions in the lease that clearly govern the intended scope of such uses. An initial list of the types and quantities of hazardous substances to be used in the tenant's operations should be provided before execution of the lease, and typically the landlord should prohibit the use of any additional substances without its prior written consent.

The landlord also needs to guard against operational costs associated with a tenant's *lawful* handling of hazardous materials. The most common concerns of a landlord in this regard are consistency with its lender's mortgage requirements concerning the handling of hazardous materials and the potential impacts on the landlord's insurance. Therefore, the landlord should consider adding provisions to the lease that specifically permit it to prohibit the tenant from using hazardous materials that are either precluded under the landlord's mortgage or would result in an increase in the landlord's insurance premiums. If such provisions are included in the lease, the tenant should seek written confirmation that the permitted uses identified in the lease, including any hazardous materials the tenant anticipates handling, would not be prohibited or trigger a premium increase.

Landlord's Representations: "As Is" Clauses

Environmental representations are valuable, both as a means of obtaining information concerning the other party's knowledge of the potential presence of hazardous substances and as a way to allocate risk for preexisting contamination.[18] In this respect, the tenant's interest in obtaining representations from the landlord may not be materially different than that of a purchaser of real property.

Although occasionally the landlord will agree to make limited representations concerning the absence of hazardous materials on the premises (usually limited to the landlord's actual knowledge and provided only to tenants commanding substantial leverage in the negotiations), often the landlord will not only disclaim all representations and warranties but also insert a provision providing that the tenant has had a full opportunity to inspect the premises and has agreed to accept the premises "as is." Although most courts will uphold contractual provisions shifting liability between PRPs through the use of contractual indemnity clauses, the courts have been more conservative in interpreting "as-is, where-is" clauses. For example, a number of cases have held that as-is provisions apply only to breach of warranty claims and not to claims arising under CERCLA or other environmental laws.[19]

Despite these potential limitations, inclusion of an as-is clause may provide important protection for the landlord. The disclaimer of the landlord's obligations may reduce the risk that the tenant will attempt to rescind the lease if it later discovers hazardous substances on the leased premises.[20] In addition, an as-is clause may be a factor in determining whether the parties intended to shift to the tenant the burden of complying with laws requiring repairs to or renovation of the leased premises.[21]

Thus, in circumstances in which its bargaining power permits it to do so, a landlord is well advised to include an as-is provision in the lease and to provide specifically that such disclaimer includes any and all liabilities associated with the presence of hazardous materials.

Issues Relating to Tenant's Operation of the Premises

Compliance with Law

Most leases contain a provision requiring the tenant to comply with all applicable federal, state, and local laws, regulations, and orders. As awareness of the potential risks associated with a hazardous material release has increased, compliance with law provisions have expanded to include express references to compliance with environmental laws, including laws governing the use, storage, and disposal of hazardous substances.

Even though many form leases will require the tenant to comply with environmental laws regulating the tenant's use of the leased premises, this type of boilerplate provision may be inadequate to allocate responsibilities effectively between the landlord and tenant if substantial structural modifications to the premises are required to address applicable environmental laws. For example, several courts have held that laws requiring the replacement of asbestos-containing materials (ACMs) are outside the scope of the compliance with law provisions of a form lease and are not alone sufficient to shift the burden of asbestos abatement to the tenant.[22] These decisions underscore the importance of drafting compliance with law provisions with an eye toward explicitly addressing any retrofitting or renovation activities that may be required under applicable law, including those that may arise due to the presence of building materials, such as ACMs, that may be considered hazardous.

The lease should also require the tenant to maintain all permits necessary to operate the tenant's business within the premises, including all permits necessary for the use, generation, storage, or disposal of hazardous materials. The lease should specifically require that the tenant file with all applicable governmental agencies any reports, business plans, notices, and other disclosures that the tenant is required to make under applicable environmental regulations. Even though no permit or license may be required to handle a certain type or quantity of hazardous material or to engage in certain activities that pose a potential threat to public health and safety, state or local governmental agencies may have adopted regulations requiring periodic disclosure. A common example is the mandatory filing of reports or business plans with a local fire department or environmental services agency so that agency can monitor the use of potentially toxic or combustible materials.

Often the reports and plans that a tenant may be required to file with a local or state governmental agency can provide a means for the landlord to monitor the tenant's compliance with lease provisions concerning the handling of hazardous materials. The lease should require the tenant to provide to the landlord, on an ongoing basis, copies of applicable environmental permits and reports as well as any notices or citations issued by applicable governmental authorities. The wording of such a provision should be carefully reviewed by the tenant to ensure that the reporting obligation does not become too onerous to implement (e.g., if every material safety data sheet or hazardous waste manifest were required). The tenant should also make certain that any technical materials submitted to a governmental agency that are classified as confidential and protected against public disclosure are provided to the landlord only under the auspices of an appropriate confidentiality agreement.

Landlord's Right of Entry and Inspection

Most leases permit the landlord to enter the premises to inspect the property, make repairs, and cure the tenant's default. These inspection rights may be particularly important as a means to allow the landlord to verify whether the tenant is complying with applicable legal requirements and lease restrictions on the use of hazardous materials. When more intensive uses of hazardous materials are involved (e.g, in the lease of a manufacturing facility or a building in an industrial park), the landlord may wish to reserve the specific right to retain an environmental consultant to audit the tenant's handling and disposal of hazardous materials. If the audit reveals that the tenant is not in compliance, the landlord may seek to assess the tenant with all audit-related costs (in addition to any costs incurred in curing any defaults).

When the landlord is particularly concerned about the potential risk of contamination of the premises—whether by the tenant, by previous tenants or owners, or from off-site migration—it may wish to reserve the right to test the soil or groundwater. Unless the lease specifically provides for this type of invasive testing, it is not clear that a general reference to "inspection" and "repair" rights would allow such tests. If a lease does provide for soil or groundwater testing, the tenant should seek assurances of the following:

1. The tenant will be notified in advance and be allowed to observe the testing.
2. The testing will not interfere unreasonably with the tenant's business operations.
3. The testing will be conducted by a licensed professional (perhaps even a consultant to be approved by the tenant).
4. The testing will be performed in compliance with all applicable laws, including any laws requiring the landlord to obtain a permit before testing (in some jurisdictions, for example, a permit is needed before groundwater testing) and to dispose of any contaminated soils or other hazardous waste materials displaced during the testing.

Alteration, Repair, and Maintenance

In many leases, the landlord's and the tenant's respective obligations in the event of a hazardous material release or threatened release are covered only generally, usually in the context of the compliance with law or indemnity provisions. These provisions typically focus on who is responsible for remediating the release or paying for the remediation. Too often, these provisions are inadequate to address the myriad issues arising in the event of an actual release, and they pay too little attention to the relationship between these risk allocation provisions and the more detailed provisions in the lease governing alteration, repair, and maintenance of the premises.

There are two sets of issues that the landlord and the tenant should consider in negotiating the alteration, repair, and maintenance provisions of a lease: (1) the "repairs" and remediation that may be required to respond to the types of hazardous material releases most likely to occur, and the roles the parties should play with respect to such remediation; and (2) the extent to which the alterations and repairs may give rise to or exacerbate a hazardous material release. The strict liability associated with most contamination issues and the regulatory requirements governing site investigation and remediation give both the landlord and tenant ample incentive to ensure their interests are protected during the course of any remediation.

Although the lease may provide that the tenant must maintain the premises in "good condition," this may not be sufficient to protect the landlord if site remediation is mishandled. Among other rights, the landlord should consider reserving the right to approve the environmental consultant selected by the tenant to investigate the extent of contamination; the right to review, before submission, any disclosure reports to regulatory agencies made by the tenant or its consultant; the right (but not the obligation) to participate in any negotiations with regulatory agencies; and, most importantly, the right to review and approve any remediation plan.

When the lease obligates the landlord to rectify specific contamination problems, the tenant should consider reserving similar rights to the extent its liability or business operations might be affected. In particular, because certain types of on-site mitigation (e.g., bioremediation or substantial excavation of contaminated soils) may disrupt the tenant's operations, the tenant should consider whether the provisions in the lease concerning the tenant's "quiet enjoyment" of the premises should be expanded to address the tenant's rights in the event the landlord begins cleanup activities before termination of the lease.

The parties also need to consider what standards to use to determine when remediation is deemed complete. This is more than an academic inquiry, since many governmental agencies are giving greater latitude to allow contamination to remain in place as long as no direct risk is posed to public health or safety.[23] Thus, unless the lease requires the tenant to restore the premises to its precontamination condition, merely requiring a tenant to comply with applicable laws or to maintain the premises in "good condition" may not be sufficient to permit the landlord to require the removal of all hazardous materials released during the tenancy. This could leave the landlord in the untenable position of accepting a surrender of the premises in a condition that impairs its market value.

In addition, the parties should consider whether alteration or repair of the premises might lead to environmental liabilities. This concern arises most often with respect to the lease of older buildings, where ACMs, lead, or other potentially hazardous building materials may be disturbed during construction activities. In these instances, the landlord should ensure that it may withhold its consent to any alterations or repairs that could damage ACMs or lead to a hazardous substance release. The tenant should ensure, before leasing the premises, that it has obtained all the information it can concerning the location of any ACM or other potentially hazardous building materials and, further, should require that the landlord provide it with information about any existing operation and maintenance program addressing the presence of ACMs.

Where local law provides (or may in the future provide) for specified retrofitting activities (such as installation of sprinklers or earthquake-related structural improvements), more attention should be paid to whether a comprehensive asbestos abatement program will be required. If removal of ACMs in those areas subject to retrofitting is more than a remote possibility, lease provisions concerning notice, vacation of the premises, abatement of rent, and condition of the premises before reoccupancy should be considered.

Assignment and Subletting

Assuming that the lease imposes specific restrictions on a tenant's ability to use hazardous materials, the landlord must ensure that these restrictions are not undermined through the tenant's subsequent assignment or sublease of the premises. This typically will not be an issue if the landlord reserves absolute discretion to approve or reject an assignment or sublease. However, where the lease or applicable law provides that these approvals cannot be unreasonably withheld or sets specific standards governing the approval, the landlord should make clear that a change of use that increases the risk of a hazardous substance release is a permissible grounds for disapproving the assignment or sublease. To ensure that this provision is not used as a pretext to limit the tenant's ability to transfer its interests, the tenant should negotiate sufficient flexibility in the use clause of the lease so that most likely transferees of the tenant's interest will be reasonably able to operate.

Indemnity Provisions

Indemnification provisions may appear in several different places throughout a lease. Unless they are carefully reviewed, they may create different, and occasionally conflicting, mechanisms for allocating contamination risks between the landlord and the tenant.

Most current lease forms contain some type of specific environmental indemnification, which, as discussed below, is often the subject of negotiations between the landlord and the tenant. However, the lease may also contain provisions dealing with compliance with law, repair and maintenance, and insurance and indemnity obligations that, if not modified to reflect the terms of the environmental indemnification provision, could be interpreted to expand the tenant's potential liability. For example, because the mere presence of certain quantities of hazardous substances in soil or groundwater may be deemed to violate applicable environmental laws, virtually any contamination occurring on the leased premises (even contamination occurring before the lease was executed) may be deemed a breach of the compliance with laws covenant in the lease and may be covered by a broadly worded general indemnity provision. Without further modifications to these and other lease provisions, confusion about who is responsible for the contamination may result.

The sophisticated tenant will typically attempt to negotiate carveouts from the broad environmental indemnity provisions contained in many leases. In particular, the tenant may attempt to exclude from the indemnity contamination that (1) existed before the term of the lease, (2) is caused or exacerbated by the landlord's active negligence, or (3) is not caused by the tenant or its agents/invitees.

Although some landlords may be willing to accept limited indemnity carve-outs addressing the first two points, the question of whether the tenant should be exculpated from hazardous material releases that occur on the premises during the lease term but are not caused by the tenant is much more debatable. Typically the landlord's response to this issue will be that, since the tenant is in control of the premises and responsible for complying with all applicable laws, it is appropriate for the tenant to be responsible for any releases occurring during the lease term, regardless of who causes the release. Even if the tenant accepts this rationale, it should be wary of including in the definition of the leased premises any property that it cannot readily control,[24] and it should also carefully review how "release" is defined in the lease, since the ongoing migration or leaching of preexisting hazardous materials may be considered a release.[25] Thus, the tenant may seek to clarify that its liability is limited to the generation or release of hazardous materials that were not present before the commencement of the lease and that are released only within that portion of the premises under the tenant's exclusive control.

While the tenant may succeed in narrowing the scope of the environmental indemnity provision, it is likely to encounter stiff resistance from the landlord in any attempt to obtain a landlord indemnification for preexisting contamination. While the landlord may already have responsibility to clean up such contamination under CERCLA and other environmental laws, if the contamination preceded the landlord's ownership of the property or was caused by other tenants or third parties without the landlord's knowledge, the landlord may feel that it is no more "responsible" than the tenant, who, under the same laws, may also be a PRP as a current operator of the premises. As with many controversial lease provisions, resolution of this issue may be determined more by the parties' respective bargaining strength than by the force of their legal arguments.

Issues Relating to Lease Expiration or Termination

Default and Termination

Although typically the tenant's failure to perform its environmental obligations under the lease will constitute a default, in many cases the lease will provide a notice and cure period before the landlord may exercise its termination rights. From the landlord's perspective, the cure period should be sufficiently short to respond to either a breach that substantially increases the landlord's exposure to environmental liability—for example, the handling of hazardous materials in violation of the use restrictions in the lease—or tenant delay in addressing a release. In both cases, the landlord should ensure that it can step in and take all appropriate steps (including, potentially, the termination of the lease and eviction of the tenant) to remedy the breach.

From the tenant's perspective, the cure rights set forth in the lease should be reasonable. In particular, where the tenant is potentially responsible for contamination it does not cause, the landlord should not be permitted to terminate the lease during the period in which the tenant is diligently and in good faith pursuing remediation of the contamination. This type of provision may be acceptable to some landlords on the grounds that little is to be gained by terminating the lease in the face of the tenant's diligent remediation, since doing so may expose the landlord to out-of-pocket investigation and mitigation costs that it might not otherwise incur.

Other landlords, however, may strongly object to any type of open-ended cure period—even if tied to the tenant's diligent remediation efforts—on the grounds that the landlord must retain the ability to reassert control over the premises if it believes that the tenant's efforts are "not diligent enough" to address the problem in a manner that minimizes the landlord's risks. In this regard, it is important to keep in mind that regulatory agencies may give dischargers fairly broad latitude in both the timing and type of remediation activities and that the tenant's idea of diligent remediation may differ sharply from the landlord's. Although many landlords will be cautious in exercising a termination right in response to a hazardous material release, in some cases in which conflicts between the landlord's and the tenant's interests preclude agreement on the pace and scope of the remediation, default and termination may be a viable means for the landlord to protect itself.[26]

The tenant likewise may need to consider whether it should reserve the right to terminate the lease as a result of contamination problems. Negotiation of a tenant termination right may be appropriate when, for example, the tenant is concerned that the potential for preexisting or off-site contamination, or other hazardous material releases that are not the tenant's responsibility under the lease, may impair the tenant's ongoing operations.

Survival of Indemnity and Other Lease Provisions Relating to Remediation of Hazardous Materials

Because remediation of serious contamination may occur over an extended period and may lead to additional litigation extending beyond the term of the lease, the landlord should provide for the survival of key hazardous material provisions in the lease, particularly the indemnity provisions. In negotiating these survival provisions, the tenant should attempt, again, to limit its liability to contamination caused by *its* activities during the lease term (under applicable law, the tenant would likely be liable for this contamination in any event) and to avoid causation issues associated with particularly stale claims by establishing some survival cutoff date.

To the extent the tenant's liability extends beyond the lease term (when it is no longer in possession of the premises), the tenant should reserve a right of access to the property to perform required investigation and remediation measures. The tenant should also seek to have some reasonable input into the nature and scope of remediation of the premises. Particularly in cases in which the contamination occurring during the tenant's possession of the premises may be relatively minor compared to contamination caused by other sources, the tenant's desire to minimize or defer remediation may conflict with the desires of other responsible parties, particularly the landlord, who may need to clean up the property before obtaining financing or re-leasing the premises. While a landlord is unlikely to turn control of site remediation over to a tenant, as long as the landlord maintains ultimate control over the cleanup standards and the timing of the remediation, it may be prepared to acknowledge some reasonable tenant review and approval rights.

Conditions of Premises upon Surrender

Even if the landlord has succeeded in providing for the survival of tenant environmental liabilities under the lease, it may still have reason to perform a second due diligence investigation before termination of the lease and resumption of the landlord's control over the premises. Inspection and inquiry before expiration of the lease may be important because the departure of the tenant and the passage of time after the lease expires make it more difficult to prove that the contamination occurred during the lease term, and more difficult to collect cleanup costs from the tenant. Once again, the scope of the due diligence will in large part be determined by the nature of the premises and the tenant's previous uses.

Regardless of the due diligence that occurs before the expiration or termination of the lease, the lease should clearly provide for the premises to be returned to the landlord in the same environmental condition that existed upon commencement of the lease term, free of any hazardous materials introduced after control of the premises was transferred to the tenant (or at least free of any hazardous materials introduced by the tenant and parties within its control). This type of provision will help prevent confusion about the standard of cleanup required if hazardous substances have been released during the term of the lease.

Conclusion

By now, most landlords and tenants are aware of the need to address environmental issues arising in the context of a commercial lease. While disparity in leverage may result in one-sided negotiations (usually with the landlord seeking to allocate all environmental risks to the tenant), many environmental issues can be resolved by identifying which risks are most likely to arise given the nature of the property and the tenant's proposed uses and by allocating responsibility based on whether the tenant or the landlord can control these risks.

In particular, by focusing on the transitional nature of control exercised by the parties during the course of the landlord-tenant relationship, the parties will be better able to anticipate which lease provisions come into play in addressing environmental issues and to determine how to protect their respective interests.

Notes

These sample provisions, like most leases, are somewhat landlord-oriented; no representation or recommendation is made by the authors as to their sufficiency for any particular lease transaction.

1. 42 U.S.C. § 9607(a) (1994). Most states have adopted environmental statutes with similar provisions. *See, e.g.*, CAL. HEALTH AND SAFETY CODE §§ 25300–395 (1994); DEL. CODE ANN. tit. 7, § 9105(a) (1993). See notes 2–11 for further discussion of circumstances in which joint and several liability and the "innocent landowner" defense may apply under CERCLA within the landlord-tenant context.

2. *See* United States v. Northernaire Plating Co., 670 F. Supp. 742 (W.D. Mich. 1987) (where harm caused by contamination is indivisible, landowner/lessor may be held strictly liable under CERCLA regardless of the fact that lessee may have been sole cause of contamination); United States v. Argent Corp., 21 Env't Rep. Cas. (BNA) 1354 (D.N.M. 1984) (because Congress deliberately omitted language from CERCLA that would have required participation in management or operation as a prerequisite to owner liability, owner may be held strictly liable for contamination caused by lessee); *C.f.*, *In re* Diamond Reo Trucks, Inc., 115 B.R. 559 (Bankr. W.D. Mich. 1991) (owner is liable for hazardous substance discharges by its tenants during its period of ownership, but is not liable for passive migration of contamination).

3. *See* Burlington Northern v. Woods Indus., Inc., 815 F. Supp. 1384 (E.D. Wash. 1993) (where lease was amended to include an additional forty-eight feet of a building later found to contain contaminated material, lessee was deemed to have sufficient control over the contaminated property to be subject to CERCLA

liability as an "owner"); United States v. SCRDI, 653 F. Supp 984, 1003 (D.S.C. 1984), *aff'd in part, vacated in part, sub nom.* United States v. Monsanto Co., 858 F.2d 160 (4th Cir. S.C. 1988), *cert. denied,* 490 U.S. 1106, 109 S. Ct. 3156, 104 L.Ed. 2d 1019 (1989) (lessee/sublessor may be held liable under CERCLA as "owner" for discharges caused by sublessee).

4. Nurad, Inc. v. William E. Hooper & Sons Co., 966 F.2d 837 (4th Cir. 1992), *cert. denied, sub-nom* Mumaw v. Nurad, Inc., 121 L.Ed. 2d 288 (U.S. 1992).

5. *Compare* Burlington Northern v. Woods Indus., Inc., 815 F. Supp. 1384 (E.D. Wash. 1993) (amendment to lease to include area that later became contaminated established sufficient control by tenant to justify imposition of liability under CERCLA).

6. *See* New York v. Shore Realty Corp., 759 F.2d 1032, 1044 (2d Cir. N.Y. 1985); Dedham Water Co. v. Cumberland Farms Dairy, Inc., 889 F.2d 1146, 1149, 1152–53 (1st Cir. Mass. 1989). However, some courts have held that to the extent a potentially responsible party can demonstrate that the harm caused by contamination is divisible and distinct, joint and several liability should not be imposed under CERCLA. *See, e.g.,* United States v. Alcan Aluminum Corp., 964 F.2d 252, 269 (3rd Cir. Pa. 1992); United States v. Marisol, Inc., 725 F. Supp. 833, 843 (M.D. Pa. 1989). While the apportionment of liability among potentially responsible parties may theoretically be available, the courts have not agreed as to when contamination should be deemed "divisible" and what standards should control apportionment. *Compare* O'Neil v. Picillo, 682 F. Supp. 706 (D.R.I. 1988), *aff'd,* 883 F.2d 176 (1st Cir. R.I. 1989) *and cert. denied,* 493 U.S. 1071 (1990) *and* United States v. Chem-Dyne Corp., 572 F. Supp. 802 (S.D. Ohio 1983) (where, in both cases, the courts applied restrictive standards for apportionment) *with* Alcan Aluminum Corp., 964 F.2d at 269 *and In re* Bell Petroleum Servs., 3 F.3d 889 (5th Cir. Tex. 1993) (where courts applied more flexible approach to apportionment).

7. CERCLA § 107(b)(3), 42 U.S.C. § 9607(b)(3)(1994). See Chapter 1 for a detailed discussion of the third party and innocent landowner defenses.

8. *See, e.g.,* United States v. Monsanto Co., 858 F.2d 160, 168–69 (4th Cir. S.C. 1988), *cert. denied,* 490 U.S. 1106 (1989) (holding that site owners could not establish the absence of a direct or indirect contractual relationship due to lease); United States v. Northernaire Plating Co., 670 F. Supp. 742, 748 (W.D. Mich. 1987) (lease agreement precludes landowner/lessor from invoking third-party defense).

9. *See, e.g.,* Westwood Pharmaceuticals, Inc. v. National Fuel Gas Distribution Corp., 964 F.2d 85 (2nd Cir. 1992) (landowner is precluded from raising third-party defense only if the contract between the landowner and the third party who was responsible for the discharge is connected with the handling of hazardous substances or allows the landowner to exert some element of control over the third party's activity).

10. *See generally* Stanley Works v. Snydergeneral Corporation, 781 F. Supp. 659, 662 (E.D. Cal. 1990) (after citing conflicting authorities as to owner and operator liability for passive discharges, court held that imposition of liability was more consistent with Congress's intent); *see also* Nurad, Inc. v. William E. Hooper & Sons Co., 966 F.2d 837 (4th Cir. Md. 1992), *cert. denied,* 121 L.Ed. 2d 288 (U.S. 1992) (holding former owner liable for passive migration); *Zoecon Corporation,* California State Water Resources Control Board, Order No. WQ 86-2 (1986) (ruling that landowner who purchased contaminated property was liable for "discharge"

of waste); *Arthur Spitzer et al.*, California State Water Resources Control Board, Order No. WQ 89-8 (1989) (ruling that hazardous waste cleanup orders may be issued to persons who have leased or purchased previously polluted land); *c.f.* Ecodyne Corp. v. Shah, 718 F. Supp. 1454 (N.D. Cal. 1989) (holding that CERCLA did not contemplate that prior owners or operators could be held liable for passive migration of contamination).

11. As discussed in Chapter 8, the scope of due diligence necessary to satisfy the "all appropriate inquiry" requirement has not been well defined and, as a result, creates uncertainty as to when the innocent landowner defense may be available.

12. *See* Mardan Corp. v. C.G.C. Music, 804 F.2d 1454 (9th Cir. Ariz. 1986); Kaufman and Broad-South Bay v. Unisys Corp., 822 F. Supp. 1468 (N.D. Cal. 1993). Chapter 11 discusses the allocation of environmental liability in detail.

13. 982 F.2d 989, 997 (6th Cir. Ohio 1993).

14. *See also* Commander Oil Corp. v. Advance Food Serv. Equip., 991 F.2d 49 (2d Cir. N.Y. 1993) (holding that ambiguities in indemnification provision necessitated review of extrinsic evidence as to parties' intent in allocating liability for environmental contamination).

15. For example, permits to operate equipment that emits criteria air pollutants may be required under applicable provisions of the Clean Air Act, 42 U.S.C. §§ 7401–7661; storm water or wastewater discharge permits may be required under the Clean Water Act, 33 U.S.C. §§ 1251–1385; and treatment, storage, and disposal permits may be required under the Resource Conservation and Recovery Act, 42 U.S.C. §§ 6901–92 (1994), and their various state analogues.

16. Cal. Health & Safety Code § 25359.7 (1994).

17. See Chapter 8 for a discussion of the potential scope of an environmental audit and other environmental due diligence.

18. See Chapter 11.

19. *See, e.g.*, International Clinical Laboratories, Inc. v. Stevens, 710 F. Supp. 466, 469–70, (E.D.N.Y. 1989) (under New York law, "as is" clause in a contract bars only breach of warranty actions and not statutory contribution claims under CERCLA); Southland Corp. v. Ashland Oil, Inc., 696 F. Supp. 994 (D.N.J. 1988) (standing alone, an "as is" provision cannot defeat CERCLA contribution claims).

20. *See, e.g.*, Commerce Redevelopment Agency v. American Home Prods. Inc., 37 Env't Rep. Cas. (BNA) 1277, 1287 (C.D. Cal. 1993) (rejecting rescission by purchaser where purchase agreement contained an "as is/where is" provision); *see also* Restatement (Second) of Contracts, § 154 (where parties are aware at the time a contract is entered into that a potential liability may arise in the future, the parties may assume such risk as an element of the contract).

21. *See generally* Annot., 22 A.L.R. 3d 521, 529–55 (1968) (discussion of cases in which tenants have been deemed to assume substantial repair obligations).

22. In Brown v. Green, 8 Cal. 4th 812, 35 Cal. Rptr. 2d 598, 884 P. 2d 55 (1994), the California Supreme Court was asked to interpret the compliance with law provisions of a Standard Industrial Lease published by the American Industrial Real Estate Association. The court held that a county order mandating the replacement of asbestos-containing materials was outside the scope of the lease provision that required the tenant to comply with laws "regulating the use by the lessee of the premises." However, after declining to adopt a rule that would have imposed

on the landlord the obligation to remove environmentally hazardous materials in the absence of explicit provisions to the contrary in the lease agreement, the court held that the language contained in the lease as a whole and the circumstances surrounding the lease transaction—including the "net" nature of the lease, its comparatively long fifteen-year term, and the burdens arising from compliance with the regulation compared to the benefits derived by the tenant under the lease—supported the conclusion that the tenant had accepted responsibility for government-mandated work unrelated to its particular use of the premises. The court expressly distinguished three other cases in which courts had held that asbestos abatement activities were the responsibility of the landlord. *Cf.*, Wolf v. 2539 Realty Assoc., 161 A.D. 2d 11, 560 N.Y.S. 2d 24 (1st Dep't 1990) (court held that a lease that required the tenant to keep the premises in good repair and to comply with laws "with respect to tenant's use and occupancy of the demised premises" was ineffective to shift the burden of abating asbestos to the tenant where asbestos abatement regulations were enacted subsequent to the date of the lease); Linden Boulevard, L.P. v. Elota Realty Co., 196 A.D. 2d 808, 601 N.Y.S. 2d 949 (2nd Dep't 1990) (holding that removal of asbestos was a "structural change," was extraordinary in scope and cost, was not required as a result of the tenant's specific use of the premises, and, therefore, was not the tenant's responsibility); Sun Insurance Servs. v. 260 Peachtree St., Inc., 192 Ga. App. 482, 385 S.E. 2d 127 (1989) (because tenant renovations would have enhanced value of landlord's property and were contemplated by terms of the lease, the landlord acted unreasonably in conditioning its consent to renovations on tenant's agreement to pay costs of asbestos removal).

23. Where regulatory agencies permit contaminated soils to remain on the premises, they often do so subject to a condition that requires any deed transferring the real property to acknowledge the presence of such materials. Obviously, this type of deed restriction may impair the marketability of property and may be unacceptable to the landlord.

24. *See* the earlier section on "Description of Premises and Liability for Releases within Common Areas."

25. *See supra* note 10.

26. The landlord's ability to terminate a lease as a result of the tenant's discharge of a hazardous substance is by no means a foregone conclusion. *See, e.g.*, Ellman v. Woo, 34 Env't. Rep. Cas. (BNA) 1969 (E.D. Pa. 1991) (after noting that lease forfeiture is looked on with disfavor and will only be upheld where termination rights are clearly set forth in the lease and exercise of such rights is not "unconscionable," court held that landlord could not terminate the lease of a tenant-dry cleaner who had not intentionally discharged solvents).

APPENDIX

Sample Lease Provisions

"As-Is" Clause

Tenant agrees that the Premises shall be leased and delivered to Tenant in its current "AS-IS/WITH ALL FAULTS" condition. Tenant hereby represents, warrants, covenants, agrees, and acknowledges that:

( ) Tenant recognizes that Landlord would not lease the Premises to Tenant except upon an "AS-IS/WITH ALL FAULTS" basis.

( ) Tenant has conducted its own independent investigation of the Premises and the physical condition thereof, including the potential presence of any Hazardous Materials on or about the Premises, and Tenant is fully aware of the condition of the Premises and the surrounding property.

( ) Landlord has made no express, implied, or other representations of any kind in connection with the physical condition of the Premises, the Building, or any other improvements appurtenant thereto, including, without limitation, the physical condition of any building materials, building systems, soils or groundwater conditions, or the presence of Hazardous Materials in, on, under, or about the Premises, Building, or the land upon which the Building is situated ("Land"), and Tenant has relied solely on Tenant's own inspection and examination of such matters.

( ) Tenant expressly assumes the risk that Hazardous Materials or other adverse environmental conditions may be present in, on, under, or around the

Premises, Building, and Land, and any risk that such conditions may affect the suitability of the Premises for Tenant's proposed or intended use, and Tenant agrees Landlord shall have no responsibility or liability with respect to any such occurrence or condition.

Covenants Governing Use of Hazardous Materials

Tenant covenants and agrees that during the term of this Lease, neither Tenant nor any of Tenant's agents, employees, contractors, invitees, assignees, or sublessees shall cause any Hazardous Material to be brought upon, kept, or used in, on, or about the Premises or Building or transported to or from the Premises or Building without the prior written consent of Landlord, which Landlord shall not unreasonably withhold so long as Tenant demonstrates to Landlord's satisfaction that such Hazardous Material: (1) is necessary or useful to Tenant's business; (2) would be used, kept, stored, and disposed of in a manner that fully complies with all laws, rules, statutes, ordinances, orders, requirements, and policies (collectively "Hazardous Material Requirements") of any governmental agency or authority or any fire insurance underwriters (collectively, "Governmental Authorities") applicable to any such Hazardous Material; (3) would not invalidate or limit the coverage or increase the premiums of any insurance policy affecting or covering the Premises or the Building; (4) would not violate any provisions of any Mortgage Documents; and (5) would not pose a material risk to any persons or property or materially increase the risk of a Hazardous Material Release. Landlord hereby consents to the specific uses by Tenant of Hazardous Materials as set forth in Exhibit ___ attached hereto. Tenant covenants and agrees that to the extent Tenant or any of Tenant's agents, employees, contractors, invitees, assignees, or sublessees shall cause any Hazardous Material to be kept, used, or present in, on, or about the Premises or the Building, Tenant shall ensure that such Hazardous Material is in full compliance with all Hazardous Material Requirements and the terms of this Lease, and that no Hazardous Material Release occurs on, under, or about the Premises or the Building.

Indemnification of Landlord

Tenant shall indemnify, defend (with counsel satisfactory to Landlord), and hold Landlord, its directors, officers, employees, agents, assigns, and any successors to Landlord's interest in the Building, harmless from and against any and all loss, cost, damage, expense (including reasonable attorneys' fees), claim, cause of action, judgment, penalty, fine, or liability, directly or indirectly, relating to or arising from the use, storage, release, discharge, handling, or presence of Hazardous Materials on, under, or about the Premises or the Building in violation of Tenant's obligations under this Lease ("Hazardous Materials Release"). This indemnification shall include without limitation (a) personal injury claims, (b) the payment of liens, (c) diminution in the value of the Premises, (d) damages for the loss or restriction on use of the Premises or the Building, (e) sums paid in settlement of claims, (f) actual attorneys' fees, consulting fees, and expert fees, (g) the cost of any investigation of site conditions, and (h) the cost of any repair, cleanup, remedial, removal, or restoration work or detoxification if required by any Governmental Authorities or deemed necessary in Landlord's reasonable judgment. Landlord shall have the right but not the obligation to join and participate in, and control, if it so elects, any legal proceedings or actions initiated in connection with the Hazardous Materials Release. Landlord may also negotiate, defend, approve, and appeal any action taken or issued by any applicable Governmental Authorities with regard to a Hazardous Materials Release. Any costs or expenses incurred by Landlord for which Tenant is responsible under this Paragraph or for which Tenant has indemnified Landlord: (i) shall be paid to Landlord on demand, during the term of this Lease as additional rent; and (ii) from and after the expiration or earlier termination of the Lease shall be reimbursed by Tenant on demand. Tenant's obligations pursuant to the foregoing indemnity shall survive the expiration or termination of this Lease and shall bind Tenant's successors and assignees and inure to the benefit of Landlord's successors and assignees.

Landlord's Right of Entry

Notwithstanding any other right of entry granted to Landlord under this Lease, Landlord shall have the right to enter the Premises or to have consultants enter the Premises throughout the Term of this Lease for the purpose of (1) determining whether the Premises are in conformity with the Hazardous Materials Requirements and other federal, state, and local statutes, regulations, ordinances, and policies, (2) conducting an environmental audit or investigation of the Premises for purposes of sale, transfer, conveyance, or financing, (3) determining whether Tenant has complied with the environmental requirements of this Lease, (4) determining the corrective measures, if any, required of Tenant to ensure the safe use, storage, and disposal of Hazardous Materials, or (5) removing Hazardous Materials (except to the extent used, stored, or disposed of by Tenant in compliance with Hazardous Materials Requirements and the terms of this Lease). Tenant agrees to provide access and reasonable assistance for such inspections. Such inspections may include, but are not limited to, entering the Premises or adjacent property with drill rigs or other machinery for the purpose of obtaining laboratory samples of soils or ground-water conditions. Landlord shall not be limited in the number of such inspections during the Term of this Lease. To the extent such inspections disclose the presence of Hazardous Materials used, stored, or disposed of by Tenant or its agents, employees, contractors, or invitees in violation of the terms of this Lease, Tenant shall reimburse Landlord for the cost of such inspections within ten (10) days of receipt of a written statement thereof. If such consultants determine that Hazardous Materials have been released, discharged, stored, or used on the Premises in violation of the terms of this Lease, Tenant shall, in a timely manner, at its expense, remove such Hazardous Materials and otherwise comply with the recommendations of such consultants to the satisfaction of Landlord and any applicable Governmental Authorities. The right granted to Landlord herein to inspect the Premises shall not create a duty on Landlord's part to inspect the Premises, nor liability of Landlord for Tenant's use, storage, or disposal of Hazardous Materials, it being understood that Tenant shall be solely responsible for all liability in connection therewith.

Notice to Landlord of Violations/Releases

Tenant shall immediately advise Landlord in writing of, and if applicable provide Landlord with a copy of: (a) any notices of violation or potential or alleged violation of any Hazardous Material Requirements that are received by Tenant from any Governmental Authorities; (b) any and all inquiries, investigations, enforcement, cleanup, removal, or other governmental or regulatory actions instituted or threatened relating to Tenant, the Premises, or the Building; (c) all claims made or threatened by any third party against Tenant, the Premises or the Building relating to any Hazardous Materials; and (d) any release of Hazardous Materials on or about the Premises or the Building that Tenant knows of or reasonably believes may have occurred.

Remediation of Hazardous Material Release

If any Hazardous Materials are released, discharged, or otherwise come to be located on or about the Premises or the Building in violation of the provisions of Paragraph __ of this Lease ("Hazardous Material Release"), Tenant shall promptly take all actions, at its sole expense and without abatement of rent, as are necessary to return the affected portion of the Premises or the Building and any other affected soil or groundwater to their condition existing prior to the Hazardous Material Release. Landlord shall have the right to approve all such remedial work, including, without limitation: (i) the selection of any contractor or consultant Tenant proposes to retain to investigate the nature or extent of such Hazardous Material Release or to perform any such remedial work; (ii) any reports or disclosure statements to be submitted to any Governmental Authorities prior to the submission of such materials; and (iii) any proposed remediation plan or any material revision thereto prior to submission to any Governmental Authorities. Notwithstanding the foregoing, Landlord's prior consent shall not be necessary if a Hazardous Material Release poses an immediate threat to the health, safety, or welfare of any persons and, despite Tenant's best efforts; it is not possible to obtain Landlord's consent before taking remedial action to abate such immediate threat; provided that: (a) Tenant shall notify Landlord as soon as possible and shall thereafter obtain Landlord's consent as otherwise provided in this Paragraph; and (b) Tenant shall take only such action as may be necessary or appropriate to abate such immediate threat and shall otherwise comply with the provisions of this Paragraph. In addition to any rights reserved by Landlord in

Paragraph ___ of this Lease, Landlord shall have the right, but not the obligation, to participate with Tenant and Tenant's consultants and contractors in any meetings with representatives of the Governmental Authorities, and Tenant shall provide Landlord reasonable notice of any such meetings. All remedial work shall be performed in compliance with all Hazardous Material Requirements. Landlord's consent to any remedial activities undertaken by Tenant shall not be withheld so long as Landlord determines, in its sole, good faith business judgment, that such activities will not cause any material adverse long-term or short-term effect on the Premises, Building, or adjacent property.

Surrender of Premises

Tenant shall surrender the Premises to Landlord upon the expiration or earlier termination of this Lease free of debris, waste, and Hazardous Materials used, stored, or disposed of by Tenant or its agents, employees, contractors, or invitees or otherwise discharged on the Premises during the term of this Lease in violation of the provisions of Paragraph __. In all events, the Premises shall be surrendered in a condition that complies with all Hazardous Material Requirements, recommendations of environmental consultants hired by Landlord, and such other reasonable environmental requirements as may be imposed by Landlord.

Operating Expense Pass-Through

Hazardous Materials.

Tenant acknowledges that Landlord may incur costs for complying with Hazardous Material Requirements that are not the responsibility of either Landlord or Tenant under this Lease, including costs in connection with the following: (a) Hazardous Materials present in the soil or groundwater under or about the Building of which Landlord has no knowledge as of the date hereof; (b) a change in Hazardous Material Requirements that makes a substance not previously considered hazardous or not previously present in violation of the Hazardous Material Requirements, whether known or unknown to Landlord, a violation of such Hazardous Material Requirements; (c) Hazardous Material that migrates, flows, percolates, diffuses, or in any way moves onto or under the Building after the date hereof; (d) Hazardous Material present on or under the Building as a result of any discharge, dumping, or spilling (whether accidental or otherwise) on the Building by other tenants of the Building or their agents, employees, contractors, or invitees, or by others. Tenant agrees that the costs incurred by Landlord for complying with Hazardous Material Requirements shall be an Operating Expense unless the cost of such compliance, as between Landlord and Tenant, is made the responsibility of Tenant pursuant to any other Paragraph of this Lease. To the extent any such Operating Expense relating to Hazardous Material is subsequently recovered or reimbursed through insurance, or recovery from responsible third parties, or other action, Tenant shall be entitled to a proportionate reimbursement to the extent it has paid its share of such Operating Expense to which such recovery or reimbursement relates.

Notwithstanding the foregoing, there shall be excluded from Operating Expenses the costs of complying with Hazardous Material Requirements that result from (1) the active negligence or willful misconduct of Landlord; or (2) the presence of Hazardous Material in the soil or groundwater or otherwise on or about the Building on or before the date of the Lease.

Covenants Governing Presence of Asbestos

( ) Tenant acknowledges that Landlord has furnished Tenant with a copy of an asbestos survey dated ______________ (the "Asbestos Survey") prepared by ________________, regarding the presence of asbestos-containing material in the Premises and the Building, and that Tenant has read and understands the report. Tenant hereby approves of the operating and maintenance recommendations set forth in the Asbestos Survey, and agrees to abide by such recommendations to the extent they relate to Tenant's use or occupancy of the Premises or the Building.

( ) Landlord's maintenance obligations as provided in Paragraph _____ of this Lease shall include the obligation to maintain, at Landlord's expense, the asbestos-containing material existing in the structural walls and roof of the Premises in accordance with the recommendations set forth in the Asbestos Survey, except for any damage or disturbance caused by any act or omission of Tenant, Tenant's employees, suppliers, shippers, customers, invitees, sublessees, or assignees and except for any alteration to the Premises performed by Tenant. Tenant agrees that Landlord shall be deemed reasonable in withholding its consent under Paragraph ____ of the Lease to any proposed alteration of the Premises if Landlord determines that such alteration would possibly disturb the asbestos-containing material or require Landlord to remove or abate the asbestos-containing material.

( ) Notwithstanding anything to the contrary contained in this Lease, Landlord reserves the right to enter the Premises at any time and from time to time during the term of the Lease, upon not less than __________ days' prior notice to Tenant, to take any action with respect to asbestos or asbestos-containing material that is necessary or desirable to comply with Hazardous Material Requirements, or to implement any of the recommendations set forth in the Asbestos Survey or in any subsequent surveys or reports prepared by Landlord's contractors or consultants (for purposes of this subparagraph, "Remedial Action"). Landlord agrees to consult with Tenant during such ______-day period prior to the taking of Remedial Action to discuss possible ways to minimize disruption to Tenant's business. Under no circumstances, however, shall the taking of any Remedial Action by Landlord be deemed or construed to be a default by Landlord under this Lease, or an actual or constructive eviction of Tenant from the Premises, and the Lease shall remain in full force and effect. Tenant hereby waives any claim for damages against Landlord, its partners, agents, and employees arising out of or related to any Remedial Action, including, without limitation, damages for any injury or inconvenience to or interference with Tenant's business, any loss of occupancy or quiet enjoyment of the Premises, and any other loss occasioned by any Remedial Action. Tenant also waives any claim for injunctive relief arising out of or related to any Remedial Action. In the event any Remedial Action renders any portion of the Premises unusable for more than ________ consecutive business days, then Base Rent shall be abated, beginning with the _____ business day after such unusability began, until the period of such unusability ends, based on the proportion of the Premises rendered unusable.

CHAPTER 13

Tax Aspects of Environmental Matters

STEFAN F. TUCKER
KATHLEEN M. COURTIS

As more information becomes available concerning the harmful effects of industrialization, taxpayers should expect to incur increasing responsibility for remediating environmental hazards. Depending on the type of hazard and the strictness of the applicable regulations, a taxpayer's decisions with respect to environmental remediation may result in unanticipated tax consequences. Unfortunately, because remediation has not been required until relatively recently, there is little case authority directly on point to provide guidance. What does exist at this writing are two Technical Advice Memoranda (TAMs) on asbestos and a Revenue Ruling and a TAM on soil remediation.

The first issue that arises with respect to remediation costs is whether such costs may be deducted in the current taxable year or must be capitalized and then, in the best of circumstances, depreciated in future years. After the determination is made whether to deduct or capitalize the costs, the taxpayer must determine when the deduction may be taken or over how many years a capitalized cost may be depreciated. The sooner a deduction is taken or the shorter the period over which depreciation occurs, the lower the after-tax cost of remediation.

This chapter first briefly discusses the theory behind the rules of capitalization and the statutory and regulatory tests for determining whether a cost is deductible or capitalized.[1] It next discusses the tax treatment of (1) the actual costs of environmental remediation, (2) legal fees associated with the remediation, and (3) penalties and fines assessed by the government. The chapter then focuses on the timing rules with respect to deductions. Lastly, it focuses on the periods over which a taxpayer depreciates capitalized remediation costs.

Background

Before examining the specific requirements of the Internal Revenue Code of 1986 (Code), as amended, and the accompanying regulations, it may be helpful to review the theory of why certain costs are deductible and others must be capitalized.

The federal income tax system theoretically imposes a tax based on a taxpayer's economic income,[2] which is measured by tracking receipts and allowing offsets for the costs of earning those receipts.[3] Because an exact measurement of this income would be complex, Congress has made certain compromises, one of which is to require that a taxpayer determine and report income at twelve-month intervals.[4] The effect of this compromise is twofold.

First, costs cannot be expensed automatically in the period in which they are incurred[5] but, instead, must be matched and deducted at the time the revenue generated by such costs is reported.[6] This matching is effectuated through capitalization, with depreciation deductions in the periods in which revenue is reported. A corollary of this principle is that, if a cost will not produce any future income, it should be expensed in the year incurred.[7]

Second, the tax system must have precise interperiod timing rules for the measurement of revenues and expenses. Imprecise rules would allow taxpayers to manipulate the reporting of their revenues and expenses, resulting in an overall decrease in tax revenues. As a result, the federal income tax system has rules to determine when revenue should be recognized[8] and when deductions should be taken.[9]

Deduction or Capitalization

Although there are no specific sections of the 1986 code that relate to the deduction or capitalization of environmental remediation costs, taxpayers have analogized these costs to repair and maintenance costs. The basic rules applicable to deduction and capitalization are found, respectively, in Sections 162[10] and 263. Deduction and capitalization are, essentially, flip sides of the same coin.

Section 162(a) requires that an expense be "ordinary and necessary" to be deducted in the year it is incurred.[11] Expenses that are appropriate and helpful for the development of the taxpayer's business are defined as "necessary." "Ordinary" distinguishes between deductible and capitalized costs.[12]

Treasury Regulation Section 1.162-4 provides that the costs of incidental repairs, which neither materially add to the value of the property nor appreciably prolong its life but keep it in an ordinarily efficient operating condition, are currently deductible. Repairs in the nature of replacements, to the extent that they arrest deterioration and appreciably prolong the life of the property, are capitalized.

Capitalization[13] is required under the Code's Section 263(a) for amounts incurred for new buildings or for permanent improvements or betterments that increase the value of any property.[14] Treasury Regulation Section 1.263(a)-1(b) denies a deduction for expenditures that (1) increase the value of property or (2) restore property for which a depreciation allowance was allowed.[15] These expenditures will generally be recognizable as capital expenditures because they (1) add to the value, or substantially prolong the useful life, of property owned by the taxpayer, or (2) adapt property to a new and different use.[16] Examples of capital expenditures include the acquisition or construction of buildings, machinery, equipment, furniture and fixtures, and similar property having a useful life substantially beyond the taxable year.[17]

How Are Increases in Value or Useful Life Measured?

In deciding whether a remediation expenditure should be deducted or capitalized, a taxpayer must determine the effect of the repair—in other words, whether it increases the property's value or extends its useful life. In making this determination, the taxpayer faces a dilemma. To assess the tax consequences of the repair, the taxpayer must ascertain the value or life of the property at two different points in time. One point, never in dispute, is after the costs have been expended to correct the problem (post-repair). In deciding on the other reference point, there are two possible choices, consisting of either the point in time after the property has become functionally impaired (post-condition) or the point in time before the occurrence of the condition necessitating the expenditure (pre-condition). If the first alternative is chosen, capitalization will always be required because the expenditures under this analysis will inevitably increase the property's value or prolong its life. This argument persuaded the tax court in *Plainfield-Union Water Co. v. Commissioner* that the appropriate time for measuring value or life was the second alternative (pre-condition).[18]

The application of this second alternative to all repair situations is in some doubt. Certain cases have required the capitalization of costs incurred to meet government regulations, which, if not complied with, would have resulted in the shutdown of the taxpayer's business.[19] In these situations, the courts held that compliance with the law increased the property's value by allowing the business to continue. In finding capitalization to be the proper treatment, these courts implicitly measured the increase in value by comparing the post-repair value with the post-condition value. The Internal Revenue Service (IRS) has argued that these cases require the capitalization of asbestos removal costs and that *Plainfield-Union* is inapplicable. Commentators have noted, however, that in all of these cases the expenditures would have been capitalized because they created separate assets with useful lives substantially beyond one year.[20]

What Constitutes an Increase in Value?

Taxpayers trying to determine the appropriate treatment for environmental remediation costs must know what constitutes an increase in value. For example, in *Plainfield-Union*, the use, strength, and capacity of pipe were the benchmarks used to determine whether the pipeline's value had increased. This type of benefit can be measured easily. Yet the IRS has asserted in the context of asbestos removal that intangible benefits, such as a safer workplace, will cause costs to be capitalized.

Definition of a New or Different Use

Because environmental remediation may result in a change in a property's use, a taxpayer must also determine whether the change in use is significant enough to require remediation costs to be capitalized. Few cases have directly addressed the question of what constitutes a new and different use. In *Plainfield-Union*, the taxpayer's water mains were originally carrying well water, and a change was made to river water. The IRS tried to argue that this was a new use, but the tax court stated that the conveyance of water, which was the primary purpose for which the pipes were used, did not change. Similarly, courts have held that there was no change in use when a pipeline was converted from manufactured to natural gas.[21] Courts have capitalized the costs involved in converting a warehouse into a manufacturing plant,[22] a personal residence into a rental property,[23] and an apartment house into a rooming house.[24] Accordingly, it appears that an asset will require a real change in function before it will be considered used for a new or different purpose.

General Plan of Rehabilitation

Superimposed upon Treasury Regulation Section 1.162-4 is a judicial concept requiring capitalization of an expenditure that is part of a general plan of rehabilitation, modernization, or improvement, even though the item standing alone may be classified as a repair.[25] The scope of this doctrine is being developed. For example, in the recent case of *Moss v. Commissioner*,[26] the taxpayer argued that the doctrine was triggered only when substantial capital improvements and repairs were made to the same asset. The Ninth Circuit noted that, although the taxpayer's theory was consistent with the case law, it chose to hold that the doctrine is invoked properly when property is being placed in efficient operating condition, and that assets must be included within the plan's scope when they are generally suitable for use in the taxpayer's trade or business. Although the IRS has treated some environmental remediation expenditures as being part of a plan of general rehabilitation, it is unclear at this writing how the IRS will apply this doctrine in the future.

Treatment of Remediation Costs as a Loss

Commentators have also suggested that remediation costs might represent a deductible loss under Section 165,[27] which allows a current deduction for losses that are not compensated for by insurance or otherwise. To recognize a loss, a taxpayer must isolate a causal event resulting, generally, in the sudden termination of the usefulness of the property and abandonment of such property.[28] In addition, losses attributable to a casualty are deductible.[29]

Taxpayers ordinarily will not satisfy the requirements of this Code section. For example, the taxpayer will not be able to isolate the nondepreciated cost of the specific item of abandoned property (e.g., asbestos insulation). In addition, it is unknown whether the passage of an environmental remediation law qualifies as a sudden event. While a strong argument can be made that a newly enacted statute banning a hazardous substance qualifies as a sudden event, the argument loses some of its persuasive power when continuous monitoring of the substance is permitted, with removal being required only if safe levels of the substance cannot be maintained. Likewise, it is unknown whether a taxpayer could demonstrate the uselessness of the property if monitoring showed nonharmful levels of the substance prior to removal. There may indeed be circumstances where remediation results in a loss deduction. However, this does not appear to be a viable position for the majority of remediation costs.

Deduction or Capitalization of Environmental Cleanup Costs

Tax Treatment of Specific Remediation Costs

This section of the chapter will analyze the IRS's arguments for the deduction of many soil and groundwater remediation costs, the capitalization of asbestos removal costs, and the deduction of asbestos encapsulation costs. In situations such as the purchase of contaminated land, leaking underground storage tanks, and lead paint, where the IRS has not promulgated specific guidance, the chapter will discuss the likely tax treatment of remediation costs.

"Necessary" Requirement

Environmental cleanup costs should meet the "necessary" threshold of Section 162(a) because leaving contamination "as is" ultimately threatens the taxpayer's investment. Nonetheless, it is possible that the IRS will assert that remediation activities not required by law are not necessary expenditures.

Remediation of Land Contaminated by the Taxpayer

Recently the IRS, in Revenue Ruling 94-38,[30] held that taxpayers may deduct most of the costs of remediating soil and groundwater contamination. This is true regardless of the type of contamination and whether the remediated land is used in the taxpayer's business or is left idle. Based on the legal analysis of the ruling, IRS personnel have also stated that remediation costs are deductible if the contamination is on property that is not owned by the taxpayer but the taxpayer is responsible for cleanup.[31]

In this ruling's fact pattern, the taxpayer purchased uncontaminated land. Hazardous waste created by the taxpayer in manufacturing processes conducted on the land was buried, contaminating the land and the groundwater. To comply with applicable and reasonably anticipated governmental requirements, the taxpayer remediated the land by excavating the contaminated soil, transporting it to a containment facility, and filling the affected areas with uncontaminated soil. The taxpayer also installed a groundwater treatment system to contain, extract, pump, treat, and monitor the groundwater.

The IRS determined that the costs to build the groundwater treatment system were capital expenditures because the system had a useful life substantially beyond the taxable year in which it was constructed.[32] However, the IRS ruled that expenditures for soil remediation and ongoing groundwater monitoring were deductible because such costs did not produce permanent improvements or otherwise provide significant benefits. In determining whether the value of the property increased as a result of the expenditures, the IRS applied the *Plainfield-Union* test, stating that the land's value was not increased because the taxpayer restored the soil and groundwater to approximately the same condition that they were in before the contamination. The IRS noted that the expenditures neither prolonged the land's useful life nor adapted it to a new and different use. The ruling stated, almost as an aside, that the land was restored, but, because land is not subject to a depreciation allowance, there was no need to capitalize the costs.

Revenue Ruling 94-38's promulgation was a radical change in the IRS's position with respect to the tax treatment of the environmental cleanup costs of land. In addition, it provides insight into how the IRS might treat other hazardous waste remediation situations, although it cannot be relied on for other types of waste or property remediation outside the fact pattern.[33]

In 1993 the IRS released TAM 9315004,[34] involving the cleanup of contamination resulting from polychlorinated biphenyls (PCBs), which required that the cleanup be capitalized. Although the costs were the same type as those at issue in Revenue Ruling 94-38, the IRS articulated five reasons why they should be capitalized.

- Courts have capitalized costs that were significant compared with a taxpayer's overall operation.
- PCB cleanup is the result of a choice to forego annual maintenance.[35]
- The replacement of soil increased the property's value because it prevented the incurrence of additional government penalties, provided a safe environment for workers and adjoining property owners, and increased the property's marketability.
- Costs are capital where modifications bring property into compliance with government regulations.[36]
- The cleanup operation constituted a general plan of rehabilitation and restoration.

The taxpayer had asserted that the *Plainfield-Union* test governed the method by which an increase in value should be tested, but the IRS stated that *Plainfield-Union* was distinguishable, since the concrete lining that had been installed in that case involved only a minor part of the taxpayer's operation and was not part of a general plan of rehabilitation.

In comparing the legal analyses of TAM 9315004 and Revenue Ruling 94-38, it appears that certain arguments will not constitute future grounds for the IRS to require capitalization with respect to other environmental cleanup costs. For example:

- The magnitude of the expenditure in relation to the taxpayer's overall business appears to be irrelevant. Although discussed in the TAM, it was not mentioned in the Revenue Ruling.[37]
- Although the intangible benefits discussed in the TAM were present in the Revenue Ruling, they did not factor into the capitalization equation. Thus, if *Plainfield-Union* is applicable, intangible future benefits are likely to be disregarded in determining an increase in value.
- Finally, compliance with government regulations did not constitute an independent reason for capitalization in the Revenue Ruling. Thus, it would appear that compliance does not pertain to the capitalization issue, but, rather, answers the question of whether the expenditures were "necessary."

The other important implication for the future is demonstrated by the following sentence in the ruling:

> Moreover, since the land is not subject to an allowance for depreciation, amortization, or depletion, the amounts expended to restore the land to its original condition are not subject to capitalization.

This sentence implies that remediation of depreciable property is capitalized. This bodes ill for the IRS changing its capitalization position on the replacement of asbestos.

Purchase of Contaminated Land

The Treasury Department has stated that Revenue Ruling 94-38 does not apply to a taxpayer's purchase of contaminated land,[38] possibly signaling that it believes remediation costs in such a situation should be capitalized. The Treasury Department has not distinguished between purchases where the contamination is known and those where it is unknown.

Purchasers who are aware of the presence of contamination before acquisition most likely will have factored the cleanup cost into the purchase price. If such purchasers are allowed a deduction, they will receive a significant undeserved tax benefit—the ability to write off part of the purchase price immediately. However, if the taxpayer who purchases without knowledge of contamination is allowed to deduct remediation costs, that taxpayer deducts a current loss that otherwise might not be recognized until disposition of the property—a benefit many could view as equitable.

In the case of a purchaser who is aware of the presence of contamination, the IRS could attack the deduction of remediation costs on the theory that, because the contamination was obvious at the time of purchase, the taxpayer's investment was incomplete until the remediation was accomplished.[39] In such a situation, the IRS might also assert the general plan of rehabilitation doctrine.

Leaking Storage Tanks

The Treasury Department has stated that Revenue Ruling 94-38 does not apply to the remediation of leaking storage tanks.[40] In a typical leaking tank situation, the taxpayer must fix or remove the tank and remediate any resulting soil or groundwater contamination. To the extent groundwater treatment facilities are constructed or the soil remediated, the tax treatment should follow the result of Revenue Ruling 94-38, but a taxpayer cannot be certain.

With respect to the storage tank, the taxpayer will either repair, replace, or remove it. The tax consequences of two of these three alternatives are clear. If the taxpayer repairs the existing tank, the cost will be deductible as a repair under Treasury Regulation Section 1.162-4. If the tank is replaced, the cost of the new tank will be capitalized as a separate asset with a useful life substantially beyond the taxable year.

The IRS has not specified the proper tax treatment if a tank is removed but not replaced. It would seem that the cost should be deducted currently because the expense will not increase the value of the property, prolong its useful life, or adapt it to a new or different use.

Asbestos

A taxpayer who finds asbestos on his or her property will generally have two alternatives, depending on the condition of the asbestos: encapsulation or removal. The IRS's current position—as stated in TAM 9240004 (the Equipment Ruling)[41] and TAM 9411002 (the Building Ruling)[42]—is that encapsulation is deductible and removal is capitalized.

ASBESTOS REMOVAL. In the Equipment Ruling, asbestos insulation in equipment (tangible personal property) was replaced with less efficient insulation. The following reasons for capitalization were given by the IRS:

- The removal increased the value of the equipment because the risk of liability to employees decreased, the equipment became more marketable, the operating efficiency of the equipment increased, and the possibility of being forced to suspend operations due to noncompliance with government regulations was reduced or eliminated.
- The removal resulted in a permanent cure.
- The value of the taxpayer's assets, other than the affected equipment, increased because removal reduced the possibility of equipment interruptions due to safety violations, reduced the time of ordinary equipment repair and maintenance, and eliminated the need for safety precautions during ordinary maintenance.[43]

In the Building Ruling asbestos removal occurred when a boiler house was converted into office space and a garage. These costs were capitalized because of the conversion of the property to a new or different use, but the IRS also stated that capitalization was required because:

- the value, use, and capacity of the boiler house increased through the elimination of health risks, which created better operating conditions and prevented any further exposure of

employees and lessees, made the property more marketable, and enabled the taxpayer to provide office space and a garage; and
- the repair was permanent.

The taxpayers in both TAMs argued that *Plainfield-Union* applied in determining whether the property's value had increased. Both taxpayers stated that the proper pre-condition value of the property was the value before asbestos was known to be a health hazard. In the Equipment Ruling the IRS stated that *Plainfield-Union* was not determinative because:

- the test only applies in circumstances where property has deteriorated progressively, which was not true here because the asbestos was not removed due to its deterioration as an insulation or fire retardant material;[44]
- the test was inappropriate in this situation because it was impossible to value the asset in its pre-condition state, inasmuch as the asset was manufactured with asbestos; and
- the increase in the value of the equipment was attributable to subjective factors and thus was incompatible with the objective test articulated in *Plainfield-Union.*

In the Building Ruling the IRS merely stated that it was impossible to determine the pre-condition value of the building.

While commentators have disagreed strongly with the IRS's position in these two TAMs,[45] the taxpayers, in responding to the IRS's position, likely were struggling to find case law that proved that their formulation was correct. The difficulty is that there is not much case law after *Plainfield-Union* dealing with repairs to assets where the latent defect existed at the asset's creation and only was found once it became patent.[46] Nonetheless, that the IRS position is wrong seems even more certain in light of its reversal on the use of *Plainfield-Union* in Revenue Ruling 94-38.

ASBESTOS ENCAPSULATION. In the Building Ruling the IRS determined that the encapsulation by wrapping of exposed and damaged pipe insulation was deductible because

- it did not result in an increase in the value or useful life of the building;
- the cure was temporary; and
- there was no general plan of rehabilitation.

According to the IRS, the encapsulation costs resembled those in *Midland Empire Packing Co. v. Commissioner,*[47] where installation of a concrete lining, designed to prevent oil seepage, was deductible. The encapsulation, like the concrete lining, did not increase the value or prolong the useful life of the property beyond what it was before the damage occurred. The IRS also stated that the cure was temporary because the wrapping reduced, but did not eliminate, the threat of exposure to airborne asbestos fibers.

The IRS clearly reached the correct result in this case because the encapsulation and monitoring do not increase the value of the property or cause the property to be used for a new or different use. What is troubling from a policy perspective is that these TAMs encourage taxpayers to encapsulate, which may or may not be the most appropriate response in all cases.

Lead Paint

Abatement of lead-based paint is generally accomplished by removal, encapsulation, or covering the affected surfaces. The IRS has not set forth any specific guidance on this point. However, the determination should be made using the tests set out in Treasury Regulation Section 1.263(a)-1 and Regulation Section 1.162-4.[48]

Legal Fees

The tax treatment of legal fees is based on a judicially created test which focuses on the "origin of the claim."[49] If the legal expenses arise in connection with a capital transaction, they will be capitalized. If the expenses arise in connection with a deductible expense, they will be deductible. Thus, the treatment of legal fees generally depends on whether the costs of the actual environmental remediation are deductible or capitalized.[50]

Fines and Penalties

The Code does not allow a deduction for any government-imposed fine or similar penalty resulting from a violation of law.[51] This rule supports a policy of not rewarding transgressors of the law. The courts have, after analysis of the legislative history,[52] interpreted the term "similar penalty" to mean a civil retributive penalty aimed at conduct that the state specifically seeks to prohibit. If the penalty is compensatory or is imposed to encourage prompt compliance, it is not similar to a criminal fine and will be deductible. Civil penalties for the violation of reporting requirements or filing deadlines and other procedural failings, which do not frustrate the primary purpose of the statutory scheme, would also be deductible.[53]

In determining the tax treatment of a penalty, it is necessary to analyze the law pursuant to which the penalty is imposed, including its legislative history, to determine whether the penalty is meant to have a retributive effect. For example, penalties under the Clean Air Act[54] and the Clean Water Act[55] are not deductible because the Supreme Court has determined that these remedies are intended as punishment, furthering retribution and deterrence. In finalizing this analysis, the Federal Circuit, in *Colt Industries, Inc. v. United States*, found pertinent the fact that the Environmental Protection Agency (EPA) was not authorized to seek compensatory damages but was limited to injunctive relief and monetary penalties.[56] In *True v. United States*,[57] the Tenth Circuit stated that, because the Federal Water Pollution Control Act[58] contained a compensatory mechanism allowing for recoupment of cleanup costs, the penalty provision had to serve as an additional sanction to deter and punish, and thus was nondeductible. In Revenue Ruling 88-46, the IRS found that a nonconformance penalty assessed by the EPA under the Clean Air Act was deductible because analysis of the act and its legislative history showed that the penalty, rather than being punitive, was designed to eliminate the competitive advantage that a nonconforming producer might have over a conforming producer. Paying the nonconformance penalty or conforming are two lawful alternative methods for obtaining a certificate of conformity.[59]

A taxpayer incurring environmental cleanup costs, legal fees, fines, or penalties must engage in some fairly thorough analysis to determine the appropriate tax treatment. It cannot be emphasized enough that advance planning and adequate documentation are essential. Taxpayers who are remediating environmental hazards for which the IRS is likely to argue that the appropriate treatment is capitalization should consider whether *bona fide* appraisals, both before and after remediation, make economic (or tax) sense. In addition, a taxpayer should be aware of, and plan for, the tax treatment of legal fees and any penalties or fines.

Timing of Deduction

Once a cost is determined to be deductible, a taxpayer must consider the proper year for taking the deduction. Generally, a deduction will be taken in the taxable year in which the taxpayer's method of accounting properly accounts for it.[60] For cash method taxpayers, this means when the expenditure is paid.[61]

Many taxpayers, however, are not allowed to use the cash method and so are on an accrual method of accounting.[62] Before 1984, accrual method taxpayers could deduct expenses when the amount could reasonably be determined and all events had occurred to fix liability (in other words, a taxpayer could not deduct a contingent liability).[63] Because taxpayers were using this rule to their advantage to deduct expenses that met these requirements but were not paid until a subsequent tax year—in effect, giving themselves a present value deduction greater than their future effective cost, Congress enacted an additional requirement: the "economic performance test."[64] This test establishes the time at which deductibility is allowed with respect to different types of costs. The proper time revolves around either payment or the provision of services (or use of property).

Under the economic performance test, liabilities arising from any tort,[65] breach of contract, or violation of law, including the settlement of such claims,[66] must be paid to the person to whom the damages are owed[67] before economic performance occurs.[68] Because of the way environmental laws are written, remediation responsibilities generally will not arise from one of these situations. However, responsibility might arise in such a manner if an adjacent property owner sued a taxpayer for environmental damage on a tort theory and the suit was settled for an amount equal to the cost of remediation.

If the liability does not arise from one of the above situations, the taxpayer determines whether it will be controlling the cleanup or will be paying a third party that will have control, such as an enforcement agency or other responsible party.

Where the taxpayer controls the cleanup, economic performance occurs as the property is remediated. If the taxpayer, or its agent, is performing the cleanup, the appropriate time for deduction is when the costs are incurred[69] Thus, a taxpayer that prepays for environmental remediation services can, nonetheless, deduct amounts only as, and when, remediation occurs.

Where the taxpayer is not in control, a taxpayer would like to have payment constitute economic performance. However, it may not fit the liability categories for which payment constitutes economic performance. If the liability is not of this type, the taxpayer must collect information about the status of the remediation and the costs incurred to know when to deduct payments. A taxpayer in this situation may be able to escape this dilemma if the liability arises out of the Comprehensive Environmental Response, Compensation, and Liability Act (CERCLA) (or Revenue Rulings or Procedures not yet released), and it contributes funds to a designated settlement fund.[70] Payment or transfer of property to such a fund in satisfaction of liability[71] generally will constitute economic performance.[72]

Determining the time for deduction may be difficult and confusing. However, these determinations should be made carefully and in advance of any remediation. This level of complexity may be frustrating, but proper awareness of the issues involved facilitates the successful coordination of tax deduction with payment and remediation.

Cost Recovery

If environmental remediation costs are required to be capitalized, the assets to which the costs will be attributed may be new assets, land, or existing buildings. Land is not depreciable. If the remediation costs are associated with nonresidential (commercial) real estate, they are recovered on a straight-line basis over thirty-nine years, or forty years if it is tax-exempt use property.[73] Costs associated with residential rental real estate are recovered on a straight-line basis over twenty-seven and a half years.[74] If a separate asset is created as part of the remediation, the period and method over which the costs may be recovered will vary, depending on the nature of the asset as realty or personalty and on the classification of the asset.[75]

While this part of the chapter merely gives the basic rules for cost recovery, this does not mean that determining the proper depreciation method is easy. Questions may arise such as whether assets created specifically to remediate property constitute separate assets or are permanently affixed to realty. As previously stated, advance consideration of these issues will help taxpayers to understand and cope with their tax situations.

Conclusion

It has been suggested that the treatment of remediation costs will be the tax issue of the 1990s. There are large amounts of money at stake, and treating removal as a deductible cost will always make it more attractive than a temporary solution. Before the release of Revenue Ruling 94-38, several members of Congress had become involved in the issue of deductibility.[76] Since the release of that ruling, interest has flagged because the ruling covers some of the most important and most costly remediation situations. However, the ruling is not applicable to real estate improvements, asbestos remediation, lead-based paint, or a host of other hazards, so concern about capitalization versus deductibility still exists for enormous numbers of taxpayers.

Resources

Anderson, Susan E. and Dinkins, Alison, "Environmental Cleanup Costs: Ordinary or Capital Expenditures." 94 TNT 135–40.

Bradford, David F. *Untangling the Income Tax*. Cambridge, Mass.: Harvard University Press, 1986.

Conjura. "IRS Reverses Course and Allows Current Deductions for Cost of Environmental Cleanup in Revenue Ruling 94-38." *Tax Management Real Estate Journal* 10 (1994): 135.

Droller. "IRS Continues Flawed Analysis of Treatment of Environmental Cleanup Costs: TAM 9411002." *Tax Notes* 63 (1994): 611.

Duffy. "Asbestos Removal Costs May Be Currently Deductible." *Journal of Taxation* 70 (1989): 290.

Efurd and Stroud. "A DRA 1984 Perspective Concerning the Deductibility of Environmental Costs." *Tax Notes* 62 (1994): 1,585.

Fox and Solomon. "Who Incurs Environmental Cleanup Costs—and Why—May Determine Deductibility." *Journal of Taxation* 76 (1992): 12.

Haig, Robert M. *The Federal Income Tax*. New York: Columbia University Press, 1921.

Holthouse and Sherry. "A Hazardous Ruling: The Service Denies Deductibility of Asbestos Mitigation Costs." *Journal of Real Estate Taxation* 20 (1993): 261.

Holthouse and Sherry. "The Tax Benefits of Toxic Waste Removal Costs." *Journal of Real Estate Taxation* 19 (1991): 8.

Horner. "Tax Treatment of Environmental Cleanup Costs: An Environmental View." 94 TNT 166–44.

Johnson. "Capitalization after the Government's Big Win in Indopco." *Tax Notes* 63 (1994): 1,323.

Note, "The Federal Tax System and the Environment: Should Payments Made Pursuant to CERCLA Be Deductible?" *Virginia Tax Review* 10 (1991): 707.

Raby. "Two Wrongs Make a Right: The IRS View of Environmental Cleanup Costs." *TNT* 93 (1993): 108–13.

Rubin and Green. "The Tax Treatment of Environmental Cleanup Costs." ALI-ABA Creative Tax Planning for Real Estate Transactions (1993) (Westlaw C865 ALI-ABA 877).

Shiao and Holthouse. "Deductibility of Environmental Cleanup Costs: The Debate Continues." *Journal of Real Estate Taxation* 21 (1993): 3.

Simons, Henry C. *Personal Income Taxation*. Books on Demand, 1938.

Slavitt. "Tax Implications of Environmental Expenses." *Tax Notes* 64 (1994): 391.

Stack. "Tax Aspects of Environmental Cleanup Costs." *New York State Bar Journal* 64 (1992): 45.

Steele. "The Tax Consequences of the Ownership and Cleanup of Environmentally Contaminated Properties." *Real Property, Probate, and Trust Journal* 26 (1991): 655.

Tucker, Stefan F. *Tax Planning for Real Estate Transactions*. Clark Boardman Callaghan, 1989, with semiannual supplements.

Yancey. "Emerging Doctrines in the Tax Treatment of Environmental Cleanup Costs." *Taxes—The Tax Magazine* 70 (1992): 948.

Notes

1. *See* STEFAN F. TUCKER, TAX PLANNING FOR REAL ESTATE TRANSACTIONS (Clark Boardman Callaghan 1989, with semiannual supplements).

2. This has been defined as the sum of consumption and increase in wealth (or savings) over a period of time. *See* ROBERT M. HAIG, THE FEDERAL INCOME TAX

(Columbia Univ. Press of New York 1921); and HENRY C. SIMONS, PERSONAL INCOME TAXATION (Books on Demand, 1938).

3. DAVID F. BRADFORD, UNTANGLING THE INCOME TAX 27 (Harvard Univ. Press, 1986).

4. IRC § 441.

5. Instead, the cost of earnings deducted in any year will be (1) those costs that are associated with revenues reported in that taxable year and no other and (2) those costs that benefit the production of revenues reported in more than one period.

6. Indopco v. Commissioner, 112 S. Ct. 1039, 1043 (1992). The Supreme Court held in *Indopco* that the creation of a separate asset was not the test for capitalization but, rather, that capitalization focused on whether the cost produced more than incidental future benefit, which must be matched to the revenue in the future year. *See* Gunn, *The Requirement that a Capital Expenditure Create or Enhance an Asset*, 15 B.C. INDUS. & COM. L. REV. 443 (1974).

7. Indopco v. Commissioner, 112 S. Ct. 1039, 1043 (1992).

8. IRC § 451; Reg. § 1.451-1.

9. IRC § 461; Regs. §§ 1.461-1, 1.461-4, 1.461-5, and 1.461-6.

10. Under IRC § 212, individuals who are not carrying on a trade or business are allowed a deduction for all the ordinary and necessary expenses paid or incurred for (1) the production or collection of income or (2) the management, conservation, or maintenance of property held for the production of income. This section was enacted because IRC § 162(a) was held to be written too narrowly to allow an individual to deduct expenses where there is an investment, but not a trade or business. The rules of capitalization or deduction are applicable to IRC § 212 expenses as well.

11. "There shall be allowed as a deduction all the ordinary and necessary expenses paid or incurred during the taxable year in carrying on any trade or business. . . ." IRC § 162(a).

12. Commissioner v. Tellier, 383 U.S. 687 (1966).

13. An ancillary effect of capitalization may be the application of IRC § 263A, which results in strict capitalization rules and costly and time-consuming record maintenance. See Reg. § 1.263A-1.

14. "No deduction shall be allowed for any amount paid out for new buildings or for permanent improvements or betterments made to increase the value of any property or estate." IRC § 263.

15. "No deduction shall be allowed for (a) any amount paid out for new buildings or for permanent improvements or betterments made to increase the value of any property or (b) any amount expended in restoring property or in making good the exhaustion thereof for which an allowance is or has been made in the form of a deduction for depreciation, amortization or depletion." Reg. § 1.263(a)-1(a).

16. Reg. § 1.263(a)-1(b).

17. Reg. § 1.263(a)-2.

18. Plainfield-Union Water Co. v. Commissioner, 39 T.C. 333 (1962), *nonacq.* 1964-2 C.B. 8. *See* Oberman Mfg. Co. v. Commissioner, 47 T.C. 471 (1967), *acq.* 1967-2 C.B. 3; and Niagara Mohawk Power Corp. v. United States, 558 F.2d 1379 (Ct. Cl. 1977).

19. *See* Teitelbaum v. Commissioner, 294 F.2d 541 (7th Cir. 1961); RKO Theatres, Inc. v. United States, 163 F. Supp. 598 (Ct. Cl. 1958); and Hotel Sulgrave, Inc. v. Commissioner, 21 T.C. 619 (1954).

20. *See, e.g., TEI Comments Regarding the Proper Federal Income Tax Treatment of Environmental Remediation Expenditures*, 93 TNT 133-76; and Letter from Lester Droller on behalf of 17 corporations to Stuart Brown, 93 TNT 124-22 (1993).

21. *See* Niagara Mohawk Power Corp. v. United States, 558 F.2d 1379 (Ct. Cl. 1977); and Connecticut Light & Power Co. v. United States, 299 F.2d 259 (Ct. Cl. 1962).

22. California Casket Co. v. Commissioner, 19 T.C. 32 (1952).

23. Pryor v. Commissioner, T.C. Memo 1954-60.

24. Hubble v. Kavanaugh, 48 A.F.T.R. 1359 (E.D. Mich. 1954).

25. *See* Wehrli v. United States, 400 F.2d 686 (10th Cir. 1968); and Stoeltzing v. Commissioner, 266 F.2d 374 (3rd Cir. 1959).

26. Moss v. Commissioner, 831 F.2d 833 (9th Cir. 1987).

27. *See* Holthouse and Sherry, *The Tax Benefits of Toxic Waste Removal Costs*, 19 J. R. EST. TAX'N 8 (1991).

28. Reg. § 1.165-2; Reg. § 1.167(a)-8(a).

29. Reg. § 1.162-7.

30. Rev. Rul. 94-38, 1994-25 I.R.B. 4.

31. Bob Kilinskis (tax specialist in the Treasury Office of Tax Legislative Counsel), Remarks at a panel discussion sponsored by American Council of Capital Formation (June 8, 1994), *reported in* BNA DTR at G-7 (June 9, 1994).

32. *See* Woolrich Woolen Mills v. United States, 289 F.2d 444 (3rd Cir. 1961).

33. A Revenue Ruling is precedential, but the IRS cautions against reaching the same conclusions in other cases unless the facts and circumstances are substantially the same.

34. Tech. Adv. Mem. 9315004 (December 17, 1992).

35. Wolfsen Land & Cattle Co. v. Commissioner, 72 T.C. 1 (1979).

36. The TAM cited these cases as support: Blue Creek Coal, Inc. v. Commissioner, T.C. Memo 1984-579; Teitelbaum v. Commissioner, 294 F.2d 541 (7th Cir. 1961); Hotel Sulgrave, Inc. v. Commissioner, 21 T.C. 619 (1954); and Cerda v. United States, 84-1 U.S.T.C. ¶ 9490 (N.D. Ill. 1984).

37. Courts hold a cost deductible based on the nature of the cost rather than its magnitude. American Bemberg Corp. v. Commissioner, 10 T.C. 361 (1948), *aff'd* 177 F.2d 200 (6th Cir. 1949).

38. Bob Kilinskis (tax specialist in the Treasury Office of Tax Legislative Counsel), Remarks at a panel discussion sponsored by American Council of Capital Formation (June 8, 1994), *reported in* BNA DTR at G-7 (June 9, 1994).

39. *See* Mt. Morris Drive-In Theater v. Commissioner, 25 T.C. 272 (1955), *aff'd* 238 F.2d 85 (6th Cir. 1956).

40. Bob Kilinskis (tax specialist in the Treasury Office of Tax Legislative Counsel), Remarks at a panel discussion sponsored by American Council of Capital Formation (June 8, 1994), *reported in* BNA DTR at G-7 (June 9, 1994).

41. Tech. Adv. Mem. 9240004 (June 29, 1992).

42. Tech. Adv. Mem. 9411002 (Nov. 19, 1993).

43. The TAM cited Electric Energy, Inc. v. United States, 87-2 U.S.T.C. ¶ 9587 (Cl. Ct. 1987).

44. The progressive deterioration argument will no longer be asserted because Revenue Ruling 94-38 modified Revenue Ruling 88-57, 1988-2 C.B. 36, to the extent that Revenue Ruling 88-57 implies *Plainfield-Union* cannot be an appropriate test in any case other than one in which there is sudden and unanticipated damage to an asset.

45. *See, e.g.*, Letter from Donald Alexander, of Cadwalader, Wickersham & Taft, to Fred Goldberg (Sept. 30, 1992), 92 TNT 198–236, and Letter from Michael Solomon and Claude Stansbury, of Ivins, Phillips & Barker, to Stuart Brown, 93 TNT 207–50 (1993).

46. Pre-*Plainfield-Union* cases include Buckland v. United States, 66 F. Supp. 681 (D. Conn. 1946), and American Bemberg Co. v. Commissioner, 10 T.C. 361 (1948), *aff'd*, 177 F.2d 200 (6th Cir. 1949). Post-*Plainfield-Union* cases include Oberman Mfg. Co. v. Commissioner, 47 T.C. 471 (1967), *acq*. 1967-2 C.B. 3, and Munroe Land Co. v. Commissioner, T.C. Memo 1966-2.

47. Midland Empire Packing Co. v. Commissioner, 14 T.C. 635 (1950), *acq*. 1950-2 C.B. 3.

48. The IRS's position, at least as expressed in General Counsel Memorandum 36828 (Sept. 1, 1976), which was written in the context of analyzing whether a medical deduction was available for the cost of lead paint removal, stated that scraping and painting would be deductible as maintenance, but that covering lead paint with a non-paint surface would be capitalized.

49. United States v. Gilmore, 372 U.S. 39 (1963).

50. It is important to note that legal fees associated with nondeductible fines or penalties are not rendered nondeductible solely because of their association with the fine or penalty. Reg. § 1.162-21(b)(2).

51. IRC § 162(f).

52. S. Rep. No. 437, 92nd Cong., 1st Sess., *reprinted in* 1971 U.S. Code Cong. & Ad. News at 1980.

53. *See* True v. United States, 894 F.2d 1197 (10th Cir. 1990); and Southern Pac. Transp. Co. v. Commissioner, 75 T.C. 497 (1980).

54. 42 U.S.C. § 7413(d).

55. 33 U.S.C. § 1319(d).

56. Colt Industries, Inc. v. United States, 880 F.2d 1311 (Fed. Cir. 1989).

57. True v. United States, 894 F.2d 1197 (10th Cir. 1990).

58. 33 U.S.C. § 1321(b)(6).

59. Rev. Rul. 88-46, 1988-1 C.B. 76. *But see* Rev. Proc. 92-21, 1992-2 C.B. 503.

60. IRC § 461(a).

61. Reg. § 1.461-1(a)(1).

62. IRC § 448.

63. IRC § 461, prior to amendment by Pub. L. No. 98-369, 98th Cong., 2nd. Sess. (1984).

64. Reg. § 1.461-1(a)(2)(i).

65. IRC § 461(h)(2)(C).

66. Reg. § 1.461-4(g)(2).

67. Economic performance does not occur as a taxpayer makes payments to another person, such as a trust, escrow account, court-administered settlement fund, or similar arrangement, but instead occurs as payments are made from that other person or fund to the person to whom the liability is owed. Reg. § 1.461-4(g)(1)(i).

68. Reg. § 1.461-4(g)(1)(i).

69. Reg. § 1.461-4(d)(4)(i). Regs. §§ 1.461-4(d)(2)(i), 1.461-4(d)(6)(i).

70. A "qualified settlement fund" is defined as any fund, account, or other arrangement that (1) qualifies as a trust under applicable state law or the assets of which are otherwise segregated from other assets of the transferor (and related persons); (2) is established pursuant to an order of, or which is approved by, a federal, state, or local governmental authority and is under the continuing jurisdiction of that governmental authority; and (3) is established in order to resolve or satisfy claims arising out of tort, breach of contract, or violation of law, or under the Comprehensive Environmental Response, Compensation, and Liability Act, or is designated in a Revenue Ruling or Revenue Procedure. Reg. § 1.468B-1(c).

71. Economic performance does not occur to the extent the transferor or a related person has a right to a refund or reversion of a transfer, if the right is exercisable currently and without the agreement of an unrelated person that is independent or has an adverse interest. Reg. § 1.468B-3(c)(2)(i)(A).

72. Reg. § 1.461-6(b).

73. IRC §§ 168(e) and (g).

74. IRC §§ 168(b)(3) and (c)(1).

75. *See* Rev. Proc. 87-56, 1987-2 C.B. 675, clarified by Rev. Proc. 88-22, 1988-1 C.B. 785, for class lives.

76. Letter from Sen. Max Baucus (D. Mont.) to Treasury Secretary Bentsen (January 25, 1994); 94 TNT 19-31.

CHAPTER 14

Assessing the Value of Environmentally Impaired Properties

JAMES A. CHALMERS
JEFFRE B. BEATTY
ROBERT B. ECKER

A former owner of a manufacturing facility released hazardous substances into the environment, thereby contaminating the groundwater. How does one ascertain whether the current owner's property value diminution claim is valid? Underground storage tanks at a gasoline station have leaked and contaminated the soil and groundwater on an adjacent ten-acre industrial property. How does one quantify the impact of the contamination on the property's value for the purpose of a property tax assessment dispute? Home owners in a residential subdivision have filed a class-action lawsuit against a salvage and storage facility, claiming that the value of their homes has diminished as a result of soil and groundwater contamination originating at the facility. How does one determine if property value diminution has resulted from the contamination in light of the fact that the residential real estate market has been soft in this geographic area?

These are a few examples of the many situations in which the contamination of real property has increasingly required attention from the legal and the appraisal professions. As a result of this increased attention, these professions are beginning to have a greater understanding of the impact of contamination on real property values, and a consensus is developing about the conceptual framework and underlying damage theory within which such valuations must take place. This chapter presents a discussion of this conceptual framework and the corresponding valuation and damage theories on which it is based.

Conceptual Framework

The issue of value diminution arises in many different contexts. These include federal and state tort claims, property tax appeals, estate tax issues, and eminent domain, to name a few.

To gain a working knowledge of the impact of contamination on real property value, one must understand the basic theory of asset valuation. This theory states that an asset's value depends on the net cash flow, or anticipated income stream, to be generated by that asset discounted by the yield necessary to attract capital to that investment in the market. The principal reason that the yield requirement associated with different assets differs is that the degree of risk associated with receiving the anticipated income differs. These two major valuation components, cash flow and risk, must be evaluated in the case of any asset (e.g., a franchise, bond, real estate, or venture capital investment) to establish its value. To prove that this value is the fair market value, appraisers try to use the sales comparison approach, which is based on actual market transactions. One must never lose sight, however, of the true determinants of value—cash flow and the rate of return necessary to attract capital to that investment. These valuation fundamentals do not change when contaminated, or previously contaminated, property is involved. However, valuing such property can be difficult because of the complexity of evaluating the effect of legal and scientific issues on cash flow and risk.

Valuation Model

The valuation of contaminated property has received considerable attention in the appraisal literature during the past few years. An early article illustrated how capitalization rates and yield rates are impacted by the effects of contamination on a property's financeability and marketability.[1] Subsequently, the concept of stigma was introduced, and it became clear that stigma can be measured by focusing on the risks associated with contaminated, or previously contaminated, property. A theory was presented arguing that the value of a contaminated property will change over time as uncertainty with respect to its condition changes and as the contamination is cleaned up.[2] Thus, the income approach to valuing property was used to illustrate how the income impairment of contaminated property and the risk premium necessary to attract capital to it combine to determine the value discount of a contaminated property relative to an uncontaminated property.[3] These theories have developed over time and are based on the general proposition that value reflects an anticipated future stream of benefits discounted at a return necessary to attract investors to that opportunity. In the case of contaminated property, value may be adversely affected if the future benefit stream is decreased or if the required returns are increased to compensate for additional risks.[4]

Terms of art have developed in the literature to define the difference between the value of contaminated property and the value of uncontaminated property that results from either direct costs, stigma, or both. "Direct costs" refers to the effect of contamination on the net cash flow to the property owner and may result from a decline in effective rents (decreased market demand for the property), remediation costs (testing, clean up, and monitoring), insurance costs, and the like. "Stigma" refers to the impact on property value that results from the increased risks associated with contaminated property and the effect of risks on marketability and financeability. Therefore, stigma does not refer exclusively to the difference between the value of an uncontaminated property and the value of an otherwise identical but once contaminated property that is fully remediated and indemnified. Stigma is a more general concept and refers to the discount, beyond direct costs, required to compensate investors or lenders for the risks associated with the contaminated property. Because of the possible existence of additional risk, the cash flow of contaminated property can be perceived to be less certain. As a result, stigma can occur before, during, or after the remediation of contamination (i.e., stigma can exist at any point after contamination is discovered).

The uncertainty relating to the cash flow of a specific contaminated property can vary over time. It is typically greatest when the contamination is discovered and little is known about its origin. As the nature and extent of the contamination is determined, however, the uncertainty associated with the property will decrease. The associated risk will typically continue to decrease as remediation strategies are evaluated and implemented. This will continue until remediation is completed to regulatory standards and a no-further-action letter is issued by the governing regulatory agency. At this point, depending on the circumstances, it is possible that stigma may still exist with regard to the property, although it is the authors' experience that "postclosure" stigma of this type is very rare.

Damages Theory

Property damages have traditionally been measured in two ways: first, as the cost of repairing the damaged property (including incidental costs such as interim loss in use during repair); and second, as the diminished value of the property. Ordinarily, the plaintiff receives one or the other; it may not recover both because that would amount to double recovery. In some states plaintiffs receive compensation for the diminution in the value of real property when the damage is "permanent" but receive the cost of repair when the harm is "temporary" and reasonably remediable. In other states, plaintiffs normally recover the lesser of the cost of repair and the diminution in value. Given the flexibility in determining "permanency" and the various exceptions to the "lesser of" rule, the practical difference between the two rules is not great.[5]

Although these general principles are well settled, the courts have not fully resolved their application in the context of toxic contamination of real property. Environmental statutes typically require remediation even when its cost may exceed the original diminution in value. Plaintiffs' entitlement to remediation and monitoring of their property and reimbursement for lost use and income during such remediation therefore seems settled, regardless of the "lesser of" principle. Furthermore, plaintiffs should be entitled to claim damages for permanent diminution in value when it is clear that the property will remain significantly contaminated and unsuitable for certain uses despite attempted remediation. This approach provides a hybrid remedy (partial repair plus residual diminution in value after that repair) that has been approved in both real and personal property damage cases.[6]

Courts have been much more reluctant, however, to award plaintiffs damages for permanent diminution in value resulting from a stigma of contamination *not* linked to demonstrable permanent physical damages resulting in health risks or limitations on use. Cases of this sort have fallen into two categories.

First, plaintiffs owning property near a contaminated site have claimed damages for diminution in value caused by stigma even though their own property was not contaminated or physically affected in any way. No matter how good the proof of diminution in value and no matter what the legal theory, the courts have consistently rejected claims for damages resulting from stigma caused by contamination elsewhere in the neighborhood.[7]

Second, plaintiffs *can* demonstrate contamination of their own property but *cannot* show that remediation to the satisfaction of governmental authorities will leave the property meaningfully physically impaired. Plaintiffs in such cases thus claim damages for devaluation caused by the permanent stigma of *former* contamination. It remains unclear whether courts will recognize this type of claim for postremediation stigma damages and, if so, whether such claims are premature before remediation is complete. In addition, the courts have not spoken on how such damages may be proved when the traditional comparable sales method of valuing property fails for lack of sufficient data. Cases on these questions are only now coming before the appellate courts.[8]

The foregoing has necessarily focused on those areas of property value diminution litigation where there is case law. This includes issues associated with the temporary versus the permanent nature of the impairment, the "lesser of" rule, and cases in which there has been permanent diminution.

It must be pointed out, however, that much of the trial court litigation at the present time deals with damages incurred by plaintiffs, above and beyond response costs, over the period of time from when contamination is first discovered to when regulatory closure is achieved (or anticipated to be achieved), that is, preremediation damages. The types of damages identified in these cases often include increased costs of capital, reduced marketability, and lost sales. The damage claims may also include business interruption or other consequential damages.

The economic principles pertinent to these claims are explained in the remainder of this chapter, but the compensability of these claims as a matter of law remains to be determined.

Commercial Property and Raw Land Applications

Property value diminution cases are generally of two types: (1) commercial property (including raw land) and (2) residential property. In the case of the former, the dominant consideration is the likelihood that the property and the contamination present a unique, or relatively unique, set of facts. As a result, the sales comparison approach to assessing market value is not often useful in this context. Commercial property or raw land would have to be similar in both real estate characteristics (property type and highest and best use) as well as contamination characteristics (type and extent of contamination, regulatory and public perceptions and evaluations, remediation strategy, liability, use limitations, etc.) before useful comparisons could be made between a specific subject property and other so-called comparable properties. Rather than try to force the sales comparison approach when in fact there is no comparability, it is the authors' experience that it is preferable to apply an income approach based on an estimate of direct costs and risk premiums associated with a given site. Whatever market evidence that does exist should then be used to test the conclusions of the income approach. Figure 1 outlines method guidelines.

FIGURE 1. Method Guidelines for Commercial Property and Raw Land

Type of Property Affected by Hazard or Contamination	Assumed Conditions	Preferred Tools	Potentially Applicable Tools
Improved commercial property or raw land	Small number of sales Effect of contamination or hazard unique, or relatively unique, to subject property	Develop case study with legal and technical input Interview market participants: users, lenders, investors	Sales comparison

Figure 2 illustrates the general process for valuing this form of contaminated property. Initially there is an investigative phase in which the nature and extent of the contamination must be fully characterized. In addition, an evaluation of the contamination from the public and regulatory perspectives must take place, and full understanding of the consequences of the problem (i.e., remediation costs and alternatives, liability, use restrictions, etc.) must be gained. The results of the investigative phase are critical throughout the remainder of the valuation process and allow one to assess preliminarily whether there may be a stigma associated with the property.

The findings from the investigative phase provide the basis for determining the direct costs associated with the property as well as for developing a hypothetical case study from which to evaluate the risk perceptions of market participants relative to the affected property. The case study becomes the foundation for assessing whether the market perceives there to be additional risk associated with the property (i.e., stigma). If the property and its contamination history are well described, it is possible to obtain definitive opinions with a high degree of consensus from users, lenders, and investors regarding the impact of contamination on their business decisions. The market feedback on risk perception provides support for deriving a risk-adjusted discount rate, which is defined as the rate of return required to attract capital to the property. As discussed earlier, the direct costs and the risk-adjusted discount rate are then used in conjunction with the anticipated future cash flow of the property to determine the property's value in a contaminated state.

FIGURE 2. Diminution in Value Resulting from Contamination

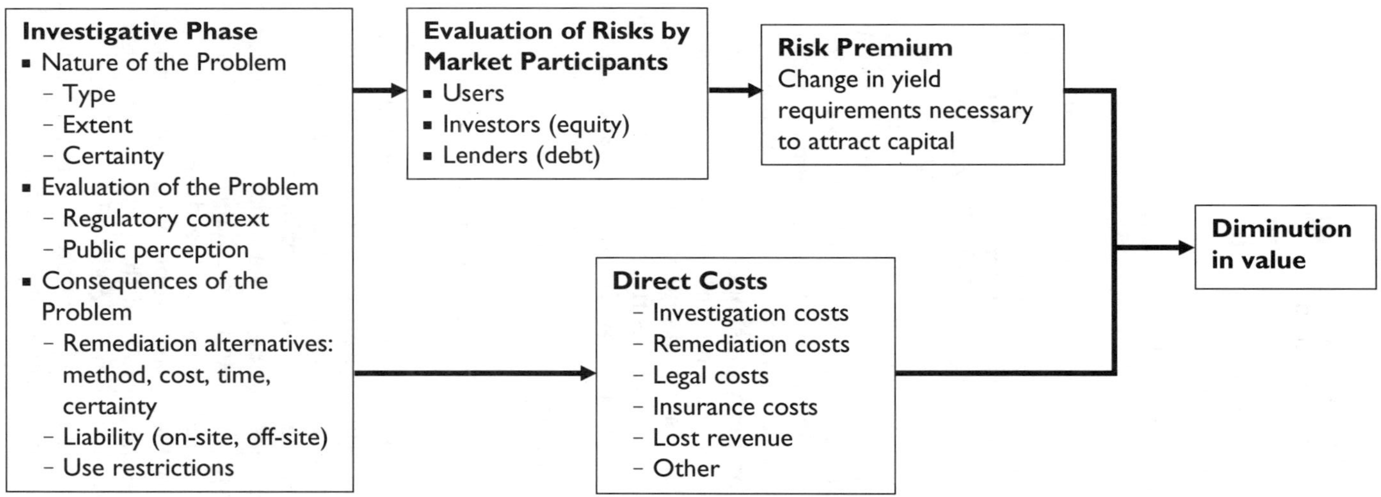

The valuation process can be summarized as the following five steps:

1. Assemble information.
2. Prepare the case study.
3. Interview market participants.
4. Estimate direct costs and risk premium.
5. Value the property.

Each part is briefly discussed below.

Assemble Information

Because of the legal and technical complexities surrounding environmental issues, collecting and interpreting information requires a team that includes both legal counsel specializing in environmental law and a qualified environmental engineering firm. Environmental engineers provide accurate and reliable information about the nature and extent of the problem. Then one must understand how the contamination is evaluated and perceived by public and regulatory agencies. Legal counsel can assist in supplying this information and accurately assessing the regulatory constraints within which the owner, or prospective owner, of the property must operate. With the information assembled, and within the team framework, the consequences of the situation can be assessed. This information can be identified: remediation alternatives and their implications from a cost, time, and certainty perspective; liability associated with on-site response costs and possible off-site claims; and possible use restrictions on the property resulting from the contamination or its remediation.

Prepare the Case Study

After obtaining the requisite information, a case study is prepared as the basis for interviewing market participants. Because no two contaminated properties are alike, the case study must reveal the subject property's peculiarities, which may include the following: current regulatory posture of the appropriate agencies; identification of the nature and extent of the contamination; liability of the potential responsible party(ies); and remediation activities or proposed remediation alternatives, including the duration and cost estimate. The exact location of the subject property remains confidential. The bottom line is that the description of the property and its current condition must disclose what an informed and knowledgeable market participant would want to know before making a decision on whether to purchase, finance, or lease the property.

Interview Market Participants

Representative market participants are identified. This process involves identifying individuals that would be interested in buying, selling, financing, or using the subject property. The appropriate participants are then further refined based on the geographic location, type, and size of the property. Upon identifying the market participants, a survey is developed to determine their attitudes and reactions toward the hypothetical property referenced in the case study. Once the survey is designed, the case study is sent to the market participants. After they have reviewed it, a structured interview is held with these individuals, either in person or by telephone, to obtain their evaluation of the environmental issue and its impact on the property and their business decision (called the structured interview approach). After a satisfactory number of quality interviews is completed (usually four to six lenders, four to six users, and four to six investors), an indication of the risk premium, if any, required by the market participants can be determined.

Estimate Direct Costs and Risk Premium

The direct costs associated with contaminated property, which are identified in the investigative phase of the valuation process, include all investigative and remediation costs. As noted in the discussion of the valuation model, it is necessary that these costs also include any impact on the present or future income-generating capacity of the property. For example, any adverse impact on effective rental rates or lost revenue from business interruption must be quantified. These market-related costs are combined with the remediation and investigation costs to derive the total direct costs resulting from the contamination.

The actual or perceived risk associated with the property is measured by the responses of the market participants surveyed. The responses to the survey indicate the market's sensitivity to the particular condition and circumstances of the contaminated property. On the one hand, the responses may indicate that there is no additional perceived risk associated with the property, or, on the other hand, they may reveal that the risk is such that no yield premium will motivate a market participant to buy, finance, or lease the property. The determination of an appropriate risk premium takes place in conjunction with reference to other market yield rates. For example, the annual rate of return required by an investor on an unimpaired property may range from 10 to 30 percent; a fully leased commercial property located in a desirable area may be at the low end of the range, while speculative raw land may be toward the high end. The market yield rates assist in determining the risk-adjusted discount rate based on the results of the market participant surveys and the professional judgment and experience of the appraiser.

Hearsay objections have been raised with respect to the admissibility of expert testimony evidence based on information obtained while implementing the structured interview approach. Hearsay is an out-of-court statement offered to prove the truth of the matter asserted. In quantifying property value diminution resulting from contamination, hearsay refers to the fact that the expert's opinion is formed from the opinions of others who are not presently testifying and thus cannot be cross-examined. The ultimate issue is whether this evidence is of a type and nature that could be reasonably relied on by an expert in forming an opinion as to a property's contaminated value. Admissibility will be decided based on whether the evidence is necessary and reliable.

Given the absence of comparable sales for contaminated property, the structured interview approach becomes a necessity, and the information obtained from performing systematic and well-planned interviews of sophisticated market participants is inherently reliable. These interviews are a vital part of the process of valuing property presently, or previously, contaminated. Also, it is well recognized that appraisers make use of interviews with market participants to develop their value opinions. As a result, from an evidentiary standpoint, there should be no concern about experts using the structured interview approach as part of the basis for their opinions regarding the computation of property value diminution by the discounted cash flow method.

Valuation of the Property

Once the above steps have been completed, valuation of the property is straightforward. The additional direct costs resulting from the contamination and remediation are deducted from the future income stream of the property in an uncontaminated state to derive the anticipated future income stream of the impaired property. The required risk-adjusted yield rate is then used to discount the income stream to determine the property's contaminated value. Damages from contamination can then be calculated as the difference between the property's unimpaired and impaired values.

Residential Property Applications

Residential property value diminution cases differ significantly from commercial property or raw land cases in that there are often enough market transactions of affected and unaffected homes to use the sales comparison approach to assess the contamination's effect on value. Issues surrounding the impact of contamination on the value of residential property arise in a variety of instances. Some of these involve overhead electric transmission lines, airport noise, freeway noise, air quality, odor, view impairment, waste dumps, nuclear waste dumps or transport routes, gas pipelines, accident or spill sites, surface or groundwater contamination, radon, and the like. Figure 3 outlines method guidelines pertaining to the valuation of residential properties.

In these cases, the issue is whether there is any evidence of systematic effect on property values resulting from the identified contaminant or hazard. Because of the relatively large number of residential transactions, statistical analysis can often be used to study the effect of different variables (i.e., lot size, location, time, etc.) on value and to isolate the effects of one variable independent of the effects of other variables. This technique is known as regression analysis, and its application in this context has been widely reported in the professional literature.[9]

However, regression analysis cannot be used if diminution in market value is asserted with respect to a future event that has not yet occurred (and therefore has had no effect on market transactions) or if the contamination or hazard is not generally known to the market. Analyzing sales transactions of contaminated property in both of these cases is similar to the commercial property case. First the nature of the contamination must be well described and then careful questioning or surveying of market participants, including buyers, seller, brokers, lenders, and appraisers, is likely necessary to gauge the market participants' sensitivity to the hazard or contamination in question.

A good example of this approach is reported in *City of Santa Fe v. Komis*.[10] The case involved the taking of property by the City of Santa

FIGURE 3. Method Guidelines for Residential Property

Type of Property Affected by Hazard or Contamination	Assumed Conditions	Preferred Tools	Potentially Applicable Tools
Residential property	Relatively large number of sales	Regression analysis	Opinion, stated behavior surveys
	Some sales affected by contamination or hazard, others not		Sales comparison Paired sales

Fe to construct a bypass around the city so that nuclear waste on its way to the Waste Isolation Pilot Project (WIPP) in Carlsbad, New Mexico, would not have to be carried through Santa Fe's center. Komis argued that because of the bypass's intended use and the perceived risk associated with the use, his remaining land was diminished in value, for which he sought, and eventually received, compensation. Because there were no other such nuclear waste bypass routes in operation at the time, the option of studying actual market behavior did not exist. Consequently, Komis commissioned an opinion survey of potential home buyers and demonstrated very strong apprehension about living close to such a transport route. If actual behavior in fact replicated the perceptions and stated behaviors reported in the survey, the marketability of the remainder land would be substantially impaired.

As a practical matter, a jury may be presented with both opinion research and regression-based market research in residential property cases. For example, in a transmission line case the plaintiff may present survey evidence consisting of market participants' perceptions and stated behaviors indicating a strong aversion to the transmission line, while the defendant may present regression-based market evidence illustrating that transmission lines have no effect on residential market values. The apparent inconsistency usually stems from one or both of the following factors. First, the information or knowledge base with respect to the transmission lines studied in the regression analysis may be different from that of the respondents to the opinion survey. In fact, the market participants may have been given specific information so that they met the theoretical "knowledgeable buyer" criteria, and this may differentiate them from the market participants on which the regression analysis was based. The second possibility is that stated behaviors may simply diverge from actual market behaviors as the result of other influences on the decision-making process not adequately accounted for in the opinion survey.

In cases in which this kind of apparent inconsistency exists between what people say they do and what they actually appear to do based on market data, it is critical that the jury be given the basis for reconciling the two sets of evidence.

Conclusion

The valuation of contaminated, or hazard-impacted, property is a process involving vital input from both the legal and the environmental engineering fields. A comprehensive understanding of the situation and the alternatives available to the owner, or prospective owner, of the property cannot be obtained without competent advice on the nature and extent of the contamination, remediation options, public perception, regulatory posture, liability issues, and similar factors.

Once the situation is fully understood, the valuation professional must assemble and obtain relevant information regarding direct costs and the risk perceptions of market participants with respect to the property. If it is determined by structured interviews that "above market" risks are associated with a contaminated, or previously contaminated, property, the owner's "bundle of rights" (the right to use, sell, lease, hypothecate, enter, or give away, or to choose to exercise all or none of these rights) has most likely been impaired. When this is the case, the diminution in value must be determined, which involves the development of a professionally supportable risk premium to be added to market yield requirements. This risk-adjusted yield rate is then applied to the future income stream of the property.

Although the economic theory is well understood, the legal perspective is unsettled. Much of the more creative work with contaminated properties over the next several years will involve the explicit recognition and quantification of risk associated with such properties. Once quantified, this risk can be traded in the market in the same way that ownership of the property can be traded. The implication is that risk or stigma effects on value will be quantified based on market transactions and the proof of these effects will be more straightforward. One suspects that as the economic dimension of these risk effects is better understood and more clearly quantified, legal theories of damages will begin to converge on a theory that is consistent with the market evidence.

Notes

1. Peter J. Patchin, *Valuation of Contaminated Property*, Appraisal J., January 1988, 7–16.

2. Peter J. Patchin, *Contaminated Properties—Stigma Revisited*, Appraisal J., April 1991, 167–72; Bill Mundy, *Stigma and Value*, Appraisal J., January 1992, 7–13; Bill Mundy, *The Impact of Hazardous Materials on Property Value*, Appraisal J., April 1992, 155–62.

3. Richard A. Neustein, *Estimating Value Diminution by the Income Approach*, Appraisal J., April 1992, 283–87.

4. Mundy, *The Impact of Hazardous Materials on Property Value*, *supra* note 2.

5. For an overview of general property damage principles and measurements, see 1 Dan Dobbs, Law of Remedies § 5.2 (2d ed. 1993).

6. *See* Restatement (Second) of Torts § 928; Wade v. S.J. Groves & Sons Co., 424 A.2d 902, 911–12 (Pa. Super. Ct. 1981). *But see* Mozzetti v. City of Brisbane, 136 Cal. Rptr. 751, 757–58 (Ct. App. 1977) (overturning award based on an instruction entitling plaintiffs to "the reasonable costs of necessary repairs," "damages

for the loss of rentals during said time," and "the difference between the market value of said property immediately before the damage and after the damage, after making any necessary repairs" because it "allowed recovery cumulatively for both the cost of repair *and* the diminution in value of the property").

7. *See, e.g.*, Berry v. Armstrong Rubber Co., 989 F.2d 822, 829 (5th Cir. 1993) (Mississippi law), *cert. denied*, 114 S. Ct. 1067 (1994); Adkins v. Thomas Solvent Co., 487 N.W.2d 715 (Mich. 1992) (Michigan law); Adams v. Star Enterprise, 851 F. Supp. 770 (E.D. Va. 1994) (Virginia law); Lamb v. Martin Marietta Energy Systems, Inc., 835 F. Supp. 959, 969 (W.D. Ky. 1993) (Kentucky law).

8. The trial court in *In re* Paoli R.R. Yard PCB Litigation, 811 F. Supp. 1071 (E.D. Pa. 1992), granted the defendants summary judgment on such a claim, reasoning that the plaintiffs had offered no credible evidence of permanent physical injury to the property. The court of appeals, however, reversed and remanded for a trial. It found some evidence of permanent physical injury and further suggested *in dictum* that permanent stigma, if proven, might itself justify an award of damages for residual diminution in value. 1994 U.S. App. LEXIS 23722 (3d Cir. 1994).

The California Court of Appeal is expected to address the availability, timing, and proof of postremediation stigma damages in Bixby Ranch Co. v. Spectrol Electronics Corp., No. B082296 (Cal. Ct. App. 2d Dist.). In that case, the trial court affirmed an award of $826,500 in postremediation stigma damages over the defendants' objections that the claim was inherently speculative, duplicative, premature, and not supported by proper expert testimony. Because remediation was not complete, the court measured damages as the difference between the property's value at the time of trial as if never contaminated and its value at the time of trial as if remediated. The award attracted nationwide attention because the contamination was not severe, the property was commercial, and the plaintiff had been indemnified against all remediation-related costs, including third-party liability.

9. Chris Zeiss and James Atwater, *Waste Facility Impacts on Residential Property Values*, 115 J. URBAN PLAN. & DEV. 123–24 (1989); V. Kerry Smith and William H. Desvouges, *The Value of Avoiding a LULU: Hazardous Waste Disposal Sites*, 68 REV. ECON. & STAT. 293–99 (1986); Hays B. Gamble and Roger H. Downing, *Effects of Nuclear Power Plants on Residential Property Values*, 22 J. REGIONAL SCIENCE 457–78 (1982); Jon P. Nelson, *Airport Noise, Location Rent, and the Market for Residential Amenities*, 6 J. ENVTL. ECON. & MGMT. 320–31 (1979); William N. Kinnard, Jr., and Mary Beth Geckler, *The Effects on Residential Real Estate Prices from Proximity to Properties Contaminated with Radioactive Materials*, REAL EST. ISSUES, 1991, 25–36; D. Kirshner and Deborah Moore, *The Effect of San Francisco Bay Water Quality on Adjacent Property Values*, 27 J. ENVTL. MGMT. 263–74 (1989); RONALD G. CUMMINGS, DAVID S. BROOKSHIRE, & WILLIAM D. SCHULZE, VALUING PUBLIC GOODS: THE CONTINGENT VALUATION METHOD (Rowman & Allanheld Publishers 1986).

10. City of Santa Fe v. Komis, 114 N.M. 659, 845 P.2d 753 (1992).

CHAPTER 15

Environmental Impairment Insurance: Practical Considerations

ROBERT J. GILBERT

Environmental risks affect virtually every type of real estate transaction, whether for commercial, industrial, or residential properties.[1] When identifying and allocating responsibility for environmental risks, parties to a real estate transaction generally employ traditional methods used for nonenvironmental risks, including performing due diligence; relying on contractual provisions, including representations, warranties, indemnities, and express assignments of risk; and modifying the price of the property to reflect the cost of contamination or remediation or establishing appropriate reserve funds. However, these traditional risk-identifying and risk-shifting tools suffer two important deficiencies. First, they require one or both parties to accept the ultimate risk of potentially catastrophic environmental liabilities. Second, they provide little protection to third parties, especially lenders, in the event the party that bears the risk of environmental liabilities is financially unable to meet its commitments.

For transactions in which neither party is willing or able to accept the risk of future environmental liabilities, or for which financing is difficult to obtain because of the lender's environmental concerns, parties may wish to consider environmental impairment (EI) insurance. Such insurance comes in a variety of forms and includes both preprinted "off-the-shelf" policies and custom-designed policies covering specifically identified risks. Coverage is available for remediation of the subject property and for adjacent properties as well as for liability to third parties for property damage or bodily injury. While some EI insurance policies provide either illusory protection or coverage that is ill-suited for particular types of risks, properly crafted EI insurance coverage may help save transactions that might otherwise fall apart as a result of environmental risks.

This chapter addresses three aspects of EI insurance: (1) the reasons for purchasing EI insurance in conjunction with a real estate transaction; (2) currently available environmental impairment products, including the scope of coverage, typical conditions affecting such coverage, and various exclusions from coverage; and (3) a discussion of procedures to follow when considering EI insurance in conjunction with a real estate transaction.[2]

Reasons for Considering EI Insurance as a Risk-Shifting Tool

Environmental risks are a unique creature in the world of real estate. Most nonenvironmental risks can be identified and either eliminated, controlled, or allocated among the parties. For example, the sale of a commercial office building involves tenant risk. Tenants may fail to renew their leases, attempt to terminate or renegotiate their leases in the event the sale of the property violates the leases' nonassignability provisions, or simply default on rent obligations. Tenant risk can be managed in a variety of ways, including due diligence (e.g., reviewing leases for assignability provisions or investigating the tenants' payment history and creditworthiness), discounting of the purchase price to account for tenant improvements necessary to retain or attract tenants, and purchase price adjustments or deferrals based on future occupancy rates. Similarly, the risk of title defects can be identified through title searches and can be allocated through representations and warranties, or it can be shifted to a third party through title insurance. Most importantly, typical real estate risks rarely involve potential liability in excess of the value of the subject property.

Environmental risks may not be susceptible to traditional means of risk control. Traditional due diligence has serious limitations in controlling or eliminating environmental risks. Environmental due diligence requires an investigation into the historical uses of both the subject parcel and nearby parcels—a so-called Phase I site assessment—and may require a Phase II site assessment (i.e., taking soil or groundwater samples), particularly at sites with a history of "dirty" uses.

Even if all of the above steps are followed, environmental due diligence may provide false security. The complete history of a site may prove elusive. A seemingly clean property may have housed industries such as machine shops or repair businesses that used solvents, petroleum products, or toxic substances. Environmental agency records may be incomplete, and the plethora of local, state, and federal regulatory agencies makes it difficult to be certain that all relevant records have been considered. Also, even complete knowledge of the past environmental practices on a property does not allow a buyer or lender to predict future enforcement actions with certainty.

Finally, the costs of an effective environmental investigation may be prohibitive, or at least incompatible with the economics of a given transaction. Adherence to industry standards almost guarantees that a Phase I site assessment will cost several thousand dollars.[3] However, failure to conduct a sufficiently comprehensive environmental investigation may result in a catastrophic failure to discover contamination. By shifting the risk of undiscovered contamination to a third-party insurer, EI insurance may reduce risks resulting from the inability of environmental due diligence to uncover all potential environmental problems.

Other traditional risk-shifting mechanisms may prove equally insufficient to control environmental risks. Real estate documents typically include indemnities, releases, and hold harmless agreements to allocate liability for various risks, including environmental risks, among the parties. However, such devices are often effective only as between the parties to the transaction and will not protect an indemnitee or releasee from primary liability to the government[4] or third parties.[5] Also, the value of an environmental indemnity or release depends on the financial resources of the indemnitor or releasor. This insecurity may destroy the economics of a real estate transaction, since the costs of defending or responding to an environmental enforcement action can be many times greater than the property's market value. EI insurance may provide the necessary financial backing to support an environmental indemnity or release.

Reserve funds and price adjustments also may provide insufficient protection because of the potentially catastrophic nature of environmental risks. Remediation costs may exceed the value of the property and may dwarf the size of a reserve fund or price adjustment. Rather than placing part of a purchase price into an environmental reserve fund, parties may wish to invest that same amount into a properly designed EI policy that provides protection against catastrophic environmental liabilities.

Even if the parties to the transaction believe that environmental risks have been adequately identified and allocated, EI insurance may be necessary to address lenders' concerns. (See Chapter 4 for a discussion of lender liability issues.) With liability under CERCLA still a source of concern to lenders, lenders have several reasons to require borrowers to obtain appropriate EI insurance.

- Ensuring that environmental liabilities do not impair the borrower's ability to repay the loan

- Protecting the security of the loan by ensuring that contaminated property will be remediated and restored to its market value in the event of a loan default
- Controlling the cost of potential "owner" liability under federal or state environmental statutes in the event a lender forecloses and assumes ownership of the property
- Protecting the lender in the event that its activities give rise to "operator" liability under federal or state environmental statutes
- Protecting the lender against a state government's possible "super lien" for environmental cleanups, which otherwise might permit the government to recover remediation costs from a bankrupt borrower's estate before secured creditors are paid

In sum, there are a number of reasons for considering the purchase of EI insurance in connection with a real estate transaction. However, care must be exercised to ensure that the EI policy provides real protection rather than illusory peace of mind.

Caveat Emptor: A Brief Survey of Environmental Insurance Products

Beginning in the early 1970s, the insurance industry has progressively reduced the amount of coverage for environmental liabilities provided under standard first-party property damage policies and third-party comprehensive general liability policies. This reduction has included the adoption of a standard exclusion for liability arising out of pollution releases that are not "sudden and accidental," subsequent cutbacks in first-party coverage for pollution-related liability, and, since 1986, the widespread use of broad-form pollution exclusions (called "absolute" pollution exclusions by some). This reduction in coverage coincided with the massive expansion of environmental laws and the accompanying increase in risk of environmental liability. The need for a risk-shifting tool such as environmental insurance burgeoned just as the general availability of such insurance started to evaporate.

The EI insurance industry developed to fill this coverage vacuum. The first EI policies, issued in the 1970s and early 1980s, typically provided third-party liability coverage for property damage or bodily injury arising from discharges of pollutants that were gradual, fortuitous, and neither expected nor intended by the insureds. Policies issued during this period provided substantial coverage to policyholders, often in excess of the premiums collected. The resulting losses led to significant restrictions in the coverage provided by EI insurers.

This less generous EI insurance failed to establish a significant market impact in the late 1980s and early 1990s, primarily because potential consumers viewed the policies as providing too little coverage at too great a price.

Many EI insurance products have now become broader in coverage and lower in price, and many EI insurance policies should now be regarded as potentially viable risk-transfer devices. Today there are wide variations in coverage available under the many different insurance products that call themselves "Environmental Impairment Insurance." As discussed below, there is no such thing as a "standard" EI policy. Moreover, the relative novelty and nonuniformity of EI policies means that policyholders do not have the ability to review judicial decisions interpreting unclear or ambiguous policy provisions. Every policy must be carefully scrutinized to ensure that meaningful coverage exists.

Purchasers of EI liability insurance must answer two basic questions: *What* coverage am I buying, and *whose* coverage am I buying? Most EI coverage, whether "off-the-shelf" policies (i.e., preprinted, nonnegotiated policies) or customized policies that are specially negotiated to meet an insured's specific needs, contains significant limitations and exclusions. Just as importantly, the purchaser of EI insurance must ensure that coverage is purchased from a financially stable insurer. For example, specialty insurers who concentrate primarily on EI coverage may prove unreliable as risk transfer partners because a glut of claims by policyholders may force the specialty insurer into insolvency. Thus, potential consumers of EI insurance must carefully consider both the product being offered and the company providing the coverage.

Who Offers EI Coverage?

A number of large, well-known insurers (or their subsidiaries) have participated in the EI market in recent years. The largest quantity of coverage has been provided by the American Insurance Group, or AIG (through Commerce and Industry Insurance Company and a number of other subsidiaries), Reliance Insurance Company, Safeco Insurance Company, United Coastal Insurance Company, and Zurich Insurance Company. Other major insurers with some degree of involvement in this market include the CIGNA group of insurers, Fireman's Fund, Lloyd's of London, St. Paul, The Home, and Wausau Insurance Company. In addition to these large, multiline national insurers, brokers may know of a number of smaller companies that specialize in EI insurance. By concentrating in EI coverage, these specialty companies may be capable of providing a more responsive insurance product, but they may also carry a greater financial risk as a result of the lack of diversification in their underwriting portfolios.

The foregoing discussion should not be interpreted either as an exclusive list of EI insurers, as an endorsement of the products offered by any insurer, or as an endorsement of the insurers themselves. It simply demonstrates that EI insurance is widely available and that potential purchasers have opportunities to shop among different insurers based on product coverage and price.

What Type of Coverage Is Available?

Every real estate transaction involves unique environmental risks. Because a variety of EI products are offered, appropriate coverage likely is available for a particular transaction. Currently available EI policies generally offer one or more of the following types of coverages.

Environmental Remediation Insurance

This coverage protects against the discovery of contamination on the subject property during the policy period. It frequently attaches at the time of the real estate transaction (e.g., sale, refinancing, or foreclosure), but it may attach at any other time. Although earlier versions of environmental remediation insurance applied only to contamination that existed but had not been identified at the time the insurance policy was issued, newer policies often cover not only prior unknown contamination but also prospective contamination (i.e., occurring during the policy period) and unknown contamination that either migrates onto or from the subject property before or during the policy period. Coverage generally is written on a first-party basis (i.e., it pays for the restoration of an insured's contaminated property) and therefore excludes liability (including defense costs) incurred with respect to claims by private parties for remediation, property damage, or bodily injury. The policy term generally lasts for three to five years, with coverage triggered by discovery of contamination during the policy period. In most environmental remediation policies, no governmental or third-party claim is required to trigger coverage. Some policies, however, may not be triggered unless an actual governmental cleanup action has been initiated.

Pollution Legal Liability Insurance

This insurance covers liability to third parties for off-site bodily injury, property damage, and cleanup costs caused by contamination emanating from a specific property. Unless negotiated separately, the policy typically does not cover remediation of an insured's own property.

Some policies provide coverage for treatment, storage, and disposal facilities. The policy covers claims made against the insured during the policy period. Some policies expressly exclude coverage for "injunctive relief," which creates a potential issue regarding coverage of cleanup costs incurred pursuant to any governmental cleanup orders or pursuant to a third-party request for affirmative injunctive relief. Most such policies agree to "pay on behalf of the insured" rather than to "indemnify" the insured, which may be important to insureds whose limited cash flow would make it difficult to advance defense or cleanup costs. Often lenders can be listed as additional insureds.

Future Contamination Coverage

Such coverage provides for remediation of contamination arising from ongoing operations of the insured. Under most policies, contamination must be discovered *and* reported to the insurer during the policy period or within a specified period after the expiration of the policy. Exclusions vary significantly from policy to policy. This coverage is increasingly being included, by endorsement or otherwise, in basic environmental remediation insurance policies or in pollution legal liability insurance policies.

Pollution Insurance for Financial Institutions

This coverage protects lenders against the risk of holding nonperforming loans secured by contaminated property. The insurer's obligation is triggered when a loan goes into default *and* the property is found to be polluted. The policy pays the lesser of the remediation costs or the loan balance. If the insurer pays off the loan, the financial institution is relieved of the need to foreclose on contaminated property and of the risk of becoming an "owner" of such property under Superfund and other environmental statutes. Such coverage is less attractive if the policy merely pays the costs of remediation, since the lender may then be forced to assume ownership and cleanup of the property to recover its full investment in the property. By doing so, the lender could incur the risk of potential additional liability as an "owner" or "operator" of the property. These policies typically exclude properties containing known pollutants and are much more expensive or difficult to underwrite for properties where potential pollutants are manufactured or stored. At least some policies cover contamination caused intentionally by someone other than the insured. Such coverage may insure an entire loan portfolio. Because such coverage often requires extensive underwriting and is comparatively expensive, an interested financial institution must have a large real estate portfolio, often in excess of $500 million, to justify and support the substantial premiums.

"Stop Loss" Insurance, or Risk Retention plus Coverage for Catastrophic Environmental Losses

This form of EI coverage, which combines traditional environmental remediation insurance with self-insurance, is useful for controlling losses at properties with known environmental problems. The policyholder and the insurance company first agree on an estimated cost for remediating the known environmental conditions. The policyholder then agrees to bear the risk of a substantial deductible or self-insured retention (the "stop loss" amount), which is calculated to be the estimated cleanup costs plus an additional amount (the "cushion") to account for cost overruns or unanticipated expenses. The insurer bears the risk of all cleanup costs in excess of the "stop loss" amount, up to the policy limit.

This "stop loss" insurance contains an important underwriting option pertaining to control of the actual cleanup. Under the first option, the policyholder retains the right to select and supervise the environmental consultants and engineers, subject to the insurer's approval. This option may be attractive to policyholders with experience in environmental remediation, since such policyholders may be able to reduce cleanup costs through close supervision of consultants and engineers.

Under the second option, the insurance company itself selects and oversees the consultants. This may be useful for parties lacking the experience or sophistication to supervise cleanup activities effectively. However, this option may result in higher cleanup costs to the insured, since the insurance company's incentive will be to ensure that costs do not exceed the "stop loss" amount, rather than to hold costs as low as possible.

Directors and Officers Pollution Insurance

These policies cover pollution-related claims against directors and officers for wrongful acts leading to contamination. In addition, many EI policies include officers and directors as named insureds.

Customized Policies

Customized policies often can be negotiated to cover specifically identified risks. Such policies can provide valuable and economical protection because coverage can be tailored to properties or risks of primary concern to insureds and some exclusions can be eliminated from the policy. Since insurers typically require an extensive site investigation before issuing manuscript EI policies, such coverage requires extra time for underwriting the policy and thus may not be feasible for real estate transactions that must close quickly.

Regardless of the specific coverage, EI insurance is nearly always written on a "claims-made" or "discovery" basis. This means that the policy will cover only those claims that meet two requirements: (1) the claim is brought against the insured (in the case of third-party claims) or the contamination is discovered by the insured (in the case of first-party claims) during the policy period, and (2) the insured provides written notice of the claim or contamination to the insurer during the policy period. In some cases the insured may purchase the "extended reporting period" endorsement, which provides the insured with an additional period after expiration of the policy in which to notify the insurer of claims arising before the policy's expiration. This option does *not* provide coverage for contamination occurring after the policy's expiration.

The claims-made nature of EI insurance represents an important limitation on coverage. First, many environmental liabilities arise from latent contamination that may not be discovered until years after a transaction is consummated. By that time the claims reporting period may have expired, resulting in a lack of coverage. In addition, claims-made liability policies frequently require the insured to have received a formal written demand from an aggrieved party during the policy period. This requirement can defeat coverage, since claimants often defer making written demands to a potentially responsible party until after completion of their environmental investigation. Such delays may result in a written claim not being made to the insured until after expiration of the policy period.

Finally, claims-made policies can result in coverage gaps even when the insured buys coverage during several consecutive years. Many EI policies exclude coverage for pollution discovered before the policy's inception. Thus, an insured may not be covered under any EI policy in the not-uncommon situation in which (1) contamination is discovered during the first EI policy period but (2) the claimant does not make a written demand upon the insured until a subsequent EI policy period. This problem can be ameliorated in part by endorsements that provide retroactive coverage for any contamination discovered, or first taking place, on or after the inception date of the first EI policy or by endorsements that provide coverage for all "prior acts" as long as the contamination was not known before issuance of the first EI policy.

Occurrence-based policies also can avoid many of the problems caused by the claims-made feature of EI insurance. An occurrence-based policy provides coverage for pollution-related property damage, bodily injury, or personal injury that occurs during the policy period, even if the harm is not discovered until years or decades after the policy has expired.[6] However, it is nearly impossible to find an insurer willing to issue EI coverage on an occurrence basis. Thus, many purchasers of EI coverage must carefully consider and plan for the limitations of the claims-made form.

In addition to the inherent limitation on coverage created by the claims-made feature, most EI policies contain numerous exclusions that may eliminate important coverage such as the following:

- Contamination happening at certain times (e.g., occurring *before* or occurring *after* the policy's inception)
- Contamination discovered during the policy period, but for which no claim was asserted until after the policy period
- Claims by third parties for property damage, bodily injury, or personal injury
- Remediation of certain property (e.g., the subject property, adjoining property, groundwater)
- Defense costs incurred in defending against governmental or third-party claims
- Consequential or economic damages (e.g., loss of profits, stigma damages, loss of marketability)
- Fines and penalties
- Punitive damages
- Natural resource damages under CERCLA
- Contamination arising from storage tanks (whether above-ground or underground)
- Contamination resulting from certain types of contaminants (e.g., asbestos, petroleum products, lead or lead-containing materials, radioactive material, natural radiation)
- Contamination resulting from specified causes (e.g., acid rain, indoor air quality, electromagnetic fields, nuclear incidents)
- Liability arising from certain types of operations
- Liability arising from a failure to comply with an applicable environmental statute, regulation, ordinance, directive, or order
- Liability arising from a post-inception change in applicable law
- Liability assumed under contract
- Claims brought by one insured against another insured
- Environmental liabilities for which the insured may be liable under worker's compensation, unemployment compensation, or disability benefits law
- Personal injury to employees arising during and in the course of employment
- Contamination causally related to automobiles, aircraft, watercraft, or other modes of transportation
- Contamination at or emanating from off-shore facilities

- Contamination at or emanating from an inactive or closed site
- Contamination causally related to an insured's products or completed operations

As more companies enter the EI insurance market, the available coverage has become broader, and many of these exclusions may disappear. Nevertheless, each EI policy must be reviewed carefully to determine whether the exclusions listed above (or many others not mentioned here) are included.

In addition to explicit exclusions from coverage, other provisions of the policy—including "definitions," "conditions," and "insured's obligations"—may also defeat or severely limit coverage otherwise expected by the insured. For instance, the amount of coverage provided by a lender's EI policy may be limited to the property's sale price or fair market value, despite the fact that remediation costs may be several times the property's value. Such a limitation may be of particular consequence to a lender facing "operator" liability by reason of its participation in the management decisions involving a property. In addition, the policy may define the actual "insured" who is entitled to policy benefits so narrowly as to exclude coverage to real parties in interest. For example, if a policy fails to identify the lender as an additional insured, the proceeds of an environmental remediation policy may flow to a bankrupt borrower's estate rather than to the lender.

Also, the policyholder should not expect to obtain coverage for previously discovered contamination. Regardless of the type of EI insurance, the insurer generally performs or commissions a preclosing audit or investigation of site conditions, issues a written report disclosing the results of the investigation, and then excludes coverage for any environmental liabilities arising from conditions identified in its report. Thus, just like the proverbial burning house, known environmental problems cannot be the subject of a new insurance policy, unless the parties specifically identify the known problem as a covered risk (i.e., pursuant to a "stop loss" policy).

Finally, purchasers of EI insurance should consider pricing issues. Potential purchasers should be aware that premium quotes are often based on educated guesswork, primarily because the quoting insurer's EI products are nonstandard, relatively new, and based on actuarial data that is less than fully developed. Thus, premiums may fluctuate significantly and are often subject to downward negotiation without a concomitant reduction in coverage. Additional savings may also be realized by agreeing either to a higher deductible or to a coinsurance arrangement (i.e., the policyholder agrees to pay a percentage of all losses above the deductible amount).

For all of these reasons, a potential purchaser of EI insurance must carefully review the scope of coverage provided, as well as the limits, all applicable definitions, conditions and exclusions, the identity of the insurer, the financial standing of the insurer, and the many factors that affect the price. Moreover, this must be done *before* purchasing the policy, since the insured who has secured an unsatisfactory EI policy may lack the ability or financial resources to replace the policy with better coverage and, in any event, may be required to pay the original insurer's costs of investigating the subject site and underwriting the policy even if the policy is canceled before expiration.

Some Practical Considerations When Purchasing Environmental Impairment Insurance

The marketplace for EI insurance is filled with a dizzying array of products of varying quality, usefulness, and value. There are several practical steps that parties to a real estate transaction should follow before and after the purchase of EI insurance.

Identify the Risks to Be Shifted

The parties should identify the likely causes of potential contamination (e.g., past uses of underground storage tanks, historic manufacturing operations, adjoining landowner's operations) as well as the likely location of such contamination (e.g., off-site, on-site, groundwater). Forethought in this area will clarify the type of coverage that should be purchased.

Quantify the Risks to Be Shifted

Before purchasing EI insurance, the parties to the real estate transaction should decide which environmental risks justify the cost of such coverage. Despite the discussion above on the limitations of due diligence, indemnities, representations and warranties, and contingency/reserve funds, such traditional devices may be sufficient for shifting many types of environmental liabilities. Because of the underwriting expenses and substantial premiums often associated with EI insurance, such coverage may be appropriate only when both (1) the potential magnitude of environmental liability justifies the costs and (2) traditional methods of risk shifting do not provide adequate protection to the interested parties in the real estate transaction. Risk quantification will also allow the parties to determine the appropriate limits of liability and the acceptable degree of self-insurance (i.e., deductibles).

Select the Right Kind of Policy

Assuming the parties have concluded that EI insurance is a sensible investment, the scope of such insurance must be determined. First, the parties should find a policy that addresses their unique environmental risks. As set forth above, different policies provide vastly different kinds of coverage. Similarly, the limits of liability should be carefully examined to ensure that the amount of coverage is neither set too low, which could result in cleanup costs in excess of policy limits being borne by the parties to the real estate transaction, nor set too high, which could result in the payment of unnecessary premiums. In selecting the limits of liability, prospective purchasers of EI insurance should bear in mind that environmental liabilities often can exceed the value of the property. Therefore, it is important to confirm that (1) the limits of liability reflect potential environmental exposure and (2) the policy does not further restrict the amount of coverage to the lesser of the actual liability or the property's fair market value.

Consult an Experienced Broker

A vast array of EI insurance products is available, and the selection is constantly changing. It is unlikely that one's regular insurance broker or agent, no matter how qualified in other areas of insurance, will have extensive experience in the environmental field. Moreover, the typical broker may not be aware of, or have access to, all available EI insurance products. The wise purchaser of EI insurance should consult a specialty broker with experience in environmental insurance coverage to ensure that the many EI insurance options have been considered.

Properly Instruct the Broker

After the decision has been made to obtain EI coverage, the party seeking such coverage should provide clear written instructions to its broker. In particular, the prospective policyholder should state in writing its understanding of the scope of coverage that will be provided and the scope of risks that are to be transferred to the insurance company. This information, commonly referred to as "insurance specifications," will assist the broker in its procurement of coverage for the insured and will also provide the insured with a potential remedy against its broker in the event the instructions are not followed and the broker fails to procure the required coverage. Conversely, the potential insured should never state in writing its understanding that exclusions in the policies will bar certain types of coverage because such writings could affect the determination of the insured's reasonable expectation of coverage and could defeat coverage even if the insured's understanding of the exclusion was incorrect.[7]

Insist on Negotiating the Terms of Coverage

Because of time or cost constraints, it may not be possible to obtain manuscript coverage (i.e., a specifically negotiated policy). Nevertheless, the insured should not hesitate to seek policy endorsements that more closely tailor coverage to the insured's needs. For example, if a property once housed storage tanks, the insured should seek the elimination of any exclusions barring coverage for contamination arising from storage tanks. Through negotiation, insureds often can ameliorate many of the substantial limitations on coverage found in most "off-the-shelf" EI policies.

Obtain an Extended Cancellation Clause

Traditionally, insurers are required to provide no more than thirty days of notice before canceling coverage prior to the policy's expiration date. Given the likely difficulty of locating suitable replacement coverage for EI insurance, policyholders should insist on a sixty- or ninety-day cancellation clause.

Investigate the Financial Condition of the Insurance Company

The value of EI coverage is only as secure as the financial condition of the insurance company. Beware of bargains. When a company offers unrealistically low premiums for broad coverage, it may be using unsound pricing practices that could result in catastrophic underwriting losses and, ultimately, the insurer's insolvency. Similarly, poor reinsurance practices can erode an insurance company's financial health. Insureds must require their brokers to investigate and disclose the financial condition of potential insurers and their reinsurers and must also obtain guidance from brokers on the soundness of a potential insurer's pricing and underwriting strategies.[8] In addition, insureds (or their brokers) should investigate the availability of "cut through" endorsements, which require an insurer's parent company to meet coverage obligations in the event of the insurance subsidiary's insolvency.

Alert Environmental Managers and Lawyers to the Existence and Content of EI Coverage

In the world of insurance, nothing is sadder than an insured who loses coverage because of a failure to comply with the policy's procedural terms and conditions. After purchasing an EI policy, the insured's risk manager or broker should prepare a written summary of the coverage provided by the policy, as well as the events necessary to trigger coverage (e.g., written demand from the claimant during policy period, timely written notice to the insurer during policy period, and other relevant policy conditions). This written summary should be distributed to environmental managers, in-house lawyers, and other personnel in a position to learn about environmental liabilities. Reminders should be sent to these personnel shortly before the expiration date of the EI policy. This proactive approach will help insureds to comply with the stringent notice and reporting provisions imposed by the claims-made nature of most EI policies. Obviously, the insured should ask a qualified insurance advisor or legal counsel to review any policy summary before it is disseminated to ensure that the summary does not contain inaccurate statements that an insurer could later use as an admission limiting the scope of coverage.

Conclusion

Environmental risks need not kill a real estate transaction. The increasing availability of environmental impairment liability insurance provides an additional mechanism to allocate the risks arising from environmental contamination, provided that buyers, sellers, and lenders use care and common sense in the procurement of such coverage.

Notes

1. The ubiquity of environmental risks is such that one cannot buy a home without confronting the issue. For example, the Massachusetts Conveyancers Association's standard-form Purchase and Sale Agreement for residential real estate now contains an express warranty regarding the absence of underground storage tanks.

2. This chapter does not address insurance products that are available to assist companies in meeting financial responsibility laws. For instance, several federal or state statutes require individuals who store or transport hazardous materials to demonstrate financial responsibility in the event these hazardous materials escape to the environment and cause bodily injury or property damage. Many companies offer "insurance" that essentially constitutes a surety bond. The

insurer merely guarantees that the handler or transporter will be able to pay damages to third parties up to the amounts required in the financial responsibility law; the handler or transporter typically is obligated to repay the insurer for any amounts paid under the policy. Such financial responsibility insurance is outside the scope of this chapter.

3. The American Society for Testing and Materials (ASTM) has developed extensive guidelines for the preparation of Phase I investigations. *See* ASTM E 1527-93 STANDARD PRACTICE FOR ENVIRONMENTAL SITE ASSESSMENTS: PHASE I ENVIRONMENTAL SITE ASSESSMENT PROCESS as well as ASTM E 1528-93 STANDARD PRACTICE FOR ENVIRONMENTAL SITE ASSESSMENTS: TRANSACTION SCREEN PROCESS. These standards are designed to permit a buyer of real property to conduct the due diligence necessary to quality for the innocent landowner defense under Section 101(35)(B) of the Comprehensive Environmental Response, Compensation, and Liability Act (CERCLA). *See* 42 U.S.C. § 9601(35)(B). One insurer has arranged for an agent or independent consultant to provide, for $400, a property inspection, interview of the owner and operator, and a check of relevant government databases. This service is advertised as being undertaken "via the ASTM Transaction Screen, which provides all appropriate inquiry, the level of inquiry required for the Innocent Landowner Defense." *See* PHW Environmental Risk Services, Inc., "Bankers Environmental Risk Insurance Summary," Program Outline at 2 (Feb. 1994). However, the insurer apparently does not regard this service as a full-fledged Phase I investigation, since it then provides that "[p]roperties with very high risk usage, such as heavy manufacturing and mining, will require a Phase I underwriting." *Id.* Chapter 8 of this book discusses the ASTM standards and environmental due diligence in more detail.

4. *See, e.g.*, Olin Corp. v. Consolidated Aluminum Corp., 807 F. Supp. 1133, 1137–39 (S.D.N.Y. 1992) ("under CERCLA, parties remain liable to the government irrespective of contractual agreement"), *aff'd in part, vacated in part*, 5 F.3d 10 (2d Cir. 1993).

5. *See, e.g.*, South Florida Water Management District v. Montalvo, 1989 Westlaw 260215 (S.D. Fla. Feb. 15, 1989) ("An indemnification agreement is only as good as the assets of the party obligating itself" and does not relieve the indemnified party from CERCLA liability to third parties).

6. Thousands of lawsuits have been filed in the last decade regarding coverage for environmental liabilities under occurrence-based liability policies issued before 1986. Parties to today's real estate transactions should be aware that older policies written on an occurrence basis may provide coverage for contamination discovered on properties that are the subject of the transaction. As an integral part of any real estate transaction involving property with potential environmental concerns, the parties should consider the transfer or assignment of rights to insurance coverage under older occurrence-based policies. The parties should ensure that any transfer or assignment of rights is structured to comply with the so-called "nonassignability" provision in most insurance policies.

For a general discussion of coverage issues that arise under the occurrence-based general liability policies issued before 1986, *see, e.g.*, N. Ballard, R. Gilbert, et al., *Insurance Coverage for Environmental Losses and Liabilities*, in 4 S. COOKE, THE LAW OF HAZARDOUS WASTE: MANAGEMENT, CLEANUP, LIABILITY, and LITIGATION (Matthew Bender & Co., 1987, cum. supp. 1995).

7. *See, e.g.*, Diamond Shamrock Chem. Co. v. Aetna Casualty & Surety Co., 1989 Haz. Waste Litig. Rep. (Andrews) 17,308 (N.J. Super. Ct. Ch. Div. April 12, 1989) (discussing insured's risk manager's expectation of scope of pollution exclusion, which was broader than exclusionary effect afforded to it by courts).

8. The most widely recognized measure of an insurance company's financial stability is A.M. Best's ratings, which evaluate companies according to six factors: (1) profitability, (2) leverage/capitalization (which measures a company's ability to withstand catastrophic losses, poor investment returns, adverse underwriting results, or poor economic conditions), (3) liquidity (which measures a company's ability to meet short-term obligations without liquidating investments in an untimely or unprofitable manner), (4) amount and soundness of reinsurance, (5) adequacy of loss reserves (which measures the amount of a company's assets that have been set aside to pay potential losses), and (6) management experience and objectives. *See* Best's Insurance Reports—Property-Casualty, Preface at x (1993). The ratings classifications include "A+" and "A" (excellent), "B+" (very good), "B" (good), "C+" (fairly good), "C" (fair), and "Omitted" (a company is eligible for a rating but fails to satisfy the basic qualifications for Best's minimum alphabetical rating). *See id.*, Preface at xi. Best's ratings are considered by most insurance professionals to be a reliable, but not infallible, indicator of an insurer's financial stability.

CHAPTER 16

SEC Requirements for Environmental Disclosures

MARGARET V. HATHAWAY

Duties to disclose environmental matters imposed by U.S. securities laws are relevant to real estate and real estate finance in several important contexts. Failure to comply with these requirements may have serious consequences.

Among the important statutes administered by the U.S. Securities and Exchange Commission (SEC) are the Securities Act of 1933 (1933 Act)[1] and the Securities Exchange Act of 1934 (1934 Act).[2] Both acts impose disclosure duties that apply generally to many types of information and to environmental disclosures particularly. SEC disclosure obligations govern information that must be disclosed in registration statements and prospectuses when offering securities for sale, in proxy statements and other communications relevant to issues subject to shareholder votes, in financial statements to be released to shareholders and prospective purchasers, and in periodic reports to be filed with the SEC.

These SEC disclosure obligations are relevant in the real estate context in several ways. First, real estate investment trusts (REITs), which are increasingly used as vehicles to invest in real property, to make loans secured by real property, or to hold and manage real property, are generally financed by publicly traded securities and are thus subject to SEC disclosure obligations.[3] Second, mortgage-backed securities are an increasingly important means of financing commercial real estate and have for many years been a major source of residential real estate financing. In mortgage-backed securities transactions, securities are issued that are not secured by real property but by full or partial interests in mortgages that are, in turn, secured by real property.[4] Third, many publicly traded corporations (e.g., banks and life insurance companies) own or finance real estate. Their potential liability for environmental matters relating to such real estate will be subject to disclosure in financial statements and periodic reports filed with the SEC as well as in any new stock offerings that meet SEC criteria for disclosure.

Because they are the source of the SEC's authority to compel disclosure, an abbreviated summary of the 1933 Act and the 1934 Act helps illuminate disclosure obligations. Generally, the 1933 Act regulates registrations of distributions of securities, while the 1934 Act regulates postdistribution trading of securities and other matters.[5] The SEC has strong enforcement powers, including authority to seek judicial orders to enjoin violations, issue cease-and-desist orders, require compliance through administrative proceedings, and impose civil and criminal sanctions for noncompliance pursuant to both the 1933 and 1934 acts.[6] There is a potentially stronger enforcement mechanism than the SEC's authority to impose remedies and sanctions, however, because both acts provide private rights of action against those who do not disclose information as required.[7] In light of the huge amounts of money often involved in environmental problems and the potential impact on a business subject to SEC disclosure obligations, private parties are likely to bring suit when they are injured as a result of nondisclosure.

The 1933 Act has several important provisions relevant to disclosure obligations. Section 5 is the primary section of the 1933 Act governing registrations and prospectuses. Registration statements must be filed with the SEC, while prospectuses must be provided to prospective purchasers. The content of registration statements and prospectuses largely but not entirely overlaps with a separate part included in registration statements.[8] Sections 11 and 12 provide for civil liability for failure to comply with SEC requirements, with such liability extending to officers and directors of issuers and to underwriters, accountants, and others.[9] In addition, Section 17 of the 1933 Act has a general antifraud provision that applies to distributions of public offerings and private placements, and Section 24 imposes criminal sanctions for violations of other sections and for willful misstatements or half-truths in registration statements.[10]

The 1934 Act requires the reporting of information necessary to keep registration statements, annual reports, and quarterly reports "reasonably current."[11] The SEC has issued regulations that call for filing of annual and quarterly reports, generally made on Forms 10-K and 10-Q, respectively. In addition, Form 8-K must be filed no later than fifteen days following certain events (e.g., a change in control, the acquisition or disposition of a significant amount of assets, bankruptcy or receivership proceedings, a change of auditors, and a director's resignation due to a policy dispute).[12] Besides these periodic reporting requirements, the 1934 Act regulates tender offers and solicitation of proxies, imposes some controls on insider trading, and imposes registration requirements additional to those of the 1933 Act.[13] Among the remedies available are the SEC's authority to suspend or withdraw registration of securities[14] and civil and criminal liability.

Because the disclosure requirements of the two statutes were confusing and overlapping, the SEC promulgated Regulation S-K[15] governing disclosure obligations under both acts for all matters, not just environmental concerns. Regulation S-K, first adopted in 1977, was substantially expanded in 1982[16] and has since been amended from time to time. Intended not to forge new law but to articulate existing law in one central regulation, Regulation S-K consolidates the reporting requirements of both acts into one document. Regulation S-K contains Item 101—Description of Business (Item 101),[17] Item 103—Legal Proceedings (Item 103),[18] and Item 303—Management's Discussion and Analysis of Financial Condition and Results of Operation (MD&A or Item 303).[19] All three items are central to an understanding of the SEC's disclosure requirements in general and environmental disclosure requirements in particular. (It should be noted that the SEC has also issued Regulation S-B, which applies a streamlined version of Regulation S-K to small businesses.)[20]

Some people believe (probably accurately) that environmental matters are being overlooked or grossly understated in financial statements and other disclosures governed by SEC laws and regulations. While he was an SEC Commissioner, Richard Roberts made a number of speeches to focus attention on this problem.[21] He has written that

> While the aggregate numbers concerning potential environmental costs are staggering, what is even more frightening is the massive amount of unacknowledged environmental cost that has yet to be reflected in corporate financial statements. Despite the growing importance of environmental issues, a 1992 survey conducted by Price Waterhouse revealed that 62% of the issuers responding to the survey have known environmental problems not yet recorded in their financial statements.[22]

Counsel should expect SEC enforcement of the duty to disclose environmental costs and liabilities to intensify. The SEC and the U.S. Environmental Protection Agency (EPA) are sharing information that may well enable the SEC to identify information that should be disclosed.[23] As Commissioner Roberts has stated, "When the [SEC] staff identifies material omissions or deficiencies relating to environmental matters, it will continue to request corrective disclosure and, in egregious cases, may refer the matter to the Division of Enforcement."[24]

This chapter describes the laws and regulations that govern SEC disclosure obligations in general and their applicability to environmental matters in particular. (Because this discussion is aimed primarily at real estate and real estate finance lawyers, it assumes little or no familiarity with SEC disclosure laws and regulations.) The chapter addresses the major regulations governing disclosure obligations under the 1933 and 1934 Acts, found in Items 101, 103, and 303 of Regulation S-K,[25] as well as SEC releases referencing disclosure of environmental matters. In addition, because environmental matters are also subject to disclosure requirements not specifically applicable to environmental concerns, the chapter addresses the SEC's general rules for disclosure of material information. Finally, the chapter addresses the practical effect of the environmental disclosure requirements of which lawyers should be aware in advising their employers and clients.

Overview of SEC Disclosure Requirements in the Context of Environmental Laws

In summary, the SEC requires disclosure of any material effects of environmental laws on the capital, expenditures, earnings, and competitive position of the issuer;[26] disclosure of administrative and judicial proceedings and activities, which must be disclosed in some cases when the government is a party whether or not the consequences are or are expected to be material;[27] and disclosure of future prospects as well as historical results in the MD&A.[28] The requirements for disclosure of future prospects for environmental costs and liabilities are particularly uncertain and troublesome, especially in light of Staff Accounting Bulletin 92 (SAB 92), issued in 1993.[29]

Environmental disclosure obligations must be assessed in the context of CERCLA's harsh liability scheme (see Chapter 1), RCRA and other federal regulatory statutes (see Chapter 1), and the many laws enacted in each state (see Chapter 3). Environmental liabilities also arise in the context of common-law causes of action such as tort liability for personal injury, death, and property damage caused by contaminants as well as nuisance and trespass laws.[30] An understanding of a company's actual and potential liabilities under environmental statutes and common law is critical to fulfilling its duties of disclosure pursuant to SEC requirements.

Review of SEC References to Environmental Disclosures

In 1971 the SEC issued its first statement specifically referring to environmental disclosures (1971 Release).[31] Though superseded by a later release, the 1971 Release essentially stated that disclosures about environmental matters are subject to the same standard of materiality that pertains to disclosures about other topics.

The Natural Resources Defense Counsel successfully challenged a 1973 release (the 1973 Release)[32] by the SEC regarding environmental disclosures. In response, the SEC proposed a new and controversial rule (the 1975 Release),[33] but in a 1976 release (1976 Release),[34] the SEC elected not to finalize most of the 1975 proposals, adding only the duty to disclose capital expenditures for environmental compliance to its existing environmental disclosure requirements. Instead, the SEC cited its existing rules as adequate in that they specifically require environmental disclosures as outlined in the 1973 Release[35] as well as generally applicable disclosure of all material information and information necessary to make other disclosed information not misleading.[36]

Subsequently the SEC instituted proceedings against U.S. Steel with regard to the company's failure to disclose its substantial expenditures for pollution control equipment required by law. These proceedings were resolved by settlement in a 1979 release (U.S. Steel Release)[37] that offers specific directives about environmental disclosures. A provision of the U.S. Steel Release that generally applies to SEC environmental disclosure obligations states that "the Commission construes its existing specific environmental disclosure rules broadly and liberally."[38] Another provision of the U.S. Steel Release with broad impact specifies that while the SEC did not choose to impose a general rule requiring disclosure of a registrant's environmental policy, there are two exceptions:

> First, if a corporation voluntarily chooses to make disclosures concerning its environmental policy, such disclosures must be accurate. And, the corporation must make any additional disclosures necessary to render the voluntary disclosure not misleading.
>
> Second, if a corporation has a policy or approach toward compliance with environmental regulations which is reasonably likely to result in substantial fines, penalties, or other significant effects on the corporation, it may be necessary for the registrant to disclose the likelihood and magnitude (thereof).[39]

Though issued before the substantial expansion of Regulation S-K in 1982, the U.S. Steel Release does not conflict with Regulation S-K and is referred to by Commissioner Roberts in his materials; thus, it should be referred to in applying Regulation S-K to environmental disclosures.

In 1982 the SEC issued the substantially revised and consolidated Regulation S-K previously mentioned.[40] In addition to Items 101, 103, and 303, Item 102 of Regulation S-K[41] requires a brief statement describing the "location and general character of the principal plants, mines, and other materially important physical properties of the registrant and its subsidiaries" as well as how the property is held (e.g., in fee or subject to encumbrance).[42] Because the regulations do not address Item 102 in the context of whether an environmental problem on a property would require listing the property for purposes of a mortgage-backed securities transaction or a REIT, the general materiality rules (discussed later in this chapter) would govern. If a property is deemed material, the regulations would require identification of the property or properties under Item 102.

More recently, the SEC issued its 1989 release "Management's Discussion and Analysis of Financial Condition Results of Operations; Certain Investment Company Disclosures" (MD&A Release). This release relates primarily to Item 303,[43] particularly the duty to discuss future prospects. (The MD&A Release is discussed in connection with Item 303 later in this chapter.) Moreover, in 1993 the staff of the SEC issued SAB 92 on the topic of environmental issues in financial statements.[44] SAB 92 has potentially far-reaching and important implications for disclosure of contingent environmental losses.

Item 101—Description of Business

Item 101 and Its Instructions

Item 101 requires a general description of the registrant's business (including business intended to be done) as well as its subsidiaries and predecessors over the past five years (longer if material). Section (c) of Item 101 calls for a narrative description of the business, including thirteen specified items. One of these specified items mandates environmental disclosure.

> (xii) Appropriate disclosure also shall be made as to the material effects that compliance with Federal, State and local provisions which have been enacted or adopted regulating the discharge of materials into the environment, or otherwise relating to the protection of the environment, may have upon the capital expenditures, earnings and competitive position of the registrant and its subsidiaries. The registrant shall disclose any material estimated

> capital expenditures for the remainder of its current fiscal year and its succeeding fiscal year and for such *further periods* as the registrant may deem material. (Emphasis added.)[45]

Thus, Item 101 requires forward-looking disclosures, in addition to disclosure of currently important environmental costs and liabilities.

Instructions accompany Item 101, and Instruction 1 defines criteria for determining what is material to an understanding of the registrant's business. Instruction 1 dictates the consideration of both quantitative and qualitative factors

> such as the significance of the matter to the registrant (e.g., whether a matter with a relatively minor impact on the registrant's business is represented by management to be important to its future profitability), the pervasiveness of the matter (e.g., whether it affects or may affect numerous items in the segment[46] information), and the impact of the matter (e.g., whether it distorts the trends reflected in the segment information).[47]

Instruction 3 allows the omission of information required by Item 101 upon written request to the SEC, provided that it is consistent with protection of investors.[48]

U.S. Steel Release, Other SEC Releases, and Item 101

In discussing the necessity to disclose the total costs of complying with environmental laws, the U.S. Steel Release disapproves earlier practices of disclosing only prior actual and presently authorized capital expenditures and addresses the role of estimates in making disclosures for future years.[49] The release states that

> where a registrant expected that additional material capital expenditures would have to be authorized . . . and had in fact developed or received estimates with respect thereto, such estimates were generally required to be disclosed.[50]

Moreover, if a registrant has estimates that go beyond the two-year period mandated by Item 101, disclosure of this fact may be necessary so that other disclosures are not misleading. The registrant may even be required to develop estimates where "the registrant reasonably expects that . . . costs for any future year will be materially higher than the costs disclosed for the mandatory two-year period."[51] When estimates are provided, it may be necessary to disclose "the source of . . . estimates, the assumptions and measurements used in reaching the estimates, and the extent of uncertainty that projected future costs may occur."[52] This release also clarifies that the Statement of Financial Accounting Standard No. 5, "Accounting for Contingencies," issued by the Financial Accounting Standards Board (FASB)[53] will apply.

The 1973 Release resembled the current Item 101, emphasizing the need to address possible future effects of environmental statutes and regulations.[54] Declining to specify how far into the future the projections must be made, the SEC did not impose a time limit on any material effect that management reasonably believes will occur.[55] The 1976 Release required disclosure of capital expenditures for environmental control facilities.[56] Item 101 now contains a more general version of this provision.[57]

Item 103—Legal Proceedings

Item 103 and Its Instructions

Item 103 requires a brief description of any "material pending legal proceedings, other than ordinary routine litigation incidental to the business, to which the registrant or any of its subsidiaries is a party or of which any of their property is the subject."[58] In addition to certain information identifying the parties and the suit, a registrant must include "a description of the factual basis alleged to underlie the proceeding and the relief sought."[59] Item 103 also dictates inclusion of "similar information as to any such proceedings *known to be contemplated* by government authorities." (Emphasis added.)[60]

Instruction 5 to Item 103 provides detailed requirements for disclosure of such proceedings when they relate to environmental issues.

> 5. Notwithstanding the foregoing, an administrative or judicial proceeding (including, for purposes of A and B of this Instruction, proceedings which present in large degree the same issues) arising under any Federal, State or local provisions that have been enacted or adopted regulating the discharge of materials into the environment or primary [*sic*] for the purpose of protecting the environment shall not be deemed "ordinary routine litigation incidental to the business" and shall be described if:
>
> A. Such proceeding is material to the business or financial condition of the registrant;
>
> B. Such proceeding involves primarily a claim for damages, or involves potential monetary sanctions, capital expenditures, deferred charges or charges to income and the amount involved, exclusive of interest and costs, exceeds 10 percent of the current assets of the registrant and its subsidiaries on a consolidated basis; or

C. A governmental authority is a party to such proceeding and such proceeding involves potential monetary sanctions, unless the registrant reasonably believes that such proceeding will result in no monetary sanctions, or in monetary sanctions, exclusive of interest and costs, of less than $100,000; provided, however, that such proceedings which are similar in nature may be grouped and described generically.[61]

Thus, Sections A and B involve a determination of materiality, but Section C requires disclosure of proceedings involving monetary sanctions and to which the government is a party, whether or not the amounts involved are material.

U.S. Steel Release, Other SEC Releases, and Item 103

The U.S. Steel Release emphasizes a general point that the duty to disclose administrative proceedings "has never been construed narrowly by the Commission."[62] It also clearly states that all Notices of Violation issued by the EPA must be disclosed.[63]

Furthermore, in the U.S. Steel Release, the "Commission interprets its rule as requiring disclosure of all administrative orders relating to environmental matters, whether or not those orders literally follow a 'proceeding'"[64] and even where the order is consented to or negotiated.[65]

The U.S. Steel Release makes it clear that proceedings must be disclosed when they are initiated by the registrant or initiated by the government.[66] (Although not specified in the U.S. Steel Release, on its face Item 103 requires disclosure of proceedings initiated by private third parties.) It cites, as an example, an adjudicatory hearing to contest provisions of an National Pollution Discharge Elimination System (NPDES) permit.[67]

With regard to the duty to disclose "the relief sought," the U.S. Steel Release explains that it is not enough to disclose that the government seeks to compel new pollution control equipment. Rather, the registrant must "*estimate the level* of expenditures required to install the pollution control equipment if the costs are likely to be material." (Emphasis added.)[68] In such an instance, a registrant may be required to develop estimates, even if it has not previously done so.

The effect of earlier releases on the current interpretation of Item 103 is unclear. With regard to divulging "the factual basis of the proceedings and the relief sought," the 1973 Release allowed disclosure of opinions of counsel regarding the merits of the claim, defenses, and cross-claims.[69] The 1976 Release required disclosure of *all proceedings* involving the government as a party, regardless of materiality.[70] The SEC refined this position in Instruction 5 to Item 103, limiting non-material disclosures to *monetary sanctions* in a proceeding involving the government. In a footnote, the SEC required disclosure of all EPA cease-and-desist orders pursuant to Item 103.[71]

Item 103's Application to Superfund Liability Addressed by the MD&A Release and the Cole Letter

The MD&A Release, which primarily governs Item 303,[72] has a footnote directly relevant to Item 103 and whether designation as a PRP under CERCLA will trigger Item 103 disclosure requirements. Footnote 30 of that release specifies that:

> Designation as a PRP does not in and of itself trigger disclosure under Item 103 . . . because PRP status alone does not provide knowledge that a governmental agency is contemplating a proceeding.[73] Nonetheless, a registrant's particular circumstances, when coupled with PRP status, may provide that knowledge. While there are many ways a PRP can become subject to potential monetary sanctions, the costs anticipated to be incurred under Superfund, pursuant to a remedial agreement entered into in the normal course of negotiations with the EPA, generally are not "sanctions" within either Instruction 5(B) or (C) to Item 103. Such remedial costs normally would constitute charges to income, or in some cases capital expenditures. The availability of insurance, indemnification or contribution may be relevant under Instruction 5(A) or (B) in determining whether the criteria for disclosure have been met.[74]

Footnote 30 refers to an interpretive letter issued by the SEC to Thomas A. Cole on January 17, 1989 (Cole letter).[75] Mr. Cole had inquired as to the meaning of the word "sanctions" in Item 103 in the context of Superfund liability and whether contributions from other PRPs could be taken into consideration in determining whether disclosure is required when a registrant has been designated as a PRP under CERCLA. The meaning of the term "sanctions" is important because it is only "sanctions" under Section (C) of Instruction 5 that must be disclosed regardless of materiality; other matters do not need to be disclosed unless they rise to the level of materiality. The Cole letter does not clearly state that being named as a PRP will not, in and of itself, trigger an Item 103 disclosure obligation but only that Instruction 5(C) is not thereby triggered because costs incurred pursuant to a remedial agreement do not constitute sanctions for purposes of Item

103. In fact, the Cole letter concludes that "where it is reasonably likely that these costs (incurred pursuant to a remedial agreement) will be material," they will need to be disclosed pursuant to Item 303, 101, or 103.[76]

The Cole letter, in fact, did not directly answer the question whether contributions (or for that matter indemnifications or insurance proceeds) could be considered an offset in determining whether a disclosure needs to be made. Rather, the Cole letter held this issue to be moot for purposes of Item 103, Instruction 5(C) (regarding sanctions in government cases) because it ruled that amounts owed pursuant to a remedial agreement were not sanctions. The Cole letter went on to specify that "the netting of insurance and contributions by other PRPs in determining materiality for Items 101 and 103 purposes must be treated on a case-by-case basis."[77] However, SAB 92,[78] discussed later in the chapter, appears to override any implication in footnote 30 to the effect that contributions, indemnifications, and insurance proceeds can be used to determine that a disclosure does not need to be made at all. Although only an SEC staff interpretation and not a regulation, SAB 92 prohibits offsetting in determining whether to accrue a liability in a financial statement, allowing only that such offsetting may be separately stated.

Item 303—MD&A

Item 303 and Its Instructions

Item 303 of Regulation S-K provides for the item known as MD&A.[79] This item is to be in narrative form and is intended by the SEC to be flexible and general.[80] It provides "a narrative explanation of the financial statements [and] . . . asks management to discuss the dynamics of the business and to analyze its financials."[81] The purpose of Item 303, as stated in Instructions to Paragraph 303(a), is "to provide investors and other users information relevant to an assessment of the financial condition and results of operations as determined by evaluating the amounts and certainty of cash flows from operations and from outside sources."[82]

MD&A generally consists of two parts. The first part provides an analysis of the company's financial statements, discussing the company's results of operations on an annual and periodic basis. The second part deals with the company's liquidity needs and the general conditions that affect its business. In recent years, the SEC has focused on the latter and encouraged registrants to provide forward-looking disclosure, particularly with respect to trends that may affect the future financial condition of their companies. The SEC has conducted close scrutiny of MD&A disclosure statements in the last few years and often comments on these disclosures.[83]

While Item 303 certainly imposes duties of disclosure, the type and extent of such disclosure is not clear from the face of Item 303 and its accompanying instructions. This lack of clarity is especially troublesome in light of Item 303's duty to look forward as well as backward in time. Section (a) of Item 303, relevant to disclosures for fiscal years, lays out the general requirement for management to "discuss registrant's financial condition, changes in financial condition and results of operations . . . ,"[84] including specified information about liquidity, capital resources, and results of operation, "and also shall provide such other information that the registrant believes to be necessary to an understanding of its financial condition, changes in financial condition, and results of operations."[85]

Item 303 specifically requires addressing three areas in the MD&A discussion: liquidity, capital resources, and results of operations. Addressing the prospective outlook in each of these areas is problematic, especially in the environmental context because environmental obligations can drastically affect all three areas and are often difficult or impossible to estimate with any accuracy at some points in time (e.g., in the early stages of designation as a PRP pursuant to CERCLA). For example, significant outlays to purchase or upgrade pollution control equipment may have more than a material impact on capital resources; potential liability under CERCLA can devastate an entity's capital, liquid resources, and income. Further, potential penalties under environmental laws for operations in violation of regulatory requirements can also affect results of operations.

Item 303 itself attempts to clarify this forward-looking duty of disclosure. With regard to prospective liquidity, Item 303 requires identification of "any known trends or any known demands, commitments, events, or uncertainties that will result in or that are reasonably likely to result in the registrant's liquidity increasing or decreasing in any material way."[86] For prospective capital resources, Item 303 requires descriptions of (i) "material commitments for capital expenditures . . . "[87] and (ii) "any known material trends, favorable or unfavorable, in the registrant's capital resources"[88] including off-balance sheet financing arrangements. Finally, for results of operations, Item 303 requires a description of "unusual or infrequent events or transactions . . . that materially affected the amount of reported income from continuing operations,"[89] as well as "any known trends or uncertainties that have had or that the registrant *reasonably expects will have* a material impact on net sales or revenues or income from continuing operations." (Emphasis added.)[90] Arguably, this duty to describe unusual or infrequent events or transactions that materially affect the amount of reported income from continuing operations encompasses the costs of complying with new statutory or regulatory environmental requirements.

In attempting to illuminate this forward-looking requirement, Instruction 3 to Item 303 states that:

> The discussion and analysis shall focus specifically on material events and uncertainties known to management that would cause reported financial information not to be necessarily indicative of future operating results or of future financial condition. This would include descriptions and amounts of (A) matters that would have an impact on future operations and have not had an impact in the past, and (B) on matters that have had an impact on reported operations and are not expected to have an impact upon future operations.[91]

Instruction 7 clarifies that "registrants are encouraged, but not required, to supply forward-looking information,"[92] but it also states that some prospective information is mandatory: "Presently known data which will impact upon future operating results, such as known future increases in costs of labor or materials . . . may be required to be disclosed."[93] Instruction 7 assures registrants that "any forward-looking information supplied is expressly covered by the safe harbor rule for projections."[94] The safe harbor rule for projections protects any statement made by or on behalf of an issuer or a registrant against allegations of fraud "unless it is shown that such statement was made or reaffirmed without a reasonable basis or was disclosed other than in good faith."[95] Thus, forward-looking disclosures must both have a reasonable basis and be made in good faith.

The instructions to Item 303 also explain that "the information provided pursuant to this item need only include that which is available to the registrant without undue effort or expense and which does not clearly appear in the registrant's financial statements."[96] On its face, the obverse of this instruction is that the registrant must exert "due" effort and expense or "due diligence" to obtain the information.

Thus, on the face of Item 303 and its accompanying instructions, it is clear that management is supposed to discuss both the past and the future, but management's duties of disclosure are unclear, particularly with regard to future projections. Nevertheless, Commissioner Roberts has emphasized the seriousness of the SEC's enforcement of the MD&A disclosure requirements, citing "In the Matter of Caterpillar Inc.,"[97] a 1992 release regarding an administrative proceeding (in a nonenvironmental context) as an example.[98]

The 1989 MD&A Release

In 1989 the SEC provided clarification of Item 303 and its duty to disclose future prospects in the MD&A Release.[99] The MD&A Release attempts to distinguish voluntary from mandatory forward-looking disclosures, and it specifically addresses the scenario of being named as a PRP in a CERCLA action. It apparently imposes on management a duty to "prove a negative" to justify not disclosing prospective information.[100] The MD&A Release clarifies that the purpose of Item 303 is "to give investors an opportunity to look at the registrant through the eyes of management by providing a historical and prospective analysis of the registrant's financial condition and results of operations, with particular emphasis on the registrant's prospects for the future."[101]

In distinguishing between optional and mandatory prospective disclosure, in addition to quoting from Item 303 and its instructions, the MD&A Release quotes an earlier SEC release:

> Both required disclosure regarding the future impact of presently known trends, events or uncertainties and optional forward-looking information may involve some prediction or projection. The distinction between the two rests with the nature of the prediction required. Required disclosure is based on *currently known trends, events, and uncertainties that are reasonably expected to have material effects*, such as: A reduction in the registrant's product prices; erosion in the registrant's market share; changes in insurance coverage; or the likely non-renewal of a material contract. In contrast, optional forward-looking disclosure involves *anticipating a future trend or even or anticipating a less predictable impact of a known event, trend or uncertainty*. (Emphasis is in MD&A Release but not in the 1987 release.)[102]

The MD&A Release goes on to explain that

> A disclosure duty exists where a trend, demand, commitment, event or uncertainty is both presently known to management and reasonably likely to have material effects on the registrant's financial condition or results of operation. Registrants preparing their MD&A disclosure should determine and carefully review what trends, demands, commitments, events or uncertainties are known to management. (Citations omitted.)[103]

In footnote 27, the MD&A Release makes the point that the traditional test for materiality of assessing both probability and magnitude, set out in *Basic Inc. v. Levinson,*[104] is not applicable to Item 303 disclosures.[105] Rather, footnote 27 emphasizes that Item 303 has its own unique test for disclosure: whether a matter is "reasonably likely to have a material effect."[106]

The troublesome language requiring a party to prove a negative is contained in this explanation:

> Where a trend, demand, commitment, event or uncertainty is known, management must make two assessments:
> (1) Is the known trend, demand, commitment, event or uncertainty likely to come to fruition? If management determines that it is *not reasonably likely to occur*, no disclosure is required.
> (2) If management cannot make that determination, it must evaluate objectively the consequences of the known trend, demand, commitment, event or uncertainty, on the assumption that it will come to fruition. *Disclosure is then required unless management determines that a material effect on the registrant's financial condition or results of operations is not reasonably likely to occur.*
> Each final determination resulting from the assessments made by management must be objectively reasonable, viewed as of the time the determination is made. (Emphasis added.)[107]

This language requires a party to prove that a known problem or uncertainty is not likely to have a disclosable effect in the future. If management cannot prove the negative, with objective reasonableness, it has a duty to assume that the uncertainty will occur and to disclose it.[108]

The SEC illustrates this explanation with a hypothetical example involving a party that has been named as a PRP with respect to cleanup costs at three sites. The party has correctly been designated as a PRP, and no statutory defenses are available. The party is at the early stages of investigation, recovery from other named PRPs and from insurance is unknown, and "management is unable to determine that a material effect on future financial condition or results of operations is not reasonably likely to occur."[109] The MD&A Release concludes that "disclosure of the effects of the PRP status, quantified to the extent reasonably practicable, would be required."[110] (A discussion of whether being named as a PRP will trigger disclosure under Item 103 is included on page 355 in this chapter.)

In making a determination whether to disclose, the MD&A Release provides that

> Facts regarding whether insurance coverage may be contested, and whether and to what extent potential sources of contribution or indemnification constitute reliable sources of recovery may be factored into the determination of whether a material future effect is not reasonably likely to occur.[111]

This language is helpful because, notwithstanding CERCLA's joint and several liability, often the practical reality is that costs are apportioned among many PRPs and sometimes insurance is available (though likely to be contested). However, this language is unlikely to allay the need for disclosure of potential full joint and several liability when, as posited by this example, recovery from other PRPs and insurance coverage are unknown (as is often the case in the early stages of investigation on an NPL site) because the PRP cannot show that recovery from such third parties is reasonably likely to occur.

Those who have been involved in determining remediation costs at an NPL site realize how impractical it often is to quantify the costs and the consequent effects of PRP status at the early stages of designation (when the remedy may not have been selected and the costs may not have been apportioned). In addition, the joint and several liability provisions of CERCLA may impose all of the response costs on a PRP, and it will be difficult at an early stage for a PRP to show, by objectively reasonable means, that other PRPs will pay their share. Thus, even if a PRP's allocable share of the contamination is minuscule, under this scenario it is arguable that a PRP, because it cannot prove the negative, would have to disclose the potential for the entire amount of remediation cost and the consequent impact on its financial condition.

SAB 92 and Environmental Loss Contingencies

Perhaps because the disclosure requirements for environmental liabilities are not clear, in 1993 the staff of the SEC issued SAB 92 on accounting and disclosures relating to loss contingencies, specifically in the context of product and environmental liability.[112] SAB 92 applies to the financial statement itself, rather than to items 101, 103, and 303, and addresses what must be included in the balance sheet. While summarized here, SAB 92 should be carefully read by counsel advising clients with regard to contingent liabilities, particularly in an environmental context, because its implications are potentially far-reaching. It should be noted that SAB 92 is an interpretation by the staff of the SEC and does not have the same force as a regulation or an SEC release.

As Commissioner Roberts has explained, SAB 92 is the staff's interpretation of the Generally Accepted Accounting Principles (GAAP) regarding contingent liabilities, an interpretation with which Commissioner Roberts agrees.[113] It is "intended to promote timely recognition of contingent losses . . . and improve environmental liability disclosure practice."[114] It addresses the issues of offsetting and discounting and, according to Commissioner Roberts, its most controversial component is that, for most situations, "contingent liabilities must be displayed on the face of the balance sheet separately from amounts of claims for recovery from insurance carriers and other third parties."[115] Thus, SAB 92 counsels against offsetting in determining whether an environmental loss contingency must be reflected in the financial statement; rather, offsets must be stated separately from anticipated losses.

SAB 92 focuses on a hypothetical situation in which a registrant "believes it may be obligated to pay material amounts as a result of product or environmental liability. These amounts may relate to, for example, clean-up [of] hazardous wastes, reclamation costs, fines and litigation costs."[116] The registrant may seek to recover the costs from an insurance carrier or other third parties.[117]

SAB 92 makes it clear that FASB's Statement of Financial Accounting Standards No. 5, "Accounting for Contingencies (SFAS 5),"[118] applies. (In light of how harsh and confusing these rules can be for disclosing environmental liabilities, it is useful to note that Commissioner Roberts has cited a new Environmental Accounting Task Force established by the American Institute of Certified Public Accountants (AICPA), which hopes "to develop an environmental liabilities guide in 1994 to assist the accounting industry in making the determinations required by SFAS 5."[119] Commissioner Roberts acknowledges that SFAS 5 is "difficult in the environmental liability area.")[120] SAB 92 paraphrases Paragraph 8 of SFAS 5 to the effect that "an estimated loss from a loss contingency shall be accrued by a charge to income if it is probable that a liability has been incurred and the amount of the loss can be reasonably estimated."[121] According to SAB 92, no offsetting will be allowed, pursuant to a consensus reached by the Emerging Issues Task Force (EITF) of FASB on EITF Issue 93-5, "Accounting for Environmental Liabilities,"[122] that an environmental liability should be evaluated independently from any potential claim for recovery. The amount of environmental liability can be reduced only if it meets certain criteria set forth in FASB Interpretation No. 39, "Offsetting of Amounts Relating to Certain Contracts,"[123] which is effective for periods beginning after December 15, 1993[124] (which criteria would rarely be met).

In addressing a hypothetical situation in which a registrant is jointly and severally liable, SAB 92 provides that it is not necessary to recognize liability apportioned to others, but if it is probable that other PRPs will not fully pay their share, the financial statement must reflect the "registrant's best estimate, before consideration of potential recoveries from other parties, of the additional costs that the registrant expects to pay."[125] SAB 92 points out that "discussion of uncertainties affecting the registrant's ultimate obligation may be necessary if, for example, the solvency of one or more parties is in doubt or responsibility for the site is disputed by a party."[126]

SAB 92 also provides that discounting to present value the environmental liability for a specific cleanup site "is appropriate to reflect the time value of money only if the aggregate amount of the obligation and the amount and timing of cash payments are fixed or reliably determinable for that site."[127] When discounting is allowed, the discount rate "should not exceed the interest rate on monetary assets that are essentially risk free" for comparable maturities.[128] Because cleanup costs at NPL sites and other sites involved in environmental litigation often take many years to determine, this directive can be harsh indeed for environmental loss contingencies, in that it may often dictate against discounting to present value when it otherwise would be reasonable to do so.

When there are uncertainties about measuring liability, remediation methods, and related costs, SAB 92 dictates that, "notwithstanding significant uncertainties, management may not delay recognition of a contingent liability until only a single amount can be reasonably estimated."[129] If there is a range, the minimum figure in the range must accrue as a liability in the registrant's financial statement because FASB Interpretation No. 14, "Reasonable Estimation of the Amount of a Loss" (FIN 14), applies.[130] If no strategy is yet determined for remediation, information about alternatives may be available, in which case SAB 92 dictates that the minimum cost must be cited.[131] SAB 92 does recognize that the liability should be measured by "currently available facts, existing technology, and presently enacted laws and regulations,"[132] inflation, and other economic factors, thus at least not requiring a prediction of changes in the law and/or technology.

In citing SFAS 5, SAB 92 requires that "detailed (financial statement) disclosures regarding the judgments and assumptions underlying the recognition and measurement of environmental and product liabilities are necessary to prevent the financial statements from being misleading and to inform readers fully regarding the range of reasonably possible outcomes that could have a material effect."[133] It cites several examples, including a duty to disclose the following:

> Circumstances affecting the reliability and precision of loss estimates.
>
> The extent to which *unasserted claims* are reflected in any accrual or may affect the magnitude of the contingency.
>
> Uncertainties with respect to joint and several liability that may affect the magnitude of the contingency, including disclosure of the aggregate expected cost to remediate particular sites that are

individually material if the likelihood of contribution by the other significant parties has not been established.

Disclosure of the nature and terms of cost sharing arrangements with other potentially responsible parties.

The extent to which disclosed but unrecognized contingent losses are expected to be recoverable through insurance, indemnification, arrangements, or other sources, with disclosure of any material limitations of that recovery.

Uncertainties regarding the legal sufficiency of insurance claims or solvency of insurance carriers.

The time frame over which the accrued or presently unrecognized amounts may be paid out.

Material components of the accruals and significant assumptions underlying estimates.[134]

Once again, these rules have a harsh effect: It may be difficult or impossible to establish the "likelihood of contribution by the other significant parties" in the early stages of designation as a PRP under CERCLA, so, apparently, disclosure of potential liability for the full amount of cleanup costs would be required. Moreover, if a party is engaged in one of the common cases of litigation against an insurer to obtain coverage for an environmental claim, the duty to disclose the uncertainty here may weaken one's case in the litigation.

A caution is provided to the effect that a statement that

> a contingency is not expected to be material does not satisfy the requirements of SFAS 5 if there is at least a reasonable possibility that a loss exceeding amounts already recognized may have been incurred and the amount of that additional loss would be material to a decision to buy or sell the registrant's securities. In that case, the registrant must either (a) disclose the estimated additional loss, or range of loss, or (b) state that such an estimate cannot be made.[135]

According to SEC staff, this provision was included to avoid statements to the effect that the amount cannot be estimated but is not expected to be material. Such a statement is internally contradictory: either no determination of materiality can be made or there is an estimate. Nevertheless, it is unclear under this caution when estimates must be developed for contingencies when those estimates do not currently exist. It seems a strict standard to require estimates except when an estimate *cannot* be made, as it could be argued that there are few instances when an estimate is absolutely impossible to develop.

For disclosures to be made outside of financial statements, SAB 92 refers registrants to Items 101, 103, and 303 as well as to two previous Commission releases[136] (i.e., the U.S. Steel Release[137] and the MD&A Release).[138] With reference to the MD&A Release, SAB 92 addresses "availability of insurance, indemnification, or contribution that may be relevant"[139] in determining whether disclosure needs to be made; in this context, SAB 92 requires consideration of "facts such as the periods in which claims for recovery may be realized, the likelihood that the claims may be contested, and the financial condition of third parties from which recovery is expected."[140] It cautions registrants to make disclosures "sufficiently specific to enable a reader to understand the scope of the contingencies."[141] Moreover, it requires *separate* discussion of the following categories:

> (a) recurring costs associated with managing hazardous substances and pollution in on-going operations, (b) capital expenditures to limit or monitor hazardous substances or pollutants, (c) mandated expenditures to remediate previously contaminated sites, and (d) other infrequent or non-recurring clean-up expenditures that can be anticipated but what are not required in the present circumstance.[142]

In addition, accrued and reasonably likely losses regarding particular sites that are "individually material"[143] may need to be disclosed separately. Further, a discussion of the different stages of investigation of costs at different sites may be required.[144] An example is provided of disclosures needed for product liability allegations relating to personal injury from asbestos products.

SAB 92 dictates disclosure of site restoration costs or what it refers to as "other exit costs that may occur on the sale, disposal, or abandonment of a property,"[145] such as postclosure monitoring commitments or other costs on sale or other disposition of a property as well as costs to be incurred before a sale or other transfer.[146] In a statement remarkable for its far-reaching implications, SAB 92 also dictates disclosure for remediation of environmental damage relating to businesses or assets previously disposed of "unless the likelihood of a material unfavorable outcome is remote."[147] On its face, this statement arguably could be interpreted to require a registrant to review every property it has ever owned or operated to determine possible remediation costs unless, once again, the registrant can prove the negative that "the likelihood of a material unfavorable outcome is remote." It is to be hoped that the ultimate interpretation of this statement will not be so harsh but will simply apply to properties for which the registrant is aware of proceedings alleging the liability of the registrant.

Finally, SAB 92 provides that the SEC staff would not object to a registrant's proposal to accrue "exit costs" (e.g., costs upon sale, disposal, or abandonment of a property) over the useful life of the asset, provided that criteria for SFAS 5 are met and that accrual is in accordance with EITF Issue 90-8, "Capitalization of Costs to Treat Environmental Contamination."[148]

General Disclosure Standard

The SEC has emphasized that the duty to disclose environmental liabilities is not limited to those regulations and releases that specifically refer to environmental issues but applies as well to anything to which SEC's general disclosure requirements apply. For example, the U.S. Steel Release provides that

> The Commission's general disclosure rules require disclosure of any additional material information, beyond that for which disclosure is specifically required, necessary to make required statements not misleading. . . . [T]he Commission has interpreted these rules as requiring that *all* material information relating to environmental matters must be disclosed. (Citations omitted).[149]

As the 1975 Release stated: "This [general disclosure rule], under appropriate circumstances, would compel the disclosure of information concerning environmental compliance, impact expenditures, plans, or violations, not otherwise specifically required, of which the average prudent investor ought reasonably to be informed."[150]

Statutory and Regulatory Requirements for Disclosure

The general duty of disclosure is found in the 1933 Act at Section 7 ("Information Required in Registration Statements"),[151] Section 10 ("Information Required in Prospectus"),[152] and Schedules A and B.[153] In addition, the 1933 Act creates, for persons injured by nondisclosures, a private right of action against

> [a]ny person who . . . (2) offers or sells a security . . . by means of a prospectus or oral communication, which includes an untrue statement of a material fact or omits to state a material fact necessary in order to make the statements, in light of the circumstances under which they were made, not misleading (the purchaser not knowing of such untruth or omission), and who shall not sustain the burden of proof that he did not know, and, in the exercise of reasonable care could not have known, of such untruth or omission.[154]

Regulation C promulgated pursuant to the 1933 Securities Act governs registrations of securities.[155] Section 405 of Regulation C defines the term "material" for purposes of disclosure as: "those matters to which there is a substantial likelihood that a reasonable investor would attach importance in determining whether to purchase the security registered."[156] Section 408 of Regulation C requires the disclosure of any "material information" necessary to make the required statements not misleading.[157] Importantly, Section 409 requires the required information to be disclosed provided only that it is "known or reasonably available to the registrant."[158] Moreover, Section 11(b) of the 1933 Securities Act provides a defense for underwriters of securities who can show that they had, "after reasonable investigation, reasonable ground to believe, and did believe . . . that the statements made . . . were true" and not misleading.[159] Both of these provisions dictate the need for due diligence in gathering information to make required disclosures. (Environmental due diligence is discussed in detail in Chapter 8 of this book.)

The 1934 Act prohibits deceptive devices and requires conformance with SEC rules (in Section 10(b)),[160] governs registrations of securities (in Section 12),[161] and requires periodic reports by issuers of securities (in Section 13) which are filed on Form 10-Q for quarterly reports, Form 10-K for annual reports, and Form 8-K when specified important events occur.[162] The 1934 Act also provides a private right of action for those injured by false or misleading statements.[163] Regulations issued pursuant to the act include the well-known Rule 10b-5, which makes it unlawful for any person, in connection with the purchase or sale of any security

> (a) To employ any device, scheme or artifice to defraud,
> (b) To make any untrue statement of a material fact or to omit to state a material fact necessary in order to make the statements made, in light of the circumstances under which they were made, not misleading, or
> (c) To engage in any act, practice or course of business which operates or would operate as a fraud or deceit upon any person.[164]

A similar regulation governs proxy statements and other communications.[165] Rule 12b governs required information in both registration statements and periodic reports.[166] Several components of the 1934 Act regulations correspond to Regulation C under the 1934 Act, including Section 12b-2, which provides a definition of the term "material" identical to that in Section 405 of Regulation C (pursuant to the 1933 Securities Act);[167] Section 12b-20, which requires disclosure of additional information necessary to make the required statements not misleading (corresponding to Section 408 of Regulation C);[168] and Section 12b-21, which requires information to be disclosed provided only that it is "known or reasonably available to the registrant" (corresponding to Section 409 of Regulation C).[169]

Materiality

Thus, the issue of what is and is not material is central to deciding what must be disclosed under both the 1933 and the 1934 Acts. The meaning of materiality is endlessly addressed in many sources, including the U.S. Supreme Court and the remarks of Commissioner Roberts.

The Supreme Court's interpretation of materiality is set forth in *TSC Industries Inc. v. Northway, Inc.*,[170] which involved a proxy solicitation and held registrants to the standard of disclosing what would be important to an objective, reasonable investor.

> An omitted fact is material if there is a substantial likelihood that a reasonable shareholder would consider it important in deciding how to vote . . . It does not require proof of a substantial likelihood that disclosure of the omitted fact would have caused the reasonable investor to change his vote. . . . Put another way, there must be a substantial likelihood that the disclosure of the omitted fact would have been viewed by the reasonable investor as having significantly altered the "total mix" of information made available.[171]

In *Basic Inc. v. Levinson et al.*,[172] the Supreme Court reaffirmed this standard of materiality, extended it to Rule 10b-5 situations, and created a rebuttable presumption that investors bringing suit relied on publicly disclosed information, thus relieving plaintiffs seeking redress for nondisclosure from the burden of proving their reliance (and imposing on registrants the obverse burden of proof).

Commissioner Roberts has pointed out that a determination of what is material is a function of qualitative as well as quantitative factors.[173] He cites FASB's Statement of Financial Accounting Concepts No. 2, issued in 1980,[174] for its insistence that determining materiality is more than just a quantitative question, observing that this document "has become a cornerstone of external financial reporting by business enterprises."[175] With regard to quantitative factors, Commissioner Roberts cites a rule of thumb used by the SEC staff as a guideline in determining materiality:

- above 10 percent—material
- 5-10 percent—may be material

- under 5 percent—usually not material . . .
- (as applied to) gross profit, net income, stockholders' equity, and the specific line item that may be misstated.[176]

So that this rule of thumb is not assumed to be applied stringently, Commissioner Roberts points out that the "percentage deemed to be material may vary from the quantitative rule of thumb as the qualitative characteristics are scrutinized."[177] (See the discussion of Instruction 5 to Item 103 for instances of when sanctions must be disclosed regardless of materiality.)[178]

Acknowledging the difficulty of judging the qualitative criteria for materiality, Commissioner Roberts points out that an important factor is whether senior management knew of or took part in the fraudulent omissions.[179] He also states that

> Usually, the smaller the quantitative impact of an incident on the financial statements, the higher the level of qualitative factors (such as fraudulent conduct by a high level of management or other egregious circumstances) should be in order to reach the level of "materiality" where there is a substantial likelihood that a reasonable investor would find the incident important in making investment or voting decisions. Conversely, the greater the impact on financial statement line item amounts, the lower the level of qualitative factors needs to be to warrant a finding that a reasonable investor would consider the incident important.[180]

Practical Effect of SEC Environmental Disclosure Requirements

Summary of Items 101, 103, 303, and General SEC Disclosure Obligations

In summary, Items 101, 103, and 303 of Regulation S-K, as well as the general duty to disclose material information, impose broad duties to disclose environmental liabilities and costs, including prospective loss contingencies. These duties are likely to be difficult to interpret or costly to comply with in many instances.

Item 101 requires prospective disclosures about anticipated environmental costs and liabilities that must be disclosed for as far into the future as there is a reasonable basis to anticipate costs. In some instances there will be a duty to develop estimates of costs that are expected to be material.

Item 103 requires disclosure not only of judicial and administrative "proceedings" but also of many other actions by a government agency that may not necessarily be considered proceedings. The duty to disclose the factual basis for relief sought by proceedings also encompasses the duty to develop estimates of costs in some instances. Proceedings involving the government that may impose sanctions must be disclosed even if they do not rise to the level of materiality. While one SEC release states that receipt of a PRP letter does not constitute sanctions that need to be disclosed, receipt of a PRP letter is nonetheless likely to be subject to disclosure requirements under other provisions of Regulation S-K or general SEC duties to disclose information that would be material to a reasonable investor.

In the MD&A disclosures mandated by Item 303, management must disclose not only the past but, in many instances, the future prospects for liquidity, capital resources, and results of operations. The MD&A Release issued by the SEC in 1989 essentially requires management to prove a negative to avoid disclosing information: unless management can prove, with objective reasonableness, that an uncertainty will not occur, it must disclose the uncertainty. On its face, in many instances this duty will require disclosing that a registrant has been designated as a PRP in a CERCLA case, particularly in the early stages after designation when remediation costs and liabilities of the various PRPs are not known. It may also require some estimate of future liability. (Footnote 30 to the MD&A Release specifies that disclosure of designation as a PRP does not require disclosure as a sanction under Item 103 but may well require disclosure under other applicable disclosure requirements.)[181]

SAB 92 (which is applicable to financial statements and is the SEC's staff interpretation rather than a regulation) governs future loss contingencies, as would be common when a party has recently been designated as a PRP, and would require accrual if it is probable that a liability has been incurred and the amount can be reasonably estimated. In making a determination of materiality, SAB 92 dictates against offsetting anticipated liabilities with anticipated insurance or indemnification proceeds; those offsets can be included in the information given but must be separately stated from the amounts of liability anticipated. In situations involving joint and several liability, if it is "probable" that other parties will not pay their share, SAB 92 counsels registrants to estimate the additional cost expected. Uncertainties—even significant uncertainties—about the magnitude of costs cannot be ignored: minimum estimates or minimum amounts of ranges of costs must be accrued in financial statements.

Even if a duty to disclose information and uncertainties about past and future environmental costs or to accrue liabilities on a financial statement is not triggered by Regulation S-K and SAB 92, environmental costs may need to be disclosed under the general duty to disclose any information that would be material to a reasonable investor, as well as information necessary to make required disclosures not misleading, and the duty to avoid deceit and fraud.[182]

Environmental Due Diligence

As noted above, regulations pursuant to both the 1933 and 1934 Acts limit the information that must be disclosed to that which is "known or reasonably available to the registrant."[183] An underwriter's defense exists for omitting information reasonably believed to be true and not misleading "after reasonable investigation."[184] Both of these provisions dictate the need for due diligence in gathering information to make required disclosures. It is not clear how these provisions relate to what those involved in real estate and financing transactions call "environmental due diligence" in non-securities contexts.

It has become common to conduct or require some sort of investigation into environmental conditions on commercial real property when that property is involved in transactions.[185] The purposes of such an environmental assessment often include taking advantage of CERCLA's innocent landowner defense which requires making "all appropriate inquiry into the previous ownership and uses of the property consistent with good commercial and customary practice."[186] (What is and is not such "all appropriate inquiry" is the subject of considerable debate.[187]) Another purpose is to assess the impact of environmental conditions on the owner or lender whose loan may be secured by real property. An owner may encounter considerable costs to comply with environmental laws or be subject to considerable penalties for non-compliance with environmental laws. Environmental conditions may erode the value of the property securing a loan on the property and environmental costs may jeopardize a borrower's ability to repay its loan.[188]

Does the common practice of conducting or requiring at least an initial environmental assessment in commercial real estate transactions for non-SEC purposes dictate such environmental assessment in order to evaluate one's SEC disclosure obligations? The answer to this question is unknown but, in light of the 1933 and 1934 Acts' duties to disclose that which is "reasonably available to the registrant,"[189] the issue is essentially a question of whether such environmental assessment is a "reasonable investigation."[190]

Even if it is likely that some sort of environmental assessment constitutes a reasonable investigation, the degree and kind of such investigation is unknown. Judging from the author's experience in reviewing hundreds of environmental site assessment reports for commercial real estate, it is common for environmental assessment reports to raise many questions and uncertainties, and it is unclear under SEC disclosure requirements what additional environmental assessment may be required and what must be disclosed. For example, a common issue in environmental assessment reports is that the subject property, although not itself the source of known contamination, is downgradient from an adjacent or nearby site known or highly suspected of being contaminated. The environmental assessment report may have language to the effect that it is "likely" or "probable" or "possible" that contaminants have migrated to the subject property although there is no observable evidence. If contaminants have migrated to the subject property, CERCLA imposes liability on the present owners and operators of the site for the full amount of cleanup of all contaminants within the designated site (which can be much larger than the subject property), whether or not those owners and operators are innocent of causing the contamination. (An exception would be if the owner or operator has a third party defense.[191]) Does the due diligence requirement mandate that soils and/or groundwater tests must be run to determine whether in fact the contamination has migrated to the subject site? The answer is unknown, but since such "Phase II" testing is not the norm for commercial real estate transactions, it is to be hoped that the SEC and the courts would not require such additional testing in order to make a determination of what must be disclosed pursuant to SEC requirements. Without additional information at this stage, it is often unknown who caused the contamination, the resources or willingness of contaminators to step up to their cleanup responsibility, the remedy to be pursued (if any), or the cost of cleanup. It may not even be known whether the government or a private party knows of the contamination and thus whether or not proceedings are likely. Under these common circumstances, it is unclear what must be disclosed pursuant to SEC disclosure requirements. Because so much of the information is uncertain, if the registrant has to "prove the negative" that it is not likely to have a material liability, a duty to disclose the potential liability might arise because at this stage it will be nearly impossible to prove the negative. If this is the ultimate interpretation of SEC disclosure requirements, the duty to disclose could be onerous indeed and result in countless additional disclosures, many of which would be disclosing liabilities that would, in fact, not materialize or would not be material if they did materialize.

Functioning with Uncertainty

Notwithstanding the releases and other communications issued by the SEC, what environmental liabilities and costs must be disclosed is not clear. Also, there is little case law addressing the duty to disclose environmental matters.[192] When practitioners make decisions regarding what must be disclosed and what does not require disclosure, there are generally several tensions between disclosing too much and disclosing too little. These tensions may create problems in the drafting of environmental disclosure provisions.

Issuers of securities realize that investors will read the prospectus as a basis for whether or not to purchase the securities and examine the financial statements as a basis for whether to retain or sell securities. Issuers want the securities to be attractive in the market. Moreover, as ratings given to securities by rating agencies affect the marketability and price of the securities, issuers do not want rating agencies to have a gloomy picture of the risks involved. On the other hand, there are serious consequences for not complying fully with disclosure obligations, a fact tending to dictate disclosing as much as possible. (Some have argued that the fear of disclosing too little sometimes results in "garbage disclosures" in which so much is disclosed that it undermines the importance of the serious disclosures.) In addition, counsel and registrants should keep in mind that the EPA and SEC are now sharing information, and failure to disclose something known to the EPA may well be discovered by the SEC.

Another tension in deciding whether to make disclosures is the understandable desire not to inform governmental authorities of possible violations of environmental laws of which the government may not be aware. Corporations are reluctant to bring to the attention of regulators matters that may lead to substantial penalties for noncompliance. Some of this fear is offset in that many environmental laws require reporting of incidents to governmental entities and provide substantial penalties for failure to do so;[193] thus, at least for some environmental problems, forces requiring disclosure independent of SEC requirements already exist. This issue has been intensely debated in the context of the growing trend for corporations to perform their own internal environmental audits of the extent of compliance with environmental laws.[194] Public policy would reasonably encourage such self-evaluation because it enables corporations to improve their environmental performance; on the other hand, if corporations are required to disclose violations discovered thereby they will want to avoid environmental audits.

Moreover, tension exists between the duty to disclose and how such a disclosure may impact anticipated or pending litigation in which a corporation understandably does not want to admit liability. When litigation is anticipated or pending, as will often be the case, care should be taken to write the disclosures to minimize use by adversaries in litigation.

Uncertainties are particularly acute for the duty to make prospective disclosures regarding the future impact of known or uncertain matters, especially in light of CERCLA's harsh liability scheme and the uncertainties inherent in determining one's liability under CERCLA. Counsel advising registrants on what must be disclosed should have thorough discussions with environmental compliance personnel of their clients; such personnel should be informed that any estimates that are developed of potential costs for environmental compliance or liabilities may well have to be disclosed, along with the source of the estimates and how they were made. Counsel should also be aware of when estimates must be developed as required by the SEC.

In making decisions about what to disclose, counsel should make sure good written records are kept of the reasons why it was decided to disclose or not to disclose a particular matter, keeping in mind that the decision must be objectively reasonable and must be made after reasonable investigation. These records are critically important for any future challenges to the disclosure decisions made, whether by the SEC, administratively or judicially, or by private parties who allege an injury from non-disclosure. Counsel should make it clear to all personnel of clients involved in environmental decision-making that memoranda or other papers describing possible losses may well be discoverable in future litigation, and thus no dire predictions should be made unless they are justified. However, because SAB 92 requires accruing the minimum amount in a range, but not necessarily the maximum, and because management needs to know the upside potential of an environmental problem, management should not avoid worst-case estimates provided that they have a reasonable basis.

Counsel who practice primarily securities law are generally the counsel who advise clients about SEC disclosure requirements in preparing registration statements, proxy statements, financial statements, periodic reports, etc. However expert they may be in securities regulations, securities lawyers often do not have a good understanding of either SEC disclosure or accrual policies as they apply to environmental matters or of the impact of environmental statutes, regulations and common law on the potential for losses. When environmental disclosures are unfamiliar to securities lawyers (in that lawyers are often reluctant to admit their lack of knowledge), their unfamiliarity with the issues may lead them to ignore or downplay the importance of environmental issues. Moreover, those who order environmental assessment reports in connection with such transactions may often know that an environmental assessment is necessary but often do not know how to order an assessment that is meaningful and how to evaluate the information generated by the environmental assessment reports. Parties often rely on environmental consultants' definitions of what is an appropriate environmental assessment, overlooking that it is environmental counsel who is the best judge of what is and is not appropriate environmental due diligence to meet a legal standard. An environmental lawyer should be on a disclosure team to advise about environmental matters in light of the SEC's environmental disclosure requirements. The environmental lawyer should be brought into the dealings early in the process. When an environmental lawyer is brought in after environmental assessments are already underway, serious mistakes may already have been made (such as grossly inadequate directives to environmental consultants that may result in environmental assessment reports that create problems rather than solve them, for example, by drawing legal conclusions that may well be invalid).

Conclusion

If the SEC continues to focus attention on SEC environmental disclosure requirements now that Commissioner Roberts's term has ended, consciousness may be raised and environmental disclosures may become more common, more appropriately thorough, and more accurate. One reason for Commissioner Roberts's speeches on this subject was presumably his belief that environmental matters are not being appropriately reflected and disclosed.[195] On the other hand, those who are tempted to use lack of clarity about what should be disclosed as an argument to defend disclosures that are less than thorough should remember the private rights of action that can result in civil liability as well as the civil and criminal enforcement powers of the SEC provided by the securities statutes.

Notes

1. 15 U.S.C. § 77a *et seq.* [hereinafter the 1933 Act or the Securities Act].

2. 15 U.S.C. § 78a *et seq.* [hereinafter the 1934 Act or the Exchange Act].

3. For an explanation of REITs and the application of securities laws to REITS, see PETER M. FASS, MICHAEL E. SHAFF, DONALD B. ZEIF, REAL ESTATE INVESTMENT TRUSTS HANDBOOK (1993) [hereinafter REIT HANDBOOK].

4. For a description and explanation of mortgage-backed securities, see Mark H. Adelson, Mortgage-Backed Securities, Origins, Structures, and Regulatory Issues, materials prepared for FFIEC Conference on Off-Balance Sheet Risk, August 1993 [hereinafter Adelson on MBS].

5. *See* LOUIS LOSS, FUNDAMENTALS OF SECURITIES REGULATION, at 35 *et seq.* and 87 *et seq.* [hereinafter Loss].

6. 15 U.S.C. §§ 77s through 77x and 15 U.S.C. §§ 78u, 78ff, respectively. *See also* Brooks Strough and L.C. Lau, Chapter 4, *Securities Filings*, materials prepared by Alan K. Austin for a November 1993 program sponsored by the Practicing Law Institute [hereinafter PLI SECURITIES FILINGS], at 136.

7. See the discussion in this chapter's section on "Practical Effect of SEC Environmental Disclosure Requirements," *infra*.

8. Loss, *supra* note 5, at 88–89, 144.

9. *Id.* at 92.

10. *Id.* at 87–88.

11. *Id.* at 433, citing Section 13(a) of the 1934 Act.

12. *Id.* at 435–36, citing Rule 13a.

13. *Id.* at 405.

14. *Id.* at 445 *et seq.*

15. 17 C.F.R. pt. 229, Standard Instructions for Filing Forms under Securities Act of 1933, Securities Exchange Act of 1934, and Energy Policy and Conservation Act of 1975 [hereinafter Regulation S-K].

16. Securities Act of 1933 Act Release No. 33-6383, Securities and Exchange Act Release No. 34-18,524, Release Nos. 35-22,407, 36-700 (March 16, 1982) [hereinafter the 1982 Release].

17. 17 C.F.R. § 229.101.

18. 17 C.F.R. § 229.103.

19. 17 C.F.R. § 229.301.

20. Loss, *supra* note 5, at 149.

21. *See, e.g.*, Remarks of Richard Y. Roberts, Commissioner, U.S. Securities and Exchange Commission, "Overview of Environmental Liability Disclosure Requirements: Recent Developments and Materiality," ABA 1993 Annual Meeting, Toxic & Hazardous Substances and Environmental Law Committee Program, New York, Aug. 9, 1994 [hereinafter Roberts's 1993 ABA Remarks]; and Remarks of Richard Y. Roberts, Commissioner, U.S. Securities and Exchange Commission, Environmental Liability Disclosure Developments, Environmental Law Institute, Corporate Environmental Management Workshop on Environmental Reporting & Accountability, Washington, D.C., June 6, 1994 [hereinafter Roberts's 1994 ELI Remarks]. It should be noted that these remarks are designated as the views of Commissioner Roberts and not necessarily those of the commission, other commissioners, or the SEC staff.

22. *See* Roberts's 1993 ABA Remarks, *supra* note 21, at 1, quoting Accounting for Environmental Compliance: Crossroad of GAAP, Engineering, and Government, a survey of corporate America's accounting for environmental costs, conducted by Price Waterhouse, 1992, at 1.

23. Roberts's 1994 ELI Remarks, *supra* note 21, at 1. *See also* Marisa C. Caputo, *SEC Environmental Disclosure Rules and CERCLA Liability*, 4 MD. J. CONTEMP. LEGAL ISSUES 97, 106–08 (Fall/Winter 1992-93) [hereinafter *Caputo*].

24. Roberts's 1993 ABA Remarks, *supra* note 21, at 2.

25. Regulation S-K, *supra* note 15.

26. Regulation S-K, Item 101 and Instructions, 17 C.F.R. § 229.101.

27. Regulation S-K, Item 103 and Instructions, 17 C.F.R. § 229.103.

28. Regulation S-K, Item 303 and Instructions, 17 C.F.R. § 229.303.

29. Staff Accounting Bulletin No. 92, Accounting and Disclosures Relating to Loss Contingencies [1993 Transfer Binder] Fed. Sec. L. Rep. (CCH) ¶ 74,141 (June 8, 1993), [hereinafter SAB 92].

30. See the discussion in Chapter 2.

31. Disclosures Pertaining to Matters Involving the Environment and Civil Rights, Securities Act of 1933 Release No. 5170, Exchange Act Release No. 9252, July 19, 1971, 1971 SEC LEXIS 20 [hereinafter the 1971 Release].

32. Compliance with Environmental Requirements, Securities Exchange Act of 1934 Release No. 34-10116 and No. 33-5386 (April 20, 1973), 1973 SEC LEXIS 2991 [hereinafter the 1973 Release].

33. Notice of Commission Conclusions and Rulemaking Proposals in the Public Proceeding Announced in Securities Act Release No. 5569 (February 11, 1975) Regarding (1) Such Further Statements, Reports, and Other Documents Required to Be Filed or Furnished to Investors Pursuant to the Securities Act of 1933 and the Securities and Exchange Act of 1934 As May Be Necessary, Consistent with the National Policy Reflected in the Federal Securities Laws, Fully to Comply with the National Environmental Policy Act of 1969; (2) Disclosure in Such Documents of Other Socially Significant Matters; and (3) Investors' Interest In and Use of Such Information, Securities Act of 1933 Release No. 5627, Securities Exchange Act of 1934 Release No. 11733 (October 14, 1975), 1975 SEC LEXIS 624 [hereinafter the 1975 Release].

34. Notice of Commission Conclusions and Final Action of the Rulemaking Proposals Announced in Securities Act Release No. 5627 (October 14, 1975) Relating to Environmental Disclosure, Securities Act of 1933 Release No. 5704, Securities Exchange Act of 1934 Release No. 12414 (May 6, 1976), 1976 SEC LEXIS 1727 [hereinafter the 1976 Release].

35. 1973 Release, *supra* note 32.

36. 1976 Release, *supra* note 34, text accompanying note 23.

37. In the Matter of United States Steel Corporation, Securities Act of 1933 Release No. 6130, Securities Exchange Act of 1934 Release No. 16223 (Sept. 27, 1979), 44 Fed. Reg. 56924 (Oct. 3, 1979) [hereinafter the U.S. Steel Release].

38. U.S. Steel Release, *supra* note 37, Section II.B.

39. U.S. Steel Release, *supra* note 37, Section II.B.3.

40. Securities Act of 1933 Act Release No. 33-6383, Securities and Exchange Act Release No. 34-18,524, Release Nos. 35-22,407, 36-700 (March 16, 1982) [hereinafter the 1982 Release]. The current version of this release is Regulation S-K, *supra* note 11.

41. 17 C.F.R. § 229.102.

42. *Id.*

43. Management's Discussion and Analysis of Financial Condition and Results of Operations: Certain Investment Company Disclosures, Securities Act of 1933 Releases No. 6835; Securities and Exchange Act Release No. 26831; IC-1691 (May 18, 1989), 54 Fed. Reg. 22,427 (1989) [hereinafter the MD&A Release]. Although this chapter focuses on environmental disclosures, counsel for lenders should note the provisions of the MD&A Release that address lenders' acquisition of other institutions or of loans from other institutions.

44. SAB 92, *supra* note 29.

45. 17 C.F.R. § 229.101(c)(1)(xii).

46. Section (b) of Item 101 requires grouping some information about the registrant into industry segments. *See* 17 C.F.R. § 229.101(b).

47. 17 C.F.R. § 229.101, Instruction 1.

48. 17 C.F.R. § 229.101, Instruction 3.
49. U.S. Steel Release, *supra* note 37, Section II.B.1.
50. *Id.*
51. *Id.*
52. *Id.*
53. ACCOUNTING FOR CONTINGENCIES, Statement of Financial Accounting Standards No. 5 (Financial Accounting Standards Board March 1975) [hereinafter SFAS 5].
54. 1973 Release, *supra* note 32.
55. *Id.*
56. 1976 Release, *supra* note 34, text accompanying note 14.
57. *See* 1982 Release, *supra* note 16.
58. 17 C.F.R. § 229.103.
59. *Id.*
60. *Id.*
61. 17 C.F.R § 229.102, Instruction 3.
62. U.S. Steel Release, *supra* note 37, Section II.B.2.
63. *Id.*
64. *Id.*
65. *Id.*
66. *Id.*
67. *Id.*
68. *Id.*
69. 1973 Release, *supra* note 32, at 2.
70. 1976 Release, *supra* note 34, text accompanying note 22.
71. *Id.* at note 22.
72. MD&A Release, *supra* note 43.
73. This statement is startling in light of the potential seriousness of a PRP letter and its common meaning that the EPA (or the private party sending a PRP letter) expects that the recipient will be held liable for response costs under CERCLA, and the Commission's broad definition of "proceedings" to include orders and other matters not necessarily related to a formal administrative or judicial proceeding (see text accompanying notes 59 and 60, *supra*).
74. MD&A Release, *supra* note 43.
75. SEC Interpretive letter to Thomas A. Cole, Sidley & Austin, from Linda C. Quinn, Director, Division of Corporate Finance, SEC, January 17, 1989, 1989 SEC No-Act. LEXIS 203.
76. *Id.*
77. *Id.*
78. SAB 92, *supra* note 29.
79. 17 C.F.R. § 229.103.
80. MD&A Release, *supra* note 43, Section IV.
81. *See* MD&A Release, *supra* note 43.
82. 17 C.F.R. § 229.303, Instructions to Paragraph 303(a), Section 2.
83. The author gratefully acknowledges that this paragraph was provided by Jack Orrick, a securities lawyer with Linowes and Blocher in Silver Spring,

Maryland. The SEC's recent emphasis on MD&A enforcement has also been noted in PLI SECURITIES FILINGS, *supra* note 6, at 118 and 137.

84. 17 C.F.R. § 229.303(a).

85. *Id.*

86. 17 C.F.R. § 229.303(a)(1).

87. 17 C.F.R. § 229.303(a)(2).

88. *Id.*

89. 17 C.F.R. § 229.303(a)(3).

90. *Id.*

91. 17 C.F.R. § 229.303, Instruction 3.

92. 17 C.F.R. § 229.303, Instruction 7.

93. *Id.*

94. *Id.*

95. 17 C.F.R. § 230.175 (pursuant to the 1933 Act) and § 240.3b-6 (pursuant to the 1934 Act).

96. 17 C.F.R. § 229.303, Instruction 2.

97. Securities Exchange Act of 1934 Release No. 30532 (March 31, 1992).

98. Roberts 1993 ABA Remarks, *supra* note 21, at 5.

99. MD&A Release, *supra* note 43.

100. The discussion of proving a negative is drawn from James G. Archer, Thomas M. McMahon and Maureen M. Crough, *SEC Reporting of Environmental Liabilities*, 20 ENVTL. L. REP. 10105, 10107 (March 1990) [hereinafter *Archer*].

101. MD&A Release, *supra* note 43, Section IV.

102. MD&A Release, *supra* note 43, Section III.B., quoting from Securities Act Release No. 6711, April 24, 1987 [hereinafter the 1987 Release]. Emphasis is in MD&A Release but not in the 1987 Release.

103. MD&A Release, *supra* note 43, Section III.B., citations omitted.

104. 485 U.S. 224 (1988). See further discussion in Section VII.B. *infra*.

105. *Id.* at note 27.

106. *Id.*

107. *Id.* at Section III.B.

108. *See Archer*, *supra* note 100.

109. MD&A Release, *supra* note 43, Section III.B.

110. *Id.*

111. *Id.* at Section III.B.

112. SAB 92, *supra* note 29.

113. Roberts's 1993 ABA Remarks, *supra* note 21, at 5 and 10. *See also* Roberts's 1994 ELI Remarks, *supra* note 21.

114. *Id.* at 7.

115. *Id.*

116. SAB 92, *supra* note 29, *Facts*.

117. *Id.*

118. SFAS 5, *supra* note 53.

119. Roberts's 1994 ELI Remarks, *supra* note 21, at 6.

120. *Id.*

121. SAB 92, *supra* note 29.

122. ACCOUNTING FOR ENVIRONMENTAL LIABILITIES, Emerging Issues Task Force (EITF) of Financial Accounting Standards Board, EITF Issue 93-5 (1993).

123. OFFSETTING OF AMOUNTS RELATED TO CERTAIN CONTRACTS, Financial Accounting Standards Board Interpretation No. 39 (Financial Accounting Standards Board March 1992), hereinafter FIN 39.

124. SAB 92, *supra* note 29, Interpretive Response to Question 1.

125. *Id.*, Interpretive Response to Question 2.

126. *Id.*

127. *Id.*

128. *Id.*, Interpretive Response to Question 4.

129. *Id.*

130. *Id.*

131. *Id.*

132. *Id.*

133. *Id.*, Interpretive Response to Question 5.

134. *Id.*

135. *Id.*

136. SAB 92, *supra* note 29, Interpretive Response to Question 6.

137. U.S. Steel Release, *supra* note 37.

138. MD&A Release, *supra* note 43.

139. *Id.*

140. *Id.*

141. *Id.*

142. *Id.*

143. *Id.*

144. *Id.*

145. *Id.*, Interpretive Response to Question 7.

146. *Id.*

147. *Id.*

148. *Id.*, Interpretive Response to Question 8.

149. U.S. Steel Release, *supra* note 37, at note 30.

150. 1976 Release, *supra* note 34, at note 23.

151. 15 U.S.C. § 77g.

152. 15 U.S.C. § 77j.

153. 15 U.S.C. § 77aa.

154. 15 U.S.C. § 77l.

155. Regulation C—Registration, 17 C.F.R. § 230.400 *et seq.*

156. 17 C.F.R. § 230.405.

157. 17 C.F.R. § 230.408.

158. 17 C.F.R. § 230.409.

159. 15 U.S.C. § 77k(b)(3).

160. 15 U.S.C. § 78j.

161. 15 U.S.C. § 78l.

162. 15 U.S.C. § 78m. This section also requires conformance with the Generally Accepted Accounting Procedures (GAAP) for any person whose methods of accounting are prescribed under the provisions of any law of the United States.

163. 1934 Act § 78r. *See also* TSC Industries, Inc. v. Northway, Inc., 426 U.S. 438, 444 (6/14/76) [hereinafter *TSC Industries*].

164. 17 C.F.R. § 240.10b-5.
165. 17 C.F.R. § 240.14a-9.
166. 17 C.F.R. § 240.12b-1 *et seq.*
167. 17 C.F.R. § 240.12b-2.
168. 17 C.F.R. § 240.12b-20.
169. 17 C.F.R. § 240.12b-21.
170. *TSC Industries, supra* note 154.
171. *Id.* at 449.
172. 485 U.S. 224 (1988).
173. Roberts's 1993 ABA Remarks, *supra* note 21, at 14.
174. QUALITATIVE CHARACTERISTICS OF ACCOUNTING INFORMATION, Statement of Financial Accounting Concepts No. 2, Paragraphs 123–132 (Financial Accounting Standards Board May 1990).
175. Roberts's 1993 ABA Remarks, *supra* note 21, at 14.
176. *Id.* at 15.
177. *Id.*
178. *See supra*, text accompanying notes 60–61 and 72–78.
179. *Id.* at 16.
180. *Id.* at 16.
181. See discussion, *supra* accompanying notes 60–61 and 72–78.
182. See discussion in Section VII, *supra.*
183. 17 C.F.R. Sections 230.409 (applicable to 1933 Act) and 240.12b-21 (applicable to 1934 Act).
184. 15 U.S.C. § 77k(b)(3).
185. See the discussion in MARGARET V. HATHAWAY & BARBARA P. BILLAUER, THE LENDER'S GUIDE TO ENVIRONMENTAL LAW: RISK AND LIABILITY § 204 (1993), and in Chapter 1 of this book.
186. 42 U.S.C. § 9601 (35)(B).
187. See HATHAWAY & BILLAUER, *supra* note 185 § 10.03, and the discussion in Chapter 1 of this book.
188. See HATHAWAY & BILLAUER, *supra* note 185, Chapter 10.
189. 17 C.F.R. Sections 230.409 (applicable to 1933 Act) and 240.12b-21 (applicable to 1934 Act).
190. 15 U.S.C. § 77k(b)(3).
191. 42 U.S.C. § 9607(b)(3).
192. For a review of the limited cases available, see *Archer, supra* note 100; Caputo, *supra* note 23; and Note, *Environmental Disclosures and SEC Reporting Requirements*, 17 DEL. J. CORP. L. 483 (1992) (authored by Risa Vetri Forman).
193. See, for example, CERCLA, 42 U.S.C. § 9603 and the Emergency Planning and Community Right-to-Know Act (EPCRA also known as SARA Title III), 42 U.S.C. § 11001 *et seq.*
194. See, for example, Wells & Lamar, Discovery of Environmental and Other Non-Financial Audits: Is There a Self-Evaluative Privilege?, Proceedings of 11th Annual Institute, Eastern Mineral Law Institute, at 1-1 (1990); and LAWRENCE B. CAHILL AND RAYMOND W. KANE, ENVIRONMENTAL AUDITS, III-1-15 (6th ed. 1989).
195. Roberts's 1993 ABA Remarks, *supra* note 21, at 1.

CHAPTER 17

Treatment of Environmental Liabilities in Bankruptcy

EDWARD C. DOLAN

There is considerable tension between enforcement of environmental statutes and the protections afforded individuals and companies in bankruptcy. The statutes that regulate the release of hazardous substances require immediate disclosure of uncontrolled releases and establish cleanup liability among a range of potentially responsible parties, focusing on eradicating the hazard to the public health and safety. When the government orders remediation of a contaminated site, the federal statute places emphasis on the cleanup effort itself and delays most judicial challenges to the government's removal or remedial action until the government brings a cost recovery action.[1]

In contrast to the sequence of events contemplated by the environmental statutes, the federal bankruptcy laws attempt to provide a financially troubled individual or company with an immediate temporary respite from creditors while normal operations are continued and the party in bankruptcy, the "debtor,"[2] either reorganizes its affairs or liquidates its assets for distribution among creditors. The federal Bankruptcy Code[3] achieves these purposes by staying most creditor actions against the debtor or its property[4] and providing for the statement,[5] objection to,[6] and allowance[7] of claims; the payment of prebankruptcy debts, some on a priority basis;[8] and the general discharge of prebankruptcy claims.[9]

If a debtor's bankruptcy were to stay enforcement of the government's cease-and-desist order or cleanup order, the environment could be further damaged. To the extent that a debtor's liability for environmental cleanup costs must be fixed before the final costs are certain,[10] the bankruptcy laws run counter to what often happens when major remedial actions must occur before liability of a party is confirmed. In bankruptcy, the actual or potential liability for cleanup costs must frequently be fixed or estimated long before the cleanup has been completed if the liable debtor is to reorganize or achieve an equitable distribution of assets.

This chapter addresses the ways in which a number of courts have resolved the sometimes inconsistent purposes of the environmental and bankruptcy statutes.

Comprehensive Environmental Response, Compensation, and Liability Act

The primary purposes of the Comprehensive Environmental Response, Compensation, and Liability Act (CERCLA)[11] are to hasten the cleanup of contaminated sites and to establish liability for cleanup costs. Although not set forth in CERCLA, courts have interpreted CERCLA liability to be joint and several among potentially liable parties.[12] A party—although it may be liable for all cleanup costs—may seek contributions from others.[13]

Response to a Hazardous Substance Release

A release of a designated hazardous substance into the environment[14] may trigger an Environmental Protection Agency (EPA) removal or remedial action. This need not be done if the EPA determines that removal and remedial action can be adequately accomplished by the owner, generator, or operator of the facility from which the release or the threat of release emanates.[15] The EPA may also pursue necessary relief in the U.S. district court in the district in which the release or threat occurs. That court has jurisdiction to grant "such relief as the public interest and the equities of the case may require."[16] To speed the cleanup of contaminated sites and minimize precleanup litigation, removal or remediation actions selected by the EPA or ordered by a district court at the EPA's instance may not be reviewed except under very limited circumstances, primarily in an action for reimbursement or an action in which the EPA has moved to compel remedial action.[17] It is important to note that the EPA's statutory right to recover response costs also includes the right to recover by any other party that incurs response costs.

Liable Parties

Persons potentially liable to the United States or to any other party that has incurred cleanup costs are: the owner or operator of a vessel or facility at which a hazardous substance was disposed of; a generator of hazardous waste; any person who arranged for disposal or treatment, or transport for disposal or treatment, of hazardous substances; and any person who transports hazardous substances, causing the incurrence of response costs.[18] Liability extends to all costs of removal or remedial action incurred by the United States, a state, or any other party as well as to any other necessary costs of response incurred and damages for injury to, destruction of, or loss of natural resources, including the reasonable cost of assessing such injury, destruction, or loss.[19]

Defenses

The three defenses to CERCLA liability for a release of hazardous substances are an act of God, an act of war, and the act or omission of an unrelated third party. In the third-party defense, however, the potentially responsible party must establish "by a preponderance of the evidence that it exercised due care and took precautions against foreseeable acts or omissions of such third party."[20] This last defense may also benefit innocent property owners who had no involvement in the contamination of the property and took title unaware of the contamination despite the exercise of due diligence.[21]

Automatic Stays in Bankruptcy

Stayed Actions

One of the initial purposes of a bankruptcy filing by a company or an individual is the benefit to be gained from an automatic stay of any proceedings under 11 U.S.C. Section 362(a). Immediately upon the filing of a voluntary or involuntary petition in bankruptcy, the Bankruptcy Code automatically stays the commencement or continuation of any action or proceeding that was or could have been commenced before the bankruptcy to recover a claim against the debtor, or against the property of the debtor's bankruptcy estate, that arose before the bankruptcy filing. In most instances, the immediate impact of the automatic stays of proceedings will be felt by creditors that may have sought collection of trade debt, commercial financing, and other similar obligations.

Police and Regulatory Exceptions

Express exceptions to the automatic stays of proceedings are found in Bankruptcy Code Section 362(b)(4) and (5) for the commencement or continuation of an action by a governmental unit to enforce that unit's police or regulatory power, including the enforcement of a judgment other than a money judgment.

Because EPA enforcement actions are exercises of the government's police or regulatory powers, it is useful to examine three aspects of those actions: first, a regulatory order or injunction constraining an individual or company from continuing or permitting a hazardous discharge; second, an order granting the EPA affirmative injunctive relief by requiring that the individual or company responsible for the hazardous discharge take immediate steps to remedy it; and third, the determination and recovery of cleanup costs reimbursable to the government by the responsible individual or company in the event that the government undertakes the cleanup in the first instance or after the responsible party has failed to act.

The injunction aspect of the police and regulatory power is perhaps the easiest to consider. If a debtor continues to operate its business in bankruptcy, the debtor must follow applicable laws, including environmental regulations.[22]

The court in *In re Becker Industries Corp.*[23] confirmed that bankruptcy was not designed to displace all of the rules and limitations applicable to a regulated industry. The Florida Land and Water Adjudicatory Commission could, without violating the automatic stays, limit the amount of phosphate ore that a Chapter 11 debtor could mine and transport. The law is not intended to confer a competitive advantage on companies in bankruptcy. The *Becker* court stated that

> Notwithstanding the desire for calm seas leeward of the rocks of regulation and for full sails, the (Bankruptcy) Code does not change the business and regulatory environment in which a debtor operates. A debtor in possession under Chapter 11 is not *pro tanto* excused by virtue of its bankruptcy from complying with valid and enforceable state and local regulations. . . . An ongoing business is not to be given a competitive edge merely by virtue of its attempt to reorganize under Chapter 11.[24]

The next issue is that of compelling remedial action to clean what has been contaminated. If the automatic stays of proceedings in bankruptcy will not stay environmental compliance actions, will the stays prevent enforcement of affirmative injunctions to clean up what has been contaminated? The answer depends on the type of bankruptcy involved, the magnitude and immediacy of the environmental risk, and the availability of assets in the bankruptcy to fund the cleanup.

A Chapter 7 bankruptcy, which can be filed by an individual or a business entity, is referred to as a liquidating bankruptcy. In Chapter 7, a business enterprise will not continue to operate, except as necessary to wind up its affairs and maximize a liquidation value.[25] An individual in Chapter 7 only rarely has the ability to undertake environmental cleanup obligations, given the amount of likely cleanup costs. Unstayed enforcement of a cleanup order would probably be pointless. A business entity in Chapter 7 is more likely to be subject to continued enforcement of a cleanup order if the business is continuing to operate (at least temporarily), a source of funds is available, and the present danger is significant.[26]

A Chapter 11 reorganizing bankruptcy can be filed by an individual or a business entity. Chapter 11 does contemplate the postbankruptcy continued existence of the business entity. If that entity is to continue to exist, it will have to do so in a regulated marketplace. No purpose would be served by permitting the business entity to excuse itself from the realities of the marketplace, including regulation, during its Chapter 11 bankruptcy. If an individual or a company is operating under Chapter 11 as debtor-in-possession, not only should the debtor be prohibited from those actions bearing on the public health and safety denied the debtor outside of bankruptcy, but the debtor should be subject to the proper exercise of police or regulatory directives to remedy transgressions. Only when the business entity is pursuing the course of a liquidating Chapter 11 or converts to a case under Chapter 7 does the focus change from the continued operation of the business to the maximizing of assets of the estate and then distribution to creditors. In that case, the bankruptcy court might stay enforcement of a cleanup order, depending on the factors described in the previous paragraph.

The court in *In re Thomas Solvent Co.*[27] considered the debtor's argument that the automatic stays of proceedings applied to bar any further actions pursuant to an order entered four months before its bankruptcy directing it to take certain actions to purify and protect groundwater contaminated by the improper storage of toxic chemicals. The court found that the State of Michigan would not be prevented by the automatic stays from postbankruptcy enforcement of the cleanup order if it were clear that the debtor continued to operate as debtor-in-possession with the intent of reorganizing. The court was, however, faced with the situation that the corporate debtor did not have long-term plans for survival and that either a liquidating Chapter 11 plan or a conversion to Chapter 7 was imminent. In that context alone, the court preliminarily enjoined further actions to enforce the cleanup order but made the record clear that the stays would be subsequently lifted to permit enforcement of the cleanup order if a liquidating plan were not confirmed or the case promptly converted to Chapter 7.[28] The requirement of 28 U.S.C. Section 959(b) that the trustee operate the debtor's business within the parameters of applicable law may not compel a liquidating trustee to clean up contaminated property or entitle the government to administrative expense priority for doing so if the trustee is not operating the debtor's business.[29]

The last step in certain enforcement actions is an attempt by the government to recover response costs. If the government can continue, postbankruptcy, to regulate certain activity and, in some cases, to direct remedial action, can the government also recover from the debtor certain response costs caused and incurred prebankruptcy without interference from the stays of proceedings? Consider the case of a prebankruptcy discharge of a hazardous substance that causes significant contamination of soil or groundwater. Assume that this discharge was discovered by the government and made the subject of appropriate prebankruptcy injunctive orders. Further assume that the responsible company failed to either stop the contamination or clean up its effects and that the government incurred those response costs and obtained a prebankruptcy judgment to recover expenses. On first examination it would appear that, distinct from prohibiting future contamination or directing that past contamination be cleaned up, the recovery of the government's response costs is nothing more or less than the continuation of a process or proceeding against the debtor that had been commenced before the bankruptcy, or an attempt to recover a claim that arose before the bankruptcy. The police and regulatory power exception to application of the Bankruptcy Code Section 362 automatic stays does not apply with respect to the enforcement of a "money judgment."

The seemingly simple term "money judgment," however, is actually more complex than it appears. The legislative history of the police and regulatory exception to the automatic stays of proceedings indicates that the exception was "intended to be given a narrow construction in order to permit government units to pursue actions to protect the public health and safety and not to apply to actions by a governmental unit to protect a pecuniary interest in property of the debtor or property of the estate."[30]

While the government might have a "pecuniary interest" in a money judgment in actions for enforcement of state consumer protection statutes, financial responsibility laws, or payment of delinquent taxes or license fees, CERCLA money judgments have been treated differently. The judgment's underlying purpose has been recognized as transcending the government recovery of response costs and serving the more important purpose of deterring other and further prohibited acts.[31] Thus, what may appear as an act to recover a prebankruptcy response cost money judgment potentially stayed under Bankruptcy

Code Section 362(a) may be treated as a proper postbankruptcy exercise of police or regulatory functions within the exceptions of Bankruptcy Code Section 362(b)(4) and (5).

Treatment of the Environmental Claim

Existence of a "Claim"

The nature of the environmental liability claim affects the progress of an individual or company through a bankruptcy in three primary contexts. The first is in the application of the stays of proceedings to the government's claim, as discussed earlier. The second is the treatment of that claim for the purposes of the bankruptcy. When does a claim cognizable in bankruptcy arise? To share in the bankruptcy's distribution to creditors, a party must have a claim, broadly described as a right to payment whether or not liquidated, fixed, matured, disputed, legal, equitable, or secured, or the right to an equitable remedy that gives rise to a right to payment.[32] The third context is that of discharge of liability, discussed later in this chapter.

The very nature of environmental liability is such that its existence is likely to become evident long before it is quantified or quantifiable. CERCLA acknowledges this reality in giving priority to accomplishing the cleanup over fixing the final cost and allocation among potentially liable parties. For bankruptcy purposes, some courts have held that the government will be regarded as having a claim once it is determined that the debtor's prebankruptcy conduct resulting in a release or threat of release could have been "fairly contemplated" by the parties to give rise to such liability.[33] The government need not have incurred the costs to have a claim for reimbursement of anticipated costs.[34] Once the government has a claim, it must file a proof of claim with the bankruptcy court to share in any payment from the bankruptcy. The amount of the government's claim must also be determined or estimated.[35] In a Chapter 11 reorganization, the amount and priority of the government's claim for reimbursement may effectively mean that the government can dominate a class of creditors and exercise what amounts to a practical veto over the reorganization process.[36]

The government frequently opposes the early estimation of cleanup claims for a variety of reasons. The government also recognizes that it may be more likely to receive a larger judgment against a potentially liable party in a court where the sole focus is on the cleanup costs. It is almost impossible for a bankruptcy court to be unmindful of the impact on distribution to other creditors of allowing any large single claim. The payout to all creditors is diluted when one claimant is allowed a comparatively large claim.[37]

Priority of Payment

Bankruptcy Code Section 507 establishes, by reference to Bankruptcy Code Section 503(a), the payment priority of administrative expense claims, including the actual, necessary costs and expenses of preserving the bankruptcy estate. The treatment of claims for reimbursement of response costs is important in bankruptcy planning for the debtor because of these administrative expense priorities. In a Chapter 7 liquidation administrative claims are paid before general, unsecured claims and may exhaust the available funds of the estate before any payment is made to holders of junior classes of claims or interests. This has a direct impact on unsecured creditors and on one of the purposes of the Bankruptcy Code, which is to obtain an equitable distribution of the debtor's assets.

Fines and penalties for postbankruptcy contamination have been accorded priority status in Chapter 11, if incurred while the debtor continued to operate. Similar postbankruptcy fines and penalties might not receive this status if incurred following conversion to Chapter 7, the rationale being that postconversion fines and penalties are unrelated to preservation of the bankruptcy estate's assets.[38]

In a Chapter 11 reorganization, a large response liability may preclude any distribution to unsecured creditors. Such liability may also directly challenge the ability of the reorganizing entity to successfully come out of bankruptcy. The Bankruptcy Code[39] requires that all holders of claims accorded administrative expense priority receive cash equal to the allowed amount of such claims as of the effective date of the reorganization plan, usually shortly after the expiration of the appeal period following the entry of an order confirming the plan. The presence in a Chapter 11 reorganization of a massive response claim that must be paid in full shortly after confirmation may effectively preclude the successful reorganization of that debtor.

The issues considered by the bankruptcy court in *In re T.P. Long Chemical, Inc.*,[40] illustrate a number of points. In that case, the individual principals of a company owned real estate on which the company conducted its rubber recycling business. A number of substances defined as hazardous under CERCLA were stored on the property both in a tank truck and in buried drums. These chemicals were the property of the corporation, subsequently the debtor in bankruptcy. The individuals' real estate was subject to a lien securing one creditor, and the personal property of the corporate debtor secured another. After default, the real estate lender successfully obtained the appointment of a receiver of the individuals' real property and scheduled a foreclosure. Approximately one year before the real estate lender's actions, the corporation filed a Chapter 11 bankruptcy, which was subsequently converted to a Chapter 7 liquidation. The bankruptcy Chapter 7 trustee arranged with the state court-appointed receiver to store the corporate debtor's personal property on the site pending an auction. A tank truck containing hazardous chemicals belonging to the corporate debtor was sold, but the buried drums were not. Subsequent to the sale but before the tank truck was removed from the operating site, a vandal released sulfur monochloride contained in it, contaminating the real property.

After the release, the EPA demanded that the trustee in the corporate bankruptcy clean the site. The trustee refused. The EPA subsequently cleaned the site and incurred total costs of approximately $38,000. The EPA then sought to recover the funds it had expended for cleaning the damage caused by the chemicals released from the tank truck as well as the costs of removing the buried drums of hazardous chemicals that had not been sold at auction. The EPA claimed that the costs were administrative expenses of the estate and entitled to priority. Although the buried drums had no value to the estate, the court found that the drums were properly included within the assets of the bankruptcy estate pursuant to Bankruptcy Code Section 541. As such, the estate could be charged with the expenses incurred by the EPA in removing the drums.[41] In considering the fairness of the impact of the EPA's administrative priority claim on creditors, the court acknowledged that the EPA's success was achieved at the expense of the creditors. While the court sympathized with those creditors, it found that "this is a risk which the creditors must bear."[42]

The matter of the costs caused by the contaminant released from the tank trunk was a much greater problem for the court. Although the tank truck and the chemicals inside had been used by the corporate debtor in its business before bankruptcy had been filed, and had been used by the debtor while it continued its operations in Chapter 11 for approximately one year before the conversion to Chapter 7, the court found that the release of the chemical, and not its storage, was the important point in determining the estate's responsibility. Because the chemical had been released only after the estate had conducted an authorized sale, the release occurred at a time when the chemicals were no longer the property of the estate of the corporate bankruptcy and the response costs could not then be properly charged against those limited assets available to pay creditors.

The decision of the Supreme Court in *Midlantic Bank v. New Jersey Department of Environmental Protection*,[43] holding that the bankruptcy court could not approve a trustee's proposed abandonment of contaminated property without adequate safeguards for the public health and safety, significantly increased the government's chances of obtaining administrative expense priority treatment for its cleanup costs where an imminent and identifiable harm to the public health can be demonstrated.[44]

A state's postbankruptcy response costs, recoverable from the debtor under federal law, may be allowable as administrative expenses in Chapter 7 when assets are available to cover those costs.[45] A claim for reimbursement of cleanup costs incurred and to be incurred by a private party entitled to reimbursement for prepetition contamination of leased premises may be treated as a general unsecured claim without priority.[46]

Surcharge Against Collateral

In the *Long Chemical* case, the EPA, faced with the court's decision that only part of its claim would be accorded administrative expense priority and that the assets of the estate were insufficient to pay that in full, then sought to recover the remainder of its claim from the proceeds of the private property collateral that secured the corporate debtor's lender. A bankruptcy trustee and, in some instances, third parties can recover from a secured creditor's collateral the reasonable, necessary costs and expenses of preserving or disposing of such collateral to the extent of any benefit to the holder of such secured claim.[47] The court noted that, where the trustee acts for the benefit of a secured creditor, generally the estate should be able to recover the costs of such action. These costs traditionally are associated with the inspection, gathering, appraisal, advertising, storage, repair, maintenance, and sale of collateral. The *Long Chemical* trustee had gathered the collateral and conducted a court-approved sale before the EPA came onto the site and removed the barrels. Because the cost of removing the barrels exceeded their value as collateral, they were not sold at the trustee's auction and the secured creditor indicated no desire to take responsibility for them. Therefore, the court concluded that "there was no value in the drums worthy of preservation."[48] The court stated that the secured creditor had to bear the burden of its initial credit underwriting when it found that it was undersecured. The court stated that it would not add to that burden by making the creditor's other collateral bear all the expenses associated with removing the drums. The court recognized that a creditor does not assume responsibility in all circumstances over collateral by the simple act of taking a security interest in it.[49]

Discharge of Environmental Claims

The issue of whether cleanup liability will ultimately be discharged as a prebankruptcy claim is of prime importance to the debtor. Frequently, a potential liability may have been identified by the EPA based on the debtor's prebankruptcy actions, but the extent of the problem may not be fully known. The EPA's first tack may be to seek an order enjoining the owner or operator from continuing ongoing pollution and requiring the facility owner or operator to remove and dispose of certain hazardous substances. Such an order, apparently entirely injunctive in nature, is convertible to a monetary obligation in part.

If the facility owner or operator does not remove existing contamination or hazardous substances that pose the threat of contamination, the EPA has the option of undertaking the cleanup activity itself. The EPA can then seek recovery of the response costs from the debtor or the debtor's estate.

These monetary obligations of the debtor owner or operator fit squarely within the Bankruptcy Code's definition of a claim in Section 101(4) as a right to payment whether or not liquidated, fixed, contingent, matured, disputed, legal, or equitable, or the right to an equitable remedy, the breach of which gives rise to a right to payment. A claim for EPA response costs incurred postbankruptcy to clean up prebankruptcy contamination will constitute a dischargeable claim in the debtor operator's bankruptcy.[50]

Continuing Injunction

An order that requires the debtor to cease or ameliorate ongoing pollution is not a claim dischargeable in bankruptcy. The debtor does not have the option to continue pollution.[51] The distinction between the dischargeable and nondischargeable parts of an environmental injunction is sometimes expressed as the difference between the affirmative order to clean up existing contamination and the negative order to cease ongoing pollution.[52] The negative order is not dischargeable. A facility owner or operator cannot maintain a nuisance, or continue to act in contravention of environmental regulations by reason of having received a discharge of liability for cleanup expenses incurred for prebankruptcy contamination.

Prebankruptcy Costs

As long as the contamination is based on prebankruptcy actions of the debtor, the eventual cleanup costs will most likely be considered claims within the bankruptcy, even if the costs have not yet been incurred or fixed with any certainty. The Bankruptcy Code's definition of claims includes those that are contingent and unmatured. Such claims can nonetheless be estimated for the purposes of the bankruptcy disclosure statement consideration and plan approval.[53] Only some courts have required that all elements of the claim for reimbursement of cleanup costs be established before the claim is includable in the bankruptcy and subsequently discharged.[54]

A possible exception to the bankruptcy discharge of an affirmative order requiring cleanup of prepetition contamination was recognized by the Sixth Circuit Court of Appeals in *United States v. Whizco, Inc.*[55] That court held that, to the extent an individual debtor retained the ability to personally reclaim some portion of a contaminated site without spending money, the affirmative injunction had not been converted to solely a monetary claim discharged in bankruptcy.

Continuing Liability

While a company might, through a Chapter 11 bankruptcy, discharge its liability as the operator of a contaminated site,[56] the reorganized company's liability as the owner of the contaminated site might continue.

An illustrative case is that of the Seventh Circuit's 1992 decision in *In re CMC Heartland Partners*.[57] The *CMC* case involved the 1977 bankruptcy of the Chicago, Milwaukee, St. Paul & Pacific Railroad. The debtor emerged from bankruptcy as CMC Heartland Partners. CMC's environmental problems involved a gravel pit, which the company had used long before its bankruptcy to provide the gravel needed for its roadbeds. Beginning in the 1950s, the railroad leased one corner of the open gravel pit to General Motors because the latter needed a place to dispose of paint sludge and coal ash. The gravel pit was so used until 1974, when it was closed in accord with Wisconsin Department of Natural Resources regulations.

Problems arose at the gravel pit in 1984 when the EPA placed the property on the National Priorities List (NPL).[58] At this time, CMC was still in the midst of its reorganization. Claims for prepetition debts could be filed for one year after the inclusion of the debtor's gravel pit on the NPL.

The EPA did not submit a claim in the CMC bankruptcy. After the confirmation of the debtor's plan of reorganization and successful emergence from bankruptcy, the EPA obtained an order requiring both CMC and General Motors to clean up contamination found at the gravel pit. CMC sought an order directing the EPA to show cause why it should not be held in contempt for violating the confirmation order's permanent injunction against actions based on discharged prebankruptcy claims. The trial court declined to issue the show cause order, and the Seventh Circuit affirmed that decision.

The decision of the Court of Appeals recognized that, because the government failed to file its CERCLA claim in the CMC bankruptcy, the environmental claim against CMC as an operator or manager of the gravel pit was extinguished under the terms of the CMC reorganization. (Although CMC's bankruptcy, having been filed in 1977, was filed under the predecessor to the current Bankruptcy Code, the relevant provisions of the predecessor law are sufficiently similar to the current statute to render the CMC decision relevant.) The court, however, distinguished an operator's discharged, prebankruptcy liability from the authority of the government to direct the current owner of contaminated property to take actions as may be necessary to address the contamination. The court said that the owner's liability is a "claim running with the land."[59]

The Seventh Circuit also declined to examine CMC's issue with respect to allocation, as between the reorganized debtor and GM of liability for particular contaminants found in the soil, noting that CERCLA defers judicial review of cleanup orders until the necessary remedial action has been taken. This is consistent with the strong public policy in favor of swift action to protect the public health and safety while leaving the EPA with ultimate liability for cleanup costs if the liability of operators or owners cannot be established.

A reorganized company may also have some continuing liability to subsequent purchasers of property contaminated before the debtor's bankruptcy unless such potential claimants were disclosed in the bankruptcy case and received some notice.[60] Where property has been transferred from a bankruptcy estate to a purchaser unaware of potential cleanup responsibilities, the Bankruptcy Court has permitted that purchaser to reassert against the debtor a private cause of action for damages and indemnification.[61] These private cause-of-action claims have even been accorded administrative priority in a Chapter 11 bankruptcy of the seller where the purchaser's liability to the EPA arose after the transfer of the property but was based on hazardous materials stored on the site before the transfer.[62]

Abandonment of Contaminated Property

Some bankruptcy trustees have attempted to avoid the risks of massive environmental liability by abandoning contaminated properties under Bankruptcy Code Section 554 as burdensome to the estate. Citing the Supreme Court's decision in *Midlantic*, the Bankruptcy Court in *In re Better Brite Plating, Inc.*[63] stated the general rule that a trustee may not abandon burdensome property in contravention of a state statute reasonably designed to protect the health and welfare of the public.

The *Better Brite* court, however, found an exception to the general rule, stating that "where the trustee has no unencumbered assets to finance the cleanup and there is no imminent harm or danger to the public, trustees have been permitted to abandon property, even though violations of state environmental laws exist."[64] In *Better Brite,* the court endorsed a settlement agreed on among the Chapter 7 trustee, the EPA, the Wisconsin Department of Natural Resources, and a creditor secured by a first-priority lien on real property contaminated and then cleaned at the expense of the EPA. In the settlement the trustee was permitted to abandon the cleaned property. The Wisconsin Department of Natural Resources and the EPA were permitted continued access to the property for the purpose of testing and monitoring and were permitted new first-priority liens on the property to assure them of payment for cleanup expenses upon any resale of the property. To deny the agencies these liens would have been to accord the secured creditor an undue windfall from the eventual sale of the now rehabilitated property.[65]

The bankruptcy courts are courts of equity. Bankruptcy Code Section 105 and its empowerment to the court to issue any "order, process, or judgment that is necessary or appropriate to carry out the provisions" of the Bankruptcy Code is often cited by litigants urging a bankruptcy court to retain its focus on achieving the broad purposes of the Bankruptcy Code and thereafter fashioning a vehicle that will take the case to its objective. In *In re Paris Industries Corp.,*[66] the Chapter 11 trustee sought to sell both the debtor's real and personal property. A sale of personal property was authorized by the bankruptcy court and yielded $475,000. These proceeds were subject to a lien securing an outstanding debt far in excess of the value of the collateral. The same creditor secured by the debtor's personal property also had a first-priority lien on the debtor's seven acres of land. The land's value was estimated to be between $500,000 and $1,000,000 if clean. The State of New York, having found contamination on the site, estimated the cost of cleaning the property at approximately $750,000. The debt owed to the first lien holder was approximately $2,000,000.

Initially, the State of New York sought an administrative expense claim against the $475,000 in personal property proceeds and first recovery from the sale proceeds of the real estate. The secured creditor, the Chapter 11 trustee, and the State of New York ultimately agreed that the personal property proceeds of $475,000 were to be paid directly to the secured creditor. The purchaser of the real estate would pay a total price of $160,000 ($75,000 of which would be immediately paid in cash to the Chapter 11 trustee and turned over to the State of New York, with the remaining $85,000 to be paid over the course of three years to the Chapter 11 trustee for ultimate distribution to creditors). The purchaser would undertake certain obligations to clean the property. The state would then cap its claims against the debtor and the secured creditor.

The court, approving the settlement, found that the Chapter 11 trustee had done a creditable job in finding a practical answer to the Supreme Court's decision in *Midlantic National Bank v. New Jersey Department of Environmental Protection* that the "bankruptcy court does not have the power to authorize an abandonment without formulating conditions that will adequately protect the public's health and safety."[67]

Notes

This chapter was developed from material and information initially gathered for Edward C. Dolan, *Treating Environmental Liabilities in Bankrupcty,* 27 MARYLAND BAR JOURNAL (September/October 1994).

1. 42 U.S.C. § 9613(h). *See* Reardon v. United States, 922 F.2d 28 (1st Cir. 1990). *See also* Lone Pine Steering Comm. v. United States Envtl. Protection Agency, 600 F. Supp. 1487 (D. N.J. 1985), *aff'd*, 777 F.2d 822 (3rd Cir. 1985), *cert. denied*, 476 U.S. 1115 (1986); and United States v. Ottati & Goss, Inc., 900 F.2d 429 (1st Cir. 1990).

2. 11 U.S.C. § 101(13).

3. The Bankruptcy Reform Act of 1978, as amended, 11 U.S.C. § 101 *et seq.* (hereinafter Bankruptcy Code).

4. 11 U.S.C. § 362(a).

5. 11 U.S.C. § 501; Federal Rules of Bankruptcy Procedure 3001, 3002, 3003.

6. Bankruptcy Rule 3007.

7. 11 U.S.C. § 502.

8. 11 U.S.C. §§ 503, 507.

9. 11 U.S.C. §§ 727, 1141, 1228, 1328, and 523.

10. The holder of an allowed claim may vote in favor of or reject a Chapter 11 plan of reorganization. 11 U.S.C. § 1126. The nature and magnitude of an environmental liability claim in Chapter 11 will determine its placement among classes of similar claims, 11 U.S.C. § 1122, and the voting rights of claimants within that class, 11 U.S.C. § 1126(c). Whereas many claims in bankruptcy are paid only in part or over time, administrative expense claims, possibly including reimbursement of government cleanup costs, must be paid in full shortly after confirmation of a Chapter 11 plan. 11 U.S.C. §§ 1129(a)(9) and 507(a). Similarly, administrative expenses are accorded priority in distribution under Chapter 7. 11 U.S.C. § 726.

11. 42 U.S.C. § 9601 *et seq.*

12. *See* United States v. Chem-Dyne Corp., 572 F. Supp. 802 (S.D. Ohio 1983); United States v. Monsanto, 858 F.2d 160 (4th Cir. 1988).

13. 42 U.S.C. § 9613(f)(1).

14. No threshold quantity is needed.

15. 11 U.S.C. § 9604(a).

16. 42 U.S.C. § 9606(a).

17. 42 U.S.C. § 9613(h).

18. 42 U.S.C. § 9607.

19. 42 U.S.C. § 9607(a). Civil penalties are set forth in 42 U.S.C. §§ 9606(b) and 9609.

20. 42 U.S.C. § 9607(b).

21. *See* 42 U.S.C. § 9601(35); International Clinical Laboratories, Inc. v. Stevens, 20 ELR 20560 (E.D.N.Y. 1990); United States v. Pacific Hide & Fur Depot, Inc., 716 F. Supp. 1341 (D. Idaho 1989).

22. 28 U.S.C. § 959(b).

23. 57 B.R. 611 (Bankr. S.D.N.Y. 1986).

24. *Id.* at 623–24. *See also* Wilner Wood Products v. Maine Dep't of Envtl. Protection, 128 B.R. 1 (D. Me. 1991).

25. In the case of an individual, the debtor surrenders all of his or her nonexempt assets (11 U.S.C. §§ 522, 541) to the estate, which is then administered by a trustee for the benefit of all creditors. Certain orders of priority are recognized with respect to the claims of creditors (11 U.S.C. § 507) and, if all of these administrative claims are paid in full, then general unsecured creditors will ultimately receive pro rata distributions. In the case of an individual, the debtor will receive a Chapter 7 discharge with certain limited exceptions. 11 U.S.C. §§ 523, 524, 727. A business entity's Chapter 7 bankruptcy is procedurally similar to that of an individual. The corporation or partnership, however, would not receive a discharge in Chapter 7 but would merely go out of existence.

26. *See* Penn Terra Ltd. v. Dep't of Envtl. Resources, 733 F.2d 267 (3rd Cir. 1984).

27. 44 B.R. 83 (Bankr. W.D. Mich. 1984).

28. *Id.* at 88.

29. *In re* Wall Tube and Metal Products Co., 56 B.R. 918, 925–26 (Bankr. E.D. Tenn. 1986). More recently, the decisions dealing with administrative priorities have eroded the certainty in *Wall Tube*.

30. 124 Cong. Rec. S17, 409 (1978), *reprinted in* 1978 U.S. Code Cong. & Ad. News 5787, 6505, 6513 (Statement of Sen. DeConcini); 124 Cong. Rec. H11, 089 (1978), *reprinted in* 1978 U.S. Code Cong. & Ad. News 5787, 6436, 6444–45 (Statement of Rep. Edwards). *See also* City of New York v. Exxon Corp., 112 B.R. 540 (S.D.N.Y. 1990).

31. *See* U.S. v. Mattiace Indus., Inc., 73 B.R. 816 (E.D.N.Y. 1987); and Penn Terra Ltd. v. Dep't of Envtl. Resources, 733 F.2d 267 (3d Cir. 1984).

32. 11 U.S.C. § 101(12). *See* Torwico Enterprises, Inc. v. Dep't of Envtl. Protection, 131 B.R. 561 (Bankr. D. N.J. 1991).

33. *See, e.g., In re* National Gypsum, 139 B.R. 397 (N.D. Tex. 1992).

34. *In re* Chicago, Milwaukee, St. Paul and Pacific R.R., 974 F.2d 775 (7th Cir. 1992); *In re* Chateaugay Corp., 944 F.2d 977 (2nd Cir. 1991).

35. 11 U.S.C. § 502(c).

36. In a Chapter 11 plan of reorganization, creditors with substantially similar claims are placed in the same class for the purpose of payment. 11 U.S.C. § 1122(a). Each class of creditors is entitled to vote for or against confirmation of a plan if that class is not to receive immediate payment in full of all claims. 11 U.S.C. §§ 1126(f), 1129(a)(10). A class accepts a plan if approved by creditors holding at least two-thirds in amount and more than one-half in number of the allowed claims in the class. 11 U.S.C. § 1126(d). If the government cleanup costs are entitled to priority in distribution under 11 U.S.C. § 507(a)(1) or (2), the government must be paid in full immediately upon confirmation unless the government agrees to other treatment.

37. *See* Gross, *Evidentiary Issues in the Estimation of CERCLA Future Cost Claims*, The 67th Annual Meeting of National Conference of Bankruptcy Judges, Educational Program, Written Materials, 4–5, 1993.

38. *See In re* N.P. Mining Co., 963 F.2d 1449 (11th Cir. 1992); and *In re* Shore Realty Co., Inc. 134 B.R. 752 (Bankr. E.D. Tex. 1991).

39. 11 U.S.C. § 1129(a)(9)(A).

40. 45 B.R. 278 (Bankr. N.D. Ohio 1985).

41. The trustee would not be permitted to abandon them as having no net value because of public policies favoring the safeguarding of the public's health and welfare. 45 B.R. 278, at 286.

42. If a Chapter 7 trustee is not permitted to abandon contaminated property, then the trustee is left with the obligation to clean it up. If the trustee fails to act and the government is left to pay the cleanup costs, these costs are properly included among those necessary to preserve the estate and are entitled to administrative expense priority. *Id.*, at 287.

43. 474 U.S. 494, 106 S. Ct. 755, 88 L. Ed. 2d 859 (1986).

44. *See In re* Charles Stevens, et al., 68 B.R. 774, 781–783 (D. Me. 1987).

45. Lancaster v. Tennessee, 831 F.2d 118, 122–24 (6th Cir. 1987).

46. *In re* Dant & Russell, Inc., 853 F.2d 700, 708 (9th Cir. 1988); and Boyd v. Dock's Corner Associates, 135 B.R. 46 (Bankr. W.D. Mich. 1991).

47. 11 U.S.C. § 506(c).

48. 45 B.R. 278, 288.

49. *See also In re* Synfax Manufacturing, Inc., 126 B.R. 30, 34 (Bkrtcy. D. N.J. 1990).

50. *See supra* note 8.

51. *See In re* Chateaugay Corp., 944 F.2d 997, 1008 (2nd Cir. 1991).

52. Ohio v. Kovacs, 469 U.S. 274, 279, 105 S. Ct. 705, 708 (1985).

53. *See In re* Jensen, 995 F.2d 925 (9th Cir. 1993); *see also In re* National Gypsum Co., 139 B.R. 397 (N.D. Tex. 1992).

54. *See, e.g.*, United States v. Union Scrap & Metal, 123 B.R. 831 (D. Minn. 1990).

55. 841 F.2d 147 (6th Cir. 1988).

56. 42 U.S.C.A. § 9606(a).

57. 966 F.2d 1143 (7th Cir. 1992).

58. 42 U.S.C. § 9605(a)(8).

59. 966 F.2d 1143, at 1146. *See* Midlantic National Bank v. New Jersey Dep't of Envtl. Protection, 474 U.S. 497 (1986).

60. Waterville Indus., Inc. v. First Hartford Corp., 124 B.R. 411, 413–14 (D. Me. 1991).

61. 42 U.S.C.A. § 9607(a)(2)(A) and (B).

62. *See In re* Hemingway Transport, Inc., 73 B.R. 494 (Bankr. D. Mass. 1987).

63. 105 B.R. 912 (Bankr. E.D. Wis. 1989).

64. *Id.* at 917.

65. *See also In re* Smith-Douglas, Inc., 856 F.2d 12, 15–16 (4th Cir. 1988).

66. 106 B.R. 339 (Bankr. D. Me. 1989).

67. 474 U.S., at 507, 106 S. Ct., at 762.

PART IV

What the Audit Revealed: Dealing with Specific Substances and Situations

~

CHAPTER 18

Underground Storage Tanks

WALTER G. WRIGHT JR.

A wide variety of businesses and governmental entities have used underground storage tanks (USTs) for years. Consequently, hundreds of thousands of active and inactive USTs are found in both rural and urban areas throughout the United States. The perception that petroleum products and chemicals were leaking from a substantial number of USTs motivated Congress to enact a federal regulatory program for USTs in 1984. Since then, owners and operators of tanks and of the properties on which tanks are located have had to make significant expenditures to fund investigations and remediations of leaks and spills as well as to upgrade UST equipment.[1]

Because USTs are found at so many facilities, they represent some of the most common environmental concerns in commercial transactions, affecting buyers, sellers, lessors, lessees, and lenders alike. All of these parties may have to comply with federal and state UST regulations and to remediate contamination from UST leaks and spills.

Fortunately, compared with other environmental regulatory programs, the federal and state UST programs are usually fairly straightforward. Because of the large number of USTs, environmental consultants and regulators have amassed a considerable amount of experience in performing and supervising UST investigations and remediation. Some states have published cleanup levels for contaminated soil and groundwater, thus clarifying remediation requirements and assisting tank owners in estimating cleanup costs. In addition, a number of states have established trust funds to reimburse tank owners for tank cleanup costs, although similar funding is unavailable to parties remediating other environmental contaminants, such as asbestos or PCBs.

USTs—The Background

Most tanks holding petroleum or chemical products that were installed in the last fifty years were placed underground, for reasons of aesthetics, space limitations, and, most importantly, fire and safety concerns. Many fire codes require the placement of storage tanks underground because many tanks hold flammable liquids and underground tanks are better protected than aboveground tanks from incidents that could cause explosions or fires.

USTs commonly contain gasoline, kerosene, diesel fuel, motor oil, sewage, chemicals, and other substances. A government report has estimated that 1.2 to 1.4 million USTs are used to store petroleum products such as motor fuel.[2] One recent report estimates there are approximately 1.3 million active USTs.[3]

USTs have been used on a wide variety of properties. Approximately 52 percent of the USTs containing petroleum are found in the retail motor fuel industry, which includes gas stations, convenience stores, refiners, and petroleum wholesalers.[4] Many entities store petroleum products in USTs for use in their own vehicles. This category includes local governments, schools, utility companies, and car dealerships and rental agencies, to name just a few. Heating-oil USTs are used in many commercial properties, including office buildings, apartment houses, and shopping centers.

It is important to note certain recent trends involving the use of USTs in the United States. Many marginally profitable service stations and convenience stores have closed in recent years, and the use of USTs has been discontinued at others. The cost of complying with UST regulations plays a role in many such facility and tank closures. For example, an auto dealership or truck terminal may not view the convenience of on-site fleet fueling as worth the perceived regulatory responsibilities or liabilities that accompany UST ownership. One report estimates that over 700,000 USTs have been permanently closed.[5]

As a result of these closures, tens of thousands of properties where USTs were used have entered the real estate market. In some cases, USTs were removed; in other cases, they were left in the ground, sometimes filled with liquid. These properties are frequently acquired or leased for conversion to other uses. Often there is no aboveground evidence of the existence, or prior use, of USTs.

Environmental Impacts of USTs

Leaks or spills from USTs can impact soil and groundwater and require significant expenditures for investigation and remediation. Tank leaks can result from corrosion, system rupture, punctures, external stress, or faulty construction and installation. Spills from the aboveground portion of tanks are typically associated with the filling of tanks.

Not all petroleum leaks or spills threaten human health or the environment. Whether or not a given leak or spill will impact groundwater depends on the time it takes to stop the release, the soil conditions, the depth of groundwater, and the characteristics of the aquifer. Even if some of a tank's contents reach the groundwater, the environmental effect will depend on the use of the groundwater, the presence of sensitive receptors, and other factors. Nonetheless, a leak or spill that has potentially affected groundwater is of particular concern because of the increased chances of the need for expensive corrective action or remediation.

Federal and State Regulatory Programs

An understanding of the UST issues that must be addressed in commercial transactions should begin with a review of the relevant federal and state statutes and regulations. As with many other environmental programs, USTs are subject to both federal and state regulatory requirements in many states. Lawyers should note that USTs may also be subject to requirements enacted by local governments.[6]

Resource Conservation and Recovery Act

Congressional Studies

In the early 1980s Congress began investigating whether leaks or spills from USTs were contaminating soil and groundwater.[7] Congress became concerned that there was no regulatory mandate for UST owners or operators to implement UST leak prevention, detection, investigation, or remediation techniques, especially because petroleum releases from USTs are excluded from the Comprehensive Environmental Response, Compensation, and Liability Act (CERCLA) regime.[8] The bar to CERCLA's use was and is still found in its petroleum exclusion.[9] Access to CERCLA funds would have allowed the U.S. Environmental Protection Agency (EPA) to address UST petroleum releases if the source was unknown or if the owner or operator was unwilling or unable to take the necessary corrective action. Because of the growing congressional support for the elimination of CERCLA's petroleum exclusion, the petroleum industry ultimately supported the development of a new subchapter under the Resource Conservation and Recovery Act (RCRA) to address petroleum and chemical USTs specifically.

Statutory Authority

MANDATE TO DEVELOP REGULATIONS. In 1983 Congress added Subchapter IX (also known as Subtitle I) to RCRA, directing the EPA to promulgate regulations applicable to all USTs containing, primarily, petroleum and chemical products designated as "regulated substances."[10] Substances classified as "hazardous waste" were already subject to a comprehensive regulatory program promulgated pursuant to Subchapter III (also known as Subtitle C) of RCRA.[11] (The RCRA hazardous waste program is beyond the scope of this chapter.)

Subtitle I required the EPA to issue design, construction, installation, and compatibility standards for new USTs as well as requirements concerning leak detection, record keeping, reporting, closure, corrective action, and financial responsibility applicable to all USTs.[12] Congress also encouraged states to develop their own UST programs by establishing state standards at least as stringent as the federal provisions.[13]

EPA RESPONSE PROGRAM: THE LUST FUND. Congress also established a $500 million Leaking Underground Storage Tank Trust Fund (LUST Fund), which in certain circumstances provides the EPA with funds for corrective action.[14] The LUST fund is financed by a 0.1 cent per gallon federal excise tax on certain petroleum products, primarily motor fuels. The EPA is authorized to use this fund to pay for corrective action costs only under limited and specifically defined circumstances, primarily when the EPA is unable to identify a solvent owner or operator.[15]

States are allowed to access the LUST Fund if they demonstrate the capability to carry out effective corrective actions (including enforcement) and have entered into a cooperative agreement.[16] Because the LUST Fund covers cleanup for petroleum UST leaks, tank owners or operators may find themselves liable to the EPA or the state for the costs incurred.[17]

Overview of the Federal UST Regulations

The EPA initially published two sets of UST regulatory requirements, codified at 40 C.F.R. Parts 280 and 281. The EPA based these requirements on industry codes developed by organizations such as the American Petroleum Institute and the National Fire Protection Association. The EPA has stated that it sought to develop a set of regulations that could be tailored to state and local needs.[18] The UST leak prevention, detection, notification, investigation, corrective action, and closure standards (cumulatively called the Technical Standards) were published on September 23, 1988, in the *Federal Register*, volume 53, at 37,081. The so-called financial responsibility regulations were published on October 26, 1988, in the *Federal Register*, volume 53, at 43,322.

Many states have by reference incorporated the federal UST regulations. Some state UST programs have provisions that are more stringent than the federal regulations.

Tanks Covered by the Regulations

The Subtitle I regulations apply to USTs containing petroleum and hazardous substances, as defined under CERCLA, 42 U.S.C. Section 9601 *et seq*.[19] Tanks holding used oil are included, although tanks with new oil are not. USTs used to store hazardous wastes regulated under Subtitle C of RCRA (i.e., listed and characteristic wastes) are excluded from regulation under Subtitle I.

A UST is defined as

> any one or combination of tanks (including underground pipes connected thereto) that is used to contain an accumulation of regulated substances, and the volume of which (including the volume of underground pipes connected thereto) is 10 percent or more beneath the surface of the ground.[20]

A "UST system" includes a UST and its "connected underground piping, underground ancillary equipment, and containment system, if any."[21]

Under the regulations, USTs do not include the following:

- Farm or residential tanks with a capacity of 1,100 gallons or less used to store motor fuel for noncommercial uses
- Tanks used to store heating oil for use on the premises
- Septic tanks
- Pipelines regulated under the National Gas Pipeline Safety Act of 1968 (49 U.S.C. App. 1671 *et seq*.), the Hazardous Liquid Pipeline Safety Act of 1979 (49 U.S.C. App. 2001 *et seq*.), or pipelines that are intrastate facilities regulated under a comparable state law
- Surface impoundments, pits, ponds, or lagoons
- Storm water or wastewater collection systems
- Flow-through process tanks
- Liquid traps and gathering lines used in oil or gas production and gathering
- Tanks that are located in an underground room, shaft, or tunnel but that are above or on the bottom surface of the room, shaft, or tunnel in which they are located.[22]

The regulations exclude or defer from regulation certain categories of USTs that would otherwise fall within the statutory and regulatory definitions of UST systems. Note, however, that some states have narrowed or eliminated some of these exemptions or deferrals. For example, some states regulate heating-oil USTs, a major issue in many commercial real estate transactions.

The regulations specifically exclude the following:

- Wastewater treatment tank systems that are part of a facility subject to regulation under Sections 307(b) or 402 of the Clean Water Act (CWA), 33 U.S.C. Sections 1317(b) or 1342
- Hydraulic lift tanks and electrical equipment tanks (often found in service stations)
- USTs with a capacity of 110 gallons or less
- USTs containing a de minimis concentration of regulated substances (this term is not defined)
- USTs used for emergency spills and overflow containment that are emptied expeditiously after use[23]

The regulations defer, for various reasons, the following categories of UST systems from all regulatory requirements, except the release response and corrective action requirements:

- Wastewater treatment tank systems
- UST systems containing radioactive materials regulated under the Atomic Energy Act (42 U.S.C. Section 2011 *et seq.*)
- USTs that are part of an emergency generator system at nuclear power generation facilities regulated by the Nuclear Regulatory Commission (10 C.F.R. Part 50, Appendix A)
- Airport hydrant fuel system distribution systems
- Field-constructed tanks[24]

UST systems that store fuel solely for use by emergency power generators do not have to meet the release detection requirements of the UST regulations but are subject to the remaining regulatory requirements.[25]

Parties Covered by the Regulations

Many federal and state environmental laws impose liabilities or responsibilities on broadly defined categories of parties without regard to fault. The UST programs are no exception. Federal and most state UST programs place the responsibility for meeting the requirements on the UST's "owner" or "operator."[26]

The term "owner" means any person who "owns" a UST used for the storage, use, or dispensing of the relevant substances.[27] The term "operator" is similarly broad and means "any person in control of, or having responsibility for, the daily operation of the UST."[28] At any given time, a tank may have more than one owner and more than one operator.[29]

Many parties are swept into the reach of these definitions. Depending on the facts of a given case, responsibility for UST regulatory compliance can be asserted against buyers, sellers, lessors, lessees, and other parties to a commercial transaction. Moreover, even though parties may agree to allocate responsibilities and liabilities among themselves, federal and state regulators may pursue any party that falls within the definitions of "owner" and "operator," regardless of the parties' agreement.

The UST regulations refer to the owner or operator of the UST as opposed to the property or facility. Lessees or purchasers of a property who do not take title to USTs thereon, and who do not "operate" them, may fall outside of the definitions. When the contract or lease does not specify whether a UST is transferred as part of the property, the issue should be scrutinized as a state property law issue. Regardless, regulators typically interpret these jurisdictional terms broadly, especially when only one potentially responsible party is available or solvent.

Technical Standards

USTs that are not exempt or deferred from regulation must meet certain requirements, as described below.

NEW UST SYSTEMS. UST systems are considered "new" if installation began after December 22, 1988. New USTs must be designed, constructed, installed, and protected from corrosion in accordance with industry codes of practice.[30] Both new and existing UST systems must be constructed or lined with materials compatible with the substances they are storing. To meet this standard, tanks may be constructed of

(1) fiberglass reinforced plastic (FRP);
(2) steel that is cathodically protected;
(3) steel-FRP composite;
(4) metal with no corrosion protection if a finding is made that the installation site is not so corrosive as to cause the tank to have a leak as a result of corrosion during its operating life; or
(5) the implementing agency (the EPA or an approved state) determines that the tank construction and corrosion protection are designed to prevent the release or threatened release of any stored regulated substance in a manner that is no less protective of human health and the environment than the previously referenced UST construction methods [in (1) through (4) above].[31]

Piping in new UST systems is subject to similar standards.[32]

Cathodically protected tanks must be coated with a suitable dielectric material, and field-installed systems must be designed by a "corrosion expert" as defined in the regulations. Dielectric material is "a material that does not conduct direct electrical current," as stated in Section 280.12. Cathodic protection systems must meet UST operation and maintenance performance standards.[33]

Spill and overfill prevention equipment is required when USTs are filled by transfer of more than twenty-five gallons at a time.[34] Owners and operators must ensure that tank filling does not result in spills or overfills, and they must investigate and clean up any spills or overfills.

EXISTING UST SYSTEMS. Existing UST systems must meet new UST system standards or be upgraded, replaced, or closed in accordance with UST regulations. Steel tanks may be upgraded by installing an interior lining, cathodic protection, or internal lining combined with cathodic protection.[35]

Tank integrity must be ensured before upgrading by one of these four methods:

(1) internal inspection before installing cathodic protection;
(2) monthly leak monitoring for tanks installed within the last ten years (by automatic tank gauging, vapor monitoring, groundwater monitoring, or interstitial monitoring in accordance with UST leak detection standards);
(3) tightness testing (in accordance with tightness testing standards) before installing cathodic protection and again three to six months afterwards; or
(4) assessment in a manner determined by the implementing agency to be as protective as items 1 through 3 above.[36]

A tank upgraded by both internal lining and cathodic protection must have the lining installed according to the UST standards for allowable repairs and must have a cathodic protection system that meets certain requirements. Spill and overfill standards also are applicable to existing USTs.

Existing UST systems must be upgraded, replaced, or closed by December 1998.[37] The EPA has expressed concern that hundreds of thousands of existing or "grandfathered" USTs have yet to be upgraded.[38] If so, the availability of equipment and competent contractors to upgrade a flood of USTs by this upcoming deadline is a real concern. However, in its public pronouncements, the EPA has stated that it does not intend to extend this deadline.

LEAK DETECTION REQUIREMENTS. The regulations impose leak detection requirements on all UST systems.[39] The Technical Standards prescribe release detection methods for tanks and piping and record-keeping requirements for release detection. The general rule for release detection is that tanks and piping must be checked for leaks at least every thirty days. Acceptable detection methods for the tank itself include automatic tank gauging, vapor monitoring, ground-water monitoring, and interstitial monitoring in accordance with the performance standards specified for each method. USTs installed after December 22, 1988 (i.e., "new tanks"), and upgraded tanks meeting new tank standards may use inventory control and manual tank gauging.

The Technical Standards allow tank tightness testing every five years, combined with either inventory control or manual tank gauging (in place of thirty-day monitoring) for new and upgraded tanks, until the later of ten years after installation or upgrading, or December 22, 1998. This provision is intended to encourage the early replacement or upgrading of USTs. At the end of the relevant period, monitoring must be performed every thirty days. For existing tanks (those installed on or before December 22, 1988) that have not been upgraded, monthly inventory control or manual tank gauging plus annual tightness testing may be substituted for monthly monitoring until December 22, 1998. By that date, tanks must be upgraded or permanently closed in accordance with the regulations.

Weekly tank gauging may be used in place of monthly monitoring if USTs are 550 gallons or less.[40] This provision is directed primarily at used oil tanks, in view of the frequent small additions to tanks holding motor oil at service stations and lube oil centers.

Owners and operators were to have upgraded their tanks to comply with applicable leak detection requirements on a five-year phase-in schedule based on the age of the UST system. The schedule was as follows:

- For UST systems installed before 1965 or a date unknown, by December 22, 1989
- For UST systems installed from 1965–69, by December 22, 1990
- For UST systems installed from 1970–74, by December 22, 1991
- For UST systems installed from 1975–79, by December 22, 1992
- For UST systems installed from 1980–88, by December 22, 1993

The Technical Standards also have specific leak detection requirements for UST piping.[41]

INVESTIGATION AND REPORTING REQUIREMENTS. Owners and operators generally must report suspected releases to the implementing agency within twenty-four hours.[42] Conditions indicative of suspected releases include: (1) the discovery of regulated substances or vapors in soils, basements, sewer and utility lines, or surface water at or near the UST site; (2) unusual operating conditions, such as sudden loss of product or the presence of water in the tank; and (3) monitoring results that indicate that a release has occurred.

Unless corrective action has started, within seven days owners and operators must investigate and confirm all suspected releases that require reporting. Tightness testing must be performed as part of this investigation.[43] If the test results indicate a release, the responsible party must repair, replace, or upgrade the UST system and begin corrective action. If the test results do not indicate a release and environmental contamination was not the cause for suspecting a release, no further investigation is required. If, however, environmental contamination was the reason for suspecting a release but tightness testing results do not indicate a release occurred, a site check must be conducted to confirm the presence and source of the release.

A site check consists of sampling performed on the site in a location where contamination is suspected.[44] If the presence of a release is confirmed, corrective action must be performed in accordance with the regulations. If no release is indicated, no further investigation is required.

Responsible parties must contain and clean up spills and overfills immediately, report to the implementing agency within twenty-four hours, and begin corrective action in accordance with the regulations if, in the case of petroleum USTs, a release of more than twenty-five gallons or a sheen on a nearby surface water occurs, or, in the case of chemical USTs, a release equal to or greater than a reportable quantity occurs.[45] Furthermore, a Section 311 CWA reporting obligation may also arise if the release reaches a water body or tributary.[46] The CWA term "waters of the United States" is broadly defined.[47]

It is imperative that the UST owner or operator or those advising that party maintain strict compliance with these detailed reporting requirements. Failure to do so can jeopardize eligibility for trust fund reimbursement, as discussed below. While the EPA or a state agency may allow extensions of regulatory deadlines, any such extensions and any oral notifications should be confirmed in writing.

CORRECTIVE ACTION. The corrective action requirements follow a site-specific approach that establishes general criteria to be followed unless the implementing agency directs otherwise.[48] The requirements outline a step-by-step process that ends when no further evidence of a release is found or when all abatement steps and reports have been completed. The steps include initial response and abatement, site check, initial site characterization, free product removal, investigations for soil and groundwater cleanup, corrective action plan, and public participation.

Within twenty days of release confirmation, the responsible party must submit a report to the implementing agency summarizing the abatement steps taken to date and any resulting data or information. An initial site characterization is due within forty-five days of release confirmation. The initial site characterization is a compilation of data concerning: (1) the nature and quantity of the release; (2) the surrounding environment, including population, soils, and water; and (3) results of the site check and free product investigations. When initial abatement measures indicate the presence of free product (i.e., the product in its pure rather than dissolved form), owners and operators must remove free product to the maximum extent practicable, as determined by the implementing agency, and file a free product removal report within forty-five days of release confirmation.

A soil and groundwater investigation is also required if previous investigations and abatement measures indicate possible impact to groundwater wells or contact between contaminated soils and groundwater or that free product removal is needed. Such an investigation is also required if the implementing agency requests it. A report on the results of the investigation must be submitted as soon as practicable.

After the required reports have been submitted for the initial response and abatement measures, including the initial site characterization, the implementing agency may require a corrective action plan for groundwater and soil contamination. A key question is what levels of contamination will require corrective action. The EPA selected a site-specific approach for setting cleanup target levels, the overriding goal of which is the establishment of cleanup standards that adequately protect human health and the environment.

Corrective action plans required by or submitted pursuant to the Technical Standards will be reviewed by analyzing the following factors:

(1) toxicity, persistence, and mobility of released substances;
(2) hydrogeology of the site and surrounding areas;
(3) proximity and uses of nearby surface and groundwater;
(4) potential effects of residual contamination on nearby surface water and groundwater;
(5) an exposure assessment; and
(6) any information assembled in compliance with the Technical Standards.

These broad guidelines afford either the EPA or the state substantial discretion in selecting the cleanup standards for a specific release. Some states review additional factors.

A number of states have or are considering adoption of uniform or statewide cleanup standards by either regulation or policy. For example, some states require the cleanup of soil with total petroleum levels above 100 parts per million (ppm) of total petroleum hydrocarbons (TPH). Such uniform standards presumably provide some certainty to the regulated community. A disadvantage of uniform standards is the failure to take into account site-specific standards.

The EPA and a number of states have recently begun developing risk-based guidelines for determining cleanup or corrective action levels for soil, groundwater, or both (dubbed "Rebecca" standards, an acronym for risk-based corrective action).[49] These guidelines provide a decision-making framework that takes into account the substances in the USTs as well as site-specific factors. The motivation for developing these standards has been the need to use available resources most efficiently in view of the fact that hundreds of thousands of UST releases are expected to be discovered over the next several years. The American Society for Testing and Materials (ASTM) has also issued a risk-based corrective action guidance document in this regard.[50]

Federal or state agency regulatory constraints also affect corrective action costs. Many states will not allow soils in which the benzene, toluene, ethyl benzene, or xylene (BTEX) content exceeds certain levels to be taken to a non-Subchapter III landfill. Further, petroleum-contaminated groundwater and soils may sometimes be classified as a "hazardous waste" under Subchapter III of RCRA, which can exponentially increase disposal costs. The EPA has chosen to exempt petroleum-contaminated soil or groundwater deemed RCRA hazardous waste because it fails the toxicity characteristic test.[51] Note, however, that soil and groundwater contaminated by petroleum releases from aboveground storage tanks (ASTs) are not exempt. The EPA has proposed expanding this exemption to include AST petroleum releases.[52]

The responsible party must implement the corrective action plan, as approved or modified, and monitor, evaluate, and report on implementation of the plan. Because prompt cleanup may minimize the extent of contamination, in some cases the Technical Standards allow cleanup to begin before approval of the corrective action plan.

CLOSURE. The UST regulations set separate requirements for temporary and permanent closure.[53] To close a UST system temporarily for less than three months, owners and operators must continue to operate and maintain corrosion leak detection systems, unless the UST system is empty, in which case no leak detection is required. The system is considered empty when not more than one inch of residue or 0.3 percent by weight of the system's total capacity remain in the system. If a UST system is closed temporarily for three months or longer, the owners and operators must also leave vent lines open and functioning and must cap and secure remaining lines and all pumps, manways, and ancillary equipment.

"Change in service" means the continued use of a UST system to store a nonregulated substance. Responsible parties must give at least thirty days' notice to the implementing agency before beginning to make a change in service or to close a UST system permanently. They must empty and clean the tank by removing all liquids and accumulated sludges. Tanks being closed permanently must be removed from the ground or filled with an inert solid material. Parties removing tanks from the ground must ensure they are complying with any state or local requirements concerning tank disposal, such as local fire and building codes.

Importantly, owners and operators must perform a site assessment to test for the presence of releases from the UST system before completing a change in service or a permanent closure. Sampling is to be performed where contamination is most likely to be present, taking into consideration the closure method, nature of the stored substance, backfill type, and depth to groundwater. Often tank closures can provide responsible parties with information that a tank has leaked in the past.

Financial Responsibility Requirements

Subchapter IX was amended in 1986 to mandate that the EPA establish financial responsibility requirements.[54] The financial responsibility regulations require an owner or operator to demonstrate financial responsibility for taking corrective action and compensating third parties for bodily injury and property damages caused by sudden and nonsudden accidental releases from petroleum USTs. This provision was and continues to be somewhat controversial because tank insurance—a means of demonstrating financial responsibility—is sometimes costly or unavailable in the case of older USTs or those that have not been upgraded.

If the owner and operator of the USTs are separate persons, only one person is required to demonstrate financial responsibility. However, as with the technical standards, the EPA may hold each party responsible if neither party complies with these requirements. The fact that the parties allocated this responsibility pursuant to a contract is irrelevant.

For purposes of covering costs of corrective actions and third-party liability, the financial responsibility requirements specify that all owners or operators of petroleum USTs at facilities engaged in petroleum marketing, refining, and the like, and UST owners with an average monthly throughput of more than 10,000 gallons, obtain financial assurance of at least $1,000,000 per occurrence.[55] Owners and operators of USTs at facilities not engaged in petroleum marketing, refining, and the like, or having an average monthly throughput of 10,000 gallons or less, need only obtain financial assurance of at least $500,000 per occurrence.

To demonstrate adequate financial responsibility, the UST owner or operator must carry a specific type of insurance or evidence of comparable coverage through a surety bond or letter of credit. Alternatively, the responsible party can pass a financial responsibility test by possessing an adequate net worth or obtaining a guarantee from a corporate affiliate. As a final option, a state may enact a trust fund to cover some or all of the financial responsibility requirements.[56]

In states without trust funds, most UST owners and operators have been forced to purchase insurance. Property and casualty insurance companies are sometimes hesitant to offer coverage for pollution exposures from petroleum USTs. Among the reasons often cited are the risks associated with older USTs and the requirements for highly specialized underwriting expertise. Even if premiums are offered, they are sometimes beyond the reach of small businesses that own or operate USTs. The insurance market should improve as the remaining USTs are upgraded, replaced, or closed by 1998.

Key UST Regulatory Requirements Affecting Commercial Transactions

The federal Technical Standards require that UST owners register their USTs with state authorities. These registration forms are available to the public and contain a variety of useful information, including the UST's age, the substances it holds, the type of leak detection used, and leak preventive measures. Further, the various record-keeping requirements mandate that the UST owner or operator track the information generated by the facility's leak detection procedures.

In a real estate transaction, this information is useful in analyzing the potential risks related to USTs. The capital costs necessitated by the required leak prevention and detection regulations may be material, depending on the number of USTs and their condition. It would seem prudent, for example, for a purchaser or tenant taking over the responsibility for USTs at a site to consider these costs.

Finally, lawyers advising clients with USTs should recognize that the various Technical Standards are detailed and often subject to short deadlines. Certain provisions require installation of leak detection methods by certain deadlines. Other provisions require reporting leaks within twenty-four hours. In all these cases, keen attention is needed to avoid noncompliance. As with other environmental statutes, noncompliance with federal and state UST programs is a serious matter, as considerable penalties can be assessed for violations.

An additional risk of noncompliance is unique to the UST programs. Most state trust fund programs make compliance with the Technical Standards a prerequisite for reimbursement. This makes it imperative that potential purchasers, lessees, and lenders who intend to rely on a state fund ensure that their USTs are in compliance before consummation of the transaction.

The closure, investigation, and corrective action requirements in the Technical Standards are especially relevant in commercial transactions. For example, in a case in which a property being transferred will not require USTs, it is important to delineate the responsibility for closure and to designate the person responsible for conducting investigation and any necessary corrective action. If required deadlines are not met because the parties are disputing these responsibilities, the resulting noncompliance may render the USTs ineligible for reimbursement under a state trust fund.

State Programs

Development of Equivalent State Programs

The RCRA UST statute and implementing regulations authorize and encourage development of state programs to operate in lieu of the federal program.[57] The EPA may approve a state program if its provisions are not less stringent than the federal program. A state with an approved UST program has primary enforcement responsibility for its program. Legislation providing authority for the development of UST programs has been enacted in almost every state.

State Reporting Issues

This chapter has already discussed a number of UST reporting requirements. Most states and the federal program limit reporting obligations to the owner or operator of the UST. However, New Jersey's regulations place a reporting obligation on any person with knowledge of a confirmed discharge. Section 7 of New Jersey's Administrative Code provides that

> [A]ny person, including but not limited to, the owner or operator of an underground storage tank system or contractor hired to install, remove, or test an underground storage tank system, shall, upon confirming a release, immediately report the release to the appropriate local health agency in accordance with the local requirements and the Department's environmental action hotline.[58]

This requirement may place a reporting obligation on persons not responsible for or in control of either the release or the actual UST.[59]

Two commentators have questioned whether this requirement places attorneys in an apparent conflict between their duty under the New Jersey Rules of Professional Conduct to keep confidential all client-related information and their potential obligation to report under the New Jersey regulations.[60] Lawyers are well advised to familiarize themselves with the reporting and notification requirements in their respective states.

State Trust Funds

Subchapter IX of RCRA allows states to set up state-sponsored financial assurance programs or trust funds to facilitate cleanup caused by UST-related contamination.[61] The realization that insurance was either unaffordable or unavailable created pressure at the state level for the development of these funds. Consequently, over forty states have created UST trust funds.[62]

Such funds may provide the mechanism for petroleum UST owners and operators to demonstrate compliance with financial responsibility requirements. A state trust fund may also reimburse parties for corrective action or third-party claims related to UST releases if owners and operators meet certain prerequisites for coverage. State trust funds vary, however, in terms of funding sources, coverage prerequisites, types, and limits of coverage and payment methods.

FUNDING. The primary methods of capitalizing state trust funds are UST registration or licensing fees and motor fuel taxes. Most states have statutory caps on the amount of revenues that can be raised.[63] Unsurprisingly, therefore, several state trust funds are experiencing financial difficulties as a result of the number and costs of UST investigations and remediations in these states. Where a tank owner or operator must rely on the fund, it is important to know the fund's viability.[64] Note that state environmental regulatory officials operating the trust funds are sometimes placed in the unusual position of seeking ways to streamline or limit costs for investigation and corrective actions because of funding shortfalls.

SCOPE AND LIMITS. Several issues arise when considering the scope and amount of costs potentially covered under a state trust fund, such as (1) type of storage tank covered, (2) type of cost covered, (3) upper limit of coverage for a particular type of cost, and (4) the deductible. While most states only permit USTs to access their funds, a few state trust funds include certain ASTs.[65] Additionally, USTs exempt from federal and state regulatory requirements may not be covered.

State trust funds typically employ two coverage options: (1) coverage for both corrective action and third-party liability claims or (2) coverage for corrective action costs only. State funds usually have maximum coverage limits. Typically, maximum coverage is $1 million per occurrence for corrective action and third-party liability amounts, but some states have lower coverage limits. An additional coverage question concerns whether the type of substances held in the USTs is eligible for trust fund proceeds.[66] Most states' funds require petroleum UST owners and operators to pay a specific deductible before coverage begins. The deductible amounts range from $5,000 to $300,000.[67]

Almost every state trust fund requires that the UST owner or operator meet certain prerequisites to be eligible to access the fund. These prerequisites often include cooperation with the state agency in addressing a release, a notification, compliance, or substantial compliance with the relevant federal and state regulations, as well as payment of fees. Funds differ regarding whether they cover existing releases, that is, those that occurred before the UST was covered by a state trust fund.[68]

A final prerequisite to trust fund eligibility is that an owner or operator must submit the claim. This seemingly simple requirement can prove problematic. Transactions may be negotiated in which the former owner retains some responsibility for addressing previously existing releases. Prior UST owners or operators who incur corrective action costs may not be able to access the trust fund because they are no longer the owner or operator. This issue must be considered in drafting the relevant provisions of the sale agreement.

PAYMENT FROM FUNDS. Four issues must be kept in mind regarding payment from reimbursement funds: (1) timing and delays of payment, (2) the state agency personnel making final decisions regarding reimbursement, (3) the procedure for submitting relevant claims, and (4) regulatory/third-party claim interaction.

The input of state regulators regarding the quality of corrective action methods warrants brief discussion. They may only provide reimbursement for cleanup necessary to decontaminate the property to a minimal level that adequately protects public health and safety. Property owners with USTs may perceive benefits in cleaning their parcels to a pristine state, but they should be prepared for reimbursement for remediation efforts to a lesser degree.

Timing. Most states provide reimbursement after corrective action costs have been incurred or the third-party claim has been paid.

Inadequate state agency staffing or a shortfall in revenues can result in considerable delays.

Personnel responsible for reimbursement decisions. The state trust funds vary in terms of the persons or groups responsible for reviewing reimbursement claims. Some states use advisory boards to review claims. The boards include appointed representatives from various interest groups such as independent petroleum marketers, service station dealers, refiners, insurance companies, and contractors. The board's decision may be subject to review by the agency supervising the trust fund. The agency or board's decision is usually subject to judicial review under the state's administrative appeal procedures.[69]

Procedures for reimbursement. Most state agencies have developed detailed procedures for reimbursement. Sometimes these procedures are addressed in published state regulations, but often they are simply found in the reimbursement application or unpublished state memoranda and guidance. A body of case law is developing in a few states that provides judicial guidance on a variety of reimbursement questions. Failure to familiarize one's self with formal and informal reimbursement procedures could result in the disallowance of some or all of a given reimbursement claim.[70]

Very few states have clearly defined reimbursement procedures regarding third-party claims for damages to person or property.[71] Some states, however, have set forth such procedures, and settlements for third-party claims should be drafted with any applicable trust fund procedures and prerequisites in mind. State regulators usually have the authority to approve a settlement that is in the best interest of the trust fund.

Regulatory/third-party claim interaction. Difficult issues are presented by the interplay between corrective action requirements, third-party claims for property damage (and in some cases bodily injury), and trust fund prerequisites. For example, consider a UST owner who is requested by a state environmental agency to perform investigative or corrective action work based on the discovery of petroleum in the area of the UST. Even if the owner suspects it is not the source of the petroleum, it may be unwilling to risk an allegation of noncompliance for two reasons. First, there is generally a significant disincentive to challenge agency requests or orders (unless the party is certain its tank is not the source). Second, such an action might later result in ineligibility for reimbursement under the state trust fund. However, agreeing to address the contamination might be viewed by a third-party claimant as an admission of liability. The UST owner may in some cases find it desirable to perform requested work pursuant to an administrative consent order in which all liability or responsibility for the release is specifically denied.

Lawyers representing parties claiming damages caused by USTs also face difficult choices. On the one hand, they have an incentive to allege, in an attempt to support a claim for negligence or punitive damages, that the UST owner did not strictly comply with the relevant regulations. Yet developing this evidence may be harmful to the UST owner attempting to convince state regulators that it should be eligible for trust fund reimbursement (i.e., that the UST is in "substantial compliance"). By cutting off the owner's access to the trust fund, especially if the defendant tank owner has few assets, the plaintiff may be creating a situation that ensures that the defendant will be unable to satisfy a judgment.

Tools for Resolution of UST Issues in Commercial Transactions: Uses and Limitations

Issues related to UST leaks can snowball into deal-breakers. Parties can, however, turn to several devices and techniques to salvage a deal that would otherwise dissolve because of UST-related issues.

State Trust Funds

A seller of a property with USTs can verify compliance with the prerequisites for state trust fund eligibility to demonstrate to potential purchasers that liability from discharges is minimized or quantified (i.e., potentially limited to the trust fund deductible). Similarly, a buyer may be better able to quantify or control its risks related to USTs if it can ensure that trust fund prerequisites are in place. The potential purchaser must, of course, maintain trust fund eligibility after consummation of the transaction. Lessors and lessees face similar state trust fund considerations, as do lenders. If the financial institution can determine that state trust fund prerequisites for coverage are in place, then upon foreclosure it would acquire title and be able to access the trust fund. The desirability of this approach will, of course, depend on the amount of the state trust fund's deductible and the value of the facility, among other factors.

Environmental Assessments

An environmental assessment provides information to purchasers and lenders regarding a property's contamination status and the degree of regulatory compliance. (For a more detailed discussion of environmental assessments, see Chapter 8.) Environmental assessments can be especially useful in the transfer of properties with USTs. The information contained in the assessment may allow the parties to verify compliance with state trust fund prerequisites. An assessment may also be used to establish a baseline at the time of the transfer (i.e., information on the environmental conditions existing at the time of closing, against which future changes can be judged). This may be particularly pertinent if, for example, a potential lessee is considering the acquisition of a lease on property where tanks were previously operated and wants to establish liability before commencing the lease.

Retention of a UST Consultant to Perform an Environmental Assessment

Environmental assessments and UST corrective actions should be performed by consulting firms with appropriate UST expertise. UST investigations and corrective actions often require hydrogeological and engineering expertise. Many states have certification requirements for consultants or firms installing, testing, or removing USTs. If the UST owner expects to pursue corrective action reimbursement pursuant to a state trust, the consultant must be familiar with this process, including reimbursement procedures, eligible costs, and allowable reimbursement rates. All UST-related work should be detailed in an appropriate scope of work. For example, if the client expects the consultant to be responsible for the trust fund reimbursement process, the scope of work should provide as such.

Contractual Allocation of UST Responsibilities

Information provided by the environmental assessment may allow the negotiating parties contractually to allocate known responsibilities and liabilities relating to USTs.

Acquisition

Parties negotiating the allocation of UST-related risks have a variety of options. For example, a seller unwilling to provide an open-ended warranty and indemnity related to soil contamination might perform the necessary remediation before marketing the property or consummating the transaction. Otherwise, the seller may be forced to discount the purchase price if there are perceived potential or unquantified problems.

A key warranty for a buyer considering the purchase of a property with USTs relates to the tanks' compliance with regulatory requirements. Such a warranty should be fairly straightforward. Regardless of whether such a warranty is provided, the purchaser will, of course, still consider the verification of compliance through an environmental assessment.

Another storage tank issue arises in an asset purchase involving real and personal property. The real or personal property status of USTs (or ASTs) can vary under different state property laws. The contract documents should specify whether or not tanks are to be acquired; otherwise, their ownership status may be unclear.

An indemnity that is triggered by noncompliance with environmental laws may not necessarily provide all the protection that is needed. The presence of contaminants on a property is not a violation of law. For example, minor spillage of petroleum over a long period of time may not be a specific violation of federal or state regulatory requirements. However, the contamination may devalue the property or subject it to a remediation order from the state.

Sellers and purchasers should carefully review contractual provisions addressing the scope of remediation obligations. While contractual language may require a party to remediate pursuant to a government standard or action level, this does not mean that the parcel will be entirely free of pollutants. Regulating agencies realize that it may not be possible or cost-effective to remediate a property so that every trace of contaminant is removed. The EPA and some states recognize it is not feasible (or necessarily desirable) to pump and treat hydrocarbon-contaminated groundwater to render it entirely free of pollutants. Thus, while a property may be cleaned up for regulatory compliance purposes, the presence of residual contaminants may still affect the purchase price. To address this situation, the parties should consider stating that the property will be remediated to allow "full economic use" or to its "previous condition."

Leases

There are special considerations for addressing UST issues in a lease. A lessee typically desires an appropriate warranty and indemnity regarding preexisting environmental conditions. In addition, the parties should clearly delineate who is responsible for any current and future environmental compliance and remediation issues.

For example, there are numerous requirements in the federal and state UST Technical Standards for which the owner or operator must assume responsibility. Because both the lessor and lessee are jointly liable for violations as owners or operators, lessors often have the incentive to ensure that lessees expediently address UST discharges on the leased premises. Thus, the lessor might consider provisions that allow it to address certain environmental issues if the lessee fails to provide a timely notification to it and to the relevant federal and state agencies. Without such incentives, the lessee's inaction may exacerbate minor problems or lead to trust fund ineligibility.

Alternatives to USTs: Aboveground Storage Tanks

The heightened regulations of USTs have led more and more tank operators to explore the use of ASTs. However, ASTs are also subject to regulation. The federal Spill Prevention Control and Countermeasure (SPCC) regulations[72] and state and local fire codes place certain restrictions and operational standards on ASTs. Lawyers should be aware that the EPA is considering revisions to the SPCC requirements, and Congress has considered bills that would set up a comprehensive federal regulatory program for ASTs.[73]

UST Secured Creditor Exemptions

On September 7, 1995, the EPA promulgated a final rule purporting to limit the regulatory obligations of persons maintaining indicia of ownership in a UST primarily to protect a security interest.[74] The RCRA UST regulatory requirements contain a security interest exemption that provides lenders a limited statutory exemption from cleanup liability for releases from petroleum USTs. This EPA rule may also be relevant to many state UST programs, since they often contain similar secured creditor exemptions. The EPA has expressed its belief that the recent District of Columbia Circuit Court of Appeals decision in *Kelley et al. v. EPA*, striking down the CERCLA secured creditor exemption, will not affect this rule.[75]

The September 7, 1995, rule sets forth criteria under which certain secured lenders may be exempted from the UST regulations. For example, the lender must hold an ownership interest in the UST or in the property on which the UST is located to protect its security interest.

The regulation describes circumstances under which a lender can be considered to be participating in the management of a UST property and therefore operating outside of the secured creditor exemption. For example, the regulation allows the lender, without losing the protection of the regulatory exemption, to monitor and investigate the borrower's collateral, business condition, and financial health on a regular basis. Lenders making loans on properties with USTs should ensure that their loan documents, and their operating procedures, comport with these regulations.

Notes

1. This chapter does not address aboveground storage tank (AST) issues in any detail. A number of the issues discussed in this chapter are, however, relevant to commercial transactions that involve ASTs. Note that, unlike USTs, ASTs are not typically subject to mandatory closure, investigatory, and remediation regulatory requirements. Nonetheless, some ASTs have been operated in a

manner resulting in minor spills. The accumulation of these releases might eventually draw the attention of an environmental agency or devalue the property or facility.

2. OFFICE OF TECHNOLOGY ASSESSMENTS, U.S. CONG., PROTECTING THE NATION'S GROUNDWATER 277 (1984).

3. Lund, *Changes in UST and LUST: The Federal Perspective*, 10 TANK TALK, No. 2 (March 1995) [hereinafter Lund].

4. GOV'T ACCOUNTING OFFICE, SUPERFUND INSURING UNDERGROUND PETROLEUM TANKS, 8 GAO/RECD-88-39 (Jan. 15, 1988).

5. Lund, at 5.

6. Local UST regulations are not discussed in this chapter.

7. Donald Feliciano, Groundwater Contamination from Petroleum Underground Storage Tanks and Associated Liability Issues, 1 (1985) (Cong. Res. Ser. 85-1040).

8. Ritter, *The Case for Including Petroleum under Superfund*, 3 ENVTL. F. 32 (August 1984).

9. The key CERCLA definition term excludes petroleum. 42 U.S.C. § 9601(14).

10. 42 U.S.C. §§ 6901–91(i).

11. 42 U.S.C. §§ 6901–21.

12. 42 U.S.C. § 6991b.

13. 42 U.S.C. § 6991c.

14. 42 U.S.C. § 6991b(h).

15. *Id.*

16. 42 U.S.C. § 6991b(h)(7)(A).

17. 42 U.S.C. § 6991b(6)(A).

18. 53 Fed. Reg. 37,096 (1988).

19. This chapter concentrates on USTs containing petroleum products rather than those containing other chemicals, since issues dealing with petroleum-containing USTs are more likely to arise in commercial real estate transactions.

20. 40 C.F.R. § 280.12.

21. *Id.*

22. 40 C.F.R. § 280.10.

23. *Id.*

24. *Id.*

25. *Id.*

26. 40 C.F.R. § 280.12.

27. *Id.*

28. *Id.*

29. In this chapter the term "responsible party" refers to the owner and/or operator responsible for compliance with the regulations. Also as used in this chapter, the term "owner" includes "operator," unless otherwise specified.

30. 40 C.F.R. § 280.20.

31. 40 C.F.R. § 280.20(a)(5).

32. 40 C.F.R. § 280.20.

33. *Id.* Cathodic protection may be provided by either sacrificial anode systems, in which the anode slowly erodes, or impressed current systems, which use alternating current as the power source.

34. *Id.*

35. 40 C.F.R. § 280.21. Cathodic protection used to upgrade existing USTs must be designed by a corrosion expert and meet the UST protection operations and maintenance requirements discussed above.

36. *Id.*

37. *Id.*

38. Lund, at 7.

39. 40 C.F.R. § 280 Subpart D.

40. 40 C.F.R. § 280.43.

41. 40 C.F.R. § 280.44. Pressurized piping must be equipped with an automatic line leak detector capable of detecting releases of 3 gph at 10 pounds per square inch line pressure within one hour. Further, pressurized piping must either have an annual line tightness test performed or be checked for releases every thirty days by using vapor monitoring, groundwater monitoring, interstitial monitoring, or an alternate method meeting prescribed standards or approved by the implementing agency. Existing pressurized piping should have had the required leak detection equipment in place by December 22, 1990, regardless of the tank or piping age. Different provisions apply for suction piping.

42. 40 C.F.R. § 280.50. There is an exception where the monitoring equipment is found to be defective and is immediately repaired or replaced and further monitoring does not indicate a release. Also, if inventory control data indicate a release but the following month's data fail to confirm it, no reporting is required.

43. 40 C.F.R. § 280.52.

44. *Id.*

45. 40 C.F.R. § 280.53.

46. 33 U.S.C. § 1321. The CWA provisions dealing with oil spills are beyond the scope of this chapter. Note, however, that in states with approved UST programs, UST leaks are routinely handled by state regulators. However, if a "navigable water" is also impacted by the release, federal regulators (often the Coast Guard) become involved, adding an additional layer of regulatory (and enforcement) complexity to the case.

47. 33 U.S.C. § 1362(7).

48. 40 C.F.R. § 280 Subpart F.

49. *Hark Rebecca Beckons*, L.U.S.T. LINE, Bulletin 21 (Ellen Frye ed., December 1994).

50. *The Model ASTM "Tiered" Approach*, L.U.S.T. LINE, Bulletin 21 (Ellen Frye ed., December 1994).

51. 55 Fed. Reg. 11,798 (1990).

52. 57 Fed. Reg. 6,154 (1992).

53. 40 C.F.R. § 280 Subpart 6.

54. 42 U.S.C. § 6991b(d).

55. 40 C.F.R. § 280 Subpart H.

56. Concern that small businesses with USTs would not be able to obtain or afford insurance to meet the financial responsibility requirements prompted a number of states to develop these trust funds.

57. Section 9004 of RCRA, 40 U.S.C. § 6991(c), authorizes the EPA to approve state UST programs.

58. N.J. Admin. Code § 7:14B–7.3(A).

59. UST regulations in the District of Columbia, although worded differently, also impose reporting obligations on parties other than tank owners and operators. D.C. MUN. REGS. T.T. 20 § 6202.1. These provisions are described in Witkin, *Subterranean Storage Tank News*, WASHINGTON LAWYER, at 36 (Nov./Dec. 1993).

60. Olson and Kneis, *Reporting Releases from Clients' Underground Storage Tank Systems: Should Attorneys Have the Hot Line on Speed Dial?* 21 SETON HALL L. REV. 104 (1991).

61. 42 U.S.C. § 6991c.

62. Lund, at 7.

63. State trust funds with statutory caps usually include a floor, allowing the funding mechanism to reactivate when reserves fall below a certain amount.

64. Every state trust fund maintains records that can provide a snapshot of its financial status.

65. Note that state trust funds covering ASTs may require their registration and that owners pay certain yearly fees. Because ASTs are not otherwise subject to comprehensive regulations in most states, their compliance with these trust fund prerequisites should be verified.

66. For example, the term "petroleum" could conceivably encompass substances other than motor fuels such as motor oils or solvents.

67. Some deductibles are tied to the size of the business or number of USTs. A few states have established trust funds that cover the first portion of the corrective action costs.

68. Many states address this issue by referencing the date of the trust fund's enactment and providing coverage for releases in which both the discovery and reporting of the release occurred after that date. A few states provide coverage for properties even after the USTs have been removed. Such a provision should help remove some of the stigma from properties for which former uses included USTs.

69. As a practical matter, state agency staff usually makes the initial recommendation on reimbursement claims. The board typically has neither the time nor the expertise to second-guess most decisions made at the staff level. Therefore, it is imperative transacting parties address all informal or formal requirements or requests by the state agency staff in the investigation, corrective action, or reimbursement procedures.

70. Consequently, consultants retained to conduct investigations and remediations should also be familiar with the reimbursement procedures. A state trust fund may not, for example, pay above a given rate per hour for a hydrogeologist. The eligibility of certain types of expenses is also important. It may not be clear, for example, whether the replacement of shrubbery is reimbursable.

71. This is likely because, compared to corrective action costs, very few third-party property damage and personal injury claims have been submitted in most states.

72. 40 C.F.R. § 112.

73. S. 389 was introduced in the Senate during the 103rd Congress. The chances for passage of such additional legislation with a more conservative Congress are uncertain.

74. 60 Fed. Reg. 46,692 (1995).

75. *Id.* The agency states at 46,695 n.3 that the recent decision by the U.S. Court of Appeals for the D.C. Circuit Court in *Kelley et al. v. EPA*, No. 93-1312 (Feb. 4, 1994), does not apply to or affect the rule.

CHAPTER 19

Asbestos

ANN PARISI MESSER
JOHNINE J. BROWN

Although asbestos in buildings is still an issue when real estate is financed, transferred, or managed, it is no longer likely to be a deal breaker. People understand better than they did a few years ago that removal of asbestos-containing materials (ACMs) is not required by law unless the only way to comply with permissible exposure limits is to remove the ACMs or unless the building is undergoing renovation or demolition that involves specific types and quantities of ACMs. The U.S. Environmental Protection Agency (EPA) does not recommend removal unless asbestos is damaged and could harm occupants. The EPA has published *Managing Asbestos in Place,* commonly called "The Green Book," which is the primary source of EPA guidance on the topic of managing ACMs in buildings.[1]

Asbestos needs to be treated with respect, not fear. There are Occupational Safety and Health Administration (OSHA) rules limiting workplace exposure to asbestos, but in buildings with undamaged asbestos OSHA[2] limits are not likely to be exceeded, and monitoring of indoor spaces is not required unless there is reason to suspect that limits have been exceeded.

There are EPA rules to limit asbestos emissions to outside air during renovation, demolition, and disposal. There are also new federal rules governing accreditation of workers for some asbestos projects. In addition, many states, cities, and counties have rules on operation and maintenance plans, notification of tenants and workers, use of trained workers, and a number of other issues.

While the authors have seen no statistics or studies on the topic, experience indicates that building owners and managers are less likely to violate asbestos regulations than they are to overreact to asbestos by removing it when it is still in good condition. Whether unnecessary removal of ACMs is overreaction or simply good management depends, of course, on one's perspective. Whatever one's approach, knowing the rules is useful to avoiding conflicts with the government, bad publicity, and unnecessary costs.

Background on Asbestos

Asbestos is a naturally occurring mineral that has historically been used in many construction materials for its strength, acoustical properties, and resistance to heat and corrosion. It was originally used in the manufacturing and shipbuilding industry. Later, from approximately 1950 to 1973, it was commonly used in the construction of buildings, including housing.

In 1973, after health concerns were raised about asbestos, the EPA banned the use of spray-applied insulation and fireproofing. In 1975, it banned the use of molded and wet-applied insulation. In 1978, it banned the use of consumer wall and ceiling patching compound and spray-applied decorative plaster. In 1989, the agency banned all new uses of asbestos flooring, cement products, pipeline wrap, roofing felts, specialty paper, rollboard, and millboard. A federal court vacated most of the 1989 rule, but it later issued a clarification that asbestos-containing products that were off the market when the rule was made in 1989 were still banned. In 1992, the EPA again banned these asbestos products from all new uses. Although asbestos is rarely used in commercial building products today, many existing construction materials still contain asbestos.

Where Asbestos Is Found

ACMs are present in many office buildings, shopping centers, and other commercial buildings, including multifamily residences. Unless material specifications are available for a building (and they are often unavailable), the materials in it that are suspected to contain asbestos must be assumed to contain asbestos until they are tested and shown not to contain it. Suspect materials fall roughly into three groups: surfacing materials, thermal system insulation, and miscellaneous materials. The types of materials in each group and the approximate dates of use are as follows:

- Surfacing materials, used from approximately 1935 to 1973, include: sprayed-on or troweled-on fireproofing on columns, beams, decks, shafts, walls, and ceilings; troweled-on plaster on walls and ceilings; textured paint on walls and ceilings;

sprayed-on acoustical ceiling material; sheetrock mud, also called joint compound; and stucco.

- Thermal system insulation, used from approximately 1926 to 1975, includes: insulation on pipes, boilers, and tanks; pipe fitting insulation (elbows, valves, tees, etc.); insulation on the interior and exterior of ducts; insulation on heat exchangers, blowers, and chillers; and blown-on insulation, as in attics.
- Miscellaneous materials include: suspended ceiling panels (dates of use unknown); glued-on ceiling tiles and mastic (dates of use unknown); floor tile and mastic (1920-89); linoleum and mastic (1950-89); roof felt and tar (1910-89); roof shingles (first date of use unknown, but continuing to 1974); transite siding, panels, and shingles (1930-89); and fire curtains and fire doors (1945-89).

Unless a building material is labeled as containing asbestos fibers, it is not possible to determine whether that material contains asbestos simply by looking at it or knowing the date of construction. To make a positive identification of asbestos, the material must be sampled by accredited persons trained in sampling techniques and then examined in a laboratory by trained workers using EPA-approved procedures.

Why Asbestos Is Regulated: Health Issues

Intact and undisturbed ACMs in buildings do not ordinarily pose a health risk to humans, property, or the environment. But in some unusual circumstances, such as when friable ACM cloth is exposed to air ducts, an ACM can pose a threat in an undamaged state. Because asbestos naturally occurs in rocks and dust and is used in such common manufactured items as brake linings, outdoor exposure to asbestos can be greater than indoor exposure. When ACMs in a building are in good condition and are properly managed and maintained, they are not likely to release asbestos fibers into the air. But when damaged, disturbed, or deteriorated, ACMs can become hazardous by releasing fibers into the air.

Friable ACMs—that is, ACMs that can be reduced to powder by hand pressure—are easily disturbed or damaged and are likely to release fibers into the air if squeezed or rubbed. Some very friable or damaged ACMs can release fibers simply by being touched. An example of friable asbestos is spray-applied ceiling texture. An example of nonfriable asbestos is floor tile. Nonfriable materials only release fibers into the air when they are damaged by chipping, breaking, sawing, sanding, grinding, abrading, and so forth.

When asbestos becomes airborne, it can be inhaled. When people breathe asbestos, some asbestos fibers remain in their lungs. There is some debate over this issue, but some experts believe the immune cells in the lungs are able to render most chrysotile asbestos fibers innocuous, and the majority of asbestos in American buildings is said to be chrysotile. The accumulation in the lungs of asbestos fibers that are not expelled or rendered innocuous may reduce breathing capacity and cause disease. Three specific diseases have been linked to asbestos exposure: asbestosis (a fibrous scarring of the lungs), lung cancer, and mesothelioma (a cancer of the lining of the chest or abdominal cavity). The relationship between exposure levels and health risk is complex. The studies of mesothelioma are less clear, but studies of workers with asbestosis show that the average person must be exposed to high levels of airborne asbestos fibers over prolonged periods for many hours a day to contract the disease. In the past, asbestosis was associated with asbestos mining and with spraying of asbestos on structural supports of ships and buildings, and smokers appeared to have had increased risk of lung disease from exposure to asbestos.

Currently, there is limited information about the health effects, if any, of exposure to low levels of airborne asbestos either inside or outside of buildings.[3] However, if ACMs are maintained in good condition in a building and are prevented from becoming airborne, the conditions for causing asbestosis in normal people do not exist. The EPA and OSHA assume that levels of airborne asbestos in buildings containing ACMs in good condition are below levels that present a risk to health or cause disease. For that reason, the agencies do not require indoor air monitoring or removal of undamaged asbestos unless there is reason to believe that airborne asbestos levels permitted by OSHA might be exceeded or unless there is a renovation or demolition that triggers the National Emissions Standards for Hazardous Air Pollutants (NESHAPS) requirements.

Jurisdictional Agencies and Asbestos Regulations Applying to Real Estate Transactions

The EPA

The NESHAPS,[4] which are implemented by the EPA, regulate the removal of asbestos, including control of emissions to the air and notifications to governmental authorities. These regulations apply to building renovation and demolition and require ACM removal when certain amounts of regulated ACMs (RACMs) will be disturbed. The NESHAPS also contain ACM disposal requirements for ACMs removed during renovation and demolition projects.[5] Owners of buildings containing ACMs who do not undertake renovation or demolition are not subject to NESHAPS, and there is no other federal law that directly requires the removal of ACMs from buildings other than schools.[6] This is an important rule to grasp because many people believe they must remove asbestos whenever it is present. They do not.

For purposes of NESHAPS, renovation means "altering a facility or one or more facility components in any way, including the stripping or removal of RACM from a facility component."[7] Demolition is "the wrecking or taking out of any load-supporting structural member of a facility together with any related handling operations or the intentional burning of any facility."[8] All buildings and other structures, with the exception of private homes and apartment buildings with four or fewer dwelling units, are potentially subject to NESHAPS during demolition or renovation.

Inspecting for RACMs

Not all ACMs are subject to NESHAPS emissions control and notification requirements during renovation and demolition. Only RACMs are subject to these requirements. Thus, the first thing a building owner must do when analyzing whether the NESHAPS requirements apply to a project is to inspect the building for RACMs. Materials are RACMs only if they fall into one of the following categories:

- Friable asbestos material (ACM[9] containing more than 1 percent asbestos that, when dry, can be crumbled, pulverized, or reduced to powder by hand pressure)
- Category I nonfriable ACM (including gaskets, packing, resilient floor tile or linoleum, and asphalt roofing products containing more than 1 percent asbestos) that has already become friable or that will or has been subjected to sanding, grinding, cutting, or abrading
- Category II nonfriable ACM (everything not in Category I that contains more than 1 percent asbestos that, when dry, cannot be crumbled, pulverized, or reduced to powder by hand pressure) that has a high probability of becoming or has become crumbled, pulverized, or reduced to powder by the forces expected to act on the material during renovation or demolition

Accordingly, Category I materials, such as ACM floor tiles, linoleum, gaskets, roofing compounds, and mastic, are not RACMs if they are in good condition. Because they are not RACMs, they are not subject to NESHAPS requirements for notice and emissions control. For Category I ACMs, it is important to use removal methods that do not make the materials friable; otherwise, they are subject to the

NESHAPS requirements. Thus, Category I materials should not be cut, sanded, ground, or abraded during renovation or demolition. Instead, they should be sliced, sheared, or removed with other methods that do not make them friable.

Similar precautions should be taken for Category II materials, such as ACM transite siding, that are not friable at the time of removal. If it is removed without breakage, the material is not subject to NESHAPS rules for notice and emission control.

Notification and Emissions Control

Under NESHAPS, the EPA and the appropriate state agency must receive written notice before any renovation project is started if the building contains RACMs in certain quantities.[10] Notification is required for all demolitions, however, regardless of the quantity of RACMs involved. NESHAPS emissions control rules also apply if certain quantities of RACMs are disturbed during renovation or demolition.[11]

For renovations, NESHAPS notification and emissions control requirements apply only if there is at least

- 260 linear feet of RACM on pipes;
- 160 square feet of RACM on other components; or
- 35 cubic feet of RACM, if the length or area cannot be measured or ACM has already been removed from the building components.

For example, if the renovation involves friable ceiling tile that will be damaged during removal but only 100 square feet of tile will be removed, there is not a regulated amount of RACM and the NESHAPS notification and emissions control requirements do not apply. But if 165 square feet of the same tile is removed, NESHAPS rules do apply. Individual states are allowed to have more stringent ACM regulations, so state law should always be reviewed before beginning a renovation or demolition involving ACMs.

For demolition projects NESHAPS rules require advance reporting regardless of the amount of RACM involved. However, the NESHAPS emissions control requirements apply only when there is at least

- 260 linear feet of RACM on pipes;
- 160 square feet of RACM on other components; or
- 35 cubic feet of RACM, if the length or area cannot be measured or ACM is already off of the building components.

For example, if the demolition involves 100 linear feet of friable pipe insulation, the EPA and the state must receive prior notice of the demolition project, but asbestos does not have to be removed from the building before demolition. Again, it is important to note that the state or local government may have other, more stringent requirements.

Once it is determined that NESHAPS requirements apply to the demolition or renovation, the steps to be taken depend on the individual project. In general, RACMs must be removed from the facility before being disturbed by demolition or renovation, and special procedures, such as wetting of asbestos before removing or stripping and careful handling of RACMs, must be followed to eliminate any asbestos emissions.[12]

There are, however, some circumstances where RACMs can be left in a building during demolition, although the emissions control and disposal procedures must still be followed.[13] RACMs can be left in a building during demolition in the following instances:

- The material is Category I nonfriable ACM that is not in poor condition and is not friable.
- The material is encased in concrete or other similarly hard material and is adequately wet down.
- The material was not accessible for testing and was not discovered until after demolition began and the material cannot be safely removed from the demolition debris. (However, all the asbestos-contaminated debris must be kept wet and treated as asbestos-contaminated waste.)
- The material is Category II nonfriable ACM and the probability is low that the material will become crumbled, pulverized, or reduced to powder during demolition.

Disposal

All ACMs (with a few exceptions that are discussed below) that are disturbed or removed during a renovation or demolition are potentially subject to NESHAPS disposal requirements.[14] There are three general areas governed by the disposal requirements, including (1) preventing visible emissions to outside air, (2) disposing of ACMs at a waste disposal site that meets the EPA standards for accepting ACM waste, and (3) keeping the appropriate records of the disposal.

The rules that prohibit the discharge of visible emissions to outside air during collection, processing, packaging, and transportation of ACMs also require that ACMs be kept adequately wet and sealed in leak tight containers and that ACM containers be labeled with the required warnings. These rules apply to all ACMs except for Category I nonfriable ACM waste that did not become crumbled, pulverized, or reduced to powder and Category II nonfriable ACM waste that did not become crumbled, pulverized, or reduced to powder. In addition, for demolished facilities at which RACMs were not removed because they were not discovered before the beginning of demolition, all contaminated materials must be treated as ACM waste after demolition and must be kept wet during handling and loading for transport. However, they do not have to be sealed in leak-tight containers and may be transported and disposed of in bulk.

The rules requiring disposal of ACM waste at a landfill that meets EPA qualifications apply to all ACMs except Category I nonfriable ACMs that are not RACMs. Many landfills accept asbestos because it is not a hazardous waste under the Resource Conservation and Recovery Act (RCRA). A landfill is handling asbestos waste properly if it prevents all visible emissions of asbestos fibers and covers the asbestos containers with six inches of soil or other nonasbestos materials or uses a dust suppressant daily.

The record-keeping requirements apply to all ACMs without exception. In general, the rules require that waste shipment records be kept for two years after disposal (although it is a good practice to keep these records indefinitely). The rules also require that a copy of the waste shipment record be given to the disposal site with the ACM waste shipment. In addition, if the disposal site does not return a signed copy of the waste shipment record, the rules require that the generator of the asbestos waste (either the building owner or its consultant) must report this to the EPA.

OSHA

OSHA worker protection rules for asbestos apply to employers in all types of working environments.[15] Many people think of OSHA standards as applying only to asbestos abatement workers. However, the standards also apply to the shopping mall employee, the apartment building maintenance person, and the factory worker.

New Developments

OSHA recently finalized new rules that, in general, lower the permissible exposure limit for asbestos to 0.1 fiber/cubic centimeter of air as an eight-hour time-weighted average; require building owners to keep records of known ACMs in the building and disclose the presence of ACMs to contractors, other employers, and employees in the building as well as to subsequent owners of the building; require specific worker training and worker protection for building custodial workers; create four classes of asbestos workers in the construction trade based on the type of work being done; and require specific worker protections depending on the class. These are all significant changes to the previous OSHA rules.

It is important to note that although OSHA has proposed indoor air quality standards they will not affect the way asbestos is regulated.[16] As currently written, the proposed rules would appear to require all nonindustrial employers to develop a written indoor air quality compliance program to protect workers from various air contaminants, including asbestos; implement the indoor air quality program through building inspections and maintenance; regulate air quality during renovation and demolition; and encapsulate or remove friable ACMs so that they do not enter the building's air distribution system. However, on August 10, 1994, in finalizing its new rules regarding worker safety, OSHA said that it intended these worker safety rules to cover all asbestos issues. OSHA made it clear that it will not create any new asbestos requirements in the final indoor air quality rules and will withdraw all references to asbestos that were in the proposed rules.[17]

For All Workers

In general, OSHA rules require employers to ensure that airborne levels of asbestos do not exceed permissible exposure limits (PELs). OSHA assumes that, unless testing proves otherwise, all thermal system insulation and sprayed- or troweled-on surfacing material and debris in work areas where that material is present contain asbestos. OSHA has called such material PACM. OSHA requires employers to perform initial air monitoring in all areas where the airborne asbestos concentrations exceed or can reasonably be expected to exceed PELs, and employers must establish a "regulated area" wherever airborne concentrations of asbestos or PACMs exceed or can reasonably be expected to exceed the PELs.[18] Employers must follow special worker safety rules in the regulated areas.

If an employer does not expect the airborne levels of asbestos in a building to exceed PELs, it does not have to follow OSHA requirements. OSHA assumes that, unless PACMs are present, office and commercial buildings are not likely to have asbestos exposure above the action level (that is, the level at which the employer must begin to take precautions lest permissible exposure limits be reached or exceeded).

Of course, if a building owner has reason to think airborne levels are above the OSHA action level, or simply wants the comfort of knowing they are not, the owner can have an expert perform air monitoring. Even though OSHA does not currently have a legal requirement to remove asbestos or to maintain asbestos in place, a building owner who has any employees must maintain asbestos in such a condition that it does not release fibers into the air above OSHA PELs. Once an ACM has become friable, usually it must be removed for the building owner to be sure of compliance with OSHA limits on airborne exposure. Employers must also undertake air monitoring, employee training, and other compliance activities.

One of the recent OSHA changes is that building custodial workers are now specifically covered under the general industry standards. Under these regulations, all building custodial workers who perform housekeeping operations in a building with ACMs or PACMs (including, for this purpose, thermal system insulation, sprayed-on and troweled-on surfacing materials, and asphalt and vinyl flooring installed no later than 1980) be provided with annual asbestos awareness training and be notified of the locations of the ACMs and PACMs in the building.

OSHA has also made another very important change to its rules, which require certain building owners to keep records and to notify other persons of ACMs and PACMs in their buildings. OSHA defines a building owner as any entity, including a lessee, that exercises control over the management and record-keeping functions related to the building if that building owner has employees or has other employers in the building (e.g., commercial tenants) who have employees. In general, these rules require that all building owners maintain records of all information known to the owner concerning the presence, location, and quantity of ACMs and PACMs. These records must be kept for the duration of the ownership and must be transferred to the next owner. In addition, building owners must inform all other employers in their building (e.g., commercial tenants) of the presence and location of ACMs and PACMs.[19]

For Asbestos Workers

In addition to general worker protection requirements, OSHA contains worker protection standards for employees engaged in demolition, renovation, and other construction activities where asbestos is present. These requirements include demarcation and enclosure of the area, restricted access, negative air pressure, air monitoring, protective clothing and respirators, hazard communication, and other worker protection practices. The type of practices that must be followed depends on the type of work being performed. OSHA has divided construction work into four classes, with Class I containing the most stringent worker protection requirements and Class IV containing the least strict standards. Class I work includes such activities as removal of thermal system insulation or surfacing materials. Class II work includes removal of asbestos-containing flooring materials, transite panels and siding, and roofing materials. Class III work is defined as repair and maintenance operations where ACMs or PACMs are likely to be disturbed. Class IV work includes maintenance and custodial-type work where employees come into contact with ACMs or PACMs, including activities to clean up waste and debris containing ACMs or PACMs in areas where other construction work is occurring. (All custodial work where construction activity is not taking place is covered under OSHA's general worker standards, as set out earlier.) Examples of Class IV work include cleanup after Class I, II, or III work; stripping or buffing of resilient flooring; or cleaning a surface where asbestos containing dust has accumulated.

The rules require that all Class I, II, and III work be conducted within a "regulated area," which is an area established by the employer where the applicable asbestos worker safety rules will be followed. Accordingly, for Class I, II, and III work, certain work practices must be followed regardless of the level of exposure to the workers. All other types of operations, such as Class IV operations, only need to be conducted in a regulated area if the airborne concentrations of asbestos exceed, or there is a reasonable possibility that they may exceed, the PEL.

In addition to the general industry notifications mentioned above, the construction standard also contains a new, comprehensive notification scheme. In summary, before work begins, the building owner must identify the presence, location, and quantity of ACMs and PACMs and must give the following persons notice of the same:

- The building owner's employees who work in or adjacent to the area containing an ACM or PACM
- Contractors bidding for work if their employees will work in or adjacent to areas containing ACMs or PACMs
- All other employers in the building who have employees that will be performing work within or adjacent to areas containing ACMs or PACMs
- Tenants who will occupy areas containing an ACM or PACM

In addition, any employer intending to perform work subject to the OSHA rules (who may or may not be a building owner) must identify the presence, location, and quantity of ACMs before the work is started. Employers must also give notice of the presence, location, and quantity of ACMs and PACMs and of the protective measures to be used to ensure that airborne asbestos is confined to the area to the following parties: owners of the building, employees who will perform the work, and employers of employees who will be working in adjacent areas.

Moreover, within ten days after the work is completed, the employer must give notice of the location and quantity of the remaining ACMs and PACMs in the area and of the final monitoring results, if any, to both the building owner and employers of employees who will be working in the area.

Finally, if any employer discovers ACMs or PACMs on a work site, the employer must, within twenty-four hours after discovery, report the presence, location, and quantity of the materials to both the building owner and other employers of employees working at the site.

OSHA has established additional rules for multiemployer work sites that will affect building owners. OSHA had stated that at multiemployer work sites the employees that may be exposed are not always the employees of the employer who created the hazard. As always, OSHA gave the employer who creates the hazard the duty to follow the rules. OSHA, however, has now said that an innocent employer, who has employees exposed to asbestos because of the failure of controls installed by the person who created the hazard, is required to either remove its employees from the area or comply with the applicable protection provisions to protect its employees. This standard imposes a duty on the innocent employer who is adjacent to a regulated area to take steps, on a daily basis, to ascertain the integrity of the enclosure and the effectiveness of the control methods used to ensure that asbestos does not enter that employer's work area.[20] Therefore, if an independent contractor is hired to do the renovation or demolition work, the contractor is responsible for meeting OSHA standards for its own workers as well as for maintaining the "regulated area" so that PELs are not exceeded outside that area. However, building owners are still responsible for ensuring that their workers are not exposed to high levels of asbestos during the project. This can be done by prohibiting employee access to the renovation or demolition project and by making it unquestionably clear through appropriate contract language that the independent contractor is responsible for following all OSHA requirements, enclosing and securing the work area, and performing air monitoring so that asbestos levels outside the work area never exceed the action level.

Asbestos School Hazards Abatement Reauthorization Act[21]

On November 28, 1992, the Asbestos School Hazards Abatement Reauthorization Act (ASHARA) became effective.[22] Although this law required that any asbestos inspection, design, or abatement work done in a "public" or "commercial building" would have to be done by an "accredited" person, there were not yet regulations implementing the law. All buildings except schools and residential buildings with fewer than ten units are considered public and commercial buildings. This includes all office buildings, stores, and shopping centers.

Under the law, the EPA was required to prepare a "model accreditation plan" (MAP), which would comprise the regulations to implement ASHARA. The EPA's regulations took effect on April 4, 1994. ASHARA and the MAP are collectively referred to as ASHARA for this discussion.

ASHARA requires that individuals be accredited to perform certain types of work with asbestos in public and commercial buildings. ASHARA applies to all ACMs inside a building and ACMs on the exterior of a building if they are in an exterior hallway connecting buildings, in a portico, or on an exterior mechanical system (such as heating and air conditioning). ASHARA does not apply to roofing materials or exterior siding materials.

Although ASHARA does not directly require anything of a building owner, the result of the regulations is that a building owner must use accredited asbestos workers for certain types of tasks.

Asbestos inspectors must be accredited. This is the case whether the material is suspected to be friable or nonfriable. This is also the case whether the inspection is visual, physical, or done by collecting samples. For instance, inspections that are done in anticipation of renovation or demolition must be done by an accredited inspector.

There are two exceptions that are important to a building owner. First, periodic surveillance of the type that is commonly performed by custodial or maintenance workers, limited only to visual observations, is exempt. However, if the person collected a sample or touched the material during the inspection that person would need to be accredited. Second, visual inspections done to confirm that a response action is complete do not require an accredited worker.

Project designers, contractors, and abatement workers working with friable ACMs must be accredited if they are working with ACMs that are friable or will become friable during the activity. A response action includes removal, encapsulation, enclosure, repair, and certain types of operations and maintenance (O&M) activities. (O&M activities are discussed in greater detail below.)

There is one very important exception here. If the work is "small-scale, short-duration" (SSSD) work, the project designers, contractors, and abatement workers do not need to be accredited. Examples of SSSD include: removal of small quantities of ACM insulation on pipes, beams, or above ceilings; replacement of an ACM gasket on a valve; installation or removal of a small section of drywall; installation of electrical conduits thought to be ACMs; removal of small quantities of ACMs only if required in the performance of maintenance activity not intended as ACM abatement.

However, this SSSD exemption does not apply if the person is conducting a response action for a major fiber release. A major fiber release is any uncontrolled or unintentional disturbance of ACM resulting in a visible emission that involves the falling or dislodging of more than three square or linear feet of friable ACM.

Operations and maintenance workers do not have to be accredited unless they are doing jobs that require accreditation, such as, for example, doing an ACM inspection that is more than just visual periodic surveillance or checking on a completed response action; designing a response action; conducting a response action, including a maintenance activity that disturbs friable ACM, unless the activity is exempt because it is SSSD; or conducting a response to a major fiber release episode.

Project monitors do not need to be accredited unless they are doing a task that otherwise requires accreditation. The typical jobs that a project monitor performs do not require accreditation, including acting as an agent or employee representing the building owner who is engaged to oversee a contractor's performance of a response action; monitoring a response action for compliance with contract/job specifications and regulatory requirements; performing visual audits of a job site before, during, and after a response action; and performing air monitoring as part of a response action, for purposes of clearing a response action, or to comply with state or local requirements. Although ASHARA does not require accreditation for project monitors, it does recommend that states voluntarily adopt such a program. Therefore, states' requirements will have to be reviewed to see if they are stricter than ASHARA and include mandatory accreditation for project monitors.

ASHARA is not a federal licensing program, and states will continue to license workers, as they have in the past. However, the state licensing programs will now have to require the type of training mandated under ASHARA to turn out accredited asbestos inspectors, designers, contractors, and workers. States may also adopt standards that are stricter than ASHARA, and many states already have licensing programs that meet or are stricter than the ASHARA requirements.

Building owners should be aware of the ASHARA program for two reasons. First, they will want to make sure that all contractors hired to inspect, repair, or remove asbestos are accredited. Second, they will want to review carefully the type of activities they allow their own workers to do. If the work falls into any of the categories of SSSD work, the worker will not have to be accredited. If, however, the work is not small scale and of short duration, the owner should hire an accredited contractor to do the work or send its worker through an accredited training program.

State Laws Governing Asbestos Removal in Buildings

Many states have adopted the federal NESHAPS in whole. However, some other states and local jurisdictions have adopted stricter standards. Before undertaking a demolition or renovation project where ACM is present, a building owner must review state and local laws to determine if there are additional emissions control, disposal, notification, or other procedures that have to be followed.

Real Estate Transactions

Leasing Property

There is now an OSHA requirement that building owners notify other employers in a building, including commercial tenants and prospective tenants, of the presence and location of ACMs and PACMs (thermal system insulation, sprayed- or troweled-on surfacing materials, and flooring materials) in a building.[23] There are no requirements governing what form of notice is required. However, before the rule, disclosure was typically made to current tenants in a special letter and to prospective tenants in a letter transmitting the lease for execution. The letters should be acknowledged in writing by the tenant and returned to the landlord for its files, or the landlord should retain proof of delivery.

Some cautious owners may want to address asbestos in the lease. However, if asbestos is addressed in a lease provision, a cautious tenant may not feel a simple notification about the presence and location of asbestos is enough. The tenant may demand to know how much asbestos is involved, what condition it is in, what monitoring has been done and where, what maintenance program is in place, and so forth. The tenant may then want the right to conduct monitoring of the premises or want the owner to conduct additional testing. The tenant may also want to negotiate other rights with regard to asbestos, including indemnification from the landlord for injury to health or property and the right to determine whether asbestos should be removed altogether. Put into a lease, asbestos suddenly becomes a subject of concern and negotiation and may require drafting of special and complex lease provisions. If asbestos is mentioned in a letter, the landlord is much less likely to have to negotiate and live with unnecessarily intrusive or onerous lease provisions.

Whether the owner or the tenant has the obligation to maintain asbestos below PELs depends on lease provisions and conditions of tenancy. In a multitenant building the landlord has responsibility at least for common spaces and will probably want to have and enforce an O&M program for those areas. Depending on market conditions and the tenant's sophistication, the landlord will have to decide whether it will require preapproval of all tenant improvements, so it can provide additional warnings before removal and monitor the removal, or whether the tenant should be given responsibility for ACMs. Landlord control over asbestos can be a plus by ensuring procedures that reduce the likelihood of harm, but it can also be a negative by increasing the landlord's liability for any harm that does result. It may be cost-effective to make commercial tenants responsible for ACM management because, as employers, they are already responsible for ensuring that their workers are not exposed to unpermitted levels of asbestos. However, even if it is the tenants' responsibility to manage asbestos, it is essential to require tenants to comply with all applicable laws so they do not make matters worse through poor management. In addition, even if it is the tenant's responsibility to manage ACMs, the tenant must give the building owner notice of the location of the ACMs, the protective measures to be taken, and, when the job is done, of the remaining ACMs at the site.[24]

Purchasing Property

In transactions in which the building owner has employees and is therefore subject to OSHA, the presence of ACMs and PACMs must be disclosed by the seller if the seller knows of such.[25] In other situations, the presence of ACMs should be disclosed by the seller if the seller knows of such to prevent later claims of misrepresentation or fraud, but there is no federal statute requiring such disclosure. Some state laws may require disclosure. Even when the seller discloses all that is known about ACMs on the property, almost all purchasers of commercial and industrial properties obtain environmental evaluations of the property through Phase I and II reports. Buyers obtain Phase I or II reports for three reasons: (1) to learn about the condition of the property to evaluate the cost of any required or voluntary remediation; (2) to try to qualify for the innocent purchaser defense under the Comprehensive Environmental Response, Compensation, and Liability Act (CERCLA), also known as Superfund; and (3) to satisfy lenders, who typically will not finance property without an environmental site assessment before financing. Environmental reports do not typically cover the presence of asbestos in buildings, unless asbestos is a concern and the purchaser or lender specifically requests an asbestos inspection.

There is no required format for a Phase I or Phase II report, but a generally accepted standard for environmental reports for commercial property has been embodied in the American Society for Testing and

Materials (ASTM) standards.[26] Interestingly, the ASTM standards do not include inspection of ACMs, indicating that asbestos is outside the scope of a standard environmental investigation.

However, there is a standard for asbestos inspections when dealing with multifamily residential properties. The Federal National Mortgage Association's (Fannie Mae) Conventional Selling: Environmental Hazards Management Procedures for Phase I and Phase II reports require testing for asbestos. According to Fannie Mae's guidelines, the presence of ACMs in areas accessible to tenants or employees of the building is considered an unacceptable condition, making the property ineligible for Fannie Mae financing if the asbestos cannot be secured or encapsulated and managed through routine inspection and maintenance operations.[27]

Even if asbestos is disclosed by the seller or identified through an investigation, it should not be a deal breaker as long as it can be managed in place through an O&M program. Typically the presence of asbestos is material to a deal only when there is a large quantity of friable ACMs in areas that are accessible to the tenants or the public or when friable ACMs are located in areas (e.g., ceilings without ducted air) that allow disturbance and dispersal of asbestos fibers through the building's ventilation system. Under these circumstances, careful consideration should be given to the cost of removal or management in relation to the value of the property.

Financing Real Estate Deals

Although this view was more prevalent during the 1980s, a few lenders still take the position that all ACMs should be removed from certain buildings they finance. Their usual reason is that removal ends tort liability for personal injury occurring after the date of removal or that the presence of asbestos may reduce the marketability of the real estate. However, ACMs need not always be removed, either as a legal or business matter. ACMs in good condition and properly maintained are not a health hazard and do not require removal independent of loan requirements.

An ACM removal that is not well designed or not properly performed can raise asbestos levels in a building and actually create a dangerous condition where none previously existed. Besides, asbestos performs many functions vital to the sound functioning of a building and its presence does not necessarily make a building less desirable. If ACMs are removed, they must usually be replaced with other materials, and the costs of removing and replacing ACMs will increase project costs and may adversely affect repayment of the loan.

Whether a lender decides to finance a building containing ACMs or insists on ACM removal is a business judgment based on evaluation of risks. The risks are that the costs of managing or removing ACMs and responding to ACM-related lawsuits may jeopardize repayment of the loan as well as that taking title to the building through foreclosure will make the lender the owner, making it liable for ACM management and consequently ACM-related lawsuits.

Most lenders recognize that refusing to make loans on buildings containing ACMs will result in a significant narrowing of the available loan market, since at least some asbestos products were installed in buildings until about 1989. In this light, the best course for a lender is not to take title to a building that contains confirmed or suspect ACMs without first assessing the risk, the management costs, and the effects on fair market value.

Building Inspections

ACMs take a variety of forms, including sprayed-on insulation and fireproofing, ceiling and floor tiles, drop-in ceiling panels, wall coverings, pipe and equipment insulation, exterior coverings, and roofing compounds. Asbestos cannot be positively identified by visual inspection alone. An expert should take samples of suspect material and have them analyzed. Whether destructive or intrusive sampling needs to be conducted depends on the caution of the owner or buyer and the cost involved. For example, taking roofing samples is destructive to the roof and someone will have to pay for repairs. Since roofing compounds, if they contain asbestos, are usually nonfriable, sampling is not usually necessary, although inspection for damage is wise. Looking for ACM insulation behind walls also requires destructive sampling and is not normally necessary unless the building is to be demolished or extensively remodeled.

The ACM survey proposal should be reviewed critically. When reviewing a survey proposal, one should make sure that unnecessary samples will not be taken, evidence that some materials in the structure are already known not to contain asbestos has not been ignored, and inconclusive laboratory methods have not been proposed. Unless there is a reason for testing a particular material, testing should be limited to suspected ACMs only, and then it may be further limited to damaged materials or those that are going to be disturbed or removed during renovation or demolition. Controlling the format of the ACM inspection report is important. It should give enough information about the materials to allow cost-effective follow-up. The report should, at a minimum, be in writing and include a description of the scope of the work (e.g., identification of those materials suspected to be ACMs); the location and form of ACMs; the estimated extent (linear or square footage) of ACMs; the location of samples; a statement as to how representative the samples are and why the sampling locations were chosen; the condition of the ACMs; and estimates of the costs of removal, replacement, maintenance, and demolition, if applicable.

No recommendations concerning abatement or other action should appear in the final report unless cleared with legal counsel. This is important because, in making a recommendation, the expert is interpreting the law and applying it to the facts of the situation, in this case the test results. This is a legal opinion. Once the expert's recommendations appear in the report, others who see the report (tenants, employees, lenders, investors, purchasers, or insurance companies) will take for granted that the expert is correct and expect his or her recommendations to be followed. In the event that the expert has misinterpreted the law, or legal counsel comes to a different conclusion, it can be difficult, if not impossible, and very costly, to convince the reader of the report that the expert's written recommendations are inaccurate or not required by law. An effective solution is to have the expert present his or her opinions in draft form (the copy must be stamped "draft") to the client or legal counsel before putting the report into final form.

Removal Projects

From a cost perspective, an owner should, whenever possible, remove ACMs only if friable and damaged beyond repair or encapsulation and should use the EPA notice and emissions control procedures only for RACMs. This requires determining in advance whether affected material is RACM. This also requires adopting an ACM removal procedure that will not make ACMs friable (e.g., popping off transite siding and not breaking it up).

If the amount of ACMs involved in a renovation is smaller than 260 linear feet or 160 square feet, the NESHAPS notice and emissions control procedures do not have to be followed. Separate renovation projects do not have to be aggregated under the NESHAPS, so if the building undergoes three separate renovations in one year, each smaller than 260 linear and 160 square feet, the NESHAPS notification and emissions control rules do not apply to any of the projects. However, if the removal is really one large project, it cannot be divided up to circumvent NESHAPS. Keep in mind that the NESHAPS disposal requirements apply in either case.

The savings from keeping projects small and not having to follow NESHAPS procedures and the savings from aggregating small projects should be compared. Doing only small projects one at a time may also produce cost savings by allowing the company to characterize the renovation expense as a normal operating and maintenance cost, which is immediately deductible, rather than as a capital expense, which is amortizable over time. The Internal Revenue Service views most asbestos removal costs as improvements that must be capitalized, but this view is widely criticized. The Treasury Department is currently trying to resolve this issue.[28]

Selecting the Consultant and Contractor

Choosing the right consultant and contractor to do the removal project is essential. Experienced, reputable, insured consultants and contractors reduce the risk that legal requirements will be violated, as well as the risk that the owner will be the only party with a deep pocket in the event of problems. In general, it is preferable to have a consultant do the investigation and design work and a contractor do any abatement work, with monitoring of the project by the consultant.

Consultants and abatement contractors should not be selected based solely on cost. Even if the best are more expensive, they may save money in the long run by doing the job right and not doing unnecessary work. The best way to select an asbestos consultant and contractor is to get a recommendation from building owners, consultants, legal counsel, or others who have experience with the industry. Look for well-trained, reputable, and accredited asbestos contractors and consultants. Interview the consultant and contractor to make sure you are comfortable with his or her approach and judgment. Although many states have no licensing or certification requirements for consultants, that should change under ASHARA, which requires use of accredited inspectors and project designers. On the other hand, most states already have licensing and certification programs for asbestos contractors and workers, and ASHARA now requires use of accredited asbestos contractors and workers.

Use contractors and consultants who understand the OSHA requirements applicable to the project. The consultant and contractor should also know and follow the NESHAPS notification, emissions control, and disposal requirements when they apply and should be required to identify and follow procedures that do not make ACMs friable, when feasible and cost-effective. The consultant (who usually prepares the report) must also be capable of preparing a streamlined ACM survey report that presents results in a format that is easily readable. For instance, a table format including the type, amount, and condition of ACMs and the ACM test results is more useful than the same information in a paragraph format.

In selecting a consultant and contractor, a building owner should also review the contractor's insurance policies, paying attention to the type and amount of coverage, the exclusions in the policies, and the rating of the insurance company. The building owner may want to obtain an endorsement in its favor for a particular renovation or demolition project.

The contracts with the consultant and contractor should also be carefully thought out and reviewed by an attorney, as with any other contract. Some of the more important issues to address in the contract are the consultant's and contractor's obligations to comply with all applicable federal, state, and local requirements dealing with asbestos removal; indemnification of the owner if those laws and regulations are not followed; certification that the consultant and contractor are adequately trained and accredited according to ASHARA and state and local laws; a written report after the work is complete; and the building owner's rights if the work is poorly, incompletely, or untimely performed.

Documentation

Documenting the asbestos abatement project is crucial if the building owner is later required to show that the abatement was done in accordance with the law. It is also important to know what materials were abated and what they were replaced with so that the replacement materials never again have to be tested for the presence of ACMs. Unnecessary testing can easily happen when adequate records are not kept and management personnel are no longer on the job or cannot remember what was done. The following records should be kept:

- A copy of the project manual, specifications, or both
- The determination made as to whether NESHAPS were applicable, for example, whether ACMs were Category I or II ACMs, whether they were friable or nonfriable, whether they were expected to become friable upon renovation or demolition, and whether they were in good or poor condition
- The amount of ACMs
- A description of the ACMs that were abated
- The waste shipment records and information about the removal and disposal methods, including the procedures used to keep ACMs from becoming friable
- Information on whether OSHA regulations applied to the project, including the reasonable basis for believing or not believing that airborne asbestos concentrations would exceed the action level

- A certification that the abatement took place in substantial compliance with applicable laws, regulations, and standard work practices
- A certification that replacement materials are non-ACM
- Air sampling results and air clearance certification, if air sampling was conducted
- A certificate of visual inspection signed by the contractor
- Licenses of all designers, inspectors, contractors, and consultants involved in the project

Managing Asbestos in Place

Because removal of ACMs is not required except for certain types and amounts of ACMs when doing a renovation or demolition or when nothing else will allow compliance with OSHA limits on airborne asbestos, ACMs can normally be left in place in a building. Unless a building is undergoing demolition or renovation, federal law does not require building owners to identify ACMs in their buildings (other than schools). Nor does federal law require building owners to have a program to manage asbestos in place.[29] Under OSHA, however, building owners who are also employers must avoid exposing their maintenance and other workers to unacceptable airborne concentrations of asbestos. In addition, while owners do not have a statutory obligation under federal law to protect tenants from high airborne concentrations, they may choose to have a program to manage asbestos in place to minimize common-law or contractual liabilities.

Programs designed to manage asbestos in place are called O&M programs. While the EPA recommends that buildings with ACMs have an O&M program, there is no federal law requiring this, and O&M plans are completely voluntary.[30] As with all voluntary manuals or programs, once they are created, they establish a standard of practice that can be expected by employees and tenants. Once this standard is created, noncompliance with the voluntary standard may lead to common-law claims if an injury or a threat of an injury occurs. For this reason, having a written O&M program and not following it may be worse than having no program at all.

Once a building owner decides to implement an O&M program, its first step is to identify all suspected ACMs. Suspect material in the building does not need to be tested, but if it is damaged or friable, testing provides useful information. Unfortunately, the owner of a building built in the last few years cannot assume there are no ACMs in the building, unless he or she has specifications for all construction materials. This is because not all uses of asbestos have been banned (like transite panels and roofing felts), and even after some materials were banned, some contractors still applied them, either by mistake or to use up inventory.

These are the basic steps in implementing an O&M program.

- Appoint the building engineer or manager (or other responsible employee) to be the O&M program manager. At the very least, the program manager should be trained to identify ACMs and deal with them in an O&M program. If the O&M program manager will also conduct asbestos inspections or design abatement projects, he or she will also have to be accredited under ASHARA.
- Make a written inventory of all suspected and known ACMs on the property, identify whether they are friable or nonfriable, and note their condition. If additional areas of ACMs are later identified, they must be added to the program.
- Include procedures for notifying all employees and tenants about where ACMs are located and advising them not to disturb the materials.
- Include policy statements in the program as to how tenants and employees are to handle ACMs. For instance, the building policy could be to prohibit tenants and employees from removing, drilling, cutting, abrading, or working in areas that are suspected or known to contain asbestos unless management approves the work and has the space inspected for the presence of ACMs before demolition or renovation begins.
- Provide for periodic inspections of suspected and known ACMs. Keep an inspection log noting the date and time of inspection and the condition of the ACMs.
- Include the building's policy on air monitoring. For owners with employees on the premises, remember that OSHA only requires indoor air monitoring if there is a reason to suspect that limits may be exceeded. An example would be heavily damaged sprayed-on fireproofing in an open area where the ventilation system continuously disturbs the asbestos fibers, dislodging and dispersing them into indoor air.
- State when ACMs in the building will be removed. For instance, the O&M plan might state that ACMs in good condition will be managed in place and that damaged ACMs will be repaired. Alternately, the O&M plan might state that ACMs in good condition will be managed in place until they become damaged or a tenant space becomes vacant, whichever occurs earlier, at which time the ACMs will be removed. Note that even though ACMs do not have to be removed, once friable ACMs are damaged, they should be repaired, encapsulated, or

removed to ensure compliance with OSHA PEL requirements and to minimize liability.

- Document all ACM removal, clearly indicating the amount, nature, and location of materials removed. It is very important to keep a running inventory of ACMs, noting removal of ACMs and replacement with non-ACM material. Keeping a record will eliminate the need for further unnecessary sampling.
- Include a policy statement about whether only qualified asbestos contractors will be allowed to work with asbestos in the building. If staff is qualified to work with ACMs, the O&M plan should contain information about the NESHAPS and OSHA standards for renovations and the ASHARA standards for accreditation.
- Provide for employee training for custodial and maintenance staff to instruct them in the use of the manual, the nature of ACMs, and the location of ACMs in the building. Training should also inform affected employees how to avoid disturbing ACMs while performing normal duties, how to identify and report any evidence of damaged ACMs, and how employees should handle minor disturbances of ACMs. Training records should be thoroughly documented.

Potential Liability for Asbestos

Building owners and managers may be liable to the government for violations of federal, state, and local laws. They may be liable to employees, guests, and tenants for personal injury and property damage. Building owners may also be liable to successor owners when they transfer property containing ACMs.

Owners may have recourse for building damage from asbestos and may be able to bring third-party claims against manufacturers if sued for personal injury or property damage. Given judicial decisions on the Superfund law, lenders probably have no statutory liability for asbestos in property securing a loan, although if they foreclose on property containing ACMs, they have all the responsibilities of any other property owner.

Claims Brought Against Building Owners

An owner engaged in a demolition or renovation project involving RACMs who does not follow the notification, emissions control, or disposal requirements under NESHAPS might face a civil enforcement action under the Clean Air Act,[31] with penalties of up to $25,000 per day of violation. If false statements are made in the required notifications to the EPA, penalties include fines of up to $10,000 and imprisonment for up to six months. Knowing violators of NESHAPS are subject to a fine of $25,000 per day of violation and imprisonment for up to one year. The EPA has been known to bring such enforcement cases against both property owners and the contractors performing the work, and even against consultants who monitor the abatement.[32]

The Clean Air Act has a citizen's suit provision allowing citizens to bring claims for violations of NESHAPS rules.[33] Such claims are rare, however, because they must allege either ongoing or intermittent violations of NESHAPS; past violations are not actionable.[34]

Personal injury lawsuits brought by affected building occupants or workers against building owners for exposure to asbestos products also are rare. This is probably because such claims are difficult to prove in light of the long exposure periods required to produce asbestos-related disease and the presence of multiple sources of asbestos exposure, both indoors and outdoors.

A building owner may, as a landlord, face liability in tort if ACMs on its property were dangerous (e.g., damaged and friable, causing excursions of OSHA limits) and it knew about the condition but failed to disclose it.[35] As to common areas, the landlord may be held responsible if it fails to warn tenants of dangers in common areas or if it fails to exercise reasonable care in maintaining the common areas of a building in a safe condition.[36] Therefore, warning tenants of the presence of asbestos may limit potential liability for asbestos-related injuries.

Landlords may also have liability based on lease provisions. Some courts have held that, because the landlord, under the lease, was required to keep the premises in a safe condition in compliance with all laws, the landlord was required to pay when asbestos had to be removed from a tenant's space before the tenant undertook renovations necessary to sublease the space.[37] However, at least one court has held the tenant responsible for the cost of removing the asbestos based on the terms of the lease.[38]

Owners who sell their property must also consider tort liability for personal injuries incurred after the transfer of property if they had actual or constructive knowledge of a dangerous condition and failed to disclose its existence to the purchaser. The general legal principal is that a seller is not liable for personal injuries sustained after transfer if the seller disclosed his or her knowledge of the existence of a property condition that presented an unreasonable risk.[39] Disclosure should limit the seller's liability.

Property owners may also incur other forms of liability resulting from the sale of property if the presence of asbestos is not disclosed. Such actions include claims for business losses or abatement costs based on theories such as fraudulent concealment and breach of warranty of habitability. Breach of warranty of habitability is a doctrine applicable to residential sales, but some courts have refused to expand the doctrine to protect buyers of commercial property.[40] While the doctrine of fraudulent concealment of defects may also be used against a seller of real property, the seller cannot be guilty of fraudulent concealment unless the seller or the seller's representative makes a false statement for the purpose of inducing the purchase of the property. So silence alone should not be the basis for fraud.[41]

Another potential form of liability for real property owners involves failure to make adequate disclosure to the U.S. Securities and Exchange Commission (SEC) if the real estate is part of a real estate investment trust (REIT) or a real estate mortgage investment conduit (REMIC). In a REIT or REMIC, properties are pooled and security interests in the pool are sold to investors. The SEC requires environmental disclosures in several sections of a prospectus for a REIT or REMIC. Recently, the SEC has increased emphasis on strict disclosure of all environmental conditions, including the presence of asbestos.[42] If the property is significantly impaired by the presence of asbestos so that there is a material impact on the value of the investment, investors may have a cause of action for securities fraud against the REIT or REMIC if the offeror did not adequately disclose the asbestos liability.[43]

Claims Brought by Building Owners

Building owners have brought claims against asbestos manufacturers for losses arising out of asbestos on their property, asking for costs for investigating, sampling, removing, and replacing ACMs and for lost profits, lost rentals, and relocation costs. These claims have been brought under a number of theories.

Owners have attempted to bring cost recovery claims against manufacturers to pay for the cost of removing asbestos from their buildings using the Superfund law, but to date this theory has not been successful. Asbestos is a hazardous substance under CERCLA, 40 C.F.R. Section 302.4. Courts, however, have rejected the notion that the sale of asbestos products for use in buildings is a "disposal" of a hazardous substance for purposes of the law.[44]

Owners have had more success bringing property damage claims for asbestos-related damages. Some courts have held that property damage occurs when the air is contaminated by asbestos and the building owner incurs repair or replacement costs.[45] Other courts have found that the diminution in value of the building resulting from the cost of removing asbestos was enough to support a property damage claim.[46]

Strict product liability claims also have been brought by property owners to recover economic losses from the presence of asbestos. These claims allege, in general, that the defendant sold a defective product that was unreasonably dangerous to the user and the product caused injury to a person or property. Manufacturers have defended on the ground that the damages constitute "economic harm," which is not recoverable. Many courts, however, have held that the damages are not purely economic in nature and have allowed recovery.[47]

Industry has also fought these claims on a number of theories, including statute of limitations and repose defenses. Most states have statutorily defined limitations periods for bringing product liability claims. Depending on which "date of loss" theory the court applies, it is quite possible that the statute of limitations will have run out on an asbestos claim. For instance, if the court holds that the date of loss is the date of installation, a claim for damages resulting from the removal of asbestos twenty years after it was installed may be time barred.

Insurance Issues

If a building owner ever carried insurance that covered liability for property damage or personal injury from asbestos, it must notify its insurers about the presence of asbestos. When that notice is to be given can be answered by reference to the individual insurance policy. Usually an insured must give notice of an occurrence as soon as practicable. Whether there is an occurrence depends on whether there is now a claim of injury or whether such a claim is likely to be made. Even if notice to insurers is not currently required because there is no occurrence, insureds have a good faith obligation to disclose material facts regarding risks either when applying for insurance or renewing an existing policy.

Clients should locate all insurance policies extending as far back in time as possible. Insurance companies are frequently unable to locate copies of policies they wrote many years ago. So it is imperative to save all insurance policies and even records of payment and other correspondence with the insurance company, in case the insured is called on to prove coverage. Although comprehensive general liability (CGL) policies covering asbestos claims are now virtually, if not actually, impossible to secure, older policies may cover losses from asbestos. Furthermore, even though a policy may not explicitly cover asbestos, if the policy does not have an asbestos exclusion (or a pollution exclusion that includes asbestos), it could arguably cover losses from asbestos-related injuries. Furthermore, even policies that have pollution exclusions have been held to provide coverage for pollution in some circumstances.

If a building owner is sued for bodily injury and has a typical CGL policy, a prerequisite to coverage is an occurrence. Because asbestos-related diseases manifest themselves over long periods of time, it has been difficult for courts to agree on the date of the occurrence. There are several "date of occurrence" approaches taken by the courts, including the date of exposure to asbestos;[48] the date the injury manifested itself;[49] the date of exposure through the date of manifestation of the injury;[50] the date the actual injury existed in the body (this could be a long time before the date of manifestation);[51] and both the time of exposure and the time of manifestation, but nothing in between.[52]

There are other issues in handling personal injury or property damage claims arising from asbestos, including whether asbestos-related damages are "property damage" within the meaning of the policy. Courts have held that they are.[53] Once property damage is established, other consequential losses, including removal and replacement costs, may also be covered.[54]

Resources

Bureau of National Affairs. *Environmental Due Diligence Guide*. Washington, D.C.: Bureau of National Affairs (1992, updated through 1995).

U.S. Environmental Protection Agency. "Asbestos NESHAP Clarification of Intent." *Federal Register* 58 (October 5, 1993): 51,784.

—. "Asbestos NESHAP Clarification Regarding Analysis of Multi-Layered Systems." *Federal Register* 59 (January 5, 1994): 542.

—. *Guidance for Controlling Asbestos-Containing Materials in Buildings*. June 1985.

—."Interpretive Rule for Roof Removal Operations under the Asbestos NESHAPS." *Federal Register* 59 (June 17, 1994): 31,157.

—. *Managing Asbestos in Place: A Building Owner's Guide to Operations and Maintenance Programs for Asbestos-Containing Materials*. July 1990.

Notes

Portions of this chapter first appeared in *Shopping Center Legal Update*, Volume 14, Number 3, and are reprinted with permission of the International Council of Shopping Centers, Inc.

1. U.S. EPA, MANAGING ASBESTOS IN PLACE: A BUILDING OWNER'S GUIDE TO OPERATIONS AND MAINTENANCE PROGRAMS FOR ASBESTOS-CONTAINING MATERIALS, July 1990.

2. In this chapter OSHA refers to the Occupational Safety and Health Administration or the Occupational Safety and Health Act, as appropriate to the context.

3. The most recent EPA study on the health risks of asbestos in buildings was conducted by Health Effects Institute-Asbestos Research in 1991.

4. 40 C.F.R. § 61.140 *et seq.* The national emissions standards are promulgated under the Clean Air Act, § 112, 42 U.S.C. § 7412.

5. 40 C.F.R. § 61.150 *et seq.*

6. States and local jurisdictions may have more stringent requirements.

7. 40 C.F.R. § 61.141.

8. *Id.*

9. However, lawyers need to check state law to be sure that the definition of ACM is the same as the definition under federal law. The more stringent state definition controls.

10. 40 C.F.R. § 61.145(a) and (b).

11. 40 C.F.R. § 61.145(a) and (c) and § 61.150.

12. *See* 40 C.F.R. § 61.145(c) (Procedures for asbestos emission control).

13. 40 C.F.R. § 61.145(c)(1).

14. 40 C.F.R. § 61.150 *et seq.*

15. 29 C.F.R. § 1910.1001 *et seq.* and 1926.1101 *et seq.*

16. 59 Fed. Reg. 15,968 (1994).

17. 59 Fed. Reg. 40,964 (1994).

18. The PELs are: the eight-hour time-weighted average (TWA) limit of 0.1 fiber/cubic centimeter of air, or the excursion limit of 1.0 fiber/cubic centimeter averaged over a thirty-minute sampling period in the work area. 29 C.F.R. §§ 1910.1001(c) and 1926.1001(c).

19. 29 C.F.R. § 1910.1001(j).

20. 29 C.F.R. § 1926.1101(d) *et seq.*

21. The section discussing ASHARA requirements is reprinted, with permission, from an article that appeared in the Fall/Winter 1994 issue of SHOPPING CENTER LEGAL UPDATE, Volume 14, Issue 3, published by the International Council of Shopping Centers.

22. In 1986, Congress enacted the Asbestos Hazard Emergency Response Act (AHERA or TSCA Title II), mandating a regulatory program to address asbestos in schools and requiring accreditation of certain asbestos workers. In 1990, Congress amended AHERA to extend some of the accreditation requirements to persons performing asbestos work in public and commercial buildings. The amended law is ASHARA. (15 U.S.C. § 2641 *et seq.*) ASHARA did not become effective until November 28, 1992. By creating the "model accreditation plan" (MAP), the EPA promulgated the regulatory changes that implement ASHARA for public and commercial buildings. (59 Fed. Reg. 5,236 (1994).)

23. 29 C.F.R. § 1901.1001(j).

24. 29 C.F.R. § 1926.1101(k).

25. 29 C.F.R. § 1901.1001(j).

26. ASTM E 1528a-93 STANDARD PRACTICE FOR ENVIRONMENTAL SITE ASSESSMENTS: TRANSACTION SCREEN PROCESS and ASTM E 1527a-93 STANDARD PRACTICE FOR ENVIRONMENTAL SITE ASSESSMENTS: PHASE I ENVIRONMENTAL SITE ASSESSMENT PROCESS.

27. Fannie Mae's procedures are published in BNA, ENVIRONMENTAL DUE DILIGENCE GUIDE, § 131.801 (1992, updated through 1995).

28. *See Environmental Cleanup Costs: Administrative or Legislative Resolution of Problem Unlikely in Near Future*, 35 TAX MGMT. MEMORANDUM 65 (1994); John S. Ross, *Environmental Cleanup Costs: Legislation Solution Unlikely; Taxpayers Await Administrative Action by IRS*. 9 TAX MGMT. REAL EST. J. 216 (1993).

29. Some states may require operations and maintenance programs under certain circumstances, and the law of the state in which the building is located should be consulted.

30. U.S. EPA, MANAGING ASBESTOS IN PLACE: A BUILDING OWNER'S GUIDE TO OPERATIONS AND MAINTENANCE PROGRAMS FOR ASBESTOS-CONTAINING MATERIALS, July 1990.

31. 42 U.S.C. § 7413.

32. United States v. Geppert Bros., Inc., 638 F. Supp. 996, 24 ERC 1609 (E.D. Pa. 1986).

33. 42 U.S.C. § 7604(a).

34. *See* Gwaltney of Smithfield, Ltd. v. Chesapeake Bay Foundation, Inc., 484 U.S. 49, 108 S. Ct. 376 (1987), which construed similar provisions under the Clean Water Act.

35. Many states have adopted the RESTATEMENT (SECOND) OF PROPERTY § 17.1 (1977), Undisclosed Dangerous Conditions Known to a Landlord, which states that

> [a] landlord who conceals or fails to disclose any condition, whether natural or artificial, which involves unreasonable risk of physical harm to persons on the leased property and which exists when the tenant takes possession, is subject to liability to the tenant . . . for physical harm caused by the condition after the tenant has taken possession if: (a) the tenant does not know or have reason to know of the condition or the risk involved; and (b) the landlord knows or has reason to know of the condition, realizes or should realize the risk involved, and has reason to expect that the tenant will not discover the condition or realize the risk.

36. *See* RESTATEMENT (SECOND) OF PROPERTY §§ 17.3, 17.4 (1977).

37. Wolf v. 2539 Realty Associates, 560 N.Y.S. 2d 24 (N.Y. App. Div. 1990), and Rapid-American Corp. v. 888 7th Avenue Assocs. Ltd. Partnership, 151 Misc. 2d 966, 574 N.Y.S. 2d 447 (N.Y. Sup. Ct. June 19, 1991).

38. *See* Brown v. Green, 20 Cal. Rptr. 2d 251 (Cal. Ct. App. 1993).

39. *See* RESTATEMENT (SECOND) OF TORTS §§ 352, 353.

40. La Placita Partners v. Northwestern Mut. Life Ins. Co., 935 F. 2d 270 (6th Cir. Ohio), *aff'd* June 19, 1991 (the seller of an office building had no duty to disclose the presence of asbestos where the buyers were sophisticated developers who conducted inspections of the property before the purchase). *See also* Hopkins v. Hartman, 101 Ill. App. 3d 260, 427 N.E. 2d 1337 (4th Dist. 1981).

41. *See* Perlmutter v. U.S. Gypsum Co., 4 F. 3d 864 (10th Cir. (Colo.) Sept 3, 1993).

42. ABA 1993 Annual Meeting, Toxic & Hazardous Substances & Environmental Law Committee Program, New York, August 9, 1993, Remarks of Richard Y. Roberts, Commissioner, U.S. Securities and Exchange Commission; *Environmental Disclosure and SEC Reporting Requirements*, 17 DEL. J. CORP. L. 483 (1992).

43. *See* Steiner v. J.F. Baxter, No. 89 809 (D. Colo. May 9, 1989); Western Federal Sav. Bank v. Western Office Partners, Ltd., No 86 CV 1341 (Denver Dist. Ct. Feb. 8, 1989).

44. Prudential Ins. Co. of America v. U.S. Gypsum, 29 ERC 1424, (D.C. N.J., No. 87-4738, March 28, 1989).

45. SSM Health Care v. Armstrong Contracting & Supply Corp., No. 85CV592 (Wis. Cir. Ct., Dane County, June 15, 1989).

46. *Asbestos Insurance Coverage Cases*, No. 1072 (Ca. Super. Ct. Aug. 29, 1988).

47. *See* Cinnaminson Township Bd. of Educ. v. U.S. Gypsum Co., 552 F. Supp. 855 (D.N.J. 1982).

48. Insurance Co. of North America v. Forty-Eight Insulations, Inc., 633 F. 2d 1212, (6th Cir. 1980), *clarified*, 657 F. 2d 814 (6th Cir.), *cert. denied*, 454 U.S. 1109 (1981).

49. Eagle-Picher Indus., Inc. v. Liberty Mutual Ins. Co., 682 F. 2d 12 (1st Cir. 1982), *cert. denied*, 460 U.S. 1028 (1983).

50. Keene Corp. v. Insurance Co. of North America, 667 F. 2d 1034 (D.C. Cir. 1981), *cert. denied*, 455 U.S. 1007 (1982).

51. American Home Products Corp v. Liberty Mutual Ins. Co., 748 F.2d 760 (2d Cir. 1984).

52. Zurich Ins. Co. v. Raymark Indus., Inc., 118 Ill. 2d 23, 514 N.E. 2d 150 (1987).

53. *Asbestos Insurance Coverage Cases*, No. 1072 (Ca. Super. Ct. Aug. 29, 1988).

54. St. Paul Fire & Marine Ins. Co. v. Sears, Roebuck & Co., 603 F. 2d 780 (9th Cir. 1979).

CHAPTER 20

Lead-Based Paint

CATHERINE A. POTTHAST

Most lawyers assume that lead-based paint is a concern only to property owners or tenants in low-income inner-city rental dwellings. Legislation passed by Congress in 1992, however, reaches far beyond the landlord-tenant context and affects buyers and sellers of real property, real estate agents, construction workers, contractors, and home inspectors. The purpose of this chapter is to provide an introduction to federal, state, and local regulation of lead-based paint in housing, with emphasis on the impact of such regulation on real estate transactions.

Lead is a naturally occurring element that has been used as an additive in paints, solders, plumbing fixtures, ammunition, gasoline, and other products. Concern about the health effects of lead has led to a variety of federal, state, and local regulations. According to the Centers for Disease Control and Prevention (CDC), there is no established safe level of lead in the human body. It has long been reported that high levels of lead exposure can result in serious disability and death. Research conducted since the early 1980s has concentrated on the effects of low levels of lead exposure. Among the reported health effects of lead exposure are damage to the brain and nervous system, interference with the formation of red blood cells, kidney damage, reproductive system damage, hearing impairment, learning disabilities, and motor coordination impairment.[1] Children under six years of age are of special concern because their nervous systems are developing and thus they are more susceptible to the adverse effects of lead. Children tend to absorb lead more readily than adults, and their normal hand-to-mouth activity increases the likelihood of lead ingestion through dust or chipping paint.[2] Recent studies have also identified pregnant women as being at special risk because lead passes through the placenta to a developing fetus.

A variety of pathways of lead ingestion have been identified. Lead was used for many years as a gasoline additive, and residual lead fallout from gasoline or industrial sources remains in many soils. Lead can be ingested through diet, canned foods, dust inhalation, water, and a variety of other sources. Because lead in old house paint is often highly concentrated, paint has been identified as one of the more significant sources of lead ingestion in both children and adults.[3] Although most health officials previously assumed that the pathway for lead ingestion from house paint was primarily from eating flaking chips of paint, the focus has recently shifted to concern over lead dust generated by paint removal, deteriorating surfaces, or friction against painted surfaces such as doors and windows.[4]

In the past, lead was used as a pigment and drying agent in alkyd oil-based paint. In the late 1960s and early 1970s, many states banned the use of lead-based paint in residential dwellings.[5] In 1971, Congress prohibited the application of lead-based paint in federally assisted residential housing, and in 1978, the Consumer Product Safety Commission (CPSC) banned the sale of lead-based paint for residential use. Most manufacturers, however, had previously ceased production of lead pigments by the late 1940s and early 1950s, when titanium replaced lead as a paint base.[6]

The CPSC has noted that lead-based paint is most often present on woodwork, doors, and windows, although it may be found on any interior or exterior surface. The regulatory authorities disagree as to the number of homes in this country that likely contain lead-based paint. The CPSC estimates that about two-thirds of the homes built before 1940 and one-half of all homes built between 1940 and 1960 contain heavily leaded paint and advises that some homes built after 1960 may also contain lead-based paint.[7] The National Lead Information Center, an information clearinghouse established by Congress, advises that "any house or apartment built before 1978 may contain lead-based paint. Most homes built before 1960 contain lead-based paint. Lead-based paint produced before 1960 contains higher concentrations of lead than paint manufactured in later years."[8] The U.S. Department of Housing and Urban Development (HUD) estimates that 75 percent of the 17 million privately owned and occupied homes constructed before 1980 contain lead-based paint.[9]

Until recently, regulation of lead paint issues had for the most part been left to local health authorities. Baltimore City has maintained a public health program designed to prevent childhood lead poisoning since the 1930s. By the 1950s, other major cities, including Boston, New York, Chicago, and New Orleans, had established active public health programs as well.[10]

Most local public health programs or regulations were founded on the assumption that children were exposed to lead primarily through chewing on painted wood or eating flaking paint chips in deteriorated houses. A typical public health program requires pediatricians to identify children likely to be at risk for lead poisoning and to arrange periodic screening for the presence of lead or lead byproducts in the children's blood. Lead poisoning is a reportable disease under many state health laws.[11] Accordingly, many states require a physician to notify the local health department upon finding an elevated blood lead level. The local health department, in turn, typically assigns a health specialist to monitor the child's medical status and assigns an environmental investigator to ascertain the source of the child's lead exposure.

Local housing or health department regulations typically prescribe housing quality standards. Many such codes do not prohibit existing lead-based paint but instead contain prohibitions against flaking lead paint or lead paint determined to present hazards on "biting surfaces" accessible to children.[12] Upon finding that a lead paint violation exists that presents a health hazard to children, many local health authorities are authorized to issue a violation notice to the property owner, requiring that the property be abated in accordance with local or state requirements. In some states the abatement regulations have changed in response to research developments.

Before the late 1980s, lead paint abatement commonly involved burning, scraping, or sanding of lead paint from "biting surfaces" or walls below the four-foot level. Medical research studies published in the mid-1980s began to note that these traditional abatement methods tended to worsen children's lead levels and created health hazards by spreading lead dust throughout a dwelling.[13] As a result, some cities and states have updated their abatement regulations to prohibit sanding, scraping, and burning of painted surfaces.[14] Detailed worker safety regulations applying to abatement, construction, and renovation work have also been promulgated in some states.[15] The Occupational Safety and Health Administration (OSHA) recently promulgated national worker safety standards governing lead in the construction and renovation industries.[16] Nevertheless, most jurisdictions either have no detailed instructions for lead abatement or have not changed the earlier local legislation that authorizes, or in some instances requires, abatement using hazardous methods.

Local public health programs that identify and monitor lead-poisoned children have been applauded as major steps toward increasing public awareness of lead poisoning prevention and toward the early identification and treatment of blood lead elevations. Nevertheless, this type of public health program has been criticized by many advocates in that it is reactive rather than proactive; unless a child is first identified as having an elevated blood lead level, no medical or environmental intervention is initiated. Perhaps due in part to these concerns, the medical community, through the CDC, has periodically lowered the definition of "elevated" blood lead levels.

Lead in blood is measured in micrograms per deciliter (ug/dl). In 1971, the CDC defined an elevated blood lead level in children to be 40 ug/dl. In 1978, the threshold was lowered to 30; in 1985, the threshold was lowered to 25; and in 1992, the current standards were promulgated. The current standards establish five classes of blood lead elevations. A blood lead level below 9 ug/dl is considered normal. Blood lead levels between 10 and 14 are considered a Class IIA elevation. No specific medical intervention is recommended for children in this class, but the CDC recommends that if a large percentage of children are identified in a community with lead levels in this range, community-wide childhood lead poisoning prevention activities should be initiated. A child with a blood lead level between 15 and 19 is considered a Class IIB, and the CDC recommends nutritional and educational intervention and more frequent screening of children in this class. Children with blood lead levels between 20 and 44 are considered Class III and require environmental evaluation, housing remediation, and a medical evaluation to assess the need for pharmacologic treatment of lead poisoning. Children with blood lead levels between 45 and 69 (Class IV) will need both medical and environmental interventions, including chelation therapy. Children whose blood lead levels are over 69 present a medical emergency (Class V) requiring immediate medical and environmental management.[17]

There has been disagreement on the number of children estimated to have blood lead levels in excess of the 1992 thresholds established by the CDC. One recent study estimated that nationally nearly 9 percent of children under age five (1.7 million children) have blood lead levels exceeding the CDC "threshold of concern" of 10 ug/dl.[18] The incidence was noted to be much higher for urban minority children (36 percent).[19] Prior studies had noted that children living in older housing containing deteriorated paint were more likely to suffer blood lead elevations than those living in housing maintained in good condition.[20]

The revised definition of elevated blood lead levels has led to earlier public health intervention, but it has drastically increased the number of children entering the system and the cost to local regulatory agencies. The revised standards have also raised concern among property owners and managers concerning liability exposure.

Personal Injury Litigation

The downward revision of the definition of lead poisoning has prompted an explosion in the number of personal injury claims alleging lead poisoning. To date, most of the litigation surrounding childhood lead poisoning has been filed by tenants against owners and managers of residential rental properties. Historically, most of the personal injury litigation, and most reported decisions, have been concentrated in jurisdictions that maintain active screening programs to detect, monitor, and prevent childhood lead poisoning.[21]

As more states adopt mandatory screening requirements, the number of claims will likely continue to increase. Moreover, passage of the federal legislation described later in this chapter, which requires that lead paint warnings be furnished to buyers and prospective tenants, will likely increase the number of claims brought outside of the landlord-tenant context.

The typical lead paint complaint against a rental property owner contains allegations founded on theories of negligence,[22] strict liability,[23] breach of express or implied warranties,[24] nuisance, violations of state consumer protection acts,[25] or various misrepresentation theories.[26] Jury verdicts in favor of tenants in some cases have been unusually high.[27] In response to the explosion of claims and the severity of claimed damages, many insurers have added lead paint exclusions to insurance policies, which exclude liability insurance coverage for bodily injury or property damage caused by lead or lead paint.[28]

Most personal injury cases allege that the property owner was negligent in failing to inspect and test for the presence of lead-based paint, failing to abate lead-based paint hazards, failing to maintain the property in good condition without flaking or chipping paint, or failing to warn tenants of the likely existence of lead-based paint. Negligence claims have been made based on the property owner's alleged failure to comply with statutes, ordinances, or housing codes. Even those property owners who have engaged in lead testing or removal efforts have been sued on the theories that the abatement itself was conducted in a negligent manner or that the property owner or abatement contractor failed to comply with local regulations or safe practices during the abatement process. Most of these cases involve allegations of inadequate postabatement cleanup of lead dust or allegations that the property owner and contractor either failed to relocate the tenants or failed to ensure that children were absent from the home during the abatement efforts.

Most jurisdictions recognize a "notice" defense to lead poisoning allegations. Some cases have been successfully defended on the ground that the property owner demonstrated that he or she did not know, or had no reason to know, of the presence of lead-based paint hazards in the property.[29]

Although most liability claims have been brought by tenants, there have been a number of cases filed between buyers and sellers of property.[30] Many of the reported decisions in this area concern federally owned or assisted housing subject to federal regulation.[31] In 1971 Congress enacted the Lead-Based Paint Poisoning Prevention Act,[32] which, among other measures, authorized HUD to issue regulations prohibiting the use of lead-based paint in residential structures constructed or rehabilitated by the federal government or supported by federal funding.[33] If, for example, a private landowner is in the Section 8 program and receives federal housing assistance funds, the federal regulations may be triggered.[34]

In addition, lead paint-related suits have been filed against inspectors of residential housing, treating physicians, and lead pigment manufacturers. Workers' compensation claims in the painting, renovation, and construction industries are not uncommon.

Title X: Federal Regulation of Lead Paint in Residential Transactions

In October 1992 Congress passed the Residential Lead-Based Paint Hazard Reduction Act (commonly referred to as Title X), which represents Congress's first attempt at regulation of lead paint issues in purely private transactions.[35] The salient feature of the act, as it concerns private transactions, is the requirement that a lead warning be furnished to all tenants and contract purchasers of residential property constructed before 1978. The act creates a statutory cause of action against property owners and real estate agents who knowingly fail to comply with the notification provisions. These notice provisions are scheduled to go into effect in 1995. At this writing, the final regulations under the act have not been released.

The act attempts to establish an aggressive national strategy aimed at eliminating lead-based paint hazards in both private and public housing as expeditiously as possible.

Public and Assisted Housing

Title X establishes grants for state and local governments, which are authorized to use the funds for testing or abating certain housing, training workers, monitoring worker safety, and pursuing a variety of other measures.[36] The act establishes a timetable for conducting risk assessments and beginning interim lead hazard control measures in housing receiving federal assistance. Priority is given to housing constructed before 1960, and full implementation of the requirements for housing constructed between 1960 and 1978 is required by the year 2002. When federal funds are provided for rehabilitation efforts, abatement is required.

The act also amends federal statutes to ensure that program funds are available for evaluation and reduction of lead-based paint hazards in housing receiving federal assistance under a variety of existing federal programs. Among the federal programs affected are the HOME investment partnerships under the Cranston-Gonzalez National Affordable Housing Act; the HOPE for public and Indian housing home ownership program established under the United States Housing Act of 1937; Section 8 rental assistance programs; and FHA-insured home improvement loan programs, rehabilitation loan programs, multifamily housing loans, and rural housing loan programs.

The act establishes a schedule for the inspection and abatement of federally owned housing and requires inspection for lead-based paint hazards before the sale of any housing constructed before 1978. If the housing was constructed before 1960, lead hazards must be abated before disposition. The effective date for the inspection and abatement requirements is January 1, 1995. The results of such inspections must be made available to prospective purchasers and must identify the presence of lead-based paint and lead-based paint hazards on a surface-by-surface basis.

The act requires federal agencies to issue guidelines for the conduct of federally supported work, including risk assessments, inspections, interim controls, and abatement of lead-based paint hazards.[37]

Task Force and Appraisal Guidelines

The act creates an interagency task force on lead-based paint hazard reduction and financing, composed of representatives from HUD, FHA, the Department of Veteran Affairs, the Federal Home Loan Mortgage Corporation, the Federal National Mortgage Association, the U.S. Environmental Protection Agency (EPA), and private representatives in the construction industry, lenders, landlords, tenants, real estate agents, insurers, and local government representatives. This task force is directed to make recommendations on a variety of subjects including: "adjusting appraisal guidelines to address lead safety"; "revising guidelines, regulations, and educational pamphlets issued by HUD and other federal agencies relating to lead-based paint poisoning prevention"; and "incorporating risk assessments or inspections for lead-based paint as a routine procedure in the origination of new residential mortgages."[38]

Required Disclosures in Residential Transactions

HUD and the EPA jointly issued proposed regulations governing the disclosure of lead hazards in the purchase, sale, or lease of "target housing." As of this writing, final regulations have not been issued but are scheduled to go into effect in October 1995.[39] The regulations will apply to housing constructed before 1978, with retirement communities excepted unless children under age six are expected to reside there. HUD is also authorized to establish, on a state-by-state basis, a date of construction earlier than 1978.

The regulations will require that, before a purchaser or lessee is obligated under any contract to purchase or lease the housing, the seller or lessor shall: (1) provide the purchaser or lessee with a lead hazard information pamphlet; and (2) disclose to the purchaser or lessee the presence of any known lead-based paint hazards in such housing and provide to the purchaser or lessee any lead hazard evaluation report available to the seller or lessor.

Also, a purchaser of pre-1978 property will be entitled to a ten-day period (unless the parties mutually agree on a longer period) to conduct a risk assessment or inspection for the presence of lead-based paint hazards.

The regulations will set forth provisions that will be required in every contract for the purchase or sale of any interest in target housing. A "lead warning statement" in the form required by the statute will be required to be attached to each such contract. In addition, purchasers will be required to sign a statement that verifies the following:

1. They have read the lead warning statement and understand its contents.
2. They have received a lead hazard information pamphlet.
3. They were given a ten-day opportunity (unless the parties mutually agreed on a different period) before becoming obligated under the contract to purchase the housing to conduct a risk assessment or inspection for the presence of lead-based paint hazards.

The statutory lead warning statement must be printed in large type on a separate sheet of paper attached to the contract and should provide as follows:

> Every purchaser of any interest in residential real property on which a residential dwelling was built prior to 1978 is notified

that such property may present exposure to lead from lead-based paint that may place young children at risk of developing lead poisoning. Lead poisoning in young children may produce permanent neurological damage, including learning disabilities, reduced intelligence quotient, behavioral problems, and impaired memory. Lead poisoning also poses a particular risk to pregnant women. The seller of any interest in residential real property is required to provide the buyer with any information on lead-based paint hazards from risk assessments or inspections in the seller's possession and notify the buyer of any known lead-based paint hazards. A risk assessment or inspection for possible lead-based paint hazards is recommended prior to purchase.[40]

The statute provides three enforcement mechanisms against persons who knowingly violate the disclosure requirements: 1) civil monetary penalties, 2) injunctive relief enforced by HUD, and 3) a private action for treble damages incurred by an aggrieved purchaser or lessee. In addition, the statute allows a prevailing plaintiff to recover court costs, attorney fees, and expert witness fees in a suit brought under the act.[41] If a seller or lessor is represented by a real estate agent in the sale or lease transaction, the statute places an additional burden of compliance on the agent.[42]

The statute specifically provides that failure to comply with its disclosure provisions does not affect the validity or enforceability of any contract for the purchase or lease of any interest in residential real property or any loan agreement, mortgage, or lien, nor does such noncompliance create a defect in title.[43]

1992 Amendments to the Toxic Substances Control Act

Congress adopted companion legislation to the Residential Lead-Based Paint Hazard Reduction Act of 1992 by incorporating amendments to the Toxic Substances Control Act (TSCA).[44] These amendments, the Lead-Based Paint Exposure Reduction Act, require the EPA to adopt regulations governing activities relating to lead-based paint and the certification of lead paint abatement contractors. In response to concern that renovation and remodeling activities may create a risk of lead exposure to workers and occupants, the EPA is required to establish guidelines for the conduct of renovation and remodeling activities, applicable to both commercial buildings and residential dwellings constructed before 1978. In March 1994 the EPA released its proposed rules governing renovation activities. Lawyers representing owners of single-family or multifamily dwellings should keep abreast of the status of those regulations, since in-house maintenance and operations employees may be considered renovators subject to the regulations.[45] The EPA is required to distribute these guidelines to the general public through hardware and paint stores, employee organizations, trade groups, and state and local agencies.

In September 1994 the EPA released proposed rules governing lead-based paint activities, training and certification requirements, and a model state program for administration and enforcement of TSCA.[46]

The TSCA amendments direct the EPA to establish threshold action levels for lead-based paint hazards and lead-contaminated dust and soil. The EPA will establish standards for sampling laboratories and is required to sponsor public education programs on lead poisoning prevention and risk assessments in housing.

The Lead-Based Paint Exposure Reduction Act also establishes a clearinghouse for technical information and directs the development of criteria for lead abatement products, testing methods, and testing products. The lead clearinghouse is now in operation and is staffed with trained information specialists who will answer questions on lead poisoning–related issues and will provide technical assistance to the general public, government agencies, and abatement professionals. The clearinghouse will provide informational materials, federal publications, selected journal articles, and summaries of lead-related federal laws and regulations.[47] A lead hot line, mandated by the statute, has been established. The hot line is operated by the National Safety Council, and its staff provides general information and state referrals to the public.[48]

The Lead-Based Paint Exposure Reduction Act directs the EPA to develop and publish the lead hazard information pamphlet referred to in Title X, which must be given to all contract purchasers and lessees beginning in October 1995. The pamphlet must also be given to occupants of both residential and commercial buildings before renovation efforts, under the EPA proposed rules governing rehabilitation work.[49] The pamphlet will describe the risks of lead exposure for children under age six, pregnant women, women of childbearing age, persons involved in home renovation, and others residing in a dwelling with lead-based paint hazards; describe the risks of renovation in a dwelling with lead-based paint hazards; provide information on approved methods for evaluating and reducing lead-based paint hazards; advise persons how to obtain a list of certified abatement contractors; recommend that a risk assessment or inspection for lead-based paint be conducted before the purchase, lease, or renovation of housing constructed before 1978; and include references to state and local regulatory agencies.[50]

Renovation and abatement efforts in older housing may generate leaded waste. Much of the leaded waste currently regulated under the

Resource Conservation and Recovery Act (RCRA) may be subject to TSCA rule making.[51] The EPA is expected shortly to outline a plan for future regulation of disposal of waste generated by abatement and renovation efforts. Improper disposal of toxic waste can result in substantial liabilities, and most of the standard liability insurance policies issued in recent years no longer provide coverage for pollution claims. Lawyers representing property owners and abatement contractors should therefore keep abreast of federal toxic waste disposal regulation.

State and Local Regulation

Disclosure Provisions

In addition to the federal disclosure requirements, many states have promulgated similar warning provisions. Maryland, for example, recently enacted legislation that provides a cap on personal injury awards against landlords who comply with the statute's requirements by undertaking interim remediation in rental properties, registering with the state department of environment all rental units constructed before 1950, and furnishing tenants with a lead paint warning and tenant rights package that is currently under development. The Maryland law requires insurers to include liability coverage for lead paint injuries up to the amount of the statutory cap, provided that the property owner is in compliance with the statutory requirements.[52]

Other states require that information about lead paint be disclosed in reports furnished to buyers under residential real property disclosure acts.[53] Common-law principles governing negligent or fraudulent omission of material facts may also be pertinent.[54] Lawyers handling residential transactions should research state and local requirements to determine whether state or local statutes, regulations, or common-law decisions impose a duty to investigate for lead hazards and whether the parties may waive any disclosure requirements.

Inspection and Remediation Requirements

Except for federally owned or subsidized properties, the specific requirements for inspection and remediation of lead paint hazards have until recently been left to the individual states and local regulatory authorities. Local health department or housing regulations in some states have set forth detailed inspection and abatement procedures. Most states lack uniform statewide regulations governing the stabilization, treatment, removal, or remediation of lead-based paint hazards.

Several states do require any remediation or abatement work to be performed by trained or licensed contractors and have promulgated statewide requirements for lead abatement projects.[55] Concern about leaded dust generated during abatement efforts has prompted several states to consider or promulgate lead dust clearance standards that must be met upon project completion. Dust standards have met with controversy, however, because exterior soil or airborne lead can contribute to interior lead dust levels.[56] In addition, some states have adopted detailed worker safety regulations governing any renovation, painting, or construction work that is likely to expose workers to lead.[57]

To date, there has been little uniformity among those states that have regulations as to the appropriate methods for stabilizing, treating, or removing lead-based paint or lead paint hazards from a property. The creation of uniform "standards of care" governing the maintenance of property or uniform approved methods to reduce lead paint hazards on residential property has been a subject of debate among regulators and advocacy groups. A HUD task force is currently considering the issue, and no real consensus among the interested parties has emerged.

Lawyers representing clients in connection with a sale or purchase of residential property should research state and local requirements to ascertain 1) whether warnings in addition to those under Title X are necessary or advisable and 2) whether any provisions, apart from federal law, specify the permitted methods of lead detection and the qualifications of lead inspectors. In addition, if lead is detected upon inspection, it will be necessary to research state or local requirements regarding the appropriate abatement methods and whether state or local requirements govern worker certification and training and worker or occupant protection requirements. Finally, lawyers should be familiar with federal and state toxic waste disposal requirements because leaded debris from an abatement project might be subject to environmental disposal and storage regulations.

The promulgation of the EPA regulations required under Title X may create some uniformity among the states as to training and certification of workers and permitted methods of testing and abating lead-contaminated properties.

Practical Issues Regarding Remediation

The present lack of uniform guidelines applicable to all lead abatement projects has caused confusion among home owners and purchasers. Because some states permit encapsulation of leaded surfaces (with specified materials) as a method of complying with lead abatement regulations, a dwelling may be deemed "lead-safe" or in compliance with state or local lead regulation and yet not be completely "deleaded" or "lead free." Further, since exterior soils and ambient air contain residual lead, which can be tracked into the home, even a home that has never been painted with lead-based paint may contain residual lead dust and not be lead free. Title X introduces the concept of interim controls, or measures that can be taken short of a complete removal of all lead-based paint, to increase the safety of a leaded house. Title X defines abatement as the permanent elimination of lead hazards (as opposed to the permanent elimination of lead paint), a standard that will be less than lead free in some cases. Other state or local regulators have permitted property owners to respond to lead violation notices merely by ensuring that painted surfaces are free from flaking paint, by covering painted surfaces below the four-foot level, or by removing paint from surfaces accessible to children.

Because of the confusion in the terminology associated with lead abatement, lawyers who prepare leases, contracts, proposals, or specifications should take care to specify which standards are referenced in their documents. Those who hire outside contractors to test or abate a property should specify the project's scope in detail and should make clear what a lead certificate of compliance entails. Is the consultant certifying that no leaded surfaces were located in the property? Is the consultant certifying instead that the painted surfaces are in good condition, inaccessible to children, or do not present any immediate hazards?

In August 1995, HUD announced the availability of its revised "Guidelines for the Evaluation and Control of Lead-Based Paint Hazards in Housing," which provides "detailed and comprehensive technical information on how to identify lead-based paint hazards in housing and how to control such hazards safely and efficiently."[58] Although the guidelines do not apply to housing having no federal connection, they have been used by many local authorities or contractors as a prototype for local compliance, particularly in the absence of any updated state regulations.

Providing detailed information on how to test or abate a property is well beyond the scope of this chapter, and regulation in this area is developing at a rapid pace. As of this writing, the EPA regulations under Title X have not been issued and the federal task force recommendations have not been published. It is important, therefore, that lawyers representing buyers, sellers, landlords, or tenants in residential transactions research the current requirements.

Lawyers representing parties to residential transactions should recognize that lead paint testing and remediation is much more expensive than, for example, a termite or radon inspection or remediation. Lead abatement is frequently a complex and time-consuming process.

The first phase of an abatement project involves the identification of lead hazards on interior and exterior surfaces in the dwelling. Title X refers to this process as an "inspection" or a "risk assessment," both of which are defined in the statute.[59] No final regulations under Title X on lead detection or laboratory standards have been issued, although the EPA recently issued its proposed regulations, which include standards for conducting lead-based paint activities such as inspections, risk assessments, and abatements.[60] In its 1990 guidelines HUD authorized only two detection methods: portable X-ray fluorescence (XRF) detection and laboratory testing of paint samples. Currently, because the cost of laboratory testing paint samples from every painted surface in a house is prohibitive, most lead testing contractors will rely heavily on XRF detection and will supplement questionable readings with paint-sample analysis.[61]

Portable XRF detection is conducted by using a portable X-ray fluorescence detector to determine lead content in paint, measured in milligrams per square centimeter (mg/cm^2). The action level under the Federal Lead-Based Paint Poisoning Prevention Act is 1 mg/cm^2. Some states, however, may have stricter standards. Maryland, for example, considers a surface leaded at a level of 0.7 mg/cm^2. The HUD guidelines prescribe detailed standards as to the number of surfaces that must be tested for valid XRF testing results. Title X requires that the EPA establish threshold action levels for lead-based paint hazards and lead-contaminated dust and soil. Critics of XRF detection methods complain that inaccurate results are possible, particularly if the operator is unskilled or the equipment is not properly calibrated. Critics have also challenged the accuracy of XRF testing methods at low action levels.

Laboratory analysis of paint samples requires the sampling of numerous painted surfaces in a dwelling and submission to a laboratory for chemical analysis. There are a variety of acceptable testing methods once the samples are in the laboratory. Careful sampling, however, is extremely important, and it is equally important that samples from different surfaces not be mixed. The federal action level for lead in paint is 0.5 percent by weight if wet laboratory methods are used. The disadvantages of paint sampling include its relatively high cost and the fact that it is destructive. Also, many samples must be taken to give an accurate picture of where lead-based paint has been used in a dwelling. Further, while XRF testing can produce immediate results, there is often a delay before the results of wet laboratory testing are available.

Test kits are commercially available that rely on sodium sulfide testing or other qualitative chemical techniques. The process involves the application of a chemical to leaded surfaces. If lead (and possibly other heavy metals) is present, a color change will occur. This method may not reveal the percentage of lead in a sample, but, if properly conducted, it can determine whether (over a given detection limit) lead-based paint is present. In its 1990 interim guidelines HUD stated that sodium sulfide testing was "not recommended as a primary testing method," since it had "not been adequately validated," but HUD also noted that the method held "some promise for expanded use in the future." Since then, the Consumer Product Safety Commission has issued some position papers on the use of commercially available sodium sulfide testing methods. At this writing, however, neither sodium sulfide nor other qualitative testing methods have met with general approval in the industry. The author recommends that this method not be used unless approved by regulatory authorities, and that positive results be confirmed by laboratory sample analysis. The EPA and the CPSC are reportedly in the process of comparing various testing techniques, and questions concerning the current status of any testing technique should be directed to regulatory authorities.

Depending on the location of lead-based paint in the dwelling and the applicable abatement regulations, an abatement project may involve as little as replacing the woodwork. On the other hand, it could involve a comprehensive remodeling including the replacement of all windows, doors, door frames, and painted surfaces. Lead paint removal, using certain limited techniques, is authorized in some states, but safe practices generally prohibit burning, sanding, and dry scraping of paint. Encapsulation of certain painted surfaces, using specified materials, has been authorized in some states. Experts recommend that the occupants of the dwelling be relocated during abatement efforts to prevent exposure to lead dust generated during remediation.

An abatement or remodeling project must comply with OSHA and local regulations governing worker and occupant safety. Adequate cleanup, on a daily basis, is essential to a safe remodeling or abatement effort. In addition, lead dust must be contained while the project is ongoing. The HUD guidelines[62] and the regulations in several states provide detailed instructions on cleanup and disposal.

Until a lead paint risk assessment is conducted and a lead remediation expert is consulted, it is nearly impossible to predict the cost of an abatement. There has been a wide range in the estimated cost of lead remediation. HUD estimates that the average cost for lead abatement in an average home is $7,700, with a range from $5,500 to $12,000. Other groups have reported much higher remediation costs.[63] Lawyers representing sellers or buyers in residential transactions should be aware that the cost of remediation, if lead-based paint is present in a dwelling, could present a huge stumbling block to negotiations and might jeopardize the transaction.

Conclusion

Current regulation of lead-based paint in housing is undergoing major revisions. The promulgation of Title X is expected to have a major impact on residential transactions. Lawyers representing landlords, tenants, and sellers and buyers of residential real estate should keep abreast of regulatory developments and will need to check the *Federal Register* for further information on federal regulation of lead paint issues.

Initially, Title X will require a threshold determination of the construction date of residential housing to determine whether the warnings must be provided. Surprisingly, this information may be difficult to ascertain from local building regulators, since public records and occupancy permits are frequently purged or archived at regular intervals. Therefore, contractors, owners, and builders should retain their own records confirming the construction date because future buyers or lenders may require proof of the construction date after the disclosure regulations become effective in October 1995. Real estate appraisers are cautioned to confirm rather than estimate the date of construction or, instead, to provide a disclaimer if the date cannot be accurately determined.

Lawyers representing residential sellers or real estate agents will need to revise their contract forms to comply with the law's disclosure provisions and the forthcoming regulations and will need to keep abreast of the EPA's efforts in developing the lead hazard information pamphlet.

More importantly, lawyers representing buyers or sellers in negotiating residential transactions will need to consider which party will bear the cost of an inspection and the risk of remediation if lead-based paint is identified.

Clients in the renovation and construction industries should become familiar with worker safety regulations and certification requirements. A number of EPA-sponsored or -approved training and certification courses are currently available.

The reader should contact state and local regulatory authorities to ascertain whether any additional state or local requirements are imposed.

Notes

1. *See, e.g.*, CENTERS FOR DISEASE CONTROL AND PREVENTION, PREVENTING LEAD POISONING IN YOUNG CHILDREN (October 1992) [hereinafter PREVENTING LEAD POISONING]; Maryland Dep't of the Environment, Lead Paint Hazard Fact Sheet #1, Health and Safety (June 1992).

2. *See id.*

3. AGENCY FOR TOXIC SUBSTANCES AND DISEASE REGISTRY, U.S. DEP'T OF HEALTH AND HUMAN SERVICES, THE NATURE AND EXTENT OF LEAD POISONING IN CHILDREN IN THE UNITED STATES: A REPORT TO CONGRESS (1988); PREVENTING LEAD POISONING, *supra* note 1.

4. *See, e.g.*, Amitai et al., *Residential Deleading: Effects on the Blood Lead Levels of Lead-Poisoned Children*, 88 PEDIATRICS (5): 893–97 (Nov. 1991); Farfel and Chisolm, *An Evaluation of Experimental Practices for Abatement of Residential Lead-Based Paint: Report on a Pilot Project*, 55 ENVIRON. RES. (2): 199–212 (Aug. 1991); Farfel and Chisolm, *Health and Environmental Outcomes of Traditional and Modified Practices for Abatement of Residential Lead-Based Paint*, 80 AM. J. PUBLIC HEALTH (10): 1240–45 (Oct. 1990).

5. *See, e.g.*, 1971 Md. Laws ch. 494.

6. *See* 42 U.S.C. § 4831(b)(1988); 16 C.F.R. 1303.1–03.5 (1994).

7. U.S. Consumer Product Safety Commission, What You Should Know about Lead-Based Paint in Your Home, Consumer Product Safety Alert (September 1990) (USGPO No. 1990-726-058).

8. NATIONAL LEAD INFORMATION CENTER, HOME REPAIRS AND RENOVATIONS: WHAT YOU SHOULD KNOW ABOUT LEAD-BASED PAINT (October 1992).

9. U.S. DEP'T OF HOUSING AND URBAN DEVELOPMENT, COMPREHENSIVE AND WORKABLE PLAN FOR THE ABATEMENT OF LEAD-BASED PAINT IN PRIVATELY OWNED HOUSING: A REPORT TO CONGRESS (1990).

10. *See generally* Fee, *Public Health in Baltimore: Childhood Lead Paint Poisoning*, 1930–70, 87 MD. HIST. MAG. 267–93 (1992).

11. *See, e.g.*, MD. REGS. CODE § 26.02.06.02.

12. *See, e.g.*, Richwind Joint Venture 4 v. Brunson, 335 Md. 661, 645 A.2d 1147 (1994) (reviewing local regulations).

13. Rey-Alvarez and Menke-Hargrave, *Deleading Dilemma: Pitfall in the Management of Childhood Lead Poisoning*, 79 PEDIATRICS (2): 214–17 (Feb. 1987); Amitai et al., *Hazards of 'Deleading' Homes of Children with Lead Poisoning*, 141 AM J. DIS. CHILD. (7): 758–60 (July 1987); M. Kawai et al., *Home Lead-Work as a Potential Source of Lead Exposure for Children*, 53 Int. Arch. Occup. Environ. Health (1): 37–46 (1983).

14. MD. ADMIN. CODE § 26.02.07.01–.14.

15. MD. ADMIN. CODE § 09.12.32.01–.16.

16. 29 C.F.R. pt. 1926.

17. PREVENTING LEAD POISONING, *supra*, note 1.

18. Brody et al., *Blood Lead Levels in the U.S. Population*, 272 J. AM. MED. ASS'N 277–83 (July 27, 1994). The population's average blood lead levels have drastically decreased since a large-scale evaluation of blood lead data from 1976 to 1980 was first conducted. Between 1976 and 1991, the average blood lead levels (including children and adults) dropped 78 percent, from an average of 12.8 ug/dl to 2.8 ug/dl. The decline in average blood lead likely results from the bans on leaded gasoline and lead solder in canned foods. Pirkle et al., *The Decline in Blood Lead Levels in the United States: The National Health and Nutrition Examination Surveys (NHANES)*, 272 J. AM. MED. ASS'N (4): 284–91 (July 27, 1994).

19. Brody et al., *Blood Lead Levels in the U.S. Population*, 272 J. AM. MED. ASS'N 277–83 (July 27, 1994); Goldman and Carra, *Childhood Lead Poisoning in 1994*, 272 J. AM. MED. ASS'N (4): 315–16 (July 27, 1994).

20. J. Schwartz and R. Levin, *The Risk of Lead Toxicity in Homes with Lead Paint Hazards*, ENVIRON. RES., 54 (1): 1–7 (Feb. 1991); C.S. Clark et al., *Condition and Type of Housing as an Indicator of Potential Environmental Lead Exposure and Pediatric Blood Lead Levels*, ENVIRON. RES., 38 (1): 46–53 (Oct. 1985); J.J. Chisolm Jr., E.D. Mellits, and S.A. Quaskey, *The Relationship between the Level of Lead Absorption in Children and the Age, Type, and Condition of Housing*, ENVIRON. RES., 38 (1): 31–45 (Oct. 1985); American Academy of Pediatrics Committee on Environmental Hazards, *Policy Statement: Pediatric Problems Related to Deteriorated Housing*, PEDIATRICS, 49 (4): 627 (Apr. 1972).

21. *See* cases cited *infra* at notes 22–25, 29–30.

22. *See, e.g.*, Winston Properties v. Sanders, 57 Ohio App.3d 28, 565 N.E.2d 1280 (1989) (summary judgment properly granted in favor of landlord, when he filed affidavit that he did not know of the existence of lead-based paint until violation notice issued, and promptly abated violation; court held that notice of peeling paint was insufficient to establish liability, that notice of lead-based paint was required before violation of municipal code was established; and that local ordinance did not create strict liability); Mahlmann v. Yelverton, 439 N.Y.S.2d 568, 109 A.D.2d 127 (1980) (strict liability not available, notice is a required element); Cole v. Bumiller, 549 S.W.2d 95 (Mo. App. 1976) (appeal of judgment in favor of landlord affirmed when jury apparently rejected plaintiff's theory that landlord violated lead-paint ordinance. Language in case suggests that no violation exists unless landlord fails to comply with lead violation notice).

23. *See, e.g.*, Bencosme v. Kokoras, 400 Mass. 40, 507 N.E.2d 748 (1987).

24. *See, e.g.*, Dunson v. Frielander Realty Corp., 369 So.2d 792 (Ala. 1979) (upholding warranty theory but dismissing negligence theory in lead-poisoning case). Such a cause of action would generally not be available in the absence of a statute or code provision providing for an implied warranty of habitability. At common law, the doctrine of caveat emptor ("buyer beware") was traditionally applied to a tenant, and no implied warranties accompanied the lease. *See, e.g.*, Smith v. Walsh, 92 Md. 518, 529–30, 48 A. 92 (1901); *accord* Martin v. Springdale Stores, Inc., 354 So. 2d 1144, 1145–46 (Ala. 1978) (complaint seeking damages for implied warranty of habitability properly dismissed); Alvarez v. DeAquire, 395 So. 2d 213, 216 (Fla. App. 1981) (complaint seeking damages for implied warranty of habitability dismissed); Cappaert v. Junker, 413 So.2d 378 (Miss. 1982); Young v. Morrisey, 329 S.E.2d 426, 429 (S.C. 1985) (summary judgment granted for landlord; no implied warranty of fitness or habitability in leases). *See* PROSSER, THE LAW OF TORTS § 63 at 435 (5th ed. 1984).

25. *See, e.g.*, Hardy v. Griffin, 41 Conn. Supp. 283, 569 A.2d 49 (1989); Richwind Joint Venture 4 v. Brunson, 335 Md. 661, 645 A.2d 1147 (1994). Most state consumer protection acts are limited to sales of goods and generally do not include the lease of real property. *See generally* Uniform Deceptive Trade Practices Act, 7A U.L.A. 265 (1966). However, several states do include leases of real property to consumers within the ambit of a Consumer Protection Act. *See, e.g.*, Maryland, MD. COMM. LAW CODE ANN. §§ 13-101–13-501; Pennsylvania, Commonwealth v. Monumental Properties, Inc., 365 A.2d 442 (Pa. 1976); Wisconsin, W.S.A. § 100.18.

26. *See* Weisman v. Connors, 312 Md. 428, 444, 540 A.2d 783 (1988), setting forth the elements required to prove a claim of negligent misrepresentation. Typical allegations of negligent misrepresentation in a lead paint case are that, by

renting an apartment, the landlord impliedly represented that the property was in compliance with all applicable rules and regulations (including those prohibiting the use of lead-based paint or prohibiting flaking or peeling paint). Whether these allegations are sufficient should be researched under local law. In Atlantis Condominium v. Whiting-Turner Contracting Co., 308 Md. 17, 41–42 (1986), the Maryland Court of Appeals held that "an involuntary warranty existing solely by law does not constitute a representation that will support a cause of action for negligent misrepresentation."

27. *See, e.g.*, *Boy Wins $10 Million for Lead Paint Injury*, 210 NEW YORK LAW J. 69 (Oct. 7, 1993); Cohen, *Low Settlement Offer Prompts $5 Million Recovery*, 22 MASS. LAWYERS WEEKLY 17 (Jan. 17, 1994) (reviewing Parker v. D'Avolio, Mass. Housing Court)).

28. Efforts by insurers to disclaim coverage on the basis of pollution exclusions have largely failed in personal injury cases. *See generally* Atlantic Mutual Insurance Co. v. McFadden, 413 Mass. 90, 595 N.E.2d 762; Generali-U.S. Branch v. Caribe Realty Corp., 1994 Westlaw 187, 189 (N.Y. Supreme Ct., April 13, 1994).

29. *See, e.g.*, Richwind Joint Venture 4 v. Brunson, *supra*; Brown v. Marathon Realty, Inc., 565 N.Y.S.2d 219 (1991) (Summary judgment should have been granted in favor of landlord when tenant failed to prove that landlord had actual or constructive notice that paint was chipping off walls and that the paint was lead-based. Tenant's allegation that landlord collected rent on occasion was insufficient to establish notice. Assertion that the use of lead-based paint in older buildings was "commonly known" was insufficient to establish notice.); Miller v. Beaugrand, 169 A.D.2d 537, 564 N.Y.S.2d 390 (1991) (upheld jury award in favor of tenant against city; jury properly found that city had notice of condition); Garcia v. Jiminez, 184 Ill. App.3d 107, 539 N.E.2d 1356, *cert. denied*, 127 Ill.2d 615 (1989) (Lack of notice is defense in lead paint case. Mere presence of paint chips does not create duty to remedy. Landlord must have actual or constructive knowledge that there are toxic paint chips and that they may be ingested by young children.); Winston Properties v. Sanders, 57 Ohio App. 3d 28, 565 N.E.2d 1280 (1989) (summary judgment properly granted in favor of landlord, when he filed affidavit that he did not know of the existence of lead-based paint until violation notice issued and promptly abated violation; court held that notice of peeling paint was insufficient to establish liability, that notice of lead-based paint was required before violation of municipal code was established; that local ordinance did not create strict liability); Mahlmann v. Yelverton, 439 N.Y.S.2d 568, 109 A.D.2d 127 (1980) (strict liability not available, notice is a required element); Cole v. Bumiller, 549 S.W.2d 95 (Mo. App. 1976) (Appeal of judgment in favor of landlord affirmed when jury apparently rejected plaintiff's theory that landlord violated lead paint ordinance. Language in case suggests that no violation exists unless landlord fails to comply with lead violation notice.); Kolojeski v. John Reisher, Inc., 429 Pa. 191, 239 A.2d 329 (1968) (mere use of lead paint did not give rise to action for negligence). *Compare* Bencosme v. Kokoras, 400 Mass. 40, 507 N.E.2d 748 (1987) (Massachusetts statute providing for strict liability of property owner allowed for liability without proof that owner knew or should have known of dangerous condition).

30. *See, e.g.*, Ford v. Goffstein Realty, Inc., 687 S.W.2d 195 (Mo. App. 1985) (dismissing complaint filed by purchasers of leaded home against vendor and real

estate agent; ordinances only applied to owners of property; negligence, nuisance, and claim based on city ordinances failed, but court allowed amendment to allege intentional misrepresentation).

31. *See, e.g.*, Pierre v. United States, 741 F. Supp. 306 (D. Mass. 1990) (purchaser of leaded house awarded damages from HUD, based on its negligent failure to remove lead-based paint prior to sale pursuant to C.F.R. regulations); Roseberry v. United States, 736 F. Supp. 408 (D.N.H. 1990) (no private cause of action for damages under Federal Lead Poisoning Act; sale of home by Veteran's Administration was "as is" and no express or implied warranties of habitability arose); Brooks v. United States, 712 F. Supp. 667 (N.D. Ill. 1989) (no liability when United States sold house and injury occurred afterwards); Ayala v. Boston Housing Authority, 404 Mass. 689, 536 N.E.2d 1082 (1989) (tenants in Section 8 housing stated viable claim against city housing authority for breach of duty to inspect for lead hazards and notify tenants of results of inspection); Prescott v. Philadelphia Housing Authority, 555 A.2d 305 (Pa. 1989) (local government immunity protected city housing authority from claim by Section 8 tenants); McCallum v. HUD, No. 85-4626 (unreported decision available at 1986 Westlaw 14217 (E.D. Pa. 1986) (denied HUD's motion for summary judgment on exhaustion; suit alleged that HUD sold property in 1978 with certification "lead paint removed").

32. 42 U.S.C. § 4831 *et seq.* (1971).

33. The regulations issued are located at 24 C.F.R. pt. 35. The provisions of 24 C.F.R. § 35.1, requiring HUD to notify tenants of "HUD associated housing" of the hazards of lead-based paint, are noteworthy.

34. Refer to 42 C.F.R. pt. 882 for the standards concerning housing quality and lead testing.

35. 42 U.S.C. §§ 4851–56 (Supp. 1993).

36. 42 U.S.C. § 4852 (Supp. 1993).

37. OSHA recently promulgated worker safety regulations governing lead in the construction and renovation industry, which are located at 29 C.F.R. pt. 1926. The EPA has issued proposed regulations governing some of the statutory mandates. Proposed regulations concerning requirements for hazard education before renovation of target housing are located at 59 Fed. Reg. 11,108 (1994). Proposed regulations concerning worker training, certification, inspection, and abatement are located at 59 Fed. Reg. 45,915 (1994). The final EPA regulations will ultimately be published at 40 C.F.R. pt. 745. HUD recently issued a detailed manual furnishing guidelines for the evaluation and control of lead-based paint hazards. *See* note 58 and accompanying text.

38. 42 U.S.C. § 4852a.

39. The proposed rules, "Lead; Proposed Requirements for Disclosure of Information Concerning Lead-Based Paint in Housing," were published on November 2, 1994, and final regulations are pending at this writing. 59 Fed. Reg. 54,984–55,004 (Nov. 2, 1994) (to be codified at 24 C.F.R. Part 38 and 40 C.F.R. Part 745). Acknowledgment and Disclosure Forms will be available through the Government Printing Office. The "Lead Hazard Information Pamphlet," which is to be distributed to contract purchasers and lessees, is now available in final form and is entitled "Protect Your Family from Lead in Your Home." Single copies are available by calling the National Lead Information Clearinghouse at 1-800-424-LEAD or the EPA Public Information Center at (202) 260-2080. The document is

available on the Internet at gopher.epa.gov. Multiple copies are available through the Government Printing Office, GPO stock number 055-000-00507-9, by calling the GPO order desk at (202) 512-2233, by panafaxing at (202) 512-2233, or by writing to the Superintendent of Documents, P.O. Box 371954, Pittsburgh, PA 15250-7954 ($26.00 per pack of 50 copies).

40. 42 U.S.C. § 4852d(a)(3) (1992).

41. 42 U.S.C. §§ 4852d (b)(3), (b)(4) (Supp. 1993).

42. 42 U.S.C. § 4852d(a)(4) (Supp. 1993).

43. 42 U.S.C. § 4852d(c) (Supp. 1993).

44. 15 U.S.C. § 2601 *et seq.*

45. The proposed rules are located at 59 Fed. Reg. 11,108 (1994) and will ultimately be codified at 40 C.F.R. pt. 745.

46. 59 Fed. Register 45,872 (1994). The final rules will be codified at 40 C.F.R. pt. 745.

47. The clearinghouse telephone number is 1 (800) 424-LEAD (424-5323).

48. Further information on local resources is available by calling the hot line at 1 (800) LEAD–FYI. Callers are mailed a basic information package containing an EPA brochure and fact sheets on lead testing, renovation and repairs, and medical issues.

49. 59 Fed. Reg. 11,108 (1994). The final rules will be codified at 40 C.F.R. pt. 745.

50. *See supra* note 39, for information on obtaining the information pamphlet.

51. *See* 60 Fed. Reg. 23,950 (May 8, 1995) (EPA TSCA regulatory agenda and agency contact person and telephone number).

52. House Bill 760, 1994 Md. Laws ch. 114 (1994) (to be codified at MD. ENVIR. CODE ANN. §§ 6-801 to 6-852; MD. REAL PROP. CODE ANN. § 8-208.2; and MD. ANN. CODE art. 48A §§ 734–37).

53. Examples include the Illinois provision, Ill. St. ch. 765 § 77/35 (1994); Wisconsin's provision, W.S.CA. § 709.03 (1993); and California's provision, Ann. Cal. Civ. Code § 1102.6 (West 1991).

54. *See, e.g.*, Ford v. Goffstein Realty, *supra* note 30.

55. MD. REGS. CODE § 26.02.07.01–.14. (1988).

56. M.B. Rabinowitz and D.C. Bellinger, *Soil Lead-Blood Bead Relationship among Boston Children*, BULL. ENVIR. CONTAM. TOXICOL. 41 (6): 791–97 (Dec. 1988); R.J. Schilling and R.P. Bain, *Prediction of Children's Blood Lead Levels on the Basis of Household-Specific Soil Lead Levels*, AM. J. EPIDEMIOL. 128 (1): 197–205 (July 1988); H.W. Mielke et al., *Lead Concentrations in Inner-City Soils as a Factor in the Child Lead Problem*, AM. J. PUBLIC HEALTH 73 (12): 1366–69 (1983); N. Schmitt et al., *Surface Soil as a Potential Source of Lead Exposure for Young Children*, CAN. MED. ASSOC. J. (11): 1474–78 (1979); F.S. Fairey and J.W. Gray III, *Soil Lead and Pediatric Lead Poisoning in Charleston, S.C.* J. S. C. MED. ASSOC. 66 (3): 7982 (1970).

57. *See, e.g.*, MD. REGS. CODE § 9.12.32.01–.16; 8 CAL. CODE REG. § 1532.1; WASH. ADMIN. CODE § 296-155-17609.

58. *See* 60 Fed. Reg. 44,362 (August 25, 1995). Copies of the Guidelines may be purchased by calling HUD USER at 1-800-245-2691 or by writing to HUD USER, P.O. Box 6091, Rockville, MD 20850 (refer to notice FR-3939 and publication title).

59. The proposed EPA regulations define an "inspection" as a surface-by-surface lead test conducted by a certified inspector under specified regulations.

A "risk assessment" is an on-site investigation conducted to "determine the existence, nature, severity, and location of lead-based paint hazards" and the "provision . . . of a report explaining the results of the investigation and providing options for reducing lead-based paint hazards." 59 Fed. Reg. 45,915 (final regulations to be codified at 40 C.F.R. pt. 745).

60. 59 Fed. Reg. 45,872–921 (1994) (final regulations to be codified at 40 C.F.R. pt. 745.

61. The cost for XRF testing of a three-bedroom row home would likely be between $275 and $700. (HUD estimates that the cost of testing averages $375 per unit.) Paint sample analysis of the same size house would require, under the 1990 HUD guidelines, numerous samples to be taken from multiple surfaces in each room. Assuming that the per sample test for lead analysis was between $15 and $30 per sample, one room could conceivably cost nearly $500 to test, if paint samples alone are relied on. Thorough testing of a sample surface in every room could thus run as much as $3,500 for an eight-room townhouse.

62. *See* note 58 and accompanying text.

63. The published reports concerning costs of a "full" abatement have not been consistent, and it is difficult to predict the cost of an abatement in any given property. In 1986 Baltimore City conducted a pilot project to compare the cost and effectiveness of various methods of abatement in a series of row homes. The study's findings were published in a report titled "Lead Poisoning Prevention Task Force Abatement Methodologies Subcommittee Report of Findings," dated November 10, 1986. According to the subcommittee report, the labor and material cost figures for a six-room house, not including profit or overhead or necessary safety equipment, start-up or cleanup costs ranged from $2,466 to $3,264. Subsequent studies incorporating the use of replacement as a lead abatement method have shown much higher costs. In its May-June 1990 newsletter, the Property Owners Association of Greater Baltimore discussed the City Pilot Program abatements. The article notes that sixty houses had been abated by city crews during the Pilot Project. It noted several row houses with cost figures in the $12,000 to $15,000 range and reported that one of the row houses, a fourteen-room three-story unit, had a final cost of $56,137 after replacement of the windows, frames, sills, and door frames.

The National Institute of Building Sciences issued a Task Force Report dated February 20, 1988, noting that the cost of identification and removal of lead-based paint "has been as large as $8,000 per dwelling unit in some cases if the lead-based paint removal is the only purpose for modifying a dwelling unit. If, however, the removal is done in conjunction with other modernization and renovation activities, the cost for only the LBP portion is decreased." On March 19, 1992, George Peek testified on behalf of the National Association of Realtors before the Senate Subcommittee on Housing and Urban Affairs. He testified that HUD estimates that the average cost per unit to remove lead is $7,700, with a range between $5,500 and $12,000. This estimate does not include the cost of testing for lead, estimated by HUD to average $375, or the cost of relocating occupants during abatement, which can be three to four weeks, and frequently longer.

CHAPTER 21

Radon's Radioactive Ramifications

ANNE RICKARD JACKOWITZ

Radon, a naturally occurring radioactive gas, is the focus of increased concern in real estate transactions and new building construction. Since the mid-1980s, public awareness and concern over radon have grown in the face of widespread press coverage of the health effects of radon exposure. Reported to be the second leading cause of lung cancer in the United States,[1] radon has attracted the attention of consumers, builders, lenders, and others who are involved in the construction and sale of residential housing, making it yet another consumer protection issue to be dealt with in the residential housing market. While some home buyers remain unaware of the mounting concern about radon, there is no question that the radon issue is being addressed more frequently in the transactional context, with consumers more frequently insisting on a radon test before buying residential property and with some lenders requiring a radon test as a condition to financing real estate.

While commercial buildings are not immune to the radon problem, concern over radon exposure has arisen primarily in the residential context for a number of reasons. First, because radon gas is produced by the decay of uranium in rock and soil, radon enters the lower levels of buildings. Indoor radon levels are therefore highest at the basement and ground-floor levels, where few occupants of commercial buildings are situated. Second, the home presents the greatest opportunity for radon exposure, since it is where most people spend the majority of their time. Thus, the presence of radon is currently not a key concern in most commercial transactions, although it should not be ignored in all cases. Radon may be an issue, for instance, in a transaction involving a commercial building in a geographic area with high radon potential.

Notwithstanding the health concerns associated with radon exposure, at this writing there is no federal regulation of indoor radon levels. The U.S. Environmental Protection Agency (EPA), however, established a program in 1985 to inform the public about radon and its perceived adverse health effects and to encourage testing and remediation as necessary. In addition to the dissemination of consumer information about radon, the agency has set a voluntary "action level" of 4 picoCuries per liter (pCi/l) of air.[2] If a building contains radon above this level, the EPA advises property owners to take steps to address the problem.

Because radon is a naturally occurring phenomenon that cannot be detected without testing, is not subject to federal regulation, and generally does not cause serious health problems without long-term exposure, many people minimize the potential health effects associated with radon and gamble on the assumption that their building will not be affected by high radon levels. However, in the sale of residential real estate or the construction of improvements on residential property, where the motive is economic as opposed to health-based, many people test for radon and remediate high radon levels if necessary.

This chapter provides background on radon and the federal action taken to date to address the radon problem; the various types of transactions in which radon issues arise; and suggestions on how to address radon issues from the perspectives of the different parties to such real estate transactions.

Background

Radon is an odorless, colorless, and tasteless radioactive gas produced as a result of the decay of uranium, which is present in many rock formations throughout the United States.[3] Radon is the nation's most serious radiation hazard contaminating air (and, to a much lesser degree, water)[4] inside homes and the lower floors of commercial buildings. According to the EPA, this radioactive gas is the second leading cause of lung cancer, resulting in between seven thousand and thirty thousand deaths each year.[5]

Radon: The Decay Chain

The significant health risk associated with radon is not the gas itself but the radioactive elements that are emitted as radon decomposes.[6] These elements are often referred to as radon decay products, radon progeny, or radon daughters. For the purposes of this chapter, the term radon will be used to refer to radon and its decay products unless otherwise specified.

The Discovery of Radon's Adverse Impacts on Human Health

As early as the 1930s, radon was recognized as a cause of lung cancer in uranium miners.[7] In the 1950s and 1960s, studies performed in the western states confirmed a high incidence of lung cancer among uranium miners.[8] However, the risk to the general population from indoor radon exposure first became an issue in the western United States when it was discovered during the late 1960s and early 1970s that uranium mill tailings had been used as construction materials in some homes or as fill dirt around residential construction sites and that some homes had been constructed on reclaimed phosphate mining land.

The magnitude of radon's dangers as a radioactive gas resulting from uranium decomposition in soil and rock throughout the United States did not receive national attention until 1984, when high levels of radon were discovered in homes located along the geologic formation known as the Reading Prong, a large deposit of low-grade uranium extending through parts of Pennsylvania, New York, and New Jersey.[9]

The Scope of the Radon Risk

Based on the results of several studies, the EPA has estimated that approximately 6 percent of all residences, or nearly 6 million homes, have annual average radon levels in excess of 4 pCi/l,[10] the action level at which the EPA recommends that home owners engage in certain mitigation activities to lower the risk of indoor radon exposure.[11] While states such as Florida, Maine, New Jersey, New York, and Pennsylvania have greater radon problems due to the presence of phosphate, granite, or certain types of shale,[12] radon affects residences in every state in the country.[13] The EPA estimates that nearly one out of every fifteen homes throughout the United States contains elevated radon levels,[14] and to date there is no way of predicting which homes contain high levels without testing each home. Studies indicate that indoor radon levels can vary greatly, not only from community to community but also from house to house.[15]

In response to the EPA's finding that geographic location is an important predictor of a building's radon levels,[16] and to the Congressional mandate that the EPA identify areas within the United States with potential for elevated indoor radon levels,[17] the EPA has compiled the EPA Map of Radon Zones,[18] which designates each of the 3,141 counties in the United States as being in one of three zones based on potential radon levels.[19] Because the map merely identifies radon potential, the EPA advises that all buildings be tested for radon regardless of geographic location or zone designation.[20]

Radon's Adverse Health Effects

While some controversy exists over the harm resulting from exposure to high levels of radon,[21] the EPA estimates that approximately fourteen thousand lung cancer deaths in the United States each year are attributable to radon. The number of deaths, however, may be as many as thirty thousand or as few as seven thousand.[22] This uncertainty stems from the fact that the assessment of radon-related health effects is extrapolated from epidemiological studies of underground uranium miners rather than from the general population.[23] The Karolinska Institute in Stockholm, Sweden, recently released the results of a study intended to increase understanding of the effects of residential radon exposure. This study, the largest residential radon case-control study to date, found that radon is a significant cause of lung cancer, that the risks associated with residential radon exposure are similar to the EPA's earlier risk estimates, and that the risks associated with residential radon increase for those individuals who smoke.[24]

Sources of Radon

Outdoor radon levels, estimated to be 0.4 pCi/l on average, are generally believed to be safe.[25] Indoors, however, radon can reach unsafe levels because the radioactive gas becomes trapped in enclosed structures. Seepage from soil is the major source of radon in buildings. Lower indoor air pressure draws air from the soil into the house.[26] Radon enters the structure through dirt floors; cracks in concrete floors and walls; gaps in suspended floors or around service pipes; floor drains; pumps; and construction joints.[27]

According to the EPA, the second source of radon in buildings is well water.[28] However, the EPA believes that water results in less than 5 percent of the overall residential radon exposure in air.[29]

Federal Radon Action

Federal Legislation

Radon in Air

Before 1985, with the exception of the statutes and regulations governing uranium mill tailings,[30] the federal government had not taken any action to deal with radon in residential or commercial buildings.[31] In

1985, however, in the wake of the sudden national concern surrounding elevated levels of radon found in homes located in the Reading Prong, the EPA created the Radon Program, a nonregulatory program designed to disseminate information to the public in an effort to enable citizens to make informed decisions on radon.[32]

To aid the EPA in its efforts to further assess the problem and to reduce the risks of indoor radon exposure, Congress included provisions dealing with radon in the Superfund Amendments and Reauthorization Act of 1986 (SARA).[33] Title IV of SARA, the Radon Gas and Indoor Air Quality Act of 1986, acknowledged the serious health threat posed by radon and authorized the EPA to conduct radon research, including performing a national radon assessment.[34] Title IV, however, did not authorize the EPA to promulgate radon regulations.

The Indoor Radon Abatement Act (IRAA) of 1988 established the national long-term goal of reducing radon levels inside buildings to the levels of radon found in outside air.[35] In view of the significant practical and economic impediments to achieving this goal in either new or existing buildings, the underlying goal of IRAA was a long-term aspiration to encourage the public to reduce indoor radon levels as much as possible.[36] Under IRAA, the EPA was provided funding[37] and directed to take certain actions to achieve the stated goal of IRAA, including publishing an updated "Citizen's Guide to Radon," which includes explanations of the health risks associated with radon, the cost and technological feasibility of reducing radon concentrations in existing and new buildings, and the relationship between short- and long-term testing techniques.[38] The EPA was also charged with developing model construction standards and techniques to control radon levels within new buildings.[39]

Radon in Water

In contrast to the voluntary, nonregulatory program for radon in indoor air, in 1991 the EPA proposed regulations under the Safe Drinking Water Act establishing a health-based mandatory drinking water standard of 300 pCi/l for radon in public water supplies.[40] Although the EPA's primary concern in regulating radon in drinking water is the risk posed by radon released from water into indoor air, the agency also recognizes that internal organs are exposed to risk by drinking water containing radon.[41] The EPA estimates that between 40 and 408 deaths per year are caused by the inhalation of waterborne radon progeny and between 11 and 212 deaths per year are caused by drinking of radon in water.[42]

Much of the controversy surrounding the proposed drinking water standard involves the issue of risk assessment and cost/benefit analysis. Because the presence of radon in indoor air poses a much greater health risk than radon in public drinking water supplies, many believe that the resources allocated to reduce radon in drinking water would produce a greater benefit if they were devoted to the goal of reducing radon in indoor air. According to the EPA, however, radon in drinking water poses a much greater risk than any other water contaminant currently being regulated.[43]

The EPA Voluntary Guideline

To date, no mandatory federal radon standard exists. However, the EPA has established a technology-based action level.[44] While only a radon level of zero can be considered safe, the agency recommends that property owners take certain actions to reduce radon levels to less than the action level of 4 pCi/l, at a minimum, and advises that efforts be made to reduce radon levels to 2 pCi/ or below. The EPA has found that elevated radon levels can be reduced to 4 pCi/l more than 95 percent of the time and to 2 pCi/l approximately 70 percent of the time.[45] By way of comparison, the average indoor radon level is estimated to be approximately 1.25 pCi/l[46] and the average outdoor radon level is approximately 0.4 pCi/l.[47]

Radon Testing

In light of the wide variation in indoor radon levels throughout the United States and even within specified areas of the country, the EPA recommends that all residents of single-family homes, housing units below the third floor in multiunit structures, and units in residential mobile homes with permanent foundations conduct a short-term test for radon.[48] If the results indicate a radon level of 4 pCi/l or higher, the agency recommends conducting a follow-up test to confirm the results. Although a long-term test is preferable because it is more likely to provide the home's average annual radon level, if results are needed quickly, as, for example, in a real estate transaction, the EPA recommends that a second short-term test be conducted.[49]

There are various measurement methods for testing radon. These methods can be characterized as long-term or short-term and active or passive. Long-term measurements are generally conducted for a period lasting between three months and one year and produce results that are closer to the actual annual radon exposure than short-term measurements. Short-term tests are conducted for a period lasting between two and ninety days depending on the device used and the time constraints imposed, although most short-term tests are conducted for less than seven days.[50]

A short-term test will not measure annual radon exposure accurately, but it will identify a radon problem. Radon levels fluctuate dramatically on a seasonal and even daily basis and are likely to be much higher in cold weather months, when doors and windows are closed. Severe storms and high winds also may affect short-term test results. A short-term test will be more reliable if all doors and windows are closed, starting at least twelve hours before the test, and if no exhaust fans or air conditioners are used during the test. At least one test kit should be placed in the lowest lived-in level of the building, at least twenty inches off the floor, in a regularly used room (with the exception of a kitchen, bathroom, or any other area with drafts, high heat, or high humidity) and away from exterior walls.[51]

Radon Mitigation

If one long-term test or the average of two short-term tests produce radon levels of 4 pCi/l or greater, the EPA advises property owners to attempt to reduce the indoor radon levels to below 4 pCi/l.[52]

Because reducing high levels of radon requires specific technical skills, the EPA urges that property owners hire a qualified contractor to perform the necessary mitigation.[53] The EPA's publication "Consumer's Guide to Radon Reduction" contains helpful checklists to aid the consumer in choosing a qualified contractor.[54]

The average cost of having a contractor install a radon remediation device is $1,200. Depending on the method chosen, however, such costs can range from $500 to $2,500. In selecting a remediation method, the following factors should be considered:[55]

- The initial radon level
- The cost of installing and operating the system
- The house size and foundation type

A building will contain elevated levels of radon only if there is a source of uranium, a pathway from the uranium to the building, a drawing force to move the radon into the building, and an opening in the building that will permit radon to enter.[56] Therefore, radon levels can be controlled either by preventing radon from entering the building—the most effective radon reduction strategy—or by attempting to remove radon after it has entered the building.

The most commonly used mitigation technology is called subslab depressurization or subslab suction. This method often reduces radon levels by more than 95 percent by removing radon from beneath the foundation and venting it outside the building. The procedure involves installing a fan and inserting a pipe through the foundation and running it to an outside point above the roof.

Submembrane depressurization is another effective method used to reduce radon levels in buildings with earth-floored crawl spaces or basements. This method involves covering the earth floor with a plastic sheet, then drawing the radon outside using a vent pipe and fan.[57]

Sealing cracks and other openings in the foundation is a basic component of most radon reduction strategies. However, the EPA recommends the use of sealing only in conjunction with another radon reduction method because sealing has not been shown to lower radon levels significantly or consistently.[58]

The EPA recommends that property owners obtain an independent follow-up radon measurement after radon reduction techniques have been employed, either by having an independent certified tester perform the test or by conducting a self-measurement.[59]

Radon-Resistant Construction Techniques

The most cost-effective means of preventing radon from entering new buildings is to ensure that those buildings include radon-resistant construction features, which usually keep radon levels below 2 pCi/l.[60] In response to the federal mandate that the EPA develop model construction standards and techniques for controlling radon levels in new buildings,[61] the EPA published final "Model Standards and Techniques for Control of Radon in New Residential Buildings" (Model Standards) in March 1994.[62] The Model Standards are designed primarily for control of radon in new one- and two-family homes and other residential buildings three stories or less in height.[63] While preliminary research indicates that implementation of the Model Standards successfully mitigates high radon levels in existing nonresidential buildings, their effectiveness in controlling radon levels in new nonresidential buildings has not yet been demonstrated fully.[64]

The Model Standards include three methods for controlling radon in new residential construction.

- Passive systems: These include the use of construction techniques that prevent radon from entering the home, reduce the pressure differential between the indoor and outdoor air levels, and facilitate the removal of radon if the barrier techniques are insufficient. Subslab depressurization or submembrane depressurization and roughed-in electrical wiring to facilitate the future installation of a fan in the vent stack and a system failure warning device are examples of passive systems.
- Active systems: These involve the installation of a passive system plus an electric fan in the vent pipe stack and a system failure warning device.[65]

- Stack effect reduction systems: These involve the installation of features such as closing air passages to reduce the upward movement of air through the structure, which in turn draws radon-containing soil gas into the lower levels of the structure.

The Model Standards attempt to balance risk reduction and cost. The recommended guidelines are based on the rationale that the installation of passive systems in areas of high radon potential (i.e., Zone 1 areas on the EPA's Map of Radon Zones), and the activation of those systems if needed, is the most cost-effective technique for newly constructed homes. In contrast, the cost of reducing high radon levels in existing homes that do not contain the construction features designed to control radon levels can range from $500 to $2,500.[66]

Impacts of Radon in Residential and Commercial Real Estate Transactions

Radon concerns may affect the purchase, sale, or lease of real estate as well as the construction of new buildings. Virtually anyone who is involved with real estate, particularly residential real estate, can expect to confront the radon issue at some point. The parties who might require advice about radon include buyers, sellers, lenders, brokers, builders, architects, mitigation contractors, landlords, tenants, home inspectors, and manufacturers.

This section reviews the contexts in which radon issues arise in real estate transactions, particularly residential transactions. Practitioners must be aware that some states, particularly those affected by a greater number of structures containing high radon levels, have enacted statutes and regulations dealing with specific concerns related to radon. The areas most commonly subject to state regulation include radon testing or disclosure of radon test results in real estate transactions; state certification of testing firms and remediation contractors; school testing; and amendments to local building codes requiring that new construction incorporate methods to prevent radon from entering the dwelling.[67]

In New Jersey, for example, by the time the purchase and sale agreement is executed, a seller of real estate must provide the buyer with the results of any radon test previously performed by the seller and evidence of any subsequent mitigation.[68] Florida,[69] Iowa,[70] New Jersey,[71] and several other states[72] require that persons who test for radon and mitigate high levels of radon be certified in accordance with the applicable state laws.[73]

A few states, such as Florida[74] and Washington,[75] have incorporated radon-resistant features in their building codes. The Washington

State Ventilation and Indoor Air Quality Code, for example, requires passive stack systems to be installed in all residential buildings located in counties designated as potential high radon areas.[76] Therefore, in addition to the precautionary measures outlined in this chapter, the laws and regulations of the applicable jurisdiction should be carefully reviewed.

The Purchase and Sale of Real Estate

Radon Testing

The EPA recommends that sellers of real estate conduct a radon test before putting a property on the market to save time during real estate transactions.[77] There are several advantages to testing at this stage, including the following:

- A seller has the opportunity to conduct a long-term test that more accurately measures the annual indoor radon exposure. Long-term results also may be more advantageous to a seller, particularly if the transaction occurs during the winter months, when a short-term test will be more likely to yield higher radon levels.
- A seller has the opportunity to employ radon reduction measures to reduce radon levels to avoid losing a prospective buyer.
- Relocation companies regularly require a radon test, and remediation if necessary, as a condition precedent to a property transfer.[78]

The disadvantages of testing before putting a building on the market include the following:

- A seller may have an obligation to disclose the radon test results.
- A buyer may perform a radon test regardless of whether a seller has tested for radon, since a buyer has no way of determining whether the seller's test was performed under conditions that would produce accurate test results.
- A buyer may wish to perform radon reduction measures that meet the buyer's personal preferences.

Some lenders have begun to require evidence that radon levels are at or below the EPA action level of 4 pCi/l.[79] The Federal National Mortgage Association (Fannie Mae), for example, has developed environmental hazards management procedures with respect to apartments, condominiums, and co-ops, requiring lenders participating in Fannie Mae's delegated underwriting and servicing program to perform an environmental assessment of the property before commitment by Fannie Mae. A property is ineligible as security for mortgages to be purchased by Fannie Mae if the property contains radon levels in excess of 4 pCi/l that can only be corrected through large capital improvements or extensive maintenance programs that are beyond the financial and technical capability of the borrower.[80] Additionally, Fannie Mae expects its appraisers to assess the potential impact of elevated levels of radon in appraisals of one- to four-family houses.[81]

Despite the imperfections of short-term testing[82] and the fact that the EPA's action level does not represent a "safe" level, some lenders are refusing to lend against property that, according to short-term test results, contains radon levels in excess of the EPA action level. Alternatively, and particularly when short-term test results reveal radon levels only slightly in excess of the EPA action level, lenders may require borrowers to indemnify the lender against any harm to borrowers and other occupants of the lenders' collateral resulting from radon exposure.

Radon Contingency Clauses

Cautious buyers may require that the purchase and sale of residential real estate or commercial real estate located in an area of high radon potential should be made contingent upon acceptable indoor radon levels.[83] In transactions where the offer to purchase and the purchase and sale agreement are two separate documents, the radon contingency clause should be incorporated into the offer to purchase. If the contingency clause was not included in the offer or has not been satisfied before the date the purchase and sale agreement is executed, the radon contingency clause should be incorporated into the purchase and sale agreement. The buyer, however, may be estopped from incorporating any such contingency into the purchase and sale agreement that was not included in the offer.

DEFINING THE ACCEPTABLE LEVEL OF RADON. Ideally, a buyer wants a radon contingency clause that permits termination of the obligations to purchase if the buyer's radon test yields results that, in the buyer's sole discretion,[84] are unacceptable, regardless of whether the test results indicate radon levels lower than the EPA's action level of 4 pCi/l.

Two cases with decidedly different results illustrate the importance of drafting unambiguous contingency clauses that will provide a buyer with maximum flexibility to determine whether a specific radon level is acceptable. In *Wong v. Mercado*,[85] the parties entered into a side agreement whereby the buyers had the option to terminate their obligations under the contract if a radon test disclosed that the home was "untenantable—i.e., not repairable." The buyers tried to exercise their right to terminate, out of concern that two of their five children would be residing in the basement, where the radon levels were highest. Even though the buyers were deemed to have acted in good faith, the Superior Court of New Jersey held that their breach of the purchase contract, due to radon levels of 2.9 pCi/l, was unreasonable because the "house was not untenantable—i.e., not repairable—within the meaning of the contract."[86]

In contrast, the Connecticut Superior Court in *Pannone v. Grandmaison*[87] held that a prospective buyer acting in good faith was entitled to terminate its obligations to purchase even though a radon test revealed that the radon level was below 4 pCi/l. In this case, however, the radon contingency clause entitled the buyer to exercise discretion in determining whether the radon test produced results acceptable to the buyer.

A seller will want to limit the discretion that a buyer can exercise in terminating a contract by setting an outside date after which, and a minimum radon level (e.g., the EPA action level) below which, the buyer is prohibited from terminating its obligation to purchase. Additionally, if an initial short-term test reveals radon levels in excess of the predetermined acceptable level, a seller may want the right to retest. If a second short-term test confirms the results of the first test, the parties can agree that no additional testing will be performed. If, however, a second short-term test produces inconsistent results, a third short-term test can be performed. The parties might agree that the indoor radon level is the average of the two highest radon levels produced from the three tests.

RADON TESTING. The parties should agree on which testing device or firm will be used, which party will pay for the testing, and under what conditions the test(s) will be performed.

In addition to the previously discussed disadvantages of short-term tests, a buyer has little or no way of controlling or monitoring the test conditions of a short-term test and a seller has a strong incentive to impair the accuracy of the test results, particularly if the seller is concerned that the building may have elevated radon levels that might jeopardize the transaction. To impair the accuracy of the test results, a seller can move the testing device to an area of the building believed to have lower radon levels, seal the testing device during all or a portion of the testing period, or increase the ventilation in the building during the testing by opening doors and windows.

There are some actions a buyer can take to ensure that a seller or other third party does not tamper with the radon testing devices. A buyer, for example, may insist that a seller maintain closed house conditions before and throughout the testing period and that the seller agree not to tamper with the testing device(s). A buyer may also require a seller to sign an affidavit under oath outlining the steps the seller took to maintain closed house conditions before and throughout the testing period and certifying that the seller did not tamper with the testing device or otherwise attempt to impair the accuracy of the test results. However, such provisions are difficult to enforce, and it is difficult to verify that a seller took steps to impair the accuracy of the test results.

In addition, the EPA's "Home Buyer's and Seller's Guide to Radon" identifies a number of ways to prevent or detect test interference, such as using motion detectors to determine whether the testing device has been moved, recording barometric pressure to identify weather conditions that may have affected the test, and taping windows shut to ensure closed house conditions.[88]

Alternatively, a buyer might insist that a continuous radon monitoring system be employed instead of the more common charcoal canister,[89] and even that the seller pay for such a radon test. This type of monitoring system measures the radon levels during the entire testing period and will generate a printout showing the radon level within the structure at various points during the testing period, thus allowing a buyer to detect suspicious variations. The disadvantages of the continuous monitoring system include the cost (which ranges from $100 to $300); the fact that a skilled professional is required to perform the test; and the difficulty in discerning whether the variations in the radon levels were caused by naturally occurring daily variations in weather and other factors affecting radon levels, or by the seller's fraudulent activity.

From a buyer's perspective, the best way to prevent a seller's temptation to impair the accuracy of radon test results and to ensure accurate test results is to escrow a small portion of the sale proceeds for remediation costs and to perform a buyer-conducted radon test(s), preferably a long-term test, after the closing date.

RADON REDUCTION MEASURES. If radon tests reveal unacceptable radon levels, the purchase and sale agreement should address what, if any, additional obligations will be imposed on the parties. Several alternatives are available.

Reduce the Purchase Price. The parties can agree to reduce the purchase price by an amount equal to the estimated radon remediation costs. A seller may require that the estimate be capped and substantiated. If the estimate exceeds the amount by which the seller has agreed to reduce the purchase price, the buyer should have the option to terminate its obligation to purchase unless the seller agrees to reduce the purchase price by the estimated amount or to accept the maximum agreed reduction to the purchase price.

Seller Performs Remediation. Alternatively, the parties might agree that the seller will perform whatever remediation is required to reduce radon levels to below the previously agreed-on acceptable levels. This resolution is advantageous from the seller's perspective because it enables the seller to implement the most cost-effective radon reduction measures. Further, relocation companies typically require sellers to perform all remediation measures as a condition precedent to the property transfer. A non-relocation-company buyer, however, at least should be able to provide input into the type of radon reduction measures employed, based on its personal preferences and proposed use(s) of the building. For example, operating costs associated with an active system range from approximately $40 and $75 annually,[90] and the buyer may not wish to incur such annual operating costs.

Escrow Funds for Remediation

Optimally, a buyer should insist that the purchase and sale agreement provide for a portion of the proceeds to be placed into an escrow account for up to one year after the closing date to fund radon remediation costs if necessary. (Chapter 11 addresses escrow provisions generally.) In drafting escrow provisions, the following issues, at minimum, should be considered.

AMOUNT OF ESCROW. While a seller obviously wants a small sum, if any, escrowed, a buyer wants an amount that will cover the maximum potential remediation costs. In a residential context, the cost of remediating a home generally ranges from $500 to $2,500.

MATERIAL TERMS OF ESCROW.

Levels of Radon That Trigger the Ability to Remediate. The parties should determine what radon level, based on long-term test results, will trigger the buyer's ability to gain access to the escrow funds. A buyer might require that the escrow funds be released to remediate the home if the long-term test produces results in excess of 2 pCi/l, a level that can be achieved approximately 70 percent of the time.[91] In contrast, a seller should insist that the escrow funds be released only if the long-term test yields results in excess of 4 pCi/l, the EPA action level, which can be achieved more than 95 percent of the time.[92]

Remediation. Assuming a long-term test produces results in excess of the level permitting the buyer to use the escrow funds to remediate, the buyer (and now owner) should insist that a proficient contractor be hired to perform the necessary remediation. Also, funds should be released to pay the mitigation contractors directly, as opposed to requiring the buyer to pay the contractor and then seek reimbursement from the escrow agent.

Follow-up Test. If after the remediation a follow-up test indicates that radon levels are above acceptable levels as defined by the parties, the buyer should be able to use all or a portion of the remaining escrow funds to engage a proficient contractor to perform additional remediation.

Timing. One year is a frequently agreed-on period in such an escrow scenario because it gives a diligent buyer sufficient time to perform a long-term test and to remediate.

Obtain Indemnification from Seller

From a buyer's perspective, a less advantageous alternative to escrowing a portion of sale proceeds is to obtain an indemnification from the seller for all reasonable costs associated with reducing indoor radon levels to a predetermined acceptable level. (Chapter 11 covers general indemnification provisions in more detail.) From a seller's perspective, it is of utmost importance that the indemnification obligation be capped at a predetermined amount and terminated after a specified length of time. Therefore, unless a seller's indemnification is unlimited in time and amount and the seller is creditworthy and likely to meet all its obligations, a buyer is more likely to recover its remediation costs if escrow funds have already been earmarked for that purpose.

Radon Disclaimers

Radon disclaimers are more likely to be enforced if they are clear, concise, unambiguous, and accompanied by general radon disclosures. If the disclaimer is drafted in this manner, a party is less able to take the position that there was unequal bargaining power and that it did not understand the nature of the risk it agreed to assume.[93] Sellers, home inspectors, builders, mitigation contractors, and landlords should consider including a radon disclaimer in all their contracts, explicitly disclaiming liability to any party for radon remediation costs. The seller should also obtain an explicit acknowledgment and understanding of the radon disclaimer by the buyer as well as the buyer's agreement to assume all liability for radon remediation costs, incurred either voluntarily or involuntarily.

The more concise the disclaimer, the more likely it will be upheld if high radon levels result in subsequent damages for the buyer. The courts, on the other hand, generally are reluctant to assume that a general disclaimer of liability resulting from environmental conditions in, on, or around the property encompasses high radon levels.[94]

General Radon Disclosure

RATIONALE FOR THE GENERAL RADON DISCLOSURE. Providing both buyers and tenants with a written general radon disclosure is a prudent step that may be taken by sellers, brokers, landlords, builders, home inspectors, and mitigation contractors with little effort and no adverse consequences. Further, written acknowledgment of the receipt and understanding of the disclosure presumably diminishes such buyers' and tenants' chances of successfully pursuing claims against such parties.[95]

CONTENTS OF THE GENERAL RADON DISCLOSURE. Similar to lead-based paint notification laws,[96] sellers and brokers might provide buyers with general information about radon and its associated health risks and a ten-day period in which to test the building for radon.

The general disclosure could read as follows:

> Radon has been identified as a problem in this state. It is a colorless, odorless, tasteless gas that can seep into homes through cracks and openings in a home's foundation. Inhalation of radon gas is associated with increased risk of lung cancer; the risk is especially high if you are exposed to high radon levels and you smoke.
>
> The Surgeon General of the United States, the United States Environmental Protection Agency, and the [name of state agency] recommend that you test your home for radon. If high radon levels are found, your home should be fixed. For more information about radon testing and mitigation, call the state radon hotline at 800-xxx-xxxx.[97]

This provision not only informs a buyer about radon and recommends that a test be performed, but it also enables a buyer to obtain additional information from a disinterested third party.

Specific Radon Disclosure

An increasing number of states are enacting laws requiring disclosure of any defect that would materially affect a property's value[98] or, even more specifically, knowledge of the presence of radon[99] or copies of all radon test results and evidence of any subsequent mitigation.[100]

Irrespective of whether a particular state has laws requiring disclosure, liability resulting from nondisclosure of high levels of radon could arise in the following contexts:

- A person, such as a seller, landlord, contractor, or builder, knows the building contains high levels of radon but is never asked about the building's radon levels and therefore never discloses his or her knowledge.

- A person knows the building contains high radon levels but, when asked if the building contains radon, either represents that he or she has no knowledge of the presence of radon in the building or that the building does not contain high radon levels.
- A person represents that high radon levels do not exist, even though no radon tests have been performed to verify the accuracy of such a representation.
- A person has no knowledge of the presence of high radon levels and therefore makes no representations regarding radon.

Under the second scenario, the representing party is likely to be held liable for misrepresentation for failing to disclose his or her knowledge of the high radon levels when specifically asked. Similarly, a party's failure to substantiate his or her representations or to disclose the fact that the representations are unsubstantiated could be deemed to be misrepresentation, thus subjecting the party to potential liability. It is less clear, however, whether a party has a duty to disclose knowledge of high radon levels or to test for radon, particularly if a general radon disclosure has been provided to the other party and that party fails to inquire about or test for the presence of radon.

Under the doctrine of caveat emptor, a seller traditionally is not liable to a buyer for preexisting conditions of the property unless an agreement expressly provides otherwise. In most jurisdictions, however, the doctrine has been eroded in the residential context, on the theory that buyers are entitled to an implied warranty of habitability. In those jurisdictions, a seller may be held liable for failing to disclose high radon levels under the rationale that a seller is required to disclose any defective condition because a buyer is less likely to learn of such a condition.[101]

Further, and equally applicable to residential or commercial real estate transactions, some courts have held that the doctrine of caveat emptor will not protect a seller who conceals or fails to disclose a condition that involves unreasonable risk to others. The seller may still be held liable to a buyer who had no reason to know of the undisclosed risk or condition if the seller knew or should have known of the condition or risk and the buyer would not have discovered it.[102] The presence of high levels of radon gas certainly poses unreasonable risk to others and is not likely to be discernible by the buyer. Therefore, if a seller knows of high radon levels, it is prudent either to take steps to remediate before marketing the property or to disclose the condition. Even if the seller's remediation measures are successful, it is advisable to disclose the prior existence of high radon levels.

Absent a state law requirement to test for radon, it is unclear whether a seller can be charged with knowledge of high radon levels or the duty to test. Such a determination would likely turn on the amount of available public information about radon and whether the area in question is an area of high radon potential. If, for example, a buyer is from an area of the country that has a low radon potential and is attempting to purchase real estate in an area of high radon potential, a seller will be more likely to be charged with knowledge of high radon levels on public policy grounds. Under these circumstances, the seller is in a better position to discover the problem. However, a general radon disclosure that warns of the health risks of radon and advises a buyer to test for radon is likely to shield the seller from liability.

The same disclosure analysis is applicable to other parties, particularly brokers.[103] A broker is subject to potential liability if he or she makes an unsubstantiated representation about radon.[104]

Leasing Real Estate

Landlords and tenants face many of the same issues as sellers and buyers. Although the issue of radon arises less frequently in leasing transactions because prospective tenants rarely test for radon, a landlord leasing residential property with high radon levels in an area of high radon potential is more likely to be held liable for any resulting damage than a seller of residential real estate, regardless of any general radon disclosure or disclaimer. Clear, unambiguous, and specific non-radon-related disclaimers, which have been enforced in sale transactions, have not been enforced in lease transactions on the theory that the landlord has superior bargaining power.[105]

With the possible exception of a landlord specifically disclosing to a tenant that the residential property contains high radon levels and a tenant knowingly and voluntarily entering into a residential lease, a landlord is subject to liability based on breach of the implied warranty of habitability if he or she leases property with high radon levels. An implied warranty of habitability signifies that the premises are fit for habitation, free of latent defects, and will be maintained in a habitable condition by the owner.

For a landlord of real estate with high radon levels, the most prudent approach is to mitigate the leased premises so that radon levels are less than or equal to 4 pCi/l, especially if any of the occupants are children, who are believed to face a greater risk from radon exposure.[106] Mitigating high levels of radon not only reduces a landlord's potential liability but also minimizes the chances, particularly in the case of a commercial landlord, of losing a prospective tenant because of high radon levels since more and more tenants perform radon tests before entering into a lease. The U.S. General Services Administration (GSA), for example, requires that any space it intends to lease be tested for the presence of radon. If the test reveals high radon levels, the GSA will not lease the space until the radon levels have been reduced to an acceptable level.[107]

New Construction

In view of the widespread knowledge about radon and its health risks and the fact that installing radon reduction measures at the construction stage is both feasible and cost-effective, builders may be subject to liability under the theory of implied warranty of habitability if damage results from high radon levels in new construction. However, in contrast to a residential lease transaction, the implied warranty in the sale of new construction can be contracted away if the disclaimers are clear, unambiguous, and specific.[108]

In addition to considering the same issues and taking similar precautions as a seller or broker of real estate, a builder should be familiar with the EPA's Map of Radon Zones and any local information to be used in conjunction therewith; the EPA Model Standards; the EPA publications "Radon-Resistant Construction Techniques for New Residential Construction"[109] and "Radon Prevention in the Design and Construction of Schools and Other Large Buildings";[110] other construction guidance documents produced by the EPA and builders' associations; and state and local building codes. Given the national attention radon has received, including the EPA's recent adoption of the Model Standards, builders are likely to be imputed with constructive knowledge of the hazards of radon and the means by which to reduce or eliminate those hazards.

In addition to familiarity with radon and the most recent technology respecting radon remediation, builders should implement the Model Standards and follow other technical guidance offered by the EPA. A buyer's refusal to purchase a passive radon control system should be documented and accompanied by a radon disclaimer and acknowledgment of such disclaimer by the buyer and a statement that the buyer accepts the building "as is," regardless of the levels of radon gas.

Cautious builders may want to reduce indoor radon concentrations to below 2 pCi/l rather than the EPA action level because the lower level is both safer and achievable through implementation of radon-resistant construction features.[111] Further, in light of the stated national goal of reducing indoor radon levels to the levels found in ambient air outside of buildings,[112] the EPA's recommendation that indoor radon levels be reduced to 2 pCi/l or below, and the adoption of the Model Rules, builders will be imputed with constructive knowledge that a lower radon level is feasible.

A buyer of new construction should always inquire about whether the building has radon-resistant features and require the builder to perform a radon test.[113] Buyers should also perform their own radon tests after the construction is complete to avoid potential conflicts of interest.[114]

Conclusion

Absent a discovery that exposure to high radon levels is more harmful than is currently believed, or the adoption of a federal or applicable state mandatory maximum indoor radon level, property owners are likely to continue to test for radon and to remediate, as necessary, primarily in the context of the purchase and sale of new or existing residential real estate. Such testing will occur either because it is a requirement of the buyer's lender or at the suggestion of the broker, the home inspector, or even the seller. Further, unless landlords eventually are held liable to tenants for damages resulting from high radon levels (as they have been in situations involving lead-based paint in residential housing), radon testing and remediation is unlikely to be performed regularly in the context of lease transactions.

Notes

1. Air and Radiation, U.S. EPA, U.S. Dep't of Health and Human Services, and U.S. Public Health Service, A Citizen's Guide to Radon (2nd ed.): The Guide to Protecting Yourself and Your Family from Radon 2-3 (Report No. 402-K92-001, May 1992) [hereinafter Citizen's Guide]; Air and Radiation, U.S. EPA, Technical Support Document for the 1992 Citizen's Guide to Radon (Report No. EPA 400-R-92-011, May 1992) [hereinafter Technical Support to Citizen's Guide].

2. According to the EPA, the average indoor radon level is 1.3 pCi/l. The EPA estimates that if 1,000 smokers and 1,000 nonsmokers are exposed to radon levels of 1.3 pCi/l over a lifetime, approximately nine smokers and one nonsmoker would contract lung cancer. By way of contrast, the EPA estimates that if 1,000 smokers and 1,000 nonsmokers are exposed to the EPA's action level of 4 pCi/l over a lifetime, approximately twenty-nine smokers and two nonsmokers would contract lung cancer. Citizen's Guide, *supra* note 1, at 7, 12. *See also* notes 10–20 for further discussion of the EPA's voluntary action level.

3. Land & Water Resources Center, University of Maine, *Radon and Water and Air*, Natural Resources Highlight 2 (rev. June 1986) [hereinafter University of Maine].

4. Office of Water, U.S. EPA, Report to the United States Congress on Radon in Drinking Water: Multimedia Risk and Cost Assessment of Radon 1-4–1-5 (Report No. EPA 811-R-94-001, Mar. 1994) [hereinafter Drinking Water Report]. The EPA estimates that between 11 and 212 lung cancer deaths

per year result from the ingestion of radon gas in drinking water. *Id.* at 1–11. *See also infra* notes 40–43 and accompanying text for further discussion of the effects and regulation of radon in drinking water.

5. CITIZEN'S GUIDE, *supra* note 1, at 2–3; TECHNICAL SUPPORT TO CITIZEN'S GUIDE, *supra* note 1.

6. UNIVERSITY OF MAINE, *supra* note 3, at 2. Radon has a short half-life (the time required for half of the atoms of a radioactive element to undergo decay) of 3.8 days and its decay products have half-lives ranging from a fraction of a second to twenty-two years. At every level of transformation from radon 222 to lead 210, emissions of energized particles damage delicate lung tissue.

7. Model Standards and Techniques for Control of Radon in New Residential Buildings, 59 Fed. Reg. 13,402 (1994) [hereinafter EPA Model Standards for New Residential Construction].

8. AIR AND RADIATION, U.S. EPA, 1989 SUMMARY OF STATE RADON PROGRAMS 5 (Report No. 520/1-91-015, Sept. 1990) [hereinafter SUMMARY OF STATE RADON PROGRAMS].

9. SUMMARY OF STATE RADON PROGRAMS, *supra* note 8, at 5. In December 1984, Stanley Watras of Boyertown, Pennsylvania, an employee at the Limerick Nuclear Power Plant, entered the plant one morning and set off radiation detection devices. After investigators were unable to detect the source of the radiation within the plant, they found traces of radioactive radon elements on Watras's clothing, which led to the search of his home. The radon levels inside Watras's home registered 4,400 pCi/l, a level one thousand times greater than the EPA suggested guideline. The radon levels measured within Watras's home had the equivalent effect of smoking 135 packs of cigarettes per day or being exposed to 455,000 chest x-rays per year. While the Watras example is extreme, it triggered national concerns over the risk of indoor radon levels. Comment, *Radon's Radioactive Ramifications: How Federal and State Government Should Address the Problem*, 16 B.C. ENVTL. AFF. L. REV. 329, 329–30 (1988) (authored by Anne Rickard Jackowitz).

10. By way of background, the Curie is the commonly used measurement for radioactivity. This unit, however, is too large to use for radiation levels discussed in radon cases. Therefore, the usual unit used is the picoCurie (pCi), which is one trillionth (1×10^{-12}) of a Curie. The amount of radon in air and water is measured in picoCuries per liter (pCi/l). Some test results are expressed in Working Levels (WL), the unit used to measure radon decay products or radioactive elements that result from the chemical breakdown of radon. Since the WL unit is generally beyond the scope of the nonscientific community's comprehension, the pCi/l is the unit more commonly used. For conversion purposes, 1WL = 200 pCi/l.

11. AIR AND RADIATION, U.S. EPA, NATIONAL RESIDENTIAL RADON SURVEY: SUMMARY REPORT 6, 9 (Report No. EPA 402-R-92-011, Oct. 1992) [hereinafter NRRS REPORT].

12. *See* Office of Public Affairs, U.S. Environmental Protection Agency, *EPA Finds Radon Problem in 10-State Survey*, ENVIRONMENTAL NEWS 2–3 (Aug. 4, 1987) [hereinafter *10-State Survey*]; NRRS REPORT, *supra* note 11, at 13.

13. While some EPA regions have been found to have a greater percentage of homes with radon concentrations above the EPA's action level of 4 pCi/l, every

EPA region was found to have a significant number of homes with radon levels above the EPA's action level. NRRS Report, *supra* note 11, at 9.

14. CITIZEN'S GUIDE, *supra* note 1, at 4. In its National Residential Radon Survey (NRRS), the EPA estimated the annual average radon concentration in the U.S. housing stock to be 1.25 pCi/l. Approximately 0.7 percent of homes within the United States have annual average radon levels greater than 10 pCi/l. NRRS REPORT, *supra* note 11, at 6, 9.

15. AIR AND RADIATION, U.S. EPA, RADON FACTS § 1 (Aug. 1987). *See also 10-State Survey*, *supra* note 12, at 2–3.

16. *10-State Survey*, *supra* note 12, at 2–3.

17. Indoor Radon Abatement Act of 1988, Title III of the Toxic Substances Control Act (TSCA), 15 U.S.C.A. §§ 2667, 2669 (West Supp. 1994) [hereinafter IRAA].

18. *See also* AIR AND RADIATION, U.S. EPA, EPA'S MAP OF RADON ZONES: NATIONAL SUMMARY I-3, Figure 1 (Report No. EPA 402-R-93-071, Sept. 1993) [hereinafter EPA MAP OF RADON ZONES].

19. Zone 1 counties have a predicted average indoor screening level of greater than 4 pCi/l; Zone 2 counties have a predicted average indoor screening level of between 2 and 4 pCi/l; and Zone 3 counties have a predicted average screening level of less than 2 pCi/l. *Id.* at I-2.

20. *Id.* at I-1.

21. *See* Cole, *Radon: The Silent Killer?*, GARBAGE 22 (Spring 1994). Leonard Cole criticizes the EPA's campaign to inform property owners about the health effects of radon and advise that all homes be tested as "aggressive and alarmist" in light of the fact that the scientific evidence of exposure to high levels of radon is based on extrapolations from the studies of underground miners. *Id.* According to the National Research Council (NRC), however, radon may be more hazardous than previously estimated. Therefore, the NRC recently issued a report recommending that the risks of radon be reassessed. The NRC is expected to complete such reassessment by the end of 1996. Lee, *Reassess Radon Risk, Panel Urges, Health Threat May Be Greater than Assumed*, WASH. POST, June 8, 1994.

22. TECHNICAL SUPPORT TO CITIZEN'S GUIDE, *supra* note 1, at 2-1–2-2. Many other national and international organizations, including, without limitation, the National Academy of Science, the Centers for Disease Control, the International Agency for Research on Cancer, and the International Commission on Radiological Protection, agree that radon causes lung cancer in humans. *Id.*

23. *Id.* at 2-8, 2-22. *See also* Page, *Radon Risks are Real*, GARBAGE 29 (Spring 1994).

24. *Residential Radon Exposure and Lung Cancer in Sweden*, NEW ENG. J. MED. 159–64 (January 20, 1994).

25. CITIZEN'S GUIDE, *supra* note 1, at 7.

26. OFFICE OF RESEARCH AND DEVELOPMENT, U.S. EPA, RADON-RESISTANT CONSTRUCTION TECHNIQUES FOR NEW RESIDENTIAL CONSTRUCTION 3 (Report No. EPA/62S/2-91/032, Feb. 1991).

27. CITIZEN'S GUIDE, *supra* note 1, at 4.

28. *Id.* DRINKING WATER REPORT, *supra* note 4, at 1-5. Radon enters the structure through water-related activities such as dish washing and showering and when water is stirred, shaken, or heated before being ingested. The radon dissolved in the water becomes airborne, further increasing radon levels inside

buildings. *Id.* As a rule of thumb, each 10,000 pCi/l of radon in water results in an approximately 1 pCi/l increase in the indoor radon level. AIR AND RADIATION, U.S. EPA, CONSUMER'S GUIDE TO RADON REDUCTION 15 (Report No. 402-K92-003, Aug. 1992) [hereinafter CONSUMER'S GUIDE]. In addition to being inhaled, waterborne radon can be ingested. CITIZEN'S GUIDE, *supra* note 1, at 4; DRINKING WATER REPORT, *supra* note 4, at 1–5.

Another possible source of radon in buildings is construction materials such as concrete, bricks, and stone. Building materials, however, are a relatively insignificant source of indoor radon. CITIZEN'S GUIDE, *supra* note 1, at 4. In the 1960s in Grand Junction, Colorado, for example, it was discovered that uranium mill tailings had been removed from waste sites and used in construction materials. SUMMARY OF STATE RADON PROGRAMS, *supra* note 8, at 5. *See* Wayne v. TVA, 730 F.2d 392 (5th Cir. 1984) (homeowners found that the phosphates slag used in concrete blocks of their house was emitting radon gas), *cert. denied*, 469 U.S. 1159 (1985).

29. DRINKING WATER REPORT, *supra* note 4, at 1-10–1-11.

30. *See* Uranium Mill Tailings Radiation Control Act of 1978, 42 U.S.C. §§ 2022, 7901–42 (1982). The Uranium Mill Tailings Radiation Control Act of 1978 regulates radon as a by-product of the mining process, including in air quality in residential and commercial buildings built over former uranium sites. *See also* 40 C.F.R. part 61, subpart B (National Emission Standards for Radon Emissions from Underground Uranium Mines). In addition, the EPA issued a national emission standard for radon emissions from phosphogypsum stacks. Phosphogypsum stacks are piles of waste or mines used to store and dispose of phosphogypsum, a waste resulting from wet acid phosphorous production. 40 C.F.R. part 61, subpart R.

31. *Cf.* The Clean Air Act, 42 U.S.C. §§ 7401–42 (1982 & Supp. IV 1986), authorizes the EPA to regulate air pollution only in "ambient air." *See id.* §§ 7409(a), 7412(a)(1), 7602(g). While the Clean Air Act does not define "ambient air," the EPA has interpreted the term "ambient air" to apply to outdoor air only. Nothing in the Clean Air Act addresses the quality of indoor air. Kirsch, *Behind Closed Doors: Indoor Air Pollution and Government Policy*, 6 HARV. ENVTL. L. REV. 339, 363–64 (1982). Therefore, unless Congress clarifies the definition of ambient air to include indoor air, the federal government does not have authority to enforce regulations regarding radon levels. Moore, *The Radon Review: The Federal and State Governments' Responses to Indoor Radon Contamination*, 7 TEMP. ENVTL. L. & TECH. J. 39, 42–43 (1988) [hereinafter *The Radon Review*].

32. TECHNICAL SUPPORT TO CITIZEN'S GUIDE, *supra* note 1, at 1-1. *See also* U.S. EPA, Report to Congress on Indoor Air Pollution and Radon under Title IV of the Superfund Amendments and Reauthorization Act of 1986, 13 (Apr. 1987).

33. Superfund Amendments and Reauthorization Act of 1986 (SARA), Pub. L. No. 99-499, 100 Stat. 1613, 1758 (codified as amended primarily in scattered sections of 42 U.S.C.).

34. Radon Gas and Indoor Air Quality Act of 1986, 42 U.S.C. § 7401 (Supp. IV 1986).

35. IRAA, 15 U.S.C.A. § 2661 *et seq.*

36. Comment, *Construction Contractors Confront the Indoor Radon Hazard: Homeowners' Private Clauses of Action and a Federal Response with the Indoor Radon*

Abatement Bill, 37 WASH. U.J. URB. & CONTEMP. L. 135, 161–62 (1990) (*citing* H.R. Rep. No. 1047, 102nd Cong., 2nd Sess. 7-8, *reprinted in* 1988 U.S. CODE CONG. & AD. NEWS 3612–13, 3617).

37. IRAA, 15 U.S.C.A. §§ 2665(f), 2666(j), 2667(b), 2668(f).

38. *Id.* § 2663.

39. *Id.* § 2664. IRAA also directed the EPA to provide technical assistance and grants to the states for radon programs, to assess the level of radon in schools and federal buildings, and to establish and operate regional radon training centers to develop and provide information regarding the health risks posed by radon and methods of radon measurement and mitigation to federal, state, and local public officials, private firms, or individuals. *Id.* §§ 2665–69.

40. 56 Fed. Reg. 33,125 (1991). Notwithstanding the fact that the EPA was under a court order to issue a final rule for radon and other radionuclides in drinking water by April 15, 1993, a final rule has not yet been issued. Further, the EPA funding bill for fiscal year 1994 precludes the EPA from working on radon regulations during 1994. However, under an agreement between the EPA and an Oregon citizens' group, a new deadline of April 30, 1995, was established for the issuance of a final rule for radionuclides, including radon, in drinking water.

41. 56 Fed. Reg. 33,074 (1991).

42. DRINKING WATER REPORT, *supra* note 4, at 1-10–1-11.

43. *Radon in Water Poses Highest Cancer Risk of Any Regulated Substance, EPA Reports*, BNA NAT'L ENVTL. DAILY (April 5, 1994). In May 1994 the Senate passed a bill to reauthorize the Safe Drinking Water Act. This legislation, if enacted into law, would set two standards for radon in drinking water: a maximum contaminant level as close to the no-health-effect level as possible; and an alternative contaminant level equivalent to average exposure from outdoor air. Under the bill, a state drinking water system could choose to meet the alternative contaminant level if it implements a program to reduce radon in indoor air or if it is located in a state that is implementing an indoor air radon program and is receiving grant assistance under IRAA. S. 1547, 103rd Cong., 1st Sess., 139 CONG. REC. S13489, S13496 (daily ed. Oct. 14, 1993). Senate Bill 1547 was reintroduced in 1994 as Senate Bill 2019 and was passed by the Senate on May 19, 1994. S. REP. NO. 103-250, 103rd Cong., 2nd Sess. (1994).

44. CITIZEN'S GUIDE, *supra* note 1, at 6–7. *See also* TECHNICAL SUPPORT TO CITIZEN'S GUIDE, *supra* note 1, at 3-3.

45. CITIZEN'S GUIDE, *supra* note 1, at 6–7, 12; TECHNICAL SUPPORT TO CITIZEN'S GUIDE, *supra* note 1, at 3-3.

46. NRRS REPORT, *supra* note 11, at 6.

47. *Id.*

48. NRRS REPORT, *supra* note 11, at 9.

49. CITIZEN'S GUIDE, *supra* note 1, at 6. *See also* AIR AND RADIATION, U.S. EPA, RADON: THE HEALTH THREAT WITH A SIMPLE SOLUTION: A PHYSICIAN'S GUIDE 11 (Report No. 402-K-93-008, Sept. 1993) [hereinafter PHYSICIAN'S GUIDE]. The EPA suggests that consumers purchase radon measurement services from organizations that have participated in the EPA's Radon Measurement Proficiency (RMP) Program, a voluntary program established in 1986 to ensure that consumers obtain reliable radon measurements. AIR AND RADIATION, U.S. EPA, RADON MEASUREMENT PROFICIENCY (RMP) PROGRAM 1-3, D-2–D-5 (Report No.

EPA 520/1-91-006, May 1994) [hereinafter RMP PROGRAM HANDBOOK]. *See also* User Fees for Radon Proficiency Programs, 59 Fed. Reg. 13,166 (1994) (to be codified at 40 C.F.R. Parts 195 and 700). While some state and local governments regulate the activities of radon measurement service organizations and/or require participation in the RMP Program, there is no federal requirement that organizations participate in the RMP Program. Organizations that meet the requirements of the RMP Program are listed as successful participants in the "National Radon Measurement Proficiency (RMP) Program—National Proficiency Report." The RMP Program does not accredit, certify, recommend, or endorse participating organizations, but the EPA and state and local governments distribute the names of participants who have demonstrated the capability for measuring radon with specific devices. *Id.*

50. RMP PROGRAM HANDBOOK, *supra* note 49, at D-2–D-5 (Radon gas measurement methods and radon decay product measurement methods are more fully described.) *See also* Bell, *Radon Primer for Practitioners Conveyancing Residential Property*, LIVING WITH TOXIC MATERIALS: EMERGING CONCERNS IN RESIDENTIAL PROPERTY TRANSACTIONS 237-41 (MCLE 91-09.02, Oct. 1990) [hereinafter *Radon Primer*] (for a discussion of the advantages and disadvantages of some of the commonly used radon measurement methods). Alpha track and electret detectors are commonly used to obtain long-term measurements. Charcoal canisters, alpha track, electret ion chamber, continuous monitors, and charcoal liquid scintillation detectors are the most commonly used short-term tests. *Id.*

51. CITIZEN'S GUIDE, *supra* note 1, at 5–6; PHYSICIAN'S GUIDE, *supra* note 49, at 11.

52. CONSUMER'S GUIDE, *supra* note 28, at 3.

53. In response to the Congressional mandate to develop a voluntary contractor proficiency program, to establish regional training programs, and to provide information on capable radon reduction contractors to state governments and the public, the EPA established the voluntary Radon Contractor Proficiency (RCP) Program in 1989 to provide the public with information about qualified radon mitigators. AIR AND RADIATION, U.S. EPA, RADON CONTRACTOR PROFICIENCY PROGRAM (RCPP) HANDBOOK AND APPLICATION 1-4 (Report No. EPA 520/1-91-021, Dec. 1991) [hereinafter RCPP HANDBOOK]. The RCP Program consists of the following elements: two days of training; the RCP Program National Radon Proficiency Exam; the National RCP Program Proficiency Report listing qualified contractors; compliance with the EPA Radon Mitigation Standards; and a biennial re-examination. *Id. See also* AIR AND RADIATION, U.S. EPA, RADON MITIGATION STANDARDS (Report No. EPA 402-R-93-078, Oct. 1993, rev. Apr. 1994) [hereinafter RADON MITIGATION STANDARDS] (for a discussion of EPA's mitigation standards). Similar to the RMP Program, there is no federal mandate that radon contractors participate in the RCP Program, although some states require successful completion of the RCP Program as a requirement for state certification.

54. CONSUMER'S GUIDE, *supra* note 28, at 5, 6, 12–13.

55. *Id.* at 7.

56. OFFICE OF RESEARCH AND DEVELOPMENT, U.S. EPA, RADON-RESISTANT CONSTRUCTION TECHNIQUES FOR NEW RESIDENTIAL CONSTRUCTION: TECHNICAL GUIDANCE 3 (Report No. EPA/625/2-91/0032, Feb. 1991) [hereinafter RESIDENTIAL RADON-RESISTANT CONSTRUCTION TECHNIQUES].

57. PHYSICIAN'S GUIDE, *supra* note 49, at 11–12.

58. CONSUMER'S GUIDE, *supra* note 28, at 11. Natural ventilation is considered a temporary approach because it causes conditioned air to be lost, increases the cost of conditioning outside air, and raises security concerns. Theoretically, the increased ventilation mixes radon with outside air, reducing indoor radon levels, and also reduces the vacuum effect, minimizing the amount of radon drawn into a building. However, ventilation may also have the effect of increasing the radon concentrations if air is drawn outside of the building by a fan, for example, because it will cause an increase in the negative pressure inside the building, thereby increasing the amount of radon entering the building. *Id.*; Crawshaw, *Radon Mitigation for Residential Property Transactions*, LIVING WITH TOXIC MATERIALS: EMERGING CONCERNS IN RESIDENTIAL PROPERTY TRANSACTIONS 179, 193 (MCLE 91-09.02, Oct. 1990).

59. CONSUMER'S GUIDE, *supra* note 28, at 13.

60. CITIZEN'S GUIDE, *supra* note 1, at 7. *See also* EPA Model Standards for New Residential Construction, *supra* note 7, at 13413, § 7.0.

61. IRAA, 15 U.S.C.A. § 2664.

62. *See* EPA Model Standards for New Residential Construction, *supra* note 7.

63. The EPA Model Standards for New Residential Construction are designed to be readily adopted by model code organizations, states, and local jurisdictions to the extent appropriate for their building code needs. *Id.* § 1.04.

64. *Id.* §§ 2.02, 5.2.

65. EPA Model Standards for New Residential Buildings, *supra* note 7. Limited research has found that passive systems are effective in reducing indoor radon levels to below the EPA action level of 4 pCi/l in homes where levels of radon would otherwise have been slightly elevated and that active systems reduce indoor radon levels to below 2 pCi/l over 90 percent of the time. The cost to builders of installing a passive system ranges from $350 to $500 per house, and the cost of the electric fan and the system failure device is about $250. Therefore, the total cost of an active system ranges from between $600 and $750. *Id.*

66. CONSUMER'S GUIDE, *supra* note 28, at 7.

67. *See* Laurel E. Lockett, Radon: The Naturally Occurring Component of the Indoor Air Quality Problem 10–11 (unpublished paper presented to the ABA Section on Real Property, Probate, and Trust Law in Washington, D.C. on May 6, 1994) [hereinafter Radon: The Naturally Occurring Component]. *See also* Foster, *Radon: An Invisible Threat*, STATE LEGISLATIVE REPORT 9 (July 1993) [hereinafter STATE LEGISLATIVE REPORT].

68. N.J. STAT. ANN. § 26:2D-73 (West 1987). *See also infra* notes 101–103 and accompanying text.

69. FLA. STAT. ANN. § 404.056(4) (West 1993).

70. IOWA CODE ANN. § 136B (West 1989).

71. N.J. STAT. ANN. §§ 26:2D-70–26:2D-72.

72. *See* RMP PROGRAM HANDBOOK, *supra* note 49, at E-3–E-8.

73. *See* ENVIRONMENTAL LAW INSTITUTE, STATE RADON LEGISLATION ISSUES AND OPTIONS 21 (Fall 1993) [hereinafter STATE RADON LEGISLATION].

74. FLA. STAT. ANN. § 553.98.

75. WASH. REV. CODE ANN. §§ 19.27.190, 19.27.192 (West 1989).

76. STATE RADON LEGISLATION, *supra* note 73, at 11.

77. Air and Radiation, U.S. EPA, Home Buyer's and Seller's Guide to Radon 6 (Report No. 402-R-93-003, Mar. 1993) [hereinafter Home Buyer's Guide].

78. Radon Division, Office and Radiation and Indoor Air, Office of Air and Radiation, U.S. EPA, EPA's Strategy to Reduce Risk of Radon 18 (June 1993).

79. Shepherd and Gayner, *Radon: A Growing Menace in Real Estate Transactions*, Real Property, Probate, and Trust J. (May/June 1989).

80. Shepherd, *Indoor Radon Rouses the Commercial Real Estate Industry*, 5 J. Real Est. Dev. 45, 49 (Summer 1989); Telephone interview with Sherri Engelman Reich, Vice President, Counsel of the Northeastern Regional Office of Fannie Mae. *See also* Fannie Mae DUS Guide § 101.04 (April 25, 1994); Fannie Mae Project Standards, Environmental Hazard Assessment § 801, 887–899.3 (January 1, 1992).

81. Fannie Mae Property and Appraisal Analysis, Special Appraisal Considerations § 303, 728–30 (January 1, 1994).

82. *See supra* note 51 and accompanying text.

83. For example, the New Jersey Realtor's Association recommends use of a radon contingency clause in every real estate transaction. *The Radon Review*, *supra* note 31, at 57–58.

84. No level of radon is safe and the health risks associated with high radon levels vary, depending on which areas of the building contain high levels of radon and the amount of time individuals will be spending in the high radon areas or in the building generally. Furthermore, the level of risk to which individuals are willing to expose themselves varies.

85. 590 A.2d 723, 726 (N.J. Super. L. 1991). *See also* Tanner v. Adams, 602 N.Y.S.2d 710, 711 (1993) (contingency clause stating "that the premises are free from any substantial structural, mechanical, electrical, plumbing, roofing, water, or sewer defects" fails to suggest that radon gas at any particular level would provide grounds to terminate the purchase contract).

86. *Id.* at 730.

87. 1990 WL 265273 (Conn. Super.).

88. *See also* Home Buyer's Guide, *supra* note 77, at 10.

89. *See Radon Primer*, *supra* note 50, at 237–38.

90. EPA Model Standards for New Residential Construction, *supra* note 7, at 13,403.

91. Technical Support to Citizen's Guide, *supra* note 1, at 3-3.

92. *Id.*

93. *Cf* T & E Industries, Inc. v. Safety Light Corp. et al., 587 A.2d 1249, 1258–59 (N.J. 1991) (purchaser can assume risk of harm from abnormally dangerous activity if it does so knowingly and voluntarily).

94. *Cf. supra* note 84.

95. *See* H.R. 2448, 103rd Cong., 2nd Sess. House Bill 2448, passed by the House on July 28, 1994, requires lessors and sellers of new and existing buildings that are frequently occupied below the third floor to make certain radon disclosures. For example, the lessor or seller must provide the lessee or buyer with a radon hazard information pamphlet; any testing results prepared for or received by lessor or purchaser and any known mitigation systems; and, in the sale of new construction located in a high radon area, disclosure that the property is located in an area of high radon potential and whether the building was constructed in compliance with model construction standards. Additionally, a purchase and sale

agreement must contain a radon warning statement and an acknowledgment by the buyer that the buyer has read the warning statement; received the radon hazard information brochure; requested and was provided with an opportunity to test for radon on acceptable terms or agreed to accept the premises without further testing; and, in the sale of new construction located in a high radon area, was informed that the property is located in an area of high radon potential and whether the building was or would be constructed in accordance with model construction standards. *Cf.* 15 U.S.C.A. § 2686 (West Supp. 1994); 42 U.S.C.A. § 4852d (West Supp. 1994).

96. 15 U.S.C.A. § 2686 (West Supp. 1994); 42 U.S.C.A. § 4852d (West Supp. 1994).

97. STATE RADON LEGISLATION, *supra* note 73, at 4. See STATE LEGISLATIVE REPORT, *supra* note 67, at 11, for a list of state radon contacts.

98. McClintock, *Home Buyer Must Look Out for Concealed Problems*, STAR TRIBUNE, May 16, 1992, at 1R (metro ed.) (In California and Maine sellers are prohibited from concealing any defect that would materially affect the property's value and desirability).

99. Becker, *Not To[o][sic] Safe at Home; Perils Pack Our Houses—From Paint and Lead Pipes to Power Lines and Radon*, CHICAGO TRIBUNE, Jan. 16, 1994, at 1 (Real Estate) (final ed.) (Illinois has a disclosure act that requires sellers to reveal structural defects as well as the presence of radon, lead, and asbestos). *See also* Radon: The Naturally Occurring Component, *supra* note 67, at 8 (Maryland, New Jersey, Ohio, Rhode Island, South Dakota, Texas, Wisconsin, and Virginia have similar statutes).

100. *See* N.J. STAT. ANN. § 26:2D-73 (West 1987) ("In the case of a prospective sale of a building which has been tested for radon gas and radon progeny, the seller shall provide the buyer, at the time contract of sale is entered into, with a copy of the results of that test and evidence of any subsequent mitigation or treatment, and any prospective buyer who contracts for the testing shall have the right to receive the results of that testing."). *See also* Radon: The Naturally Occurring Component, *supra* note 67, at 8 (Montana has a similar disclosure requirement).

101. I*n re* Modern Laundry & Dry Cleaning Co., Inc., et al. v. Coyne, 1993 WL 235505, at 4 (E.D. Pa.).

102. *See* T & E Industries, Inc. v. Safety Light Corp. et al., 587 A.2d 1249, 1259 (N.J. 1991).

103. *See also* Comment, *Clearing the Air on Radon Testing: The Duty of Real Estate Brokers to Protect Prospective Homebuyers*, 15 FORDHAM URB. L.J. 767 (1987).

104. Several jurisdictions (including Alaska, the District of Columbia, Illinois, Maine, Texas, Utah, Washington, West Virginia, and Wisconsin) hold brokers liable for losses a buyer suffers due to a broker's innocent representations. Additionally, brokers might be held liable for innocent misrepresentation under some states' consumer protection laws or real estate licensing laws. Kornreich, *Dealing with the Invisible Trap of Radon Liability*, PRAC. REAL EST. LAW 17, 29–30 (Sept. 1987) [hereinafter *The Invisible Trap of Radon Liability*]. *See also* Radon: The Naturally Occurring Component, *supra* note 67, at 8 (in Colorado, it is a deceptive trade practice for a person to knowingly misrepresent the results of a radon test or the need for radon mitigation in the course of the person's business, vocation,

or occupation). A broker also may be charged with knowledge of high radon levels irrespective of the broker's actual knowledge, on the theory that the broker has an affirmative duty to conduct a reasonably thorough and diligent inspection and to disclose material facts revealed by such an investigation. *The Invisible Trap of Radon Liability, supra,* at 28, citing Easton v. Strassburger, 152 Cal. App. 3d 90, 199 Cal. Rptr. 383 (1984). The California law on duty to inspect has been clarified to require a broker to conduct a reasonably competent and diligent *visual* inspection of residential real property offered for sale and to disclose to a buyer all facts materially affecting the value or desirability of the property. However, it is unclear the extent to which limiting inspections to visual inspections protects a broker from liability for failing to discover and disclose elevated radon levels. *Id.*

As a practical matter, brokers should provide buyers with a general radon disclosure. In addition, if a broker is relying on information obtained from a seller, the broker might require the seller to provide a statement setting forth the seller's radon representations and a certification that all such representations are true and correct. The broker also should require the seller to provide the broker with an indemnification in favor of the broker against all liability that results from any untrue representations. *Id.* at 30.

105. Comment, *Radon Gas: Ramifications for Real Estate Transactions in Pennsylvania,* 91 DICK. L. REV. 1113, 1149–50 (Summer 1987) [hereinafter *Radon Gas Ramifications*].

106. CITIZEN'S GUIDE, *supra* note 1, at 11.

107. Shepherd, *Drafting Radon Contingency Clauses,* 6 PRAC. REAL EST. LAW 43, 44 (Jan. 1990).

108. *Radon Gas Ramifications, supra* note 105, at 1148–50, citing Tyus v. Resta, 328 Pa. Super. 11, 21, 476 A.2d 427, 432 (1984). *See also* Comment, *Construction Contractors Confront the Indoor Radon Hazard: Homeowners' Private Causes of Action and a Federal Response with the Indoor Radon Abatement Bill,* 37 J. URB. & CONTEMP. L. 135 (1990).

109. RESIDENTIAL RADON-RESISTANT CONSTRUCTION TECHNIQUES, *supra* note 56.

110. OFFICE OF RESEARCH AND DEVELOPMENT, U.S. EPA, RADON PREVENTION IN THE DESIGN AND CONSTRUCTION OF SCHOOLS AND OTHER LARGE BUILDINGS (Report No. EPA/625/R-92/016, Jan. 1993).

111. CITIZEN'S GUIDE, *supra* note 1, at 7.

112. IRAA, 15 U.S.C.A. § 2661.

113. CITIZEN'S GUIDE, *supra* note 1, at 7.

114. *See* CONSUMER'S GUIDE, *supra* note 28, at 13.

CHAPTER 22

Polychlorinated Biphenyls

BRIGID E. KENNEY

Polychlorinated biphenyls (PCBs) present serious problems for buyers, sellers, and managers of real property. Because PCBs and PCB-containing equipment are heavily regulated by some states and the federal government, an owner or user of PCB-containing equipment must grapple with a burdensome and complicated regulatory scheme. In addition, certain types of PCB-containing equipment that were once legal to own and use are prohibited under current regulations. As a result, a client acquiring property where such equipment is located may be buying an enforcement action as well.

Moreover, PCBs, like hazardous waste, cannot be disposed of cheaply because they present a risk to human health and the environment, particularly in the event of fire. PCB-related fires are extremely dangerous and expensive to clean up because of dangerous residual contaminants in the smoke and soot. The products of the incomplete combustion of PCBs are thought to be even more dangerous than PCBs themselves.

Depending on the type and location of equipment in which PCBs are present and the concentration of PCBs within that equipment, any of the following may be true:

- The continued presence and use of the equipment is illegal, and it must be disposed of promptly at considerable cost.
- The equipment may continue to be used, but with many restrictions, including labeling, inspection, and registration with the fire department and owners of nearby buildings.
- The equipment can continue to be used with no special restrictions until the end of its useful life, when it must be disposed of properly.

Even if PCB-containing equipment no longer exists on a property, the fact that such equipment was present in the past is a source of concern if the equipment leaked or otherwise caused a release of PCBs.

A real estate lawyer representing a client in a land transaction must first determine whether PCBs are present on the property. Next, if PCBs are present, the lawyer must ascertain whether they are being used legally. If the use is illegal, the PCBs should be removed and responsibility allocated for their future management and ultimate disposal. Where PCB releases have previously occurred, the lawyer should verify that those spills have been remediated in accordance with the Spill Cleanup Policy promulgated by the U.S. Environmental Protection Agency (EPA) or ensure that they will be cleaned up properly.

This chapter provides background information on PCBs and discusses ways to determine whether PCBs are present. It also addresses responsibility for PCBs and PCB spills and explores ways to allocate that responsibility. A summary of PCB regulations is included.

What Are PCBs?

PCBs are a class of man-made compounds consisting of two joined six-member carbon rings with one to ten chlorine atoms attached.[1] They can take the form of flowing yellow oils, viscous liquids or resins, or even waxy solids. They have low volatility;[2] are very stable even at high temperatures; and have low flammability, good chemical resistance, and low conductivity.[3]

Because PCBs possess these desirable properties, they were widely used, after their introduction in 1929, as dielectric fluid[4] in electrical equipment such as transformers and capacitors. Later, industries found other uses for PCBs, including use in heat transfer and hydraulic systems, paints, inks, lubricants, sealants, plasticizers, and carbonless copy paper. In 1979 the government imposed stringent restrictions on the manufacture and distribution of PCBs in the United States. Nonetheless, PCBs continue to be present on real property. They are occasionally still in use but are more often in storage or in the form of contamination from past use or disposal. The continued presence of PCBs in the environment can be attributed to their widespread use, low solubility in water, and tendency to adhere to soil and sediment particles. The illegal disposal and "reuse" of PCB-containing products—for example, the use of PCB-contaminated oil for dust control—has resulted in widespread PCB contamination.[5]

While in use, PCBs were sold under a variety of names. Among the generic names were Askarel (PCB liquids in transformers and capacitors), Therminol (PCB liquids in heat transfer systems), and Pydraul (PCB liquids in hydraulic systems). Among the most common trade names were Aroclor, Chlorinol, and Inerteen.[6] One of these words on the nameplate of a transformer or capacitor should put a real property owner on notice that the equipment in question may contain high levels of PCBs.[7]

Health and Environmental Effects

There is considerable controversy over the possible adverse effects of PCBs on human health and the environment. Some investigators have stated that PCBs are regulated more stringently than dictated by the level of risk they present.[8] On the other hand, PCBs have been shown to be toxic to the human liver and to cause chloracne, a painful and disfiguring skin disorder. Moreover, PCBs have been proven to cause cancer in laboratory animals exposed to high levels of PCBs during their lifetimes. While these laboratory findings are inconclusive, it is widely believed that chemicals that cause cancer in laboratory animals may also increase the risk of cancer in humans subjected to long-term exposure to the same chemicals.

In addition, it is well documented that PCBs "bioaccumulate," meaning that ingested PCBs tend to be stored in the body rather than metabolized or excreted. As a result, PCB concentrations in organisms tend to be higher than concentrations in the environment. Animals higher on the food chain tend to have higher body burdens because they consume organisms that may, in turn, have consumed PCB-contaminated plants or animals. For example, eating fish is thought to be a primary source of humans' exposure to PCBs. For this reason, PCB-contaminated sediment in rivers and harbors is of special concern.

Determining Whether PCBs Are Present

Environmental engineers are generally resourceful in investigating the possible presence of PCBs during Phase I environmental site assessments. Nevertheless, owners, real estate managers, and even lawyers can learn a great deal from inspection and questioning. The person responsible for maintenance at the facility probably possesses the determinative facts, although he or she may not be aware of the legal significance of that information. Obvious though it may seem, it is worth noting that both the lawyer and the client should look, but not touch. If anything suspicious is found, the services of both an electrician and an environmental consultant will probably be required.

Where to Look

The first step in ascertaining whether PCBs exist on a property is to locate the property's source of electricity, beginning with overhead lines. The utility supplying power to the property is usually the legal owner of pole-mounted transformers and transformers in electrical substations[9] and can provide information on the presence of PCBs in that equipment. However, pad- and roof-mounted transformers may be owned either by the utility, the real estate owner, or the building occupant.

If no transformers are visible on the outside or on the roof of the building, the building's interior should be checked. If a transformer is found, read the nameplate and label, if there is one, and note all information, including the year of manufacture and type of dielectric fluid contained in the transformer. If one of the trade names for PCB dielectric fluid appears, assume that the transformer is a PCB Transformer,[10] that is, that it contains at least 500 parts per million (ppm) of PCBs. If the nameplate does not mention the name of the dielectric fluid but the transformer is filled with oil not known to be mineral oil, the EPA takes the position that one must assume the transformer is a PCB Transformer.

One should also look for oil-filled capacitors,[11] circuit breakers, and switches. If any of these or any transformers are filled with mineral oil, assume that the equipment is PCB-contaminated, that is, that it contains at least 50 but less than 500 ppm PCBs. This assumption, of course, can be defeated by further information or by testing.

In addition to the electrical equipment, look for hydraulic systems, heat transfer systems, electromagnets, and voltage regulators. Be suspicious of any accumulations of waste oil in tanks or containers, especially if there is evidence of past use of hydraulic or heat transfer systems.

Testing

It is not difficult to test oil in tanks or containers. Testing electrical equipment that is in use, on the other hand, can be difficult and dangerous. Ordinarily, the equipment must be taken out of service while a sample is withdrawn. This can be a serious inconvenience, as when, for example, the elevators in a high-rise building are powered through the transformer.

Fluorescent Light Fixtures

Fluorescent light fixtures contain ballasts that include small capacitors. Since January 1, 1979, federal regulations have required that all PCB-containing equipment containing a PCB small capacitor be marked at the time of manufacture with this statement: "This equipment contains PCB Capacitor(s)." The regulations further require that fluorescent light ballasts manufactured between July 1, 1978, and July 1, 1998, that do not contain PCBs must be marked by the manufacturer with this statement: "No PCBs." The marks must be as durable and readable as other marks, such as the manufacturer's name. The marks must be on the exterior, where they can be easily read by a person inspecting or servicing the item. Thus, it should be fairly easy to determine whether fluorescent light fixtures contain PCBs.

Disposal of PCB fluorescent light ballasts, however, poses a peculiar problem under the Comprehensive Environmental Response, Compensation, and Liability Act (CERCLA), commonly known as Superfund. The applicable PCB regulations under the Toxic Substances Control Act (TSCA) are clear: "Fluorescent light ballast" means a device that electrically controls fluorescent light fixtures and that includes a capacitor containing 0.1 kilogram (kg) or less of dielectric fluid.[12] Unless one manufactured PCB-containing equipment and acquired PCB capacitors in the course of that manufacturing, one may dispose of small PCB capacitors, including those in fluorescent light fixtures, as municipal solid waste.[13]

PCBs, however, are considered a hazardous substance under CERCLA.[14] CERCLA Section 103 requires that the person in charge of a facility notify the National Response Center (NRC)[15] upon learning of a release (other than one that is federally permitted) of more than the reportable quantity of a hazardous substance from the facility. Disposal is considered a type of release. Because of this, one EPA region has apparently taken the position that the disposal of relatively few light ballasts (such as the typical quantity resulting from a demolition or remodeling project) would require reporting under Superfund.[16] This interpretation may be disputed. In any event, one way to avoid the problem would be to dispose of the ballasts in a chemical waste landfill.

State regulations also may have an impact. If a state regulates PCBs as hazardous waste, the fluorescent light fixtures generated in the course of some demolition and remodeling projects may be governed by the hazardous waste regulations that deal with storage, manifesting, and disposal.

If PCBs Are Present, Who Is Responsible?

Some PCB regulations under TSCA are worded in a way that makes clear what must be done but not *who* must do it.[17] It is not unusual for PCB-containing equipment to be owned by one person, used by another, and located on land or in a building owned or occupied by a third. Consider, for example, a shopping mall that is owned by a partnership and operated by a management company. PCB-containing transformers in an electrical substation owned by the partnership serve the shops in the mall, but an anchor tenant in a free-standing building installed its own roof-mounted transformers, and an on-site muffler shop uses PCB-containing hydraulic fluid. Who is responsible for labeling, inspection, and emergency response? Some regulations specifically state that the owner of the equipment shall comply, but other regulations are phrased in a way that permits more than one interpretation.

The EPA's Position

In 1982 the EPA published a TSCA Compliance Program policy statement to clarify who is responsible for TSCA compliance when PCB-containing equipment is owned by one party but used by another or is located on the property of someone other than the owner.[18] The document is a statement of compliance program policy and is not intended to affect the rights or liabilities of any person under law or private agreement. The EPA's position is that persons may not absolve themselves from liability for noncompliance with the PCB rules by contractual agreements. However, the agency will consider such agreements in making a determination of liability. The statement provides, in pertinent part, as follows:

> As a matter of compliance program policy, the Agency intends to hold the owners of PCB-containing equipment responsible for compliance with the PCB Rule. However, in all cases involving PCBs used by a person not the owner, or located on property owned by a person other than the owner of the PCBs, the Agency will consider the facts of each case to determine whether the user or landowner should be held responsible for compliance, either in addition to, or instead of, the owner of the PCB-containing equipment. In determining responsibility for compliance, the Agency will consider, without limitation, the following factors:
>
> - *Written agreements between the parties.* Contracts that provide that the user will service the equipment, or that the user agrees to comply with all laws, argue in favor of the user's being responsible.
> - *Prior actions by the parties.* If one of the parties has traditionally serviced the equipment, or taken responsibility for compliance with regulations on the equipment, this will influence the Agency's decision on liability.

- *Access to the equipment.* If one party has restricted or no access to the equipment, this argues strongly against that party's responsibility for compliance.
- *Reasonable actions in emergencies.* Even where the other factors indicate that the owner is responsible for regulatory compliance, the Agency expects users of PCB-containing equipment to act reasonably in the event of a rupture or other environmental emergency. Thus, the failure by a user to notify the owner promptly of any rupture might subject the user to liability under TSCA.

As dictated by the specific instance, the Agency will also consider any other pertinent factors in determining who should be held accountable for compliance with the law. Any person who uses PCB-containing equipment or has such equipment on his property, and is uncertain about his responsibility for compliance is strongly urged to contact the owner of the equipment to reach an agreement on this subject. . . .[19]

Of course, determining ownership of PCBs or PCB-containing equipment is not always easy. The specific question of whether transformers are fixtures that are transferred with real estate may be determined by local law.

If PCBs Are Present, What Should Be Done?

An individual's options are limited if PCBs are found stored or in use on real property he or she owns or leases. The first step should be to determine, as precisely as possible, the type of equipment and the level of concentration of PCBs. If PCB regulations allow the particular use, it must either conform to those regulations or cease. If regulations do not allow the use, it must be discontinued. PCBs not in use must be properly stored and be disposed of within a year of initial storage.

Under some circumstances, PCB use may be legal but undesirable because of the potential for liability or the economic burden associated with such use. Under these circumstances, it may make sense to convert the equipment to a less regulated class by reducing the concentration of PCBs. This process is referred to as retrofilling and reclassifying the equipment. Certain companies specialize in this task, which essentially involves repeatedly draining and refilling the equipment over a period of several months, sometimes with proprietary chemical mixtures, until the PCB concentration drops to the desired level. Verification testing must be done after the equipment has operated for several months. The alternative to this process is to retire and replace the equipment.

Legal Structuring of Liability

From a liability perspective, it is, obviously, preferable not to own or use PCBs or to have them on one's property. Thus, in any property acquisition it is desirable to obtain a preclosing assurance that past PCB spills have been adequately remediated and that all PCBs have been removed from the site. Because this removal may require the retirement and expensive disposal of electrical equipment with significant remaining useful life, however, this is frequently a costly solution.

In a leasing situation, the landlord might insist that the tenant not own or use PCBs. An alternative to such a contractual prohibition on PCB use is to assign responsibility for compliance with PCB laws and regulations to either of the parties to the lease transaction. The lease provisions alone, however, will not be determinative of responsibility in the event of a PCB-related mishap. The parties should be cognizant of the fact that their course of performance will be taken into account if a dispute arises from the use of PCBs. Moreover, an indemnity agreement may be necessary to protect the party seeking to avoid responsibility, since the EPA retains enormous enforcement discretion.

Who Is Responsible for Cleanup of PCB Contamination?

Instead of finding PCBs in storage or in use, one might discover that there have been on-site releases of PCBs in the past. Must the contamination be cleaned up and, if so, by whom?

The EPA's Policy

Spills and leaks are deemed illegal disposal under PCB regulations[20] and, as such, are punishable civilly or criminally under TSCA. The EPA has developed and codified a PCB Spill Cleanup Policy.[21] The agency has described the effect of compliance with this policy as follows:

> (a) Although a spill of material containing 50 ppm or greater PCBs is considered improper PCB disposal, this policy establishes requirements that EPA considers to be adequate cleanup of the spilled PCBs. Cleanup in accordance with this policy means compliance with the procedural as well as the numerical requirements of this policy. Compliance with this policy creates a presumption against both enforcement action for penalties and the need for further cleanup under TSCA. The Agency reserves the right, however, to initiate appropriate action to compel cleanup where, upon review of the records of cleanup or EPA sampling following

> cleanup, EPA finds that the decontamination levels in the policy have not been achieved. The Agency also reserves the right to seek penalties where the Agency believes that the responsible party has not made a good faith effort to comply with all provisions of this policy, such as prompt notification of EPA of a spill, recordkeeping, etc.
>
> (b) EPA's exercise of enforcement discretion does not preclude enforcement action under other provisions of TSCA or any other Federal statute. This includes, even in cases where the numerical decontamination levels set forth in this policy have been met, civil or criminal action for penalties where EPA believes the spill to have been the result of gross negligence or knowing violation.[22]

The EPA also notes, however, that

> This policy does not affect cleanup standards or requirements for the reporting of spills imposed, or to be imposed, under other Federal statutory authorities, including but not limited to, the Clean Water Act (CWA), the Resource Conservation and Recovery Act (RCRA), and the Comprehensive Environmental Response, Compensation, and Liability Act of 1980 (CERCLA) as amended by the Superfund Amendments and Reauthorization Act (SARA). Where more than one requirement applies, the stricter standard must be met.[23]

This policy applies to all spills that have occurred since May 4, 1987, except that the numerical cleanup standards do not apply to spills directly into surface waters, drinking waters, sewers, grazing lands, and vegetable gardens.[24] Cleanup levels for these spills will be established by the EPA regional offices.

Spill Response

Like CERCLA, TSCA places cleanup liability on the "responsible party," defined as "the owner of the PCB equipment, facility, or other source of PCBs or his/her designated agent (e.g., a facility manager or foreman)."[25] The policy establishes notification requirements for some, but not all, spills. Cleanup standards vary depending on the following factors: the concentration of PCBs spilled; the magnitude of the spill; and the use, accessibility, and characteristics of the area where the spill occurred. In some cases, postcleanup sampling is required to verify that cleanup levels have been achieved. This requirement sometimes raises difficult issues of sampling and statistical analysis. These issues are addressed in helpful literature available from the TSCA Assistance Office.[26]

Although TSCA responsibility for the cleanup of any PCB spill falls on the "responsible party," anyone may perform the cleanup or verify that a prior cleanup achieved the standards set forth in the PCB Spill Cleanup Policy. The latter should enable one to argue for the benefit of the presumption that no further cleanup would be required under TSCA.

Federal and State Regulation of PCBs

TSCA,[27] passed in 1976, explicitly directs the EPA to regulate the manufacture, processing, distribution in commerce, use, disposal, storage, and marking of PCBs.[28] Most PCB regulations apply only if the PCBs are present in concentrations above a specified level (e.g., 50 ppm and above). However, one cannot escape regulation by dilution.[29]

Some states have imposed additional restrictions on PCBs, and some even regulate PCBs as hazardous waste. TSCA contains a section on preemption, but the application of that provision turns on facts specific to each state or local regulation.[30] If the state or local law is not preempted, anyone managing PCBs must comply with both the federal and the state or local law. For example, if a state has listed PCBs as a hazardous waste, the generator of that waste may accumulate it only for a short time (usually 90 days) before shipping it off the site, unless the generator obtains a hazardous waste storage permit. The TSCA regulations generally allow storage for up to one year.

The TSCA Regulations[31]

The federal regulations, found at 40 C.F.R. Part 761, contain a sweeping prohibition on the use, manufacture, processing, or distribution in commerce of any PCB or PCB item, but they also include exceptions, called authorizations.[32] Activities not permitted by the authorizations, or not carried on in conformance with their terms, are illegal. Storage and disposal also are regulated closely. Violations of the TSCA regulations are subject to penalties of up to $25,000 for each violation.

Classification Based on Concentrations

The regulations divide PCBs into categories based on concentration: less than 50 ppm, at least 50 ppm but less than 500 ppm, and 500 ppm or more. Different regulations apply to the different categories. Transformers, for example, are classified as follows: non-PCB (containing less than 50 ppm PCBs); PCB-contaminated (containing 50 ppm or greater PCBs, but less than 500 ppm PCBs); or PCB (containing 500 ppm or greater PCBs). Certain assumptions apply if the concentration is unknown.

The Nameplate Presumption

The EPA takes the position that a transformer must be assumed to be a PCB Transformer if the nameplate indicates that the transformer contains PCB dielectric fluid (e.g., if the nameplate lists one of the generic or trade names for PCB dielectric)[33] or the owner or operator has any reason to believe that the transformer contains PCB dielectric fluid.[34] In addition, the EPA maintains that if a transformer does not have a nameplate or if there is no information about the type of dielectric in the transformer, it must be presumed to be a PCB Transformer unless it is tested and determined to have less than 500 ppm PCBs.[35]

Presumption for Mineral Oil–Filled Electrical Equipment

On the other hand, the regulations provide that oil-filled transformers and other oil-filled electrical equipment (other than circuit breakers, reclosers, and cable) with unknown concentrations of PCBs must be assumed to be PCB-contaminated electrical equipment.[36] Despite the unqualified wording of the regulations, the EPA maintains that this applies only to *mineral* oil-filled transformers and electrical equipment.[37]

Presumptions Regarding Capacitors

Capacitors are categorized as (1) large or small and (2) high-voltage or low-voltage. The regulations define "large" as containing three or more pounds of dielectric fluid. The regulations allow an assumption to be made about the weight of dielectric fluid, based on the total volume of the capacitor.[38]

Use Authorizations and Mandatory Phaseout

Federal regulations closely govern the use of PCBs but, in general, allow electrical equipment containing PCBs to continue to be used for the remainder of its useful life. One exception is for PCB Transformers that pose an exposure risk to food or feed. Another deals with certain transformers that are in or near commercial buildings. A third exception forbids the use of many large PCB capacitors. A summary of use prohibitions and restrictions for transformers in given in Figure 1.

EXPOSURE RISK TO FOOD OR FEED. Transformers that pose an exposure risk to food or feed were prohibited as of October 1, 1985.[39] "Posing an exposure risk to food or feed" is defined to include any location where released PCBs would have a potential pathway to human food or animal feed, except when the food or feed is used or stored in private homes. Typical forbidden locations are retail stores and grazing lands.

FIGURE 1. Summary of Use Prohibitions and Restrictions on Certain PCB Transformers in 40 C.F.R. Section 761.30(a)(1)

Activity	Type of PCB Transformers	Location	Prohibition/ Restriction	As of/By	Subsection
Use and storage for reuse	All	Posing exposure risk to food or feed	Prohibited	Oct. 1, 1985	(i)
Use	Higher secondary voltage network	In or near commercial buildings	Prohibited	Oct. 1, 1990	(ii)
Use	Lower secondary voltage network	In or near a commercial building and also located in a sidewalk vault	Remove from service	Oct. 1, 1993	(iv)(D)
Use	Lower secondary voltage network	In or near a commercial building but not located in a sidewalk vault	Protect against high current faults *OR* Register with EPA and remove from service	Oct. 1, 1990 Oct. 1, 1993 Oct. 1, 1993	(iv) (iv)(C) (iv)(B)
Use	Higher secondary voltage radial	In or near commercial buildings	Remove from service *OR* Protect against high current faults	Oct. 1, 1990	(iv)
Use	Higher secondary voltage radial	In or near commercial buildings	Protect against low current faults	Oct. 1, 1990	(v)
Use	All	In or near commerical buildings	Register with building owners	Dec. 1, 1985	(vii)
Use	Lower secondary voltage radial	In or near commerical buildings	Protect against high current faults	Feb. 25, 1991	(iv)

IN OR NEAR COMMERCIAL BUILDINGS. Certain types of transformers in or near commercial buildings[40] were required to be phased out between 1990 and 1993 unless they were equipped with certain types of electrical protection and met other requirements. Some were prohibited outright. (See Figure 1.) This prohibition forced many schools, hospitals, shopping centers, and other public buildings to replace PCB Transformers that had significant remaining useful lives.

The concept of "in or near commercial buildings" is defined in the regulations and is also addressed in guidance from the EPA. The regulations provide as follows:

> "In or Near Commercial Buildings" means within the interior of, on the roof of, attached to the exterior wall of, in the parking area serving, or within 30 meters of a nonindustrial non-substation building. Commercial buildings are typically accessible to both members of the general public and employees, and include: (1) public assembly properties, (2) educational properties, (3) institutional properties, (4) residential properties, (5) stores, (6) office buildings, and (7) transportation centers (e.g., airport terminal buildings, subway stations, bus stations, or train stations).[41]

The EPA has acknowledged that some buildings serve more than one purpose and that a dual-purpose building may be either commercial or industrial, depending on factors such as the proportion of space allocated to commercial versus industrial uses; whether access to the building by the general public is restricted; whether the PCB transformer is visible to workers during the routine conduct of their work; and whether there is disconnect equipment and persons trained to use it.[42]

OTHER USES. Since October 1, 1988, large PCB capacitors have been prohibited unless they are in restricted-access substations or contained indoor installations.[43] Small PCB capacitors can continue to be used.

PCBs at concentrations of less than 50 ppm can be used in heat transfer[44] and hydraulic systems.[45] PCBs of any concentration may be used, subject to certain conditions, in electromagnets, switches, and voltage regulators[46] and in circuit breakers, reclosers, and cable.[47]

Registration of PCB Transformers

When use of a PCB Transformer (one over 500 ppm PCBs) may continue, elaborate regulations apply. For one, the transformer must be registered with the *local* fire department. The EPA interprets this requirement literally—enforcement actions have been brought because the notice was sent to the city fire department rather than to the local fire house. The regulations specify what the notice must include.[48]

In addition, the owner of a PCB Transformer in use in a commercial building must register it with the building owner of record. The owner of such a transformer must also register it with all owners of buildings located within thirty meters of the PCB Transformer. The regulations set forth the required contents of the notice.[49]

Combustible Materials, Inspections, Records, Leaks, and Fires

Combustible materials may not be stored within five meters of a PCB Transformer.[50] The transformer must be inspected quarterly,[51] and records documenting the inspections must be kept for at least three years after the transformer's disposal.[52] The regulations specify the steps that must be taken if the transformer is found to be leaking or is involved in a fire-related incident.[53] The leak must be contained and inspected, the leaking material cleaned up and properly disposed of, and the transformer repaired or replaced.[54]

Labeling and Marking

The transformer must be marked with a label. The vault door, machinery room door, fence, hallway, or means of access other than grates or manhole covers also must be marked.[55] The label is specified by the regulations.[56] In addition, this label must be affixed to large high-voltage capacitors, PCB containers, storage areas, and other equipment such as heat transfer or hydraulic systems.[57] Electrical equipment that is merely PCB-contaminated (50 to 500 ppm PCBs) need not be labeled.[58]

Servicing

The servicing of in-use PCB equipment also is regulated.[59] The regulations typically allow or disallow certain types of repairs, restrict the types of fluid that can be used to replenish the dielectric fluid, and impose controls on the handling and disposal of wastes generated.[60]

Disposal

Disposal of PCBs and PCB spill cleanup materials is heavily regulated.[61] In general, high-concentration PCBs must be disposed of in an approved incinerator, chemical waste landfill, or high-efficiency boiler, or by an EPA-approved alternate method. Equipment that held high-concentration PCBs must be drained, filled with a solvent, and allowed to sit for a period of time, then drained again. The liquid must be disposed of properly. Some types of drained equipment can be landfilled as municipal solid waste, and other types may only be buried in an approved chemical waste landfill. Some equipment that held low-concentration PCBs may be drained and landfilled. Again, the liquid must be managed and disposed of properly.

Upon incineration or landfilling, the owner or operator of the disposal facility must prepare and send to the generator a certificate of disposal. This is the generator's proof that the PCBs have been handled properly.

Storage

Storage also is closely regulated under TSCA. Generators of PCB wastes[62] may store the PCBs without individual approval by the EPA if the generators store in accordance with the regulations.[63] Items stored for disposal must be disposed of within one year from the date they are first placed into storage.[64] Storage facilities must have an appropriate floor, curbing, walls, and roof.[65] The storage area must be marked and inspected periodically and any spills or leaks must be cleaned up. Proper storage containers must be used, and equipment such as forklifts cannot be removed from the storage area unless they are decontaminated. In addition, the PCB articles and containers must show the date they were placed in storage, and records must be kept.[66] Commercial storers of PCB wastes, those who store PCB wastes generated by others or removed from servicing equipment owned by others and brokered for disposal, are subject to additional requirements.[67]

Shipping

As of 1990, generators of PCB waste must obtain EPA identification numbers and use manifests when shipping PCB wastes for off-site storage or disposal.[68] Generators may offer their wastes only to transporters, disposers, or commercial storers of PCB waste who have received EPA identification numbers. New generators who operate PCB storage facilities must notify the EPA of their activities before starting to handle PCBs. The regulations contain detailed requirements concerning the information required on the manifests and in the notices. Manifests must be retained for at least three years.[69] There are provisions for manifest discrepancies and exception reporting similar to those in the hazardous waste regulations.

Record Keeping

The regulations contain detailed record keeping requirements for both generators and persons in the business of storing and disposing of PCBs generated by others. Generators who at any one time use or store 45 kg or more of PCBs in PCB containers, one or more PCB transformers, or fifty or more large capacitors must develop and maintain annual records and a written log of the fate of the PCBs. The records must include manifests and certificates of disposal.[70]

Conclusion

Except for the extraordinary complexity of the regulations, PCBs are very much like other "compliance with laws" issues in the law of real property. Noncompliance must be cured, the costs of continued use in compliance with the regulations must be weighed against the costs of PCB disposal and equipment replacement, and the effects of past releases must be addressed.

Notes

1. Because the number and location of the chlorine atoms can vary, there are ten different chemical formulas for PCBs and many different arrangements of the same formula. These arrangements are called isomers; a total of 209 isomers are possible. Often the results of chemical analyses of samples for PCBs identify which isomer was analyzed for and detected.

2. That is, they do not readily evaporate.

3. That is, they do not readily conduct electricity and are therefore good insulators.

4. Dielectric fluid is liquid that does not transmit direct electric current.

5. For example, hundreds of miles of soil alongside rural roads in North Carolina were contaminated in the 1970s by the dumping of PCB-contaminated transformer oil.

6. In addition, the following trade names were used for the fluid in transformers and capacitors: ALC, Apirolio, Asbestol, ASK, Capacitor 21, Chlorextol, Clophen, Clorinol, Diaclor, DK, Dykanol, EEC-18, Elemex, Eucarel, Fenclor, Hyvol, Inclor, Kanechlor, Magvar, MCS 1489, Nepolin, Non-Flammable Liquid, No-Flamol, Phenoclor, Pyralene, Pyranol, Pyroclor, Saf-T-Kuhl, Santotherm, Santotherm FR, and Santovac 1 and 2.

7. This is referred to as the "nameplate presumption."

8. PCBs are tightly regulated under the Toxic Substances Control Act and are also mentioned in regulations under these federal statutes: the Clean Water Act, Safe Drinking Water Act, Resource Conservation and Recovery Act, Comprehensive Environmental Response, Compensation, and Liability Act, Superfund Amendments and Reauthorization Act, and Hazardous Materials Transportation Act.

9. Pole-mounted transformers are generally cylindrical metal objects, while other transformers are usually metal boxes, some with cooling fans.

10. When used in this chapter, "PCB Transformer" means a transformer that contains 500 ppm or more PCBs.

11. A capacitor is a device for accumulating and holding a charge of electricity and consists of conducting surfaces separated by a dielectric. Capacitors are generally box-like in shape and larger than a bread box.

12. 40 C.F.R. § 761.3.

13. 40 C.F.R. § 761.60(b)(2).

14. 42 U.S.C.A. §§ 9601–75.

15. The NRC, located at U.S. Coast Guard Headquarters, is a national communications center, continuously staffed for handling activities related to spills and emergency response. The NRC acts as the single point of contact for all pollution incident reporting. The telephone numbers are (800) 424-8802 and (202) 267-2675.

16. Memorandum from Robert W. Jackson, Chief, Toxic Substances Control Section, EPA Region VII, to TSCS Staff (July 18, 1991).

17. For example, "As of December 1, 1985, all PCB Transformers . . . must be registered. . . ."

18. TSCA Compliance Program Policy No. 6-PCB-1 (March 4, 1982).

19. *Id.*, at 2–3.

20. The regulations define disposal to include the intentional or accidental discarding of PCBs, including spills and leaks. 40 C.F.R. 761.761.3.

21. 40 C.F.R. Subpart G.

22. 40 C.F.R. § 761.135.

23. 40 C.F.R. § 761.120(e).

24. Notification must still be provided.

25. 40 C.F.R. § 761.123.

26. The documents are "Verification of PCB Spill Cleanup by Sampling and Analysis," and "Field Manual for Grid Sampling of PCB Spill Sites to Verify Cleanup." 40 C.F.R. § 761.130(e).

27. 15 U.S.C.A. §§ 2601–92.

28. TSCA § 6(e), 15 U.S.C.A. § 2605(e).

29. 40 C.F.R. § 761.1(b).

30. 15 U.S.C.A. § 2617. *See also* Edward A. Nolfi, Annot., *State or Local Regulation of Toxic Substances as Preempted by Toxic Substances Control Act* (15 U.S.C.A. §§ 2601 *et seq.*), 84 A.L.R. FED. 913 (1987).

31. EPA has proposed extensive revisions to the TSCA PCB Regulations. 59 Fed. Reg. 62,788 (1994).

32. 40 C.F.R. §§ 761.20, 761.30.

33. The so-called nameplate presumption.

34. 44 Fed. Reg. 31,514, 31,517 (1979).

35. *Id.*

36. Testing may establish that equipment thought to be PCB-contaminated is actually below 50 ppm or above 500 ppm PCBs. In the case of a mineral oil transformer, the EPA has provided a schedule for bringing the transformer into compliance once it is determined that it is actually a PCB Transformer. 40 C.F.R. § 761.30(a)(1)(xv).

37. 56 Fed. Reg. 26,738, 26,741 (1991) (discussion in an advance notice of proposed rule making).

38. 40 C.F.R. § 761.3.

39. 40 C.F.R. § 761.60(a)(1)(i).

40. 40 C.F.R. § 761.60 (a).

41. 40 C.F.R. § 761.3.

42. Letter dated May 3, 1990, from Tom Baney, Chief of the Chemical Regulation Branch, to Edward L. Meyer.

43. 40 C.F.R. § 761.30(l).

44. 40 C.F.R. § 761.30(d).

45. 40 C.F.R. § 761.30(e).

46. 40 C.F.R. § 761.30(h). Under Section 761.30(h), the use of electromagnets that contain 500 ppm or more PCBs and that pose an exposure risk to food or feed was prohibited as of October 1, 1985.

47. 40 C.F.R. § 761.30(m).

48. 40 C.F.R. § 761.30(a)(1)(vi).

49. 40 C.F.R. § 761.30(a)(1)(vii).

50. 40 C.F.R. § 761.30(a)(1)(viii).

51. A reduced frequency of inspection is allowed if the transformer has adequate secondary containment or if it contains less than 60,000 ppm PCBs. 40 C.F.R. § 761.30(a)(1)(xiii).

52. 40 C.F.R. §§ 761.30(a)(1)(ix) and (xii).

53. 40 C.F.R. §§ 761.30(x) and (xi).

54. 40 C.F.R. § 761.30(a)(1)(x).

55. 40 C.F.R. §§ 761.40 (a), (c), and (j).

56. 40 C.F.R. § 761.45.

57. 40 C.F.R. § 761.40.

58. 40 C.F.R. § 761.40(a)(2).

59. 40 C.F.R. § 761.30.

60. *Id.*

61. 40 C.F.R. § 761.60.

62. A generator is a person whose act produces regulated PCBs; whose act first causes the PCBs to be subject to the disposal requirements; or "who has physical control over the PCBs when a decision is made that the use of the PCBs has been terminated and therefore is subject to the disposal requirements." 40 C.F.R. § 761.3.

63. Certain short-term storage is permitted outside of approved storage areas. 40 C.F.R. § 761.65(c).

64. 40 C.F.R. § 761.65(a).

65. 40 C.F.R. § 761.65(b).

66. 40 C.F.R. § 761.65(c).

67. 40 C.F.R. §§ 761.65(d)–(h).

68. 40 C.F.R. § 761.202.

69. 40 C.F.R. § 761.209.

70. 40 C.F.R. § 761.180.

CHAPTER 23

Indoor Air Pollution

FRANK B. CROSS

Indoor air pollution could well be *the* environmental problem of the next decade. Exposure studies have found levels of major air contaminants to be consistently higher indoors than outside. Many of these pollutants are subject to extensive regulation that restricts emissions into the ambient air.[1] Yet the higher indoor levels of these pollutants have been the subject of very little government attention or regulation. As recognition of indoor air quality problems grows, this situation is certain to change. Regulatory action moves forward very slowly, but many cases are being filed for recovery under common-law principles. These cases are generally settled, so neither rules nor precedents provide much guidance to building owners.

Indoor Air Quality Problems

Indoor air quality problems arise in all types of buildings and from countless types of contamination. While much attention has centered on residential buildings, this chapter focuses on the particular indoor air quality and liability problems of commercial buildings.

There are two central types of indoor air quality problems. The term Building-Related Illness (BRI) refers to a clinically diagnosable illness that can be traced to a specific contaminant in the building. Legionnaire's disease and hypersensitivity pneumonitis are examples of BRI. This category encompasses various distinct illnesses attributable to differing contaminants. A second category of indoor air quality problems is commonly known as Sick Building Syndrome (SBS). SBS is an imprecise term that customarily describes a white-collar environment in which a significant number of building occupants report symptoms, often including headaches, nausea, eye irritation, and other immediate effects. These symptoms cannot be scientifically attributed to a specific contaminant or contaminants in the building, yet the symptoms usually diminish or disappear when the occupant leaves the building. Most SBS problems are thought to be multifactorial in nature—that is, people may be reacting to a number of factors in the building, which may include chemical and biological pollutants, but which may also include other factors, such as temperature, odor, lighting, ergonomics, stress, and other influences.

There are no authoritative estimates of the extent of BRI and SBS in the nation's building inventory. OSHA believes that 10 to 25 percent of nonindustrial buildings have SBS and another 15 to 30 percent of such buildings suffer other indoor air pollution problems, such as BRI. The World Health Organization estimates that as many as 30 percent of new or remodeled buildings have high rates of sick building complaints. While these are imprecise, "off the cuff" estimates, they indicate that the problem is widespread.

Ironically, the nation's most notorious SBS problem was found at the Waterside Mall headquarters of the U.S. Environmental Protection Agency (EPA) in Washington, D.C. Of the 5,500-person workforce, 10 to 20 percent complained of symptoms that they attributed to indoor air pollution. Nineteen employees sued the building owners and managing company for $35 million, and a jury ultimately returned a verdict for $948,000 in favor of five plaintiffs whose case was heard first. The complaint alleged use of toxic cleaning products, failure to provide adequate ventilation, and failure to protect occupants from toxic materials used in renovation.

Probably the major commercial indoor air pollution problem derives from biological contamination. Such microbial contamination of the air is generally traceable to sources of moisture, which facilitates the growth of microorganisms. In office buildings, the contamination is typically due to microbial growth in air conditioning systems, cooling towers, or wet furnishings such as carpets. The problem can be exacerbated by low levels of the ventilation that could clear the air of the contaminants. Microbes can produce a wide range of illnesses, including flu, allergies, and asthma. More seriously, indoor microbial contamination is a source of Legionnaires' disease, which reportedly causes the deaths of five to seven thousand persons each year. Mold and mildew problems are especially common in humid regions of the South, where misplaced vapor barriers can increase indoor humidity, which in turn breeds microorganisms.

Chemical contamination represents another indoor air quality problem. Modern products emit a broad range of chemicals in a process known as "off-gassing." Some indoor chemical pollution problems are attributable to volatile organic compounds (VOCs), formaldehyde, and certain carpet-associated chemicals. The chemicals can often be traced to pressed-wood furniture, solvents, and general building materials. Ozone may emanate from photocopying machines. There are many other potential sources of chemical contamination, ranging from the ventilation system's circulation of outdoor vehicle exhausts to ordinary perfumes and air fresheners. Recent research suggests that fiberglass commonly found in acoustical tiles and insulation may cause cancer or SBS symptoms. Even carbonless copy paper and correction fluid have been implicated in exposing workers to hazards. This general contamination is also aggravated by a lack of ventilation.

Another major source of indoor air contamination is environmental tobacco smoke (ETS). Secondhand smoke is a combination of the smoke exhaled by smokers and the smoke given off by the burning end of a cigarette. Government research implicates ETS in thousands of deaths each year from cancer and heart disease, plus hundreds of thousands of cases of respiratory problems in young children.[2] (The legal implications of ETS are explored in Chapter 24.)

An indoor air pollution problem arises from a source of contamination, such as those described above, combined with a lack of dilution in the indoor air. Insufficient ventilation can concentrate the pollutants and may also create a general atmosphere of "stuffiness." About 50 percent of SBS cases are attributed by the National Institute for Occupational Safety and Health to some ventilation problem, often inadequate ventilation.[3] Energy conservation efforts in the 1970s and 1980s reduced ventilation in most buildings. Temperature also may play a role in causing SBS, as higher temperatures are associated with discomfort that may contribute to the syndrome. Ergonomic stress may contribute to SBS, and some believe that many sufferers' symptoms may merely be psychosomatic. Plainly, it will be difficult to ascertain the precise cause of a health problem for many indoor air-related complaints. An attack on the indoor air pollution problem probably requires both control, or elimination, of pollution sources and concern for ventilation levels.

The American Society of Heating, Refrigeration, and Air-Conditioning Engineers (ASHRAE) has promulgated minimum ventilation design standards to protect indoor air quality, and these require more ventilation than found in the typical office building. In 1989 ASHRAE updated its Standard 62 on ventilation to call for increased ventilation. While different standards apply to different settings, office space and conference rooms are to provide at least 20 cubic feet per minute per person of ventilation, a substantial increase from the earlier 1981 standard of 5 cubic feet per minute. Reception areas are to provide at least 15 cubic feet per minute per person of ventilation. Even higher ventilation can be required, depending on occupancy and other characteristics. Smoking lounges must have 60 cubic feet per minute of ventilation. As an alternative to the minimum ventilation, ASHRAE provides an optional method that directly controls contaminants and limits them below specified maximum levels in indoor air. The ASHRAE standard also establishes maintenance requirements for ventilation systems and other building systems. ASHRAE further recommends that relative humidity be maintained between 30 percent and 60 percent to limit the growth of microbial pathogens.

The ASHRAE standards are only guidelines, however, and are not legally enforceable. Some building codes incorporated the earlier ASHRAE standard, but these required the lower level of ventilation and applied only to new construction. Thus, the uniform building code generally calls for a minimum of 5 cubic feet per minute per person. Buildings constructed in the past could not meet these ventilation standards without substantial and costly renovation. However, the total cost of indoor air pollution illnesses is itself substantial—the EPA estimates that such contamination causes tens of billions of dollars in lost white-collar productivity per year. Moreover, ASHRAE 62-89 may be used in common-law liability litigation to establish a standard of care for building owners and operators.

This chapter focuses on the above indoor air quality problems. Other indoor air pollution is caused by radon and asbestos, which are the subjects of their own specific government programs. (Asbestos and radon are considered in detail in Chapters 19 and 21, respectively.)

Common-Law Liability

Litigation over indoor air problems has become commonplace. However, relatively few of these cases have produced opinions. Many cases are still pending and many others have been settled out of court. Some potentially successful theories of common-law liability are nevertheless emerging.

Potentially Liable Parties

Indoor air liability may arise in a variety of scenarios, each of which has distinct legal implications. Before considering the specific legal claims, it is important to understand these scenarios. Individual occupants of a building may suffer symptoms and file suit. These persons could bring an action against their employer, though their recovery in such an action generally will be under workers' compensation. The occupants may have a more promising negligence claim against the building owner, the architect, construction contractors, and others responsible for the poor indoor air quality. The occupants may also have a strict liability or negligence claim against any manufacturers of products that caused the indoor air problem. Commercial lenders can become liable, particularly if they foreclose on the building.

A second scenario arises when the commercial tenant is the plaintiff, suing for economic damages that arose from poor air quality. Under the economic loss rule, the tenant may not have negligence claims but does have a variety of contract-based claims. For example, the tenant may sue for breach of express or implied warranties or under the doctrine of mistake. In tort, the tenant may be able to bring actions for fraud or negligent misrepresentation, depending on the facts and the law of the forum.

Yet a third scenario involves a building purchaser bringing suit against the entity that sold the structure. The basic claims in this scenario will again be contract claims, supplemented by possible fraud and negligent misrepresentation actions. The application of principles or duties and the nature of warranties, however, will be different from the tenant/landlord action. The purchaser may also have an action against the commercial real estate broker who put together the sale.

Theories of Liability

Because very few indoor air pollution cases have yielded a published opinion, the extent of potential liability for commercial buildings remains unsettled. Some general principles can be identified and certain legal theories may be promising to plaintiffs.

Negligence

The plaintiff in negligence has three preliminary barriers to overcome: establishing the presence of a duty of care, establishing that such duty was breached, and proving causation. Under traditional landlord/tenant law, occupants suing a building owner should be able to establish a duty of care, as long as the source of the contamination was within the control of the building owner. The existence of a duty to future building occupants is less established for other potential defendants, such as architects, contractors, and brokers. The nature of such a duty is not clearly defined, but general principles of a duty not to harm foreseeable victims could be applied to create a duty on the part of this category of defendants. Some doctrines limit the scope of such a duty. For example,

> where work of an independent contractor is completely turned over to and accepted by an owner, the contractor is not liable to

third persons for damages subsequently suffered as a consequence of his workmanship, even where the contractor was negligent.[4]

Landlords are particularly susceptible to negligence suits by building occupants arising from indoor air pollution. Recent cases have considerably broadened the scope of landlords' duties. For example, landlords are being held liable for foreseeable criminal acts against tenants on the property.[5] By analogy, these cases would make landlords quite vulnerable to indoor air litigation.

Even assuming the presence of a duty of care, a plaintiff may face difficulty in demonstrating that such a duty was breached. It may be difficult to establish negligence for older buildings because the defendants probably had no reason to be aware of a potential indoor air problem. In the case of newer construction, proving negligence will be easier because SBS has been well known for a number of years. Proving duty and breach should be easier in ETS cases because smoking is under the ongoing control of an employer and possibly a building owner. Courts have held that an employer has a duty to provide a workplace free of damaging ETS[6] and granted injunctive relief to protect a plaintiff from future ETS exposures.[7]

Yet another substantial hurdle for plaintiffs will be proof of causation, which has two constituent parts. First, plaintiffs must demonstrate that their physical symptoms were caused by indoor air contamination. Second, plaintiffs must show that the indoor air contamination was proximately caused by the defendant's negligence.

The difficulty inherent in tracing symptoms to certain pollutants imposes a heavy burden on the plaintiff in satisfying the causation test. Expert witnesses may be able to draw this link, but such proof will be complicated by alternative causes for the symptoms. Numerous toxic tort actions have failed on causation, though success is possible. In one case involving indoor air quality issues, *Bloomquist v. Wapello County*, Iowa state office building occupants sued the government after a pesticide (Dursban LO) was absorbed by office carpeting and circulated through a negligently maintained heating, ventilation, and air-conditioning (HVAC) system. After a verdict granting the three plaintiffs $1 million in compensatory damages, the state court entered judgment notwithstanding the verdict (JNOV) for failure to demonstrate causation. After several years, the JNOV was reversed on appeal.[8] Another case involving residential exposure to pesticides in indoor air yielded a punitive damages award against the exterminators from an Arizona court.[9] Conversely, businesspersons lost a trial verdict on their claim that a carpet produced their multiple chemical sensitivity, apparently due to their failure to prove causation.[10] The evidence on the harms of the challenged carpet material (4-phenylcyclohexene) was not conclusive, and there is considerable debate regarding the existence of the syndrome known as multiple chemical sensitivity.

A plaintiff must also show that the defendants' negligence was the proximate cause of the contamination. This requires identifying the offending pollutant and tracing it to its source. The plaintiff may also be expected to demonstrate that nonnegligent action would have prevented the problem from occurring.

A typical negligence action is illustrated by *Call v. Prudential*, a case in which occupants of a new office building suffered headaches and other symptoms attributed to inadequate ventilation that permitted the buildup of certain irritant fumes. The plaintiffs sued the building, the management company, the architect, and several construction contractors. This case was settled during trial for an undisclosed amount.[11]

A distinct scenario applies to commercial real estate broker negligence. This type of case may be brought by a large company that purchased or rented space in a contaminated building. Brokers are potentially liable if they fail to exercise the care expected of a reasonable professional real estate broker. A broker will be liable for failure to disclose known material hazards and may be liable for failure to investigate, though the scope of this liability remains ambiguous. A broker could also be liable for negligence in recommending an inspection service.

Workers' Compensation

A building occupant who suffers from SBS or BRI may opt for workers' compensation, which will bring a lesser recovery but will free the claimant of the burden of proving negligence. Whether recovery under workers' compensation will, in fact, be available depends on the jurisdiction. Most workers' compensation statutes require that the compensable injury occur as a result of an accident. Many states have deemed an occupational disease, such as SBS, to be such a covered "accident," but other states have not so extended their statutes. Workers' compensation is generally an exclusive remedy against an employer, so if such a statutory action is available, the employer will not be liable in common-law tort.

States in which employees have recovered under workers' compensation statutes for diseases stemming from indoor air pollution include Wisconsin and Florida, but a New York court held that an on-the-job allergy caused by indoor air pollution was not a compensable accident under that state's statute.[12] Some states have passed specific occupational disease statutes to address this uncertainty. A possible downside of going for a workers' compensation remedy is the fact that the claimant must prove causation and may have to meet a higher standard of proof to satisfy this burden. A Pennsylvania case, for example, denied a worker's effort to recover for Legionnaire's Disease, holding that the connection between the workplace and the disease "must be established by unequivocal medical testimony."[13] The Nevada Supreme Court dismissed an ETS workers' compensation case on the ground that the smoke was not incidental to the character of the business (required for recovery under that state's law),[14] and an Illinois court similarly dismissed a claim that indoor air pollution caused chemical hypersensitivity due to the uncertain linkage of indoor air contamination and the claimed symptoms.[15]

Strict Liability

The application of strict liability is limited, and seldom will a commercial building qualify as an abnormally dangerous activity, which would invoke strict liability. However, strict liability for products will often apply to manufacturers and sellers of products that produce indoor air contamination. Such strict liability will be unavailable against other potential defendants, such as employers.

The availability of an action for strict product liability hinges on the definition of "product." While some courts have held that prefabricated residential homes may in some circumstances be considered products, there are no reported decisions suggesting that large commercial buildings are themselves products subject to strict liability. However, specific components of a building obviously qualify as products. Carpet, for example, is a product, as is carpet backing, furniture, and many other sources of indoor air pollution. It is unclear whether an entire HVAC system will qualify as a product for purposes of strict liability.

Fraud

Fraud is a common basis for claims brought by purchasers or renters of buildings with indoor air quality problems. Essential elements of a fraud cause of action include a material misrepresentation by a seller or landlord or an omission accompanied by a duty to disclose. The plaintiff must also establish justifiable reliance on the misrepresentation and resultant damages. A general seller/landlord representation that the property is "safe" might fulfill this requirement, but no reported cases have so held. A more specific and inaccurate representation regarding indoor air would certainly qualify. Therefore, a buyer or prospective tenant should always inquire about indoor air quality because a directly responsive comment could form the basis for a fraud action.

It may be more common to allege a defendant's material omission of bad indoor air quality. In an arm's-length transaction, a seller traditionally did not owe a general duty to disclose to a buyer under the doctrine of caveat emptor. However, if the seller has special knowledge of a latent defect not obvious to the buyer (as is possible in the case of indoor air quality), the seller may have a duty to disclose under either common-law or state statutes. Under the Restatement of Torts, such a seller is responsible for disclosing information that the seller knows or could discover upon reasonable inspection.[16] In addition, a broker has a general affirmative duty to disclose known material facts that would bear on a purchaser's decision to enter into transaction, rendering brokers vulnerable to suit.[17]

Fraud also requires *scienter*, an intentional or possibly reckless misrepresentation or omission. A seller or landlord who is unaware of the indoor air contamination will raise his or her ignorance of the problem as a defense. States have incorporated recklessness into *scienter* in varying degrees, and such a defendant may still be liable under a fraud theory for reckless failure to ascertain the existence of indoor air pollution. Historic unawareness of indoor air contamination probably will not be considered recklessness, but growing public and professional awareness of the problem renders current and future ignorance potentially reckless. Moreover, if the seller is aware of contamination, it may be liable in fraud even if it sold the building "as is."[18]

The *scienter* problem is illustrated by a residential action in which individuals built their home with radon-contaminated concrete blocks. After discovering this problem, the home owners sued the producers of the blocks, claiming fraudulent concealment of the hazard. The U.S. Court of Appeals for the Fifth Circuit rejected this claim because knowledge of potential radon problems was not generally available in 1968, when the blocks were purchased, so the defendants could not have committed fraud.[19]

Warranty

Violations of express warranties about indoor air quality can obviously give rise to litigation. An implied warranty of merchantability action may be available if the contamination can be traced to a product subject to Section 2-314 of the Uniform Commercial Code. This section creates the implied warranty that products are of ordinary quality and fit for their generally intended use. Carpets, insulation, and other products may not be deemed fit for their intended use if they create a serious indoor air quality problem.

An evolving cause of action for commercial tenants is the implied warranty of habitability. Under this doctrine, a building would contain an implied warranty that it was constructed in a workmanlike manner and suitable for occupation. A serious indoor air pollution problem could breach an implied warranty of habitability or of suitability for intended use. Traditionally this implied warranty applied only to residential sales and did not protect commercial buyers or renters. The rule is increasingly being extended to the commercial context. Texas, for example, has established that commercial landlords may be liable for breach of this warranty, even if a tenant is considered negligent in failing to discover the defects itself in a prelease inspection.[20]

Procedural Issues

In addition to the substantive requirements of a plaintiff's cause of action, the indoor air pollution litigant will face the full range of procedural issues characteristic of any lawsuit. Thus, plaintiffs must comply with applicable statutes of limitations and repose, which have been a major barrier to toxic tort litigation, particularly for latent diseases such as cancer. Another key issue will be whether a group of individual plaintiffs all suffering varying symptoms may maintain a class action. The lone reported opinion on this issue certified a class and held that the symptoms and claims of the named plaintiffs were reasonably typical of the entire class.[21]

An unlitigated but potentially significant issue is that of injunctive relief. One suffering from serious health problems attributable to indoor air contamination presumably will have suffered irreparable harm. An injunction requiring the correction of the indoor air quality problem could prove distinctly more expensive than paying damages to the victim. An unreported New Jersey Superior Court case presented the interesting issue of an apartment dweller suing her downstairs neighbors to compel them to stop smoking. The "stench" was allegedly seeping upstairs. The judge declined to order the requested relief but issued an interim order directing the defendants to purchase the best available air cleaner for their apartment.

Government Regulation

When compared with outdoor air pollution, indoor contamination is scarcely regulated. Traditional environmental legislation, such as the Clean Air Act and the Comprehensive Environmental Response, Compensation, and Liability Act, has generally not been applied to indoor air pollution. The problems of indoor air are receiving increased government attention, however, and some new requirements have emerged. In addition, more regulations can be expected in the future and numerous bills are pending before Congress. Most relevant regulation will be issued by the Occupational Safety and Health Administration (OSHA), the EPA, and analogous state bodies.

OSHA

OSHA has historically focused on the risks of accident and disease in blue-collar workplaces and, until recently, has shown little concern for the quality of indoor air in office buildings. This approach changed dramatically on March 25, 1994, when OSHA announced a proposed rule for indoor air contamination in nonindustrial workplaces.[22] This proposal would apply to over 4.5 million buildings, including office buildings, as well as to offices, cafeterias, and other nonindustrial areas within otherwise industrial work sites. Although adoption of a final, binding rule is unlikely until 1996 or 1997, advance action can ease the burden of ultimate compliance with the regulation. The proposed rule provides fines of $70,000 for each willful violation and $7,000 for each lesser violation.

OSHA's proposed standard first requires the development of indoor air quality compliance programs. These are written operations plans that cover management and operation of HVAC systems to ensure that they comply with reported design criteria. These plans must include minimum outside air ventilation rates, humidity controls, and provision for retrofitting when design occupancy levels are exceeded. HVAC maintenance plans also are required. This provision of the regulation further compels employers to keep records of illnesses and identify a designated person with responsibility for indoor air quality.

The second and most costly provision of the OSHA proposal is the indoor air quality operation and maintenance program itself. The HVAC system "should provide at least the outside air ventilation rate based on actual occupancy, building code, mechanical code, or ventilation code and that carbon dioxide concentration does not exceed 800 parts per million."[23] Employers must also take specific protective measures to control employee exposure to specific contaminants, including ETS. To control microbial contamination, employers must routinely inspect for water leaks and repair any leaks that are found. In addition, employers are expected to take other measures to remove visible contamination in ductwork, humidifiers, and elsewhere. Additional requirements are aimed at preventing contamination during remodeling, renovation, and similar activities. OSHA estimates that the total annual cost of this provision will exceed $6 billion nationwide, with well over $2 billion in cost for each of the wholesale and retail trade and service industries.

A third central requirement of the OSHA proposal is training for HVAC maintenance workers and an information program for other employees. These training programs must include instruction on how to maintain adequate ventilation of contaminants generated during building cleaning and maintenance and how to minimize adverse effects on indoor air quality during the use and disposal of chemicals and other agents. OSHA would also require record keeping, including a log of employee complaints. This provision alone will cost more than $1 billion per year, according to the agency. Overall, the owner of a 100,000-square-foot building would have to pay $21,000 per year on average to implement OSHA's proposed rules. OSHA expects that its provisions will eliminate at least 80 percent of indoor air quality complaints.

The EPA

The EPA has traditionally evinced little concern over indoor air pollution. While the agency arguably has authority under the Toxic Substances Control Act, it has not developed a regulatory approach to indoor contamination. Nor does the agency anticipate receiving explicit regulatory authority over indoor air quality. Rather, the EPA has issued comprehensive guidance in *Building Air Quality: A Guide for Building Owners and Facility Managers,* which instructs parties on how to prevent and resolve indoor air quality problems in commercial and public structures. The agency is proceeding with a voluntary program that stresses source management and good operation and maintenance of building systems. The EPA also conducts extensive outreach, training, and research on indoor air pollution.

Unless Congress passes new legislation, the EPA is likely to remain relatively inactive on the regulation of indoor air problems. Legislation has been introduced in Congress during each of the last several years, but none of these bills has come close to enactment. Importantly, even if such a bill were to pass, it would not contain strict mandatory standards for ventilation or minimum air quality in buildings. The pending legislation takes an information approach to private buildings but would require some response actions in federal buildings, including those leased from private property owners. The one area of existing regulation is in EPA requirements for pesticide applications that affect indoor air under Federal Insecticide, Fungicide, and Rodenticide Act authority. The funding of the EPA's Indoor Air Division is so low ($4 million) that little regulatory action can be expected.

The EPA is developing a voluntary program called the Building Air Quality Alliance. Under this program, building owners and operators will voluntarily adopt and implement problems to preserve and improve the quality of indoor air. This program will function in consultation with the private sector and may be of interest to building owners and managers.

State and Local Regulation

Considerable state and local regulation bears upon indoor air pollution, but the nature of these rules varies considerably across the country. Local building codes contain components that govern indoor air quality, frequently containing minimum ventilation and related requirements. These codes are generally limited to new construction or renovation, however, and do not affect existing problems. Furthermore, most codes do not incorporate the stricter ventilation standards of ASHRAE 62-89.

The area of greatest state activity is ETS, where states and local governments have restricted smoking in public places and some private businesses, such as restaurants. Other states, such as New Jersey, Maine, and New Hampshire, have adopted indoor air quality standards for buildings where public employees work. The New Jersey regulations adopt ASHRAE guidelines as the standard for indoor air quality and provide that a building owner can be required to retrofit to comply with ASHRAE guidelines. California is moving toward establishing ventilation standards for commercial buildings. Washington law also regulates residential houses and provides that it is a defense in a civil action that a builder complied with the state's requirements.[24] In general, state and local regulation is haphazard and limited.

Conclusion

The law has been slow in responding to the substantial risks of indoor air pollution. As a result, building owners are confronted with considerable uncertainty about their duties and potential liabilities. Any company that ignores the problem, however, faces considerable legal risk.

The OSHA standard, though only a proposed rule at this time, represents a significant breakthrough. Because an OSHA nonindustrial indoor air quality rule is likely to become final in some form, businesses should begin preparing now for its eventual promulgation. These businesses may also be able to use the proposed OSHA rule as a shield in private litigation. Alternatively, businesses may demonstrate good faith nonnegligence by complying with EPA guidelines on indoor air quality. Moving to comply with the rule even before its finalization should be viewed as a good faith effort to resolve indoor air quality problems and as strong evidence of nonnegligence. Ultimately, legal guidance will depend on the specifics of a given indoor air contamination problem.

Resources

Cross, Frank B. *Legal Responses to Indoor Air Pollution*, Westport, Conn.: Quorum Books, 1990.

Cross, Frank B., and Murray, Paula C. "Liability for Toxic Radon Gas in Residential Home Sales." *North Carolina Law Review* 66 (1987): 687.

Eden, Barbara J. "Toxic Indoor Air: Commercial Real Estate Transactions May Be Hazardous to Your (Fiscal) Health." *Tulsa Law Journal* 24 (1989): 449.

Harrison, Andrew J. "An Analysis of the Health Effects, Economic Consequences, and Legal Implications of Human Exposure to Indoor Air Pollutants." *South Dakota Law Review* 37 (1992): 289.

Kirsch, Lawrence S. "Liability for Indoor Air Pollution in the Work Place," in *Indoor Pollution and Toxic Torts*, New York: Law Journal Seminars Press, 1987.

Kornreich, Mary Rose. "Minimizing Liability for Indoor Air Pollution." *Tulane Environmental Law Review* 4 (1990): 61.

Loewy, Steven A., Kelly, George W., and Nathanson, Martha D. "Indoor Pollution in Commercial Buildings: Legal Requirements and Emerging Trends." *Journal of Environmental Law* 3 (1993): 29.

Meckler, Milton. *Indoor Air Quality Design Guidebook*, Englewood Cliffs, N.J.: Prentice Hall, 1990.

Note, "Indoor Air Pollution: An Impetus for Environmental Regulation Indoors?" *Brigham Young University Journal of Public Law* 6 (1993): 295.

U.S. Environmental Protection Agency. *Building Air Quality: A Guide for Building Owners and Facility Managers* (1991).

—. "Report to Congress on Indoor Air Quality" (1989).

—. "Targeting Indoor Air Pollution: EPA's Approach and Progress" (1993).

Notes

1. *See* U.S. EPA, Report to Congress on Indoor Air Quality (1989).

2. National Institute for Occupational Safety and Health, Environmental Tobacco Smoke in the Workplace: Lung Cancer and Other Health Effects (1991).

3. James Melius et al., *Indoor Air Quality—The NIOSH Experience*, 10 Ann. Am. Conf. Gov. Ind. Hyg. 3 (1984).

4. Mary Rose Kornreich, *Minimizing Liability for Indoor Air Pollution*, 4 Tulane Env. L. Rev. 61, 67 (1990). The author notes that an exception to this doctrine may be created for imminently dangerous conditions created by contractor negligence.

5. *Id.*

6. McCarthy v. Department of Social & Health Services, 759 P.2d 351 (Wash. 1988).

7. Smith v. Western Electric Co., 643 S.W.2d 10 (Mo. App. 1992).

8. Bloomquist v. Wapello County, 500 N.W.2d 1 (Iowa 1993).

9. Hooper v. Truly Nolen of America, Inc., 832 P.2d 709 (Ariz. App. 1992).

10. Frank B. Cross, Legal Responses to Indoor Air Pollution (1990), at 168.

11. Helen Einstein, *The Impact of the "Call" Case*, Indoor Pollution L. Rep. (December 1990), at 5–7.

12. Legal Responses to Indoor Air Pollution, at 171.

13. May Department Stores v. Workmen's Compensation Appeal Board, 525 A.2d 33, 34 (Pa. Commw. 1987).

14. Palmer v. Del Webb's High Sierra, 838 P.2d 435 (Nev. 1992).

15. Weekley v. The Industrial Comm'n, 615 N.E.2d 59 (Ill. App. 1993).

16. *Id.*

17. Easton v. Strassburger, 152 Cal. App. 3d 90 (1984).

18. Prudential Insurance Co. of America v. Jefferson Associates, Ltd., 839 S.W.2d 866 (Tex. App. 1992) (sale of building containing asbestos).

19. Wayne v. Tennessee Valley Auth., 730 F.2d 392 (5th Cir. 1984), *cert. denied*, 469 U.S. 1159 (1985).

20. Paula C. Murray, *The Evolution of Implied Warranties in Commercial Real Estate Leases*, 28 U. Richmond L. Rev. 145 (1993).

21. Klocke v. A & D Limited Partnership, 629 N.E.2d 49 (Ohio App. 1993).

22. 59 Fed. Reg. 15,967 (1994).

23. 59 Fed. Reg. at 16,014.

24. R.C.W.A. § 4.24.560.

CHAPTER 24

Environmental Tobacco Smoke

JEFFERY R. BERRY

For a long time nonsmokers have complained about breathing air filled with tobacco smoke. Only recently, however, have they begun to realize that exposure to secondhand or passive tobacco smoke may endanger their health. This realization has made secondhand smoke, or, as it is frequently called, environmental tobacco smoke (ETS), a full-blown legal issue.

In the past few years the risks associated with exposure to ETS have been well publicized. What many people do not yet understand, however, is that ETS exposure occurs not only from breathing the tobacco smoke of a person in the same room but that the indoor air quality throughout a building can be affected whenever smoking occurs in a part of the building that is not separately ventilated to the outside.

The concentration of ETS in the air within a particular part of a building depends on many factors, including the amount of smoking and the air flow patterns in the building; the type of heating, ventilation, and air conditioning (HVAC) system used in the building; and the rate of exchange between indoor and outdoor air. The more outside air that is brought inside a building, the less likely it is that concentrations of ETS or other pollutants will accumulate. Ironically, energy conservation efforts during the 1970s and early 1980s increased the chance for a buildup of concentrations of ETS and other indoor air pollutants because so-called "tight" buildings were designed to have decreased air exchange with the outside to reduce energy costs.[1]

Once a concern only for building occupants, ETS is a growing issue for building owners and operators as well. The U.S. Environmental Protection Agency (EPA) has labeled ETS a known carcinogen.

Although there is not yet any binding federal regulation of ETS, at this writing the U.S. Occupational Safety and Health Administration (OSHA) is considering action on the issue, and many states and hundreds of municipalities already have laws and regulations that restrict smoking in public places. Building owners and operators must simultaneously comply with these provisions and accommodate the desires of tenants. Moreover, owners and operators must be cognizant of the potential liability for ETS exposure that they may face in private litigation brought by building occupants.

This chapter examines the legal issues associated with ETS and the resulting implications for the real estate industry. Scientific, medical, and legal developments involving ETS are occurring at an astonishing pace; thus, much of the information in this chapter is subject to change. Nevertheless, the chapter aims to provide useful background and reference information concerning ETS and identify significant trends affecting the real estate industry.

The EPA's ETS Report and Other Scientific Developments

The potential dangers associated with ETS exposure first received widespread coverage in 1986, when the Surgeon General concluded that ETS can cause lung cancer in adult nonsmokers and that children of parents who smoke face an increased risk of respiratory problems.[2] The Surgeon General's report prompted several major public and private studies of the ETS issue and led to some governmental regulation of smoking in public places, particularly at the state and local level.

Perhaps the most significant ETS development occurred in January 1993, when EPA issued a report titled *Respiratory Health Effects of Passive Smoking: Lung Cancer and Other Disorders* (ETS Report).[3] The ETS Report concluded, based on a review of various studies, that ETS is a Class A carcinogen "responsible for approximately 3,000 lung cancer deaths annually in U.S. nonsmokers" and that ETS causes bronchitis or pneumonia in 150,000 to 300,000 children annually as well as many cases of childhood asthma.

The ETS Report was widely publicized in the news media. It could play a major role in ETS litigation because it provides plaintiffs with support for the proposition that ETS is harmful.[4] As the following discussion will show, the ETS Report has already had a tremendous influence on both governmental and private sector ETS regulation.

Moreover, the ETS Report has attracted the concern of the tobacco industry, which has filed a lawsuit in the U.S. District Court for the Middle District of North Carolina, seeking to have the ETS Report declared null and void. The industry contends that the EPA lacked the authority to classify ETS as a carcinogen and that, in any event, the scientific studies relied on in the ETS Report are flawed. The government's motion to dismiss this case was denied on July 20, 1994.[5] This case is pending at this time. The tobacco industry has also conducted a major public relations offensive against the ETS Report, taking out frequent full-page advertisements in newspapers with national circulation that attempt to discredit the report's conclusions.[6]

The EPA has responded to these advertisements in its publication *Setting the Record Straight: Second-hand Smoke Is a Preventable Health Risk,* which asserts that the conclusions in the ETS Report are "absolutely" correct and are supported by several more recent epidemiology studies.[7] Indeed, two recent studies published in major medical journals support the EPA's conclusion that ETS injures and kills nonsmokers. A study titled *Environmental Tobacco Smoke and Lung Cancer in Nonsmoking Women* was published in the *Journal of the American Medical Association* on June 8, 1994. This study concluded that nonsmoking women's exposure to ETS *as adults* increases the risk of these nonsmokers developing lung cancer. The second study, published in the *Journal of the American College of Cardiology* in August 1994, looked not at lung cancer or respiratory effects but at whether ETS exposure causes heart disease. The study concluded that, in 1994 alone, ETS exposure will cause an estimated 47,000 heart disease deaths and about 150,000 nonfatal heart attacks among nonsmokers in this country.

Legal Developments

Federal Law and Regulation

Despite the federal government's endorsement of the scientific conclusion that ETS exposure is harmful, to date there is very little federal regulation of smoking. There is a federal law banning smoking on all domestic airline flights.[8] Congress's only attempt to deal with the ETS problem in public buildings, however, occurred only recently, in the education reform bill known as Goals 2000: Educate America Act, which went into effect on March 31, 1994. This law bans smoking in public kindergarten, elementary, and secondary schools and in private schools that receive federal money.[9]

The EPA currently has no statutory authority to regulate smoking. Nevertheless, the agency began the process of developing a voluntary program called the Building Air Quality Alliance, which would enlist the cooperation of building owners and operators in adopting good indoor air quality practices, including protecting building occupants from exposure to ETS. The most recent draft of the Alliance program would call on Alliance members to establish a smoking policy that bans smoking except in separately designated smoking rooms that are maintained under negative air pressure, ventilated directly to the outside, and provide at least 60 cubic feet per minute (CFM) of makeup (or transfer) air per smoker. At this time, it appears EPA has postponed efforts to implement the Alliance due to concerns raised by various interest groups.

Even before the ETS Report labeled ETS a carcinogen, OSHA was under pressure to limit workplace exposure to ETS. In 1992 Action on Smoking and Health (ASH), a Washington, D.C.–based nonsmokers advocacy group, filed a petition against OSHA in the U.S. Court of Appeals for the District of Columbia Circuit, seeking to force OSHA to place a total ban on smoking in the workplace. This petition was still under review by the court when, on March 25, 1994, more than a year after the ETS Report was issued, OSHA issued a proposed smoking regulation. This regulation, which OSHA issued as part of broader proposed indoor air quality (IAQ) regulations, would require virtually all "employers" in the United States (including bars, restaurants, and hotels) to protect workers from ETS exposure by either banning smoking altogether or permitting it only in "designated smoking areas [that] are enclosed and exhausted directly to the outside, and are maintained under negative air pressure (with respect to surrounding spaces) sufficient to contain tobacco smoke within the designated area."[10] Under the proposed regulation, in multitenant buildings a building owner who controls the HVAC system is defined to be the "employer" of *everyone* in the building, including employees of the building's tenants.

OSHA has pledged to implement its proposed smoking regulation quickly, but both this regulation and the general IAQ regulations of which it is a part have generated considerable controversy. OSHA conducted public hearings on these regulations for several months. OSHA is currently considering the comments it received and it is not known whether OSHA will promulgate final regulations or issue new proposed regulations. In either case, it could be several years before there is any binding OSHA regulation of ETS. To keep pressure on OSHA, ASH has vowed to continue legal action seeking a total ban on smoking in the workplace.[11]

Ironically, the proposed OSHA IAQ regulations (including the smoking regulation) do *not* apply to federal buildings. This is reportedly because of concerns about the "multimillion-dollar cost of revamping the ventilation systems in federal buildings to meet the new standards."[12] At this time, the only regulation in effect governing smoking in federal buildings is a General Services Administration (GSA) regulation that essentially authorizes each federal agency to set its own workplace smoking policy.[13] Several federal agencies have responded to this regulation by banning or restricting smoking. For example, beginning on April 8, 1994, the Pentagon banned smoking in all indoor spaces on military bases around the world, except in restaurants and barracks.[14] President Clinton has banned smoking altogether in the White House[15] and is reportedly considering an executive order that would ban smoking in virtually all federal buildings.[16]

Congressional Activity

The paucity of federal ETS regulation has not escaped congressional attention. Several antismoking bills were considered by House and Senate committees in the last Congress, the most well known of which was sponsored by Rep. Henry Waxman (D-Calif.).[17] The Waxman bill would require building owners and tenants to ban smoking in all nonresidential buildings in the United States (including federal buildings) that are entered by more than ten people at least one day per week. The only exception to the no-smoking policy would be for smoking in separately designated smoking areas where: (1) the air is "directly exhausted to the outside" and not allowed to "recirculate or drift to other areas" of the building; and (2) nonsmokers never have to enter for any purpose. Building owners would be responsible for implementing the no-smoking policy, except in areas of the building that are leased to tenants, where the implementation would be the tenant's responsibility.

Legislation similar to the Waxman bill was introduced by Sen. Frank Lautenberg (D-N.J.).[18] In addition, there were bills proposed in both the House and Senate that would ban or severely restrict smoking in federal buildings[19] and in buildings where federally funded children's services are provided.[20]

None of the proposed ETS legislation was enacted in the last Congress. Given the Republican takeover of Congress, the prospect for legislative action on ETS in the current Congress, convened in January 1995, is even more unlikely. Indeed, Rep. Thomas Bliley, Jr. (R-Va.), the new chair of the House Commerce Committee (which has jurisdiction over smoking issues), has publicly stated that he does not see the need for any more investigations of the tobacco industry.

State and Local Law and Regulation

To date, most ETS regulation has been enacted at the state and local levels. Even before the ETS Report was published, numerous states and hundreds of municipalities had enacted laws banning or restricting smoking in certain places. Since publication of the report, the amount of state and local regulation of ETS has exploded. Most states (other than those in the tobacco-belt) have some type of law restricting smoking. Historically, Hawaii, Minnesota, New Hampshire, New York, and Vermont have probably had the most comprehensive anti-smoking laws, although, as discussed below, several states have recently passed even more restrictive statutes.[21]

State and local antismoking ordinances vary widely in scope. The first generation of ordinances, enacted in the 1970s and early 1980s, generally required no more than the setting aside of smoking (or non-smoking) areas in certain limited environments, such as schools and some other public facilities. Many of the ordinances passed in the 1990s, particularly since the ETS Report, are much tougher. These more recent laws either ban smoking altogether in a much broader range of environments, including offices, restaurants, and other public places (such as museums, malls, retail stores, recreational facilities, and common areas of hotels and motels), or limit smoking in such places in a way that more effectively ensures that ETS does not migrate into nonsmoking areas. The clear trend is toward more comprehensive and restrictive regulation of smoking in workplaces, restaurants, and other public places.[22]

For example, New York City has had smoking restrictions for some time, but on December 21, 1994, its City Council passed an even tougher ordinance that requires employers to ban smoking altogether or to limit smoking to separately ventilated smoking rooms or private offices occupied by no more than three people. The ordinance also forbids smoking in dining areas of restaurants seating more than thirty-five customers, though smoking would still be permitted in bar areas and separate smoking lounges. Under the ordinance, smoking is also banned in many other public places, including outdoor recreational facilities and sports arenas.[23] The New York City ordinance was signed by Mayor Rudolph Guiliani and became effective April 10, 1995.

On February 1, 1994, a San Francisco ordinance banning smoking in offices went into effect. This ordinance also bans smoking in restaurants beginning January 1, 1995. The San Francisco ordinance is a 100 percent smoke-free ordinance because it does not permit exceptions for separate smoking rooms. Much of the San Francisco ordinance has now been preempted by a California state law.[24]

The tobacco industry has been attempting, with some success, to persuade states to enact less stringent smoking laws that *expressly* preempt local regulation of smoking. Several states, including Connecticut, Florida, Illinois, Iowa, Louisiana, Nevada, New Jersey, North Carolina, North Dakota, and Oklahoma, have enacted state laws that expressly preempt local regulation of smoking. These preemption statutes, however, generally do not apply to preexisting local ordinances. North Carolina's statute preempts local ordinances, even though it contains *no* restrictions on smoking in the workplace or in public places.

In California, Proposition 188, a ballot initiative supported by the tobacco industry that would have preempted local smoking laws, was voted on in the November 1994 election. Proposition 188 would have repealed all local smoking ordinances and preempted any future ordinances and replaced them with a single, less restrictive statewide ordinance. Proposition 188 would have allowed smoking in any designated smoking area in workplaces, restaurants, and other public places as long as the area met ventilation standards set by the American Society of Heating, Refrigerating, and Air Conditioning Engineers (ASHRAE).[25] It would *not* have required smoking areas to be enclosed, maintained under negative air pressure, or separately ventilated directly to the outside. Proposition 188 was defeated by a margin of more than 70 percent to 30 percent.

Even though Proposition 188 and its preemption provisions failed, the California Assembly recently enacted a law, Assembly Bill 13, effective January 1, 1995, that itself preempts local regulation of smoking in most enclosed workplaces in California. Unlike Proposition 188, however, this law is one of the most restrictive state smoking laws passed to date and bans smoking in most workplaces, including restaurants, except in "employee breakrooms," which must have separate ventilation to the outside and comply with any applicable federal and state ventilation standards.[26] The few workplaces not covered by this California law are still subject to local smoking regulations.

Washington state's Labor and Industries Agency adopted a regulation effective September 1, 1994, that bans smoking in all indoor workplaces except in designated smoking rooms that have "sufficient negative air pressure . . . to prevent smoke migration" and are mechanically "exhausted directly outside."[27] Similarly, Utah recently enacted a law banning smoking not only in offices but also in restaurants, malls, stores, child-care facilities, and the common areas of hotels and motels. The only exception allowed by Utah's ban is for separate smoking areas within private workplaces as long as smoke is prevented from getting into the rest of the building.[28]

On August 1, 1994, Maryland's Division of Labor and Industry enacted a regulation banning smoking in all enclosed public places, including malls, restaurants, bars, and stores, and in all indoor public and private workplaces. Originally, the only exceptions were for tobacco stores, smoking-research laboratories, and single-person vehicles, though a few other exceptions were added, including exceptions for bars and limited areas of restaurants in enclosed rooms.[29] This antismoking regulation was met by an immediate state court challenge from the tobacco industry, which obtained an injunction from a judge in Talbot County, Maryland. This injunction was subsequently vacated by the Court of Appeals of Maryland and the regulation went into effect.[30]

Smoking Regulation in Multifamily Residential Properties

One environment that smoking regulation at all levels seems to have overlooked is multifamily residential properties. Government's reluctance to intrude on the decision of whether to smoke in the privacy of one's own home is understandable, although the question has been raised in custody disputes about whether children should be protected from ETS generated by parents who smoke or allow smoking in the home.[31] However, what about the common areas within multifamily residential properties?

Although the jurisdiction of OSHA and state safety agencies generally does not extend to such places, it is somewhat surprising that state and local smoking laws have not extended protections to those areas.[32] Even the Waxman bill, which otherwise would cover nearly all buildings in the country, expressly would not apply to "any building or portion thereof regularly used for residential purposes." Thus, even if the Waxman bill were enacted, people would be free to smoke not only in their own living quarters but anywhere in the lobbies, hallways, and other common elements of apartment buildings, condominiums, cooperatives, retirement homes, nursing homes, and other residential properties.

Case Law

In 1976 a court ruled for the first time that an employer has a common-law duty to provide its employees with a smoke-free working environment.[33] Since then, some courts have held that employees are entitled to collect unemployment,[34] disability,[35] and workers' compensation benefits[36] from their employers for injuries caused by ETS exposure. Moreover, some courts have allowed employees to pursue damage claims against employers for ETS injuries under common-law theories such as negligence[37] and assault and battery.[38] Other courts, however, have ruled against employees seeking benefits arising out of alleged ETS-related injuries.[39]

In addition, numerous ETS cases have been brought, with varying degrees of success, against employers under the Americans with Disabilities Act (ADA)[40] on the theory that sensitivity to ETS constitutes a handicap. Also, ETS cases have been brought against restaurants and a nightclub under the ADA for failure to provide nonsmoking facilities for ETS-sensitive persons. The restaurant cases have been dismissed;

the nightclub case went to trial, but was decided against the plaintiffs by a federal judge in Texas.[41]

Prisoners have frequently sued prison officials over ETS exposure. In 1993 the U.S. Supreme Court ruled that a prisoner could state "a cause of action under the Eighth Amendment['s prohibition against cruel and unusual punishment] by alleging that [prison officials had], with deliberate indifference, exposed him to levels of ETS that pose an unreasonable risk of serious damage to his future health."[42] This is the only case in which the right to be free from ETS exposure has been recognized as a constitutional concern. Other constitutional claims by nonsmokers have consistently been denied.[43]

Smokers, on the other hand, generally have not succeeded with constitutional challenges to ordinances banning or restricting smoking.[44] Moreover, they will not be able to make an argument that antismoking laws and regulations constitute discrimination against them under the ADA, as that statute expressly states that it is not intended "to preclude the prohibition of, or the imposition of, restrictions on smoking in places of employment . . . , in transportation . . . , or in places of public accommodation. . . ."[45]

Although arguments based on constitutional rights have not fared well on either side of the ETS debate, the tobacco industry has begun to face ETS-related personal injury claims. A Mississippi state court, for example, has allowed a barber to proceed against several tobacco companies for injuries he allegedly suffered as a result of long-term exposure to ETS from customers who smoked.[46] In addition, the Florida Court of Appeals has allowed a group of airline flight attendants who alleged that they had been injured as a result of being forced to breathe ETS in aircraft cabins to pursue a class action lawsuit against several tobacco companies.[47]

To date, most ETS cases have involved employers, prison officials, or the tobacco industry. The author knows of no litigation involving the owner of a commercial office building or retail property. However, several ETS cases have been brought against residential landlords, demonstrating that even the real estate industry is not immune from ETS-related liability concerns.

For example, in 1991, in a Massachusetts housing court, a tenant sued her landlord for nuisance, breach of warranty of habitability, breach of covenant of quiet enjoyment, negligence, battery, and intentional infliction of emotional distress due to exposure to ETS in her apartment coming from another apartment (where the defendant landlord lived). The tenant alleged that the ETS caused her to suffer asthma attacks, labored breathing, wheezing, prolonged coughing bouts, clogged sinuses, and frequent vomiting. The case was later settled.[48]

In 1992, in an Oregon state court case, a landlord was sued for moving a known smoker into an apartment below the plaintiff, a nonsmoker, who began to suffer nausea, swollen membranes, and respiratory problems as a result of the cigarette smoke entering her apartment. The suit alleged breaches of the statutory warranty of habitability and the covenant of quiet enjoyment implied in the lease. The jury reduced the plaintiff's rent by 50 percent and awarded her damages to cover her medical bills. The landlord in the case moved for a judgment notwithstanding the verdict. At this writing, the disposition of that motion is unknown.[49]

Finally, in a recent New Jersey case, a nonsmoking couple allegedly injured by smoke coming into their apartment for over a year brought ETS claims not only against the smoking tenant but also against the property management company and the tenant association for not taking action to stop the smoke migration.[50]

Private Regulation of Smoking

Unless legislation such as the Waxman bill is enacted at the federal level or OSHA finalizes its proposed ETS rule, state and local ETS regulation is likely to remain subject to wide variation. In the meantime, the issuance of the ETS Report (and perhaps the threat of ETS lawsuits) has caused such a surge in private regulation of smoking that governmental regulation may eventually prove superfluous.

In fact, the ETS Report only increased the tendency of businesses to ban, or at least severely restrict, workplace smoking. A survey of businesses conducted by the Bureau of National Affairs in 1991—two years before the ETS Report was issued—revealed that 85 percent of responding businesses had already imposed some form of smoking restriction on employees. More than one-third of the respondents reported that their buildings were smoke-free.[51] Graphic evidence of the number of companies regulating smoking can be found in the groups of smokers huddled outside office buildings across the country.

In 1994, McDonald's, Taco Bell, and several other fast food chains announced with great fanfare that their restaurants were becoming smoke-free. These companies were undoubtedly prompted to act by lawsuits filed on February 16, 1994, by the Texas attorney general against members of the fast food industry, alleging that the restaurants used playgrounds and special meals to attract children into their establishments and then failed to protect them from ETS. The lawsuits claimed it was false, misleading, and deceptive to suggest that a nonsmoking section protects the public from ETS when the smoke is simply recirculated within the restaurant.[52]

Implications for the Real Estate Industry

What are the implications of the ETS issue for the real estate industry? The good news is that ETS appears to pose considerably less of a threat to property values than other environmental issues that often require costly remediation, such as soil and groundwater contamination, asbestos, and lead-based paint. The bad news is that, unlike those issues, ETS affects *every* building, regardless of age or use.

The Impact of ETS on Value

The ETS issue will threaten real estate values only if building owners are forced to provide smokers with specially ventilated smoking rooms or otherwise retrofit their buildings to mitigate ETS. Complying with such a mandate could be very expensive, depending on the size of the building and the extent of retrofitting required. Consider, for example, the impact of a law requiring each apartment in a complex to be separately ventilated so that no air is exchanged between apartments, or a law requiring a separately ventilated smoking lounge on every floor of a high-rise commercial office building.

If the negative public attitude toward smoking continues as the prevailing trend, it is unlikely that future law or regulation will saddle building owners and operators with the obligation of making expensive building alterations to accommodate smokers. The author is aware of no current or proposed smoking law or regulation that mandates construction of separately ventilated smoking facilities for building occupants who wish to smoke.[53] Moreover, all the major new federal government initiatives, including the proposed OSHA smoking regulation, the EPA's Alliance, and the Waxman bill, expressly provide building owners and operators with the option of implementing an outright smoking ban.

In addition, without a specific lease provision addressing smoking, it is unlikely that a tenant will be able to force a landlord either to permit smoking or to provide special smoking facilities. Such a claim cannot be made under the ADA with respect to a nonresidential commercial building because, as noted earlier, the statute expressly sanctions the prohibition of smoking.[54] Further, an ADA claim by a residential tenant will not lie because residential facilities are not covered by the statute.[55] To assert a right to smoke or to be provided with special smoking accommodations, a residential tenant would likely have to rely on the Fair Housing Act (FHA) Amendments of 1988, which preclude housing discrimination based on a "physical or mental impairment which substantially limits one or more of such person's major life activities."[56] The desire to smoke, or even an addiction to smoking, would not appear to fall within the scope of this definition. Moreover, the FHA expressly states that it does not require "that a dwelling be made available to an individual whose tenancy would constitute a direct threat to the health or safety of other individuals. . . ."[57] Thus, given the EPA's conclusion that ETS is a carcinogen, the refusal to lease to a smoker would not appear actionable, even if smoking were deemed to be an "impairment."

Transactional Due Diligence Concerning ETS

Even if property values are not likely to be affected by ETS, real estate investors should consider, as part of their pretransaction environmental due diligence, inquiring about the applicable smoking ordinances in the location where they are considering a new loan or acquisition. In addition, investors should consider investigating each of the following:

- The ability of the building's mechanical systems to control ETS buildup and migration
- Whether separately ventilated smoking facilities exist and, if they do not, the cost of installing them
- The building's current smoking policies
- Whether the leases of existing tenants contain smoking-related covenants that could potentially limit the landlord's flexibility in coping with the ETS issue

The Risk of ETS Liability

Assuming that expensive alterations are not required in leases, by law or to satisfy tenant demand, the most significant ETS risks facing building owners and operators are claims by building occupants alleging injury from ETS exposure. (The potential exposure of real estate lenders to such ETS claims appears to be remote, as long as lenders avoid involvement in property operations.)

Although most ETS cases to date have involved claims against employers, prison officials, or the tobacco industry, the lawsuits against residential landlords discussed previously in this chapter should concern building owners. Moreover, as more tenants ban workplace smoking, building occupants may begin to look to landlords for protection against ETS migrating from other parts of the building. It is not inconceivable that a court might extend the rationale of the negligence, battery, or ADA cases against employers and impose a duty on commercial building owners and operators to maintain a safe indoor environment, free from the hazards of ETS. Thus, particularly in light of the ETS Report findings, it may be only a matter of time before commercial building owners and operators begin to face serious ETS claims.

Not surprisingly, the industry is concerned. The Building Owners and Managers Association (BOMA) International has been a vocal supporter of the Waxman bill because passage of the legislation would relieve nonresidential building owners and operators of the decision whether to institute smoking policies. BOMA International has not only testified in favor of the Waxman bill but has also publicly supported the smoking provisions in OSHA's proposed IAQ regulations and issued a resolution supporting a total federal ban on smoking in the workplace—with the proviso that building owners and managers be absolved of responsibility for policing the law and of any liability for injuries caused by noncompliance.

Avoiding ETS Liability

What, if anything, should real estate owners and operators consider doing to avoid ETS liability?

First, they should consider becoming aware of the smoking laws and ordinances that apply where their buildings are located and ensure that their buildings are in compliance. Depending on the jurisdiction, instituting a smoking ban may be the single action required to bring a building into "compliance." An outright ban will go a long way toward reducing, or even eliminating, liability exposure for ETS injury claims. If such a ban is not legally mandated, however, imposing one voluntarily may have collateral consequences, such as violating existing leases. Even if permitted under existing leases, a total ban may negatively affect tenant relations (and, ultimately, occupancy rates).

An alternative to a blanket prohibition might be a ban on smoking anywhere in the building except for designated, enclosed smoking rooms made available by the landlord. Maintaining these rooms under negative air pressure and exhausting them directly to the outside will minimize the possibility of ETS migrating into the general building atmosphere. One significant downside to this approach, of course, would be the cost of such building alterations. In the preamble to its proposed IAQ regulations, OSHA has estimated that it would cost $25,000 to retrofit a single one thousand-square-foot room to accommodate up to sixty-five smokers.[58]

Another option would be for the landlord to provide smoking areas that are physically separated but not retrofitted with negative air pressure and a separate ventilation system. The most obvious downside to this approach would be that ETS could still migrate into other portions of the building. This strategy, of course, would not suffice in jurisdictions that have banned smoking except in separately ventilated rooms. Indeed, for most nonresidential properties, the option of merely segregating smokers from nonsmokers would be foreclosed if the Waxman bill were enacted or OSHA's proposed smoking regulation became final as written.

Still another option—one that is being considered by an increasing number of office building owners and operators—is to ban smoking in all enclosed public and common areas, including rest rooms and stairwells.[59] In this scenario, individual tenants would continue to decide for themselves how smoking should be regulated within their premises, subject to federal, state, and local laws. The principal downside to this approach is that, unless the building is designed so that each tenant's space is separately ventilated and no air is exchanged with other tenant spaces, there is no way to stop ETS from circulating throughout the building.

The Apartment Owner's Dilemma

Of all building owners, apartment owners may face the most perplexing dilemma. Although many of the apartments in this country are in low-rise buildings without a common ventilation system, a considerable number of high-rise buildings have mechanical ventilation systems that distribute "shared air" throughout the building, similar to the systems found in commercial buildings. Such a system may permit ETS to circulate easily from apartment to apartment, but it also allows air exchange within the building that may remove ETS before it accumulates to a potentially dangerous level. In apartments with no ventilation system, there is less potential for migration of smoke into the apartments of nonsmokers. If ETS does get into such apartments, however, it is not easily removed or diluted with fresh air.

Smoking regulation generally does not now apply to residential properties and is not likely to be so extended in the future. Although regulation may eventually cover the common areas of residential properties, it is unlikely to be extended to the interior of individual apartments. Therefore, in contrast to commercial properties, where decisions over the tenant's right to smoke in their leased premises are increasingly being taken out of the hands of landlords, apartment owners will still be forced to navigate on their own through the minefield of potential ETS liability. As noted earlier, liability for ETS exposure has been imposed on at least one residential landlord, and another ETS case brought against a landlord has been settled. Compounding the difficulty for apartment owners is the fact that children are likely to be among their tenants. Children, according to the ETS Report, are particularly susceptible to injuries from ETS exposure.

Although residential landlords possess the ability to ban smoking in their buildings entirely, the disadvantage inherent in this rather drastic measure is that smokers are likely to feel strongly that they should be able to smoke in their own homes. Such a ban could eliminate a significant portion of the residential rental market. Restricting smoking to separately ventilated smoking lounges within apartment buildings is likely to be equally unpopular with tenants and potential tenants who smoke.

For owners of residential buildings, the optimal way to stave off liability without affecting occupancy rates would be to provide smoking tenants with separately ventilated apartments. Unfortunately, the prohibitive cost of retrofitting existing apartments renders this solution impractical in most cases. Still, it is worth considering at the design phase for new multifamily residential buildings.

Perhaps the residential landlord's most practical alternative is to prohibit smoking in common areas, or at least to limit common area smoking to separately ventilated smoking lounges provided by the landlord, and to be as responsive as possible to tenant concerns about smoking. The residential landlord should also consider situating smokers and nonsmokers in different parts of the apartment building if possible. In buildings with mechanical ventilation systems, the landlord should consider whether the air exchange meets applicable ASHRAE standards and adequately eliminates smoke odor in nonsmokers' apartments. The landlord should also consider whether good maintenance procedures are being followed on filters and other elements of the HVAC system. In difficult cases, structural or mechanical alterations may have to be considered.

Conclusion

None of the alternatives for dealing with ETS that confront building owners and operators is perfect. At a minimum, each owner should consider implementing a rational smoking policy that takes into account the type of building, its mechanical systems, the nature of the building's tenancy, and the ETS regulations that exist where the building is located. Whatever policy is decided on could be set forth clearly in all new leases and lease renewals. Beyond that, building owners and operators should hope that eventually federal legislation or final federal regulation will be enacted that will provide clear guidance on controlling ETS.

Notes

The views expressed herein are the author's own and do not necessarily represent the views of Aetna Life and Casualty Company or its affiliates.

1. For a discussion of the components of ETS and how ETS can circulate through a building, *see* Allison D. Schwartz, *Environmental Tobacco Smoke and Its Effect on Children: Controlling Smoking in the Home*, 20 B. COLLEGE ENVTL. AFF. L.R., 135, 138–42 (1993).

2. U.S. Dep't of Health and Human Services, The Health Consequences of Involuntary Smoking, A Report of the Surgeon General (1986).

3. EPA/60016-901006F.

4. *See, e.g.*, Gordon v. Raven Systems & Research, Inc., 462 A.2d 10, 15 (D.C. 1983) (in dismissing plaintiff's ETS claims, court noted plaintiff's failure to provide "scientific evidence of the deleterious effects of tobacco smoke on nonsmokers").

5. Flue-Cured Tobacco Cooperative Stabilization Corp. v. United States Envtl. Protection Agency, 857 F. Supp. 1137 (1994).

6. *Philip Morris Plans an Attack on EPA Report*, WALL ST. J., June 24, 1994, at B1. *See also Send Regulations Up in Smoke*, WALL ST. J., June 3, 1994, at A14 (editorial in which a Harvard economics professor and fellow at the Hoover Institution at Stanford University argues that "the statistical evidence for health risks from [ETS] is extremely weak . . . ").

7. A copy of this publication can be obtained by calling (800) 438-4318.

8. 49 U.S.C. App. § 1374(d)(1)(A) (1993 Supp. Pamphlet).

9. P.L. 103-227, Sec. 1043, 1994 U.S. CODE CONG. & AD. NEWS, Vol. 2, 108 STAT. 271.

10. The proposed OSHA IAQ regulations have been published in the *Federal Register*. *See* 59 Fed. Reg. 15,068, 16,035–39 (1994). The lengthy preamble to the regulations contains a detailed discussion of the background surrounding the ETS issue.

11. The court has dismissed ASH's petition without prejudice on the ground that it was mooted by OSHA's issuance of its proposed smoking regulation. Action on Smoking and Health v. Dep't of Labor, 1994 WL 32675, at 3 (D.C. Cir. July 12, 1994). But the court held that ASH could "renew its petition if OSHA fails to pursue its rulemaking with due dispatch." *Id.*, at 5.

12. *Periscope*, NEWSWEEK, April 4, 1994, at 4.

13. 41 C.F.R. § 101-20.109–10 (1994).

14. *Cracking Down on Smokers*, N.Y. TIMES, March 17, 1994, at B3.

15. *Smoking Shifts to the Front Burner of Property Issues*, CHICAGO TRIBUNE, May 16, 1993, Real Estate Section, at 1.

16. In 1991 a proposed executive order was drafted for President Bush that would have banned smoking in all interior spaces of property owned, rented, or leased by the federal government except for residential facilities and buildings leased to the private sector. This order was never signed. It has been redrafted and is reportedly now being considered by President Clinton.

17. H.R. 3434, 103rd Cong., 1st Sess. (1993).

18. S. 1680, 103rd Cong., 1st Sess. (1993).

19. H.R. 881, 103rd Cong., 1st Sess. (1993); S. 262, 103rd Cong., 1st Sess. (1993).

20. H.R. 710, 103rd Cong., 1st Sess. (1993); S. 261, 103rd Cong., 1st Sess. (1993).

21. A publication titled STATE LEGISLATED ACTIONS ON TOBACCO ISSUES, which summarizes all state laws regulating smoking, can be obtained for $7.50 from the Coalition on Smoking OR Health, a Washington, D.C.-based advocacy group, at (202) 452–1184. A synopsis of local smoking laws and ordinances can be found in a publication titled MONOGRAPH 3: MAJOR LOCAL TOBACCO CONTROL ORDINANCES IN THE UNITED STATES, National Institutes of Health, National Cancer Institute (NIH Publication No. 93-3532).

22. For an article discussing recent state and local regulation of smoking, see *Nationwide, Reins on Smokers' Freedom Tighten*, N.Y. TIMES, March 22, 1994, at A1.

23. *Butt Out, Smokers Told*, NEWSDAY, December 22, 1994, at A15. The original version of this ordinance, proposed by the city council on March 16, 1994, contained even stronger smoking restrictions. The final version was revised to some extent in response to concerns raised by restaurant owners and the tobacco industry. *Foes of Ban on Smoking Win Changes*, N.Y. TIMES, October 13, 1994, at B1.

24. CAL. LABOR CODE § 6404.5 (Assembly Bill No. 13).

25. The benchmark standard for building ventilation is ASHRAE Standard 62-1989. This is a voluntary standard that is not legally enforceable and, among other things, sets minimum ventilation rates for various indoor air spaces.

26. CAL. LABOR CODE § 6404.5 (Assembly Bill No. 13).

27. WASH. ADMIN. CODE § 296-62-12005 (1994).

28. UTAH CODE ANN. §§ 26-38-1–26-38-9 (1994).

29. MD. REGS. CODE tit. 09 § 12.23.

30. Fogle v. H&G Restaurant, Inc., 654 A.2d 449 (Md. Ct. App. 1995). *See also Maryland Smoking Ban*, WALL ST. J., July 25, 1994, at B5.

31. The issue of protecting children from ETS exposure in the home is addressed at length in Schwartz, *supra* note 1, at 138–42. Some state smoking laws have extended their reach into private homes that are being used as day-care facilities for children. *See, e.g.*, CAL. HEALTH & SAFETY CODE § 1596.795 (1993); ME. REV. STAT. ANN. tit. 22, § 262-1542 (1993).

32. Statutes in a few states do extend smoking restrictions to the common areas of condominiums and retirement homes, FLA. STAT. ANN. §§ 386.201–386.211 (1992); of elderly housing complexes, R.I. GEN. LAWS §§ 23-20.6-1–23-20.6-2 (1993); and of nursing homes, VT. STAT. ANN. tit. 18, § 1742 (1993). They do not, however, extend to living quarters within these kinds of properties.

33. Shimp v. New Jersey Bell Tel. Co., 368 A.2d 408, 416 (N.J. Super. Ct. Ch. Div. 1976). *Accord* McCarthy v. Dep't of Social and Health Services, 759 P. 2d 351, 354 (Wash. 1988); Smith v. Western Electric Co., 643 S.W.2d 10, 13 (Mo. Ct. App. 1982).

34. Alexander v. California Unemployment Ins. Appeals Bd., 163 Cal. Rptr. 411, 412–13 (Cal. Ct. App. 1980).

35. Parodi v. Merit Systems Protection Bd., 690 F.2d 731, 751 (9th Cir. 1982).

36. Johannesen v. New York City Dep't of Housing Preservation and Dev., No. 89 (N.Y. Ct. App. June 21, 1994); Pechan v. Dynapro, 622 N.E.2d 108, 121 (Ill. App. Ct. 1993); Schober v. Mountain Bell Tel., 630 P.2d 1231, 1236 (N.M. Ct. App. 1980).

37. *See, e.g.*, McCarthy v. Dep't of Social and Health Services, 759 P. 2d at 358 (negligence claim allowed to proceed because compensation for ETS injury had been denied under workers' compensation statute).

38. *See, e.g.*, Portenier v. Republic Hogg Robinson, Inc., Case No. BC 028990 (Cal. Super. Ct., County of Los Angeles, Central Jud. Dist. 1994) (in an unwritten decision, court denied defense motions for summary judgment on ETS battery claim against employer and ruled that workers' compensation is not plaintiff's exclusive remedy); Richardson v. Hennly, 434 S.E.2d 772, 776–77 (Ga. Ct. App. 1993) (currently on appeal to the Georgia Supreme Court, which granted *certiorari* on December 6, 1993) (employee can state claim for battery against both co-employee who smoked and employer who permitted it); Leichtman v. WLW Jacor Communications, Inc., No. C-920922, 1994 WL 19097, at 2 (Ohio Ct. App. January 26, 1994) (court held that smokers can themselves be sued for battery).

39. *See, e.g.*, Palmer v. Del Webb's High Sierra, 838 P.2d 435, 437 (Nev. 1992); Billman v. Sumrall, 464 So.2d 382, 386 (La. Ct. App. 1985).

40. 42 U.S.C. § 12101 *et seq.* (1993 Pamphlet).

41. *Smoking and Disabilities*, WALL ST. J., February 2, 1995, at B7. A current synopsis of the ETS cases brought under the ADA, as well as other ETS case law, is available from the Tobacco Control Resource Center, Inc., 102 The Fenway, Boston, MA 02115, (617) 373–2026.

42. Helling v. McKinney, 113 S. Ct. 2475, 2481 (1993).

43. *See, e.g.*, Gasper v. Louisiana Stadium and Exposition Dist., 577 F.2d 897, 899 (5th Cir. 1978), *cert. denied*, 439 U.S. 1073 (1979); Kensell v. State of Oklahoma, 716 F.2d 1350, 1351 (10th Cir. 1983).

44. *See, e.g.*, Grusendorf v. City of Oklahoma City, 816 F.2d 539, 543 (10th Cir. 1987); Rossie v. State of Wisconsin/Dep't of Revenue, 395 N.W.2d 801, 806–07 (Wis. Ct. App. 1986); Fagan v. Axelrod, 550 N.Y.S.2d 552, 559 (N.Y. Sup. Ct., 1990) (court held that "[t]here is no more a fundamental right to smoke cigarettes than there is to shoot-up or snort heroin or cocaine").

45. 42 U.S.C. § 12201(b) (1993 Pamphlet).

46. Butler v. R.J. Reynolds Tobacco Co., No. 92-73-361, slip op. (Miss. Cir. Ct., 1st Jud. Dist., Hinds Cty. January 24, 1994) (court denied defendant tobacco companies' motion for summary judgment on plaintiff's claims for conspiratorial fraudulent omission, conspiratorial fraudulent misrepresentation, breach of express and implied warranty, manufacturing defects, and strict liability. The barber, Earl Butler, has since died and his case has been refiled in Jones County, Mississippi, as a wrongful death action. Discovery is proceeding).

47. Broin v. Philip Morris Cos., No. 92-1405, 1994 WL 81712, at 2 (Fla. Dist. Ct. App. March 15, 1994). The district court judge recently certified a class of sixty thousand flight attendants in this case. *See Cigarette Suit Approved*, WALL ST. J., December 13, 1994, at B11.

48. Donath v. Dadah, No. 91-CV179 (Mass. Housing Ct., Worcester Cty. 1991).

49. Fox Point Apt. v. Kippes, No. 92-6924 (Or. Dist. Ct., Lackamas Cty. 1992).

50. Pentony v. Conrad, Morris County Ct. (N.J. 1994). This case is discussed in an article titled *Dover Couple Rebuffed on No-Smoking Demand*, STAR-LEDGER, April 29, 1994. *See also* Lipsman v. McPherson, 6.2 TPLR 2.345, 19 M.L.W. 1605 (No. 90-1918) (Mass. Super. Ct., Middlesex 1991) (nonsmoking tenant's claim

against smoking tenant for nuisance and negligence arising out of smoke seeping into the nonsmoker's apartment dismissed because three to six cigarettes per day "is not substantial and would not affect an ordinary person").

51. *Workers Forced Outdoors to Catch a Smoke*, ALBANY (NEW YORK) TIMES-UNION, January 3, 1994, at B1.

52. *'Smoke Free' Challenged*, NATIONAL LAW JOURNAL, February 28, 1994, at 25.

53. North Carolina, however, has a law that *requires* that smoking be permitted in at least 25 percent of the indoor space of state government buildings, even if no enclosure or separate ventilation is used. N.C. GEN. STAT. ch. 14 § 1 (1993).

54. *See supra* note 45 and accompanying text.

55. *See* 1990 U.S. CODE CONG. & AD. NEWS, Vol. 4, 101st Cong., 2nd Sess., P.L. 101-336, at 383 (discussion in legislative history of the definition of "public accommodation").

56. 42 U.S.C. § 3602 (h) (1) (1994 Pamphlet).

57. 42 U.S.C. § 3604 (f) (9) (1994 Pamphlet).

58. 59 Fed. Reg. 15,068, 16,017 (1994).

59. A survey by BOMA/Chicago last year found that 20 percent of the office buildings in the Chicago Loop prohibit smoking entirely and another 42 percent prohibit smoking in lobbies and corridors. *Smoking Shifts*, *supra* note 15.

CHAPTER 25

Electric and Magnetic Fields

I. LEO MOTIUK
HARRY M. BAUMGARTNER

Debate is intensifying over the possible adverse health and safety impacts of electric and magnetic fields (EMFs), which are often collectively referred to as electromagnetic fields. Despite inconclusive scientific evidence, personal injury and property damage lawsuits are increasing, creating a broad range of novel legal issues. Accordingly, real estate practitioners are well advised to familiarize themselves with the technical aspects of EMFs and to be prepared to advise clients engaged in real estate ownership, development, leasing, management, and financing activities on how to anticipate and mitigate potential adverse business consequences.

What Are EMFs?

EMFs are separate but interrelated forces created by the presence and movement of electric charges.[1]

Electric fields are produced by electric pressure, or voltage, in a charged conductor (e.g., wire). Magnetic fields are created by the flow of charges, or current, that moves back and forth through a conductor. Thus, electric fields are present whenever a conductor is energized (e.g., when an electrical device is plugged in), but magnetic fields are present only when the electrical device is turned on.[2]

The strength of an electric field is determined by the voltage applied to a conductor. The higher the voltage, the stronger the electric field.[3] The strength of a magnetic field is determined by the strength of the current, which is measured in amperes. As current increases, the magnetic field increases.[4] Field strength drops rapidly with distance from the conductor.[5]

Electric fields are measured in volts per meter (V/m); magnetic fields are measured in a unit called a gauss. "Gaussmeters" indicate the strength of a magnetic field in terms of a thousandth of a gauss, or milligauss (mG).[6] Electric fields primarily create charges or current near the surface of the body. Magnetic fields induce electric currents within the body.[7] It is relatively easy to shield electric fields from human exposure. Magnetic fields, however, can pass through virtually anything.[8] For these and other reasons, most research on EMFs has focused on magnetic fields.[9]

EMFs exist throughout the "electromagnetic spectrum." Ordinary electricity is transmitted in the United States at a frequency of 60 hertz (Hz), which is within the 0–300 Hz extremely low-frequency (ELF) range of the spectrum.[10] At the opposite end of the spectrum, in the extremely high-frequency range, are gamma rays and x-rays.

EMFs from 60-Hz electric power are sometimes referred to as "nonionizing radiation." Unlike "ionizing" radiation, such as that associated with x-rays, nonionizing radiation does not have the capacity to alter atomic structure.[11] Radio waves and microwaves, which are at the midpoint of the electromagnetic frequency spectrum, are forms of high-frequency nonionizing radiation.[12]

EMFs interact in high-frequency ranges, rendering their effects inseparable.[13] At low frequency, EMFs have separate and distinct effects.[14]

The earth's core generates a natural magnetic field that averages approximately 500 mG at the earth's surface.[15] By comparison, high-voltage electric transmission lines typically produce magnetic fields ranging from 30 mG to 183 mG within a utility's right of way, depending on line strength and level of use.[16] Electric tools or appliances can generate much higher mG levels. For example, some can openers generate a 1,500-mG reading at a distance of six inches.[17] Hair dryers, power tools, and industrial equipment also generate readings at close range.[18] Readings of 500 mG have been recorded in the passenger compartments of electric rail lines.[19] Field strength drops exponentially as distance from the source increases.[20] For instance, a vacuum cleaner's 300 mG at a distance of six inches falls to 60 mG at one foot, 10 mG at two feet, and one mG at four feet.[21]

EMFs and Health Risks

Scores of studies have addressed the possible health impacts posed by EMFs. These studies include: (1) epidemiological studies of human populations exposed to EMFs at work or home; (2) studies of tissues or cell cultures exposed to EMFs (*in vitro* studies); and (3) studies in which laboratory animals are exposed to EMFs and health and reproductive patterns are observed (*in vivo* studies).[22]

To date, neither *in vivo* nor *in vitro* studies have revealed an affirmative health risk.[23] Some epidemiological studies have indicated a positive association between EMFs and health risks, but on the whole, epidemiological research remains inconsistent, contradictory, and inconclusive.[24]

Epidemiological Research

EMFs first became a concern in the United States after publication of a 1979 epidemiological study by Nancy Wertheimer and Ed Leeper, which reported that children living near high-current power lines died of leukemia at a rate greater than children not so exposed.[25] The study was criticized, however, as suffering from significant methodological flaws.[26] A year later, in 1980, a study by J.P. Fulton and others failed to confirm an EMF-cancer association.[27] In 1982, Wertheimer and Leeper published a second study, which reported increased cancer mortality among adults living near high-current power lines.[28] In 1986, a Swedish study failed to confirm a statistically significant link between EMFs and leukemia.[29]

Interest was rekindled in 1988 after publication of a study by David Savitz, which improved on the Wertheimer-Leeper methodologies. The Savitz study reported that children living near high-current power lines were more likely to develop cancer.[30] In 1991, however, a study by S.J. London and others showed no statistically significant relationship between cancer and EMFs.[31] A Swedish study, published in 1992, received widespread publicity and focused broad new attention on the issue. The study, by Anders Ahlbom and Marie Feychting, reported that the incidence of leukemia in children increased proportionately with the strength of magnetic fields generated by high-current power lines.[32] According to Ahlbom-Feychting, that incidence increased nearly threefold for children exposed to the strongest magnetic fields.[33]

Critics emphasize that the Swedish study, like previous epidemiological efforts, relied not on actual EMF exposure measurements but on imprecise historic estimates, or "surrogates," of magnetic field strength.[34] Others note that epidemiological studies are flawed in general, since they fail to account for other possible cancer causes, such as chemical exposure (e.g., radon gas, benzene emissions) or genetic history, and because they can only demonstrate possible associations, not cause-and-effect relationships.[35] Other critics note that there is no biologically plausible explanation for the purported association between EMFs and cancer, particularly since naturally occurring EMFs from the earth's magnetic field far exceed EMFs from man-made sources.[36] The lack of demonstrable carcinogenic effect in laboratory studies also weakens epidemiological inferences, they state.[37]

As with general population studies, occupational studies of power line workers, electricians, and others also have yielded inconsistent results.[38] For instance, a 1992 Swedish study, headed by Birgitta Floderus, indicated an association between workplace exposure and chronic lymphocytic leukemia that increased with the estimated magnitude of EMF strength.[39] Yet a 1993 study of electric utility workers in Southern California found no link between workplace exposure and leukemia or other cancers.[40] A 1994 French-Canadian study also found no link between EMF exposure and common cancers, but an association was noted with one type of adult leukemia.[41] A large-scale study of electric utility workers published in 1995, by Savitch and Dana Loomis, failed to identify a link between EMFs and leukemia but noted a possible correlation between exposure to high levels of EMFs and brain cancer.[42]

All told, more than eighty epidemiological studies have been conducted.[43] Numerous comprehensive peer reviews of these studies also have been published.[44] While the reviewers differ in their evaluation of specific reported results, their consensus is that epidemiological evidence of an EMF-cancer link remains inconclusive.[45] As noted by Savitch and Loomis, "Firm conclusions regarding whether magnetic fields cause cancer, based on our study alone or on the entire literature, are not yet possible."[46]

Cellular and Whole Animal Research

It is generally accepted that electric power EMFs generate insufficient energy to initiate cancer.[47] As a result, cellular studies have been directed at determining whether EMFs may contribute to the promotion or acceleration of cancers.[48] These studies indicate demonstrable biological effects of EMFs, but they have not, to date, determined that EMFs induce or promote cancer.[49]

The biological effects noted from significant exposure to EMFs include altered flows of ions and protons across cell membranes, changes in the permeability of cellular membrane calcium, changes in cell division and endocrine tissues, effects on the synthesis of DNA in the cell nucleus and the transcription of RNA outside the nucleus, lower growth rates in bean roots, effects on cellular responses to hormones and neurotransmitters, and effects on immunological responses.[50] However, these studies have been deemed inconclusive because they are not consistent and, according to one commentator, "have been conducted in conditions that are not comparable to day-to-day exposure—specifically, [high] exposures that are not realistic."[51]

Long-term whole animal studies are incomplete.[52] Interim studies of animals exposed to EMFs reveal certain effects on biological rhythms and neuroendrocrinial processing, certain effects on central nervous system development, and behavioral effects, such as EMF avoidance.[53] As with cellular studies, the results are inconsistent, and many scientists remain skeptical of any lasting biological effects caused by EMFs.[54] As noted by one scientist, "It seems foolish to be worrying about the conceivable effects of these minuscule magnetic fields when you're immersed in bigger [naturally occurring] fields, though random, all the time."[55]

The Legislative Response

In response to the substantial debate surrounding EMFs, Congress in 1992 passed the Electric and Magnetic Field Research and Public Information and Dissemination Act.[56] This act, which was incorporated into the Energy Policy Act of 1992[57] and signed into law on October 24, 1992, authorized a five-year $65 million research program on EMFs. The act also requires the National Institute of Environmental Health Sciences (NIEHS) to coordinate research on possible health effects caused by EMFs and to report its findings by June 1, 1995.[58] In addition, the act assigns to the Department of Energy responsibility for research on technologies to characterize, measure, and manage exposure to EMFs.[59] It also directs the National Toxicology Program to coordinate long-term animal studies.[60] Such studies began in June 1993.[61]

Pending federal legislation includes the Children's Electromagnetic Field Risk Reduction Act,[62] which would require public schools or day-care facilities built, accredited, or opened after the bill's enactment to be located in areas where magnetic field levels do not exceed a daily 2-mG average, and the Electromagnetic Labeling Act of 1993,[63] which would establish uniform labeling requirements for products that emit EMFs. Pending state legislation covers the EMF front. In New York, for instance, a bill would establish maximum EMF exposure levels.[64] In Pennsylvania, a bill would provide compensation for landowners whose property is within five hundred feet of a power-line right of way.[65] In California, a bill would require electric utilities and telecommunications companies to notify customers annually of current research regarding EMFs.[66] Numerous states also have proposed bills mandating research on the potential health impacts of EMFs.[67]

Municipalities also are responding. For instance, a 1990 East Greenwich, Rhode Island, ordinance mandated a three-year ban on the construction of certain high-voltage transmission lines. However, the Rhode Island Supreme Court declared that ordinance an unconstitutional burden on interstate commerce.[68] Ordinances in Lake Villa, Illinois, and Brentwood, Tennessee, restrict "spillage" of EMFs onto adjoining properties.[69] In San Diego, sellers of property are required to disclose the location of power lines.[70]

The Regulatory Response

Federal

Federal regulatory efforts, led by the Environmental Protection Agency (EPA), have been directed primarily toward coordinating the work of various agencies undertaking to formulate and issue guidelines, standards, and regulations for workplace and general population exposure to EMFs.

Such efforts began in the 1970s when the Occupational Safety and Health Administration adopted guidelines for worker exposure to nonionizing radiation.[71] In 1979, the Federal Communications Commission (FCC) entered the fray when it issued a notice of inquiry regarding whether the National Environmental Policy Act (NEPA) required the FCC to include EMF-related concerns as part of its environmental analysis obligations under the act.[72] Ultimately, the FCC adopted regulations requiring the preparation of an environmental assessment when a proposed activity exceeded radio-frequency protection guidelines established by the American National Standard Institute (ANSI).[73] In 1993, the FCC issued a notice of proposed rule making in which it announced its intent to incorporate into its regulations the 1992 ANSI standards, which are more restrictive than the standards currently in place.[74]

In March 1993, the EPA announced that it had contributed $1.8 million to the NIEHS to support EMF research efforts. Before making the contribution, the EPA's Office of Research and Development had released a draft report that indicated support for an EMF-cancer link.[75] However, this report was criticized by numerous commentators as well as by the EPA's own Science Advisory Board, which recommended further research before a final report was issued.[76]

The Food and Drug Administration (FDA) also has independent authority to define "performance standards" for electronic products pursuant to the Radiation Control for Health and Safety Act of 1968.[77] To date, however, the FDA has issued such standards only for microwave ovens.[78] Currently, the FDA is working with various industries to establish voluntary guidelines for emissions from electric blankets, police radar units, cellular phones, video display terminals, and other products.

States

States have chosen among four basic regulatory options directed primarily toward the electric power industry: (1) prudent avoidance, (2) moratoria on new transmission lines, (3) adoption of numerical field strength standards, and (4) preservation of the status quo.[79]

Prudent Avoidance

Recognizing the uncertain science surrounding EMFs, "prudent avoidance" is defined as the balancing of strategies designed to minimize human exposure to EMFs while spending only a reasonable level of funds to achieve such minimization.[80] Several state commissions have adopted this policy when considering new applications for transmission lines or for upgrades to existing lines.[81]

The New Jersey Board of Regulatory Commissioners (BRC), for instance, is in the prudent-avoidance camp. In 1993, in *Re Atlantic City Electric Co.*,[82] the BRC, in approving the siting of an electrical distribution station despite the objection of a town planning board, articulated its "prudent avoidance/prudent field management" policy, stating that utilities should engage in reasonable efforts at appropriate cost levels to manage EMF exposure. Such efforts include the design of transmission lines to reduce EMF levels, using existing rights of way, avoiding the siting of new facilities in heavily populated areas, and other measures.[83] The planning board's appeal of the BRC's decision was rejected by an appellate court.[84]

Construction Moratoria

A "construction moratorium" completely prohibits construction of power lines.[85] To date, only Rhode Island has implemented this option solely on the basis of EMF-related concerns. Its Act Relating to Health and Safety—High Voltage Lines prohibits for a period of three years the construction of lines greater than 60 kV.[86] Critics insist that construction moratoria actually increase risk to the public by requiring current flowing in older power lines to be increased to meet customer demands, thereby increasing EMF emissions.[87]

Field Strength Standards

A third option is to regulate EMF emissions from high-power electric lines. Several states have adopted such "field strength standards," including New York and Florida.[88] In 1989 the Florida Environmental Regulatory Commission became the first state agency to adopt magnetic field emissions standards formally. Its rules basically allow utilities to decide how to meet the standards.[89] Options include wider rights of way, raising the height of transmission towers, burying the cable, or arranging lines to enhance field cancellation.[90]

Status Quo

Some states, such as Texas and Connecticut, have opted to do nothing until more conclusive data are developed.[91]

The Legal Response

Legal issues surrounding EMFs are being raised in a variety of forums, including condemnation proceedings, inverse condemnation and diminution-of-value lawsuits, personal injury and product liability actions, workers' compensation cases, and administrative proceedings regarding the siting of power lines, electric substations, microwave transmission towers, and other facilities. These cases have raised novel legal issues such as recovery for "cancerphobia" and the application of "junk science" to prove legal damages.

Property Damage Cases

EMF lawsuits in the property damage arena typically involve property owners seeking compensation from utilities in right-of-way condemnation proceedings. Increasingly, however, property owners located near existing power lines are filing inverse condemnation or diminution-of-value lawsuits against utilities, claiming that power-line EMFs, coupled with increased public fear of EMFs, have decreased the value of their property.

Condemnation, Inverse Condemnation, and Diminution of Value

In a condemnation proceeding a plaintiff must demonstrate a compensable "taking." The issue then focuses on the adequacy of compensation for both direct, physical confiscation of land and indirect loss of use without actual confiscation.[92] These types of cases have existed since the earliest days of right-of-way appropriation.

One form of inverse condemnation claim arises when the value of a landowner's property not the subject of an eminent domain proceeding has been reduced by action (including formal condemnation) against another, nearby property. The inverse condemnation claim is that the plaintiff's nearby parcel has, in effect, been constructively condemned. Thus, even though eminent domain proceedings were not taken against the parcel, just compensation may be required.[93]

Diminution-of-value claims are akin to inverse condemnation proceedings insofar as they involve actions against trespassers, nuisances, or off-site stigmas that effectively devalue property.[94]

CANCERPHOBIA. Relatively new to the EMF property damage arena is "cancerphobia," that is, that the fear that EMFs may cause cancer, even in the absence of affirmative proof, is compensable. Three distinct views on the compensability of property value lost as a result of EMF "cancerphobia" have developed.[95]

One view holds that because the fear of EMFs has an impact on the market value of property, landowners must be compensated even if they fail to prove the scientific reasonableness of that fear.[96] The middle view holds that diminution of value resulting from public fear is compensable only if such fear is reasonably grounded in recognized science.[97] The third view denies any compensation for diminution of value associated with EMFs because such fear is as yet scientifically unjustified.[98]

New York's highest court addressed the cancerphobia issue in *Criscuola v. Power Authority of the State of New York*.[99] In *Criscuola*, the Power Authority had appropriated a 6.6-acre right of way across the plaintiff's 100-acre lot. The plaintiff argued that the condemnation rendered the entire lot unmarketable because of public fear of EMFs. The Power Authority argued that such fear was unreasonable because it was not grounded in generally accepted science. The court found for the plaintiff, holding that the existence of the fear alone, rather than the reasonableness of the fear, could affect property value and thus was compensable:

> We are satisfied that there should be no requirement that the claimant, as a separate and higher component of its market value proofs, must establish the reasonableness of a fear or perception of danger or of health risks from exposure to high voltage lines. The issue in a just compensation proceeding is whether or not the market value has been adversely affected. . . . This consequence may be present even if the public's fear is unreasonable. Whether the danger is a scientifically genuine or verifiable fact should be irrelevant to the central issue of the market value impact.[100]

Thus, under the New York view, which is shared by Florida, Kansas, and other states, no proof of actual EMF-related danger is required to recover damages for lost value. However, the *Criscuola* court also held that a plaintiff's subjective fear was not enough; rather, a plaintiff must demonstrate evidence of public fear in the community at issue.[101]

The plaintiffs in a California case, *McCartin v. San Diego Gas & Electric*,[102] did not fare as well. The plaintiffs, who lived near existing power lines, alleged they should be compensated for lost property value based solely on the perceived risk posed by EMFs. Before trial, claims based on trespass, nuisance, intentional and negligent infliction of emotional distress, negligent and strict product liability, and diminution of value were dismissed, leaving only an inverse condemnation claim. The case was tried to conclusion, and on May 16, 1994, the jury issued an advisory verdict, later adopted by the court, finding that the power lines did not constitute a taking or warrant other damages.[103]

Siting Proceedings

Also on the rise is citizen intervention in administrative siting proceedings for new or upgraded power lines, electric substations, microwave transmission facilities, and other sources of EMFs. For example, a recent proposal by a utility to build an interstate power line between Pennsylvania and New Jersey became the most heavily contested utility project in New Jersey history. Some nine thousand complaints regarding the project were filed with state regulators, principally from home owners who expressed concerns about health effects and diminution of property values. Ultimately, state regulators rejected the plan without addressing the EMF issue.[104]

Duty to Warn

There may be developing a seller's duty to warn prospective purchasers of potential toxic tort problems, including EMFs. For instance, in another New Jersey case, the New Jersey Supreme Court found that, due to its potential impact on property value, real estate brokers had a duty to disclose the existence of a nearby landfill unknown to the buyer.[105]

Breach of Warranty of Habitability and Constructive Eviction

In a pending New York case, a business tenant contends that EMFs emitted from nearby utility equipment and the lessor's internal power distribution network forced the tenant to move out as the result of interference with its computer systems.[106] The tenant refused to pay rent due under its lease, claiming constructive eviction, and the lessor sued. Similar cases also are pending in New York, alleging, in addition to constructive eviction, claims based in trespass, negligent siting of transmission equipment, loss of use, breach of warranty of habitability, and fraud.[107] Future constructive eviction claims may also arise over "fear" issues.

Personal Injury Cases

Personal injury actions are more difficult to prove than property damage cases, given the plaintiff's burden of establishing an affirmative link between EMF exposure and the actual injury suffered. Nonetheless, lawsuits are being filed in increasing number against power companies, cellular phone manufacturers, manufacturers of magnetic resonance imaging (MRI) equipment, owners of microwave transmission facilities, manufacturers of video display terminals, radar equipment firms, and others. One recent case also seeks recovery against an employer and the owner of the building in which the employees worked.

Negligence, Nuisance, and Strict Liability Cases

In *Zuidema v. San Diego Gas & Electric Co.*,[108] the Zuidema family alleged that their young daughter contracted a rare form of cancer as a result of EMFs emanating from nearby transmission and distribution lines.[109] The plaintiffs were permitted to present to the jury two causes of action: (1) negligence, in essence, whether San Diego Gas & Electric was negligent in failing to warn the Zuidema family about possible health effects from EMFs; and (2) nuisance, in essence, whether EMFs emitted from the company's power lines affected the Zuidemas' use and enjoyment of their property.[110] The Zuidemas also sought recovery for diminution-of-value damages. The defense argued, among other things, that scientific evidence failed to establish a cancer link and that epidemiological studies only noted associations with cancers different from the cancer suffered by the plaintiff.[111] On April 30, 1993, the jury returned a verdict in favor of San Diego Gas & Electric, finding, essentially, that not enough scientific evidence existed to hold the company liable.[112]

In a Georgia case, a jury also found in favor of an electric company, which had been sued by a woman who alleged that power-line EMFs caused her cancer.[113] As in *Zuidema*, the company's defense was based on the lack of scientific proof regarding causation.[114]

In another personal injury action, a nineteen-year-old woman filed suit in December 1991 in Connecticut state court against Connecticut Light & Power and its parent, Northeast Utilities, alleging that EMFs radiating from a power substation and distribution lines located near her home caused her malignant brain tumor.[115] The complaint contained counts typical of EMF personal injury suits—namely, failure to warn, negligence, strict liability, and ultrahazardous activities.[116] In addition to punitive damages and compensatory damages for the woman's injuries and her mother's emotional distress, the plaintiff also seeks to enjoin emissions of electromagnetic radiation and to compel the release to the public of information on the dangers posed by EMFs.[117] The case is pending trial, as are other similar cases brought against electric utilities.[118]

Product Liability Actions

EMF issues have also arisen in the context of product liability actions. For example, in January 1993 a federal jury in California found for the defense in the first trial against a radar-gun manufacturer by a police officer who alleged that long-term exposure to EMFs emanating from the equipment caused his cancer.[119] Other cases against manufacturers and distributors of radar equipment are pending.[120]

In a case involving cellular phones, the plaintiffs included in their complaint counts for breach of implied warranty of merchantability, breach of implied warranty of fitness for particular purpose, breach of express warranty, violation of the Magnuson-Moss Warranty Act, negligent and strict product liability, consumer fraud, and deceptive trade practices.[121] The case was ultimately dismissed on grounds that cellular phone safety was preempted by the FCC and the FDA. Soon thereafter, an employee of Motorola Inc. filed a lawsuit against the company alleging that his brain cancer was caused by his work on prototype cellular phones.[122]

Worker's Compensation Claims

EMF issues are also being raised in worker's compensation claims. In fact, the only known adjudicated claim in any forum that resulted in an award for EMF-alleged personal injury occurred in a worker's compensation case. In that case, the Washington Department of Labor and Industry upheld the claim of a Kaiser Aluminum employee who alleged that his non-Hodgkin's lymphoma resulted from occupational exposure to EMFs while working in a "pot room" involving electrochemical processes.[123] The company has said it will appeal.

Not long after that decision was rendered, however, another state agency in Washington rejected a similar worker's compensation claim, in which a widow of a utility worker alleged that her husband's leukemia had been caused by exposure to EMFs.[124] The decision was upheld by the Washington State Board of Industrial Appeals.[125]

Employee Claims Against Employers and Building Owners

Finally, in cases of particular significance to real estate practitioners, employees have filed lawsuits against their employers, lessors, and others, alleging that workplace exposure to electrical transformers and other EMF sources caused their illnesses.

For instance, in *Marano v. Consolidated Edison of New York*,[126] an employee of a broadcasting and entertainment company alleges that her cancer was caused by EMF emissions from electrical transformers located in the building in which she worked. Named as defendants are the electric utility supplying the building with power as well as the manufacturer of the transformers. Similarly, in *Johsz v. Kall Co.*,[127] three employees of a Southern California real estate brokerage firm filed a lawsuit against their employer, the owner of the building in which they worked, and the local electric utility, alleging that their cancers were caused by excessive exposure to EMFs emanating from interior electrical equipment and nearby power lines.[128] If the plaintiffs in these actions are successful, the boundary of potential EMF personal injury defendants may be expanded to include building owners, lessors, and all employers, regardless of whether they are directly responsible for EMF emissions.

The Advent of "Junk Science"

Proving causation is the major difficulty facing plaintiffs in EMF personal injury cases. Such plaintiffs must prove what has not yet been generally accepted by scientists—a causal link between EMF exposure and illness. Moreover, each plaintiff faces the additional hurdle of proving that his or her particular illness was caused by a particular EMF source. Given the courts' general bar on expert scientific opinion that has not been widely accepted in the scientific community, no plaintiff has thus far been able to prove the causal nexus to a jury. However, the trend in both federal and state courts is to liberalize the admissibility of expert testimony, thus allowing the introduction of a broader range of scientific opinion.

Daubert v. Merrell Dow Pharmaceuticals is illustrative.[129] In *Daubert*, the plaintiffs alleged that birth defects were caused by prenatal ingestion of an antinausea drug. The trial court dismissed the case essentially on grounds that the opinions of plaintiffs' experts were not based on scientific conclusions that were generally accepted by the relevant scientific community. The Court of Appeals for the Ninth Circuit affirmed,[130] but the Supreme Court reversed.[131]

Rejecting the "generally accepted" common-law rule for admissibility of expert opinion, the Supreme Court ruled that Federal Rule of Evidence 702 superseded that standard. Rule 702 applies a broader standard of admissibility, the court ruled, by allowing the admissibility of opinion testimony as long as the expert's methodology is reasonable and the expert's testimony is both "relevant" and "reliable."[132] Given this broader standard, which has been adopted by some states, testimony regarding the alleged EMF-cancer link may now be admissible, regardless of whether such conclusions are accepted by the scientific community at large.[133]

The "Preemption" Defense

As noted, utilities, manufacturers, and other companies have been successful in defending EMF cases principally on grounds that a scientifically accepted nexus between exposure and illness has not been shown to exist. Defendants also have been successful in obtaining early favorable summary judgment determinations on certain causes of action (e.g., strict product liability on grounds that electricity in transit is not a "product" or, even if a product, is not in the "stream of commerce"). Of increasing importance is the "preemption" defense, which maintains that personal injury or property damage claims may not be brought against utilities or certain manufacturers because they are preempted by governmental regulation or laws.

For instance, in 1995 the Court of Appeals of the State of California, in a case alleging diminution of property value resulting from proximity to electric transmission lines, ruled that such actions could not be maintained because they would impermissibly interfere with the exclusive jurisdiction of the state public utility commission (PUC) in regulating and controlling public utilities.[134] Finding that the PUC had extensively studied EMF issues and had articulated energy policy centered on its view that there was insufficient scientific evidence that EMFs threatened public health, the court said that it would be inappropriate to allow judicial intervention on the safety of electrical transmission systems constructed in accordance with PUC regulations.[135] To award damages for traditional tort causes of action, the court held, would mean that courts "would have to come to conclusions contrary to those reached by the PUC in considering the same issue."[136]

Facing the Uncertainty

Selecting an appropriate course of action in response to the EMF controversy is no easy task, given the scientific uncertainty surrounding EMFs, fast-changing and often-conflicting legislative and regulatory environments, and the enormous potential costs associated with EMF abatement. At the same time, however, entities involved in real estate ownership, development, leasing, management, and financing must weigh the potential for significant legal liabilities. Such liabilities already exist to a limited extent as a result of "cancerphobia" and diminution-of-value cases, and they have the potential to escalate rapidly in personal injury actions if "junk science" theories prevail, if future studies provide an accepted causal link between EMFs and health risks, or if plaintiffs begin to prevail despite the lack of an accepted scientific link.

All of these factors weigh in favor of incorporating a "prudent avoidance" approach into business strategies. Proactive strategies—such as implementation of mitigation technologies, labeling, reducing occupational exposure, disclosure, and employee and public communication efforts—have the capacity to assist in the defense of future property damage, personal injury, and siting cases. At the same time, companies must be careful in how they position their efforts, lest such efforts be used against them as unwarranted admissions.

Electric Utilities, Communications, and Other Companies

Any company engaged in the transmission of energy or information (even in a state that has not yet adopted the prudent avoidance standard) is well advised to adopt a prudent avoidance strategy. Given the uncertain science surrounding the causal connection, if any, between EMFs and health risks, as well as the growing acceptance of prudent avoidance as an appropriate interim solution, such a strategy, at minimum, may assist in the defense of negligence, duty-to-warn, or related claims. It certainly may prove instrumental in avoiding punitive damages based on claims of reckless, intentional, or willful misconduct.

Prudent avoidance may involve a variety of actions, including increasing buffer zones around power lines, transmission facilities, or other sources of EMFs; ensuring that such facilities are not located near schools or other areas populated by children; avoiding high-population areas if practical; and implementing mitigation technologies. On the latter score, EMF strength from transmission lines may be reduced by "reverse phasing," which entails the arrangement of power lines to effect partial magnetic field cancellation. EMF exposure also may be reduced by increasing the height of transmission lines. In addition, utilities are investigating the use of buried cables, which does not in itself cancel magnetic fields but, in combination with cable alignment, may diminish EMF strength.[137] Burying cable, however, is an extremely costly solution.

Corollaries to the prudent avoidance approach include participation in EMF research efforts and regular dissemination of information to constituents regarding the status of that research. The electric utility industry, for instance, has contributed multiple millions of dollars toward EMF research efforts, and many utility companies have deployed extensive community education programs. Copious records of such efforts should be maintained.

Real Estate Agents

An official of the National Association of Realtors recently opined that real estate brokers are not obligated to disclose EMF-related information to buyers who do not inquire about the issue.[138] However, courts throughout the United States increasingly are eroding the principle of caveat emptor, or "let the buyer beware," particularly where environmental contamination is concerned. As a matter of self-interest, real estate agents must remain apprised of the evolving state of the law on this issue in their jurisdictions.

Clearly, if a prospective purchaser inquires about the location of power lines or other facilities, brokers must, to the extent such information is known or readily ascertainable, provide that information. Additionally, if a broker is aware of a particular source of EMFs that may be publicly at issue in a given community, that information should be supplied to avoid a downstream duty-to-warn claim.

Given the potential impact on property values, and the increasing coverage of these issues in the popular and trade press, the most prudent course for brokers to follow may be to make a positive disclosure to prospective purchasers of nearby EMF sources and to provide informational booklets to such parties. Maximum protection from downstream claims may be provided by including provisions in real estate contracts that both provide such notice and disclaim broker liability.

Real Estate Builders and Developers

The above recommendations to real estate brokers apply with equal force to real estate developers or builders also involved in the sale of property, either to interim owners (i.e., investors) or ultimate purchasers. It also may be prudent for builders and developers who are constructing facilities near EMF sources to implement avoidance strategies. Such strategies may include the construction of open space between EMF sources and offices or dwellings or the construction of limited exposure areas, such as parking lots or roads, between the EMF source and the occupancy zone.

In addition, builders and developers may find it prudent to construct office or manufacturing facilities in ways that avoid unnecessary human exposure to internal EMF sources, such as power closets. From an economic standpoint, it also may be prudent to conduct prepurchase audits of external EMF sources to account for, and perhaps avoid, future diminution of value, regulations, or personal injury claims.

Lessors and Managers of Existing Structures

Lessors or real estate management firms dealing with existing properties within the range of EMF sources face perhaps the most difficult choices. At minimum, they may be well advised to follow the lead of power companies by providing information on the current status of the scientific debate or by offering to arrange for EMF measurements. Consultants also are available to provide "topographical mapping" of EMF readings in the office environment. Again, these measures may assist in defense of downstream duty-to-warn claims.

As mentioned, office buildings frequently have internal sources of EMFs, such as power cabinets or other high-voltage equipment. Some building owners and lessors have attempted to minimize workplace exposure to these sources by relocating work stations at a "safe" distance from such sources. Whether or not they own a structure, employers also need to be concerned because of possible exposure to, and claims by, employees.

Financial Institutions

The effect of EMFs on property values poses a unique quandary for lenders. At minimum, such institutions must weigh the potential economic effect of EMFs in their evaluation of projects. Until more is known about the health effects of EMFs, lenders may also wish to allocate expressly to borrowers all potentially adverse economic effects. This may include indemnification clauses in the mortgage or separate indemnification agreements requiring the borrower to hold the lender harmless against monetary loss associated with EMFs or to implement mitigation activities should such activities ultimately be required. A separate indemnity agreement may give the lender the option of suing on that agreement rather than foreclosing on the mortgage. For particularly risky projects, the pledge of other collateral and personal guarantees may be advisable.

Tax Issues

States differ in their assessment policies for contaminated properties, with some allowing a lower assessment based on a reduction in market value. To the extent a property affected by EMF sources has been devalued by market conditions, property owners may seek to lower their tax assessments.

Zoning Issues

Some jurisdictions have attempted to rezone parcels of land or have implemented other use restrictions to avoid construction of potential EMF sources such as power lines or microwave transmission towers. This can be a thorny issue, however, given constitutional and other concerns that may give rise to claims of arbitrary and capricious conduct by zoning authorities. A potential defense to such claims may be to assert that such uses would have a detrimental impact on a community's tax base, given the potential devaluation of neighboring properties.

Insurance Issues

Lastly, considerable controversy is being raised over whether historic and current general liability insurance policies cover EMF-related claims. Such policies often contain "pollution exclusions" or other provisions that may bar coverage, depending on the language of the provisions and applicable state law. Some insurers are currently offering policies that explicitly cover EMF claims, and entities that believe they face EMF-related exposure may wish to consider this protective option.

Notes

1. New York State Dep't of Law, Environmental Protection Bureau, *Electromagnetic Fields—What You Should Know* (August 1993).

2. Gordon Hester, *Electric & Magnetic Fields: Managing an Uncertain Risk,* 34 ENVIRONMENT 1, at 7 (Jan.–Feb. 1992).

3. U.S. EPA, Office of Radiation and Indoor Air, *EMF in Your Environment,* at 3–4 (Dec. 1992) [hereinafter EPA ORIA]; Public Utility Commission of Texas, *Health Effects of Exposure to Powerline Frequency Electric and Magnetic Fields,* at 1-1 (March 1992) [hereinafter Texas PUC]; M. Graner Morgan, Carnegie Mellon University, *Electric and Magnetic Fields from 60 Hertz Electric Power: What Do We Know about Possible Health Risks?,* at 1 (1989).

4. *Id.*

5. EPA ORIA, *supra* note 3, at 14, 24.

6. *Id.* at 9; Texas PUC, *supra* note 3, at 1-1.

7. EPA ORIA, *supra* note 3, at 9–23.

8. *Id.* at 6.

9. *Id.*; Texas PUC, *supra* note 3, at 3–6.

10. EPA ORIA, *supra* note 3, at 6.

11. *Id.* at 7–8; *See also* Note, *Lethal Lines: Establishing a Personal Injury Case Against a New Jersey Utility for Harm Caused By Electromagnetic Fields,* 20 RUTGERS COMPUTER & TECH. L.J. 663, 665–66 (1994).

12. EPA ORIA, *supra* note 3, at 4–7.

13. Hester, *supra* note 2, at 8.

14. *Id.*

15. *Id.*

16. EPA ORIA, *supra* note 3, at 23–24.

17. *Id.* at 14.

18. *Id.* at 13–21.

19. *Id.* at 25.

20. *Id.* at 11.

21. *Id.* at 17.

22. Leonard A. Sagan, *Epidemiological and Laboratory Studies of Power Frequency Electric and Magnetic Fields,* 268 JAMA 5, at 625 (August 5, 1992); Nachman Brautbar, *Electromagnetic Fields, Exposure and Cancer: Fact or Myth?,* TRIAL LAWYER at 33 (March 1994).

23. Sagan, *supra* note 22, at 627–28.

24. *See* Carol Ezzell, *Power-Line Static: Debates Rage Over the Possible Hazards of Electromagnetic Fields*, SCIENCE NEWS, at 202 (Sept. 28, 1991); Leonard A. Sagan, *EMF Health Effects Research: Problems and Current Status*, PUB. UTIL. FORT. (July 19, 1990); Harold R. Piety, *What We Don't Know About EMF*, PUB. UTIL. FORT. (Nov. 15, 1991).

25. Nancy Wertheimer and Ed Leeper, *Electrical Wiring Configurations and Childhood Cancer*, 109 AM. J. EPIDEMIOLOGY 273 (1979).

26. *See* Comment, *AEP Researcher Casts Doubt on Earlier EMF Study*, PUB. UTIL. FORT. (Feb. 15, 1993).

27. J. Fulton et al., *Electrical Wiring Configurations and Childhood Leukemia in Rhode Island*, 111 AM. J. EPIDEMIOLOGY 292 (1980).

28. Texas PUC, *supra* note 3, at 3–10.

29. *Id.* at 3–12.

30. David A. Savitz, *Case-Control Study of Childhood Cancer and Exposure to 60-Hz Magnetic Fields*, 128 AM. J. EPIDEMIOLOGY 21 (1988).

31. S.J. Landon et al., *Exposure to Electrical and Magnetic Fields and Risk of Childhood Leukemia*, 134 AM. J. EPIDEMIOLOGY 923–37 (1991).

32. Maria Feychting and Anders Ahlbom, *Magnetic Fields and Cancer in Children*, AM. J. EPIDEMIOLOGY (Oct. 1, 1993).

33. *Id.*

34. Leonard A. Sagan, *Epidemiological and Laboratory Studies of Power Frequency Electric and Magnetic Fields*, 268 JAMA 5, at 626 (August 5, 1992); *see also* Texas PUC, *supra* note 3, at 3–5.

35. *See* Gary Taubes, *Electric Emissions: Dangerous or Not?*, N.Y. TIMES, June 22, 1993, at C1; Brautbar, *supra* note 22 at 33.

36. Taubes, *supra* note 35, at C8.

37. Brautbar, *supra* note 22, at 37.

38. National Radiation Protection Board Advisory Group, *Electromagnetic Fields and the Risk of Cancer: Report of an Advisory Group on Non-ionizing Radiation*, London, England (1992).

39. *See* B. Floderus et al., *Occupational Exposure to Electromagnetic Fields in Relation to Leukemia and Brain Tumors: A Case Control Study in Sweden*, 4 CANCER CAUSES AND CONTROL 465–76 (1993); *see also* R. Stone, *Polarized Debate: EMFs and Cancer*, 258 SCIENCE 1724 (Dec. 11, 1992).

40. *See*, *Utility Finds No Relation between On-The-Job Exposure to EMF and Cancer Deaths*, 93 OCCUPATIONAL SAFETY & HEALTH REP., at 1955 (April 7, 1993).

41. 94 TOXICS L. REP. 1249, *Canadian-French Study Finds No Link between Exposure and Common Cancers* (April 6, 1994); *but see* 94 TOXICS L. REP. 70, *Study Suggests Higher Breast Cancer Risk among Certain Female Electrical Workers* (June 22, 1994); 91 TOXICS L. REP. 181, *Study Finds Increased Risk of Leukemia in Employees Working on Telephone Lines* (July 10, 1991).

42. D. Savitz and D. Loomis, *Magnetic Field Exposure in Relation to Leukemia and Brain Cancer Mortality among Electric Workers*, 141 AM. J. EPIDEMIOLOGY (1995).

43. Texas PUC, *supra* note 3, at 3–10.

44. *Id.*

45. *Id.* at 3-10–3-12; Taubes, *supra* note 33.

46. Savitz and Loomis, *supra* note 42.

47. *See* Hester, *supra* note 2.

48. *Id.*

49. Kristopher D. Brown, *Electromagnetic Field Injury Claims: Judicial Reaction to an Emerging Public-Health Issue*, 72 B.U.L. REV. 325 (March 1992); John W. Gulliver and Christine C. Vito, *EMF and Transmission Line Siting: The Emerging State Regulatory Framework and Implications for Utilities*, NR&E (Winter 1993); Taubes, *supra* note 35; United States Environmental Protection Agency pamphlet, *Questions and Answers About Electric and Magnetic Fields* (Dec. 1992).

50. Hester, *supra* note 2, at 26; Brautbar, *supra* note 22, at 34.

51. *Id.*; *see also* Taubes, *supra* note 35; Roy W. Kreiger, *On the Line*, A.B.A. J. (Jan. 1994), at 40.

52. 7 TOXICS L. REP. 1048 (Feb. 10, 1993).

53. Hester, *supra* note 2.

54. *See* B. Aurecchione, *EMF Regulation: Is Congress Riding the Wave of Paranoia?*, 18 SETON HALL LEGIS. J. 261 (1993).

In addition, the world's largest group of physicists, the American Physical Society, has stated that it can find no evidence that EMFs that radiate from power lines cause cancer. After reviewing EMF research for several years, the society has concluded that the preponderance of existing research does not substantiate studies reporting adverse health effects. In its one-page statement, the society added that groundless public fears about a possible link between power lines and cancer were diverting billions of dollars into mitigation work and that the "burden of cost placed on the American public is incommensurate with the risk, if any." William J. Broad, *Cancer Fear Is Unfounded, Physicists Say*, N.Y. TIMES, May 14, 1995, at A14.

55. Taubes, *supra* note 35, *quoting* Yale physicist William Bennett.

56. 42 U.S.C.A. § 13478 (West Supp. 1993); 42 U.S.C.A. §§ 13201–556 (West Supp. 1993).

57. 42 U.S.C.A. §§ 13201–556 (West Supp. 1993).

58. *Id.*

59. *Id.*

60. *Id.*

61. 7 TOXICS L. REP. 1048 (Feb. 10, 1993).

62. H.R. 1494, 103d Cong., 1st Sess. (1993).

63. H.R. 1665, 103d Cong., 1st Sess. (1993).

64. New York Assembly Bill No. 5230 (1993).

65. Pennsylvania House Bill No. 382 (1993).

66. California Bill No. 2028 (1993).

67. *See, e.g.*, California A.B. 2028 (1993), Florida H.B. 1751 (1993), Illinois H.B. 2368 (1993), Indiana S.B. 370 (1993), Kansas H.B. 2307 (1991), Massachusetts H.B. 3709 (1993) and H.B. 5263 (1993), New Jersey S.B. 164 (1992), New York S.B. 8831 (1993), and Rhode Island H.B. 572 (1994); *see also* Virginia Senate Joint Resolution 278 (1993).

68. Town of East Greenwich v. O'Neil, No. 91-477 (Dec. 4, 1992).

69. Lake Villa, Ill., Ordinance 92-3-1, Subsection 6.5-B-9; *see also* UTILITY ENVIRONMENTAL REP. (April 19, 1991) regarding Brentwood, Tenn., ordinance.

70. Daniel P. Delaney, Preparing for State and Local EMF Regulations, unpublished paper delivered at conference on Anticipating, Avoiding, and Managing EMF Claims, Washington, D.C. (Sept. 20–21, 1993).

71. 29 C.F.R. § 1910.97.

72. Docket No. 79-144 (June 7, 1979).

73. 47 C.F.R. § 1.1301; ANSI C95.1-1982.

74. Federal Communications Commission Notice of Proposed Rulemaking, *In the Matter of Guidelines for Evaluating the Environmental Effects of Radio Frequency Radiation*, ET Docket No. 93-62, FCC Rcd. 2849, 1993 FCC LEXIS 1822 (March 11, 1993).

75. *See* 5 TOXICS L. REP. 996 (Jan. 9, 1991).

76. Report to EPA Administration from EPA Science Advisory Board (May 11, 1992).

77. Incorporated into Food, Drug, and Cosmetic Act, 21 U.S.C. § 360 kk.

78. 21 C.F.R. § 1030.

79. *See* Gulliver, *supra* note 49 (evaluating the four prevailing EMF regulatory philosophies and specific programs adopted by states); *see also* Aurecchione, *supra* note 54, at 285–92.

80. *See* U.S. Congressional Office of Technology Assessment report titled "Biological Effects of Power Frequency Electric and Magnetic Fields, Background Paper" published in 1989; *see also* Gulliver, *supra* note 49; Aurecchione, *supra* note 54, at 285–92; 129 PUB. UTIL. FORT. 6, at 26 (March 15, 1992).

81. The concept of "prudent avoidance" is also being invoked, generally, as a business strategy. For example, companies are now marketing video display terminals that do not emit the very low frequency electromagnetic radiation produced by conventional cathode ray tube monitors. *See* Peter H. Lewis, *No Pie in the Sky: I.B.M.'s New "Green" Machine*, N.Y. TIMES, May 23, 1993, at F8; Todd Woody, *EMF—Plaintiffs' Bar Ought to Be a Huge Market For This Product*, THE RECORDER, July 19, 1993.

82. Agency Docket No. EE91111747, OAL Docket No. PUC 154-93, 1993 WL 241916 (Feb. 3, 1993).

83. *Id.* Ohio, Wisconsin, Colorado, California, and other states also have adopted prudent avoidance regulatory strategies.

84. *I/M/O Appeal of Atlantic City Electric Co.*, No. A-5046-92T2, unpublished opinion (June 8, 1994).

85. *See* Gulliver, *supra* note 49; *see also* Aurecchione, *supra* note 54.

86. 1002 R.I. Pub. Laws 92-439 (effective July 21, 1992); *see also* Comment, *Electromagnetic Fields*, PUB. UTIL. FORT. (June 15, 1993) (noting that West Virginia Commission had not found enough evidence of health risk to warrant moratorium on construction of new electric transmission facilities).

87. *See* Gulliver, *supra* note 49.

88. *See* Kristopher D. Brown, *Electromagnetic Field Injury Claims: Judicial Reaction to an Emerging Public-Health Issue*, 72 B.U.L. REV. 325 (March 1992); Comment, *Dealing with Presumed Health Risks from High-Voltage Transmission Lines*, PUB. UTIL. FORT. (Aug. 3, 1989); Aurecchione, *supra* note 54, at 285–92.

89. *See* Lisa N. Mulhall, *The Transmission Line Siting Act: Balancing Power and People*, 20 STETSON L. REV. 909 (Summer 1991).

90. *See* Aurecchione, *supra* note 54, at 285, n. 108.

91. *See* Gulliver, *supra* note 49.

92. *See* Michael Freeman, *The Courts and Electromagnetic Fields*, PUB. UTIL. FORT. (July 19, 1990); *see also* Todd D. Brown, *The Power Line Plaintiff & The Inverse Condemnation Alternative*, 19 B.C. ENVTL. AFF. L. REV. 655 (Spring 1992).

93. *See* Krieger, *supra* note 51.

94. *Id.*

95. *See* Brown, *supra* note 92.

96. *Id.*

97. *Id.*; *see also* Hicks v. United States, 266 F.2d 515 (6th Cir. 1959).

98. *See, e.g.*, Linnebur v. Public Service Co. of Colorado, 716 P.2d 1120 (Colo. 1986).

99. 81 N.Y. 2d 649, 602 N.Y.S. 2d 588, 621 N.E. 2d 1195 (1993).

100. *Id. See also* Florida Power & Light Co. v. Jennings, 518 So.2d 895 (Fla. 1987); Ryan v. Kansas Power & Light Co., 815 P.2d 528 (Kan. 1991); San Diego Gas & Electric Co. v. Daley, 253 Cal. Rptr. 144 (Cal. App. 1988).

101. 621 N.E. 2d at 1197.

102. No. 69949 (Cal. Sup. Ct., Orange County, May 16, 1994).

103. *See* 8 Toxics L. Rep. 1450 (May 25, 1994).

104. Peter J. Shelly, *Power Line Plan Killed by Ruling*, Patriot News, Dec. 9, 1993; *see also* Dverson v. East Kentucky Power Cooperative, Inc., 843 S.W. 2d 340 (Ky. Ct. App. 1992); East Greenwich v. O'Neil, 617 A.2d 104 (R.I. 1992).

105. Strawn v. Canuso, A-56/57 (September Term 1994).

106. Darby & Darby, P.C. v. Klackner Chemical, Inc., No. 32130/92 (Sup. Ct., New York City).

107. Marine Midland Bank v. IR VistaRealty Corp., No. 20624/90 (Sup. Ct., New York City); Watermark Assocs. v. Hudson Tower Housing Co., Inc., No. 33790/92 (Sup. Ct., New York City).

108. No. 638-222 (Calif. Sup. Ct. San Diego County).

109. *See* John Simpson and Lori A. Burkart, *Utility Wins EMF Trial*, Pub. Util. Fort. (June 1, 1993); E. Gregory Barnes, *A Blitz Fails*, Pub. Util. Fort. (July 1, 1993).

110. *Id.*

111. Krieger, *supra* note 51, at 45.

112. *Id.*

113. Jordan v. Georgia Power Co., No. 91-4103SS-296 (Ga. Sup. Ct., verdict May 11, 1994).

114. *Id.*

115. Bullock v. Northeast Util., No. 32-6697 (Conn. Super. Ct. New Haven Jud. Dist., complaint filed Dec. 19, 1991); *see also* 6 Toxics L. Rep. 927 (Jan. 8, 1992); Leonard S. Greenberger, *Meadow Street Family Files EMF Suit*, Pub. Util. Fort. (Feb. 15, 1992).

116. 6 Toxics L. Rep. 927 (Jan. 8, 1992).

117. *Id.*

118. *See also, e.g.*, Walston v. Northeast Utilities, No. 32-7441 (Conn. Super. Ct. New Haven Jud. Dist., complaint filed Jan. 24, 1992); Glazer v. Florida Power & Light Co., No. 94-01279 (Fla. Cir. Ct., Dade Cnty., complaint filed Jan. 20, 1994).

119. Bendure v. Kustom Signals, Inc., No. C-91-1174 (D.N.Cal., complaint filed June 2, 1992); *see also* 7 Toxics L. Rep. 984 (Jan. 27, 1993).

120. *See, e.g.*, Edwards v. Kustom Signals, Inc., No. 51038 (Ohio Ct. of Common Pleas, complaint filed June 2, 1993).

121. Verb v. Motorola, Inc., No. 93 CH 969 (Ill. Cir. Ct., Cook County).

122. Kane v. Motorola Inc., No. 93 L 15256 (Cook County Circuit Ct., Ill. County Dep't, complaint filed Dec. 13, 1993).

123. *In re* Brewer, No. T-74341 (Wash. Dep't of Labor & Industry June 29, 1994); 8 INDOOR POLLUTION L. REP. 3 (August 1994); 9 TOXICS L. REP. 188 (July 20, 1994).

124. *In re* Robert Pilisuk, No. 92-2051 (Wash. State Bd. of Indus. Ins.).

125. 9 TOXICS L. REP. 188 (July 20, 1994); 8 INDOOR POLLUTION L. REP. 5 (Oct. 1994).

126. No. 129740193 (N.Y. Sup. Ct. N.Y. Co.).

127. No. 726765 (Cal. Sup. Ct. Orange Co.).

128. *See also* ORANGE COUNTY (CA) REGISTER, March 17, 1994.

129. 113 S. Ct. 2786 (1993).

130. 951 F.2d 1128 (9th Cir. 1991).

131. 113 S. Ct. 2786 (1993).

132. *Id.* at 2795.

133. *But see* 9 TOXICS L. REP. 9, at 252 (August 3, 1994) (discussing fact that many post-*Daubert* decisions still reject unsubstantiated expert testimony); additionally, see Reynard v. NEC Corp., No. 94-825-CIV-T-21E (M.D. Fla. May 17, 1995), applying *Daubert* in rejecting plaintiffs' expert testimony in case involving emissions from cellular telephones.

134. San Diego Gas & Electric Co. v. Superior Ct. of Orange County, No. G016256, slip. op. (Cal. Sup. Ct., 4th App. Dist. Feb. 28, 1995), *appeal pending,* Covalt v. San Diego Gas & Electric Co., No. 5045854 (review granted, May 11, 1995); *see also* 9 TOXICS L. REP. 861 (Jan. 18, 1995).

135. *Id.* at 13–14.

136. *Id.* at 13. Separately, the court also disallowed the plaintiffs' personal injury claims on ground that public fear of potential illness absent corroboration of actual harm by reliable medical and scientific opinion was not compensable. *Id.* at 8–9.

137. *See, e.g.,* Hester, *supra* note 2.

138. Sharon Tomecek, *Concerns about Power Lines Loom over Sales—Power Lines Spark Buyer Fears about Safety,* REAL ESTATE TODAY, at 20, 21 (Nov.–Dec. 1992).

PART V

Environmental Issues Affecting Real Estate Development

~

CHAPTER 26

Takings: What Does It Take to Make a Take?

JOHN J. DELANEY

Among the most significant national phenomena of the last decade have been the environmental movement and the private property rights movement. Each has enjoyed major success in raising the public's consciousness regarding its concerns, and each has sought the aid of the courts when necessary to protect its core values.

One of the principal causes espoused by property rights advocates is the Fifth Amendment right of landowners to be compensated when a regulatory action results in a taking of their property. Whether a regulation effects a taking of property or a mere noncompensable diminution of value to promote public health, safety, or welfare is a question that has pitted the two movements against each other on many occasions. Indeed, both of the major Supreme Court decisions on regulatory takings in the 1990s, *Lucas v. South Carolina Coastal Council*[1] and *Dolan v. City of Tigard*,[2] involved environmental regulations. In *Lucas*, the landowner was denied a building permit for a residential dwelling on beachfront property based on a Beachfront Management Act designed to prevent erosion of a sensitive barrier island and to protect the habitats of threatened species of plants and animals. In *Dolan*, approval of a building permit was conditioned on the landowner dedicating a portion of her property for a public greenway to minimize flooding of an adjacent creek.

Environmental laws have long been at the center of regulatory takings disputes. For example, in *United States v. Riverside Bayview Homes*,[3] the Supreme Court addressed the issue of whether denial of a permit under Section 404 of the Clean Water Act gave rise to a compensable takings claim. Permitting actions affecting wetlands were also the subject of two significant 1994 regulatory takings decisions of the U.S. Court of Appeals for the Federal Circuit, *Loveladies Harbor v. United States*[4] and *Florida Rock Industries, Inc. v. United States.*[5] Cases arising under the Endangered Species Act also have presented takings issues. For example, in *Christy v. Hodel,*[6] a rancher whose sheep had been eaten by grizzly bears unsuccessfully argued that the protected status of the bears prevented him from protecting his sheep and thus amounted to a taking. In another case, mitigation measures required by the Fish and Wildlife Service to protect endangered and threatened species' habitats have given rise to claims of *Dolan*-mandated proportionality requirement violation and *Lucas*-style deprivation.[7] In Maryland, enforcement of a state airport noise regulation has apparently left an owner of twenty-seven platted residential lots near Baltimore-Washington International Airport without any viable use of his property.[8]

It is apparent, therefore, that regulatory takings and other property rights issues may be present whenever environmental regulations are promulgated or enforced. These issues may arise in the form of traditional "total taking" claims of the type raised in *Lucas* or as a result of mitigation or regulatory exaction programs such as in *Dolan*. This chapter attempts to explain the separate lessons of *Lucas* and *Dolan* and the legal analysis employed by the Supreme Court in each case.

The Supreme Court Background

Throughout the 1980s the Supreme Court bobbed and weaved its way through several land use cases, trying to decide whether an overly oppressive police power regulation could result in a taking of private property that entitled the owner to compensation. Some thought this issue had been resolved in 1922, in the famous case of *Pennsylvania Coal v. Mahon.*[9] However, the Court's ruling in that case was not to be given effect for another sixty-five years.

Before 1987 there were numerous false starts in which the Court found itself thwarted on ripeness grounds. These cases included *Agins v. City of Tiburon;*[10] *San Diego Gas & Electric Co. v. City of San Diego;*[11] *Williamson County Regional Planning Commission v. Hamilton Bank of Johnson City;*[12] and *MacDonald, Sommer & Frates v. Yolo County.*[13] It finally decided the question affirmatively in 1987 in *First English Evangelical Lutheran Church v. County of Los Angeles.*[14] *First English* was accompanied in the same year by two other significant regulatory takings decisions, *Keystone Bituminous Coal Association v. DeBenedictis*[15] and *Nollan v. California Coastal Commission.*[16]

Takings mavens, who had despaired that the Supreme Court would ever face up to the question, were overjoyed. The 1987 "trilogy" spawned a tidal wave of seminars, treatises, and articles, as commentators on both sides of the question attempted to sort out what the court had done. No sooner had reaction to the 1987 trilogy begun to ebb when *Lucas v. South Carolina Coastal Council*[17] was decided in 1992, breaking more new ground and precipitating yet another round of commentary. In 1994, hard on the heels of *Lucas*, the Court established additional precedent in yet another takings case, *Dolan v. City of Tigard*.[18]

The following sections discuss the sometimes confusing jurisprudence that has emerged from the Supreme Court over the past seventy years and attempt to distill it into an understandable statement of principles regarding regulatory takings and the remedy of compensation. Other relevant court decisions are also discussed.

Basic Principles of Regulatory Takings

Basis of Regulatory Takings Law: The Fifth Amendment

The Fifth Amendment to the Constitution, as applied to the states through the Fourteenth Amendment,[19] provides that "no person shall be . . . deprived of life, liberty or property, without due process of law, nor shall private property be taken for public use, without just compensation." The key phrases are the Due Process (or "Depriving") Clause, which is directed to the exercise of police power, and the Takings Clause, which is directed to the exercise of eminent domain. In diagrametrical form, the Fifth Amendment can be described as shown in Figure 1.

FIGURE 1. The Fifth Amendment

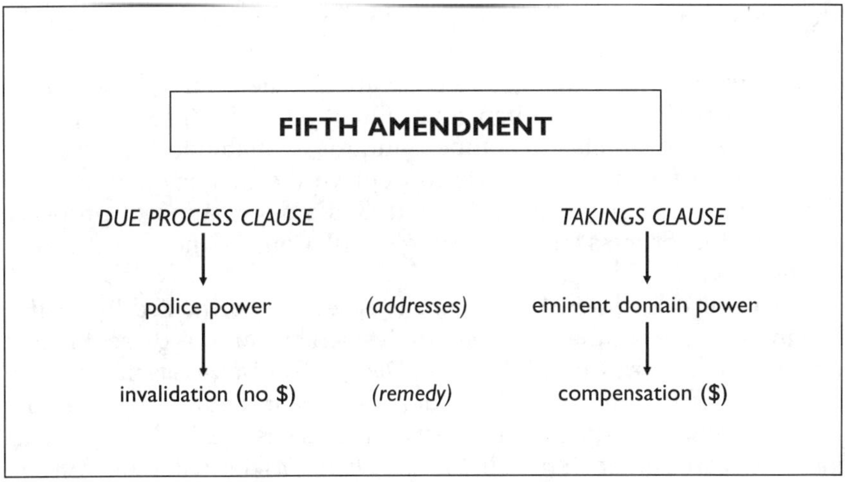

It looks simple enough, but generations of Supreme Court justices and legal scholars have disagreed as to whether the remedy of compensation—in addition to invalidation—should be available when due process violations occur.

Can an Overreaching Police Power Regulation Ever Constitute a Compensable Taking?

Justice Oliver Wendell Holmes appeared to have answered this question affirmatively in *Pennsylvania Coal v. Mahon* when he said: "[W]hile property may be regulated to a certain extent, if a regulation goes too far, it will be recognized as a taking."[20] Thus, in Justice Holmes's view, two remedies—invalidation and compensation—were available to the owner whose property had been "taken" through overreaching regulation. Justice Brandeis disagreed, arguing that no matter how egregious the regulatory act, invalidation was the only remedy available to the property owner.[21] In Brandeis's view, the Due Process and Takings Clauses of the Fifth Amendment were disjunctive in character, addressing entirely separate and distinct governmental activities: the exercise of police power on the one hand and eminent domain on the other. Never could an overreaching regulatory action to promote the public health, safety, or welfare transmute into a compensable event.

For the next sixty-five years, courts throughout the country followed the Brandeis dissent in *Pennsylvania Coal* rather than the Holmes majority opinion. No money damages were awarded to injured property owners, regardless of how injurious the police power action was. A typical example of this reasoning is found in the case of *Fred F. French Investing Co. v. City of New York*,[22] in which a city regulation creating an open space park on private property, leaving virtually no income-productive uses available to the property owner, was invalidated. However, no damages were awarded. The Court of Appeals of New York reasoned that when government acts in its "arbitral" capacity to resolve conflicts, no compensation is available to the property owner, even when the result is to deprive the owner of reasonable income productivity. Although invalid as a deprivation of property without due process, the offending regulation did not constitute a taking.[23]

Several years later, *Fred French* was severely criticized by Justice Brennan as an example of flawed analysis in his famous dissent in *San Diego Gas & Electric Co. v. City of San Diego*.[24] *San Diego Gas* marked the beginning of the end of the Brandeis view that invalidation was the only available remedy in regulatory takings cases. Justice Brennan was joined by three other justices in his *San Diego Gas* dissent, which, citing

Pennsylvania Coal, argued that compensation, in addition to invalidation, was an available remedy when the state overreaches in exercising its police power. A fifth justice would have joined the dissenters in *San Diego Gas* but for the fact that he felt the case was not ripe for adjudication.

Thus, *San Diego Gas* became the harbinger of *First English*, which reestablished the Holmes view in *Pennsylvania Coal* that the remedy of compensation is also available when a regulation effects a taking of private property. *First English* also holds that even a temporary taking requires just compensation, although "normal delays" in obtaining a building permit will not be regarded as a taking.[25]

Regulatory Takings Analysis: Two Separate Formulations

In conducting a regulatory takings analysis, one must remember that a regulation can effect a taking under either of two distinct circumstances. A regulation may take private property for public use if it (1) "does not substantially advance legitimate state interests" or (2) "denies an owner economically viable use of his land."[26] Different formulas must be used evaluating each type of taking claim, as discussed below.

Formula for Evaluating Economic Deprivation Claims

When a regulation is alleged to have denied economically viable use of land, the court must examine three primary factors:

- The character of the governmental action
- The economic impact of the regulation on the claimant
- The extent to which the regulation has interfered with distinct investment-backed expectations[27]

When the challenged governmental action goes beyond mere regulation and results in physical invasion of private property (e.g., through flooding or low-level overflight of aircraft), the court's focus is limited to the character of the governmental action. If there is physical occupation, a *per se* taking occurs, and no further analysis of the economic impact on the landowner or of the public interest basis for the government's action is necessary.[28]

The Lucas *Categorical Rule*

In *Lucas v. South Carolina Coastal Council*,[29] the Supreme Court established a threshold "categorical rule" for examining takings claims. Plaintiff Lucas owned two beach lots on a barrier island, the "Isle of Palms," located off the South Carolina coast. The lots were surrounded by beach homes, some of which had existed for many years. In 1988, after Lucas purchased the lots in question, the South Carolina legislature enacted the Beach Front Management Act, which expanded the previously defined "critical area" within which construction of occupiable dwellings on the island was prohibited. Lucas sued, contending that the act, even though properly and validly promulgated to preserve South Carolina's beaches, denied him all economically viable use of the lots and was thus a taking.

The Court held that two categories of regulatory action are compensable without the usual three-pronged case-specific *Penn-Central*–type inquiry into the public interest allegedly advanced by the regulation:

- where a regulation compels a property owner to suffer a physical invasion of his property; and
- where a regulation denies all economically beneficial or productive use of land.[30]

The Court reasoned that confiscatory regulations are to be accorded the same treatment as permanent physical occupations of land.

However, in setting forth the second prong of the categorical rule, the Court acknowledged that it has never clarified the "property interest" against which the loss of value is to be measured. It suggested that the answer may lie in how the owner's investment-backed expectations have been shaped by the state's law of property.[31] The question, sometimes described as the "denominator" issue,[32] is illustrated by this example: When a wetlands regulation totally precludes development of 5 percent of one's property but allows development of the remaining 95 percent, has the owner been deprived of all economically beneficial use of the burdened 5-percent portion or merely suffered a noncompensable diminution in the value of the entire tract?

In *Loveladies Harbor v. United States*,[33] this question was answered in favor of the property owner, who claimed a total deprivation as to 5 percent of a 250-acre tract that was burdened by the denial of a wetlands permit. The facts indicated that the entire tract, including the burdened 5-percent portion, had been acquired more than twenty years earlier—before enactment of the wetlands regulation in question—and most of it had since been developed. Thus, the developer never had the opportunity to decide at the outset whether its investment-backed expectations, under the later-enacted regulatory environment, could be achieved.[34]

Facts to Be Determined in Analyzing Economic Deprivation Claims

When a regulation is claimed to have denied the landowner economically viable use of land, the *Penn Central* test, as updated in *Lucas*, is applied. *Lucas*, however, holds that in applying the test the court is not bound to give credence to "artful" legislative findings of harm prevention to justify the challenged actions.[35] Conclusory findings that the landowner's proposed use is inconsistent with the public interest will not suffice.[36]

Helpful guidance in making the economic deprivation analysis is provided in *Reahard v. Lee County*.[37] The court sets forth eight essentially factual questions to be analyzed in addressing a regulatory taking claim when, as in *Lucas*, a regulation is conceded to be valid, but is nevertheless alleged to have denied the claimant economically viable use of property, entitling the claimant to just compensation.

At the outset, the reviewing court must determine whether there has been a denial of all or substantially all economically viable use. To do this, the court must analyze the economic impact of the regulation on the claimant and the extent to which the regulation has interfered with the claimant's investment-backed expectations. This analysis is facilitated by considering the following factors:

1. What is the history of the property?
   - When was it purchased?
   - How much land was purchased?
   - Where was the land located?
   - What was the nature of title?
   - What was the composition of the land?
   - How was the land initially used?
2. What is the history of development?
   - What was built on the land?
   - Who built it?
   - How was it subdivided?
   - To whom was it sold?
   - What plats were filed?
   - What roads were dedicated?
3. What is the history of zoning and regulation?
   - How and when was the land classified?
   - How was its use proscribed?
   - Were there changes in zoning classification?
4. How did development change when title passed?
5. What is the present nature and extent of the property?
6. What are the owner's reasonable expectations under state common law?
7. What are the neighboring landowners' reasonable expectations under state common law?
8. What is the diminution of the owner's investment-backed expectations, if any, after passage of the regulation?

Although the *Reahard* guidelines are helpful, some appear to unduly favor the proactive owner or developer over the passive investor. Courts using the guidelines might well be drawn into a vesting analysis, which does not appear to be the intent of *Lucas*. The investment-backed expectations of one who buys property for long-term family investment, such as retirement or education of children, but who is content to await the arrival of planned public facilities and infrastructure would not seem protected to the same degree as those of a more active investor who proceeds to spend money on development activity. Whether this makes the passive investor's expectations less investment-backed, and thus less deserving of protection, remains to be seen.

The Concept of a Partial Taking

The Supreme Court in *Lucas* expressly left the door open to the concept that a landowner need not have suffered a total deprivation of economic use to prove a taking.[38] While such a person would not have the benefit of the Court's "categorical rule," the extent to which a regulation may have interfered with the owner's "distinct investment-backed expectations" is characterized by the Court as "keenly relevant" to a takings analysis.[39]

In *Florida Rock Industries, Inc. v. United States,*[40] the Circuit Court of Appeals for the Federal Circuit referred specifically to this *Lucas* analysis in recognizing the concept of a compensable "partial taking" when a landowner is deprived of a substantial part of, but not necessarily all of, the economic value or use of its property.[41]

The facts in *Florida Rock* indicated an after-regulation reduction of economic use to approximately 40 percent of the subject property. Under traditional economic deprivation analysis (i.e., looking at what is left to the landowner), this would clearly not amount to a taking.[42] However, the court in *Florida Rock* held that the Fifth Amendment "prohibits uncompensated takings of private property without reference to the owner's remaining property interests."[43] This formulation represents a significant departure from traditional takings jurisprudence, which has always focused on what is left to the property owner after the regulatory action rather than what has been taken away. Under this analysis, the amount of just compensation should be "proportional to the value of the interest taken as compared to the total value of the property," whether the taking results from physical occupation or regulation.[44] In remanding, however, the court acknowledges the "difficult task of resolving when a partial loss of economic use of the property has crossed the line from a noncompensable 'mere diminution' to a compensable 'partial taking.'"[45] It directed the lower court to examine the "after imposition" value of the land to determine if a taking had occurred.[46]

Narrowing of the "Nuisance Exception" to the Compensation Requirement in Regulatory Takings

PRE-LUCAS. The nuisance rule states that one's property may not be used in a way that will "create a public nuisance" or cause harm or injury to neighboring properties.[47] The nuisance rule evolved in a series of cases dating back to 1887, including *Mugler v. Kansas*[48] (statute prohibiting manufacture of intoxicating liquors upheld); *Hadacheck v. Sabastian*[49] (ordinance prohibiting manufacture of brick upheld); *Miller v. Schoene*[50] (statute requiring infected cedar rust trees to be cut down to save neighboring apple orchards upheld); and *Goldblatt v. Town of Hempstead*[51] (ordinance banning excavation of sand and gravel below the water line upheld).

In its original application, the "nuisance exception" held that when a regulation prohibits only noxious or injurious uses of private property, it is exempt from scrutiny under the normal regulatory taking analysis.[52]

POST-LUCAS. While confirming the existence of a nuisance exception to the requirement that compensation be paid when police power actions prevent economically viable use of land, the Supreme Court in *Lucas* narrowed the exception significantly.[53] For a regulation that deprives land of all beneficial use to fit within the nuisance exception, "the proscribed use interests" must not have been "part of [the owner's] title to begin with."[54] To come under the exception, the restrictions on use must inhere to the owner's title itself, that is, in restrictions that "background principles of the State's law of property and nuisance have already placed upon land ownership."[55] The nuisance addressed by the regulation must be a traditional type of nuisance under state law (i.e., one that was "always unlawful"), such as a restriction on the filling of a dry lake bed.[56] The Court concluded that nuisance law may be invoked to prohibit all economically viable use of land without compensation only when the property owner, at the time of acquisition, could have had no reasonable expectation to use the property productively. The court also noted, however, that changed circumstances or new knowledge may make what was previously permissible no longer so.[57]

The Lucas Total Taking Inquiry

Recalling the reasoning normally accompanying the application of state nuisance law, *Lucas* enunciated a "total taking inquiry" in which it established the following three factors to be considered by reviewing courts:

- The degree of harm to public lands and resources, or adjacent private property, posed by the claimant's proposed activities

- The social value of the claimant's activities and their suitability to the locality
- The relative ease with which the alleged harm can be avoided through measures taken by the claimant and the government (or adjacent landowners)[58]

The total taking inquiry offers the opportunity to weigh the landowner's proposed "competing use" against the state's "use interest" in an environment that the Supreme Court believes should be more "objectively reasonable" than in the past.[59] The Court seems to be suggesting a more searching judicial review in these circumstances, one aimed toward avoiding total regulatory wipeouts where possible, and employment of a gentler test that would inquire whether the perceived harm or injury to the neighbors or the public can be obviated through less draconian measures taken by the property owner, the government, or adjacent landowners.

Formula for Evaluating Claims that the Government Action Fails to Substantially Advance a Legitimate State Interest

The Nollan/Dolan *Double Nexus Analysis*

As noted, economic deprivation is not the only barometer by which regulatory takings claims are measured. A regulation that does not necessarily result in denial of economically viable use of private property may still effect a taking if it fails to "substantially advance legitimate state interests."[60] *Nollan* and *Dolan*, both permit exaction cases, are prime examples of this aspect of regulatory takings law, although each case also had trappings of physical occupation.

In *Nollan*, the landowners challenged a California Coastal Commission requirement for a public access easement through the rear of their beachfront property as a condition of approval of a permit to construct a new dwelling that would replace an existing smaller beach home. The permit exaction, if upheld, would not have deprived the Nollans of all economically beneficial use of their property because they could still have built and lived in the new dwelling. Thus, the issue was not whether the Nollans could put their land to economically beneficial use but whether the permit condition furthered a legitimate state interest. The commission argued that conditioning approval of the building permit in this manner was necessary to foster visual access to the beach and to overcome perceived psychological barriers to citizens wanting to use the beach as they drove along the street in front of the Nollans' property. However, since the condition was an easement for lateral access to allow persons already on the beach to traverse the Nollans' property while walking from one public beach to another, the required "essential nexus" between the permit condition and the public purpose asserted by the commission to justify it was missing, thereby precipitating a taking.[61]

Nollan further teaches that the standards for evaluating takings and due process challenges are not the same. In a due process claim, the court need only inquire whether the agency "could rationally have decided" that the regulation would achieve the stated public purpose.[62] This is a standard that invokes only a minimal level of court review.[63] If there is substantial evidence to support the agency decision, and the issues are deemed to be fairly debatable, the regulation will be upheld. On the other hand, legislative findings that may be sufficient to overcome a substantive due process claim may be entirely irrelevant in determining whether the challenged police power action has effected a taking by failing to "substantially advance" a legitimate state interest . . . or by denying an owner "economically viable use" of his or her land.[64] *Nollan* also provides a reminder that the right to build on one's own property, even though subject to legitimate permitting requirements, "cannot remotely be described as a governmental benefit."[65]

The "essential nexus" test announced in *Nollan* is further enhanced and refined in *Dolan*. There, the city of Tigard conditioned approval of a building permit to expand a plumbing and electric supply store upon Dolan's dedication of certain of her land adjoining and partly within an adjacent floodplain for improvement of a storm drainage system. It also called for dedication of an additional fifteen-foot strip of her land adjacent to the floodplain as a pedestrian and bicycle pathway. The required dedications encompassed approximately 10 percent of the owner's 1.67-acre parcel. The city's planning commission made generalized findings regarding the relationship between the required exactions and the anticipated impacts of the proposed development. These included findings that the new development would likely result in increased traffic congestion and that the increased impervious surface, including an enlarged and newly paved parking lot, would increase the amount of storm water runoff. The city's action was upheld by the state courts.[66]

In reversing, the Court, building upon *Nollan*, established the following two-step nexus test:

- First, the *Nollan*-required "essential nexus" must exist between the asserted "legitimate state interest" and the permit condition exacted by the government.[67]

- Second, if the required nexus exists, the next step is to analyze the "degree of connection" between the exaction and the "projected impact" of the proposed development.[68] There must be "rough proportionality" between the two.[69]

Importantly, the burden of proof, at least in the second phase of the *Dolan* analysis, is on the government, not the property owner.[70] No "precise mathematical calculation" is required, but the regulator must make "some sort of individualized determination" that the exaction "is related both in nature and extent to the impact of the proposed development."[71] It must make an effort "to quantify its findings" in support of the action.[72] The "rough proportionality" standard is analogous to the "reasonable relationship" test and is intended to invoke a higher level of court scrutiny than the minimal level of scrutiny that would occur under the "rational basis" test.[73] This is consistent with the heightened scrutiny standard required by *Nollan* where approval of a permit is conditioned on the conveyance of land.[74]

Figure 2 shows The *Nollan/Dolan* two-pronged nexus test for regulatory exactions in diagrametric form.

FIGURE 2. The *Nollan/Dolan* Double Nexus Test

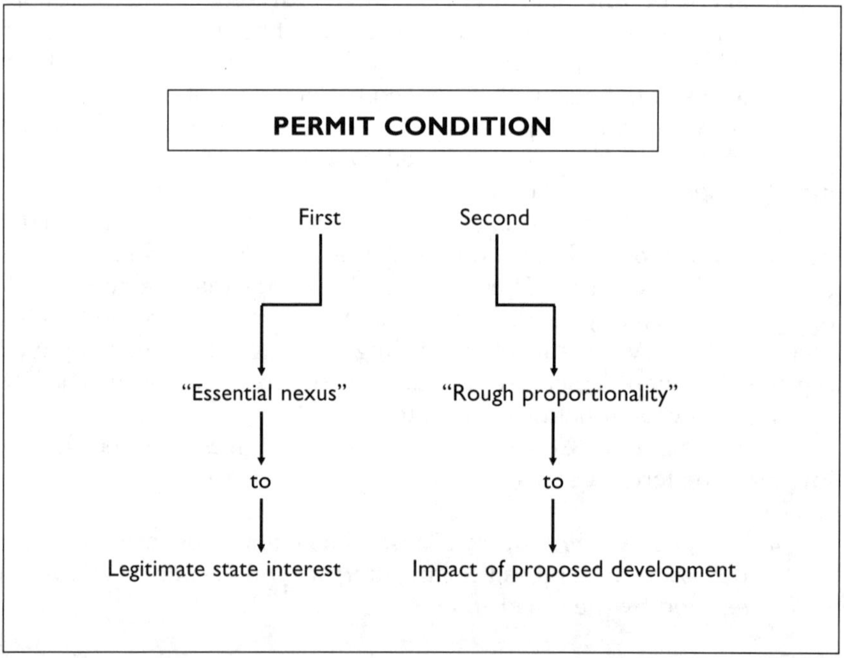

Applicability of the Nollan/Dolan *Test to Exactions*

As noted, the Supreme Court in *Nollan* and *Dolan* was obviously influenced by the fact that the required exactions had elements of physical invasion as well as regulatory taking. The *Nollan* opinion notes that the Court will be "particularly careful" when the conveyance or dedication of property is made a condition of permit approval.[75] *Dolan* reaffirms this view in observing that permit conditions such as those in *Nollan* were not simply limitations on use but, rather, a requirement that the landowner "deed portions of the property" to the city.[76]

Some courts have distinguished *Nollan* on this basis.[77] Based on the Supreme Court's disposition of *Ehrlich v. City of Culver City*,[78] however, there is reason to believe that the *Nollan/Dolan* double nexus requirement and heightened scrutiny will be applied to other forms of land use exactions, including development fees. In *Ehrlich*, the owner of a defunct private health and tennis club sought a building permit to construct a condominium townhouse project on the site. Culver City approved the permit, conditioned upon the applicant paying a number of fees, including a fee of $280,000 to enable the city to build public tennis courts that would replace the recreational facilities lost with the demise of the club and a fee of $33,200 to provide art in public places. Ehrlich sued, contending that the fee exactions bore no relationship to any impact caused by the proposed townhouse project and that the public arts fee violated his First Amendment right of free speech. He was unsuccessful in state court,[79] and he petitioned for *certiorari* in the Supreme Court. In granting *certiorari*, the Court vacated the judgment of the lower court and remanded "for further consideration in light of *Dolan*."[80] Doubtless this is not the end of this issue.

Conclusion

It is now well established that a police power regulation that denies a landowner economically viable use of land or fails to advance the asserted legitimate state interest substantially is compensable under the Fifth Amendment. Invalidation is not the property owner's only remedy.

A categorical taking exists whenever a regulation results in physical occupation of private property or denies the landowner all economically viable use of land. Even temporary takings are compensable, although normal permitting delays are not regarded as temporary takings. Partial takings, where the landowner is not divested of all use or value of the property, may also be compensable, but this depends on the facts. Partial loss of economic use of property may only be a noncompensable diminution in value.

Courts reviewing takings claims based on economic deprivation will focus on the character of the governmental regulation, its economic impact on the claimant, and the extent to which it has interfered with the claimant's investment-backed expectations. Regulatory exactions, especially those requiring conveyance or dedication of property to the public, as well as development fees and exactions having only a remote connection to the development's projected impact will be subjected to higher than minimal scrutiny, with the burden of proof being on the government instead of the property owner. Exactions of this nature will be invalidated as noncompensated takings unless a two-fold nexus requirement is satisfied. First, a nexus must exist between the government-asserted legitimate state interest and the exaction. If this nexus is found to exist, government must then demonstrate that some quantifiable rough proportionality exists between the exaction and the expected impact of the proposed development.

The right to build on one's own land is a protected property right under the Fifth Amendment. Although subject to legitimate permitting requirements, this right cannot be described as a benefit conferred by government.

Comment: Regulatory Exactions after *Dolan*—The California Experience and Predictions

In December of 1994, after this article was originally written, a divided California appellate court, on remand of *Ehrlich,* in a lengthy, unpublished opinion, stuck to its guns and again denied relief to the developer.[81] The rationale of the California court is that a regulatory exaction will not be regarded as a taking unless it fails on two fronts. First, it must fail to advance a legitimate state interest substantially, and second, it must also deprive the landowner of all viable use of land. The same rationale is apparently being applied by California appellate courts in other post-*Dolan* cases.[82] This conjunctive approach is directly contrary to the disjunctive rule for regulatory takings announced in *Agins* and confirmed in *Keystone* and *Lucas*.[83] *Agins* clearly states that a taking will occur when a regulation fails to "substantially advance legitimate state interests *or* denies a landowner economically viable use" of land.[84] One of the major flaws in the reasoning of the California court is its obvious inference that a regulation that promotes "legitimate" public purposes can never result in a compensable taking. This contradicts repeated Supreme Court holdings to the effect that, even when the legislative purpose is "laudable," compensation must be paid to the landowner if a taking of private property results.[85] Conversely, under this analysis, compensation would be withheld even where an admittedly bad regulation failed to advance its asserted public purpose, so long as the landowner (e.g., Mrs. Dolan) is not totally deprived of all beneficial use of her land. The conjunctive interpretation of *Agins* seems also to have been adopted by the Ohio Supreme Court on a closely split vote.[86]

The California Supreme Court is reviewing the appellate court's decision in *Ehrlich.*[87] Since that court's views on regulatory takings have often been at odds with those of the U.S. Supreme Court, one can only speculate whether, and to what extent, it will apply *Dolan* to Ehrlich's claim. Thus, unless the Supreme Court again reviews *Ehrlich,* or another regulatory takings case, the issue will likely remain in doubt in California.

However, *Dolan* is being applied by other courts,[88] and it is reasonable to conclude that landowners will receive greater protection from onerous regulatory exactions, including development fees, in the future. This is especially true when government is acting "adjudicatively" in determining site-specific land use approval requests, such as subdivision, site plan, or building permit applications. The Supreme Court in *Dolan* was careful to point out that in reviewing the owner's building permit application the city was not making a legislative determination but was acting in an adjucative manner.[89] Exactions imposed ad hoc in these circumstances are apt to receive closer scrutiny. There may be less protection for landowners when government acts "legislatively" on matters affecting entire areas of a county or city. This would include carefully constructed exaction ordinances establishing standardized fee schedules tailored to the different types of developments involved.[90]

Notes

Major portions of this chapter originally appeared in *The Urban Lawyer,* volume 27, number 1, winter 1995 and were subsequently reprinted in *Exactions, Impact Fees, and Dedications: Shaping Land-Use Development and Funding Infrastructure in the Post-*Dolan *Era* (American Bar Association, 1995).

1. 505 U.S. ______, 112 S. Ct. 2886 (1992).
2. ______ U.S. ______, 114 S. Ct. 2309 (1994).
3. 474 U.S. 128 (1985).
4. 28 F.3d 1171.
5. 18 F.3d 1560.
6. 857 F.2d 1324 (9th Cir. 1989), *cert. denied, sub. nom.* Christy v. Lujan, 490 U.S. 1114 (1989).
7. *See* Babbitt v. Sweet Home Chapter of Communities for a Great Oregon, ______ U.S. ______, 115 S. Ct. 2407 (1995). Briefs of Amici Curiae, Nationwide Public Projects Coalition et al.; American Farm Bureau Fed'n et al.; National

Cattleman's Ass'n et al.; Florida Legal Foundation et al.; and Institute for Justice (reviewing Sweet Home Chapter of Communities for a Great Oregon v. Babbitt, 17 F.3d 1463 (D.C. Cir. 1994)).

8. *See* Maryland Aviation Admin. v. Newsome, 652 A.2d 116 (Md. 1995).

9. 260 U.S. 393.

10. 447 U.S. 255 (1980).

11. 450 U.S. 621 (1981).

12. 473 U.S. 172 (1985).

13. 477 U.S. 340 (1986).

14. 482 U.S. 304 (1987).

15. 480 U.S. 470 (1987).

16. 483 U.S. 825, 107 S. Ct. 3141 (1987).

17. 505 U.S. ____, 112 S. Ct. 2886.

18. ____ U.S. ____, 114 S. Ct. 2309 (1994).

19. Penn Central Transportation Co. v. City of New York, 438 U.S. 104, 121 (1978).

20. 260 U.S. 393, 415 (1922).

21. *Id.* at 417–22 (Brandeis, J. dissenting).

22. 350 N.E.2d 381, 385–86 (1976).

23. *Id.* at 388.

24. 450 U.S. 621 (1981).

25. 482 U.S. at 321.

26. Agins v. City of Tiburon, 447 U.S. 255, 260 (1980); Nollan v. California Coastal Comm'n, 483 U.S. 825, 837 (1987); Keystone Bituminous Coal Ass'n v. DeBenedictis, 480 U.S. 470, 484–85 (1987); Lucas v. South Carolina Coastal Comm'n, 112 S. Ct. 2886, 2894 (1992); Dolan v. City of Tigard, _____ U.S. _____, 114 S. Ct., 2309, 2317 (1994).

27. Penn Central Transportation Co. v. New York City, 438 U.S. 104, 122 (1978).

28. Loretto v. Teleprompter Manhattan CATV Corp., 458 U.S. 419 (1982).

29. 112 S. Ct. 2886 (1992).

30. *Id.* at 2893.

31. *Id.* at 2894, n.7.

32. *Id.*

33. 28 F.3d 1171 (Fed. Cir. 1994).

34. *Id.* at 1174.

35. 112 S. Ct. at 2898, n.12.

36. *Id.* at 2901. *See Dolan,* 114 S. Ct. at 2321–22.

37. 968 F.2d 1131, *vacated and remanded,* 978 F.2d 1212 (11th Cir. 1992).

38. 112 S. Ct. at 2895, n.8.

39. *Id.*

40. 18 F.3d 1560, 1568 (Fed. Cir. 1994).

41. *Lucas,* 112 S. Ct. at 2895–2900.

42. Penn Central Transportation Co. v. City of New York, 483 U.S. 104, 131 (1978).

43. 18 F.3d at 1568. The court pointedly noted that if the government took only five acres of a hundred-acre tract for a park, "there would be no question that the owner was entitled to compensation for the parcel taken." *Id.* at 1569.

44. *Id.*

45. *Id.* at 1570.

46. *Id.* at 1573.

47. *Pennsylvania Coal*, 260 U.S. at 417 (Brandeis, J., dissenting); *Keystone*, 480 U.S. at 491 n.20, 511 (Rehnquist, C.J., dissenting).

48. 123 U.S. 623, 663, 669 (1887).

49. 239 U.S. 394 (1915).

50. 276 U.S. 246 (1928).

51. 369 U.S. 509 (1962).

52. *Penn Central*, 438 U.S. at 144–46 (Rehnquist, J., dissenting); *Keystone*, 480 U.S. at 488–93 (1987).

53. For an insightful discussion of the nuisance rule before and after *Lucas*, *see* Robert M. Washburn, *Land Use Control, The Individual, and Society: Lucas v. South Carolina Coastal Council*, 52 MD. L. REV. 162 (1993).

54. *Lucas*, 112 S. Ct. at 2899.

55. *Id.* at 2900.

56. *Id.* at 2900–01.

57. *Id.* at 2901.

58. *Id.*

59. *Id.* at 2898–99, 2901–02, n.18.

60. *Nollan*, 483 U.S. at 837; *Dolan*, 114 S. Ct. at 2316; *Keystone*, 480 U.S. at 484–85; *Lucas* at 2894; *Agins*, 447 U.S. at 260.

61. *Nollan*, 483 U.S. at 836. The *Nollan* court would have upheld permit conditions related to the public's ability to see the beach, such as height or width restrictions on the new house, or a ban on fences. Even requiring a viewing spot on the Nollans' property from which the public could observe the ocean would be appropriate. *Id.* How the latter condition would square with the Nollans' right to "exclude others"—described as "one of the most essential sticks in the bundle" of property rights, *id.* at 831, quoting *Loretto*, 458 U.S. at 433—is hard to fathom unless payment of compensation for the taking of the viewing spot is implied.

62. *Nollan*, 483 U.S. at 835, n.3, 843 (Brennan, J., dissenting).

63. *See Dolan*, 114 S. Ct. at 2319.

64. *See Agins*, 477 U.S. at 260; *Nollan*, 483 U.S. at 837; *Lucas*, 112 S. Ct. at 2894; *Dolan*, 114 S. Ct. at 2317.

65. *Nollan*, 483 U.S. at 834, n.2.

66. *See* Oregon Court of Appeals decision at 832 P.2d 853 (1992), and Oregon Supreme Court decision at 859 P.2d 437 (1993).

67. *Dolan*, 114 S. Ct. at 2317. *See also Nollan*, 483 U.S. at 837. The *Dolan* Court found no *Nollan*-type "gimmickry" on the part of the defendant city. Rather, the required nexus was found to exist between preventing flooding and limiting development in the flood plain, and between reducing traffic and providing alternative means of transportation. *Dolan*, 114 S. Ct. at 2317–18.

68. *Dolan*, 114 S. Ct. at 2317.

69. *Id.* at 2311.

70. *Id.* at 2319–20, n.8.

71. *Id.*

72. *Id.* at 2322.

73. *Id.* at 2319.

74. 483 U.S. at 841. *But see* Ehrlich v. City of Culver City, *infra*, for the premise that heightened scrutiny may also apply to other forms of regulatory exactions, including development fees.

75. *Nollan*, 483 U.S. at 839.

76. *Dolan*, 114 S. Ct. at 2316.

77. *See, e.g.*, Offen v. County Council for Prince George's County, 625 A.2d 424, at 434 (Md. App. 1993), *rev'd on other grounds*, 639 A.2d 1070 (Md. 1994).

78. 114 S. Ct. at 2731 (1994).

79. Ehrlich v. City of Culver City, 15 Cal. App. 4th 1737 (1993).

80. *Ehrlich*, 114 S. Ct. at 2731 (1994); Justices Blackmun, Stevens, Souter, and Ginsberg voted to deny *certiorari*.

81. 15 Cal. App. 4th 1737, 19 Cal. Rptr. 2d 468, *review granted*, 95 C.D.O.S. 1988 (Cal. 1995). The dissent found that the *Dolan* rough proportionality test had not been met.

82. *See particularly* Del Oro Hills v. City of Oceanside, 31 Cal. App. 4th 1060, 37 Cal. Rptr. 2d 677 (1995); Jones v. County of Tuolumne, Calif. Court of Appeals, Fifth Dist. F018725, Nov. 3, 1994. *See also* Daniel J. Curtin, *The Status of "Takings" After Dolan: Recent California Decisions That Uphold Impact Fees,* CAL. LAND USE L. & POL'Y, Vol. 4, No. 5, p. 100 (January 1995).

83. The California appellate court cites *Nollan* as authority for its conjunctive rule. *Nollan* expressly cites the *Agins* rule as its authority, but in so doing it uses "and" instead of "or" (483 U.S. at 837). The same is true in *Dolan* (114 S. Ct. at 2316). However, it is clear that in *Nollan* and *Dolan*, the court is merely describing the two circumstances in which a regulatory taking may occur. Nowhere does *Nollan* or *Dolan* require that both circumstances must be present to have a taking. Both *Keystone* and *Lucas* actually quote the *Agins* rule, using the disjunctive "or" (Keystone, 480 U.S. at 485; *Lucas*, 112 S. Ct. at 2894).

84. *Agins*, 447 U.S. at 260 (emphasis added). *See also Lucas*, 112 S. Ct. at 894.

85. *See Dolan*, 114 S. Ct. at 2322, *Pennsylvania Coal*, 260 U.S. 393, 416 (1922).

86. *See* Gerijo Inc. v. City of Fairfield, 638 N.E.2d 533 (Ohio 1994); *cert. denied*, 115 S. Ct. 1101 (1995).

87. *See* note 81.

88. *See, e.g.*, Christopher Lake Development Co. v. St. Louis County, 35 F.3d 1269 (8th Cir. 1994); Menocherian v. Lenox Hill Hospital, 616 N.Y.S.2d 473, 640 N.E.2d 140 (1994); *cert. denied*, 115 S. Ct. 1961 (1995).

89. *Dolan*, 114 S. Ct. at 2316.

90. *See, e.g.*, Home Builders Ass'n of Central Arizona v. City of Scottsdale, 1 CA-CV 92-0210, Court of Appeals of Arizona, Div. One, Dept. B, filed Feb. 16, 1995. (However, this is yet another split decision. The dissenting judge argued that the legislative character of the City's action did not excuse it from complying with the rough proportionality mandate of *Dolan*.) *See also* Parking Ass'n of Georgia v. City of Atlanta, 450 S.E.2d 200 (Ga. 1994); *cert. denied*, 115 S. Ct. 2268 (1995). But for a case invalidating a broad legislative enactment of a transportation impact fee program for failure to comply with *Dolan, see* Northern Illinois Homebuilders v. County of DuPage, 649 N.E.2d 384 (Ill. 1995).

CHAPTER 27

Wetlands: Avoiding the Swamp Monster

MARGARET N. STRAND

You get an urgent message from your construction manager: "We've got the crew on-site leveling the back of the lots and the concrete is ready to pour for the sidewalks, but a few minutes ago somebody showed up saying she was from the Corps of Engineers. There's a guy with her wearing an EPA hat, taking a bunch of photos and talking to the men. When I told them to get away from my workers, they handed me a letter and told me we are illegally filling wetlands in violation of federal law. They said that I had to stop all work on the lots. You know the costs we'll face if we stop work. What do you want me to do?"

This nightmare—identification of wetlands on property long after investments have been made—occurs far too frequently. It is possible to have regulated wetlands on real estate and not know it without expert help. The consequences of making such a mistake can be severe. Therefore, identification of wetlands, by experienced professionals, should be a routine part of real estate transactions. Early evaluation of potential wetlands is the best way to avoid surprises that can derail a transaction. Wetlands are subject to protection and use limitations under the law. There is no legal restriction against owning wetlands, and it is not illegal to buy or sell wetland property. However, federal law does restrict a person's ability to alter wetlands (or any other body of water, such as a creek, stream, or pond). Under Section 404 of the federal Clean Water Act (CWA),[1] a permit is required to place any material into wetlands. Thus, wetlands affect real estate transactions because limitations on altering them impact the development potential of the land.

From the buyer's perspective, four questions must be answered before a transaction should proceed:

1. Are there wetlands? To answer this question, one must have an understanding of the legal and technical definitions and be familiar with the process for obtaining a wetland delineation.
2. Can an authorization to alter the wetlands be obtained? Depending on the planned activities, wetlands alteration may be authorized by an exemption, a nationwide or general permit, or an individual permit. Familiarity with the permit criteria enables the buyer to assess whether development of the land will be authorized and under what conditions.
3. Is any enforcement action pending? Some liabilities for wetlands violations will be recorded or may run with the land. Buyers need to know the consequences of any past liabilities or possible future enforcement.
4. What happens if the wetlands must be preserved? There may be remedies for an owner who is denied permission to alter wetlands. Moreover, wetland acreage may have value in its natural state if it is incorporated into the buyer's plans.

Before addressing these four questions more fully, it is important to know who regulates wetlands. This chapter focuses on the federal CWA wetlands program. However, many states have wetlands protection laws, and federal law does not preempt state law. Wetlands laws may be found in different places in the various state codes. While the federal CWA addresses wetlands protection as part of water pollution controls, some states include wetlands under natural resource management provisions or land use requirements rather than pollution laws. On the federal level, most wetlands law is found in regulations rather than statutes. This also will vary among the states. The range of practices reflects the hybrid nature of wetlands law, which involves both pollution control and private property regulation.

While most of the authority to administer the CWA is vested in the U.S. Environmental Protection Agency (EPA), the federal wetlands program under Section 404 is run primarily, but not exclusively, by the U.S. Army Corps of Engineers (Corps). The CWA preserved coordination roles for several other federal agencies, including an oversight role for the EPA. This scheme gives rise to one of the frustrating aspects of the federal wetlands program: the involvement of multiple agencies with different responsibilities. These include the following:

The Corps: It makes decisions on individual permits; reviews predischarge notification for certain nationwide permits; makes wetland delineations; issues wetlands program regulations in consultation with the EPA; and enforces against violators.[2]

The EPA: It issues CWA Section 404(b)(1) regulations setting environmental standards for permits; may "veto" Corps permit decisions under CWA Section 404(c); enforces against violators; and may elevate disputes with the Corps under CWA Section 404(q) to headquarters for review.[3]

U.S. Fish and Wildlife Service (FWS): It reviews and comments on permit applications; may elevate disputes with the Corps under CWA Section 404(q) to headquarters for review; and develops and maintains National Wetland Inventory maps.[4]

National Oceanic and Atmospheric Administration (NOAA): It reviews and comments on permit applications and may elevate disputes with the Corps under CWA Section 404(q) to headquarters for review.

States: They make water quality certification determinations under CWA Section 401 and may comment on permits.

Others: Many other agencies may consult or comment, depending on the resources at issue in a particular situation (for example, historic preservation).

Because multiple agencies are involved, a person who intends to alter wetlands is wise to accept the invitation extended by the Corps regulations to have an *early* informal consultation regarding potential activities that may affect wetlands.[5]

With this brief background, the four categories of information identified in this introduction can be more fully explored.

Are There Wetlands on the Parcel?

CWA Jurisdictional Wetlands

Wetlands subject to federal control are often referred to as "jurisdictional wetlands" because they are within the regulatory jurisdiction of federal law. Regulation of wetlands arises from the combination of several legal and regulatory terms that result in wetlands being treated as "waters of the United States" under the federal CWA. Several definitions must be linked together to explain federal regulation of wetlands.

The CWA prohibits the "discharge of any pollutant by any person."[6] The "discharge of a pollutant" means, in pertinent part, "any addition of any pollutant to navigable waters from a point source."[7] The key jurisdictional phrase, "navigable waters," is defined by the CWA as "the waters of the United States, including the territorial seas."[8] Congress left it to the EPA and the Corps to further define the scope of "waters of the United States." After an initial period during which the limits of this term were expanded gradually,[9] the current federal regulations provide a very broad definition of "waters of the United States." The regulations state that the CWA applies to

- all traditionally navigable waters;
- all interstate waters, including interstate wetlands;
- all waters, including wetlands, the use, degradation, or destruction of which could affect interstate commerce; and
- wetlands adjacent to other waters within the definition.[10]

There is little question that the regulations encompass wetlands adjacent to other bodies of water. Courts have had no problem finding that protection of such adjacent wetlands is consistent with the goals of the CWA to preserve and protect the nation's waters.[11] It does not matter if a wetland has been artificially created.[12] CWA jurisdiction has been upheld over areas created by the unauthorized activities of others,[13] highway construction,[14] government ditches,[15] and artificial canals.[16] Intermittent and seasonal waters are also CWA jurisdictional.[17] Moreover, the CWA prohibition against filling applies year-round, not just during the wet season.

Jurisdiction over isolated wetlands has been and remains hotly contested, although the U.S. government maintains that isolated wetlands are subject to CWA jurisdiction.[18] Isolated wetlands are included as jurisdictional under the regulations if the government can establish a nexus between the wetlands and interstate commerce. The regulations include examples of appropriate connections to interstate commerce, such as waters

- that could be used by travelers for recreational or other purposes;
- that are used for commercial fisheries; or
- that are used by industries that are in interstate commerce.[19]

Although not listed in the regulations, the U.S. government maintains that wetlands that support migratory birds have a sufficient nexus to interstate commerce because such birds support interstate commercial and recreational activities, such as hunting and bird watching.[20] The U.S. Court of Appeals for the Fourth Circuit has held that the government cannot rely on bird or wildlife usage as a basis for the commerce nexus until it formally amends its regulations.[21] In contrast, the U.S. Court of Appeals for the Seventh[22] and the Ninth Circuits[23] have said that bird and wildlife usage can be the basis for a connection between wetlands and interstate commerce under the existing CWA regulations. The government must prove the connection and cannot rely on the "potential" for birds to use an isolated wetland.[24] Perhaps reflecting some judicial discomfort with the breadth of the CWA, the Seventh Circuit recently held that an artificial retention pond, unconnected to any other surface waters, was not jurisdictional under the CWA.[25]

In sum, the government maintains that virtually all wetlands, whether adjacent to other waters or isolated, are presumptively subject to CWA jurisdiction. If a wetland is small and unconnected to other surface waters, it is possible that it may be outside of CWA jurisdiction. This is a "cutting edge" area of the law where landowners, with expert help, must tread carefully. A review of the property by experts qualified in habitat studies is necessary, since the landowner will face strong government opposition if he or she maintains that an isolated wetland is not jurisdictional.

Physical Definition of Wetlands

While most wetlands will be subject to CWA jurisdiction, identifying the physical features that are characteristic of a wetland involves application of a separate regulatory definition. The Corps and the EPA define wetlands as:

> areas that are inundated or saturated by surface or ground water at a frequency and duration sufficient to support, and that under normal circumstances do support, a prevalence of vegetation typically adapted for life in saturated soil conditions. Wetlands generally include swamps, marshes, bogs, and similar areas.[26]

This definition is referred to as a "three parameter" test, in which wetlands are characterized by hydrology (water at or near surface for a sufficient time); hydrophytic vegetation (plants adapted to saturated soils); and hydric soils (specified soils and conditions). These three parameters are exhibited on the ground in myriad physical circumstances.[27] A wetland, under the standards applied by federal agencies, must exhibit *all three* of these characteristics. Locating the boundaries of a wetland on the ground is called wetland delineation.

A similar three-part wetland definition is found in the Food Security Act (FSA).[28] The definition applies for purposes of administering two related FSA programs: "Swampbuster" and the federal wetland reserve program. Under "Swampbuster," farmers who drain or fill wetlands are ineligible for agricultural benefits on that land. The wetland reserve program authorizes payments to farmers who enroll wetland property in a preservation program via the sale to the government of a ten-year conservation easement.[29]

The FSA wetlands programs are administered in coordination with the CWA programs, under a 1994 Memorandum of Agreement between the Corps, the EPA, the FWS, and the Natural Resources Conservation Services (NRCS), formerly the Soil Conservation Service (SCS). Some agricultural practices are exempt from the CWA, and the FSA has a different set of exemptions. These special provisions for agricultural wetlands are not covered in detail in this chapter. Persons working with agricultural property should consider the FSA as well as the CWA in evaluating wetlands issues. While the definition of a wetland is similar under both programs, the legal requirements, exceptions, and exemptions vary under the two statutes.

The regulatory definition of "wetland" omits many details. For example, it does not specify how long an area must be saturated or inundated, how a prevalence of wetland vegetation is measured, or which kinds of soils can support a wetland ecosystem. To fill in these interstices, the federal agencies have developed wetland delineation manuals.[30] Currently, federal CWA wetland delineation is conducted in accordance with the Corps's 1987 *Wetlands Delineation Manual*.[31] This manual provides guidance on methods for evaluating the required hydrology, plants, and soils needed for a wetland. Hydrophytic vegetation is identified by using the National List of Plant Species That Occur in Wetlands, which is maintained in regional segments by the FWS.[32] Hydric soils are specified by reference to the Hydric Soils List developed by the National Technical Committee for Hydric Soils (NTCHS) under the auspices of the U.S. Department of Agriculture's NRCS.[33] The Corps manual identifies acceptable indicators of wetland soils, vegetation, and hydrology and addresses problem areas, such as wetlands disturbed by unauthorized activities. The manual is not "self executing" but should be used in consultation with properly trained experts.

Often there is little question that a land feature is a wetland, identifiable by standing water or saturated soil and clearly identified plants. Under the Corps manual, the minimum time wetlands must be inundated or saturated at or near the surface (i.e., in the root zone) is between 5 percent and 12.5 percent of the growing season. Thus, an area that exhibits hydric soils and hydrophytic vegetation may be visibly wet for only a few weeks of the year and still be regulated as a wetland year-round.

Wetlands may exhibit many types of vegetation, including large forested areas. Myriad combinations of wetland vegetation, soils, and hydrology can occur. While wetlands may develop under many different physical circumstances, topography offers important clues to wetland identification. Even if a location is dry for much of the year, low-lying areas, depressions, areas near sources of water, or areas exhibiting special wet season vegetation all are likely to exhibit wetland characteristics.

Delineation of Wetlands

Wetlands are delineated on a site-specific basis. Delineation is not a simple matter of applying cookbook standards from the Corps manual. It takes a trained professional to identify clearly the place on the land where the wetland characteristics—hydrophytic plants, hydric soils, and sufficient hydrology—begin and cease.

Wetlands are delineated so that the property owner knows where he or she may carry on construction (or other earth moving) without a CWA permit. Thus, wetland delineations may be done for private planning purposes to mark the "safe" areas for construction. The delineation may result in changing plans so that activities occur solely in the uplands and thus avoid all wetlands. The delineation will also help inform the owner whether he or she qualifies for an exemption or for a general permit, subjects that are addressed below.

If a parcel contains wetlands, the owner may seek approval to alter those wetlands by obtaining a permit. In that case, a wetland delineation will be required as part of the application for an individual permit. In some instances, a wetland delineation must also accompany the predischarge notification required to qualify for certain of the nationwide permits.[34]

The Corps and the EPA are not required to provide a wetland delineation to a property owner at his or her demand. While Corps offices are authorized to do so,[35] they may be too understaffed to perform wetland delineations upon demand. Hence, instead of waiting for the Corps to conduct the delineation, property owners generally rely on private consultants.[36]

When the Corps does conduct a wetland delineation, it must be in writing.[37] As a general rule, final wetland delineations by the Corps are valid for three years, although five years may be justified if the Corps receives appropriate information. The Corps reserves to itself the authority to change a wetland delineation if new information warrants it.

The practices vary among Corps offices when a wetland delineation is performed by a private consultant. In theory, the Corps must conduct a site visit to review a privately conducted delineation. In fact, some Corps offices may accept wetland delineations from some consultants based on an "office review," looking at the delineation and perhaps maps or photographs of the site. This should not, however, be the normal practice. Regardless of who conducts the initial delineation, when it is approved by the Corps it is valid for the same term described above.

There is currently no uniform system to train or certify wetland delineators, either public or private, but that situation is changing. In 1993 the Corps commenced a pilot program for certification of wetland delineators.[38] The agency intends to use this program as the basis for a permanent certification program. As the program is envisioned, a certified wetland delineator will have to pass a two-part Corps test, in the classroom and in the field. The tests are based on application of the Corps manual in various difficult situations. Persons who successfully completed the certification tests in the pilot program have been "conditionally certified." When the program is final, successful students and those who passed the pilot program will be eligible to be permanently certified. A delineation by a certified wetland delineator should be valid and acceptable to the Corps for regulatory purposes.

A number of private organizations (including consulting firms and universities)[39] offer wetland delineation training and certification. At this time, there is no official recognition by the federal agencies of any particular private training or certification programs.

Wetland delineations can be as specific or as general as the person requesting the delineation desires. For example, a property owner often will want to determine wetland boundaries in a general fashion for planning purposes. However, for certain properties, it will be necessary to draw a precise line marking the boundaries of the jurisdictional wetlands, complete with the placement of flags on the ground and lines on a map. The property owner must specify the type of wetland delineation desired when contracting with a consultant.

Identification and delineation of wetlands on real estate should be a part of any environmental audit conducted for a transaction. As with other audit provisions, the party contracting for the audit needs to specify the degree of detail desired.

Sources of Assistance for Wetland Delineation

While the government is not required to delineate wetlands for private parties, the Corps and other federal agencies encourage early consultation with regard to wetlands.[40] Frequently a property owner will inform the Corps that a consultant is conducting a wetland delineation, and a representative of the Corps, the EPA, or both, will accompany the consultant and provide feedback. Often the Corps has conducted other wetland delineations in the area, which serve as a useful starting point.

The NRCS also maintains information about wetlands, such as soil maps for all areas of the United States, identifying the general location of hydric soils. While all areas with hydric soils are not wetlands, a wetland must have hydric soils, so these maps are useful starting points.

In addition, the FWS maintains a series of maps known as the National Wetland Inventory (NWI) maps, which identify wetlands on a map scale of 1:24,000. FWS intends to map the wetlands of the whole country, and the project is ongoing. While some of the NWI maps are out of date, others are very accurate, and even the older maps can provide a good starting point for identifying wetlands. NWI maps, however, do not have regulatory effect. The FWS used a different definition of wetlands for the NWI than the regulatory definition used by the Corps and the EPA, which means that the NWI maps may designate more (or different) areas as wetlands than are defined by the Corps and the EPA.

Another source of wetlands information is an EPA program known as the Advanced Identification (ADID) program.[41] Where the EPA has conducted an ADID, it works with the local community to identify wetlands and to designate wetland areas that are and are not suitable for development. Identification of a wetland in the ADID program does not substitute for a site-specific wetland delineation, but it does provide useful information for general planning of land uses.

Other land planning programs may identify wetlands in a community. The federal Coastal Zone Management Act,[42] for example, provides states with a source of funding for coastal planning. States may develop Special Area Management Plans (SAMPs) to guide development in sensitive areas of the coastal zone. Wetlands may be the subject of a state SAMP. The Corps has issued a guidance letter to all field offices, encouraging them to work with states in the development of SAMPs.[43] A property owner in the coastal zone may find useful information if a SAMP has been developed.

How Can Wetland Property Be Developed?

The Corps is authorized to issue permits allowing placement of fill in wetlands or other CWA jurisdictional waters. Conceptually, therefore, wetlands may be filled and developed if the owner obtains a CWA permit. In addition, there are a few statutory exemptions from the permit obligation. The regulations of both the Corps and the EPA apply to the permit process. The Corps regulations set forth the procedures and basic requirements, while the EPA regulations establish substantive environmental standards.

What Activities in Wetlands Are Regulated?

Section 404 of the CWA authorizes the Corps to issue permits for the discharge of "dredged or fill material" into jurisdictional areas.[44] The regulations define fill material very broadly, as any material that changes the bottom elevation of a water area or converts an aquatic area to dry land.[45] Therefore, filling a wetland, by placing dirt, rocks, sand, or similar substances into the wetland, is a regulated activity.

Cases have arisen in which landowners have claimed that redeposit of existing indigenous materials is not regulated filling. Generally, however, these claims have been rejected. Land-clearing activities involving redeposit of soil and debris are regulated.[46] Moving stream channels also is a regulated activity.[47] The fill material does not have to come from some location other than the wetland.

In contrast, the placement of pilings for bridges and piers generally is not treated as filling, unless the pilings are placed so closely together as to accomplish the same purpose as filling.[48] Conceptually, pilings allow water to continue to circulate and generally do not change the bottom elevation of the body of water.

The Corps traditionally maintained that activities other than filling that destroyed a wetland were not regulated by the CWA.[49] Thus, draining a wetland without depositing fill or dredging material from a wetland without depositing fill were not regulated activities. In August 1993 the Corps and the EPA changed their regulations to regulate activities such as dredging and draining. Such activities that have minimal movement of fill materials and incidental fallback (such as drippings from dredge buckets) but nonetheless result in a substantial change to the wetland (or other water body) now require a Section 404 permit.[50] This rule has been challenged in court.[51]

Permit Exemptions

The CWA exempts certain activities from the permit requirement. Most of the exemptions concern agriculture and silviculture practices.[52] Routine, ongoing farming activities, including growing crops in areas that might qualify as wetlands, fall under these exemptions. The courts have tended to construe the CWA exemptions narrowly.[53] For example, while many farming activities are exempt, converting a wetland to new farmland or other new agricultural use is not.[54] The exemptions are aimed at routine, ongoing activities, in contrast to major changes in use of the land.

A few of the exemptions pertain to general, nonagricultural construction. For example, the statute exempts activities conducted "for the purpose of construction of temporary sedimentation basins on a construction site which does not include placement of fill material into the navigable waters."[55] This does not mean that new drainage basins can be constructed in wetlands. It means that such temporarily wet construction basins may be constructed and destructed on dry land, notwithstanding the temporary wetland traits.

Maintenance and emergency repairs of structures such as dikes, dams, levees, groins, riprap, breakwaters, causeways, bridge abutments, and transportation structures also are exempted.[56] Again, this does not allow new construction but does permit maintenance of existing serviceable structures.

General or Nationwide Permits

If an activity is not exempt, it must have a permit. The Corps has regulations setting forth nationwide general permits,[57] which identify activities that can proceed without an individual permit, as long as the activity is carried out consistent with nationwide standards. Nationwide permits are essentially "permits by rule," designed for situations that the Corps has determined have minimal adverse effects, separately and cumulatively.[58] There are thirty-six nationwide permits established by the regulations. Corps district offices are authorized to develop general permits, effective for their districts, for activities with minimal impacts that may proceed without an individual permit.[59]

Nationwide permits are not exemptions. If a person believes that an activity is authorized by a nationwide permit, the conditions and standards for that activity must be observed carefully. Although one does not have to apply for a nationwide permit, certain nationwide permits require the filing with the Corps of a predischarge notification (PDN), providing extensive information about the planned discharge.[60] A wetland delineation must be filed along with the PDN, and the Corps may impose conditions on the application of the nationwide permit to a particular site. The Corps has authority to decide on a case-by-case basis that an activity otherwise subject to a nationwide permit requires an individual permit if there are significant environmental or other concerns.[61]

Several nationwide permits are pertinent to real estate with wetlands. For example, Nationwide Permit 12 authorizes utility line backfill and bedding. Required best management practices are set forth, including limits on what constitutes a utility line, how long the fill can remain in place, and the degree of disturbance allowed. Nationwide Permit 14 authorizes fill of less than one-third of an acre for road crossings. Best management practices are established, and a PDN, with a wetland delineation, is required.

Nationwide Permit 26 allows limited discharges to headwaters and isolated waters where up to ten acres will be impacted. For impacts between one and ten acres, a PDN, with a wetland delineation, is required. Headwaters are nontidal areas where flow is less than 5 cubic feet per second.[62] Nationwide Permit 26 can be used only once on a project; the Corps will not allow aggregated small fills under this permit.

Nationwide Permit 26 has long been subject to considerable controversy, as some environmental groups maintain that significant amounts of wetland acreage have been lost under this authorization. Although the Corps revised the nationwide permit regulations in 1991 and did not significantly change Permit 26,[63] the Corps is considering possible changes to this regulation.

General permits are similar to nationwide permits, except that they are issued by Corps districts for application in that district or a particular state. Owners of property containing wetlands should determine whether their Corps district has issued any general permits for the activities they seek to undertake.

Individual Permits

Obtaining a permit authorizing the filling of wetlands can be expensive and time-consuming[64] for a number of reasons. Permit applications are subject to public notice.[65] Mitigation will be required for any wetland filling that is allowed. Wetland habitat functions may prompt several different federal agencies to become involved in setting the permit terms. Thorough review of environmental impacts is required by the Corps's regulations and by the National Environmental Policy Act (NEPA). Moreover, looming over a Corps decision to issue a permit is the EPA's power to veto the permit on environmental grounds.[66] Knowing these obstacles in advance enables the property owner to plan development accordingly.[67]

Three sets of regulations apply to individual wetland permit applications. The Corps has regulations governing the application process[68] as well as separate regulations establishing substantive guidance for permit review, known as the "public interest" regulations.[69] The Corps also is bound by the EPA's regulations, which establish environmental considerations for Section 404, known as the 404(b)(1) guidelines.[70]

Information and Application Form

The Corps has a standard permit application form.[71] The applicant must provide a wetland delineation and enough information about the proposed activity to enable the Corps to assess the activity's probable impact. Permit applications are processed through informal notice and comment proceedings. The Corps provides public notice of a permit application when the application is complete. The Corps district engineer has discretion to determine whether to hold a hearing, and hearings are not trial-type.[72] The Corps generally relies on the applicant to respond to comments received on the permit application, and the applicant may take the initiative to address the concerns or objections of other persons.

Currently, the Corps is supposed to process routine permit applications within sixty days, although the deadline is frequently extended, particularly in the case of major projects.[73] Indeed, timely processing of wetland permits is a contentious policy issue.[74] The Clinton Administration has promised to modify the regulations to require permit decisions to be issued within ninety, rather than sixty, days in the apparent belief that the ninety-day deadline will be met in most cases, thus improving the process by reducing uncertainty.[75]

Interagency Consultation

The CWA contemplates interagency consultation with regard to wetland permits. Section 404(q) requires that the Corps enter into memoranda of agreement (MOA) with the EPA and several other agencies to minimize "duplication, needless paperwork, and delays in the issuance of permits" under Section 404.[76] The statute says these MOAs are designed to assure that permits can be issued no later than ninety days after publication of the public notice of the application. The Section 404(q) MOAs establish procedures and deadlines for elevation of disputes from the field level to the headquarters of each agency. In 1992 the Corps executed revised MOAs with the EPA, the FWS, and the NOAA, modifying the procedures for addressing disagreement between these agencies and the Corps. The 1992 MOAs distinguish between issues associated with particular permits and general policy issues, aiming to avoid situations in which permit applicants become hostages to interagency policy disputes. The Corps is the ultimate decision maker under Section 404(q).[77]

Substantive Environmental Standards

The Corps "public interest" regulations address the type of information concerning environmental impacts that a permit applicant must provide. These regulations cross-reference many other federal statutes that may apply to a particular permit application depending on the facts, such as the Endangered Species Act or the National Historic Preservation Act.[78] The burden on the permit applicant will vary, depending on the size and location of the wetlands as well as the surrounding environment.

The EPA Section 404(b)(1) guidelines establish rigorous environmental standards for wetland permits. The "practicable alternative" test in the Section 404(b)(1) guidelines provides that filling of wetlands cannot occur if there is a practicable alternative with less adverse impact on the aquatic ecosystem.[79] The burden is on the applicant to show that there are no practicable alternatives.[80] This provision has often been the subject of dispute between the Corps and other agencies, resulting in a number of Section 404(q) elevation decisions that provide guidance on the meaning of these regulations.[81]

The Section 404(b)(1) guidelines also classify wetlands as "special aquatic sites,"[82] for which there is a regulatory presumption of alternatives for non-water-dependent activities.[83] "Non-water-dependent activities" refers to projects that do not have to be located in or near water, such as housing or commercial facilities. Not only do the rules presume that there are alternative sites for these activities, but there also is a presumption that any alternative not in a special aquatic site is environmentally preferable. The applicant can overcome these presumptions only with a strong showing that the activity should be located in a wetland or that there are no practicable alternatives to locating in the wetland.

The Corps will review a permit application to ensure that the proposed development activity will not "cause or contribute to significant degradation of wetlands."[84] Appropriate steps must be taken to minimize adverse impacts. This effort is known as mitigation.[85] Mitigation involves a process known as "sequencing," or taking the following three steps in sequence:

- Avoiding damages
- Minimizing adverse impacts
- Compensating for unavoidable losses[86]

The applicant must consider modifying a project to avoid adverse impacts on wetlands and to minimize unavoidable impacts. When, and if, development on the condition of compensatory mitigation is authorized, the required mitigation may be on-site, if possible, or off-site. Off-site compensatory mitigation generally must be undertaken within the same watershed where the filling occurs. The amount of mitigation required by the Corps may be greater than a one-to-one acre ratio of harmed wetland acres to acres replaced, depending on the nature of the wetlands being destroyed. Some Corps districts presume at the outset that a greater than one-to-one ratio should be required.

State Water Quality Certification

Under Section 401 of the CWA a permit applicant must provide the Corps with a water quality certification from the state indicating that its proposed activity will comply with state water quality criteria. This can be a complete stopper—the Corps will not "second-guess" a state decision to deny a water quality certification.[87] The Section 401 water quality certification is separate from any other state regulation of wetlands that might apply to particular activities.

The EPA Veto Authority

The EPA has authority under Section 404(c) to "veto" a Corps permit decision if it finds the permit would have an "unacceptable adverse effect on municipal water supplies, shellfish beds and fishery areas . . . wildlife, or recreational areas."[88] The EPA's veto authority has been used infrequently,[89] but it is the source of great concern. An applicant for a major project may find that, even though the Corps is satisfied with a proposal, there can be extensive delay if the EPA is not. The EPA's regulations for Section 404(c) are procedural, describing the notice and comment procedure that the EPA will follow if it decides to exercise a veto.[90] As a substantive matter, the EPA can veto a permit on environmental grounds alone, without balancing any other factors.[91] In many cases, the veto decision involves the EPA applying the Section 404(b)(1) guidelines differently than the Corps, with the permit applicant suffering the burden of the interagency dispute.[92]

NEPA and Section 404 Permits

The Corps, like any federal agency, is subject to NEPA.[93] Permit decisions will require compliance with NEPA; however, this does not mean that every permit requires an environmental impact statement (EIS). In fact, the Corps has relatively few permit actions in any year that require an EIS. Nationwide permits were subject to NEPA review when the Corps issued the nationwide permit regulations. Thus, decisions concerning application of the nationwide permit rules to particular fills, such as review of a predischarge notification, should require no further NEPA investigation.

The Corps also has rules that categorically exclude from NEPA's scope certain routine activities that have a minimal impact on the environment.[94] Minor utility lines, minor maintenance dredging using existing disposal sites, and boat launching ramps are examples of activities categorically excluded from NEPA by the Corps.

Most Section 404 permit actions will be subject to an environmental assessment under NEPA. The environmental assessment, which often takes the form of a checklist, examines the overall environmental impact of an activity. If the activity in question does not cause significant impacts, the Corps will incorporate a Finding of No Significant Impact (FONSI) into its record of decision on the permit application.

Major projects may call for an EIS, in which case the permit process is likely to take a year or more. An EIS must include information about all environmental impacts potentially resulting from a project, identify alternatives to the project, and identify possible mitigation for the anticipated impacts. A draft EIS will be circulated for public comment, and the final EIS must contain the Corps's response to the public comments that are received.

NEPA does not require that the federal agency select the most environmentally protective alternative, only that the agency take a hard look at environmental consequences before it issues a permit and explain its reasoning in the record of decision. However, in the case of Section 404 permits, environmental problems identified in an EIS are likely also to be issues under the Section 404(b)(1) guidelines. Thus, the permit applicant whose project is subject to an EIS under NEPA may have to make adjustments based on the NEPA review because, while NEPA itself does not require the applicant to mitigate environmental consequences, the NEPA review may uncover issues that have to be dealt with to comply with Section 404. Amplification of NEPA and Section 404 permits is found in the Corps regulations and an extensive body of case law.[95]

Permit Transfers

Federal wetland permits may be transferred, subject to Corps notification.[96] The Corps standard permit conditions provide that if the property is sold, the new owner must sign the permit and a copy must be sent to the Corps. The transferee will sign a declaration as follows:

> When the structures or work authorized by this permit are still in existence at the time the property is transferred, the terms and conditions of this permit will continue to be binding on the new owner(s) of the property. To validate the transfer of this permit and the associated liabilities associated with compliance with its terms and conditions, have the transferee sign and date below.[97]

The regulations do not directly address any permit transfer other than in association with sale of the property. The rules, however, authorize modification of permits at the request of the permittee.[98] Transfer of the permit would be a modification of the named permittee, which the Corps could, in its discretion, allow.

Several states have construed their state wetland permits as running with the land rather than as personal holdings of the permittee.[99] These decisions view the wetland permits as equivalent to zoning variances and give the wetland permits the same legal effect as staying with the land. Of course, issues of state wetland permit transfers must be addressed by consulting the particular state's laws and cases.

Is There Any Enforcement Concern?

The enforcement tools for prosecuting wetlands violations are strong and numerous. Far and away the greatest amount of enforcement involves filling or altering a wetland without a permit. Although often the landowner is unaware that certain lands are wetlands, wetlands violations have been subject to severe penalties in recent years. To achieve lasting protection of wetlands, the government may require the placement of a real estate restriction, such as a conservation easement, on the property. In this manner, consequences of wetlands enforcement may run with the land.

The Enforcement Arsenal

The CWA authorizes enforcement with administrative orders,[100] administrative penalties,[101] judicial civil actions seeking remedies and penalties,[102] and criminal actions.[103] In most cases, the first enforcement document a person sees is a Corps "cease-and-desist letter," informing the landowner of a violation and directing him or her to stop. Sometimes the notice letter is styled a Notice of Violation, and it may come from the EPA. More formal enforcement steps could follow, such as an administrative complaint. The CWA authorizes civil penalties of up to $25,000 per day, while criminal sanctions include fines of up to $25,000 for misdemeanor negligence crimes, fines of up to $250,000 for felonies, and incarceration. The level of penalties and fines has increased in recent years, and wetlands violators have served time in federal prison. The statute also authorizes citizen enforcement actions, in which injunctions and civil penalties may be awarded at the request of private individuals or associations.[104]

The CWA imposes strict liability for violations, which means that the defendant is liable for his or her actions regardless of intent.[105] The prosecutor only has to prove that the defendant committed the prohibited act (the filling), not that the defendant knew that it was wrong. There are no statutory defenses, as provided for in some other federal laws.[106] The government generally enforces not only to punish a violator but also to obtain injunctive relief to stop a violation, to restore the environment to its prefill status, and to "send a message" that will deter other violations. Comprehensive injunctions requiring restoration and mitigation have been entered by courts.[107]

The U.S. Supreme Court has held that defendants in civil wetlands enforcement actions have the right to a jury trial.[108] The jury may decide liability for civil penalties, but the court decides equitable issues such as whether to impose an injunctive remedy. The court also decides the amount of the civil penalty.[109] A jury is always available to the criminally charged defendant.

Enforcement consequences are personal to the defendant. As a general matter, a wetlands enforcement order operates against named persons and does not run with the land. However, the government may file a lien against real property as part of its enforcement action. In addition, recordation of property restrictions may be made part of the permanent remedy.[110]

Who Can Be Held Liable?

Any person involved with illegal filling can be liable for a CWA violation.[111] For criminal violations, this specifically includes any responsible corporate officer,[112] a term that generally covers the line of supervision up through a company. Persons held liable for wetlands violations include the owner of the property, a nonowner who discharges fill, and the contractors (or other personnel) conducting the filling. Consulting and design engineers involved in illegal filling also have been held liable.[113]

For the most part, violations of wetlands laws are personal to the violator and do not run with the land. Remember that the CWA prohibits the act of discharging fill without a permit. The actor who conducts the illegal filling is the one who commits the violation. Thus, subsequent purchasers of land on which wetlands have been filled would not be violating the CWA (unless they did additional filling).

There is only one reported case in which a subsequent purchaser was required to continue the removal of illegal fill placed by a predecessor in title. In *United States v. Norris*,[114] a bank acquired by foreclosure (after default on a note) property on which an illegal levee had been constructed. The prior landowner had settled his enforcement problems by agreeing to take out the levee, but he had not completed the work. With the levee removed, the property had a much lower value, so the bank claimed it was an innocent purchaser that should not have to respond to the prior owner's violation. Impressed more by the fact that the bank did not investigate the property and its illegalities before it gave the mortgage than by the enforcement structure of the CWA, the court required the bank to allow the removal of the levee. The court stated: "If the bank lent more than a quarter of a million dollars without inspecting the property . . . the bank acted imprudently. It acted no less imprudently . . . if it saw the new levee and failed to satisfy itself that the necessary permit had been issued."[115]

Another private, subsequent purchaser, who unhappily found a number of undisclosed environmental problems, including illegal filling of wetlands, on land purchased for $1.2 million, was not able to use the citizen enforcement section of the CWA to recover against the seller. In *Brossman Sales, Inc. v. Broderick*,[116] the court followed Supreme Court precedent[117] and held that a violation actionable under the CWA citizen suit section requires that the violator be "in violation" at the time of the suit. The seller in *Brossman Sales*, who no longer owned the land, was no longer filling or conducting actions "in violation." The purchaser was thus left to contend with the consequences of the seller's actions, which not only diminished the value of the property but also required remediation because of continued contamination problems.

Norris and *Brossman Sales* may indicate the future trends in wetlands enforcement litigation. In cases like these, illegal wetland fill is a substantial concern for land purchasers. Although subsequent purchasers of land are not the ones placing the fill, the government may engage in creative efforts to hold them liable for remedying prior violations. In addition, the buyer may find he or she cannot use the CWA to pursue illegal actions committed by the seller. Even between purchaser and seller, as wetland conditions are incorporated into the process of transactional due diligence, wetlands violations as well as wetland conditions could play a major role in the deal.

Making Lemonade: Protecting and Recouping Investments

So what's the good news for those who have wetland property? There are remedies and opportunities for wetlands owners. The courts provide some avenues for relief. Most government decisions about wetlands can, eventually, be appealed, and a small but emerging body of case law recognizes a compensation remedy for the landowner when regulations prevent all economic use of property. While litigation can be tough, citizens can take on the government in court and prevail.

The court of public opinion offers other avenues for relief. As the country becomes more sensitive to environmental needs, the value of wetlands in their natural state grows. This makes development that accommodates wetlands more attractive and valuable. Wetlands left undeveloped may provide valuable recreational property for hunting, fishing, and bird watching. Enhancing and restoring wetlands to preserve diverse natural communities can also be profitable if community conditions support development of a wetland mitigation bank.

Challenging Government Regulatory Decisions

Final actions by the Corps or the EPA concerning wetlands may be challenged in court. With the exception of an EPA administrative enforcement order, the CWA does not have an explicit judicial review provision for Section 404 decisions.[118] Rather, government wetland actions are reviewed in U.S. district courts under the general "federal question" jurisdiction of 28 U.S.C. Section 1331 and are measured by the "arbitrary and capricious" standard of the Administrative Procedure Act.[119]

At the time of this writing, the Corps regulations do not provide for any administrative appeal of either wetland delineations or permit decisions. However, the Corps was developing changes to its regulations to establish an administrative appeal system,[120] including having the administrative appeal available for permit decisions. However, the government's position on appeal of wetland jurisdictional delineations had not been settled as of press time. Another major issue for the administrative appeals is whether anyone other than the permit applicant, such as citizen's groups or permit opponents, should be authorized to bring an administrative appeal. Again as of this writing, the Corps's position is that only the applicant should be able to appeal a permit decision. All of these issues, including the Corps response to public comments, will have to be resolved in the Corps regulations.

A Corps decision to issue or deny a permit may be reviewed in a federal district court. When a permit is issued, the applicant's acceptance (signing) constitutes acceptance of all conditions.[121] Therefore, a permit seeker who is unsatisfied with some or all proposed permit conditions must decline to take the permit to challenge the Corps's decision. Persons other than the applicant also may bring suit to challenge issuance of a Corps permit. Thus, a citizen's group or any other party may challenge a Corps permit in court. Generally the permit holder also will be sued or will seek to intervene in the suit to protect his or her permit. The EPA Section 404(c) veto decisions, when final, are also subject to review in federal district courts.

Judicial challenges can be very costly, and several factors counsel that the permit applicant think very carefully before bringing a lawsuit against the federal government. The government's regulatory action will be reviewed on the basis of the administrative record made before the lawsuit.[122] This means that the plaintiff generally will not obtain a trial *de novo* or be allowed to introduce witnesses and evidence to the reviewing court. Naturally, this requires the permit applicant or other interested party to make sure that the administrative record is complete by submitting all necessary information to the Corps in writing while the permit is pending.

Second, the arbitrary and capricious standard of review favors the government. It means that a Corps or EPA decision can be set aside only if it lacks a reasonable basis or is otherwise not in compliance with governing law. There is room for the exercise of considerable discretion and judgment by the government before a decision will be struck down. It is difficult to get a court to reverse a government decision under this standard, even if the decision does not make much sense.

In addition, the reviewing court has limited remedies, since the court does not have the power to issue the permit. Instead, the court can "set aside" unlawful action but must remand the matter to the agency so that the agency can decide what action to take.[123] Private parties need to be sensitive to the fact that even if they "win" in court against the Corps or the EPA, they will find themselves facing that same federal agency for another round of administrative proceedings. Furthermore, the government can make the same decision a second time, giving itself stronger support on the record.

Finally, it is important to remember that judicial review is available only for *final* agency action. The government has successfully argued that certain Corps actions are not final, even though they may have heavy impacts on a property owner. Thus, the courts have held that judicial review is not immediately available for cease-and-desist letters or other enforcement notices.[124] Wetland delineations by the Corps also are not immediately reviewable,[125] although that may change if the Corps allows an administrative appeal of wetland delineations in its anticipated regulations.

The Compensation Remedy for Takings

In certain instances, the government denial of a Section 404 permit may so deprive a landowner of the economic value of property that the action will constitute a taking of property compensable under the Constitution. The Fifth Amendment provides that "no . . . private property [shall] be taken for public use without just compensation."[126] This "takings clause" protects private property owners from the physical appropriation of their land. In recent years, courts and commentators have investigated the prospect that government regulation may go so far as to be the equivalent of a physical taking warranting compensation. There remains considerable uncertainty in the regulatory takings case law.

A takings claim is not a defense to Section 404 or wetlands enforcement.[127] Rather, the property owner must comply with the CWA but may pursue the money remedy. The government is not required to stop its enforcement action because it causes a taking, but it must pay compensation. Exclusive jurisdiction for takings claims over $10,000 is in the U.S. Court of Federal Claims (formerly Claims Court), sitting in Washington, D.C.[128] Generally a takings claim is not ripe for adjudication until the government has made a final determination concerning restrictions on the property. For example, a wetland delineation alone is not likely to support a takings claim, since the property owner might be able to develop some or all of the property by obtaining a permit.

The wetlands regulatory program has been a focus of the takings discussion because approximately 70 percent of the nation's remaining wetlands are on private property. Notwithstanding this fact, there have been relatively few wetlands taking cases brought, and those decisions split almost fifty-fifty between awards to landowners and victories by the government. Of course, wetland regulation is not the only government regulation being addressed in takings litigation. The property owner contemplating a takings remedy must evaluate other contemporary takings decisions in addition to the wetlands cases.

Regulatory takings cases involving a variety of public health regulatory programs had resulted in a judicial takings test balancing the economic harm (loss) to the citizen against the legitimate governmental interests advanced by the regulation.[129] The Supreme Court had already recognized that wetland regulation could constitute a taking[130] before its landmark decision in *Lucas v. South Carolina Coastal Council*,[131] which brought substantial publicity to the regulatory takings arena. In *Lucas*, a property owner who was denied permission to build on a coastal lot, as a result of coastal protection laws enacted after he bought his land, was held to have a right to compensation. While its impact is hotly debated in legal circles, *Lucas* held that where there is a total deprivation of economic use of property, there must be compensation, unless the proposed use was prohibited by the existing law at the time the land was acquired. Ongoing takings litigation will establish the nuances and bounds of these standards.

In the wetlands cases, the government defeated most early takings claims.[132] Since the mid-1980s, however, takings have been found in four cases involving denial of a Section 404 permit. The only one of these cases that is final is *Formanek v. United States*,[133] where a complete taking of the property was found as a result of denial of a Section 404 permit.

Other wetlands takings cases, in various stages of litigation, reflect a range of outcomes. One well-known wetlands takings case, *Florida Rock Industries v. United States*, has been in litigation for over fourteen years, and twice has gone to the Court of Appeals.[134] Florida Rock sought and was denied a permit to dig limestone in 98 acres of its 1,560-acre wetland but has yet to see a penny of compensation. *Loveladies Harbor, Inc. v. United States*[135] involved the denial of a Section 404 permit to develop homesites on approximately 12 acres, which were part of an original 250-acre parcel, most of which had been developed and sold before the CWA took effect. A taking was found, and the trial court awarded Loveladies compensation of $2.5 million plus interest. The U.S. Court of Appeals for the Federal Circuit, after entering a decision on jurisdiction,[136] subsequently affirmed the award.[137] The Court of Federal Claims found a permit denial to be a taking in *Bowles v. United States*,[138] and it is not clear at this point whether there will be an appeal. The same court found no taking from a Section 404 permit denial in *Plantation Landing Resort v. United States*.[139] Finally, the same court held that the EPA's veto of a permit did not constitute a taking in *Creppel v. United States*[140] on the grounds that the suit was filed too late.

Issues other than permit denials arise in the takings arena. For example, delay in issuing a Section 404 permit, even a delay of several years, was held by the Federal Circuit not to constitute a compensable taking in *Tabb Lakes v. United States*.[141] In addition, Section 404 permits may incorporate certain conditions such as a requirement that the permit holder compensate for the destruction of wetlands. These kinds of compensatory conditions may be influenced by another regulatory takings lawsuit from Oregon recently decided by the U.S. Supreme Court. In *Dolan v. City of Tigard*,[142] the Court held that the city's dedication requirements, which conditioned authorization of expansion of a store and parking lot on dedication of a public greenway and bike path, constituted a taking of property without compensation. The court held that permit conditions must have an "essential nexus" to the subject of the permit. If there is no such nexus, the condition may be a compensable taking.

The checkered pattern of wetlands takings litigation provides several practical lessons. First, it is time-consuming and expensive to bring a takings action. The property owner must be prepared to wait years to obtain compensation. However, the government must pay interest on that award from the time of the taking, which, in the Section 404 context, generally will be the time of the agency's denial of the permit. Recently, the Court of Federal Claims held in *Bowles v. United States* that this interest is compound interest, not simple interest.[143]

Second, the rules of the game remain unsettled. Although a number of judges on the Court of Federal Claims are quite willing to award compensation for regulatory takings, until recently the Federal Circuit did not routinely uphold those decisions. The takings litigant enters into a world of great uncertainty, in which a particular judge may determine the outcome as much as anything else. Moreover, the government will stay in the case for the long haul, as reflected in the many years that the *Florida Rock* and *Loveladies Harbor* cases have been litigated.

Although the constitutional remedy for a taking has been defined largely by the courts, the executive and legislative branches have become interested in the protection for private property afforded by the Fifth Amendment. In 1988 President Reagan signed the so-called "Takings Executive Order,"[144] which was intended to make federal agencies aware of the potential that their actions would result in a monetary award of compensation. To achieve this, the agencies were to prepare a "takings implication assessment" (TIA) for their actions. However, there was no private remedy under the executive order, and the possibility of causing a taking did not seem to change government behavior when the Reagan executive order was in effect. Thus, as a practical matter for the property owner, the status of the executive order is of minimal importance.

Congress also has weighed in on the takings issue, with a number of members supporting various bills that would provide remedies for perceived regulatory takings of private property. For example, some of the bills introduced to amend the CWA wetlands provisions have included compensation remedies for private owners of wetlands. Rep. Jimmy Hayes (D-La.) introduced legislation that would, among other features, establish a classification system for wetlands and guarantee compensation to landowners of "high" value wetlands that could not be developed.[145] Remedies for interference with private property rights have also received considerable attention in other recent environmental legislation.[146] In the 104th Congress, takings legislation was introduced as part of the "Contract with America." As of this writing, no takings legislation has been enacted.

Private Remedies in Wetlands Transactions

There are no special rights or remedies between buyer and seller in circumstances involving property with wetlands. The purchaser of such property may use any of the existing remedies that ameliorate the otherwise applicable principle of caveat emptor. Federal wetlands law provides no such remedies, but it is possible that state environmental disclosure laws may.

Generally, states that have laws requiring sellers to identify or disclose "environmental conditions" on property before sale do not include wetlands as an "environmental condition." In addition, wetlands may not be automatically included as part of an environmental audit or otherwise as part of any environmental disclosure requirements of real estate sales contracts. A purchaser should determine whether the property contains wetlands; whether there were any alterations or filling of wetlands within the past five years; whether there are or were any wetland permits applicable to the property; and whether there has been any wetlands enforcement action in connection with the property. The purchaser should ensure that this information is explicitly disclosed in the sales contract as part of the seller's representations and warranties. It should be included as an "environmental condition" that the buyer can cite as a reason to walk away from the sale.

The few federal cases that have addressed the matter indicate that the buyer of land that contains wetlands will be charged with knowledge of the condition of the land. *Norris*, for example, provides the Sixth Circuit's view that a prudent purchaser will have investigated the site before purchase. This standard for a prudent purchaser's knowledge of environmental conditions is derived from situations and cases involving other conditions visible on reasonable inspection. To the extent that a buyer tries to argue that wetlands constitute a serious condition impacting property value, that buyer will be held to a standard of due diligence with respect to inspection before sale.

The buyer must approach the transaction with this in mind. The contract should include wetlands within the definition of the "environmental conditions" for which an inspection will be conducted. The due diligence environmental audit should include wetlands as an item to be identified and preliminarily delineated by the auditor. This may create difficulties for some companies that perform environmental audits, since their personnel may not be trained in wetland delineation. Traditionally, wetlands environmental consulting has been a specialty area marked by a few small firms. Increasingly, however, the larger, "full service" consultants have developed the capacity to identify wetlands. In land transactions in "wet" locations, or where the wetland delineation is critical to the value of the parcel, a buyer should hire a qualified wetland delineator rather than relying on general environmental auditors or surveyors.

While wetlands consultants to date have not been singled out for liability, there is an emerging body of case law holding environmental consultants liable for errors in their studies or reports.[147] If wetland identification is part of the consultant's duties, failure to identify the wetlands properly could subject the consultant to a claim for damages by the purchaser.

Of course, the precise language of any contract provisions addressing wetlands will depend on and be tailored to the nature of the property and the buyer's objectives for the purchase. Unlike some environmental matters, however, there are no federal (and few state) statutory protections for the buyer in transactions involving wetlands, so the buyer must protect himself or herself with appropriate contract terms.

Utilizing Wetlands as Wetlands

Wetlands have important value in their natural state because they perform significant functions relating to water purification, flood control, wildlife habitat, and recreation. As society becomes increasingly aware of these benefits, developers, rather than attempting major alterations of nature, are adjusting their development plans to coexist with natural features of a parcel. The resulting properties often have enhanced aesthetic attributes, which translates into increased value and prices.

There is no single source of information on development projects that were subject to federal wetlands laws but employed wetlands preservation strategies from the inception. The Urban Land Institute, however, has published a monograph describing a number of successful projects that have integrated wetland planning.[148] For example, there are instances in which construction was planned around greenways, including wetlands, to provide wildlife habitat corridors and run-off basins. In other locations, development was authorized to destroy some wetlands but the developer replaced those areas with enhanced and expanded wetlands elsewhere on the parcel. The local and national Home Builders' Associations also have monographs and other materials describing land developments that used wetlands and were both environmental and economic successes.

Local zoning ordinances and state law must be consulted to determine what impact using wetlands as community greenways will have on the developable density of a parcel. Some state laws require buffer zones near wetlands, significantly reducing the areas available for development. Even though it may be a complicated route through the various applicable laws, many developers find it more profitable to plan to use the wetlands in a natural state rather than to try to obtain a federal permit to fill them.

In some communities, wetland mitigation banking may be a profitable use for large wetland parcels. A wetland mitigation bank is a location that is available to satisfy a requirement under a Section 404 permit for off-site compensatory mitigation. The bank generally is a restored or enhanced wetland (previously degraded in some manner). The developer of a wetland mitigation bank sells credits; purchasers of credits are other persons who are allowed by a Section 404 permit to fill their wetlands if they perform mitigation elsewhere.

Mitigation banking can be used by a single entity as a source of wetland mitigation for a variety of planned future activities. For example, state highway administrations have developed wetland mitigation banks in anticipation of their long-term needs for highway development. The Home Builders' Associations in some states have provided wetland mitigation banks to serve members. Other mitigation banks have been developed by entrepreneurs planning to sell credits on the open market. For example, the Florida Wetlands Bank is a private company operating an entrepreneurial wetland mitigation bank in Broward County, Florida.[149] Any Corps district office should be able to tell landowners if there are wetland mitigation banks within their locale.

The Corps and the EPA have issued a policy providing guidance to their field offices on wetland mitigation banking.[150] It provides interim guidance until the agencies issue a formal guidance document, subject to public notice and comment. Under the interim policy, mitigation banks are encouraged as ecologically advantageous over smaller, isolated wetland mitigation habitats. The interim policy statement lists various considerations for wetland mitigation banks, including: location; goals and objectives of the project; development and maintenance plans; systems for allocating credits; monitoring requirements; adequate funding; and perpetual maintenance.

Conclusion

Wetlands law as it exists at this writing must be viewed as unsettled, and it should be analyzed with care by property owners and their counsel. Comprehensive changes to Section 404 were under consideration by both houses of Congress in 1995, and significant amendments were passed by the House.[151] Depending on the outcome of that legislative effort, wetlands regulation could become either more strict or more favorable to private landowners. Thus, when dealing with wetlands, it is always a good practice for the real estate lawyer to stay abreast of regulatory and legislative developments, including those that may occur between the contract execution and settlement.

Wetland regulation can severely affect real estate development. As with other aspects of a land transaction, knowledge is the key. A developer, and his or her lawyer, should make it a point to learn about the possible wetland areas on a parcel and should plan a purchase accordingly. Remember that wetland regulation is a specialized area that historically has not been addressed in most Phase I environmental audits. Wetlands should be part of the purchaser's "contract checklist" and should be considered when drafting the sales agreement, contracting for the due diligence audit, conducting site inspections, and closing the sale.

If you learn too late about a wetland, like the builder in the opening paragraph of this chapter, don't give in to your instinct to throw the Corps and the EPA investigators off your property. The landowners who are guided by anger become the names in the cases held up as examples of record fines, penalties, and jail time. Make sure that your name is cited only as an example of success in working with wetlands.

Notes

1. 33 U.S.C. § 1344.

2. The Corps runs the regulatory program in a decentralized manner, with day-to-day operations arising in the thirty-eight Corps district offices. *See*

Margaret Strand, FEDERAL WETLANDS LAW ch. 17, WETLANDS DESKBOOK at 89–93 (Environmental Law Institute 1993).

3. The EPA runs its wetland programs out of its ten regional offices. *See id.* at 95–96.

4. The Fish and Wildlife Service has eight regional offices. *See id.* at 97–98.

5. 33 C.F.R. § 325.1(b).

6. 33 U.S.C. § 1311(a).

7. 33 U.S.C. § 1362(12).

8. 33 U.S.C. § 1362(7).

9. *See, e.g.*, Natural Resources Defense Council, Inc. v. Callaway, 392 F. Supp. 685 (D.D.C. 1975), which required that the definition be extended beyond traditionally navigable waters. The expansion was phased in, as provided for in 1977 regulations. 42 Fed. Reg. 37,122 (1977).

10. 33 C.F.R. § 328.3.

11. *See* United States v. Riverside Bayview Homes, Inc., 474 U.S. 121 (1985).

12. Leslie Salt Co. v. United States, 896 F.2d 354 (9th Cir. 1990), *cert. denied*, 498 U.S. 1126 (1991), *on remand. reconsideration denied*, 820 F. Supp. 478 (N.D. Cal. 1992); Swanson v. United States, 789 F.2d 1368 (9th Cir. 1986).

13. United States v. DeFelice, 641 F.2d 1169, 1175 (5th Cir. 1981), *cert. denied*, 454 U.S. 940 (1981).

14. Track 12, Inc. v. District Eng'r, 618 F. Supp. 448, 449 (D. Minn. 1985).

15. United States v. Bradshaw, 541 F. Supp. 880, 883 (D. Md. 1981).

16. Wieszmann v. District Eng'r, 526 F.2d 1302 (5th Cir. 1976).

17. Quivira Mining Co. v. United States EPA, 765 F.2d 126 (10th Cir. 1985), *cert. denied*, 474 U.S. 1055 (1986); United States v. Phelps Dodge Corp., 391 F. Supp. 1181 (D. Ariz. 1975).

18. There has been litigation over the federal authority to regulate isolated wetlands. *See* Hoffman Homes, Inc. v. United States EPA, 961 F.2d 1310 (7th Cir. 1992), *vacated, reh'g granted*, 975 F.2d 1554 (7th Cir. 1992), *supplemental op.*, 999 F.2d 256 (7th Cir. 1993); Leslie Salt Co. v. United States, 896 F.2d 354 (9th Cir. 1990), *cert. denied*, 498 U.S. 1126 (1991), *on remand, reconsideration denied*, 820 F. Supp. 478 (N.D. Cal. 1992); Tabb Lakes, Ltd. v. United States, 715 F. Supp. 726 (E.D. Va. 1988), *aff'd without op.*, 885 F.2d 866 (4th Cir. 1989), *reported in full*, 30 Env't Rep. Cas. (BNA) 1510 (4th Cir. 1989).

19. 33 C.F.R. § 328.3(a)(3).

20. *See* Memorandum from Francis S. Blake, General Counsel, U.S. EPA, to Richard E. Sanderson, Acting Assistant Administrator, Office of External Affairs (Clean Water Act jurisdiction over isolated waters) (Sept. 12, 1985), *reprinted in* Environmental Law Institute, WETLANDS DESKBOOK (1993).

21. Tabb Lakes, Ltd. v. United States, 715 F. Supp. 726 (E.D. Va. 1988), *aff'd without op.*, 885 F.2d 866 (4th Cir. 1989), *reported in full*, 30 Env't. Rep. Cas. (BNA) 1510 (4th Cir. 1989).

22. Hoffman Homes, Inc. v. United States EPA, 961 F.2d 1310 (7th Cir. 1992), *vacated, reh'g granted*, 975 F.2d 1554 (7th Cir. 1992), *supplemental op.*, 999 F.2d 256 (7th Cir. 1993).

23. Leslie Salt Co. v. United States, 896 F.2d 354 (9th Cir. 1990), *cert. denied*, 498 U.S. 1126 (1991), *on remand, reconsideration denied*, 820 F. Supp. 478 (N.D. Cal. 1992).

24. Hoffman Homes, Inc. v. United States EPA, 999 F.2d 256 (7th Cir. 1993).

25. Village of Oconomowoc Lake v. Dayton Hudson Corp., No. 93-3380, 1994 U.S. App. LEXIS 11263 (7th Cir. May 18, 1994).

26. 33 C.F.R. § 328.3(b); 40 C.F.R. §§ 230.3(t), 232.2(r).

27. The Supreme Court eloquently captured the dilemma of wetlands identification in its landmark decision upholding the federal authority to regulate wetlands:

> Our common experience tells us that [wetlands delineation] is no easy task: the transition from water to solid ground is not necessarily or even typically an abrupt one. Rather, between open waters and dry land may lie shallows, marshes, mudflats, swamps, bogs—in short, a huge array of areas that are not wholly aquatic but nevertheless fall far short of being dry land. Where on this continuum to find the limit of "waters" is far from obvious.

United States v. Riverside Bayview Homes, Inc., 474 U.S. 121 (1985).

28. 16 U.S.C. § 3801(a)(16).

29. The agricultural programs are described more fully in Strand, *supra* note 1, at ch. 11.

30. Development of a wetland delineation manual has been very controversial in recent years. In 1989, the Corps, EPA, FWS, and SCS issued a *Joint Manual for Wetland Delineation*, to reduce differences in the methods applied by the four federal agencies. This 1989 manual was criticized as expanding the definition of wetlands, bringing extensive new acreage within the regulatory program. After policy level review, proposed revisions to the delineation manual were published in 1991. 56 Fed. Reg. 40,446 (1991). This proposal was criticized for lacking scientific foundation and for eliminating vast areas from wetlands regulations. Finally, Congress directed that the Corps continue to use its 1987 manual, Energy and Water Development Appropriations Act, Pub. L. No. 102-04, 105 Stat. 510 (1991); Energy and Water Development Appropriations Act, Pub. L. No. 102-377, 106 Stat. 1315 (1992), and that the National Academy of Sciences conduct a study of the scientific bases for wetland delineation, Departments of Veterans Affairs and Housing and Urban Development, and Independent Agencies Appropriations Act, Pub. L. No. 102-389, 106 Stat. 1571 (1992).

31. Envtl. Lab. for Dep't of the Army, Technical Report Y-87-1, Corps of Eng'rs Wetlands Delineation Manual (1987), *reprinted in* WETLANDS DESKBOOK at 495 (Jan. 1993).

32. The Hydrophytic Plant List segregates plants based on the likelihood of a plant occurring in a wetland. The categories are:

Obligate Wetland Plants	= OBL	= 99% in wetlands
Facultative Wetland	= FACW	= 67% to 99% in wetlands
Facultative	= FAC	= 33% to 67% in wetlands
Facultative Upland	= FACU	= 1% to < 33% in wetlands
Obligate Upland Plants	= UPL	= < 1% in wetlands

33. The NRCS, formerly the SCS, maintains the official list of hydric soils and their characteristics, developed by the National Technical Committee for Hydric Soils. This list may be obtained from the NRCS, P.O. Box 2890, Washington, D.C. 20013.

34. As described within, the commonly used Nationwide Permit 26 requires submission of a wetland delineation.

35. 33 C.F.R. § 325.9.

36. *See* WILLIAM L. WANT, LAW OF WETLANDS REGULATION § 4.02[3]–4.02[4] (Clark Boardman Callaghan, envtl. law series release #5, June 1994).

37. Regulatory Guidance Letter 90-06 (Aug. 14, 1990), *reprinted in* 57 Fed. Reg. 6591 (1992).

38. *See* 57 Fed. Reg. 62,312 (1992).

39. For example, Rutgers University includes several courses on wetland management, including Methodology of Delineating Wetlands, Hydric Soils, Plant Identification for Wetland Delineation, and others, as part of its Cook College Short Courses in Environmental Management. Other universities around the country offer similar courses of one to three days.

40. *See supra* note 5.

41. 40 C.F.R. § 230.80.

42. 16 U.S.C. §§ 1451–64.

43. Regulatory Guidance Letter 92-3 (Aug. 19, 1992), *reprinted in* 58 Fed. Reg. 17,219 (1993).

44. 33 U.S.C. § 1344(a).

45. 33 C.F.R. § 323.2(e). The EPA's definition is similarly broad, 40 C.F.R. § 232.2(i).

46. Avoyelles Sportsmen's League, Inc. v. Marsh, 715 F.2d 897 (5th Cir. 1983), *later proceeding*, 786 F.2d 631 (5th Cir. 1986).

47. United States v. Sinclair Oil Co., 767 F. Supp. 200 (D. Mont. 1990); United States v. Zanger, 767 F. Supp. 1030 (N.D. Cal. 1991).

48. 58 Fed. Reg. 45,008, at 45,038 (1993) (to be codified at 33 C.F.R. pt. 232.2).

49. Save Our Community v. United States EPA, 741 F. Supp. 605 (N.D. Tex. 1990), *rev'd*, 971 F.2d 1155 (5th Cir. 1992); Salt Pond Associates v. United States Army Corps of Engineers, 815 F. Supp. 766 (D. Del. 1993).

50. *See* 58 Fed. Reg. 45,008 (1993).

51. American Mining Congress v. United States Army Corps of Eng'rs, Civ. No. 93-1754 (D.D.C. filed Aug. 24, 1993).

52. 33 U.S.C. § 1344(f)(1)(A), (C), (E). *See also* 33 C.F.R. § 323.4, the Corps regulations addressing the exemptions.

53. United States v. Akers, 785 F.2d 814, 819 (9th Cir. 1986), *cert. denied*, 479 U.S. 828 (1986); United States v. Huebner, 752 F.2d 1235, 1240–41 (7th Cir. 1985), *cert. denied*, 474 U.S. 817 (1985).

54. Hobbs v. United States, 947 F.2d 941 (4th Cir. 1991), *cert. denied*, 112 S. Ct. 2274 (1992).

55. 33 U.S.C. § 1344(f)(1)(D).

56. 33 U.S.C. § 1344 (f)(l)(B).

57. 33 U.S.C. § 1344(e); 33 C.F.R. pt. 330.

58. 33 U.S.C. § 1344(e).

59. 33 C.F.R. § 325.2(e)(2).

60. 33 C.F.R. pt. 330 app. A(C)(13)(e).

61. 33 C.F.R. § 330.4(e)(2). *See* Riverside Irrigation Dist. v. Andrews, 758 F.2d 508 (10th Cir. 1985).

62. 33 C.F.R § 330.2(d).

63. 56 Fed. Reg. 59,110 (1991).

64. This chapter only summarizes the individual permit process, hitting some of the highlights in a general fashion. Shepherding an application through the permit process requires careful and thorough review of the pertinent regulations, regulatory guidance letters, memoranda of agreement, and prior decisions of the Corps and of the Courts.

65. In addition to individual permits, the Corps may also issue a "letter of permission," which is an individual authorization for an activity, issued in a more abbreviated fashion than an individual permit. 33 C.F.R. §§ 325.2(e)(1), 325.5(b)(2). Letters of permission involve interagency coordination and review under the regulations but do not involve publication of notice to the public.

66. The Corps issued a regulatory guidance letter in 1992 reiterating that it was responsible for permit decisions and that other agencies had only consulting roles, except when the EPA exercises its veto power. Federal Agencies Roles and Responsibilities, Regulatory Guidance Letter 92-1 (May 13, 1992), *reprinted in* 59 Fed. Reg. 5182, 5183 (1994).

67. Some examples of major real estate developments that incorporated wetlands into the planning are described in DAVID SALVESEN, WETLANDS: MITIGATING AND REGULATING DEVELOPMENT IMPACTS (Urban Land Institute 2d ed. 1994).

68. 33 C.F.R. pt. 325.

69. 33 C.F.R. pt. 320.

70. 40 C.F.R. pt. 230. Although referred to as guidelines, the EPA's standards are binding regulations.

71. ENG Form 4345. A $100 fee must be paid for commercial projects, and a $10 fee for noncommercial activities.

72. Buttrey v. United States, 690 F.2d 1170 (5th Cir. 1982), *cert. denied*, 461 U.S. 927 (1983).

73. 33 C.F.R. § 325.2.

74. One study of the Corps permit program found that the average time to process permits was 373 days and that 93 percent of the individual permit applications exceeded the 60-day standard. V. Albrecht and B. Goode, *Wetland Regulation in the Real World* (Beveridge & Diamond, Feb. 1994). The Corps and the EPA maintain that this report is not accurate. Letter from John H. Zirchky, Acting Assistant Secretary of the Army, and Robert Perciasepe, Assistant Administrator for Water, to Senator Max Baucus (Mar. 29, 1994).

75. WHITE HOUSE OFFICE ON ENVTL. POLICY, PROTECTING AMERICA'S WETLANDS: A FAIR, FLEXIBLE, AND EFFECTIVE APPROACH 6 (Aug. 24, 1993).

76. 33 U.S.C. § 1344(q).

77. These Section 404(q) MOAs are reproduced in the WETLANDS DESKBOOK (1993), *supra* note 2.

78. *See* 33 C.F.R. pt. 320.

79. 40 C.F.R. § 230.10(a).

80. The practicable alternatives test of the 404(b)(1) guidelines has been often litigated and should be approached with caution. *See, e.g.*, Bersani v. Robichaud, 850 F.2d 36 (2d Cir. 1988), *cert. denied*, Bersani v. United States EPA,

489 U.S. 1089 (1989), and *cert. denied*, Robichaud v. United States EPA, 489 U.S. 1089 (1989); Borough of Ridgefield v. United States Army Corps of Eng'rs, [1990] 20 Envtl. L. Rep. (Envtl. L. Inst.) 21,387 (D.N.J. July 2, 1990).

81. These Corps decisions are reprinted in the WETLANDS DESKBOOK, *supra* note 2.

82. 40 C.F.R. § 230.41.

83. 40 C.F.R. § 230.10(a)(3).

84. 40 C.F.R. § 230.10(c).

85. 40 C.F.R. § 230.10(d).

86. Memorandum of Agreement Regarding Determination of Mitigation under the Clean Water Act § 404(b)(1) guidelines, effective Feb. 7, 1990, U.S. EPA-U.S. Dep't of the Army, *reprinted in* WETLANDS DESKBOOK; *supra* note 73, at 331. See Municipality of Anchorage v. United States, 32 Env't Rep. Cas. (BNA) 1199 (D. Alaska Oct. 15, 1990), *aff'd*, Avella v. United States Army Corps of Eng'rs, 916 F.2d 721 (11th Cir. 1990), and *reconsideration granted*, Municipality of Anchorage v. Reilly, 32 Env't Rep. Cas. (BNA) 2007 (D. Alaska Jan. 4, 1991).

87. 33 C.F.R. § 325.2(b). *See* United States v. Marathon Dev. Corp., 867 F.2d 96 (1st Cir. 1989).

88. 33 U.S.C. § 1344(c).

89. There have been eleven vetoes. See WETLANDS DESKBOOK, *supra* note 2, at 48. The Corps processes approximately ten thousand permit applications a year.

90. 40 C.F.R. pt. 231.

91. James City County v. EPA, 12 F.3d 1330 (4th Cir. 1993), *petition for cert. filed*, 63 U.S.L.W. 3009 (U.S. June 22, 1994) (No. 93-2045).

92. Bersani v. Robichaud, 850 F.2d 36 (2d Cir. 1988), *cert. denied*, Bersani v. United States EPA, 489 U.S. 1089 (1989), and *cert. denied*, Robichaud v. United States EPA, 489 U.S. 1089 (1989); Russo Dev. Co. v. Thomas, 735 F. Supp. 631 (D.N.J. 1989), *supplemental op.*, [1990] 20 Envtl. L. Rep. (Envtl. L. Inst.) 20,938 (D.N.J. Mar. 16, 1990), *dismissed, remanded, summ. judgment granted*, Russo Dev. Corp. v. Reilly, [1991] 21 Envtl. L. Rep. (Envtl. L. Inst.) 21,345 (D.N.J. May 17, 1991); James City County v. United States EPA, 758 F. Supp. 348 (E.D. Va. 1990), *aff'd and remanded*, 955 F.2d 254 (4th Cir. 1991), *on remand*, [1992] 23 Envtl. L. Rep. (Envtl. L. Inst.) 20,228 (E.D. Va. Aug. 4, 1992), *rev'd*, 12 F.3d 1330 (4th Cir. 1993), *petition for cert. filed*, 63 U.S.L.W. 3009 (U.S. June 22, 1994) (No. 93-2045).

93. 42 U.S.C. §§ 4321–70d.

94. The Corps's general NEPA categorical exclusions are at 33 C.F.R. § 230.9. Categorical exclusions in the Section 404 permit program are found at 33 C.F.R. pt. 325 app. B(6).

95. 33 C.F.R. pt. 325 app. B sets out the Corps's NEPA procedures.

96. 33 C.F.R. pt. 325 app. A.

97. 33 C.F.R. pt. 325 app. A(A)("special conditions")(6).

98. 33 C.F.R. § 325.7.

99. *See, e.g.*, Fromer v. Two Hundred Post Associates, 631 A.2d 347 (Conn. App. Ct. 1993); County of Imperial v. McDougal, 564 P.2d 14 (Cal. 1977), *appeal dismissed*, 434 U.S. 944 (1977); Northpointe Plaza v. City of Rochester, 457 N.W.2d 398 (Minn. Ct. App. 1990), *aff'd*, 465 N.W.2d 686 (Minn. 1991).

100. 33 U.S.C. § 1319(a)(3) authorizes EPA compliance orders for any violations. 33 U.S.C. § 1344(s) authorizes Corps enforcement of Section 404.

101. 33 U.S.C. §§ 1319(g)(1)(B), 1344(s)(4).

102. 33 U.S.C. § 1319(d).

103. 33 U.S.C. § 1319(c).

104. 33 U.S.C. § 1365(a)(1).

105. United States v. Sinclair Oil Co., 767 F. Supp. 200 (D. Mont. 1990).

106. *See, e.g.*, 42 U.S.C. § 9607(b) (Superfund defenses).

107. United States v. Van Leuzen, 816 F. Supp. 1171 (S.D. Tex. 1993); United States v. Malibu Beach, Inc., 711 F. Supp. 1301 (D.N.J. 1989).

108. Tull v. United States, 481 U.S. 412 (1987).

109. United States v. M.C.C. of Florida, Inc., 848 F.2d 1133 (11th Cir. 1988), *reh'g granted*, 863 F.2d 802 (11th Cir. 1989), *appeal after remand*, 967 F.2d 1559 (11th Cir. 1992).

110. *See* United States v. VanLeuzen, 816 F. Supp. 1171 (S.D. Tex. 1993).

111. "Person" is defined broadly to include individuals, businesses, and state government entities. 33 U.S.C. § 1362(5).

112. 33 U.S.C. § 1319(c)(6).

113. United States v. Board of Trustees of Florida Keys Community College, 531 F. Supp. 267 (S.D. Fla. 1981), *later proceeding*, 19 Env't Rep. Cas. (BNA) 1167 (S.D. Fla. July 27, 1982).

114. 937 F.2d 286 (6th Cir. 1991).

115. 937 F.2d at 288.

116. 808 F. Supp. 1209 (E.D. Pa. 1992).

117. *See* Gwaltney of Smithfield, Ltd. v. Chesapeake Bay Found., Inc., 484 U.S. 49 (1987), *on remand*, 844 F.2d 170 (4th Cir. 1988), *on remand*, 688 F. Supp. 1078 (E.D. Va. 1988), *aff'd in part and rev'd in part, remanded*, 890 F.2d 690 (4th Cir. 1989).

118. EPA administrative enforcement penalties under Section 309 are made reviewable in either the District Courts or the Courts of Appeal, depending on the size and class of the penalty. 33 U.S.C. § 1319(g)(8).

119. 5 U.S.C. § 706.

120. This was one of the policy changes set in motion by the Clinton Administration's wetlands program, issued August 24, 1993. PROTECTING AMERICA'S WETLANDS, *supra* note 75.

121. 33 C.F.R. pt. 325 app. A(A)("special conditions")(6).

122. *See, e.g.*, Bailey v. United States, 647 F. Supp. 44 (D. Idaho 1986).

123. *See, e.g.*, Sierra Club v. Sigler, 695 F.2d 957 (5th Cir. 1983), *reh'g denied*, 704 F.2d 1251 (5th Cir. 1983); *but see* 1902 Atlantic Ltd. v. Hudson, 574 F. Supp. 1381 (E.D. Va. 1983).

124. Hoffman Group, Inc. v. EPA, 902 F.2d 567 (7th Cir. 1990); (EPA enforcement order); Fiscella & Fiscella v. United States, 717 F. Supp. 1143 (E.D. Va. 1989) (Corps cease and desist letter).

125. Route 26 Land Dev. Ass'n v. United States, 753 F. Supp. 532 (D. Del. 1990), *aff'd without op.*, 961 F.2d 1568 (3d Cir. 1992).

126. U.S. Const. amend. V, cl. 4.

127. United States v. Riverside Bayview Homes, Inc., 474 U.S. 121 (1985).

128. 28 U.S.C. § 1491(a)(1). This court has exclusive jurisdiction for takings claims over $10,000; jurisdiction is shared with federal district courts for takings claims under $10,000. 28 U.S.C. § 1346(a)(2).

129. Keystone Bituminous Coal Ass'n v. DeBenedictis, 480 U.S. 470 (1987); Agins v. Tiburon, 447 U.S. 255 (1980); Nollan v. California Coastal Comm'n, 483 U.S. 825 (1987).

130. United States v. Riverside Bayview Homes, Inc., 474 U.S. 121, 126–27 (1985).

131. 112 S. Ct. 2886 (1992).

132. *See, e.g.*, The Deltona Corp. v. United States, 657 F.2d 1184 (Ct. C1. 1981), *cert. denied*, 455 U.S. 1017 (1982); Jentgen v. United States, 657 F.2d 1210 (Ct. C1. 1981), *cert. denied*, 455 U.S. 1017 (1982).

133. 18 C1. Ct. 785 (1989).

134. 8 C1. Ct. 160 (1985), *aff'd in part, vacated in part and remanded*, 791 F.2d 893 (Fed. Cir. 1986), *cert. denied*, 479 U.S. 1053 (1987), *on remand*, 21 C1. Ct. 161 (1990), *vacated and remanded*, 18 F.3d 1560 (Fed. Cir. 1994), *reh'g, en banc, denied*, 1994 U.S. App. LEXIS 16257 (Fed. Cir. June 21, 1994).

135. 21 C1. Ct. 153 (1990), *mot. denied, remanded*, 1994 U.S. App. LEXIS 11842 (Fed. Cir. May 24, 1994), *aff'd*, 1994 U.S. App. LEXIS 14768 (Fed. Cir. June 15, 1994).

136. Loveladies Harbor v. United States, 1994 U.S. App. LEXIS 11842 (Fed. Cir. May 24, 1994).

137. Loveladies Harbor v. United States, No. 91-5050, 1994 U.S. App. LEXIS 14768 (Fed. Cir. June 15, 1994).

138. 31 C1. Ct. 37 (filed Mar. 24, 1994).

139. 30 C1. Ct. 63 (1993), *appeal docketed*, No. 94-5064 (Fed. Cir. Feb. 2, 1994).

140. 30 C1. Ct. 323 (1994), *appeal docketed*, No. 94-5070 (Fed. Cir. Feb. 15, 1994).

141. 10 F.3d 796, 801 (Fed. Cir. 1993).

142. 854 P.2d 437 (Or. 1993), *mot. granted, cert. granted*, 114 S. Ct. 544 (1993), *mot. granted*, 114 S. Ct. 1185 (1994), *mot. granted*, 114 S. Ct. 1395 (1994), *and rev'd. remanded*, 1994 U.S. LEXIS 4826, 62 U.S.L.W. 4576 (1994).

143. 31 C1. Ct. 37 (filed Mar. 24, 1994).

144. Exec. Order No. 12,630, 3 C.F.R. 554 (1989), *reprinted in* 5 U.S.C. § 601.

145. H.R. 1330, 102d Cong., 1st Sess. (1991).

146. H.R. 3875, 103d Cong., 2d Sess. (1994).

147. Chapter 9 of this book discusses environmental consultants in more depth.

148. WETLANDS: MITIGATING AND REGULATING DEVELOPMENT IMPACTS (2d ed. 1994).

149. A recent survey of wetland mitigation banks is the Environmental Law Institute's *Wetland Mitigation Banking* (1993).

150. U.S. EPA and U.S. Dep't of the Army, Memorandum to the Field, Establishment and Use of Wetland Mitigation Banks in the Clean Water Act Section 404 Regulatory Program (Aug. 23, 1993).

151. H.R. 961, 104th Cong., 1st Sess., May 3, 1995. Many of the issues addressed in this chapter would change under this legislation including wetlands definition, delineation, permit standards, and private property compensation.

CHAPTER 28

The Endangered Species Act

J.B. RUHL

The Endangered Species Act (ESA) has the potential to stop real estate development projects dead in their tracks. The nation's primary wildlife conservation law is deceptively noble in purpose and simple in structure. While few would take issue with the goal of protecting plants and wildlife threatened with extinction, the regulatory framework of species protection law can be exceptionally problematic for landowners and developers.

The ESA authorizes the Secretaries of the Interior and Commerce to "list" species whose continued existence is "endangered" or "threatened," to develop plans to promote the eventual "recovery" of listed species, to acquire and preserve the "habitat" of such listed species, and to regulate any "take" of certain listed species. On its face, this approach seems to have little to do with real estate development. However, anyone doubting the potency of the ESA in that arena can contact the local Home Builders Associations and other real estate professionals of Southern California, Austin, San Antonio, Las Vegas, and many other major cities for firsthand accounts of the "train wreck" experience that accompanies urban encroachment into protected species habitat.

Although Southern California continues to present landowners and developers with the most numerous and controversial challenges under the ESA, the region is by no means alone. Since 1982, when the statute was strengthened by amendments, the number of species extended protection under the ESA has expanded steadily—to over 900—most with ranges outside of California. In particular, Texas, Florida, and the northwestern and southeastern states contain large numbers of protected species. Like other environmental laws designed to protect limited resources, such as the wetlands protection provisions of Section 404 of the Clean Water Act, the ESA operates wherever a protected species is found. All it takes, then, is one protected species in the vicinity of a proposed land use—even if the species is merely migrating through the area—and a potential constraint exists. With over 2,500 species throughout the nation classified as "candidates" for ESA protection, if the pace of new additions to the protected species lists continues, it will be difficult by the end of this decade to develop any property without having to ensure proper compliance with the ESA. The ESA may not have come to your town yet, but you should assume it will.

The ESA is being implemented in ways having direct and immediate effects on individual development projects around the nation. Just as no knowledgeable developer today would think of purchasing or developing land without first surveying for contaminated soils, wetlands, archaeological sites, and other well-known potential development constraints and liabilities, no project should proceed without careful surveys and planning efforts directed toward identifying and dealing with ESA issues and obstacles.

Hence, despite its laudable goals and straightforward approach, the ESA has become the center of a national debate between wildlife conservationists and property rights advocates. The reasons for and substance of that debate are of vital importance to all real estate professionals. Collisions between the interests of developers and endangered species have occurred with increasing frequency throughout the nation, often with dramatic effects on local building and real estate markets. The potency of the ESA's enforcement provisions, coupled with the relative inadequacy of federal funding for species recovery, has made the statute a weapon of choice for opponents of development. The successes the ESA has brought development opponents in parts of the nation have raised a new awareness within the building and real estate industries of the need to participate in the ESA programs that potentially regulate development. In other words, the ESA's regulated community has finally awakened to the fact that it is being regulated.

Although Congress clearly intended the ESA to operate broadly and powerfully, many would argue that the law, as implemented, has been propelled beyond what Congress ever intended, in that the act is being used by federal agencies and citizens' groups to regulate matters normally subject to local and regional natural resource and land use management decisions. An understanding of the structure and history of the ESA is a necessary predicate to a discussion of the problems inherent in attempts to use the ESA to regulate such development. Each of the major ESA regulatory programs, which are described in detail in the next section of this chapter, presents significant concerns for any real estate development project.

The purpose of this chapter, however, is not to evaluate or resolve the philosophical and political disputes currently raging over the ESA. Those are for Congress to deal with in its ESA reauthorization process, which is expected to unfold within the next several years, and for the courts to decide. Rather, this chapter is intended to give real estate professionals an overview of the ESA, with particular emphasis on its potential impact on real estate development, and to suggest steps that can be taken to minimize the regulatory constraints posed by the ESA and to maximize compliance with those that are unavoidable. The first section of the chapter provides a detailed summary of the major ESA statutory and regulatory provisions and policies affecting the building and real estate industries. The next section provides a brief background of the statute and identifies the features of the regulatory program that pose the greatest potential impact on development projects, with examples from recent experience. The final section outlines an ESA "checklist" of development strategies to be implemented beginning at the earliest stages of a project and following through the project's conclusion and beyond.

Statutory and Regulatory Overview

Congress enacted the ESA in response to its key finding that various species "have been rendered extinct as a consequence of economic growth and development untempered by adequate concern and conservation."[1] Congress's major purposes for enacting the ESA were to "provide a means whereby the ecosystems upon which endangered species and threatened species depend may be conserved [and] to provide a program for the conservation of such endangered species and threatened species."[2]

To accomplish those goals, the ESA encompasses several basic programs that Congress has authorized the Secretaries of the Interior and Commerce to administer:

- Listing of species as endangered or threatened, and planning for their recovery
- Prohibitions against the killing, hunting, injuring, harming, or other "take" of certain listed species
- Administrative permitting of otherwise prohibited takes of listed species, if the permitted activities are incidental to a lawful purpose
- Enforcement

The Secretary of the Interior is responsible for implementing these programs for terrestrial and freshwater species and has delegated that authority to the U.S. Fish and Wildlife Service (FWS). The Secretary of Commerce is responsible for implementing the ESA with respect to marine species and has delegated that authority to the National Marine Fisheries Service (NMFS). (The FWS and the NMFS are sometimes referred to collectively as the Service.)

Species Listing and Recovery Planning

Section 4 of the ESA establishes the listing and recovery planning authorities, requiring the Secretaries of Interior and Commerce to designate any species that is "endangered" or "threatened" as a result of virtually any "natural or man-made factors affecting its continued existence."[3] "Endangered species" means "any species which is in danger of extinction throughout all or a significant portion of its range."[4] "Threatened species" means "any species which is likely to become an endangered species within the foreseeable future throughout all or a significant portion of its range."[5] Congress envisioned that "[t]he listing process under section 4 is the keystone of the Endangered Species Act."[6] The FWS is required to publish lists of all listed species.[7]

Congress directed that listing decisions be made "solely on the basis of the best scientific and commercial data available."[8] The FWS and NMFS have jointly promulgated species listing regulations consistent with that scope of review[9] and have published complete lists of endangered and threatened species.[10] There are over 900 listed endangered and threatened animal and plant species existing in the United States as well as over 2,500 species that FWS and NMFS consider "candidates" for listing at some future time.

Section 4 also requires the Service, at the time of the listing of a species, to designate "critical habitat" for the species "to the maximum extent prudent and determinable."[11] Critical habitat constitutes "specific areas within the geographical area occupied by the species,"[12] but it expressly "shall not include the entire geographical area which can be occupied."[13] Rather, the specific designated areas must be those that are "essential to the conservation of the species and . . . may require special management considerations."[14]

The Service can initiate a species listing or critical habitat designation through a proposed rule either on its own or by "the petition of an interested person."[15] Most listings are initiated by a petition. Upon receipt of a petition, the agency must, within ninety days, notify the public whether the petitioned action may be warranted, which is a relatively low threshold for keeping the petition alive.[16] Within one year of receipt of the petition, the agency must make the harder decision whether to propose to list the species or to deny the petitioned action.[17] The agencies are almost always late in making both of those decisions, which adds to the time the species, and developments potentially affected by its listing, remains in limbo.

Regardless of whether the process is initiated by petition or from within the agency, listing must be based on five factors: (1) the present or threatened destruction, modification, or overutilization of the species's habitat or range; (2) the overutilization of the species for commercial, recreational, scientific, or educational purposes; (3) disease or predation; (4) the inadequacy of existing regulatory mechanisms; and (5) other natural or man-made factors affecting the species's continued existence.[18] Any single factor is a sufficient basis for listing, though historically the first factor—habitat loss and range reduction—has served as the principal basis for listings. The agency must also take into account the efforts of states and other nations to protect the species.[19] Except in cases of an "emergency posing a significant risk to the well being of any species,"[20] in which case a listing becomes immediately effective for up to 240 days, the listing process requires the promulgation of a proposed rule, within one year of which the Service must issue a final rule designating the species as endangered or threatened.[21]

Listed species may be the subject of a plan designed to promote recovery of the species to nonendangered and nonthreatened status.[22] Notwithstanding that most recovery plans require more implementation funds than are available, once approved, the terms of a recovery plan are potentially enforceable against the agency if it fails to implement the essential steps detailed in the plan. The FWS and NMFS can also promote the ESA's species listing and recovery planning purposes by exercising their authority under Section 5 to acquire land in connection with a species conservation program.[23] Under Section 6, the FWS and NMFS can cooperate with states to establish conservation area management agreements or programwide cooperation agreements.[24] When a recovery plan involves steps affecting privately owned land, the impact of recovery planning cannot be underestimated.

If the species listing process seems ponderous, that is because it is. Also, it is heavily weighed in favor of the agency's decision. Although judicial review of the agencies' listing decisions is available, the courts measure these decisions under an administrative law standard of deference as required under the Administrative Procedure Act. As a result, no decision to list a species or designate critical habitat has been overturned on the ground that the decision was not supported by substantial evidence, and only one decision not to list has been overturned.[25] One increasing focus of ESA litigation in recent years, however, has been on challenges to listing and critical habitat designations. It may develop that some courts apply closer scrutiny of those Section 4 actions.

Section 4 case law provides an important lesson for landowners and developers: Don't count on overturning a listing decision on substantive grounds unless the agency was clearly wrong, and do count on an uphill battle in establishing the agency's error. On the other hand, several listing decisions have been overturned on procedural, rather than substantive, grounds.[26] On more than one occasion the agencies have been held to be in violation of deadlines, public comment and notice provisions, and other mechanical requirements of the statute. Landowners and developers should carefully monitor the listing agency's procedural compliance. Even when a procedural defect or glaring substantive error is detected, however, not all courts will recognize the standing of development interests to challenge an ESA listing.[27] Overall, although most courts appear willing to allow development and other economic interests into court to contest listing and critical habitat decisions, the fight will be an uphill battle.

Take Prohibitions

Once a species is listed, Section 9 of the ESA prohibits certain acts, depending on whether the species is a plant, fish, or wildlife and on whether it is listed as threatened or endangered. The most protected class is endangered fish and wildlife. The strongest proscriptive feature of the ESA is found in Section 9(a)(1), which provides that

> with respect to any endangered species of fish or wildlife listed pursuant to section 1533 of this title it is unlawful for any person subject to the jurisdiction of the United States to . . . take any such species within the United States or the territorial sea of the United States.[28]

The take prohibition can extend to *threatened* fish and wildlife species if the Service deems it "necessary and advisable to provide for the conservation of such species."[29]

Section 9(a)(2) protects endangered plant species. However, the "take" prohibition affecting plants extends only to plants on federally controlled lands or to plants that are protected from being taken by state law.[30] Although listed plant species do not receive the same degree of protection as fish and wildlife species under the statute, under certain circumstances the prohibitions and other limitations associated with plants can be significant obstacles to a development project.

Depending on how broadly "take" is defined—an issue that has recently received extensive attention in the courts—development within the identified habitat of a listed endangered or threatened species of fish or wildlife can be severely restricted. This issue has been of greatest relevance in cases in which a project is located in or near a listed species's purported habitat, but the construction and operation of the project cannot be linked to any direct physical force affecting individuals of the species. Most of the components of the take definition imply some direct contact with the species (e.g., hunt, shoot, capture), but the "harm" component is not clear in that respect. The agencies, however, have defined harm, which is not defined in the statute, as including

> an act which actually kills or injures wildlife. Such act may include significant habitat modification or degradation where it actually kills or injures wildlife by significantly impairing essential behavioral functions, including breeding, feeding or sheltering.[31]

Thus, the agencies have defined harm so as to link take to habitat modification without direct physical contact with individual members of the species.

An example from Austin, Texas, illustrates how the agencies' definition of harm has broadened the take prohibition. The golden-cheeked warbler, an endangered songbird, nests exclusively in central Texas, primarily around Austin, in dense, mature woodlands that also happen to offer prime development opportunities. The bird's nesting territory is relatively easy to locate in season, and it migrates to Central America in the winter. Any development, therefore, could avoid causing direct injury to a warbler by mapping and avoiding the nesting territories or, even safer, by waiting to build until the birds migrate south. FWS, however, has asserted that the harm definition precludes development activity in purportedly "suitable" warbler habitat at any time of the year because of the possibility that reduced habitat might interfere with nesting in subsequent seasons. FWS goes so far as to restrict activities near warbler habitat because of secondary impacts such as introduction of predators and noise. The difference in the amount of regulated land, between regulating only nesting territories and regulating all "suitable habitat" areas, is tens of thousands of acres.

It is important to note, however, that FWS's position regarding the harm definition and theories of secondary and speculative takes have met with mixed results in the courts. Ironically, though they publicize their position regarding the breadth of the harm definition, FWS and NMFS have rarely sued to enforce the definition in a case involving only habitat modification and no "dead body" evidence of a take. Rather, suits by citizens' groups have been the principal forum in which harm purportedly associated with habitat modification has been alleged.

Two early decisions suggested that the courts would embrace the agencies' broad definition of harm. In *Sierra Club v. Yeutter* and *Palila v. Hawaii Department of Land and Natural Resources*, the U.S. Courts of Appeal for the Fifth and Ninth Circuits, respectively, found that a take had occurred when evidence correlated statistical declines in a species's populations with a diminishing habitat base.[32] With the exception of those two cases, however, the harm definition has been applied very narrowly against finding of a take in cases of alleged speculative or secondary impact. Indeed, no reported case, other than *Palila* and *Yeutter*, has found that a "habitat modification" take has occurred under the harm definition.[33] Hence, although *Palila* and *Yeutter* remain influential cases, the track record of the harm definition in court has been fairly limited in effect. The definition and its scope remain sufficiently amorphous, however, to keep the threat of litigation ever present.

Even the threat of litigation under the harm definition would have diminished significantly if a 1994 decision of the U.S. Court of Appeals for the District of Columbia Circuit, in *Sweet Home Chapter of Communities for a Great Oregon v. Babbitt*,[34] had become the law of the land. That court of appeals held that the agencies' harm definition exceeds congressional intent because, unlike the plain meaning of all the other terms included in the statutory definition of take, the harm definition does not require direct application of physical force to a species individual in order for take to occur. If the reasoning of that case were to be applied throughout the nation, the protective scope of the harm definition for many species would be minimal. For example, in the situation of the golden-cheeked warbler discussed earlier, the court of appeals' approach in *Sweet Home* would appear to have allowed unrestricted habitat clearing after the songbird has migrated south, or even during nesting season, as long as active nests are not destroyed.

Perhaps because of those dramatic potential consequences, the Supreme Court in June 1995 reversed the court of appeals and reinstated the harm definition.[35] In so doing, however, the Supreme Court focused on the "actually kills or injures wildlife" phrase in the rule, and advised that there must be solid evidence of proximate causation between the habitat effects and such actual death or injury.[36] Which result Congress intended—the narrow construction to cover only "physical impact" as opposed to the opposite extreme that FWS has adopted—is likely to be clarified when the ESA is reauthorized. Until then the case law on the harm definition suggests that it would be difficult to challenge a well-planned development designed not to affect listed species individuals directly and physically. If, however, the type of habitat impact involved in the development is taking place regionally and is statistically linked to a decline in the species' population, then *Palila* and *Yeutter* would provide a stronger enforcement arsenal. Hence, a suit to challenge the development under the harm definition would likely not be deemed frivolous simply for lack of "dead body" evidence. Therefore, because the threat of protracted litigation is often sufficient to suppress development altogether, the harm definition as it exists today has a very real effect, regardless of its stingy application by the courts.

Incidental Take Authorities

The strict prohibitions in Section 9 of the ESA are tempered by permitting provisions designed to allow certain otherwise prohibited takes of listed species, provided the takes are incidental to a lawful activity, such as real estate development. Actions that any federal agency funds, authorizes, or carries out directly are eligible for incidental take permitting under Section 7 of the ESA, which imposes a broad array of additional duties on federal agencies generally. The scope of Section 7 is actually quite broad, extending to projects that do not on their face appear "federal" in nature, because granting of other federal permits is considered "authorizing" under the ESA. For those actions that have no such federal nexus, Section 10 of the ESA authorizes FWS and NMFS to issue incidental take permits if the project applicant prepares a "habitat conservation plan" demonstrating how it will avoid, minimize, and mitigate otherwise prohibited takes. Although these two permitting procedures are similar in many respects, there are also important differences that may influence whether a project applicant wishes to have a federal nexus that triggers Section 7 or to forgo federal involvement, if possible, and proceed under Section 10.

Incidental Take Authorizations in Section 7 Consultations

Ironically, the more important of the two incidental take procedures for purposes of real estate development has been the Section 7 procedure for federal agency projects, since Section 7 extends to any project that requires any form of federal permit for its completion. A Corps of Engineers permit under Section 404 of the Clean Water Act, an Environmental Protection Agency Clean Air Act permit, or a National Pollutant Discharge Elimination System permit would trigger the duty of the federal agency issuing the permit, known as the "action agency," to consult with the FWS or NMFS under Section 7. When that occurs, the developer, who probably never thought of the project as "federal" in nature, must proceed with the action agency through the

Section 7 process. Thus, the number of Section 7 consultations historically has exceeded Section 10(a) permits many times over, although Section 10(a) is increasing in importance.

Section 7 requires that federal agencies consult with the Service to carry out species conservation programs and to ensure that agency actions or prospective actions do not jeopardize the continued existence of any listed or proposed species or result in destruction or adverse modifications of any designated or proposed critical habitat.[37] The Section 7(a)(2) "consultation" process for existing listed species and designated critical habitat imposes a formal relationship between the Service and the federal action agency. For major projects, the action agency must provide the Service with a biological assessment of the impact of the agency action.[38] Based on the biological assessment, the FWS or NMFS issues its written biological opinion "setting forth the Secretary's opinion, and a summary of the information on which the opinion is based, detailing how the agency action affects the species or its critical habitat."[39]

On rare occasions the Service concludes that the proposed action is likely to jeopardize the continued existence of the species or cause adverse modification of critical habitat, in which case the Service must suggest "reasonable and prudent alternatives" to the proposed agency action that will allow the agency to go forward without violating Section 7.[40] Such jeopardy opinion can be the death of a development project.[41] Although in the statute Congress has not elaborated on what would be "reasonable and prudent alternatives" in response to a finding of jeopardy or adverse modification, the agencies have defined that term broadly.[42]

If the Service issues a "no jeopardy" opinion, or if the federal action agency accepts the "reasonable and prudent alternative" in a jeopardy opinion situation, the Service will also issue a statement authorizing the federal agency to carry out or allow "incidental taking," subject to conditions on the manner of taking and any other suggested conservation measures.[43] Through this incidental take statement procedure FWS is able to impose mitigation measures on the underlying development through the federal action agency. Hence, although jeopardy opinions are rare, the Section 7 consultation process has nonetheless resulted in significant changes to many development projects. The Service has promulgated complex, and occasionally vague, regulations to guide other federal agencies through the consultation and incidental take statement processes.[44]

Several aspects of the Section 7 process of vital importance to development interests are its extension to plants, the trigger threshold applied for consultations, and the duty to conserve. First, the consultation provisions of Section 7(a)(2) are not limited to listed fish and wildlife species, as is the take prohibition in Section 9(a)(1). Thus, a development project proceeding under Section 7 must consider impacts on listed plants.

Second, consultation is required whenever the action agency concludes that the project "may affect" a listed species, either adversely or beneficially, and the threshold for "may affect" is very low. Often the action agency does not challenge FWS or NMFS when they take an aggressive position on the "may affect" determination, dragging the permit applicant into a consultation process even when the perceived impacts are negligible or nonexistent.

Finally, even when the action agency, with or without FWS or NMFS concurrence, decides that a project will not affect the species, Section 7(a) requires all federal agencies to "conserve" listed species, which includes promoting their recovery. Arguably, the duty to conserve is therefore broader than the duty not to take, meaning that an agency may need to deny or limit a project permit if the project might restrict recovery of a listed species, even if no take can be demonstrated. The lesson is that a project that involves a federal nexus within the meaning of Section 7 inherits all the burdens of the federal action agency when dealing with the ESA.

Section 10(a) Authorizations

In the case of projects that are not federally authorized, funded, or carried out, Section 10(a) authorizes the Service to issue a permit allowing a taking that is "incidental to, and not the purpose of, the carrying out of an otherwise lawful activity."[45] Before the Service can issue such a permit, the applicant must provide a conservation plan specifying the impact of the taking, the applicant's efforts to minimize and mitigate such impacts, and the reasons why alternatives to the taking are not being used.[46] To issue a Section 10(a) permit, the Service must find that the taking will indeed be incidental, that its impacts will be minimized and mitigated to the maximum extent practicable, and that the taking will not appreciably reduce the likelihood of the survival and recovery of the species in the wild.[47] The Service must also be satisfied that the conservation plan will be adequately funded and implemented.[48]

These and other requirements of the Section 10 permitting process are only loosely defined in the statute. Because the current implementing regulations merely repeat the statutory language, they fail to give meaning to the various criteria imposed.[49] Guidance documents, currently in the drafting stages, attempt to fill some of those gaps by requesting that the permit applicant provide voluminous amounts of information responsive to numerous issues. However, they fail to describe the regulatory criteria in any useful detail.[50]

The Section 10(a) permitting experience has been limited thus far. Southern California has been a focal point for "regional" permits issued to multiple parties or a public authority as an umbrella permit for a defined region, while a number of individual property permits have been issued in Austin, Texas. (The regional permitting effort begun there in 1988 has failed to produce any usable permit to date.) In all, however, only several dozen Section 10(a) permits have been issued nationally as of this writing. While that number is expected to increase steadily, there is not yet enough experience under Section 10(a) to avoid having to reinvent the wheel with each new project.

Section 7 versus Section 10(a): Pros and Cons of Each

Although it may not always be possible for a project to choose which permitting procedure it can use, it is often possible to create or eliminate the federal nexus that triggers Section 7 through project redesign. For example, a project with a sewer line crossing in a water of the United States, and thus requiring a Corps of Engineers permit under Section 404 of the Clean Water Act, might be in a position to move the line out of the waters, and thus eliminate that Section 7 trigger. It is useful, therefore, to appreciate the practical differences between the two procedures.

One important distinction is that Section 7 requires consideration of plant species, whereas Section 10(a) does not unless the proposed project is on land owned or controlled by the federal government or state law requires plants to be considered. Hence, a wider array of potential species of concern exists when proceeding under Section 7.

Another distinction involves the decision to contact the Service about the project. Under Section 7, the action agency decides whether the project may affect a listed species, and if so, the action agency must consult with the Service. Under Section 10(a), by contrast, there is no consultation step. Nonfederal projects must simply avoid a take under Section 9, or they must seek permits when a take cannot be avoided. A nonfederal project, therefore, need not initiate any contact with the Service unless a take is expected to occur, which is a much higher threshold than the Section 7 "may affect" standard. Thus, careful project design may provide the justification for concluding that no take will occur. Of course, the nonfederal project may have this greater leeway, but it also bears the risk of enforcement when FWS or NMFS is not contacted before development. That risk often causes developers and project financiers to seek the certainty offered by contacting FWS or NMFS and, if necessary, obtaining a Section 10(a) permit, notwithstanding the time and cost involved.

Another difference between the Section 10(a) and Section 7 procedures is that the developer must negotiate with the Service through the action agency under Section 7. Although there is a procedure for designation of the project proponent as a nonfederal representative of the action agency, ultimately the action agency calls the shots and makes the difficult decisions. By contrast, under Section 10(a) the project proponent deals one-on-one with the Service, allowing the developer to take stronger negotiating positions without the "filter" of the action agency that exists under Section 7.

On the other hand, the detailed procedural record, extensive track record, and clear time lines under Section 7 are superior to the undefined process that takes place under Section 10(a). The project proponent in a Section 7 context inherits the action agency's burdens, but it also inherits the agency's protections. Because the procedural regulations are not well-developed under Section 10(a), FWS and NMFS can almost make up rules as the project goes along.

Most significantly, because the conservation duties imposed on federal agencies under Section 7(a) exceed those imposed on nonfederal entities, the applicant in a Section 7 proceeding inherits those extra issues. The only duty nonfederal entities (not triggering Section 7) have is not to take listed species in violation of Section 9. Conservation, which carries with it the duty to promote recovery and not to take steps that prevent recovery, is broader than the take prohibition. No court has imposed the conservation duty on a nonfederal entity acting without a federal nexus triggering Section 7.[51]

Moreover, the *Sweet Home* controversy and the possibility that Congress may some day alter the result the Supreme Court reached may cause FWS and NMFS to focus on other means of influencing species protection efforts by federal and nonfederal entities. For example, the federal agencies' duty to conserve, which is broader than the duty not to take, could provide an alternative means of forcing federal agencies to promote species protection. Also, FWS and NMFS might consider using the Section 4 critical habitat designation process more often and more broadly, since federal agencies' Section 7 duty not to modify critical habitat adversely does operate independently of the Section 9 take prohibition and, thus, would not be affected by the scope of the harm definition. Jeopardy opinions, which also operate independently of the take prohibition, may also become more common in Section 7 consultations, and notions of the type of federal actions that trigger Section 7 may be revisited. In short, by broadening and strengthening Section 7, FWS and NMFS may go a long way toward minimizing the impact of future litigation and legislation on the reach and effect of their efforts through Section 9 to regulate development projects. Thus, it could come to pass that the distinctions between Section 7 and Section 10(a) become merely theoretical.

Also, if it is clear that the project requires incidental take authorization, and if the potential action agency under a Section 7 scenario is in favor of the project, it may help to have a federal entity negotiating with FWS or NMFS on behalf of the project. Under Section 10(a), by contrast, the negotiating takes place exclusively between the project proponent and the FWS or NMFS.

Enforcement and Other Programs

The ESA's Section 11 also provides FWS and NMFS with a strong array of enforcement tools, including administrative penalties, criminal sanctions, and injunctive relief. A citizen suit provision in Section 11(g) has proven to be a more potent enforcement mechanism, however, as conservation groups around the nation have sued alleged violators of the ESA, as well as the FWS and NMFS, with increasing frequency and success. A more recent trend has been suits by property rights interests suing the agencies for exceeding statutory authority, also with a number of successes. Hence, while the agencies have strong enforcement authorities, the ESA enforcement story has been written mostly by citizen suits coming from diverse perspectives.

Section 11 provides the agencies with various civil and criminal enforcement options to ensure that Sections 7, 9, and 10 are properly followed.[52] Citizens may also enforce the ESA through a citizen suit provision[53] or by providing information to the FWS or NMFS that leads to successful federal enforcement.[54] Under the citizen suit provision, a citizen may sue to enjoin a violation of the ESA or any regulation adopted thereunder.[55] In addition, a citizen may sue the Secretary to require enforcement of the ESA's taking prohibitions or to perform any nondiscretionary act or duty related to the determination of whether a species is endangered.[56] ESA also allows the Secretary to pay a reward to a citizen who provides information leading to a criminal conviction, civil penalty assessment, or forfeiture of property pursuant to the ESA from the fines collected or property forfeited.[57]

As the experience under the harm definition previously described suggests, citizens' groups have been responsible for most of the attempted enforcement against development projects alleged to present a take of listed species, usually under the harm definition. This author is aware of no reported cases involving enforcement under the harm definition by FWS or NMFS against a real estate development project, though on many occasions the agencies have initiated enforcement investigations based on alleged harm resulting from habitat modification.

Pitfalls for Development Projects

Among environmental laws, the ESA involves a unique intersection between law and science. Although the goal of species protection could not otherwise be served, this feature of the ESA poses many pitfalls to the practical world of real estate development. An examination of the statute's impact in some recent cases from around the nation illustrates the need for a greater understanding of the ESA's workings from the development community.

No Grandfathering

Perhaps the principal source of concern for readers of this book, and the primary reason for the statute's potential influence as a source of land use regulation, is that, when a species of fish or wildlife is listed pursuant to Section 4 of the ESA, the take prohibitions grab hold with no regard to the status of a particular development. Thus, a developer who diligently surveys for listed species before property acquisition could nonetheless face an unanticipated endangered species issue at the groundbreaking ceremony, or even during the development process, if a species found in the project area is listed after the survey. The ESA provides no relief in such situations because the take prohibitions apply wherever and whenever a take will occur, and no provision is made for any resulting economic loss to the developer. The most infamous example is the snail darter case, in which the nearly built Tellico Dam was shut down because of an alleged take of an endangered fish below the dam. (Congress eventually exempted the project by special law, and the fish was later found to be abundant elsewhere.) Even the smallest real estate development project could face the same fate.

This feature of the ESA requires real estate professionals to stay abreast of all the ESA programs. For example, the listing of the Delhi sands flower-loving fly in 1993 threatened the viability of several public projects in California's San Bernardino County, including a major public hospital project and a lower income area economic redevelopment effort, because the projects were allegedly located in or near some of the last remaining habitat areas of the fly. Only through costly project redesign was the public hospital able to avoid the concern that its construction would cause a take of the species. Similarly, in Austin, Texas, developers of many half-built subdivision projects that failed during the economic downturn of the 1980s found they were delayed in taking advantage of the upturn of the 1990s because several species had been listed in the interim. The fact that the development projects were substantially underway at the time the species were listed offered no safe harbor from the ESA's reach.

The Listing "Black Box"

For real estate professionals the listing process is the most challenging aspect of the ESA, mainly because it is so difficult to monitor and participate in it. The ESA essentially demands hard conclusions about species populations, a subject often open to intense scientific debate. The legal criteria for listing focus principally on the threats posed to a species, which are often amorphous. The statute limits the listing review process to consideration of only the "best available" scientific data (whatever that may be). The funding necessary to compile even satisfactory data, much less the "best," is simply not available in all cases. In short, the listing process is driven by an inexact science and is underfunded. The result is that listing decisions often appear to be based on incomplete, disputed, or downright incorrect information.

It is the job of the FWS and NMFS to evaluate the body of available information, no matter how much it is disputed; to sift through it for the "best" information; and to measure that information against the listing criteria. To the layperson the agencies' review processes and decisions often appear inscrutable and open-ended. Without hiring a battery of lawyers and biological consultants, it is often difficult for a developer whose real estate project that might be affected by a proposed listing to plug into the listing process, comment meaningfully and within the specified time frames on the information the agency is considering, and supply either supporting or challenging information.

A fitting example is the Barton Springs salamander, a subterranean aquatic species proposed for listing in the Austin, Texas, area in 1993. The species has been popularized because of its presence in Austin's featured seminatural public swimming hole. FWS and virtually every researcher who has had any input into the study of the species agree that very little is known about it. No one knows how many there are, whether their population has declined, or what the full extent of their geographic range is. Except for evidence that a single event involving the dumping of chlorine into the species' surface habitat may have killed some of them—and the surface population quickly rebounded—there is no concrete evidence that any natural or human-induced thing, other than the researchers who collect the salamanders, has ever harmed a single individual of the species. Yet because the salamander depends on water from a surrounding aquifer, and because FWS perceives that aquifer as subject to water quality degradation by development, FWS has proposed to list the species. Because the listing of the species could threaten development in a 355-square-mile watershed area, local developers commented on the listing proposal at every stage with what they believed to be relevant scientific data, if not the "best" data, only to be largely ignored by FWS. Hence, other than to point out how little is known about the species, the regulated community has found it pointless to comment on the proposed rule, except to build a record in the event of later challenges to the listing decision.

Responding to the criticism about the species listing process, in July 1994 FWS and NMFS issued policies under which the agencies will solicit the expert opinions of three appropriate and independent specialists for each species under consideration for listing. The specialists will be consulted regarding such matters as taxonomy, population models, and other biological and ecological information.[58] The agencies will also use, review, and respond to primary and original data sources, including those that conflict with the agency's proposal, as the principal basis for recommending listing actions.[59] It remains to be seen whether this step will add clarity or confusion to the process.

The Post-Listing Paradox

One common phenomenon in the ESA world is to find that after a species has been listed, things were not as they seemed at the time of the listing. Information compiled by academic researchers may initially suggest the species has a small range or population and may identify threats to that entire range or population. Often, however, information later compiled by federal agencies and other entities conducting property surveys in an effort to avoid a take of the species reveals a much larger range or population. In such circumstances the FWS and NMFS tend to enforce the species's listed status as if it applies wherever the species is found, and no matter in what numbers, and to resist appeals to reconsider the listing.

A classic example is the case of several cave-dwelling invertebrate species located in Williamson County, Texas. The species were listed in 1988 under FWS's repeated insistence that they existed only in seven closely situated caves. Almost immediately after the listing, however, FWS suggested that development in the general region around those caves must undergo predevelopment surveys to ensure that no unauthorized take of one of the species would occur. By early 1992, researchers had uncovered scores of caves spread out over hundreds of square miles in which some of the species had been identified. FWS correspondingly expanded the area subject to its predevelopment survey requirement. Whereas in 1988 members of the real estate industry in Austin paid little attention to the proposed listing because of its narrow geographic scope, by 1992 they were up in arms, and the county sued FWS over the matter.[60] Hence, while it is true that some species are not listed until it is "too late" because of a misconceived belief that their population was higher than it in fact was (the salmon runs of the West Coast provide an example), many examples exist of species being listed "too early" and thereby causing economic dislocations without sufficient biological evidence to support the listing.

Of "Secondary" and "Speculative" Takes

Once a species is listed and it is known that it or its habitat exists on or near a proposed development, it can be difficult to determine what activities associated with the development might run afoul of the take prohibition. FWS and NMFS interpret the take prohibition to extend far beyond activities that involve obvious, direct, and immediate physical impact to the species. Injury that might occur secondarily, or sometime in the future, also might be the subject of the agencies' scrutiny. The activity could be very remote in time and location from the point of impact under this approach, and the causal link between the injury and the activity might appear tenuous at best. The result is a vast gray area of potential regulation that is as broad as the creativity of those who believe in the secondary and speculative impacts theories. This regulatory cloud can create vexing problems for development because new businesses and lenders may shy away from an area until the development constraints and compliance methods become more certain.

A prime example of the stretch involved in some alleged take scenarios involves the Peridido beach mouse, which inhabits beach dunes along the Alabama Gulf coast. A development project proposed for an area adjacent to known mouse habitat was challenged under the ESA by citizens' groups, on the grounds that the area to be developed was potential habitat of the mouse and that the development would introduce predators of the mouse, such as cats and birds, to its known habitat across the road. The court in that case, as in many others involving similar claims of future, secondary impact, rejected the assertion of ESA jurisdiction because of the lack of definitive evidence.[61] Nevertheless, real estate developments in similar circumstances can suffer from delays and increased expenses as a result of such litigation. One developer in Austin, for example, was so stymied by assertions that his proposed project would result in a secondary and speculative take that he has sued FWS and several agency officials for conspiracy to deprive him of civil rights and to take his property without just compensation.[62]

The uncertainty surrounding the take question thus poses difficulties well before an enforcement action is imminent. The mere filing of a citizen's petition to list a species can inhibit development in the area alleged to be within the species's range, for fear that the species will be listed and projects will grind to a halt. While ESA issues embroiled Austin, Texas, in the early 1990s, more than a few subdivisions, with roads and utilities in and half the lots built out, sat idle as mortgage lenders refused to lend without written confirmation from FWS that the construction of a home on a lot would not harm an endangered species. FWS was stingy with its letters in certain areas and required extensive biological surveys to support many of the few letters that were issued.

A policy that the Service issued in July 1994 is supposed to require the agencies to identify, to the extent known at the time of listing, specific activities that will or will not result in a take of the listed species.[63] However, there is as yet no track record to show how helpful that policy will be for defining the rules of development. For now, the huge twilight zone of determining what is a take continues to boggle many development projects.

The Permitting Maze

For projects that must confront the issue of a take of a listed species, permitting under the ESA is a costly, time-consuming venture. There are no "general permits" under the ESA, as there are in the Clean Water Act Section 404 fill permitting program, so the most limited take of a species is potentially subject to full-blown permitting procedures. In federal projects (carried out, funded, or authorized by a federal agency), though controlled by well-defined time frames and regulatory procedures, applicants may have to monitor and mediate between the action agency and FWS or NMFS to protect their interests. Participants in nonfederal projects have the luxury of dealing with FWS or NMFS one-on-one, but without any defined regulatory procedure or time frame. The cost side of the equation, besides the expense of legal and scientific consultants and project delay, comes at the point FWS or NMFS demand "mitigation" in return for the take authorization. The agency often requires compensating land conservation (at ratios greater than 1:1 and usually closer to 3:1) and scientific studies.

The experience in Austin, where more nonfederal project permit applications for individual development projects have been filed than anywhere in the nation, suggests the experience development projects elsewhere could face. Projects that have received permits in Austin have involved additional costs associated with permitting negotiation and mitigation estimated in a University of Texas economic study to exceed $9,000 per acre. Most of the permits have involved more than a year of FWS processing time from the time of application submittal. The result has been gridlock in the development community.

An ESA Checklist for Development Projects

Evaluating and dealing with ESA issues can be fraught with pitfalls and complications of vexing proportions. It is difficult to avoid these problems altogether, but there are measures a developer can take to identify and evaluate potential impacts under the ESA and to address efforts by citizens' groups and the FWS and NMFS to subject land or land uses to ESA control. The following steps could help a development project avoid conflicts with the ESA and increase the chances of compliance in cases in which the ESA's regulatory web cannot be avoided. It is important to note that, because the ESA essentially involves plugging imprecise scientific determinations into a rather black-and-white legal context, none of these steps should be taken without obtaining input from qualified biological and legal consultants. The overall compliance strategy is divided into three areas of concern: (1) before and during project design; (2) during ESA permitting, if a permit is needed; and (3) in the event of a petition or proposed rule to list a species not previously accounted for in the project design.

Before and During Project Design

1. The most important step any project participant can take is to survey the property for all listed, proposed, petitioned, and candidate species, preferably before property acquisition or as early thereafter as possible. One way to start is to contact the local office of FWS or NMFS and request information regarding all listed proposed, candidate, and petitioned species whose range includes the project area. If the agency is not forthcoming with information, a Freedom of Information Act request can be filed. Once this information is received, qualified biologists should survey the property for the presence of the species in question and for habitat appearing to be suitable for them. Note that if it is likely that a listed species may be in the area, the surveyors may need a research permit from the agency to look for the species, and the results and location of the survey must be part of the researcher's annual report to the agency. That confidentiality concern does not exist for unlisted species.
2. Once the species and habitat survey results are available, consider their impact on the project in terms of where develop-

ment might intrude on species' habitat. This process should not be limited to listed species unless the developer is confident it can build out the entire project before proposed, petitioned, and candidate species with habitat in the project area are actually listed. Beware of the potential for overnight emergency listings made in response to fear of overnight clearing of habitat.

3. Once the areas of project intrusion into habitat areas are known, it may be possible to "self permit" the project by adjusting development areas to avoid the habitat and to reduce secondary impacts on the habitat to a minimum. This step recognizes that, under the case law interpreting the take prohibition, in the event of agency or citizen opposition to the project, the opposition must offer definitive proof that a take will occur before an injunction can be obtained. If the survey information was thoroughly compiled and the project was designed with competent biological input, it may be possible to reduce the risk of a successful ESA challenge to acceptable levels and thus forego the need to obtain a permit. However, financial backers and potential buyers often require the increased certainty afforded by a permit.

During the Permitting Phase

1. Assuming that the conclusion of the "self permitting" step is that the project cannot be completed without considerable risk of a take of a listed species at some point in the project's completion, it may be necessary to explore ESA permitting options. The first step in this process is to determine the flexibility and desirability of proceeding under Section 7 versus Section 10(a). First, list all possible connections to other federal agencies, such as financial assistance and permits, that may trigger Section 7. If Section 7 is deemed undesirable for the reasons discussed above, consider whether any of the bases for the Section 7 trigger can be avoided.
2. Once the likely permitting pathway is determined, begin preparing the necessary scientific documentation to allow for internal review well ahead of the schedule for dealing with the agency. Generally, FWS and NMFS do not have the resources to research and confirm all aspects of the project's documentation, so the more thorough the documentation, the more likely that the agency will use it. Consider the presentation regarding the extent of a take and possible mitigation. With respect to this analysis, remember the creed of "avoid, mini-

mize, then mitigate." FWS and NMFS will push first for project alterations that will avoid a take and will view minimization of adverse effects and mitigation of unavoidable adverse effects as second and third choices, respectively.

3. Once confident that it has a firm grasp of the ESA impacts of the project, the developer should approach the relevant agency (FWS or NMFS in the case of Section 10(a), or the Service and the action agency in the case of Section 7) to discuss the project and request a "reality check" on time frames for permitting.
4. If the project must proceed under Section 7, the developer should request that the action agency appoint the developer as the designated nonfederal representative for purposes of initial contacts with the FWS or NMFS, and the developer should immediately begin preparing a draft of the action agency's biological assessment for the action agency's review. Most action agencies do not have the resources to negotiate with FWS and NMFS or to prepare a timely, thorough biological assessment. The action agency may have conducted other consultations for the species of concern. If this is so, the developer should obtain the biological assessments and the biological opinions involved to determine what has been decided in the past with regard to take and mitigation under similar circumstances.
5. If the project is proceeding under Section 10(a), the developer should collect permits that FWS or NMFS has already issued for the same species to determine what agency findings have been made in similar circumstances with regard to take and mitigation.
6. The developer should adopt a polite "squeaky wheel" approach to the FWS or NMFS once the Section 7 or 10(a) documentation has been submitted. Without becoming a pest, the developer should monitor the progress of the project through the agency's review process, supply necessary supplemental information quickly, and generally do whatever can be done to usher things along.

Dealing with Newly Listed Species

1. At any time during the project construction or operation, the listing of a species could disrupt that progress. Hence, the developer should contact the FWS or NMFS during project development to obtain copies of any petitions that have been filed for species in the area and to obtain any ninety-day or twelve-month findings on petitions or proposed listing rules.

2. If listing of a previously unaccounted-for species appears possible, the developer should repeat all the steps called for at the predesign stage. If it appears that the project might be affected by the listing, the developer should consider monitoring and commenting at each stage of the administrative process—the petition, the ninety-day finding, the twelve-month finding, or the proposed rule. In many cases, this can be done without expensive new scientific field research by having qualified biologists peer-review the agency's documentation. If significant holes appear in the agency's data, however, new field research might be influential. If more time is needed to conduct the review and research, the developer should contact local, state, and federal political offices to request more time.
3. In connection with commenting on a possible listing, the developer should consider the recent FWS and NMFS policy of describing activities that will or will not result in a take. It may be very difficult to halt a listing action—for one thing, the species may legitimately require protection—so the more fruitful strategy may be to offer input to the listing agency regarding activities important to the development industry and that should not be constricted unnecessarily by the listing.

Conclusion

The ESA is a potent weapon for shaping and restricting land uses in developing areas. Virtually overnight, the statute can burden any development project with significant expenses and delays. Moreover, it is often difficult to determine what constraints the ESA may impose on a particular project and what measures will be necessary to ensure compliance.

Listing activity by the FWS has increased in recent years, and with thousands of "candidate" species in line for status review, an increase in new listings is likely to be the trend. Hence, property owners, developers, and builders can no longer assume that endangered species issues will not affect their projects. Taking the steps described in this chapter to understand and cope with the ESA regulatory process will assist property owners and developers in making well-reasoned decisions about property acquisitions, development plans, and project designs. If, even after taking a reasonable, cooperative approach with environmentalists and the government over listing and permitting issues, the developer has no option but to litigate, these measures will at least put the developer in the best position to marshall credible evidence and make well-reasoned legal arguments.

Notes

1. 16 U.S.C. § 1531(a)(1). *See also* H.R. REP. No. 567, 97th Cong., 2d Sess. 9-10, *reprinted in* 1982 U.S. CODE CONG. & AD. NEWS 2807, 2809–10. This chapter focuses exclusively on the federal ESA. Readers should be aware that many states have enacted state species protection laws, some of which go beyond the federal law in terms of restricting activity affecting protected species. For the most part, however, the compliance strategies discussed in this chapter will apply even for those broader state laws, though in all cases the state law should be consulted.

2. 16 U.S.C. § 1531(b).

3. 16 U.S.C. § 1533(a)(1)(E). A species may be "any subspecies of fish or wildlife or plants, and any distinct population segment of any species of vertebrate fish or wildlife which interbreeds when mature." 16 U.S.C. § 1532(16).

4. 16 U.S.C. § 1532(6). Insects determined to be pests are excluded.

5. 16 U.S.C. § 1532(20).

6. House Report, *supra* note 1, at 8, *reprinted in* 1982 U.S. CODE CONG. & AD. NEWS 2807, 2810.

7. 16 U.S.C. § 1533(c)(1).

8. 16 U.S.C. § 1533(b)(1)(A).

9. 50 C.F.R. § 17.

10. 50 C.F.R. §§ 17.11 (wildlife), 17.12 (plants).

11. 16 U.S.C. § 1533(a)(3).

12. 16 U.S.C. § 1532(5)(A)(i).

13. 16 U.S.C. § 1532(5)(C).

14. 16 U.S.C. § 1532(5)(A)(i). The Service can designate specific areas outside of the occupied geographical area only if such areas are determined to be essential for conservation of the species. 16 U.S.C. § 1532(5)(A)(ii). Even an area fitting those narrow criteria can be denied critical habitat designation if the Service finds that, after considering the economic impact, the designation is not necessary to prevent extinction and "that the benefits of such exclusion outweigh the benefits of specifying such area as part of the critical habitat." 16 U.S.C. § 1533(b)(2). In that sense the critical habitat designation differs substantially from endangered and threatened species *listing*, which may not take cost/benefit analysis into account. 16 U.S.C. § 1533(b)(1)(A). The Service has published its designations of critical habitat. *See* 50 C.F.R. §§ 17.95 (wildlife), 17.96 (plants).

15. 16 U.S.C. § 1533(b)(3).

16. 16 U.S.C. § 1533(b)(3)(a).

17. 16 U.S.C. § 1533(b)(3)(B).

18. 16 U.S.C. § 1533 § (a)(1)(A)–(E).

19. 16 U.S.C. § 1533(b)(1)(A).

20. 16 U.S.C. § 1533(b)(7).

21. 16 U.S.C. § 1533(b)(5)–(6). The Service may extend the one-year period once by up to six months if it finds that there is disagreement regarding the biological data. 16 U.S.C. § 1533(b)(6)(A)–(B). Critical habitat is designated concurrently with the final listing rule unless the Service decides that additional time of up to one year is needed. 16 U.S.C. § 1533(b)(6)(C).

22. 16 U.S.C. § 1533(f). Recovery plans often designate areas in which the species will be studied and in which the species is expected to find habitat as it

recovers, thus marking areas of concern for potential developments. Draft recovery plans must be published for comment before final approval.

23. 16 U.S.C. § 1534.

24. 16 U.S.C. § 1535.

25. *See* Northern Spotted Owl v. Hodel, 716 F. Supp. 479 (W.D. Wash 1988) (invalidating decision not to list the spotted owl because no person consulted by the FWS had concluded the species was not endangered or threatened).

26. *See, e.g.,* Idaho Farm Bureau Fed'n v. Babbitt, 839 F. Supp. 32 (D. Id. 1993) (invalidating listing of snail species because FWS had not rendered its final rule by the conclusion of the mandatory statutory time period); Endangered Species Comm. v. Babbitt, 852 F. Supp. 32 (D.D.C. 1994) (agency must supply public complete information during public comment period, including backup data supporting reports upon which agency relies for its decision).

27. *Compare* Pacific Northwest Generating Co-Op v. Brown, 25 F. 3d 1443 (9th Cir. 1994), Region 8 Forest Timber Purchasers Council v. Alcock, 993 F.2d 800 (11th Cir. 1993), and Trinity County Concerned Citizens v. Babbitt, 1993 WL 650393 (D.D.C. Sept. 9, 1993) (economic interests insufficient to establish standing to challenge listing and critical habitat designation decisions), *with* Alabama-Tombigbee Rivers Coalition v. FWS, 1993 WL 646409 (N.D. Ala. 1993), *aff'd* 26 F.3d 1103 (11th Cir. 1994) (standing must be granted in cases involving economic injury as a result of ESA listing decision).

28. 16 U.S.C. § 1538(a)(1). "Take" is broadly defined as "to harass, harm, pursue, hunt, shoot, wound, kill, trap, capture, or collect, or to attempt to engage in any such conduct." *Id.* § 1532(19). Section 9(a)(1) also proscribes other activities with respect to such species, such as importation and sale in commerce.

29. 16 U.S.C. § 1533(d). The Service has implemented this "Section 4(d)" authority through a general rule extending endangered species protection status to all threatened species unless specifically stated otherwise in the species's listing rule (50 C.F.R. § 17.31(a)). That general rule has been upheld as a valid exercise of the authority. Sweet Home Chapter of Communities for a Great Oregon v. Babbitt, 1 F.3d (D.C. Cir. 1993), *modified on other grounds,* 17 F.3d 1463 (D.C. Cir. 1994), *rev'd on other grounds,* 115 S. Ct. 2407 (1995).

30. 16 U.S.C. § 1538(a)(2).

31. 50 C.F.R. § 17.3.

32. *See* Sierra Club v. Yeutter, 926 F.2d 429 (5th Cir. 1991); Palila v. Hawaii Dep't of Land and Natural Resources, 852 F.2d 1106 (9th Cir. 1988).

33. *See, e.g.,* Pyramid Lake Paiute Tribe v. Dep't of the Navy, 898 F.2d 1410 (9th Cir. 1990); American Bald Eagle v. Bhatti, 9 F.3d 163 (1st Cir. 1993); National Wildlife Fed'n v. Burlington Northern R.R., 23 F.3d 1508 (9th Cir. 1994); Morril v. Lujan, 802 F. Supp. 424 (S.D. Ala. 1992); Swan View Coalition v. Turner, 824 F. Supp. 923 (D. Mont. 1992).

34. 17 F.3d 1463 (D.C. Cir.), *reh'g denied,* 30 F.3d 190 (1994), *rev'd,* 115 S. Ct. 2407 (1995).

35. Babbitt v. Sweet Home Chapter of Communities for a Great Oregon, 115 S. Ct. 2407 (1995).

36. *Id.*

37. Four separate consultation processes are established for actions carried out, authorized, or funded by federal agencies. Section 7(a)(1) requires federal

agencies to "utilize their authorities in furtherance of the purposes of this chapter by carrying out programs for the conservation of endangered species and threatened species." 16 U.S.C. § 1536(a)(1). Consultation with respect to any federal agency action is required for listed endangered or threatened species under Section 7(a)(2), 16 U.S.C. § 1536(a)(2), and for species proposed for listing under Section 7(a)(4) (known in that context as a "conference"). 16 U.S.C. § 1536(a)(4). Section 7(a)(3) authorizes "early consultation" with respect to any *prospective* federal agency action if there is reason to believe the action might affect a listed endangered or threatened species. 16 U.S.C. § 1536(a)(3).

38. 16 U.S.C. § 1536(c).

39. 16 U.S.C. § 1536(b)(3)(A).

40. *Id.*

41. No objective criteria for making the jeopardy determination exist in the statute or regulations, and thus it can be very difficult to challenge a jeopardy opinion. The statute defines neither "jeopardy" nor "adverse modification," and the Service has only conceptually defined those terms in connection with its regulations implementing the consultation processes. 50 C.F.R. § 402 (1991). Under those regulations, "jeopardize the continued existence of" means "to engage in an action that reasonably would be expected, directly or indirectly, to reduce appreciably the likelihood of both the survival and recovery of listed species in the wild reducing the reproduction, numbers, or distribution of that species." 50 C.F.R. § 402.02 (1991). "Destruction or adverse modification" means

> a direct or indirect alteration that appreciably diminishes the value of critical habitat for both the survival and recovery of a listed species. Such alterations include, but are not limited to, alterations adversely modifying any of those physical or biological features that were the basis for determining the habitat to be critical.

50 C.F.R. § 402.02 (1991). The Service has explained that, rather than assign generally applicable numerical or other objective criteria to the "survival" standard embodied in those two definitions, the analysis must be conducted "on a case-by-case" basis, taking into account the particular needs of and the severity and immediacy of threats posed to a listed species." 51 Fed. Reg. 19,926, 19,934 (1986) (codified at 50 C.F.R. § 402.02).

42. The regulation covers an alternative action identified during formal consultation that can be implemented in a manner consistent with the intended purposes of the action, that can be implemented consistent with the scope of the federal agency's legal authority and jurisdiction, that is economically and technologically feasible, and that the [Service] believes would avoid the likelihood of jeopardizing the continued existence of listed species or resulting in the destruction or adverse modification of critical habitat. 50 C.F.R. § 402.02 (1991). If the alternative is not acceptable to the federal agency, it may seek an exemption from the ESA by petitioning the Endangered Species Committee. 16 U.S.C. § 1536(e)–(m) (1985).

43. 16 U.S.C. § 1536(b)(4). "Incidental take," although not the subject of a specific statutory definition provision, is described elsewhere in the statute as a take that is "incidental to, and not the purpose of, the carrying out of an otherwise lawful activity." 16 U.S.C. § 1539(a)(1)(B). The Service has adopted this meaning for purposes of its regulations implementing Section 7. 50 C.F.R. § 402.02.

44. 50 C.F.R. § 402. The regulations for formal consultation procedures, *id.* at Subpart B, are poorly organized and contain many terms and concepts not included in the statutory language. For a complete understanding of the procedures, it is essential to refer to the preamble of the final adoption rule. 51 Fed. Reg. 19,926 (1986). In general, the process is initiated through an "informal consultation" designed to determine whether the proposed action may affect a listed species or its designated critical habitat. 50 C.F.R. § 402.13. Depending on the outcome of that procedure, "formal consultation," which involves the action agency's preparation of a biological assessment and delivery by the FWS/NMFS of a biological opinion in response thereto, may be necessary. 50 C.F.R. § 402.14. The regulations apply similar procedures for the "early consultation" process the Service employs for prospective applications under Section 7(a)(3) of the ESA. 50 C.F.R. § 402.11.

45. 16 U.S.C. § 1539(a)(1)(B). Congress added the Section 10(a) incidental take permitting procedure to the ESA in 1982 to resolve "the concerns of private landowners who are faced with having otherwise lawful actions not requiring Federal permits prevented by section 9 prohibitions against taking." H.R. Conf. Rep. No. 835, 97th Cong., 2d Sess. 29, *reprinted in* 1982 U.S. Code Cong. & Ad. News 2860, 2870 [hereinafter Conference Report].

46. 16 U.S.C. § 1539(a)(2)(A).

47. 16 U.S.C. §§ 1539(a)(2)(B)(i)–(ii), (iv). Congress expressly intended that "[t]he Secretary will base his determination as to whether or not to grant the permit, in part, by using the same standard as found in section 7(a)(2) of the Act, . . . that is, whether the taking will appreciably reduce the likelihood of the survival and recovery of the species in the wild." Conference Report, *supra,* note 40, *reprinted in* 1982 U.S. Code Cong. & AD. News 2807, 2870. Indeed, because issuing a Section 10(a) permit involves federal agency approval of an action, the Service maintains that consultation with itself is required before issuance. *See* 50 Fed. Reg. 39,681, 39,683–84 (1985) (codified at 50 C.F.R. pts. 13, 17).

48. 16 U.S.C. §§ 1539(a)(2)(B)(iii), (v).

49. *See* 50 C.F.R. §§ 17.22(b). The Service has described its rules as "largely identical to the express language of section 10(a)." 50 Fed. Reg. 39,681, 39,682 (1985) (codified at 50 C.F.R. §§ 13, 17).

50. *See* FWS, Preliminary Draft Handbook for Habitat Conservation Planning and Incidental Take Permit Procession (Sept. 15, 1994).

51. *See, e.g.,* National Wildlife Fed'n v. Burlington Northern R.R., 23 F.3d 1508 (9th Cir. 1994).

52. 16 U.S.C. §§ 1540(a) (civil penalties), (b) (criminal violations), and (e)(6) (civil injunctions). Civil penalties for knowing violations of Section 9, or of permits or regulations issued thereunder, other than reporting requirements, may be as high as $25,000 per violation. 16 U.S.C. § 1540(a)(1). For certain lesser offenses, a maximum civil penalty of $500 per violation may be assessed. 16 U.S.C. § 1540(a)(1). A person guilty of a knowing violation of Section 9 or of permits or regulations issued thereunder, other than reporting requirements, may be fined up to $50,000, imprisoned for not more than one year, or both. 16 U.S.C. § 1540(b). For certain offenses, the maximum punishment is a fine of $25,000, imprisonment for six months, or both.

53. 16 U.S.C. § 1540(g).

54. 16 U.S.C. § 1540(d).

55. 16 U.S.C. § 1540(g)(1)(A).

56. 16 U.S.C. § 1540(g)(1)(B) and (C). Except in emergency circumstances, before bringing the suit, the citizen must provide sixty days' written notice to the Secretary of Interior and any alleged violator. 16 U.S.C. § 1540(g)(2)(A) and (C). In the event the Secretary takes certain actions in response to the notice, the citizen's suit will be barred. 16 U.S.C. § 1540(g)(2)(B).

57. 16 U.S.C. § 1540(d).

58. 59 Fed. Reg. 34,270 (1994).

59. 59 Fed. Reg. 34,271 (1994).

60. Williamson County Commissioners Court v. Babbitt, No. A-94-CA-219-SS (W.D. Tex.) (complaint dismissed for lack of standing), *app. pending*, No. 95-50034 (5th Cir.).

61. Morril v. Lujan, 802 F. Supp. 424 (S.D. Ala. 1992).

62. *E.g.*, Four Points Utility Joint Venture v. United States, No. A-93-CA-655-55 (W.D. Tex.) (complaint dismissed for failure to exhaust administrative procedures).

63. 59 Fed. Reg. 34,272 (1994).

CHAPTER 29

Storm Water Regulation of Construction Activities

RICHARD S. DAVIS
MICHELLE A. WENZEL
GEOFFREY T. CULLEN

And soon I heard a roaring wind:
It did not come anear;
But with its sounds it shook the sails,
That were so thin and sere.

The upper air burst into life!
And a hundred fire-flags sheen,
To and fro they were hurried about!
The wan stars danced between.

And the coming wind did roar more loud,
And the sails did sigh like sedge;
And the rain poured down from one black cloud;
The Moon was at its edge.

The thick black cloud was cleft, and still
The Moon was at its side:
Like waters shot from some high crag,
The lightning fell with never a jag,
A river steep and wide.

—Samuel T. Coleridge, "The Rime of the Ancient Mariner," pt. V

In thinking about the concept of "storm water," one envisions thunderstorms, hurricanes, and other weather patterns that inundate the land with water. One might imagine children playing in the rain, making small ships out of leaves and twigs and launching the ships in streams of rainwater that cascade past. As water released from rain and snow clouds reaches the ground, some is absorbed into the earth and the rest runs off, moving downslope at a speed that varies in relation to the topographical and surface characteristics of the area. This runoff is "storm water."

The Environmental Protection Agency (EPA) is authorized by Congress to regulate storm water discharges from a variety of sources, including certain construction sites. The agency defines storm water as "storm water runoff, snow melt runoff, and surface runoff and drainage."[1] The key to the agency's definition is the notion of "precipitation event": runoff deriving from a precipitation event such as a rainshower or hail storm qualifies as storm water, whereas other sources of runoff carrying de minimis quantities of pollutants, such as landscape irrigation, diverted stream flows, foundation drains, roof drains, and water from crawl space pumps, are not categorized as storm water. This distinction may seem excessively technical, but it is important to understand that in permitting storm water, Congress did not intend to regulate all overland discharges. Rather, storm water permits authorize discharges of storm water only; other runoff sources are either unregulated or must be permitted through nonstorm water programs.

At the present time, the EPA requires Clean Water Act (CWA) permits for discharges of storm water from construction sites where activities such as clearing, grading, and excavation result in disturbances of five or more acres of land. Smaller sites may also be regulated if they are part of a common plan of development or sale that encompasses a minimum of five acres. Construction site operators must file for general or individual storm water permits and must design and implement storm water pollution prevention plans for their sites. These plans should incorporate erosion and sediment controls as well as measures to manage storm water flows over the sites.

In advising clients whose construction projects meet the five-acre or common-plan requirements, it is vital to inform them of their obligations under the storm water program. Unpermitted discharges are prohibited and subject the discharger to administrative penalties, civil enforcement, and criminal prosecution.[2] In addition, a construction operator that is required to obtain a storm water permit and fails to do so may be enjoined from proceeding with construction operations until such time as the operator applies for and receives a permit. In such cases, developers will incur easily avoidable carrying costs by becoming embroiled in application processes that should have been completed far in advance of groundbreaking. Plainly, these potential consequences of noncompliance provide significant incentives for developers to factor into development planning the time, effort, and expense involved in obtaining storm water permits.

This chapter discusses the procedures that must be followed by construction site operators to obtain storm water permits. It first provides a brief overview of the statutory and regulatory history of the storm water program, with a special emphasis on the components of the program affecting construction sites. It then defines the scope of construction activities subject to storm water permitting and specifies the conditions under which site owners, contractors, or developers must apply for permits. Next, the chapter discusses the application procedures and types of permits (general and individual) available for construction operations and describes the typical contents of those permits. Lastly, a number of potential future developments in storm water permitting are explored.

One final introductory note: The requirements mentioned in the preceding paragraphs represent minimum federal standards for implementation of the storm water permitting program. They are applicable, as is, in the minority of states and territories that have not assumed responsibility for administering CWA permitting. In the majority of states that have assumed the federal program, storm water standards and permit requirements may be more stringent than the federal specifications. As an example, certain states may routinely require storm water permits for parcels smaller in size than five acres. Most state programs, however, track federal requirements relatively closely, and, consequently, this chapter focuses on explaining the federal standards. Clearly, practitioners should always check specific state program requirements for projects located in states with independent permitting authority.

Recent Developments

As this book was going to press, the EPA promulgated a new rule that brings smaller, currently unregulated storm water sources—notably construction sites of less than five acres—into the storm water program. The rule requires the EPA (or a state exercising delegated permitting authority) to identify sources that "contribute to a violation of a water quality standard or [are] significant contributor[s] of pollutants to waters of the United States."[3] These dischargers must apply for a permit within 180 days of receiving notice from the permitting authority, unless permission for a later date is obtained. The rule also provides that all other sources of storm water will be required to apply for a permit by August 7, 2001,[4] unless Congress decides in the interim to change the existing regulating scheme.[5] In the meantime, EPA will explore a numbr of non-permit control strategies designed to reduce regulatory burdens by targeting the most significant environmental risks.

This chapter has not been rewritten to reflect the new rule's provisions. Consequently, the chapter refers repeatedly to construction projects that meet the five-acre or common-plan requirements as being the only projects subject to federal storm water regulation. Care should be taken to read this chapter with the new rule firmly in mind. The rule, as it now stands, significantly expands the scope of storm water regulation of construction activities.

Applicability of the CWA Storm Water Program to Construction Activities

Historic Posture of Storm Water Discharges

In 1972 Congress made sweeping changes to the CWA for the stated purpose of restoring and maintaining the chemical, physical, and bio logical integrity of the nation's waters.[6] Congress targeted "point source" pollution as an entity in particular need of control. A point source is

> any discernible, confined and discrete conveyance, including but not limited to any pipe, ditch, channel, tunnel, conduit, well, discrete fissure, container, rolling stock, concentrated animal feeding operation, or vessel or other floating craft, from which pollutants are or may be discharged.[7]

Some common examples of point sources include pipelines or channels through which industrial wastewater or municipal sewage is discharged into lakes, rivers, or streams. Outfalls from sewer systems that are devoted solely to storm water (i.e., "separate" storm sewers, as distinguished from multipurpose sewers that drain into municipal sewage treatment facilities) also qualify as point sources.

In the 1972 amendments, Congress established the National Pollutant Discharge Elimination System (NPDES) as a means to control point source pollution. The NPDES program requires permits for any discharge of pollutants from a point source into waters of the United States.[8] In addition, Congress granted the EPA authority to establish effluent limitations for a variety of pollutants.[9] NPDES permits must be conditioned to ensure that these effluent limits are not exceeded.

By adding these provisions to the CWA, Congress effectively authorized the EPA to regulate storm water discharges from point sources. In the early years of the NPDES program, however, the EPA declined the opportunity to oversee storm water, preferring instead to focus on regulating industrial process wastewater and municipal sewage discharges. In the 1970s these concentrated releases were perceived as posing the greatest threat to water quality. Consequently, storm water was relegated to ad hoc permitting achieved either as a result of permit writers' decisions to apply EPA effluent limits to storm water discharges at individual facilities, or through implementation of a handful of effluent guidelines that contained storm water runoff standards.

As environmental degradation caused by industrial process wastewater and sewage discharges abated in response to the development and installation of pollution control measures, it became increasingly apparent that other, more diffuse contaminant sources, including storm water runoff, were significant causes of water pollution. To investigate these sources, from 1978 to 1983 the EPA funded a series of water pollution projects called the Nationwide Urban Runoff Program (NURP). NURP demonstrated that storm water contains many of the same conventional and toxic pollutants that are present in process outfalls and municipal sewage discharges. In addition, other studies revealed that storm sewers are frequently riddled with illicit connections that allow municipal, commercial, and industrial wastes, such as used oil, to be improperly disposed through the storm sewer system.

These findings were supplemented by efforts to track the effect of construction activities on waters of the United States. In one study sponsored by the EPA and the Association of State and Interstate Water Pollution Control Administrators, data gathered at the state level indicated that construction site runoff is a major contributor to water quality impairment. Construction activities typically generate an abundance of common storm water pollutants, such as fertilizers, pesticides, petroleum products, construction chemicals, and solid wastes. All of these substances have adverse effects on aquatic organisms and impair water's suitability for drinking, bathing, swimming, fishing, and boating. In addition, storm water washing over construction sites dissolves large quantities of soil and carries that soil away as sediment. Sediment is deemed a pollutant because, in high volumes, the material can smother underwater plant and animal life and alter watercourses and aquatic habitats by choking off streams and filling wetlands.

In light of these findings, numerous parties urged the EPA to use its existing CWA authority to regulate all storm water discharges from point sources. In the context of construction, runoff released through separate storm sewers or via discrete, traceable points such as channels or culverts would qualify as point sources, so the industry would have been affected by an affirmative EPA decision on this matter. The EPA acknowledged that storm water posed nontrivial pollution problems, but after estimating that all storm water point sources taken together would number in the hundreds of thousands, the agency decided that its limited resources would be better expended on other, more narrowly focused projects.

The 1987 Amendments to the CWA

By the mid-1980s, Congress became aware of the mounting evidence against storm water and recognized that regulation of the problem had lagged badly behind other water pollution initiatives. Consequently, in the 1987 amendments to the CWA, Congress devised a compromise: the EPA would be required to issue permits for storm water discharges, but the agency could regulate in phases the anticipated legions of sources. To implement this compromise, Congress added Section 402(p) to the CWA. This section lists five categories of storm water discharges thought to be highly contaminated and requiring immediate permitting. Those categories include:

1. Discharges covered by an existing NPDES permit;
2. Discharges "associated with industrial activity," which the EPA defined by regulation to include many industrial categories by Standard Industrial Classification (SIC) code, as well as certain other activities, notably construction activities;
3. Discharges from municipal separate storm sewer systems serving populations of 250,000 or more;
4. Discharges from municipal separate storm sewer systems serving populations between 100,000 and 250,000; and
5. Discharges identified by the EPA Administrator or a state as contributing to a water quality standard violation or as significantly contributing pollutants to waters of the United States.[10]

Congress temporarily excused from permitting all other storm water discharges, with the caveat that the EPA would report to Congress by a later date as to what, if any, action the agency would recommend with respect to those discharges.[11] Meanwhile, Congress directed the EPA to establish a permitting program to ensure that storm water discharges in the first five targeted categories would immediately be placed under NPDES permits.

1990 and Subsequent Regulations

On November 16, 1990, the EPA fulfilled a portion of its statutory obligation to regulate the priority storm water categories by promulgating the Storm Water Application Rule, which contains permit application criteria for those categories.[12] The rule describes, in great detail, the types of facilities that are subject to the permitting program and the ways in which those facilities may obtain storm water permits.

In an effort to streamline the permitting process and infuse it with flexibility, the EPA established two types of storm water permits and three types of permit application methods for use by regulated facilities.

The two types of storm water permits are individual permits, which are narrowly tailored to fit the unique needs of individual facilities, and general permits, which are broadly drawn instruments that provide coverage for a large number of facilities. The three types of application methods include individual, group, and general procedures. The individual method tends to be the costliest, in terms of both time and money, because a considerable amount of information must be compiled on a facility's potential storm water discharges and other features. The group application method, on the other hand, is an EPA innovation intended to facilitate the permitting of multiple industrial facilities that have similar characteristics. Given the uniqueness of real property, construction applicants may not make use of group applications, but the method is useful for some entities and results in an individual or general permit for each of the facilities included in a group. Finally, the general permit application process is the simplest, requiring only a minimal amount of data from an applicant. The November 16th regulations set forth requirements, including deadlines, for the individual and group permit applications and lay initial groundwork for general permits.

On April 2, 1992, the EPA issued the Storm Water Implementation Rule, the second in its series of storm water permitting regulations. The implementation rule builds on a number of themes discussed in the application rule.[13] For example, the implementation rule addresses the EPA's long-term permit issuance strategy for storm water discharges associated with industrial activity, modifies the minimum monitoring and reporting requirements imposed in such permits, and explores the parameters of the general permit application process. On the latter point, the EPA explains that the qualifying conditions for filing an application to be covered by a general permit, called a Notice of Intent (NOI), are established on a case-by-case basis.[14] The rule delineates minimum federal requirements for NOI contents and sets the stage for the EPA's issuance of "baseline" general permits.[15]

Baseline general permits play a central role in the EPA's tactical approach to regulating the ever-expanding universe of storm water discharges. The EPA anticipates that, in every discharge category, separate baseline permits will be promulgated for each state in which the EPA administers the NPDES program. In states where state permitting agencies oversee NPDES permitting, the EPA foresees that the state agencies will design general permits based on the EPA models. On September 9 and 25, 1992, the EPA implemented a portion of this agenda by publishing baseline general permits for storm water discharges from construction sites.[16] With the issuance of these permits, the EPA completed its statutory obligation to create a regulatory framework for construction discharges as part of the priority industrial activity storm water category.

Which Construction Activities Are Subject to Permitting?

In the storm water application rule issued in 1990, the EPA defines the term "storm water discharge associated with industrial activity" to include discharges from construction operations, such as clearing, grading, and excavation, that result in the disturbance of five or more acres of total land area.[17] Operations affecting smaller parcels of land may also be included within the rule's scope if the parcels are considered part of a "larger common plan of development or sale" that covers five or more acres. The EPA explains that a "larger plan" of this type is meant to indicate a "contiguous area where multiple separate and distinct construction activities may be taking place at different times on different schedules under one plan."[18] For example, if a developer purchases twenty-five acres of property for a residential subdivision and prepares the property by building roads or installing sewer lines, any subsequent development of portions of that property, either by the original owner or by a subsequent purchaser, is subject to the storm water permit rule because the smaller parcels were included on the original site plan.[19]

As another example, imagine a situation in which a developer is engaged in the partial rehabilitation of a shopping center that covers five acres, but only three acres are affected by the rehabilitation efforts. Technically, the developer's activities will not result in the disturbance of five or more acres of land, so this operation does not require a storm water permit. However, if an existing storm water permit covers the entire shopping center site, the developer must file for a modification of the existing permit.

The key question to analyze in this context is whether construction activities will *result* in the *disturbance* of *five or more acres* of *land*. "Disturbed" land is land, specifically soil, that is exposed to the elements through the removal of surface vegetation, rocks, pavement, and buildings by means of bulldozing, grading, excavation, demolition, discing, or similar earth-invasive operations. The operations must yield a minimum of five acres of "invaded" soil (with the exception of small parcels subject to the larger-common-plan rule). Thus, a construction operation that exceeds five acres in size will not trigger the permitting requirement if it will disturb only one or two acres of soil. For example, if an existing forty-acre parcel is paved or covered by buildings, an operator's plan to repave (and consequently disturb) two acres of that parcel will not require a new permit.

The EPA's rationale for regulating construction under the rubric of industrial activity is based on the agency's assessment that developers' use of bulldozers, cranes, dump trucks, and dynamite to fill and level land, along with their routine installation of roads, drainage systems, and holding ponds, is prototypical industrial activity.[20] The EPA cites the highly degraded quality of construction site runoff as further evidence of construction's industrial nature. According to the agency, storm water runoff from construction sites typically carries sediment at a rate ten to twenty times higher than runoff from agricultural lands and one thousand to two thousand times higher than runoff from forest lands. These dramatic statistics led the EPA to conclude that "[e]ven small construction sites may have a significant negative impact on water quality in localized areas. Over a short period of time, construction sites can contribute more sediment to streams than was previously deposited over several decades."[21]

The EPA's assertions that construction operations have significant detrimental effects on water quality encouraged a nonprofit organization, the Natural Resources Defense Council, to challenge the agency's exemption from the industrial activity category of construction resulting in disturbances of less than five acres. In *Natural Resources Defense Council, Inc. v. EPA*,[22] the U.S. Court of Appeals for the Ninth Circuit reviewed the under-five-acre exemption (among other disputed storm water issues) and found it to be baseless. The court noted that the EPA had provided no information to support its determination that construction activities on less than five acres are nonindustrial in nature. Accordingly, the court held the EPA's choice of a five-acre limit to be arbitrary and capricious and invalidated that portion of the storm water rule exempting construction sites of less than five acres from permitting requirements.[23] In addition, the court remanded the case to the EPA for further rule making.

Interestingly, the EPA interpreted the *NRDC* decision as allowing the under-five-acre exemption to stand, at least until such time as the agency was able to revisit the storm water application rule.[24] As discussed earlier, the EPA has now done so and has issued a rule that subjects construction sites smaller than five acres to regulation.

Who Must Apply?

In general, storm water permits must be obtained by "operators" of regulated facilities or activities.[25] In the construction context, the EPA defines an operator as the entity (or entities) responsible for designing, modifying, and implementing specifications for a particular site and, in addition, for exercising day-to-day control over site operations, particularly over those involving earth-moving functions.[26] If these tasks are distributed among several parties at a particular site, those parties are required to become "co-permittees" for the site. For example, if a developer wields operational control over site specifications and a general contractor supervises day-to-day construction activities and permit compliance measures, the developer and the general contractor will be co-permittees for that site. Similarly, if these oversight responsibilities are further subdivided between the developer, general contractor, and subcontractors, all parties must be co-permittees. Under storm water permits co-permittees bear individual responsibility for those portions of a project that they operate.

When applying for a general permit, each party qualifying as a site operator must submit an NOI to the permitting authority. The NOI should be accompanied by photocopies of the other operators' NOIs or should reference the general permit number assigned to the project. Importantly, the existence of multiple operators and multiple NOIs for a site does not mean that multiple pollution prevention plans must be generated for the site. Rather, co-permittees under a general permit are obliged to cooperate in the design and implementation of a single, comprehensive pollution prevention plan for the construction site.

Similarly, in cases in which an individual storm water discharge permit is mandated, the owner or developer of a construction site will typically file the initial permit application. When a contractor is selected at some later point and the operator of various components of the site concomitantly identified, these parties may sign on to the individual permit application as co-permittees rather than submitting new applications. Again, only one pollution prevention plan will need to be created for the construction site, although the plan would have to be modified in the event that material changes were made in construction operations or plans.

How Are Permits Obtained?

Permitting options for construction operators differ depending on whether the state in which a project is located has been delegated to operate its NPDES program. In states that do not have NPDES authority, permitting is administered by the appropriate regional EPA office.[27] Construction applicants in these states may apply for individual storm water permits or may submit NOIs to be covered by the federal baseline general permits promulgated by the EPA in September 1992. In states with NPDES authority, permitting is administered by EPA-approved state offices. Construction applicants in these states may apply for individual permits and, if the state also has EPA-delegated authority to issue general permits, may apply for state general permits that are modeled after the federal baseline permits.[28] Finally, in states with NPDES authority but without general permit authority, construction applicants may apply only for individual permits.[29]

General Permits

Federal Baseline General Permits or "Permit-by-Rule"

The optimal course for a construction operator to pursue is to submit an NOI to be covered by a general permit. In relative terms, NOIs require only a modicum of data, including such prosaic information as the location of the construction site; the names, addresses, and telephone numbers of the site owners and operators; an identification of receiving waters; and a listing of existing NPDES permit numbers (if any) for other discharges from the site.[30] In addition, if an applicant possesses sampling data that describe the concentration of pollutants in a site's storm water discharges, the applicant must indicate in the NOI that such information exists. However, the EPA does not require that existing sampling data be reported in the NOI, nor does the agency mandate that new pollutant monitoring be performed for purposes of the NOI. NOI applicants must provide estimates of project start and completion dates and the number of acres of the site on which soil will be disturbed. Finally, the most rigorous component of the NOI process is a prerequisite to the NOI itself: applicants are required to design storm water pollution prevention plans for their sites. Applicants must certify in their NOIs that such plans have been prepared and that the plans comply with the general permit criteria and any applicable state and local sediment, erosion, and storm water management specifications.[31]

Plainly, NOIs are useful tools for storm water dischargers because the universe of information that must be submitted to the EPA is relatively narrow. NOIs are also advantageous because fees for their filing are nonexistent, and filing deadlines are nearly as liberal. Construction operators need to submit NOIs only two days before the commencement of clearing, grading, excavation, or other construction activities.[32] If the operator at a construction site changes, a new NOI must be filed, but again, only two days before the new operator commences work at the site. Of course, the compilation of thoughtful, workable storm water pollution prevention plans will in most cases take longer than several days, and these plans must be completed before the NOI filing. In theory, however, and perhaps in practice, the entire NOI process could be completed in as little time as several weeks.

Beginning two days after the postmark date on a properly executed NOI, the applicant is authorized to discharge storm water from the subject construction site under the terms and conditions of the general permit, unless notified otherwise by the EPA.[33] The EPA will review the NOI submittal and may deny coverage under the general permit. In such a case, the agency will require the site operator to file for an individual NPDES permit. Importantly, the site will be covered by the general permit until such time as the operator's individual permit is issued or denied, at which point general permit coverage automatically terminates.[34]

In cases where a general permit is found to be appropriate, permit coverage continues from two days after filing through the course of construction, up to a maximum of five years. If construction continues beyond five years, the operator must apply for a new permit.[35] To terminate permit coverage, the operator must file a Notice of Termination (NOT).[36] For construction activities, an NOT can be filed when all disturbed areas are "finally stabilized." The EPA defines final stabilization as the situation that exists when all soil-disturbing activities are completed and a uniform perennial vegetative cover with a density of 70 percent is established. Equivalent stabilization measures in the form of geotextiles or mulches can also be used to "finally stabilize" an area until vegetation is established at the 70 percent rate. Other equivalent measures include situations in which a site is completely covered by impervious structures and therefore is not susceptible to soil erosion from precipitation events.[37]

All of the data used to complete the NOI, as well as copies of the site's storm water pollution prevention plan and any other reports required by the permit, must be retained by the operator for three years after the completion of final site stabilization.[38] Upon final stabilization and the filing of an NOT, however, the operator's responsibility for storm water discharges from the site under a general permit is ended.

State General Permits

The federal baseline general permits are not available for use in states that have assumed responsibility for the NPDES and general permitting programs. Instead, a construction operator in one of those states is obliged to apply for a state general permit. As indicated earlier, the EPA intends that delegated states use the federal baseline permits as models for creating state general permits. To a large extent, states have used the baseline permits in that way. However, applicants with construction sites in these states should consult their particular state's regulations to determine the precise format and timing criteria of the state's general permit application or NOI process.

Individual Permits

Finally, construction operators may be required to submit applications for individual storm water permits. As a rule of thumb, individual permits will be required when (1) the EPA or a state permitting authority determines that the discharge is contributing to the violation of a water quality standard or is a significant contributor of pollutants to waters of the United States; or (2) the discharge has previously been regulated under an individual permit. Individual permits tend to be viewed with some distaste because of the rigors involved in compiling the permit application and also because an operator has heightened pollution control obligations under individual permits. In addition, rather than providing a two-day lead time similar to the one used for federal general permits, individual applications must be submitted at least ninety days before the commencement of construction.[39]

Under the federal rules, individual permit applications must include detailed information on a site's general characteristics, drainage patterns, and proposed pollution controls. These requirements are the federal government's minimum standards; as always, delegated states may levy more exhaustive information obligations. The required federal data include a map indicating the site's location; the nature of the construction activity; the total area of the site and the area that will undergo excavation during the life of the permit; proposed measures, including best management practices, to control pollutants in storm water discharges during construction, accompanied by a brief description of applicable state and local erosion and sediment control requirements; proposed measures to control pollutants in storm water discharges that will occur after construction operations are completed, again including a brief description of state and local erosion and sediment control requirements; an estimate of the site's runoff coefficient (the fraction of total rainfall that will appear as runoff) and the increase in impervious area after construction is completed; the nature of fill material and existing data describing the soil or the quality of the discharge; and the name of the receiving water.[40]

Contents of Storm Water Permits

While individual permits and state general permits differ somewhat from one another in content, they generally follow the form of the federal general permit. That permit contains five primary components: (1) NOI requirements; (2) a prohibition on discharging non-storm water; (3) requirements for handling hazardous substance releases that exceed reporting quantities; (4) a storm water pollution prevention plan; and (5) site inspection requirements.[41] With the exception of the NOI criteria, which have already been discussed, each of these components is briefly described below.

Prohibition on Discharging Sources of Nonstorm Water

The EPA makes clear that, as a general proposition, the federal general storm water permits do not authorize discharges of nonstorm water, whether the nonstorm water is mixed with storm water or is discharged alone.[42] However, certain types of nonstorm discharges will be authorized if they are specifically mentioned in a storm water permit. These nonstorm water releases are referred to as "conditionally authorized nonstorm water discharges."[43] Storm water pollution prevention plans must identify and ensure the implementation of appropriate pollution prevention measures for any nonstorm water components in a site's discharge stream.

Requirements for Releases of Hazardous Substances or Oil in Excess of Reporting Quantities

Over the course of a construction project, certain types of hazardous substances or oil may be used to complete various portions of the project. The EPA has promulgated rules pursuant to the CWA that require NPDES-permitted facilities to report any spills of these substances in quantities that exceed specified limits.[44] If a reportable release occurs during the construction period, the site operator must immediately notify the National Response Center in Washington, D.C., of the spill. Within fourteen days after the spill, the operator must submit to the permitting authority a written description of the release, providing the date and circumstances of the release and the steps that will be taken on the site to prevent a similar release. Finally, the operator must modify the site's storm water pollution prevention plan to include the information submitted to the permitting authority.[45]

Storm Water Pollution Prevention Plans

Purpose and General Contents

In general, storm water pollution prevention plans are intended to fulfill two important purposes. First, the plans act as a kind of detective service for regulatory agencies in that they provide a vehicle by which various forms of water pollution can be traced to storm water discharges from particular facilities. Second, pollution prevention plans are just that: plans aimed at identifying and implementing measures to reduce pollutants in storm water discharges, thereby ensuring permittees' compliance with the terms and conditions of their permits.[46] The pollution prevention plans are required to contain four primary components: (1) a site description, (2) a description of pollution controls that will be installed at the site, (3) a description of maintenance and inspection procedures, and (4) a description of pollution prevention measures for any nonstorm water discharges existing at the site.

Site Description

In terms of site description, storm water pollution prevention plans must contain the following minimum information:

- a description of the nature of the construction activity, including the ultimate use of the project (e.g., shopping mall, horse farm, highway);
- a description of the intended sequence of major activities that will disturb soils on significant portions of the site;
- estimates of the total area of the site and the total area expected to be disturbed by excavation, grading, or other activities;
- estimates of the runoff coefficient of the site after construction activities are completed, as well as existing data describing the quality of any discharge from the site or the soil;
- a site map indicating drainage patterns and approximate slopes anticipated after major grading activities, areas of soil disturbance, location of major structural and nonstructural controls, location of surface waters including wetlands, location of areas where stabilization practices are expected to occur, and locations where storm water is discharged to a surface water; and
- the names of receiving waters.[47]

Storm Water Pollution Controls

Storm water pollution controls form the heart of pollution prevention plans. Permittees must design and implement four classes of pollution controls: (1) erosion and sediment controls; (2) storm water management controls; (3) a specified set of other controls; and (4) any applicable controls specified in state and local sediment, erosion, and storm water management programs.

Erosion and sediment controls are used to minimize the flow of storm water over areas where soil has been disturbed and to remove sediment from water before the water flows off the site.[48] These controls include "stabilization practices," such as seeding and mulching, and "structural practices," such as silt fences, earth dikes, drainage swales, check dams, subsurface drains, level spreaders, and sediment traps. The federal general permits require that stabilization measures be initiated on disturbed areas as soon as practicable, but no more than fourteen days after construction activity on a particular portion of the site has temporarily or permanently ceased. Limited exemptions exist for cases in which construction activities will resume within twenty-one days or in which snow cover or arid conditions preclude the initiation of stabilization measures altogether.[49] Further, the federal permits require that structural practices be implemented to the degree "economically attainable."[50]

Storm water management measures, the second class of pollutant controls, consist of such entities as wet ponds, infiltration trenches, sand filter systems, man-made wetlands, and velocity dissipation devices. These measures control the volume and velocity of storm water discharges during construction and can also reduce the amount of pollutants discharged after construction operations are completed. In cases in which storm water flows exceed predevelopment levels, the pollution prevention plan must explain the technical and economic reasons used to select the particular storm water management measures installed on site.[51]

Other classes of pollutant controls, such as measures to minimize a site's generation of dust and the off-site tracking of sediment by trucks and cars, as well as measures to ensure site compliance with state and local sewage and waste disposal rules, must also be addressed in pollution prevention plans.[52] In addition, measures to implement state and local controls governing erosion, sediment, and storm water management must be incorporated into the plans.[53]

Maintenance and Repair Procedures

To ensure that erosion, sediment, and storm water management control structures such as sediment basins, silt fences, drains, and filter devices remain in working order, the EPA requires that construction site operators include routine maintenance and repair procedures in storm water pollution prevention plans.[54]

Nonstorm Water Discharges

As mentioned above, if a site is particularly susceptible to certain classes of nonstorm water discharges, those classes may be conditionally authorized under the site's storm water permit. In such cases, the classes of nonstorm water discharges must be specified in the site's storm water pollution prevention plan, and appropriate pollution prevention measures must be identified and implemented to control the discharges.[55]

Inspection Procedures

In general, the EPA requires regulated entities to monitor the contents of their storm water discharges. In the construction context, however, the EPA has concluded that the many discharge points and erosion and sediment control structures installed at sites make monitoring impractical. Therefore, in lieu of monitoring pollutant output, the EPA requires that construction operations undergo periodic inspections.

Accordingly, storm water pollution prevention plans for construction sites must identify areas at a site that will be inspected by qualified discharger-provided personnel a minimum of once every seven calendar days and within twenty-four hours after any storm event of greater than half an inch of rainfall.[56] Less frequent inspections are mandated in some arid areas and when sites have been temporarily or finally stabilized. Targeted inspection locales include areas that host disturbed soils, structural control measures, and vehicle entrance or exit points. If an inspection reveals inadequacies in the pollution prevention measures governing any of these areas, the measures must be modified. The inspection reports must be retained as a part of the pollution prevention plan for at least three years after the date of inspection.

In practice, complying with the inspection requirement 100 percent of the time can be frustratingly difficult. Operators of large sites with multiple control structures and discharge points are hard pressed to compile adequate written reports on a weekly, or perhaps a daily (if it rains every day), basis. Confusion reigns over what standards of inspection are applicable. For instance, an inspection after a storm might reveal that a site's sediment fences are up but that the site is spitting mud. Is the site in compliance? Inspectors have to make judgment calls and document their decisions as best they can in such cases. As with any violation of storm water permitting criteria, noncompliance with EPA inspection and documentation requirements subjects a discharger to potential administrative, civil, and criminal penalties. Given the difficulty operators have in complying with this particular component of the storm water program, practitioners should take special care to clarify the inspection and documentation expectations with the relevant permitting agency and the client.

The Future

At present, federal and state regulation of storm water discharges from construction sites is expanding to include smaller sites, as discussed earlier. In addition, several relatively new issues are gaining attention and may, in the near future, lead to further revisions to storm water regulatory schemes.

For instance, states are beginning to look for ways to regulate storm water discharges into "sensitive streams." Sensitive streams include unique natural resource waterways that are designated "wild and scenic" under the Federal Wild and Scenic Rivers Act or state analogues. Waters receiving "elevated use" designations, such as cold water fisheries that are extremely responsive to turbidity conditions, also qualify as "sensitive streams." If discharges of storm water into sensitive streams have significant potential to cause violations of water quality specifications, states may require individual permits for those discharges. Accordingly, operators of construction sites located near sensitive waterways would do well to factor the timing and compilation cost criteria of the individual permit application process into their long-term planning schedules.

A related development involves the ever-present risk that a spill will occur on a construction site. Under federal and state environmental laws, spills of hazardous materials and petroleum products trigger reporting obligations. Once federal and state spill-control authorities are alerted to the fact that a spill of a hazardous substance or oil has occurred, those authorities will notify the relevant storm water permitting office. That office may respond in a number of ways, none of which are particularly palatable to construction operators.

First, no operator in the country is permitted to discharge oil or hazardous materials via storm water flows, so dischargers of such substances are in violation of their storm water permits. A permitting office may act to correct such a violation by immediately terminating the operator's general storm water permit and enjoining further operations at the site until an individual permit can be obtained. Second, spills of hazardous materials or oils left untreated for a period of time may trigger permitting requirements under other environmental laws. For example, a site may be classified as a hazardous waste "treatment, storage, and disposal facility" (TSDF) by virtue of the fact that hazardous waste is left sitting on the ground for a specified number of days. In such cases, the site operator will be required to obtain TSDF permits under the Federal Resource Conservation and Recovery Act or analogous state laws. In light of these consequences, spill control's importance cannot be overemphasized. If the condition of a site changes materially, the site operator can expect an increased level of regulatory interference at the site. Consequently, site operators should manage their sites extremely carefully to avoid even de minimis spills of hazardous substances or oils.

Finally, a wide range of issues potentially affecting storm water permitting are currently being discussed in the ongoing efforts to reauthorize the CWA. These discussions may result in future regulatory additions to storm water permits, such as significant monitoring of effluent quality, standardized treatment system criteria, and numerical limitations on pollutant loadings. In 1994, Congress explicitly considered mechanisms to regulate storm water discharges to groundwater, and in 1995, the House of Representatives has proposed to overhaul the storm water program completely, replacing it with voluntary controls similar to those found in the non-point provisions of CWA Section 319. While it is by no means certain that any of these initiatives will survive the legislative process, it is important to be aware of their existence and attempt, to the extent it is possible and cost-effective, to incorporate their foreseeable requirements into the planning process for construction projects.

Resources

Stormwater Permit Manual. Vols. 1–2. Thompson Publishing Group, Washington, D.C. (1995).

U.S. Environmental Protection Agency, Office of Wastewater Enforcement and Compliance. "NPDES Storm Water Program: Question and Answer Document." Vol. I. EPA Doc. No. 833/F-93-002 (March 1992).

—-. "NPDES Storm Water Program: Question and Answer Document." Vol. II. EPA Doc. No. 833/F-93-002B (July 1993).

—-. *Overview of the Storm Water Program.* EPA Doc. No. 833/F-93-001 (March 1993).

—-. "Storm Water General Permits Briefing." EPA Doc. No. 833/E-93-001 (Sept. 1992).

U.S. Environmental Protection Agency, Office of Water. "Storm Water Management for Construction Activities: Developing Pollution Prevention Plans and Best Management Practices." EPA Doc. No. 833-R-92-001 (Oct. 1992).

Water Pollution Control: BNA Policy and Practice Series. Washington, D.C.: Bureau of National Affairs, Inc. (1995).

Notes

1. 40 C.F.R. § 122.26(b)(13) (1994).

2. *See* CWA § 309(b), (d), 33 U.S.C. § 1319(b), (d) (civil penalties); CWA § 309(c), 33 U.S.C. § 1319(c) (criminal penalties); CWA § 309(g), 33 U.S.C. § 1319(g) (administrative penalties).

3. 60 Fed. Reg. 40,230, 40,235 (1995) (to be codified at 40 C.F.R. § 122.26(g)(1)(i)); *see also* 60 Fed. Reg. 17,950 (1995) (direct final rule) (withdrawn).

4. 60 Fed. Reg. at 40,235 (to be codified at 40 C.F.R. § 122.26(g)(1)(ii); *see also* 60 Fed. Reg. 17,950 (1995).

5. *See* 60 Fed. Reg. at 40,230 (sources must "apply for permits by the end of six years, but only if the . . . regulatory program in place at that time requires permits").

6. CWA § 101(a), 33 U.S.C. § 1251(a).

7. CWA § 502(14), 33 U.S.C. § 1362(14).

8. CWA § 402(a), 33 U.S.C. § 1342(a).

9. CWA § 301, 33 U.S.C. § 1311.

10. *See* CWA § 402(p)(2)(A)–(E), 33 U.S.C. § 1342(p)(2)(A)–(E); 40 C.F.R. § 122.26(a)(1)(i)–(v).

11. CWA § 402(p)(5)–(6), 33 U.S.C. § 1342(p)(5)–(6).

12. *See generally* 55 Fed. Reg. 47,990 (1990) (preamble and final rule) (codified in scattered sections of 40 C.F.R. pts. 122–24).

13. *See generally* 57 Fed. Reg. 11,394 (1992) (preamble and final rule) (codified in scattered sections of 40 C.F.R. pt. 122).

14. *Id.* at 11,404.

15. *See* 40 C.F.R. § 122.28(b)(2)(ii); 57 Fed. Reg., at 11,404–07.

16. *See* 57 Fed. Reg. 41,176 (1992); 57 Fed. Reg. 44,412 (1992).

17. 40 C.F.R. § 122.26(b)(14)(x).

18. U.S. EPA, Office of Wastewater Enforcement and Compliance, EPA Doc. No. 833/F-93-002B, NPDES STORM WATER PROGRAM: QUESTION AND ANSWER DOCUMENT VOLUME II 11 (July 1993) [hereinafter EPA QUESTION AND ANSWER Vol. II].

19. *Id.* at 12.

20. *See* 55 Fed. Reg., at 48,033–36.

21. *Id.* at 48,033.

22. 966 F.2d 1292 (9th Cir. 1992).

23. Natural Resources Defense Council, Inc. v. EPA, 966 F.2d 1292, 1305–06 (9th Cir. 1992).

24. *See* EPA QUESTION AND ANSWER VOL. II, *supra* note 18, at 14.

25. *See* 40 C.F.R. § 122.21(b).

26. *See* 57 Fed. Reg. 41,176, 41,190–91 (1992); EPA QUESTION AND ANSWER VOL. II, *supra* note 18, at 11.

27. As of August 1995, ten states—Alaska, Arizona, Idaho, Louisiana, Maine, Massachusetts, New Hampshire, New Mexico, Oklahoma, and Texas—have federally run NPDES programs. In addition, the District of Columbia and the territories of American Samoa, Guam, Johnston Atoll, Midway Island, Puerto Rico, and Wake Island have federally administered permitting programs.

28. As of August 1995, all forty states not mentioned in note 27, *supra*, have assumed the NPDES program and have obtained general permit authority as well.

29. As of August 1995, only the Virgin Islands falls into this category.

30. *See* 40 C.F.R. § 122.28(b)(2)(ii); 57 Fed. Reg., at 41,180, 41,218.

31. 57 Fed. Reg., at 41,180, 41,218.

32. *Id.*

33. *Id.*; *see also* EPA QUESTION AND ANSWER VOL. II, *supra* note 18, at 18.

34. 57 Fed. Reg., at 41,224.

35. U.S. EPA, Office of Wastewater Enforcement and Compliance, EPA Doc. No. 833/F-93-002, NPDES STORM WATER PROGRAM: QUESTION AND ANSWER DOCUMENT VOLUME I 15 (Mar. 1992).

36. 57 Fed. Reg., at 41,192–93, 41,224–25.

37. *Id.* at 41,192.

38. *Id.* at 41,185–86, 41,222.

39. 40 C.F.R. § 122.26(f)(2), (5).

40. *Id.* § 122.26(c)(1)(ii)(A)–(F).

41. 57 Fed. Reg., at 41,179–80, 41,217–29.

42. *Id.* at 41,181, 41,219.

43. Nonstorm water discharges that may receive conditional authorization include: discharges from firefighting activities; fire hydrant flushings; waters used to wash vehicles or control dust in accordance with permit requirements; potable water sources including waterline flushings; irrigation drainage; routine external building washdown that does not use detergents; pavement washwaters where spills or leaks of toxic or hazardous materials have not occurred (unless all spilled material has been removed) and where detergents are not used; air conditioning condensate; springs; uncontaminated groundwater; and foundation or footing drains where flows are not contaminated with process materials such as solvents. *Id.*

44. *See* 40 C.F.R. §§ 110, 117, 302.

45. 57 Fed. Reg., at 41,182, 41,219.

46. *See id.* at 41,181–85, 41,219–22.

47. *Id.* at 41,181–82, 41,220.

48. *Id.* at 41,182–83, 41,220.

49. *Id.* at 41,183, 41,220.

50. *Id.* at 41,182–83, 41,220.

51. *Id.* at 41,183–84, 41,220–21. *See generally* U.S. EPA, Office of Water, EPA Doc. No. 833-R-92-001, STORM WATER MANAGEMENT FOR CONSTRUCTION ACTIVITIES: DEVELOPING POLLUTION PREVENTION PLANS AND BEST MANAGEMENT PRACTICES (Oct. 1992).

52. 57 Fed. Reg., at 41,184, 41,221.

53. *Id.*

54. *Id.*

55. *Id.* at 41,181, 41,184–85, 41,219, 41,221.

56. *Id.* at 41,184, 41,221.

ORDER FORM

Mail to: American Bar Association, Order Fulfillment, P.O. Box 10892, Chicago, IL 60610-0892
Fax: 312/988-5568 (24 hours a day) Phone: 312/988-5522

___ I am a member of the Section of Natural Resources, Energy, and Environmental Law and am eligible for the reduced member prices listed on this form.

___ I wish to join the Section of Natural Resources, Energy, and Environmental Law and take advantage of the member price now. I have enclosed a separate check for $25 (payable to American Bar Association—SONREEL). Please send the publications I have indicated at the member prices. I am an ABA member.

SONREEL Books

Qty	Title	SONREEL price	nonmember price	Amount
	Environmental Aspects of Real Estate Transactions (5350052)	$94.00	$104.00	$
	The Natural Resources Manual (5350051)	$75.00	$80.00	$
	Water Law (5350050)	$70.00	$75.00	$
	Underground Storage Tanks: A Primer on the Federal Regulatory Program, Second Ed. (5350048)	$55.00	$60.00	$
	The Environmental Law Manual (5350035)	$75.00	$80.00	$
	What to Do When the Environmental Client Calls, Second Edition (5350043)	$55.00	$60.00	$
	The Clean Water Act Handbook (5350045)	$75.00	$80.00	$
	The Clean Air Act Operating Permit Program: A Handbook for Counsel, Environmental Managers & Plant Managers (5350040)	$75.00	$75.00	$
	The RCRA Practice Manual (5350044)	$84.95	$94.95	$
	The RCRA Policy Documents: Finding Your Way Through the Maze of EPA Guidance on Solid & Hazardous Waste (5350037)	$55.00	$60.00	$

SONREEL Monographs

On oil & gas issues

Qty	Title	SONREEL price	nonmember price	Amount
	Gas Dispatch, Allocation, and Balancing Agreement—A Proposed Form #22 (5350047)	$29.95	$39.95	$
	Drafting Indemnity Provisions in Oil and Gas Contracts #21 (5350046)	$29.95	$39.95	$
	Legal Research Checklists for International Petroleum Operations #20 (5350042)	$29.95	$39.95	$
	Federal Oil and Gas Appeals in the Department of the Interior #18 (5350036)	$29.95	$39.95	$
	Legal Aspects of the Purchase & Sale of Oil & Gas Properties #17 (5350034)	$29.95	$39.95	$
	International Oil & Gas Joint Ventures #16 (5350033)	$29.95	$39.95	$
	Improved 1989 Joint Operating Agreement #15 (5350030)	$29.95	$39.95	$
	Drafting Oil & Gas Exploration Agreements #14 (5350029)	$19.95	$29.95	$
	Package: 1989 Joint Operating Agreement and Drafting Oil & Gas Exploration Agreements (5350031)	$39.95	$49.95	$
	An Analysis & Evaluation of Rules and Policies Governing OCS Operations #13 (5350027)	$29.95	$39.95	$
	Drafting Natural Gas Contracts After Order 436 #11 (5350021)	$19.95	$29.95	$

Federal Oil & Gas Leasing Reform Act of 1987 #9 (5350018)	$29.95	$39.95	$
Protecting Oil & Gas Lien and Security Agreements #6 (5350014)	$19.95	$29.95	$
Offshore Bidding Agreements #3 (5350010)	$19.95	$29.95	$
1982 Joint Operating Agreement #2 (5350008)	$19.95	$29.95	$
Standard Form Farmout Agreements #1 (5350007)	$19.95	$29.95	$
Package: 1982 Joint Operating Agreement and Farmout Agreement (5350009)	$29.95	$39.95	$

On land patents

Railroad Land Grants #4 (5350011)	$29.95	$39.95	$

Environmental Issues

The Application of RCRA and CERCLA to Wastes Produced by Oil & Gas Operations #19 (5350039)	$29.95	$39.95	$
Identification of RCRA-Related Substances #8 (5350016)	$19.95	$29.95	$
Checklists for Preparing NEPA Documents #5 (5350013)	$19.95	$29.95	$

The Year in Review. Information on pertinent legislation, adminstrative, and regulatory actions in such areas as oil; natural gas; electric power; alternate energy sources; water, marine, and forest resources; air, water, and environmental quality; and solid and hazardous wastes.

1994 Year in Review (5350049)	$29.95	$39.95	$
1993 Year in Review (5350041)	$29.95	$39.95	$
1992 Year in Review (5350038)	$29.95	$39.95	$

SUBTOTAL	$________
TAX*	$________
HANDLING**	$________
TOTAL	$________

*IL residents add 8.75%; DC residents add 5.75%; MD residents add 5%

** For orders of $10-24.99 add $3.95; orders of $25-49.95 add $4.95; orders of $50 or more add $5.95.

Name

Firm/organization

Street address (no box numbers please)

City/State/Zip — Day phone number

Payment

___ Check enclosed, payable to ABA ___ Bill me Charge to: ___ VISA ___ MasterCard

Card number — Expiration date

Cardholder signature

If for any reason you are not satisfied with your purchase, you may return it within 30 days for a refund of the purchase price.